Music and Culture in
Eighteenth-Century Europe

MUSIC & CULTURE
—IN—
EIGHTEENTH-CENTURY
EUROPE

—A SOURCE BOOK—

ENRICO FUBINI

Translated from the original sources by
WOLFGANG FREIS
LISA GASBARRONE
MICHAEL LOUIS LEONE

Translation edited by
BONNIE J. BLACKBURN

THE UNIVERSITY OF CHICAGO PRESS
CHICAGO AND LONDON

ENRICO FUBINI is professor of the aesthetics of music at the University of Turin. BONNIE J. BLACKBURN is an Oxford-based musicologist who has taught at the State University of New York at Buffalo.

The University of Chicago Press, Chicago 60637
The University of Chicago Press, Ltd., London
© 1994 by The University of Chicago
All rights reserved. Published 1994
Printed in the United States of America
03 02 01 00 99 98 97 96 95 94   5 4 3 2 1

ISBN (cloth): 0-226-26731-8
ISBN (paper): 0-226-26732-6

Originally published as *Musica e cultura nel Settecento europeo,* © 1986 E.D.T.
Edizioni di Torino

Library of Congress Cataloging-in-Publication Data

Musica e cultura nel Settecento europeo. English.
    Music and culture in eighteenth-century Europe : a source book /
Enrico Fubini ; translated from the original sources by Wolfgang
Freis, Lisa Gasbarrone, Michael Louis Leone ; translation edited by
Bonnie J. Blackburn.
        p.   cm.
    Includes bibliographical references and index.
    ISBN 0-226-26731-8. — ISBN 0-226-26732-6
    1. Music—Europe—18th century—History and criticism—Sources.
I. Fubini, Enrico.   II. Blackburn, Bonnie J.   III. Title.
IV. Title: Music and culture in 18th-century Europe.
ML240.3.M8613   1994
780'.9'033—dc20   93-36066
                                                       CIP
                                                       MN

∞ The paper used in this publication meets the minimum requirements of the
American National Standard for Information Sciences—Permanence of Paper for
Printed Library Materials, ANSI Z39.48-1984.

Contents

Editor's Preface

FOR MUSIC HISTORIANS accustomed to thinking of the periodization of music by ages with the familiar, though ever less satisfactory, titles of "Middle Ages," "Renaissance," "Baroque," "Classicism," and "Romanticism," it may come as something of a surprise to find an anthology of writings collected under the rubric "Eighteenth Century." Categorization by century is common in Italian scholarship, and it offers advantages in the present book, since many of the topics covered do not lend themselves to the adjectives "Baroque" and "Classical." Debates over the relative role of words and music in opera, the related question whether instrumental music has any expressive power, and the nature of music itself continue right through the century; the nuances are different, the arguments change, but the issues remain constant. The eighteenth century was indeed a very argumentative age, as the excerpts in this anthology amply attest.

For this English translation Professor Fubini has added a new chapter on the revaluation of instrumental music and new excerpts to Chapters 4 (Brown, Sharp, and Baretti) and 6 (Mattheson on musical taste). When the anthology was published in Italy, few of the excerpts chosen by Professor Fubini were accessible in Italian translation; a number, however, were already available in English, either in Oliver Strunk's *Source Readings in Music History* (New York: W. W. Norton, 1950 and 1965; references in this anthology are to the original edition) or in translations of complete treatises. But to have eliminated such duplications would have seriously limited the value of the anthology. No excerpts have therefore been omitted. The source note at the end of each excerpt gives the location in the original source and, where such exists, a recent modern edition; English translations are also noted.

All the translations have been made from the original sources, following the original paragraphing unless sections were unduly long; the spellings of proper names have been normalized. A literal translation has been sought, but not at the expense of readability—a fine line that is not easy to draw (a translation into eighteenth-century English would have been easier). Certain terms have at times been left untranslated to avoid ambiguity; perhaps the most frequently used is *sinfonia* or *symphonie,* a generic term for instrumental music, which sometimes means an overture, but not (in these excerpts) a symphony. The term "opera" is used side by side with *drame lyrique, melodramma, teatro lirico,* and *dramma per musica.* In all cases these words were translated as "opera," since there is no good alternative in English (and least of all "melodrama"). *Poème lyrique* was more problematic; it means "libretto," and yet translating it as such removes some of its resonance: it is not merely the text set by the composer but the dramatic poem (in French "poème" is more likely to refer to a long work) written to be set to music. Thus, depending on the context, "lyric poem" has sometimes been used instead.

In the Italian edition, few of the excerpts were annotated. In addition to supplying more annotations, I have restored all the original footnotes, several of which had been omitted. In many the titles were abbreviated; these have been expanded (and corrected where necessary) and publication information added. Some of the original annotations may seem less germane to the topic, but by omitting the frequent references to classical sources we miss an essential aspect of eighteenth-century culture, and one that cannot be assumed in the modern reader. For the many classical references that were not identified in the original I have relied on the goodwill of Leofranc Holford-Strevens; his annotations bear the initials LAH-S. Professor Fubini's annotations are labeled EF, my own BJB.

A number of people who needed identification were mentioned in more than one excerpt; to avoid duplicate annotations I have supplied a biographical dictionary; the brief entries are intended to do no more than to set the writers and musicians in context. The dictionary also includes all authors of excerpts.

I am greatly indebted to Kathleen K. Hansell, who answered many questions in a field in which she is far more expert than I and gave me much helpful information. She has added occasional annotations, labeled KKH, and revised and updated the bibliography.

B.J.B.

Introduction

COMPILING AN ANTHOLOGY of writings on music in eighteenth-century Europe presents at least two sets of problems: the enormous number of writings concerning music produced during the Enlightenment, and the apparent uniformity of the tone, the subject matter, and the discussions among the various authors. It is difficult to orient oneself, to choose, to discard, to distinguish what is essential from what is superfluous, to single out the real problems from those that are merely fictitious or simply the product of passing fashions, to distinguish between those disquisitions and debates that have left their mark and profoundly affected the history of European musical culture and those that were merely frivolous or academic. The boundaries between these two areas are often rather ambiguous and blurred.

In fact, even to the most casual observer, quantity is the most striking change presented by the vast panorama of eighteenth-century musical writings. Perhaps for the first time in Western history music claims its rightful place in the world of culture, in the widest sense of the term, abandoning for the most part its traditionally specialist nature to the extent of becoming a topic of discussion in aristocratic salons and in learned academies of all kinds. At times it even becomes a cultural fashion, making music and the many *querelles* it sparked during that century a favorite subject of polemicists, writers, intellectual circles, aspiring musicians, poets, and literati, and of the authors of thou- of pamphlets.

In this respect, France was undoubtedly in the vanguard. However, during the course of the century, this trend quickly spread from France to the whole of Europe. Even a product purely of fashion deserves a place and merits evaluation, whether positive or negative, and it would be unfair if such material were not documented, albeit to a limited extent, in an anthology of the eighteenth century in Europe. But beyond doubt, the world of music assumed a relevance and, above all, a cultural significance unknown in preceding centuries. In the eighteenth century there were also learned specialist treatises on harmony, on problems of acoustics, and on the music of the ancients, but they were over-shadowed by pamphlets on the polemics then in fashion, usually written by philosophers, literati, critics, poets, mathematicians, and the learned, rather than by musicians. Even when the protagonists of the music world themselves took part, musicians or performers preferred to assume a popular tone, approximating everyday language in an attempt to make themselves accessible to men of average culture, rather than enclosing themselves in an ivory tower, or rather in the iron cage they had been shut up in for so long. There are relatively few exceptions, and these only serve to prove the rule. A new interest in music was born, and especially in opera, the century's most popular theatrical form. The number of people with any interest in music grew enormously, and, despite appearances to the contrary, there was a parallel increase in the discussion of music and related problems by men of culture. Thus, as the musician began to come out into the open, to take up pen and paper, and to make himself into a man of letters as an able polemicist and a writer who can speak of his art with cultured men, and not just his colleagues, so too did the man of letters realize that music had become a part of his world, and that the problems of music could and should interest him directly.

Hence the difficulty in giving everything its just due in an anthology of eighteenth-century musical culture. To whom should one allow more space? To the literati who wrote of music, to the critics, or to musicians, who in ever greater number took up the pen? To the mathematicians, to the physicists who devised new theories on acoustics and harmony, or to the philosophers and scholars of the fine arts, who by now did not fail to devote at least one chapter of their treatises to music? Then there are the journalists, those who wrote for the first music journals, the historians who attempted to draft the first histories of music, the musicians who wrote didactic treatises on their favorite instruments, the travelers who were often interested in music, a phenomenon that was becoming increasingly widespread and significant from a socio-historical point of view. Not all can be included in a volume designed to offer the reader something more than a few lines by each author. Therefore, a compromise has been struck, since any anthology that privileges one category of writings above another would offer a distorted view of the eighteenth century. The idiosyncrasy of the century is precisely its eclecticism. An attempt has therefore been made, within the given limits, to provide the reader with a first-hand awareness of how music evolved from a specialist concern to a subject of interest to the most disparate categories of intellectuals. Thus the broadest possible sampling of authors and subject matter has been sought. At times the number of authors has been limited in order to give more space to themes; at times the number of passages was reduced in favor of a selection of broader and more exhaustive ones, sufficient at least to supply the reader with a sampling of both authors and subject matter that is not too fragmented.

When approaching the world of eighteenth-century musical culture, as already mentioned, we are at first disoriented by the enormous quantity of writings, which might also prove disappointing at the outset due to a certain uniformity and even paucity of the subjects treated. Some broad themes are stressed more in one country than in another, and this only increases the impression of the basic uniformity of musical thought. The majority of French treatises, for example, is dominated right from the very first years of the eighteenth century by the great *querelle* concerning the supremacy of French music over Italian, or vice versa. Italian musical treatises are dominated by the problem of the relationship between music and poetry, and by the tendency on the part of literati and literary critics to stress the dependence of music on poetry in opera, thus condemning the frivolous musical tendencies of the contemporary theater. German musical treatises are more closely involved with strictly musical themes, and therefore more concerned with didactic problems linked to instrumental music and to instrumental performance practice. A category somewhat apart seems to be that of the musicians, mathematicians, and physicists interested in strictly technical problems concerning harmony and acoustics.

Viewing the century as a whole, one becomes aware that as its second half approaches, those themes that at the beginning of the century appeared isolated and were treated almost exclusively in countries where they aroused the greatest interest little by little began to intertwine. Exchanges among nations increased, the cultural scene grew more complex, and music became the focus of ever more articulate and diversified interest, in which philosophical, political, literary, historical, and anthropological problems, among others, found a common ground.

The *querelle* between the supporters of French and Italian music aroused passions throughout Europe, even though it was central to French culture for almost a century, from the first debate between the Abbé Raguenet and the nobleman Lecerf de la Viéville in the very first years of the century to the last *querelle* between the supporters of Gluck and Piccinni. In fact, the first skirmishes of this controversy can already be found in the seventeenth century in the columns on music in the *Mercure Galant* and other journals. It may seem surprising, at first, how a world that displayed the cultural liveliness of the century of the *philosophes* in France could with such passion and at times with such dogged tenacity debate a problem whose terms appear in retrospect to be rather futile, if not unreal. However, we have only to begin to penetrate the recesses of this debate to realize that it is to be read as a code, and that other more provocative problems underlie the age-old controversy whether the French or the Italians are the better musicians. As in the *querelle* of the ancients and the moderns, where all the important issues of the century of Enlightenment surfaced, or rather took shape, similarly in the musical *querelle*—to a large extent derived from the former—the aesthetic problems related to music were more precisely defined. This happened as well with larger themes, such as the concept of nature, of genius, of spontaneity and creativity, the function of rules, the weight of tradition and innovation, the value of imagination, of taste, of melody and harmony, the relationship between words and music, the momentous problem of the origin of language, and, lastly, even political issues, leading to the threshold of the French Revolution.

These and perhaps even other problems are to be found in the crannies of the monotonous *querelle* on the Italians and the French, in which all cultured Frenchmen participated in one way or the other—musicians and non-musicians, experts and non-experts, people who were deeply interested in musical problems and others who had only a fleeting contact with the world of music. In this panorama, which at close range is in fact extremely varied and multiform, two figures stand out who differed greatly but who were equal in importance: a musician-philosopher, Jean-Philippe Rameau, and a philosopher and aspiring musician, Jean-Jacques Rousseau. Their importance proved decisive not only for French culture but for all European musical culture, and their philosophical legacy went far beyond the boundaries of their century.

But let us follow more closely, albeit in general terms, the themes that emerge from the background of the *querelle*.

In the very first years of the century, in 1702, upon returning from a voyage to Italy, the Abbé Raguenet wrote the *Paralèle des Italiens et des Français, en ce qui regarde la musique et les opéras*. This brief, brilliant, and incisive pamphlet gave birth to the long *querelle* that was to divide France for a century; with it the myth of Italian music was born—and, in the end, its stereotype. In Raguenet's pamphlet we can find all the attributes that, up to and beyond Rousseau, will serve to characterize Italian music in contrast to French. We must not expect to find analyses of Italian or French music, stylistic or formal comparisons, and so forth; what we do find are generic attributes of genius, originality, and melodic inventiveness, and praise for the Italian musicians' capacity to move, to entertain, and to delight. Conversely, Raguenet deplored the monotony, the uniformity, the heavy-handed harmony, the inability to touch the listener's heart, and the cold inventiveness of French musicians.

Raguenet, and subsequently all those who participated in the *querelle*, referred these judgments almost exclusively to opera, the genre *par excellence*, the most beloved and popular, in the face of which all instrumental music, which was also produced in great quantity during the century, was cast into shadow. In the comparison between French and Italian music, the central issue was the word–tone relationship, between the libretto and the music. Both sides agreed unanimously that the French excelled in writing dramas to be set to music, whereas Italian librettos were notoriously poor. Even this appraisal, which in general was never supported by detailed analyses or examples, soon became a myth, but at its root there always lay a musical rather than a literary problem: does the literary quality of an operatic text influence the final result, or is what counts in the end the musical invention, the beauty of the arias totally absorbing the libretto? What is more important, the clarity of the recitative—the place where by choice the drama unfolds—or the musicality of the aria, the place where the characters display their own feelings? And finally, the basic problem around which the entire *querelle* revolves: are genius, inventiveness, and the unfettered flow of feelings worth more than rules, tradition, and regularity? In other words, the moderns or the ancients?

The comparison between French and Italian music can thus be considered the musical equivalent of the dispute between the ancients and the moderns, although, as it continued through the eighteenth century, it would take on more specific characteristics and be enriched by new and more specifically musical themes, such as the confrontation between instrumental and vocal music. Thus, in light of the philosophical and aesthetic background from which it arose, the entire *querelle* proved to be strongly conditioned by ideological considerations. The motivations and choices on either side were never based on historical or empirical observations, but were usually predictable in light of the particular partisan allegiance that inspired them.

As proof, it is sufficient simply to leaf through the *Comparaison de la musique italienne et de la musique française,* that long, weighty, and bombastic essay that Lecerf de la Viéville, Seigneur de Freneuse, great admirer of Lully and French opera, wrote in 1704 in response to Raguenet's pamphlet. Using the form of a drawing-room conversation among aristocrats, the host (that is, the author) politely answers his guests' questions, pointing out the rules governing good musical taste. As usual, he is forever at odds with Raguenet, the constant target of his barbs. Lecerf typifies the moderate conservative, and his all-out defense of French, as opposed to Italian, music establishes a solid ideological link between a conservative mentality, the defenders of the ancients, the classicists, and French music and opera. For them, what in reality ought to be eliminated from opera is precisely its musical element. However, since this basic aspiration of French classicism—also shared by Italian classicism—is by definition impossible, the musical component should be kept to a bare minimum, just enough not to obscure the clarity of the drama, which is entirely dependent on the verbal rather than on the musical element.

Music, therefore, assumes the aspect of an inconvenient factor, upsetting and disturbing in many ways because one is hard put to make it coincide with the linear canons of reason. One feels that its semantic value is ambiguous, forever fleeting, that it is that "je ne sais quoi," evanescent but at the same time present to a sufficiently powerful degree to disturb the rationalist, for whom beauty is synonymous with truth and pure reason. In this perspective, Italian music, and especially Italian opera, is hailed as a triumph of fantasy, or, to use an expression of the time, of "artifice"—in a word, of "art." At the opposite pole from artifice stands nature, which is synonymous with reason, clarity, and nobility, and therefore with beauty. Lecerf expresses the concept very effectively when he says: "Art is the enemy of nature. It represents something of which one can neither explain the function nor the necessity. We submit to its whims and its charms with amazement and distrust, but we subject it to reason and thus reduce it to the minimum." In this ideal reduction of art to the minimum a quantitative factor is introduced as a critical element: enlightened common sense will suggest the right and tolerable quantity, proportionate to good taste, to a happy medium. There should be no ornate and jagged melodies, no bold harmonies, no gaudy colors, no trills, no vocal or instrumental daring; monotony (an ideal unacknowledged, but clearly inferable from the context) should barely be broken by embellishments, which should not always be improvised.

The essentially negative attitude of French culture to music and musicality in the first half of the eighteenth century is common above all to philosophers and critics of classical bent, and is based on a double motivation, moralistic and rationalistic. Music represents "languor" and "voluptuousness," which creeps into the virility of a tragic representation, corrupting it from within, altering its spirit, its very essence, and transforming it into an enticement for the eyes and a pleasure for the senses. On the other hand, if music represents the triumph of irrationality, of fantasy, of fiction, of improbability, then reason is betrayed, the intellect clouded, and truth is covered by a soft and deceitful cloak.

From Bossuet to Saint-Évremond, from Boileau to Fontenelle and Voltaire, all concur in considering opera a corrupt product of modern times, a spectacle that misguides the spirit and betrays reason. However, the virulence of these critics' aversion to opera should not mislead us. It is not that they do not understand music, much less that they underestimate its power and strength. Rather, their critical attitude is one of fear and hostility toward a form of expression at odds with their concept of art. Music is a force, albeit a fearful one; it is given over to evil because it is irrational; it is anything but a harmless or insignificant embellishment: "Music," Bossuet states, "awakens in us some indefinable, restless, and vague inclination toward pleasure; it aspires to nothing and to everything . . . and it produces a secret inclination to that intimate disposition that enfeebles the soul and inclines the heart toward all that is perceived through the

senses. One no longer knows what it is one wants."[1] The subtle powers of seduction attributed to music will in turn constitute a premise for its revaluation
in a not too distant future, when there will no longer be moralistic prejudices
against feeling, emotions, and everything related to expression, and against everything that does not coincide with the traditional categories of reason.

Therefore, at first the problem was simply that of limiting as much as possible the "social" damage brought about by operatic music, realizing that opera
could no longer be eliminated from the European scene, where its triumphs
overshadowed in popularity all other types of theatrical representation. Inevitably, opera came to be considered a by-product and a corruption of tragedy,
lacking any autonomy as an artistic genre. On the one hand we have the
noble, austere, and rational tragedies of Corneille and Racine; on the other, the
corrupt and degenerate tragedies of Quinault, and the even more corrupt ones
of the Italians. At least Lully's music did not wreak such serious and irreparable
damage on the text (the only thing that counted) of Quinault's tragedies, as did
the contorted operas of the Italians.

The antimusical controversy of the French literati and philosophers, not dissimilar to that of their Italian counterparts, was thus aimed primarily at the
degeneration of tragedy, rather than at music as such, whose subtle and perverse
effects were in fact recognized, while any value in terms of beauty was denied it.
Nevertheless, already in the first half of the century, voices were evident in European culture suggesting new outlooks paving the way to a consideration of
opera as an autonomous genre, endowed with its own artistic specificity. The
new ideas, already contained in Raguenet's pamphlet in the form of a defense of
Italian music—but in reality a defense of music *tout court*—and the legitimacy
of the pleasure it produced, were taken up again and developed with greater
philosophical insight by the Abbé Dubos, author of the *Réflexions critiques sur la
poésie, la peinture et la musique* (1719). It is not by chance that at the root of the
defense of music, and especially of opera, there was a tendentially empirical
mentality. Even for Raguenet, the yardstick with which to judge the superiority
of Italian music was one's own taste, the ability to listen to the flow of pleasure
that music produces, and not reasoning or logical deduction. Even Dubos acknowledged that music gives us pleasure and moves us, thus achieving the aim
of all the arts. Nevertheless, compared with the other arts, music affects the
passions in a much more direct way, since it represents their "natural traits."
Poetry, on the other hand, represents their arbitrary, or, as we would say today,
their conventional traits. But the intuition most promising for the future of

1. Jacques Bénigne Bossuet, *Maximes et réflexions sur la comédie* (1694), ch. 3.

eighteenth-century musical thinking was the discovery of the complementary relationship between music and poetry, based on their common origin. Perrault had already suggested the idea that singing was simply a way of emphasizing poetry. Dubos, however, went further and did not hesitate to affirm that music was the proper language of the emotions, and that one resorted to music "particularly on those occasions in which the power of words would not be capable of arousing the same emotions." There is thus an "operatic" poetry, fit for setting to music; it already has potential musicality because it "contains emotions," whereas that which "contains painting" does not lend itself to setting to music.

The rationalistic tradition's concepts of verisimilitude, of art seen as a means to instruct and edify, were completely meaningless from Dubos's new empirical and sensist perspective. Thus, opera was no longer considered an unnatural or unlikely aggregate of poetry and music, a futile embellishment, or a corruption of the nobler and more instructive genre of tragedy. Opera's antecedent was not to be sought in classical tragedy, but in song. Dubos added that the realization "that words of songs had quite a different force when they were sung than when they were recited gave rise to setting entire stories to music on the stage, and we came round gradually to singing an entire dramatic piece. These are our operas."[2]

The revolutionary scope of the Abbé Dubos's thinking was fully grasped, often unwittingly, only in the second half of the eighteenth century. Only the Encyclopedists, and especially Rousseau, Diderot, and Grimm, would be the ones to reap his legacy by coherently developing the idea of the common origin of music and poetry in primitive man's first songs.

This controversy, pitting the two opposed factions of the traditionalists against the innovators, the rationalists against the empiricists, the supporters of a classicizing taste against those of the new galant style, the advocates of harmony against those of a freer melody, the humanists and literati against the musicians, continued to take shape throughout the eighteenth century in the opposition between French and Italian music. Such considerations, which are more conceptual than real, always take on the value of stereotypes. If Raguenet, before writing his lively and effective pamphlet, had undertaken a journey to Italy and had tested for better or worse and listened before passing judgment, the other polemicists generally spoke, discussed, and delivered irrevocable pronouncements in favor of one or the other side on the basis of ideologically slanted stereotypes. In fact, what was at stake was not so much the superiority or inferiority of the music of the one or the other as certain aesthetic and philosophical values, such as tradition, taste, nature, genius, fantasy, freedom from

2. *Réflexions critiques,* ch. 1, sec. XLV.

rules, the preeminence of emotions over reason, and lastly the basic problem, which in some way subsumes all the others, the relationship between verbal and musical expression. Thus, a certain basic monotony, which surfaces from these endless discussions on the merits and defects of the music of France and Italy, takes on a brighter coloring and a broader interest if these disquisitions, which always seem to turn abstractly on the same subject, are in some way decoded and referred back to the more important and compelling underlying issues.

In the rich and at times picturesque panorama of these controversies, in the numerous pamphlets and counter-pamphlets, the writings of Jean-Philippe Rameau, composer, but also a theorist of harmony, philosopher, and polemicist, warrant special consideration. His profound aspiration to be not only a musician but a philosopher and a man of culture and science sets him apart from his French and Italian contemporaries, who were generally distant from the world of ideological disputes, immersed in their hectic craft, and traditionally alien to the world of culture. Rameau had a high regard for his own work as a musician, but he also wanted to discover a solid and unshakeable philosophical and scientific foundation for music itself. This is why he had little in common with the French literati and classicists of his time, although his contemporaries classified him as a traditionalist, a supporter of French music and opera, and an adversary of Italian melody. Primarily, what emerges with extraordinary force in his writings is a marked desire to free music from the limbo not only of the insignificant and purely emotional, but also from the realm of the irrational, where it had been relegated. When, in 1722, he published his first and carefully thought out *Traité de l'harmonie réduite à ses principes naturels,* followed in 1726 by the *Nouveau système de musique théorique,* the basic principles of his thinking were already clear. In his numerous treatises written during the following decades, and in his controversy with the Encyclopedists, he only confirmed his basic theoretical principles. Music is founded on harmony and not on melody. Indeed, the former is rational and therefore natural; the latter is dependent on the taste of a single individual or people, and is thus an arbitrary and inessential variable. For Rameau, how was music to be rationalized and thus rescued from the limbo in which it had been confined by classicism? As is well known, the phenomenon of harmonics offered the scientific and rational basis for showing that harmony was both fundamental and natural. Rameau was not the first to have studied the phenomenon, which had been previously observed by Joseph Sauveur, the mathematician who succeeded in calculating the absolute number of vibrations in a sound and in providing a scientific explanation of overtones. The model for Rameau's reasoning was Descartes: start with a sound principle, the evidence of which is clear, and which is rationally beyond debate. "Enlightened by the method of Descartes, whom fortunately I

had read and by whom I had been impressed, I began to look within myself."[3]
Descartes's "I think" is for Rameau the phenomenon of a sounding body's resonance; the first overtones it produces give us a perfect major chord. All the possible variety of chords can be reduced to this sole principle, which is both simple
and rational, and provided by nature itself. "How marvelous is this principle in
its simplicity!" Rameau exclaims with enchanted and almost religious awe in
his *Traité de l'harmonie*. "Such variety of chords, of beautiful melody, this limitless variety of such beautiful and right expressions, of such well-rendered emotions: all these derive from two or three intervals arranged in thirds, which all
originate from only one sound!"

This principle, presented at this point without any mention of its implications for developing a functional theory of harmony, is interesting in the present context as it constituted an attempt to base the autonomy of music on
rational grounds. In this way, music no longer need resort to other arts in order
to achieve its expressive capacity. Music's harmonic foundation helps rescue
it from previous accusations of its being arbitrary, hedonistic, and a useless ornament of poetry, its supposed elder sister. Music can exist in its own right;
indeed, it is autonomously expressive precisely in terms of its own musical
means, that is, because of harmony. Saying that music is a science does not imply depriving it of its power to express or imitate emotions, but rather grounds
it in a solid and rational principle capable of safeguarding it against the whims
of men, the variety of tastes and styles, and changes in fashion. Rameau is therefore able to conclude that music is the science of expression, and the variety of
chords can constitute a sort of dictionary of the emotions and passions, the
meanings of which are fixed and unalterable both in time and place. Art and
science, emotion and reason, sensibility and rationality are therefore not opposite and irreconcilable principles: in Rameau's musical philosophy they are perfectly reconciled and solidly allied.

Obviously, in this light the obstreperous *querelle* between the advocates of
French and Italian music becomes devoid of all meaning. For Rameau, music
has no nationality; it is a universal language that remains constant. Its relationship to poetry is non-essential, accessory, and of no theoretical interest. A
strange fate was to befall Rameau: he was attacked on one side by the classicists
as a betrayer of the noble and austere French tradition, of the glorious school of
Lully, Campra, and Destouches, and for being sensitive to the whims and liberties taken by Italian opera composers; and on the other by the theorists of aesthetics, by the Encyclopedists, and by the lovers of Italian melody for being a
sullen and stern guardian of a classical tradition no longer in step with the

3. *Démonstration du principe de l'harmonie, servant de base à tout l'art musical théoretique et
pratique* (Paris, 1750), 7–8.

times. It certainly cannot be concluded that because of this Rameau represents a middle course; in reality, his position is different from both that of the classicists and of the *philosophes,* and clearly runs countercurrent. It is not by chance that Rameau had no immediate followers, but remained isolated. In an age when throughout Europe, and not just in France, attempts were under way to deepen and radicalize the split between art and science, taste and reason, sensibility and rules, it sounded at least false and out of place to insist with such obstinacy on the unity of head and heart, of reason and sense. This theology of music, this exclusive attention to the eternal and immutable in the world of sounds, mirroring the divine unity of things, would only be taken up some decades later by the Romantics.

European musical thought followed another route in the eighteenth century. If Rameau set a solid foundation for the future rehabilitation of pure instrumental music, most Enlightenment thinkers focused their attention on opera and on the unresolved, age-old problem of the relationship between words and music. We have seen how classicist rationalism could not accept opera as other than a devious compromise, on account of its improbability, its hedonism, its unacceptable bringing together of two basically irreconcilable languages, music and poetry, its logical absurdities, and the fantastic and unreal world it evoked. The new aesthetic, with its subsequent revaluation of the sphere of feelings and emotions, in terms of both their autonomy and legitimacy in the face of reason, had to confront the challenge of explaining opera, the rage in theaters all over Europe, despite the insults hurled against it, despite the immoral behavior of singers, musicians, poets, and impresarios, and despite its pandering to the public's exceedingly banal taste—ills that were universally deplored. It was a question of finding a philosophical and theoretical legitimation so that Italian opera, which was loved by everyone and especially by the *philosophes,* would no longer be judged as a mere matter of taste, a pure source of enjoyment, albeit for intellectuals, or as a futile pastime. Italian opera was no longer to be considered an inessential diversion: digging deep into its structure and reclaiming its origins should reveal its true essence, an authentic expression of man, a manifestation of an unalienated existence.

Italian and French opera became once again abstract ideological reference points in the famous *querelle des Bouffons.* Rousseau's personality and his encumbering presence prevailed unchallenged throughout the second half of the century. There was no musician, theorist, polemicist, librettist, or music historian who in some way did not have to reckon with the Genevan philosopher, or who was not influenced by him in some way. We are accustomed to identifying the eclectic and diverse thinking of the Encyclopedists, from Voltaire to d'Alembert, from Diderot to Grimm, from de Jaucourt to Marmontel, with Rousseau's revolutionary thought, much in the same way that we tend to consider his thought as being exclusively linked to the defense of the "bouffonistes." Even if the occasion that stimulated Rousseau to take up music—to the extent of becoming a musician and composer of the perhaps too famous one-act opera *Le Devin du village*—was accidental, his ideas on music went far beyond the limits of the ensuing polemic and became a basic reference point for the musical aesthetics of the following decades. Therefore, what counts more than a few pamphlets occasioned by the raging polemics, such as the famous *Lettre sur la musique française* of 1753, are the more reflective and wider-ranging albeit less well-known writings, like his *Essai sur l'origine des langues,* published posthumously in 1781, but presumably written between 1756 and 1762.

At least in part, Rousseau's ideas on music are linked to some of the Abbé Dubos's happy intuitions on the musicality of poetry and on its intrinsic relationship with the world of emotions. Beyond his sympathy, shared by almost all the *philosophes,* for Italian music, known more as a stereotype than as a reality, he aimed at redeeming music and musicality in a way totally different from, if not opposed to, that of his formidable antagonist, Rameau. Rousseau neither wanted to nor was interested in rehabilitating music through reason, but through recognizing in it an echo of a mythical original language of primitive man. In his *Essai sur l'origine des langues* he stated that "poetry developed before prose," since the passions and emotions should prevail over reason; nor was he in favor of a division between the two spheres, whereby the emotions would fall within the purview of art, reason within that of science or philosophy. Rather, Rousseau dreamt of a harmonious and instinctive agreement between the two faculties, coming about solely in this mythical original language, which, however, should continue to represent a reference point for the musician. Primitive man's language was born of his passions, and not of his needs; that is why it is song, which is a total human expression. Insofar as it is melody, it includes and embodies the articulation of language. Words and melodious sound originated within man's original expression, and only the development of civilization was able to break this unity: ". . . progressively as needs develop, as affairs become more complex, and as enlightenment spreads, language changes character. It becomes more exact and less passionate; it substitutes ideas for emotions; it no longer speaks to the heart, but to reason. As a consequence, stress diminishes, articulation is extended; language becomes more exact, clearer, but slower, duller, and colder."[4]

This is not the place to investigate in depth the concept of nature central to all of Rousseau's thinking. It is sufficient to recall that his appeal to nature has a totally different meaning from Rameau's. For the latter, music is natural in that

4. *Essai sur l'origine des langues,* ch. 5.

its underlying harmony precisely reflects a physical law that is natural because it is eternal and immutable. This is why music is a universal language. For Rousseau, the emotions and passions are natural. Nature, in fact, "inspires songs and not chords; it teaches melody, not harmony." To identify nature no longer with harmony but with melody had manifold consequences. Harmony universalizes, while melody individualizes; to affirm the supremacy of melody meant to affirm that of the subject, of individual emotions, of what is particular. Universality, which is proper to reason, became a negative element for Rousseau. Universality is that which is always the same, that never changes: it is harmony. Melody, however, is what gives every music its specific, peculiar, and distinguishing character. It varies, as all languages vary, from one people to another, from one climate to another, from one age to another. It represents nature as subjectivity, as an outburst of individual expression, of life in its variegated mobility, at the pole opposite to harmony's empty and abstract universality.

The analysis of melody, however, could not be separated from the parallel analysis of the melodiousness of language, because melody could not exist as an abstract musical quality, but only melodiousness as song. Civilization had ruptured this original unity, giving rise to the language of words on the one hand, and the sounds of music on the other. Languages also changed from country to country, while they conserved, in varying degree, the memory of their sweet ancient ringing. There were countries, like the Nordic ones, where the predominance of reason over emotion had despoiled words of all musical character. Music consequently had completely divorced itself from words and had survived in an arid and abstract way; melody had become barren and harmony prevailed in its empty universality. The same thing had happened in the French language and music. Conversely, Italian, in keeping with the character of its people, had remained "sweet, sonorous, harmonious, and accentuated more than all others, and these four qualities are precisely the ones that befit singing" (*Lettre sur la musique française*). Now, to affirm that the Italian mode of singing was more beautiful, more melodious, more pleasing, and more expressive than the French was no longer a mere matter of taste but had a historical and philosophical basis. According to Rousseau, the French do not have, nor can they ever have, an expressive mode of singing, as their language does not allow it. Song survived only in Italy and in other southern countries, whose languages had preserved something of their primitive and original melodiousness.

In this context, opera finds a profound justification: it is no longer a genre among others, no longer the staging of unlikely events or a corrupt tragedy, but the only form in which music, or rather musicality, can in some way survive. For Rousseau, then, opera is not a more or less successful aggregate of diverse elements—music, poetry, painting, dance, etc.—but man's only complete and organic expression. It can exist only where the basic concept survives, where the thread that links heart and mind, music and language, is not yet totally severed. Italian *opera buffa,* which Rousseau could have known through the performances that the Italian troupe had brought to the Théâtre des Italiens in 1752, represents man's last chance, in the modern world, to preserve an authentic form of expression.

In the ancient world, the mythical reference point, for Rousseau as well as for all the Encyclopedists, there was Greek theater. Onto it were projected all the aesthetic ideals of the time, the desire for a strong and expressive art form embodying powerful collective ideals, for a music intimately united with poetry, for a total art form wherein words and music would be completely integrated. In the imagination of the *philosphes,* the music of Greek tragedy had all the fascination and power of the primitive: "Our music," Rousseau affirmed, "is without doubt more learned and more pleasant. However, I believe that Greek music was more expressive and more forceful . . . they only aimed at moving the soul, while we only desire to please the ear . . ." (article on *Music* in the *Encyclopédie*).

At the root of this idealization, however, there was not only an aesthetic, but also an ethico-political choice: if music in the form of song is man's most powerful means of expression and communication, it presupposes that it can only exist in a climate of freedom. In fact, music strengthens the meaning of language as a tool to address the masses. The decadence of music in his time, according to Rousseau, paralleled the crisis of society, of civil liberties, and of a democratic participation in life. The crisis affecting artistic modes of expression was not just an intrinsic phenomenon; it was also related to the changes taking place within society itself:[5]

> There are languages favorable to liberty; these are the sonorous, prosodic, harmonious languages, whose discourse may be recognized from a great distance. Our languages are suited to the buzzing voices of drawing-room society. . . . Among the ancients, it was easy to make oneself heard by the people on the public square; one could talk to them all day long without tiring. . . . Today, an academician who reads a paper in a public assembly is scarcely heard at the far end of the hall. . . . Therefore, I say that any language in which one cannot make oneself heard in a public gathering is a servile language; it is impossible for a people to speak that language and remain free.

This extension of an aesthetic and musical problem to the political sphere, in a broad sense, was not an isolated instance. Other Encyclopedists also followed Rousseau along this path, which, if examined closely, is linked to the

5. Ibid., ch. 20.

entire aesthetic tradition of the Enlightenment. Throughout the century it was always affirmed that art should not only entertain but also instruct. Therefore, music too was to have content and convey some message. Where music was thought to be insufficient, the lack was to be supplied by words. Rousseau's great revolution was to have pointed out this new direction to aesthetic intellectualism: it is true that art, to be such, must not be frivolous, but must contain a rich and expressive message; music and words are both inadequate in this respect. Free expression, which is proper to free men in an integrated society, proper to beings who are not divided and alienated in their faculties, can be achieved only through the modulated word, that is, through song, where music and words recover their original unity.

In this way, discussions of music and opera became far-reaching. Once having mythicized Greek democracy and popular theater as realized in ancient Athens, the next logical step was to criticize eighteenth-century society and the ancien régime, which had been undermined, well before the Revolution, by the seemingly harmless performances of the Bouffons. To be sure, *La serva padrona* became a myth, a standard-bearer, and today we can hardly believe how such a charming little opera, which moreover is similar to many other little works and intermezzos composed in the first half of the eighteenth century, could have divided France and taken on so many political, aesthetic, and philosophical implications. However, the potency of myths and symbols is beyond discussion: we can only acknowledge the power that certain apparently unimportant events have to become focuses of interests, meanings, experiences, and concepts far outstripping their real scope.

D'Alembert was still inclined to consider opera as a union of disparate elements, its success dependent primarily on the quality of its ingredients. Perhaps less interested than Rousseau in music, he nevertheless was acutely aware of the political significance of the musical *querelles* that enlivened his time. The relationship between music and freedom is central to his essay *De la liberté de la musique* (1759), in which he ironically observed that although difficult to believe, "in certain people's idiom, *bouffoniste,* republican, frondeur, atheist—I was about to forget materialist—are so many synonymous terms." However, irony aside, in the same essay he retraced the logic whereby the ruling class rejected the nimble, merry, disenchanted, often caustic intermezzos of the Italian comic troupes:[6]

> You are very shortsighted, our great politicians reply; all freedoms are linked together and are equally dangerous. Freedom of music presupposes that of feeling; freedom of feeling leads to that of thought; freedom of thought to that of action,

6. *De la liberté de la musique,* ch. 9.

and freedom of action is the ruin of nations. Let us therefore preserve opera as it is, if we wish to preserve the kingdom, and let us curb the license to sing, if we do not want the license to speak to follow soon after.

Here again the basic assumption is always the same, although the conclusions reached are different and new: art, and thus opera, is not and must not be an innocuous pastime, but it can be used for ends outside art, such as education, morality, and politics, and can thus become, for better or for worse, an instrument of power. Preference for either Italian or French opera, therefore, is not a mere matter of taste—for Dubos taste was not a matter for discussion—but a choice of sides: the ancien régime or democratic freedom, tyranny or freedom of expression.

More subtle and problematic, less keen on the *querelles* raging at the time, but more committed to investigation of the important ideological and philosophical themes of those years, is the figure of Diderot, the principal mind behind the awesome undertaking of the *Encyclopédie*. Conversant with music —among other things he was the author of all the entries on musical instruments in the *Encyclopédie*—Diderot tackled the problem of music from manifold perspectives, without, however, favoring any one in particular. On one hand, the problem of the origin of language and of the primordial nature of song fascinated him (see *Lettre sur les sourds et les muets*); on the other, he was aware that the pure language of sounds had its own expressive autonomy that had to be founded philosophically, and perhaps had its roots in the more obscure but deeper recesses of our being. In this respect, Diderot seems to waver between two explanations, only apparently contrasting. Recalling Leibniz's famous definition, "musica est exercitium arithmeticae occultum nescientis se numerare animi" (music is the hidden practice of arithmetic by a mind unaware that it is counting), Diderot delineated an aesthetics of beauty as perception of mathematical relations. He elaborated this theory in his *Principes généraux de la science du son,* and shortly afterwards in the entry on "Beauty" in the *Encyclopédie*. Harmony, which more than any other musical parameter reveals the mathematical side of music, was thus rescued precisely by an Encyclopedist from the disdain in which it was held by the *bouffonistes* and by the followers of Rousseau, who saw it as a symbol of dull French rationalism. The mathematical relations present in chords are not the result of abstract numerical formulas, nor the product of arid and hypertrophic reason: they are linked instead to unconscious elements, primordial relations that make up the original and instinctive part of our being. These are certainly closer to emotion than to discursive reason, if these two terms are really to be set in opposition.

To perceive such relations and thus to be a connoisseur of music does not mean to know, but rather to "feel" them. Therefore, the relations present in music seem to express the world and our being at the most elemental level, but also perhaps the deepest and most general one. Our perception of them brings us back to an original, direct, and immediate element, which is present before and beyond any linguistic convention.

Can we still say that music is an art that imitates the passions and emotions? Yes and no. In fact music, the art least tied to the appearances of the external world, "by showing objects less directly gives more power to our imagination" and "speaks more mightily to our soul" (*Lettre sur les sourds et les muets*).

If this is what the concept of "beauty as a perception of relations" means, it neither contrasts with nor diverges from the well-known evaluation of music as a "cri animal." All classicism has accustomed us to considering art and music as a function of civilization, as a triumph of progress, an expression of the age of Enlightenment. In the darkness of the Middle Ages, the arts languished and declined. With the spread of culture, progress, and the light of reason, the arts too flourished again and progressed. This was still Voltaire's perspective, but no longer that of Diderot and Rousseau. The arts, but especially music, are primitive man's most authentic mode of communication. Music and civilization diverge markedly; they certainly do not converge: "Poetry demands something enormous, barbarous, and wild," Diderot stresses in his *Discours sur la poésie dramatique*.

In his celebrated satire *Le Neveu de Rameau*, Diderot broadened his considerations on music as a "cri animal," forcefully underscoring his opposition to the poetics of classicism: "No expressions of wit, no epigrams, no seductive thoughts; all such things are too removed from genuine nature"; "only the animal cry of passion can dictate the line of thinking that suits us." Obviously, it is Italian music that takes on, for the last time before Gluck's reform, the role of genuine nature, which embodies the ideal of expressive truth, of the authenticity of the popular in opposition to the artificiality of the salons and the affectedness of the false and artificial pseudo-nature of the courts. It marks the definitive waning of the poetics of an ancient art, "of witty phrases, light, tender, and delicate madrigals" (*Le Neveu de Rameau*). The "cri animal" represents an appeal to nature as a vital force, as an unfettered outpouring of the instincts, an affirmation of the right to exist not only of the "strong passions," but also of the obscure animal core buried in man and hidden by the thick cloak of civilization.

Both Rousseau's thinking and that of Diderot radically transformed the way of conceiving music, its relation to words, and its social function. Undoubtedly, though, such a profound upsetting of musical categories, and not only of rationalism but also of eighteenth-century sensism and empiricism, had its roots in a totally new philosophy and conception of the world that paved the way for new ideals in the social and artistic sphere, as well as in that of thought. Not for nothing did Rousseau's thoughts on music, whether accepted or rejected, remain an explicit reference point throughout the second half of the eighteenth century, although no one developed them further in a significant way. As regards music, a Rousseauian school of sorts was to be formed, and would continue some features of the master's thinking, but usually uprooted from the ideological context that gave them meaning. Only the Sturm und Drang movement in Germany was to take up Rousseau's philosophy of music in a productive manner, developing it further and stamping it with new characteristics. These considerations, however, lead us beyond the chronological limits of our investigation.

Many other Encyclopedists were interested in music; they have left writings, critical essays, musical entries in the *Encyclopédie,* pamphlets, etc. Yet even if many gathered the innovative stimuli, present especially in the thinking of Rousseau and Diderot, few made contributions that were anything more than eclectic. They wavered between positions that were still conservative, and others that were closer to sensism and to the aesthetics of taste. The focus of interest continued to be opera, and even in this respect the positions assumed range from those, such as de Jaucourt or Cahusac, who still essentially considered opera as a heterogeneous spectacle, a more or less happy aggregate of parts that ought to strike a proper balance, to Grimm, who, closer to the spirit of Diderot and a fervent partisan of the *Bouffons,* took up the idea of the supremacy of music as the dramatic intensification of expression. Thus the work of the Encyclopedists is fundamental in order to understand problems concerning music around the middle of the century. Although not one of them was a professional musician, they all were competent connoisseurs, a qualification more than sufficient for them to feel authorized to take part in the debate. The 1,600 musical entries in the *Encyclopédie,*[7] in addition to the numerous other writings, often of remarkable literary quality, that appeared in those years, are all proof of how alive and important was the debate over problems relating to music, language, and opera, the latter being central to Enlightenment civilization. The Encyclopedists' thinking, in its variety and internal articulations, faithfully mirrors the contradictions and the ferment of those years of crisis and profound renewal in European thought preceding the Revolution.

Although as regards music France was undoubtedly the most fertile country in terms of developing a broad cultural debate, the other European countries also

---

7. Initially Rameau had been entrusted with writing the musical entries, but, as a result of disagreements with the Encyclopedists due to profound ideological differences, he gave up the assignment, which was then taken over by Rousseau.

contributed meaningfully and with originality. Albeit with less energy, Italy, Germany, England, and Spain each tackled the problems of music from different perspectives, referring back to their own cultural traditions, and becoming less involved in the *querelles* that so impassioned French men of culture.

Amidst the variety of positions, Italian culture for the most part remained anchored in the humanist tradition and in the concept of poetry's supremacy as an art form and as a privileged mode of expression. In this perspective, it becomes problematic to accept and justify opera, and even more so instrumental music, in theoretical terms. Curiously enough, it was eighteenth-century Italy that went down in history as the country of *bel canto* and one where the principal instrumental schools flourished. Yet it was not in general musicians who discussed musical matters—Benedetto Marcello and Giuseppe Tartini are among the few exceptions—but rather the literati. Although the numerous theaters were always packed, the austere Italian literati, from Muratori to Alfieri, seemed to scorn this frivolous, inane, and unedifying type of spectacle. Rarely did they come to a compromise, and even more rarely, perhaps with the sole exception of Verri, did they make an effort to understand and accept opera's artistic singularity. Basically, the Italian literati who wrote about music always considered opera as tragedy accompanied by music, that is, with an added element that was largely inessential if not disturbing. The intellectual element was closely joined to the moralistic one, as had already occurred with many French literati, and the boundaries between the two often became blurred. A rigidly rationalistic mentality perceives a basic incompatibility between poetry and music, inasmuch as the two art forms speak different languages: the former addresses reason, the latter the senses, and between the two no reconciliation is possible. After having attended an opera performance, Muratori felt duty-bound to deliver a judgment with censorial severity:

> The spectators are filled neither with solemnity nor with noble emotions, but only with a feminine softness, unworthy of virile spirits and of wise and valorous people. . . . Certainly, modern theatrical music is supremely harmful to the morals of those who, in listening to it, become increasingly base and inclined to lasciviousness.

This rigorously moralistic stricture was combined with an intellectual one not dissimilar to that already sounded by Saint-Évremond, Boileau, Fontenelle, etc. Furthermore, Muratori's fear of the harmful effect of theatrical music did not conceal his awareness of opera's power to pervert. Opera is absurd because it is not realistic, obviously according to the criteria of reason:[8]

---

8. *Della perfetta poesia italiana*, bk. 3, ch. 5.

Now, when are men ever seen singing in the midst of their activities and while engaged in serious matters? Is it humanly likely that a person, beset by anger, full of sorrow or anguish, or talking seriously about his affairs, can sing? If such behavior is not in keeping with the way people really behave, what can come of it on the stage, where nature and man's true actions and habits are to be imitated as far as possible?

Gian Vincenzo Gravina was not much kinder to opera, even though he cherished a mythical Greek tragedy in which entertainment and instruction were on an equal plane, and where the functions of poet and musician did not conflict, as was the case in the corrupt theater of his time. This corruption arose above all from what could be called an eclipse of reason in favor of pleasure, the latter understood as a primary and self-sufficient element: ". . . Pleasure today is produced first of all by the lack of the true idea, and then incidentally by any movement of voice capable of enticing and appeasing man's animal nature, which is sense alone, without the participation of reason . . ." (*Della tragedia*).

Among these criticisms on the literary side, which all tended in the same direction, the satirical pamphlet *Il teatro alla moda* of Benedetto Marcello, one of the few voices representing the musical camp, stands out. Well known in its own century and beyond, even today it can confound our attempts to understand the real scope and importance of operatic performances. In fact, although Marcello aims his barbs against the degeneration of operatic theater, we must not be led to think that the latter was reduced to the degraded portrayal that emerges from his caustic satire. *Il teatro alla moda* spares no one. Ignorant poets, presumptuous musicians, vain singers, greedy impresarios all contribute to create a kind of performance that lacks unity and is shoddily put together only to whet the most undiscerning appetites of an ill-educated public. Yet it suffices to think of librettists like Zeno, and especially Metastasio, to understand that, despite widespread immorality in the domain of opera, there existed in and outside Italy, especially at the Viennese court, a theater that embodied a sober awareness of the peculiar nature of this complex but unique representational genre. Thus it is precisely opera's special theatrical reality—the subtle dialectic between what is realistic and what is not, the imaginary space created by the absurd events contained in librettos that acquires meaning uniquely in the sphere of music—that proved difficult if not impossible to understand in the rationalistic and humanistic mentality of Italian intellectuals, for whom the language of poetry was after all the only form of expression allowed in the realm of the fine arts. Poetry was a supremely privileged mode of expression because it clearly and manifestly evinced its relationship to reason, and therefore its moral content, its edifying and pedagogical design.

Only in the writings appearing in the second half of the century do new ideals begin, albeit timidly, to surface. They are attempts to create conceptual and aesthetic structures that would make it possible to accept and better understand opera and, to a lesser degree, instrumental music. Among the Encyclopedists, Rousseau was perhaps the most widely read on matters musical, and his influence began to make itself felt. The interest of literati such as Algarotti, Planelli, Eximeno, and Arteaga continued to focus on opera, on agreement or disagreement as regards its components, on comparisons between the Greek and the modern theater. Eximeno and Arteaga were Spanish, but, having been expelled from their country of origin because they were Jesuits, they are properly considered as belonging to Italian culture. Nevertheless, some of the writings of these literati began to show the influence of new perspectives imported from beyond the Alps, such as Condillac's sensism, the aesthetics of feeling, English empiricism, and, last but not least, interest in mathematics and in problems related to harmonic theory, after the example of Euler and Rameau.

The venerable Padre Martini of Bologna, although moving within an ambit of erudition that at times was an end in itself, had already manifested interests diverging rather markedly from the Italian tradition. No longer was opera at the center of his attention, but the music of the ancients, the rules that governed the glorious polyphonic tradition, the very origin of music. His work displays an even keener interest as regards the beginning of musical historiography. Giuseppe Tartini, the great composer and theorist, had a more modern approach. The inspiration underlying his impressive treatises is quite similar to that of Rousseau: music and harmony—which constitutes its basic structure— are governed by natural laws and consequently rest on precise, eternal, and unchangeable mathematical formulae. Therefore, the fundamentals of the music of the Greeks must be the same as those of his time. This interest in the mathematical foundation of music, which also led to important discoveries such as the so-called "combination tone" (resulting from the simultaneous generation of two other sounds having a frequency equal to the difference in frequency between the generating sounds), places Tartini in a sphere far removed from that of the literati of his time. The center of his attention was no longer on opera, on problems inherent in the encounter between poetry and music, on the *querelles* that so impassioned his contemporaries, but rather on the nature of sound, on instrumental music, of which he was one of the most fertile authors, on compositional techniques, embellishment, harmony, and so forth. Approximately at the same time, another instrumental composer, Francesco Geminiani, wrote theoretical treatises on problems related to performance practice and the use of instruments (*Regole per suonare con buon gusto*, 1739; *L'arte di suonare il violino*, 1740; *L'arte dell'accompagnamento*, 1755–56), pointing to and confirming the existence—albeit marginal—of interests in Italy (the homeland of Humanism) that were not linked to opera.

Yet the mainstream of Italian musical culture was still derived from literature. Men with a humanistic background, such as Algarotti and Planelli, were to direct their attention to opera, forgoing, however, the moralistic acrimony of Muratori or Gravina. Rejection was replaced by cautious acceptance. One now spoke of reforming opera, of correcting abuses, of limiting excesses, while at the same time hoping that the poets would keep theatrical performances under control. Greek theater continued to be cited as an unsurpassable model, to which all were to look, albeit with the awareness of its unattainability. But the Greek model mythicized by Rousseau and, in part, by Grimm, d'Alembert, and other Encyclopedists, was not that of the Italian literati. The latter saw in Greek theater not so much the triumph of democracy, the voice of the people extended freely in the huge open amphitheaters beneath the Mediterranean sun, or the triumph of original expression intact in its power of persuasion, but rather its solid plot structure and its manner of keeping music in check, not indulging the virtuosity of the singers, and above all subordinating it to the dramatic intentions of the tragedian. Music, therefore, was to be accepted and recognized; it was no longer to be exorcised but led back to its function as an accompaniment to words.

All speak of "abuses," which compromise imitation, as the virtuous aim of tragedy; but once composers were again instructed in the proper use of their art, the abuses would be eliminated. Unfortunately, Algarotti affirmed in his *Saggio sopra l'opera in musica* (1755), composers today "cannot conceive of the idea of subordination, and that the greatest effect of music derives from its being subordinated and ancillary to poetry." The concept of music and poetry as having a common origin in an original human form of expression is one Algarotti barely touches on, but he fails to draw the necessary conclusions from it; at best, the concept is used to overcome the current prejudice against lack of realism, of which opera had been accused for so many decades. If it is true that to die while singing can seem absurd, all things considered, it is almost equally absurd to die while reciting verses! The lack of realism in such a situation is heightened only by music that does not "suit" the poetry. In laying down the criteria of this so-called "suitability," which only means subordination, the "dependence of Lully on Quinault, and Vinci on Metastasio," it is difficult not to think of the future reform of opera that Calzabigi and Gluck were to carry out in the years immediately following.

If the general tone of Algarotti's essay still remains linked to a rationalistic mentality, which essentially views opera as "tragedy recited through music," Antonio Planelli's essay *Dell'opera in musica* (1772) is undoubtedly closer to the spirit of Gluck's reform and to the ideas of the Encyclopedists. In fact, Planelli presents ideas that are much more advanced in respect to those of his predecessors. By now, Gluck's reform had become a reality, the authority of which was felt not only in France, thus bringing about with artistic effectiveness many of the Encyclopedists' ideals. Planelli drew from it its most important feature: opera's most characteristic dimension, the expression of pathos. For Planelli, the function of criticism and the elimination of "abuses" was not that of heightening the poets' verses, but of exalting the "style of theater music," which "is bound to sustain the words and to move the emotions." Such a style consisted in avoiding too many notes, useless ornaments, bravura vocal pieces, repetition within arias, notes that go either too high or too low, all with the aim of giving drama "greater strength," while rendering the "pathetic element," the basic component of theatrical style, with the greatest effectiveness.

Calzabigi's famous preface to *Alceste,* written under Gluck's name a few years earlier, in 1769, although extremely concise, says nothing different, but it defines with great precision the main points of their reformist platform and its justifications. They too wanted to proscribe "abuses." By then there was a set repertory so that one knew in advance what the "abuses" were: "da capo" arias that interrupt the action and the flow of expression in the moments that ought to be most intense and charged with emotion; "breaks that are too abrupt" between arias and recitatives; unjustified virtuoso pieces unrelated to the action; overtures that do not "presage the subject," etc. There was nothing particularly new in the guidelines of this "reform"; it echoes the problems bemoaned by Benedetto Marcello half a century earlier, along with all the ills that beset Italian opera. What had changed was the way of considering music, which was no longer, as Algarotti said, "subordinated and ancillary to poetry," but an "art that must help poetry strengthen the expression of emotions and bolster interest in the situations."

Previously, in other writings echoing Rousseau's ideas, Calzabigi hinted at an intrinsic musicality of poetry, which the musician need only rediscover, exalt and stress. In a letter to the *Mercure de France* in 1784 he affirmed:

> The only music that befits dramatic poetry, and especially the aria and dialogue that we call action, is that which to a greater extent suits a natural, animated, and energetic declamation. In itself, declamation is only imperfect music. We could truly notate it only after having devised a sufficient number of musical signs capable of rendering the almost infinite variety of tones, inflections, raisings, lowerings, and nuances the voice assumes when declaiming . . .

These, Calzabigi added, are the guiding ideas of his reform, and correspond to the task that he assigned to Gluck, and which the latter musician diligently carried out.

Not only Rousseau, but also Diderot and Grimm appear in these pages of Gluck's libretto; and Gluck also seems to concur with the basic ideas of the Encyclopedists: "The union between words and song," he writes, "must be so close that the poetry has to appear to have been patterned on the music no less than the music on the poetry" (Gluck's open letter to La Harpe, in the *Journal de Paris*, 1777). If, on one hand, the idea of opera as an art endowed with its own specific sphere of action (what Planelli was effectively to designate as the "pathetic" element, which has its own intrinsic coherence, wherein music and poetry are intimately fused and subservient to theatrical and operatic expression) undoubtedly derives from the Encyclopedists; on the other, that of a powerful art, charged and pregnant with meaning and deeply touching the heart, together with the desire to do away with the "abuses," derives from the Italian humanistic tradition.

Ideally, Gluck's and Calzabigi's reformist ideas were an attempt to go beyond the traditional *querelles*, accepting and assimilating the criticism that practically all eighteenth-century intellectuals leveled at opera. At the same time, however, they yielded neither to the temptations of simple moralistic censure, as Alfieri would still do in his famous preface to *Abele*, nor to the traditional concept of opera as a debased version of tragedy. By now, after Rousseau, opera had carved a significant niche for itself, even in aesthetic and philosophical terms. Consequently, the polemic on whether music was superior to poetry, or vice versa, had lost meaning, in the same way as the polemic on the superiority of melody or harmony. Music and poetry represented the dismembered parts of an organic body that recovered its lost unity in drama. Therefore, the last *querelle*, that between the followers of Gluck and Piccinni, appears slightly artificial, a resurfacing of old themes and arguments already supplanted by new ideas and the new theater.

Strangely, in this last *querelle* the traditional positions between the supporters of Italian music (this time it was that of Piccinni) and the supporters of French music (now that of Gluck) seem completely reversed. The former assumed the role of traditionalists, the latter that of innovators. Instead of Gluck's dramatic intentions and his "strong art," which derived from the harshness and expressive power of Greek tragedy, Piccinni's supporters preferred the classical ideals of a beautiful and polished art that moved the soul without troubling it, essentially an art diametrically opposed to Diderot's "cri animal." La Harpe and Marmontel championed this latter sweetened and softened version of Italian *bel canto*, and Piccinni had to assume a position that perhaps did not really suit him. La Harpe asserted that he did not want "to go to the theater to listen to a man who is suffering," and if a scene truly required a grieving man, it was up to the composer to find "sorrowful but not unpleasant accents, capable of gratifying the ear while insinuating themselves into the heart" (*Journal de politique et de littérature*, October, 1777).

Gluck and his supporters, in the wake of the Encyclopedists, chose instead an all-engaging art, one that would constitute an authentic message conveying true and therefore strong emotions, without fearing to border on ugliness, since what they aimed at was not the beautiful but the expressive.

It was no longer the sanguine Italian *opera buffa* that embodied such ideals. Compared with the times of *La serva padrona*, Italian comic opera had now fallen in line; and toward the end of the century it had become a soft, drawing-room sort of bel canto, with no harshness or roughness, nor with any polemic undertones either in the libretto or in the music. "Opera," as Marmontel effectively put it, "is the theater of illusions, and of pleasant illusions." Thus the ideal of neoclassical beauty, embodied in the melodious, polished, and sweet singing of late eighteenth-century Italian comic operas, is confirmed. The powerful and incisive expression of Gluck's post-reform operas is quite removed from this model. Tragedy "in its austerity is not suited to opera," Marmontel added, thus defining this disagreement with Gluck and confirming a traditional ideal of French and Italian classicism, according to which music's function remains that of pleasing. It is an inessential and ornamental art, and as such is fit for subjects that are light and of scant intellectual content. Serious and demanding subjects, and tragic theater with its austere rituals, must not be contaminated by this inherently frivolous art, which is more suited to the tenuous, graceful, and drawing-room-like plots of Italian comic opera, meant to please, to delight the ear and the heart, and certainly not to express dynamically man's great emotional conflicts.

The last *querelle* marks the close of a historical period in eighteenth-century thought and musical culture. It has been noted that Gluck's and Piccinni's supporters inverted the roles traditionally held by the advocates of French and Italian music; perhaps it would be more accurate to say that the so-called reform of Gluck and Calzabigi incorporated the most valid and vital aspects of both sides. Classicists and innovators, rationalists and empiricists, French and Italian taste are all reconciled, and the positive seeds that took more than a century to germinate come to fruition in Gluckian opera. Precisely because his personality typified the century in which he lived, in light of his conciliatory role, the *querelle* occasioned by his music was also the most artificial and unimportant. The classicists, those who rejected the hedonism that to a great extent characterized eighteenth-century theater and the theatrical mores it engendered, could by then identify with Gluck. But also the innovators, who rejected "tragedy recited through music," preferring musical drama in which music and poetry could recover their original and natural unity, in which the spectators' deepest emotions would be engaged, and in which emotions would be authentic, instead of frigid inventions, found that their aspirations were fully realized in Gluckian opera. In fact, all expressed satisfaction, from the classicist and rationalist Voltaire to Rousseau and Grimm.

Gluck, however, closed an age; he did not pave the way for new ideas. Mozart, instead, was the one to mark a new direction for opera. Although he left very few theoretical guidelines, his operas from *Don Giovanni* to the *Magic Flute* are in themselves sufficiently eloquent for us to perceive the dawning of a new era. The problems of Romantic opera are of another type, and Mozart's last works go beyond the traditional distinction between comic and serious opera, the logic of which is still fully accepted by Gluck.

If the *querelles* occupied a place of prime importance, both quantitatively and qualitatively, in the realm of significant eighteenth-century musical literature (particularly Italian and French), other interests, destined to prove fruitful in the following decades, are revealed upon closer scrutiny of the century's musical literature. First of all, the importance of the birth of musical historiography should be stressed; in the beginning timid and uncertain, as it developed it became more lively and fully conscious. It is well known that music, among the arts, is the one in which, for a variety of more or less evident reasons, an awareness of its own history develops later. The loss of all ancient Greek and Roman music, the problems linked to deciphering medieval and Renaissance music, and especially the fact that musical compositions were destined to be short-lived contributed to rendering a reconstruction of the historic fabric of a fragmentary and obscure past all the more difficult. The eighteenth century still required composers to produce material in great quantity, meant to be consumed immediately and then forgotten. It suffices to recall that Charles Burney, one of the first great music historians, on a trip to Italy in 1772 was unable to collect any evidence in Venice, either direct or indirect, of the existence of Vivaldi. The first music histories, therefore, sprang from virgin soil. There was no musical tradition to refer back to, nor were there any points of reference. Consequently, the need to trace a musical history of the past, with the available means, and to draw a qualitative comparison between the music of the present and that of the past, developed concomitantly with the *querelle des anciens et des modernes*. Furthermore, the notion of progress championed by Enlightenment figures provided further impetus for historical research. The fact that music was also subject to this universal tendency sparked interest and curiosity aimed at understanding just what musical progress consisted of, and on what its superiority over that of the past should be based. This new discipline developed on a limited scale, hesitantly and informally in the first half of the century, in Italy, France, England, and Germany. It gained momentum in the second half of the century, and during the Romantic era it crystallized into a true and proper discipline.

The first attempts at historiography of music are to be found in treatises on a very wide variety of topics. Within this welter of facts, especially as regards more remote periods, there is a wealth of fanciful or even mythical accounts. The latter, however, are significant in their own right, although they do not provide information in the modern sense of the term. Among the first histories of this type, at the beginning of the century, the one left unfinished by Bourdelot and continued by his nephew Jacques Bonnet deserves to be mentioned. Aware of the novelty of his undertaking, Bonnet naively writes in his preface that no one "has ventured to write the history of music . . . either because of the uncertainty of success, or for want of having thought to do so, which has reduced me to writing it solely according to the rules of common sense." Perhaps common sense is not enough for a budding science. In fact, the themes preferred by these pioneer historians are the pseudo-historical problem of the origin of music on one hand, and, on the other, after rapidly traversing the millennia, the comparison between French and Italian music. About fifty years after these first attempts at music historiography, we already find the first truly erudite studies of a more or less remote historical past, which reveal genuine historical research. The material culled by many foreign travelers, especially in Italy, proved particularly useful as an initial collection of data for subsequent historians. Italy, in fact, was a veritable mecca, attracting an uninterrupted flow of people no longer in search only of ancient Greco-Roman artistic traces, but also of the much more recent and current musical events for which the country of bel canto had made such a reputation for itself in Europe. Travel accounts such as those by de Brosses, Sharp, Delalande, Reichardt, and others provide a wealth of information, especially in terms of the historical reconstruction of the most up-to-date music.

Among the true historians of the second half of the eighteenth century, that is, among the founders of history understood in modern terms as methodological research into the past, it is possible to distinguish two different attitudes, which in turn also produced two different results. On one hand, there were those who, not at all bedazzled by the wisdom of the present, both out of taste and ideological choice held up the music of the past as an unsurpassable model, and especially as source of those rules that had governed and would always govern music composed according to the correct criteria of good taste. On the other hand, there were those who believed in the victorious and unstoppable development of progress; they were confident in the enlightened civilization of the present, which would forever dispel the barbarous obscurity of the past. Obviously, such different attitudes would give rise to equally different types of history. Padre Martini, the learned Bolognese musician, a lover of antiquity and admirer of severe polyphonic rigor, was among the pioneers of the new discipline and has left us a monumental history of music in three volumes. Published respectively in 1757, 1770, and in 1781, these volumes constitute a typical example of the first manner of understanding music and its history.

Padre Martini's lengthy and painstaking work, which was to have comprised a complete history of music, from its origins to his own time, not surprisingly did not go beyond the section devoted to the ancients; as a man of great erudition, his preference lay here, especially since he believed it represented the eternal foundation for all other kinds of music. Significantly, he conducted his research mainly using the texts of the ancient theorists. (The rich library Padre Martini left is still preserved in Bologna.) With his third volume, Martini's history only got as far as the music of the Jews in the Temple! However, in his *Esemplare, ossia saggio fondamentale pratico di contrappunto sopra il canto fermo* (1774–75), he extended his field of investigation to counterpoint, his favorite subject, and to the Palestrina style. In the same vein as Padre Martini's antiquarian learning is the research of Martin Gerbert, who, among other things, has left us a monumental collection of documentary sources concerning medieval music. This work, *Scriptores ecclesiastici de musica sacra, potissimum ex variis Italiae, Galliae et Germaniae codicibus manuscriptis collecti et nunc primum publica luce donati* (1784), continues to be of fundamental importance. Gerbert, like Padre Martini opposed to the Enlightenment, was more interested in the remote and dark Middle Ages than in the sparkling galant and rococo music of his day.

This is not the place to mention the many authors who, even in treatises not specifically devoted to music history, have nevertheless left evidence and research that has proved helpful to subsequent scholars, such as Marpurg, Mattheson, Charles-Henri de Blainville (*Histoire générale critique et philologique de la musique,* 1767), etc. It is more worthwhile to focus our attention on three major late eighteenth-century historians: Charles Burney and John Hawkins, both English, and Johann Nikolaus Forkel, a German. Burney's *General History of Music from the Earliest Ages to the Present Period,* in four volumes (1776–89), and Hawkins's *General History of the Science and Practice of Music,* in five volumes (1776), constitute the two major works that are usually contrasted, at times in too Manichean a fashion, because of their basically different approaches. They are to be considered the first true and proper music histories, in the modern sense of the term: not anecdotal, but systematic, they cover history in its entirety, from the ancients down to the authors' own time, even though the attention they devote to different historical periods varies greatly. Both works are based on an explicitly stated methodology and serve as models for the future development of music historiography. Although exactly contemporary, they develop from contrasting historical perspectives. Burney's work is informed by an empirical outlook, by a lively curiosity about music and the manifestations of culture and customs associated with it throughout history, by the desire to have first-hand knowledge of everything he was to be a witness to, and to listen to as much music as possible. As a convinced advocate of the age of reason and of the progress of music, he was led to pay proportionately greater attention to the music that was closer to his time. Such an ideological and existential approach brought him, already advanced in years, to face the discomfort and adventures of a long voyage that was to take him, on two different itineraries, across all of Europe in search of musical scores and documents. He committed himself to listening to every type of music, from peasant songs in the country to the leading singers in the most important theaters, from the refined musical concerts in aristocratic salons to the orphan girls of Neapolitan and Venetian conservatories. The concept of progress represents both the guiding principle and the unifying element of his broad research. In fact, in his four volumes his narrative becomes broader, clearer, and progressively more descriptive as he approaches his own period than was the case in times past. What makes this work modern is his vision of music not as a science, but rather as a culture, solidly integrated in its social, political, and historical context. Such a perspective explains the author's keen interest in all elements related to music: audience, performers, lives of composers, publishers, conservatories, patronage, etc. Complementary to his history of music are the two diaries he wrote during his musical travels: *The Present State of Music in Italy and France* and *The Present State of Music in Germany, the Netherlands and United Provinces*, from which emerge with even greater clarity and spontaneity, in the freshness of his diary jottings, his humanistic and historical vision of music.

The complete title of John Hawkins's *History* is in itself an indication of the different orientation of Burney's major rival. No longer simply a "general history of music," Hawkins's title includes "of the science and practice," thereby adding an element, science, that is totally absent from Burney's studies. "The principles of harmony," Hawkins claims, "are general and universal . . . the proportions in which it consists are to be found in those material forms, which are beheld with the greatest pleasure . . . and constitute what we call symmetry, beauty, and regularity" (Preliminary discourse). Even though he claims to believe in progress and in creative genius, his musical history, in keeping with the above mentioned principles, unfolds according to proportions and criteria quite the reverse of Burney's. What really interests Hawkins is the music of the past; he devotes much greater attention to it than to the music of his day, for which he has little liking. The laws governing musical science are more easily found in the great models of the past than in the frivolous music of his time. Therefore, his *General History* is based more on books, treatises, and data culled from other texts than from direct sources. It is not for nothing that Hawkins never thought of going on musical travels to listen to new music and gather data firsthand.

Despite these profound differences in the basic criteria that guided the two rival musicologists, their works—one a product of an empiricist mentality, the other of a rationalistic approach—remain monumental and mark the beginning of a new school. Even today, after more than two centuries, their respective *General History* can still be read with interest. Furthermore, they strike the reader as being modern history texts, and as such quite different from the primitive, abstract, and mythological approaches of their predecessors.

A few years later, the German musicologist and composer, Johann Nikolaus Forkel, published his *Allgemeine Geschichte der Musik* (1788–1801). Forkel was very familiar with Burney's and Hawkins's works, and made good use of them. His *Allgemeine Geschichte,* however, is already pre-Romantic. Unfortunately, this important work was never completed and does not extend beyond the Renaissance. Of the third volume, which was to complete his historical outline up to his time, there remains a biography of Bach, the composer Forkel considered as the model of musical genius, thereby anticipating the coming Bach revival of the Romantic era. What is striking in the first two published volumes is the work's extraordinary scope, which includes all music history from its mythical beginnings. Steeped in Encyclopedist culture, in English sensism as well as German rationalism, Forkel combined both orientations, thus laying the foundations for an approach that divides history into major periods (as will be customary in the Romantic era), placed in succession and progression towards artistic perfection, which is realized in close connection and collaboration with all the other arts and with human civilization in its entirety. "Arts and sciences grow to perfection, like all creations of nature, only step by step," Forkel wrote in the introduction to his history, where he delineated the three ages of music. However, it is not as important to follow these rather fanciful divisions as it is to understand the guiding ideas behind this concept. Familiar with the ideas of Rousseau, Forkel translated the principle of the original unity of music and language into a historical category, suitable for interpreting music's development throughout civilization. "The surest guide in this investigation," Forkel continued in his introduction, "may be offered by the similarity traceable between man's language and his music, which reaches back not only to their origins but extends throughout their entire development from their beginning to their highest perfection." Rousseau's concept of the positive mythicizing of origins is transformed here through the Enlightenment and Romantic concept of a necessary and uninterrupted process of perfection, which should carry humanity and its loftiest expressions—such as music—to ever higher goals. Thus, the various elements that make up music—rhythm, melody, and harmony— are no longer placed on an abstract scale of values, but viewed in terms of a progressive historical development in which, over the three ages, they become reciprocally integrated in ever more complete and expressive forms.

With Forkel, historiography left its infancy behind and opened itself to new and more complex points of view. There are several reasons why Forkel's work is already closer to early Romanticism than to the age of Enlightenment. This is

due not so much to the results he reaches as to his general approach, the unprecedented attention he devotes to the major creative figures, the homogeneous
nature of his method and his way of dividing history into epochs, which, rather
than hearkening back to Vico's cyclic vision of historical development, seem to
foreshadow Hegel's dialectical triads. Indeed, the stimulating ideas already contained in Forkel's *Allgemeine Geschichte der Musik* were to be further developed
by German musicology and historiography.

In the eighteenth century, critical and historical musical research developed not
only through the abovementioned major works, not only in the myriad polemical pamphlets and treatises of every nature and kind, but also through nascent newspaper criticism. It suffices to recall Addison's *Spectator* at the beginning of the century, the Verri brothers' *Il Caffè*, or the numerous French
newspapers and magazines, such as the famed *Mercure de France* or the *Journal
de Paris*, or the even more significant exclusively musical magazines, such as
Hamburg's famous *Der critische Musikus* (1737–40), edited by Johann Adolf
Scheibe. Such writings, prompted by particular occasions and related interests,
at times gave rise to new themes, which were then further expanded upon in
subsequent essays and treatises, no less significant and stimulating. If these occasional writings in Italy, France, and England were mostly connected to the
usual themes of the by now well-known *querelles*, in Germany new topics arose,
which would be developed further only later. Instrumental music had only
occasionally aroused the attention of a few theorists, such as Rameau, Euler,
Tartini, Padre Martini, and a few others who were profoundly interested in
problems of harmony and its underlying mathematical structure. Men of culture devoted scant attention to the subject. Perhaps the only exception was Germany, where, parallel to an opera tradition mostly imported from Italy, an
ancient and strict instrumental tradition still prevailed. But what distinguished
German musical culture was not only the existence of an impressive performance tradition, which could also be found in Italy, but also a theoretical and
didactic interest in it. The Lutheran tradition had to a large extent freed music
in general from the prevalent moralistic fetters that still obtained in Italy. Consequently, men of culture and musicians themselves could express interest in
instrumental music, not only from its didactic and pedagogical aspects, but also
its attendant philosophical and aesthetic problems, without being subject to
self-criticism.

Therefore, the panorama presented by German musical literature was somewhat anomalous with respect to the other European countries. The scant interest
in the traditional problems of opera and in the *querelle* raging between Italians
and French was offset by a keen interest in the many aspects of instrumental
music. Above all, there was greater consideration of the technical problems con-

nected with music, both as regards composition and performance. Thus, it is not surprising that the best-known *querelle* to be debated in Germany, that between J. S. Bach's supporters and his adversaries, focused more on technical and stylistic points than on philosophical and ideological ones. The debate in fact developed between those who favored the contrapuntal style and those who instead preferred the new harmonic-melodic style and its manifestation in the galant and rococo styles. This is not to say that ideological motivations were absent from these two positions; it is simply that, for the most part, they were implied and rarely made explicit. Johann Mattheson's numerous writings (see especially *Der vollkommene Capellmeister*, 1739, a compendium of all the musical knowledge of the time), those by Friedrich W. Marpurg, founder of the magazine *Der kritische Musicus an der Spree* (1749–50), and especially those by Johann Adolph Scheibe, editor of the weekly *Der critische Musikus* (1737–40), offer rich documentation of the diverse cultural climate that enlivened the German musical world. Scheibe's violent polemics with Bach are particularly significant. While acknowledging Bach's great accomplishments as an organist and harpsichord virtuoso, Scheibe challenged his talent as a composer. In Scheibe's opinion, Bach lacked pleasantness and naturalness; his music was dominated by "artfulness," an art perhaps "too great," to the point of becoming "obscure."

Bach was out of step with his time and was accused, in the name of reason, or rather, of reasonableness, of being an old-fashioned composer. Because of his austere religiosity and his contrapuntal style, he was charged with being anchored to the canons of an art that was by then outmoded, and which at any rate had lost ground to the competition of the younger and more aggressive musicians of the time, such as Graun, Hasse, Quantz, Mattheson, Telemann, and others, whose fame was then so much greater than Bach's.

The poetics of simplicity, of easy sentimentalism, of melody with uncomplicated harmonization, of galant pleasantness undoubtedly prevailed at midcentury. This drawing-room musical ideal, in which melody prevails over harmony, and all the more so over counterpoint (which by then served merely as learned quotation), was favorably received by German musicians and theorists of the eighteenth century. In light of this ideal, and in accordance with the Doctrine of the Affections (*Affektenlehre*), the musicians' aim was to imitate and represent emotions by means of suitable melodic figures capable of moving the listener. Bach's case became a mere polemical reference point useful to assert contrasting musical and aesthetic ideals. Arguments not dissimilar to those put forward by Scheibe are to be found in the writings of Mattheson, who was particularly fond of "reasonable music," which, precisely on this account, can "touch the heart."

Their aesthetic horizons and orientations in terms of taste were not very different from those of French critics and musicians of the same years. What differed was the particular focus on instrumental music, considered as completely autonomous and a self-sufficient expressive mode, capable of imitating affections and conveying emotions and sentiments. In reality, the *Affektenlehre* was not new, as it had already formed the basis for the Florentine Camerata's poetics of opera, founded by Bardi with Galilei and Caccini. What was new was that this theory was now applied to instrumental music, which was considered as having fully come of age and therefore capable of imitating and representing the entire range of the emotions, and thus of moving the listener without the support of poetry and dramatic action. The *Affektenlehre* is not to be found so much in treatises on aesthetics dedicated to the subject as it is in numerous pedagogical treatises on instrumental performance. If we read the *Versuch einer Anweisung die Flöte traversiere zu spielen* (1752) by Johann Joachim Quantz, the famous flutist, composer, and performer at the court of Frederick the Great of Prussia, or the essay *Versuch über die wahre Art das Clavier zu spielen* (1753–62) by Carl Philipp Emanuel Bach, one of Bach's sons, or the *Versuch einer gründlichen Violinschule* (1756) by Leopold Mozart, Wolfgang's father, we become aware that the detailed instructions about performance practice are never an end in themselves, but are intimately linked not only to a theory of interpretation, but also to an entire aesthetic based on the *Affektenlehre*.

Although the taste of these composers was clearly oriented toward the galant or rococo style, it did not prevent them from transcending the circumstances of their time. Quantz's treatise is particularly interesting precisely because of his specifically aesthetic observations. According to Quantz, the only sure guide to assessing art objects, and music in particular, is "good taste." Nothing, however, is more difficult to define. In the language of the time, "good taste" is everything that runs counter to rules and tradition; it is everything that refers to the rights of the individual and his freedom to judge, to the validity of feeling and of impressions against the empty universality of reason. This, however, did not prevent Quantz from giving advice and providing, if not rigid rules, at least precise directions to composers and performers, ever mindful of the principle that the ultimate aim of music is to arouse the listener's emotions and passions. Both the composer and the performer can properly achieve this aim by observing certain rules suggested by "good taste," such as a judicious amount of contrasts, proper balance among the various parts, avoidance of excesses, particularly counterpoint, which is conceived "more for the eye than for the ear." This typically Enlightenment ideal of music, representing a compromise between Italian and French tastes, between the excessive learning and severity of old-fashioned counterpoint and the frivolity of certain rococo music, overladen with useless and arbitrary embellishments, was typical of German taste; it was an ideal advocated by most German treatise writers around the middle of the century. This ambition to achieve a supranational music, profiting from the best accomplishments of the various schools (d'Alembert had previously expressed the same ambition), was in line with the cosmopolitan ideals of progress and good taste pursued by all cultivated men of every country.

In this respect, the essay of Carl Philipp Emanuel Bach mentioned earlier is also extremely interesting, although it focuses mainly on interpretation. The performer's aim is to reveal "the true content and emotion of a composition" to the listener. This can happen only if the performer is able to identify with the emotions that the composer wanted to represent. Therefore, even if there are many rules governing correct performance, and even if much advice can be given the performer, only if the latter "feels" the emotions of the music can he execute with "good taste" that which constitutes its meaning. Only in this way can the performer avoid lowering himself to the rank of those "who do nothing more than play notes." Thus there arose the concept of something lying beyond and below the notes, which only an act of empathy, first by the performer and then by the listener, could discover and bring out. It was an intuition all the more important and revolutionary if applied to instrumental music, which was by tradition asemantic and insignificant, or, at best, an inessential embellishment.

In this variegated panorama of eighteenth-century musical culture, which only a superficial and hasty glance can view as uniform and monothematic, there were essentially two significant paths that music would follow on its way toward Romanticism. On one hand, there was Rousseau and his fundamental intuition that music is a part of man's original expressive mode, one that rational civilization threatens to destroy. On the other, there were the various investigations of instrumental language, aimed at discovering the origins of its self-sufficiency, its meaning, and the reasons for its autonomy. Romantic thought, in parallel with the development of instrumental music and with the invention of the more complex and articulated modes of Classical sonata form, would develop these themes both from a literary and a philosophical perspective. Yet it would always be indebted to the rich musical heritage that eighteenth-century Europe bequeathed to the world born of the French Revolution and of Sturm und Drang.

*Historically, the beginnings of instr. involvement in "emotions" lie in the moth openings?

Chapter One

The First Polemics on Opera in Italy

IT IS SYMPTOMATIC THAT Italian literati, like the French, devoted some attention to music and to opera in their works on tragedy. Evidently, opera was considered a sub-species of tragedy, and music an ingredient of this strange and corrupt theatrical form of modern times. Comparison with ancient tragedy was usual and modern opera commonly appeared as a debased version of ancient theater. Thus Gravina considered the spectacle of opera as an "empire of the senses," and music as being largely responsible for this barbarizing process.

The idea that animated ancient tragedy had been lost, and poetry and music had been corrupted to such an extent as to have become sterile. The moderns had given up the concept of "imitation," and pleasure no longer derived from it, but now issued from "any vocal modulation capable of enticing and appeasing man's animal nature," that is, "sense alone, without the participation of reason."

Muratori's attack on opera appears even more radical. The selection chosen from his vast work entitled *Della perfetta poesia italiana* stresses, with particular emphasis, his moral condemnation of a theatrical form based on lasciviousness, not only from an ethical but also from an intellectual standpoint. No reform is possible because opera is corrupt to its very foundations. Poetry cannot and must not be mixed with music, since the latter, as is well known, provides only delight to the senses.

A satirical criticism of opera, or rather of its "abuses," is Benedetto Marcello's well-known *Teatro alla moda*, written in 1720. His approach is neither theoretical nor philosophical; the lashing criticism of the musician is directed above all against the most obvious aspects of theatrical immorality. His short chapter on composers touches on a theme of considerable importance, both from a social and musical point of view: the composer's isolation, his ignorance in poetical matters, and his lack of cultural sensitivity, which will inevitably lead him to compose musical banalities, availing himself only of the scant crafts-manship he has acquired through the practice of composing.

In the panorama of Italian writers from the early part of the eighteenth cen-tury, Pier Jacopo Martello's case is unique. In his work *Della tragedia antica e moderna,* published in 1715, it is difficult to comprehend fully where serious-ness begins and irony ends. In the form of a dialogue between the author and Aristotle, it discusses among other things the problems of modern opera. Com-pared with the humanistic and classical approaches of other Italian literati, Martello's embodies a perspective that is already quite close to sensism, in that it gives a positive assessment of music precisely on the strength of its capacity to convey pleasurable sensations. Although opera is a monstrosity from the point of view of reason, the pleasure it gives is beyond all criticism and frustrates any attempt at moralizing. Martello acknowledges that opera, notwithstanding all good intentions to the contrary, is dominated by music. On the other hand, this art "was invented to delight and to unburden the human soul." The traditional viewpoint on opera appears ironically reversed in Martello's imaginary dialogue with Aristotle: "Musical composition is the essence of opera; all other compo-nents are incidental, even including poetry" (!).

GIAN VINCENZO GRAVINA
from *On Tragedy* (1715)

I
THE PURPOSE OF POETRY

The wise have long debated whether poetry was invented to delight or to in-struct. Such a dispute would easily have been resolved had the origin of poetry been distinguished from its development. In fact, the early creators of civilized society were constrained, in order to instruct the people, to avail themselves of the very same poetic forms that the people themselves had contrived for their own pleasure. Being aware that the sweetness of song enraptured the human heart, and that the measured discourse of the laws was conveyed more readily through the ears to the soul to soothe the passions, the ancient sages thought well to express instruction through poetry, that is, through harmonious speech, and so they coupled poetic to vocal harmony, and called it music. Therefore, the sages themselves, turning over in their minds the norms of human life, by transmuting these salutary precepts into poetry, and adapting the poetry to vocal harmony, united in one profession, and in one person, that of the philosopher, the poet, and the musician. Subsequently, as these professions became separated, each was weakened, because the philosopher without the support of poetry and the poet without that of music are unable to employ their talents for the utility of all. Thus the philosopher remains confined in his schools, the poet in his academies, while theater-goers are left only with pure voice, devoid of all poetic eloquence and philosophical content. As a consequence, harmony no longer ministers to words, nor words to feelings, but only at the service and support of harmony do they flow in theaters; whence the ear is appeased, but the soul reaps harm rather than benefit. Surrounded by fanciful chimeras and inured to feelings and expressions far removed from nature and truth, it neither knows nor can do anything but conceive and express falsehoods, and then proceed to behave strangely, pursuing vain and false passions, from which it often escapes either through hasty retreats or suicide, all of which is a source of infamy. Poetry, therefore, which is at present a harmful minister to even more harmful music, was originally a true and popular inducement to pleasure. Then the philosophers, who professed both poetry and music, converted poetry to general utility at banquets, festivities, and games, and especially in public theaters, where tragedy, above all other representational modes, appeared as a supreme life-instructing force. Its image, as a rose in the bud, was hidden within dithyrambic poetry, which, performed by a chorus of musicians playing, dancing, and singing during Bacchic festivities, sang the praise of the god Bacchus. The sages, drawing on such pleasure and popular participation, gave tragedy to the people, culled from the heart of the dithyramb, first in the form of satire directed at reproaching the vices and violence of those who held greater power, and then as a form in its own right, where, more than in any other human activity, one distinguishes the power and variety of the passions and the fickleness of fortune; and where eloquence is more often proportional to the artfulness, diversity, and nobility of expression. Therefore, by restricting tragedy to its true essence, the people were given the fruit of philosophy and eloquence to correct their morals and manner of speaking. In our theaters, the latter are corrupted instead of being corrected. . . .

XXXIII
OF MELODY, THE FIFTH PART OF QUALITY

We could by now go on to discuss the parts of quantity, as all poetic imitation is concerned with story, moral behavior, sentiment, and speech. Melody is imitation and is the work of music; ornamentation, that is, the stage set, is the work of architecture. However, as onto these two is grafted much information from antiquity, which also sheds light on poetry, we shall briefly discuss these two parts, although Aristotle dispensed with them as, in his time, they were familiar to one and all. Not only the uneducated and the ignorant, but even many learned people will find it strange that ancient tragedies and comedies were sung. According to the testimony of many, and especially of Plato, ancient music excited and assuaged the passions, cured unhappy dispositions, and modified behavior. Since that ancient music, which so animated and regulated natural expression, and so effectively touched the human heart, has been lost, the music heard in theaters today, quite unlike that of the ancients, lacks such effects. Nowadays our theaters mostly extol that harmony which, as it entices softened and discordant dispositions, anguishes those whose senses are guided by reason, for instead of expressing and imitating, it extinguishes and erases all semblance of truth. We should not rejoice, therefore, if instead of expressing human emotions and passions, and imitating our actions and ways of behaving, it resembles and imitates, as it often does with its much admired trills, the warblings of goldfinches and canaries. In our day, there are some able and reasonable singers who, guided by instinctive good judgment and intelligence, often imitate nature, despite the general corruption of our times. However, they would imitate it even more if the ancient art of music could once again lift its head from a remote and tenebrous past.

It is not surprising that, as poetry has been corrupted, so too has music. As I mentioned in my *Ragion poetica,* all the imitative arts have a common concept that, once altered, causes all the others to be altered. Music in particular changes with alterations to the poetry, just as the shadow changes with the body. Poetry, therefore, being corrupted by an excess of ornaments and figures, has also contaminated music, by now so full of figures as to have lost its natural expression. Because it delights the ear is no reason to consider it suited to tragedy, as the delight proper to dramatic music is that born of imitation. Pleasure today, however, is produced first of all from the lack of the true idea, and then incidentally from any movement of voice capable of enticing and appeasing man's animal nature, which is sense alone, without the participation of reason, just like the singing of any goldfinch or nightingale, or like the liveliness and variety of color of Chinese paintings, which delight without imitating truth, or like Gothic statues and crude mosaics, which were pleasing before true design was rediscovered.

From *Della tragedia* (Naples, 1715), sec. I, "Fine della Poesia," p. 73, and sec. XXXIII, "Della melodia, quinta parte di qualità," pp. 98–99; modern edition in *Scritti critici e teorici,* ed. Amedeo Quondam (Bari: Laterza, 1973), 507–8, 555–56.

LUDOVICO ANTONIO MURATORI
from *On Perfect Italian Poetry* (1706)

ON THE DEFECTS THAT CAN BE OBSERVED IN MODERN OPERAS.
THEIR MUSIC, PERNICIOUS TO MORALS. CRITICIZED ALSO BY THE
ANCIENTS. POETRY IS THE SERVANT OF MUSIC. THE PURPOSE OF
TRAGEDY CANNOT BE REALIZED BY MEANS OF THESE OPERAS.
OTHER DEFECTS OF POETRY FOR THE THEATER,
AND VARIOUS INCONGRUITIES

A much debated matter, as interesting to unravel as it is difficult to resolve, is whether the ancient tragedies and comedies were sung not only in the choruses but also during the acts, and with real music. What may be said or conjectured on this topic I have already expounded in a lengthy dissertation, which cannot be included in the present essay. For now, suffice it to say that, even if it were true that those dramas were sung entirely, modern theater music could not therefore expect to be exonerated or defended by the authority of the ancients. First of all, there is no doubt that the music of the past was very different from that of today. The Abbé Giusto Fontanini, who espouses the opinion that both tragedies and comedies were once entirely sung, has nevertheless written me a most erudite letter, in which he states: "As regards the music in modern operas, I do not believe it would occur to anyone to think it is similar to ancient music, which was all solemn and learned. And, even if someone did so believe, he could easily be disabused by perusing the works of Galilei and Doni."[1] Secondly, even if this were not certain, it cannot be denied that our present theater music has become unduly effeminate, and thus more apt to corrupt the souls of those in the audience than to purge and improve them, as did ancient music. This is the primary defect of modern operas, nor would it be necessary to go to great lengths to provide evidence of this assertion, were the matter not so pressing. We all know and feel what emotions are sparked within us when we listen to skillful musicians in the theater. Their singing always inspires a certain softness and sweetness, which secretly contributes to further debasing the common people, turning them toward lowly vices, as they drink in the affected languor of the singing voices, and savor the vilest passions, seasoned with unwholesome melodies. What would the divine Plato say if today he could hear

---

1. Vincenzo Galilei, *Dialogo di Vincentio Galilei nobile fiorentino della musica antica, et della moderna* (Florence, 1581); Giovanni Battista Doni, *De praestantia musicae veteris libri tres* (Florence, 1647). [BJB]

our theater music, he who in the books of his *Republic* so forcefully censured that manner of music which, in his day, inspired a certain softness, deeming it highly pernicious to public morals?[2] And yet the music of the ancients, even when soft, could never be compared to that of the moderns, which, as I believe, perhaps contains a greater amount of counterpoint than the ancient,[3] and exudes effeminacy from every pore, contaminating the theaters. Spectators thus never leave the theaters feeling high-minded and nobly inspired, but only full of feminine tenderness, unworthy both of virile spirits and of wise and valorous people.

Although counterpoint never reached such a degree of sophistication with the ancients as music has today, nevertheless Cicero, in his second book of *On the Laws,* attests that many Greek cities, having forsaken the solemnity and austerity of music, and having given themselves up to soft and effeminate music, became full of vice and vile luxury. Cicero further laments the fact that Rome no longer honored the virile and robust melody that was in vogue in the days of Livius Andronicus and Naevius.[4] After Cicero, however, the vice of sloth increased among the Romans. Having highly praised (as it deserves to be praised) the use of music, Quintilian goes on to say that indeed he does not praise, nor recommend, the music which was then allowed in theaters, because it deprived

---

2. *Republic,* bk. 3, 398C–405A; see the translation in Strunk, *Source Readings,* 4–11. [BJB]

3. If by "the ancient" is meant the renewal made by Guido d'Arezzo, I concede this. But if it means the music of ancient Greece, where all gentlemen studied music and knew music, so that Themistocles, a famous Athenian citizen, was shamed because he did not know how to play (and therefore was considered ill-bred and ignorant), I deny it. If it would be possible to hear their music, as today we can see and admire their statues, I suspect that everyone would have a different opinion whether he would be disillusioned. Only the enharmonic genus shows the subtlety of the Greek genius in music, in dividing the tone or voice into four parts, which because of its difficulty and effort even came to be neglected in antiquity, as Plutarch testifies in his book on music; it has been revived in our times by the late Francesco Nigitti, the celebrated Florentine musician and organist at our cathedral; he invented and constructed a harpsichord, or keyboard instrument, with four orders or ranks, which he called omnisonorous instrument (*strumento omnisono*), where every tone is divided into four parts; he keeps it at home, and it is played by his talented disciple and successor, the Florentine priest Giovanni Maria Casini, chaplain of the Most Serene Princess of Tuscany, Violante Beatrice of Bavaria. The writings of the ancients, the multiplicity of stringed and wind instruments, the practice and study of this art, which was highly venerated by them, the prizes and honors that nourished it, and all those reasons adduced by the Florentine gentleman Giovanni Battista Doni in his golden and extremely elegant treatise *De praestantia veteris musicae* [Florence, 1647] that one can see there, make it possible to give an honest opinion of the matter. The choruses of the ancients one might perhaps call simpler and less artistic than ours, because they were neither concerted nor in counterpoint, but everyone sang in unison; however, this was more natural, and more true to life, as we do today with plainchant. But this simplicity was compensated for by other refinements that we do not have. Our music today dates from the time of the barbarians, and just before the year 1,000 or thereabouts, it was patched up on the ancient model by Guido d'Arezzo, mentioned above.

4. *De legibus* 2.15.38–39. [LAH-S]

the Romans of what little remained of their former courage, spirit, and manly valor. Instead, he commends that kind of music once used to sing the praises of heroes, that the heroes themselves sang, and that so forcefully moves and placates men's passions.[5] . . .

Thus, if the ancient sages deplored that effeminate and dissolute music because of its corrupting effect on the people, how much greater should be our condemnation of modern music, which is perhaps unprecedentedly softer, more tender, and which renders its listeners softer and more lascivious? Whether this effeminacy is caused by an excessive use of eighth notes, sixteenth notes, and the smallest rhythmic values, which break the solemnity of the melody, or is produced by the voices of the singers, who are all either naturally or artificially womanlike, and consequently inspire undue tenderness and languor in the souls of the audience; or whether it stems from the use of ariettas in operas, which induce excessive enjoyment in anyone who listens to them, or from the words, which often lack integrity and abound in lasciviousness, or from the practice of using women singers in theaters; or from all these reasons put together: it is a fact that modern theater music is exceedingly harmful for public mores, in that people become ever baser and prone to lasciviousness when listening to it. No longer does one cultivate that art which, as Quintilian stated and is attested to by all the ancient writers, taught how to move, temper, and mitigate men's passions with song.[6] All the effort is put into delighting the ear, and the deplorable modern taste will not suffer operas whose music is not joyful, soft, and tender. . . . But wiser times will come (so I hope) that will reform music and restore its majesty and that honest decorum it so needs if it is to provide us with wholesome delight. People will then heed the words of those zealous pastors of God's church, who have so often banned that music which has made its way from theaters into the sacred temples, where, under the guise of devotion, it dominates—not decorating but contaminating—the solemnity of the divine hymns, and particularly some sacred poems, which are called oratorios. Thus moderated and reformed, music will become most useful socially, and pleasing to our heavenly Father, for whom, and to whose honor, it was invented, music in itself being something most divine, sweet, and praiseworthy.

This is the first shortcoming of modern operas, which also happens to be the most considerable, although the least attention is paid to it. To this, others would add the tremendous damage to the cities caused by the musicians themselves, whose behavior, be they men or women, matches the lasciviousness and effeminacy of their singing, and not without the displeasure of pious men and wise citizens. However, as this, properly speaking, is not a fault of music or of

---

5. *Institutio oratoria* 1.10.31. [LAH-S]
6. Ibid. 1.10.23. [LAH-S]

operas, I shall refrain from speaking of it. Let us then go on to consider other defects, focusing on the poetry that makes up the operas. It should not be thought that I wish to speak ill of poets. In fact, I sympathize with them, as the art they profess is today condemned to be subservient to the demands of theater. Nowadays this happens with such little integrity, indeed with such discredit to them, that I dare say poetry has been placed in bondage. Indeed, where once music was both a servant and minister to poetry, today poetry is a servant to music. If we were to attempt something of this nature, I do not know what fame or glory poets could hope to obtain by writing such harmonious operas. Today nothing is more obvious than the ancillary position that poetry occupies with respect to music. From the start, the number of characters and their vocal roles are imposed on the poet. In accordance with a composer's whim, a poet is asked to write, alter, add, or exclude ariettas and recitatives. Further, every performer claims the authority of telling the poet what to do, and of having him write verses according to the dictates of the performer's imagination. Also, it is necessary to distribute the roles in the opera suitably, and to divide the verses carefully among them, so that no singer will complain of having been assigned a part that is shorter or inferior to those given the other performers. Thus, poets are constrained to lay out and embellish their operas, not as art and the particular subject matter would demand, but in accordance with the dictates of music.

Let us add that, to comply with the wishes of the theater directors, it is at times necessary to suit the plot and the verses to some stage machine, or set design, which they of course wish to include and show to the audience. All this, however, could easily be tolerated. But, on stage, what utility or glory accrues to poetry? It is of course true that the verses are recited, but in such a way that either the melody or the ignorance of the performing musicians rarely allows the meaning to come through, and quite often not even the words themselves, as they alter and transform the vowels. Some composers consider this charming, and they speak of "diphthonged singing,"[7] as if not only grammar, but also music had its diphthongs. If the audience did not have before its eyes, in printed form, what is being sung,[8] I am certain that they would understand nothing of the action or of the story that is being staged. Should the people in

---

7. That is, giving a syllable as many beats as the notes to which it is set, which draws out a passage, whereas the ancients, obeying the laws of meter, gave it two beats if it was long, but one if it was short (something that Doni, in the abovementioned book, considered of enormous importance); it makes it difficult to grasp the whole word, and in those wandering and confused tremolos, trills, and passages one loses track of the words, and so understanding is confounded.

8. Here it would be opportune to say that since painting in the most ancient times was so crude and imperfect that, as Aelian testifies [*Varia historia* 10.10], it was necessary to write underneath the figures: "This is a dog; this is a horse," so imperfect was that recitation that, in order to be understood, it had to be read.

the audience lack the *libricciuolo* (as it is called), they only see and listen to some performers who alternately go on and off stage, and in turn sing, without being able to make out what they are singing, nor what the story is all about. Thus music is what stands out in modern operas. As for poetry, today theaters demand only that it act as a means and an instrument for the music, whereas it used to be, as it should be, the main end. In fact, today's tastes have determined the music to be the very essence of these operas, and the selection of skillful singers to be the most important objective. This is the only reason why people flock to theaters. They certainly do not go to delight in the efforts of poets, whose verses, printed in the librettos, they deign hardly worth a glance. Furthermore, it may be said that the verses are not even recited, as they are uttered by those who do not understand them and who, moreover, I would almost say, are not capable of conveying their meaning to the audience precisely because of the modern manner of singing. In addition, it is well known that those dramas which have enjoyed particular fame are those whose music has been fortunate enough to delight audiences. It matters little whether the story itself and the poet's verses are excellent or if they merit derision. For this reason, many dramas written by the cleverest poets elicit no applause, while applause is offered to others that were horribly defective in terms of their poetry. In fact, composers are not fond of those librettos that are overwrought and contain excessively contrived sentiments, as it is not easy to set their verses and ariettas to music. Only sweet, sonorous words are desired; little does it matter—in fact the composers prefer it—if the ariettas lack strong emotions and profound reflections, as long as their words are harmonious and beautiful.[9] In truth, however, I cannot blame these people for demanding such things, for if only, or at least mainly, musical delight is sought in operas, it follows logically that, when writing them, poets will follow the tastes and the demands of the music, and not their own talents and creativity. They will be in a position of subservience, not of command.

This said, two conclusions may easily be drawn. The first is that poets cannot write something perfect in the tragic genre by contriving such operas. The second is that, even if a perfect opera is written, when it is sung in the theater, as is the practice today, the true aim of tragedy will not be achieved. The first consequence may seem rather dubious: how will poets ever be able to apply the rules of their art in such compositions, and follow the power of their own genius, if they are constrained to serve and obey the demands of music? The latter's dominion fetters poets and places a thousand obstacles in their path. If, in

9. I should have added the reason; that is, that what works very well for poetry, such as the occasional aspirate or harshness, to make the style more imposing, or to suit the chosen subject, is exceedingly inappropriate for music, which is completely sweet, syrupy, and languid with caresses.

order to serve the singers and the theater directors, the poet is obliged to introduce sham and unnecessary characters; if he must divide the scenes and the
verses in keeping with the performers' requests, and not as art and his subject
would instruct; if finally he has to change, add, and delete lines according to
others' desires, how can he ever hope to write something perfect in the tragic
genre? Furthermore, poetry's forced subjection to music impoverishes the writing itself, making it rife with improprieties and causing it to lack all verisimilitude. A good number of people in opera are involved in the ariettas, which
means in unnecessary words; others are occupied with similarly superfluous
verses that poets are often constrained to add for the pleasure of others. Then,
having to ensure brevity, so as to prevent the music accompanying the dramas
from going on endlessly, poets have little opportunity to explain those concepts
that are necessary to the understanding of the story itself. They are thus obliged
to abridge the action, be unduly laconic, and condense in a few lines what verisimilitude would warrant be stated at length. Thus the plot cannot be brought
to a close with the necessary decorum and logic. Modern tastes have reached
such a point that many people can no longer tolerate recitatives, considering
them tedious, although it is precisely in recitative, and not in the ariettas, that
the plot, development, and the very essence of the story lie. If we compare these
imaginary tragedies with real ones, we see that between the two there is absolutely no similarity. . . .

Let us allow, however, that a perfect opera libretto could be written. Even so,
when it is sung, the poet will nevertheless fail to achieve the stated aim of tragedy and art. The reason for this failure is that, when dramas are sung, no terror,
no compassion, indeed no noble sentiments are awakened in the listener. The
poet may do his utmost to stir emotions by his verses and his story, and he may
perhaps succeed if his libretto is only read. However, he ought never aspire to
achieve such glory on the stage, since the length and quality of the modern way
of singing, together with its lack of verisimilitude, are such that all emotions not
only languish, but are deprived of their very soul, as experience teaches us.
Without doubt, music in itself is sufficiently powerful to stir passions. Ancient
history, in fact, relates various miraculous instances of just such a power. There
are times when we also feel that moving and powerful sentiments, sung by a
talented performer, strike our heart in a more forceful way than if they were
simply recited. Normally, however, music does not produce such a lofty effect
in operas, both because of its own shortcomings and those of the singers themselves. Today, no one either studies or uses the sort of music that stirs the emotions. Perhaps we have even lost all knowledge of it, being familiar only with
the names of the modes, such as Phrygian, Lydian, Aeolian, Dorian, Hypo-
phrygian, and the like. The ancients took great pains to learn the art of these

modes, whereby the various sentiments of the listener were either awakened or placated. Today, the sole aim is to delight the ear; nor is any attention paid to the salutory regulating effects of music on the emotions, as only its practice, divorced from the science of harmony, has been revived. Yet, though there are some competent composers (some of whom I know) who can skillfully match the music to the particular sentiment expressed in the verses, for the most part their endeavors, as well as the poet's intentions, are betrayed by the singers. Few of them understand the power of words; fewer still know how to express that power. Instead, they concentrate their efforts on techniques of singing, while ignoring those of acting, which is quite different and most essential if things and emotions are to be well represented. . . .

Now, when are men ever seen singing in the midst of their activities and while engaged in serious matters? Is it humanly likely that a person beset by anger, full of sorrow or anguish, or talking seriously about his affairs, can sing? If such behavior is not in keeping with the way people really behave, what can come of it on stage, where nature and man's true actions and habits are to be imitated as far as possible? Certainly, if we consider the opera house, we are sooner moved to laughter than to any other emotion in observing those who seek to imitate and represent serious individuals, who treat matters of state, plan betrayals, assaults, and wars, or go to their death; or who complain and bemoan some terrible mishap; or who perform other such deeds, all the while singing sweetly, warbling, and with the utmost composure producing a prolonged and sweet trill. Is this not rather a way of belying, through deeds and actions, what is being said with the words? Who could ever claim that by acting and performing dialogue and manners in such a way truth and nature are imitated? This consideration, which would also pertain to the dramas of the ancients, had they also been sung in the same way as the modern ones, has always led me to believe that the former were sung differently, especially in light of the great care with which ancient tragedy imitated nature.

Verisimilitude has decreased even more in our theaters, since ariettas, or canzonettas, which are totally extraneous and indeed contrary to the concept of imitation, were introduced in operas. I shall refrain from considering the quality of the verses and rhythms, or meter, which could never suit tragedy (which imitates the changing patterns of human life, and its solemnity). I say simply that it is a travesty of verisimilitude to want to imitate real people, and then interrupt their serious and heated dialogues with such ariettas: the other singer has to remain idle and silent, listening to the former's beautiful melody, when in fact the very nature of the situation and of civil conversation would have him go on with the matter at hand. Whoever saw anyone, in informal speech, repeating and singing the same word, or expressing the same feeling, over and over again, as happens in ariettas?[10] What could be more ridiculous than to observe two people who sing while duelling, or who prepare for death, or bemoan some terrible misfortune with a gentle and calm arietta, or who take so much time to repeat the music and words of one of these canzonettas, when the plot would warrant a prompt departure, and not wasting time on chatter? If we cannot apply the term solecism to define such imitations, whatever else deserves to be called thus? However, without wasting any more words, anyone familiar with the matter under discussion knows very well how many drawbacks and unlikely situations occur on account of these ariettas, or rather of this interspersing of dramas with song. We need not wonder, therefore, why these modern tales, well devised, do not awaken various passions in the listeners; for not only do the many unlikely situations, which distort reality, deprive the emotions represented of their authority and likelihood, but the undue length and inappropriateness of the singing of ariettas either causes the passions to languish or extinguishes whatever spark may have been ignited in the listeners. How can we take seriously someone who sings his problems, misfortunes, or disdain with such measured and studied melodiousness?[11] It can never seem that he is speaking in earnest; consequently, he can neither move us nor touch our hearts. This is to say nothing of the unsuitability of the voices, since the leading parts must be performed by sopranos, while the heroic roles, instead of having virile, deep voices, disconcertingly appear speaking in a markedly weak and effeminate tone of voice.[12] Thus, among the many shortcomings of dramas, tragedy's real aim, which is to move and purge human passions, is frustrated. Such an effect is ordinarily achieved by tragedies that are well contrived and well acted, but not sung; experience teaches us that the people who leave such performances do so with feelings of compassion, terror, scorn, and other such emotions. Notwithstanding, these tragedies today are either ignored or disdained, since music and operas have prevailed.

However, as we cannot expect modern operas to achieve the results and offer

10. If only musical repetition were limited to natural restraints, as one limits poetic and rhetorical repetition, which ordinarily does not exceed two times, or three at the most [follow examples from Dante and Cicero], although one would do. But to keep repeating "a voice that is so prodigiously one" [Horace, *Ars poetica* 29] is too disconcerting and unnatural. Grace displayed beyond the fitting becomes graceless.

11. Muratori cites two passages from Persius' Satire 1. [BJB]

12. St. Cyprian, in bk. 2 of his Epistles, no. 10 [= *Ad Donatum* 8, ed. W. Hartel (Corpus scriptorum ecclesiasticorum Latinorum, 3/1 (Vienna, 1868)], discussing abuses in the theaters: "Men are unmanned; the entire dignity and vigor of their sex is made effeminate by the disgrace of their effeminated body, and the more a man breaks his manhood into womanhood, the more he is applauded in the theater." [The reference is not to castration of actors, but to shameful performances on stage. LAH-S]

the benefits of true poetry, they should at least be able to provide us with the fruits of their only, or main, purpose, which is that of delighting us with song. But herein they are also defective, for we can usually say that the tedium they produce is greater than the enjoyment, as those who go to the theater have readily experienced for themselves. The reason for this is the disproportionate length of the music, since it takes at least three, often four, and even five or six hours to perform an opera. Although music is an extremely sweet thing, it nevertheless shares the liability of other sweet things, which, having been born to delight the senses, soon engender satiety. No food is more satiating than honey and milk. Aristophanes, who derived the idea from Homer, says wittily in his *Plutus*[13] that music, like all things and all foods, produces boredom and satiation. The ear, to the satisfaction of which the sweetness of music is itself directed, is rapidly filled with it. Then, little by little, that same sweetness begins to turn sour as, by continuing to taste the same flavor, our appetite, or taste, is no longer inclined to receive it. Nor is it possible to keep filling what has already been filled more than once. Real tragedies, on the other hand, when well performed, hold their audience's attention; nor are they easily inclined to tedium, since their delight is aimed at satisfying not the ear but the soul, whose capacity is limitless. Furthermore, by instructing and stirring the various emotions, tragedies contain variety, which is the mother of delight. It cannot be denied that the actors' singing is also varied; but this variety is limited and generates only one pleasure and one emotion in just one of man's senses, thus easily producing satiety. It follows that rarely if ever can one bear to listen attentively to an entire opera, especially having already heard it once, and even more so if both the music and the performers are not excellent. The audience's attention is captured only when a well-known arietta is about to be sung. For this reason, public gambling and continuous chatter have found their way into the theater, as everyone seeks a way of defending himself against the idleness and tedium that he experiences when hearing music that goes on for much too long. What recreation, what delight do our famous operas provide if, while listening to them, the audience has to look elsewhere for enjoyment and delight? Thus operas, besides not being of much use, are even less enjoyable to the public.

From *Della perfetta poesia italiana* (Modena, 1706), bk. 3, ch. 5; modern edition by Ada Ruschioni (Milan: Marzorati, 1971–72), 573–83.

13. The passage is given in a footnote. [BJB]

PIER JACOPO MARTELLO
from *On Ancient and Modern Tragedy* (1714)

"This type of theater relieves the soul of all cares and envelops it in a carefree and satisfying tranquillity. In this way, the spectator leaves the theater so restored by the harmonies and the sights perceived that he is fortified and better disposed toward all human activities. Thus, such theater is both physically and morally useful to a republic, no less than satire, comedy, and tragedy.

It is, however, necessary to assume that, in such fine theatrical performances, music occupies a preeminent position. Music is the soul of these performances, and those who are called to contribute to it, either with poetry or stage design, are to show it the greatest respect. It is not my intention here to give you a lesson in music, especially as I am perhaps ill equipped to do so; or, should I succeed, I would have to use terms that are obscure in themselves, perhaps even to those who happened to invent them. I will say only that if you have heard people lament the loss of ancient music, tell these worshippers of antiquity from me that they are impostors. Judge the music of the Jews and of the other Orientals by their instruments, which were horns, drums, and trumpets. The zither, the harp, the lyre, and the pipe delighted their ears, as they did those of all Greece. Yet he who hears nothing better becomes accustomed to perceiving as excellent that which would prove extremely bad if compared with the perfection of modern music, accompanied by the subtle refinement of so many well-tempered instruments that at present enrich and fill our orchestras.

I also intend, at least for the present occasion, to avoid comparisons between French and Italian music. Each has its own rules, and each has its own supporters. I will only say, albeit in confidence, that I have seen the French derive much pleasure on hearing sung in the middle of their performances an arietta whose poetry and style are in the Italian fashion. This, however, proves very little, as I have also seen Italians similarly delighted when a French song is included in their operas. What is certain, however, is that both the Germans and the English prefer Italian music, and these two countries pay the most renowned musicians very high salaries. And I, being Greek, will not easily change my mind. What is more, the French author of the foreword to a printed collection of the most select French ariettas also credits you Italians with preeminence in this type of musical representation. At least your language, being sweeter and abounding in more prolonged sounds, is more suited to the vagaries of passage-work and the delicate nuances of ornamentation. Now we have embarked. Let us see if we can find some harbor in this sea new to me.

I shall attempt to establish whether, in order to please, opera requires the aid of words and poetry. I sincerely maintain that it does not. I find that at night, while listening to one or more nightingales singing, almost conversing with one another in song, the drama of those unseen birds delights me and removes me from every care, so that I sit for long periods listening to them. Yet their warbling is by nature limited to certain airs that are uniform, if not always the same. A serenade, even if performed only with instruments, makes a person go out onto the balcony and lose himself there for hours, if it lasts that long. The delight experienced is so much greater insofar as the players, with their various instruments, produce symphonies that are as diverse among themselves as those of the aforementioned nightingales were uniform. Furthermore, as we prefer to listen to birds vying in song and to the intermingling of instruments in a green wood, or within view of a pleasant garden, similarly, listening to voices singing in a charming and pleasantly adorned place gives us greater enjoyment. Therefore, the marvelous variety of scenes that are interspersed with singing cannot but increase our pleasure. And the more beautiful and graceful the bird is, the more we appreciate its singing—all the more so if it is adorned with pleasantly mottled feathers—so we experience even greater satisfaction when listening to a lute or flute that is also pretty to look at. The richness of mother-of-pearl and ivory-inlaid instruments makes them all the more perfect. Thus, a singing voice will please us even more if it issues from a well-proportioned mouth, complemented by a finely complexioned and beautifully featured face, which is in turn sustained by a gracefully craned neck. Such a voice will be particularly gratifying if it comes from a woman who, lifting her bosom with her breathing, which rises up through her throat where it becomes song, lets you anticipate what the musical outcome will be by the heaving of her breast. Our enjoyment will be all the greater then if she appears on stage with her beautiful body clad in rich, charming, and colorful clothes. These will be her feathers and her marquetry, as those I have praised in birds and instruments. Thus, the type of performance we are discussing, which is delightful in its own right, will be all the more so because of the stage design, and of the attractiveness of the performers and their costumes.

How insatiable we are, especially when we are immersed in pleasure! As we know how birds whistle, and how instruments play, and how man alone reasons, we also want the sweetness of human singing to be complemented by that of words capable of conveying the emotions of the soul. Finally, we come to another delight that further enhances this type of performance, namely that of poetry. In opera, however, poetry sustains a paltry role, whereas both in tragedy and in comedy it occupies a preeminent position. As regards these last, it acts as a master; in opera it acts as a servant. Let us not, however, debase poetry by honoring servile verse with its name; I freed the name of poetry from Empedocles' versification with far less reason. They are not poets, therefore, but versifiers; and not even versifiers because, since dramatic action is also required, something more than simple versification is necessary. Therefore, not mere versifiers, and not true poets. Nor would I know how to call some who are more than the former, while less than the latter. Uninvited, they volunteer to cater to the needs of opera as did the chorus directors to the material needs of tragedy.

Scene designs have to be varied and grand. The number of trees should be kept to a minimum, as knotty tree trunks and leaves are not suited to scene painters. Besides, in candlelight trees look rough and unpleasant. Instead, what is needed is architectural variety, giving impressions of length and width far greater than those of real places and buildings. Gardens with real fountains artfully recreated on the stage; marine vistas with foamy undulating waves; and let us not forget a Gothic temple or a rustic prison, as these are the most frequent subjects of scene changes.

Castratos are selected not only for their agile and beautiful voices, but also for their gracious presence. Women are chosen for their gentle faces and especially for the expressiveness and gracefulness with which they move. Their clothes should be bejeweled and embroidered, simulating silver and gold, and of regal cut. Their voices should be such, and of such strength, that the composer can intermingle them so that one enhances instead of overwhelming the other. If these instructions are followed, the profit of the impresarios or producers of operas is assured.

As regards verses, what can be done to make them pleasing to the composer, to the musicians, to the audience, and, God willing, to the versifier himself? This last should also be the composer, as was your famous contralto Pistocco, no less renowned for having refined singing than for having combined notes in such a way that they spread with much distinction to Italy's greater glory, and particularly that of your home region. In Germany, he wrote both the music and words to an opera that proved the delight and marvel of the Prussian court, and mine. How divine did those verses, so embodied in notes, appear to me! And yet later, when reading them in a printed libretto, how insipid and weak did they seem to me! At any rate, those sentiments were simple, smooth, and relaxed only to the degree the music required, and no more, as perhaps the composer on that particular occasion thought necessary for musical symmetry. Music, moreover, was never subordinate to verse; the latter served the former, and willingly, not in a servile manner. I should furthermore like the composer to be a poet of average ability, which would benefit the opera in that he could first outline mentally, and then set down on paper, the entire musical composition from the beginning to the end of the drama. He would decide first where forcefulness, where tenderness, where recitatives and where arias are more appropriate; whether a soprano, bass, a contralto, or a tenor is more suited for binding together and interweaving perfect harmony. Then he would adapt the events, either taking them from Greek fables, or inventing them completely from his own imagination, together with simple words and verses, steady and sonorous. In this manner, he would draw from the mouths and purses of the listeners no fewer bravos than coins.

Although, unfortunately, few *maestri di cappella* are able to understand verses, let alone write them, the versifying poetaster is likely at least to be somewhat conversant with notes and music, so that he can conform his invention and verses, as much as possible, to the composer's idea. In the same way, a painter adapts his colors to the figural and representational requirements of stage machinery designed by a theater architect. Such painting will always be permitted as long as, without betraying the architect's intention, it does not hamper the effect either of the ropes or the pulleys, which are essential if the machine is to be lowered or suspended. I have known such "loaders" [*caricatori*] (as you call them) of notes, the most versatile men in the world, capable of composing easily articulated words at the harpsichord, words abounding in vowels that suit the beauty of the passagework, and at times mean little or even nothing. Nevertheless, when properly sung they can please a whole host of literati, even those who thrive on criticizing the most distinguished and solemn poetry.

These fortunate dramatists should not draw their subjects from history but from fables, being mindful of the barbarity of brazenly deforming the truth of events recorded by Livy, Justin, Sallust, or any other ancient and revered writer, realizing that some manipulation would be inevitable in order to include elements in an opera satisfying to the composer, the male and female singers, the architect, the machinist, the set decorator, and even the impresario. This will also be difficult, but not impossible, to achieve with subjects drawn from fables, as in any case the versifier has the same authority as our forebears had to invent wild stories, and to add Italian lies to those of the Greeks. Furthermore, leaving aside the ancient ones, he can invent modern fables, which are even more suited to stage machinery and performance; the French do this very successfully, and so shall the Italians. And since his name is not destined to outlive the performances themselves, all the same he will have the pleasure of hearing himself addressed at the great courts with the title of Poet, a title he deserves as much as the castratos and female singers deserve that of Virtuosi. What is more important, he can play the know-it-all, passing judgment with authoritative disdain on the works of the great poets in every language and nation, and receive in return resounding plaudits from the blathering mouths of young girls and buffoons. He can sit down to lavish dinners and fill his treasure chest with necklaces, jewels, and money, and enjoy himself. All this is no mean reward; indeed, it is ample recompense for the scorn he will receive from the Arcadians and the purists of the Crusca, when they read his librettos.[1] Thus, no matter what, the poetaster will compose bad tragedies for music, but tragedies nonetheless, for otherwise they would not suit the pomp of the splendid royal garments that adorn impresarios' wardrobes (which you call costumes), if the characters imitated in his works were anything less than kings or demigods. As proof, you can see that pastoral scenes are rarely set to music, as they are ill suited to richness of apparel and lots of extras, and are alien to powerful dramatic action and certain heightened interpretations that enliven this type of musical performance.

Thus, you see to what extent anyone wishing to furnish commercial operas with acceptable verses must be hampered. There will be a few who will write for some prince who, not for gain but out of pomp and liberality, prefers to regale the nobility, rather than the people, with a celebrated and graceful representation with music. Then a versifier too can be a poet, but woe betide him if he does not distance himself from the rigid, strict rules of tragedy." . . .

"Therefore, I expect you to draw up a system in which a competent poet can compose a drama not only to be read, but also to be listened to."

Then Aristotle said: "Since you want me to give you some rules for a kind of composition which, in order to please, should be entirely without rules, I shall give you some based more on observation and experience than on reason. To please you, I shall also mix as much as possible the duties of the choragus, of the composer, of the musician, and of the poet, almost forgetting that I am a philosopher. And here I am ready to satisfy you.

If ever, then, the ridiculous folly of writing an opera should cross your mind, before determining the plot, you must first assess the theater's capacity, the composer's renown, and the quantity and quality of the singers hired by the impresario. . . .

Having divided the action into acts, you must then think of dividing each act into scenes, something that will prove no mean task. First, you must determine the number of leading singers, in order to allot them equal roles. Otherwise, you can imagine what quarrels will ensue among those bold females and those spirited castratos! You must also pay attention to the voices, interweaving them so as to enhance rather than undermine the composer's intention. But before you divide the acts into scenes, I urge you to discuss what you are doing with the composer, asking him what voice, according to his taste, you should introduce at the beginning, middle, and end of each act. You must, however,

1. The Accademia della Crusca (founded 1582 in Florence) was dedicated to preserving the Tuscan purity of the Italian language; the Arcadian academy, founded in Rome in 1690, was devoted to cultivation of the fine arts. Gian Vincenzo Gravina, the author of the first extract in this chapter, was one of the founding members. Martello himself helped found the Bologna branch of Arcadia in 1698. [BJB]

agree with the composer, and he will readily consent, that each act contain one of those so-called forceful scenes, be it for some violent and unusual clash of contrasting emotions, or for some encounter and event not foreseen by the audience. Having so divided your work, you can be assured that your opera will be successful. All that remains is to put your drama into verse.

It needs to be completely divided in recitatives and ariettas, otherwise called canzonettas. Each scene must contain only recitative or only an arietta, or at most one followed by the other. All narration, or emotionless expression, should be conveyed by means of recitative verse. However, whatever is prompted by passion, or is somehow more violent, is best expressed by the canzonetta. It is preferable that recitatives be short enough not to provoke tedium, and long enough not to be unintelligible. Their sentences and structures are to be agile, concise rather than lengthy, so as to suit the composer, the singer, and the listener: the composer, because he will be able to give greater life to the inherently dead recitative by varying the cadences; the singer, because he will be able to catch his breath while uttering the words and sentences, thus exploiting the rests to renew the vigor of his voice; and the listener, because, being unaccustomed to music, which alters the normal sound of words, he will have no great difficulty perceiving their emotional charge, even though they are couched in convoluted and circuitous language. It should be set in seven- and eleven-syllable verse, both alternating and mixed, whatever is more suitable, and where at least in the cadences one can achieve harmony with consonance and rhyme. In this manner, the lubricious nature of music will be enhanced. What I said about the brevity of recitatives suffers some exception in those scenes I have called "forceful," where the recitatives should prevail over the ariettas because the former confer greater vigor and draw greater attention to the action. In such cases, the poet can to some extent give free play to a moderate sample of his talent. The prudent composer should make allowances for such a display; the singers, who are likewise experienced in matters of staging, should not have any objection, and the impresario should be gratified.

Canzonettas are either simple or compound: the former are sung by one voice, the latter by two or more. Those sung by two voices we shall call duets; those with several voices are called choruses. Regarding the simple arias, some are called entrance arias, others exit arias, and others mid-scene arias. Their functions can be inferred from their names. Entrance arias are sung when a character comes on stage, and are particularly suited to soliloquies. The rhetorical figure of the apostrophe is essential to them. However, you are to make use of them sparingly. The mid-scene arias should be used with equal parsimony, as they have a lifeless effect each time singers who are silent are obliged to remain standing in the middle of a scene while listening to someone else singing unhurriedly. That is why such scenes are best accompanied by action, which at least forces the other singers to some activity and does not leave them completely idle, and thus they are capable of producing excellent effects. Only in the mid-scene arias can the rhetorical figure of interrogation sometimes be used; in all others it is abhorrent because it does not offer the opportunity for any musical variety. The exit arias must close each scene, and a singer ought never leave the stage without an ornamented canzonetta. Whether or not this accords with ver-isimilitude is of little importance, as hearing a scene ended spiritedly and with liveliness is all too exciting. However, be careful, when ending a scene with an exit aria, not to begin the following one with an entrance canzonetta. This would deprive the music of the chiaroscuro effect: the instrumental ritornellos (*ricercate*) would clash with one another, and instead of having a supportive role, they would overwhelm one another. For this reason, entrance arias are generally suited only to the beginnings of acts. Duets in the middle of a scene are always welcome, as they enable several actors at a time to interact. In fact, I would also prefer to have another one at the close of the second act. At the end of the last act choruses are inevitable, as audiences enjoy listening to all voices they had applauded separately during the course of the opera now joined to-gether. The noise of the voices and instruments makes everyone stand up and leave the theater in high spirits and eager to return.

These ariettas, or canzonettas, have to be distributed in equal number among the leading singers, whose competitiveness is extreme and never-ending. Furthermore, the performance is itself enhanced when the best voices are perceived in equal degree of excellence by the audience. These ariettas are made up of several meters, to use the Italian term. The eight-syllable meter, which is the most sonorous, should prevail over all the others. An example is:

Innamora amor le belle.[2]

This can be varied by alternation or truncation; a *tronco* line is the most pleas-ant to hear, especially when one wishes to effect a cadence, such as:

Per chi gode il tempo vola;
per chi pena ha tardo il pié.

or

Augellin lascia in obblio
antri opachi, argenteo rio,
bosco, volo e libertà.

---

2. The examples have not been identified. Piero Weiss assumes that they are by Martello him-self; "Pier Jacopo Martello on Opera" (see source note), 395, note 20. [KKH]

This verse line can be further split into two four-syllable verses. The quadri-syllabic verse is graceful, even when alternated with an octosyllabic verse rhyming in the middle with a quadrisyllable:

> Già la tromba
> là dal lido
> ne rimbomba: al mare, al mare.

However, bear in mind that in each aria there be an *intercalare,* or refrain. This is what the teachers call the first part of an aria, which is then repeated by the singer. The composer is also happy to have it repeated, as it displays the mastery of his art. Furthermore, it pleases both the singers and the audience. Therefore, the first part must be no longer than three lines if it is octosyllabic, and no longer than four if it is quadrisyllabic. This rule is to be stringently observed when composing canzonettas, in accordance with the length and brevity of their lines. The octosyllable is followed by the heptasyllable, which should also preferably be *tronco* rather than *piano* at the end of the stanza. It can then be *tronco* on the stressed vowel or by leaving the last consonant without the following vowel. In this way, it more clearly distinguishes itself from recitative verse:

> Cangiano moto gli astri
> varia d'aspetto il ciel.

The lines of six-syllable verse usually end in *sdruccioli* (dactyls); however, at times they can also be *tronchi.* The former could be:

> Ma già più languide
> le stelle girano.
> Già fosco e pallido
> si asconde il sol.

The latter:

> Chi non sa amar beltà
> non ha nel petto il cor.

Do you want an example of a five-syllable verse?

> Voglio un amore
> tutto di core,
> che vi sia nato
> sol per pietà.

Lastly, would you like an example of a ten-syllable verse? Here is one:

> La speranza mi va consolando,
> ma' sanarmi bastante non è.

Your versifiers, however, have devised many discordant rhythms, so incapable of producing pleasant harmony that I certainly should not advise you to use them. The meters I have discussed will prove more pleasing if you adapt them to the emotions that are best suited to them. Fury, for example, is best, indeed almost solely, conveyed with ten-syllable verses, where it can express all its frightfulness. This is especially so if you use *sdruccioli* up to the cadences, which should always be either *piano* or *tronco,* as in the following example:

> Sibillanti dell'orride Eumenidi
> veggio in campo rizzarsi le vipere,
> minacciando di mordermi il sen.

A *sdrucciolo* six-syllable verse is particularly suited to portraying the debilitated state of someone giving himself up to amorous languor:

> Le luci tenere
> della mia Venere
> mi fan languir.

The others are interchangeable and can be used to express any other emotion that is less forceful than fury. Do not attempt to rhyme *sdrucciolo* verses unless you are sure of their effectiveness; it will suffice to rhyme the cadences. In the others, however, despite the grumbles of the more permissive poetasters, I prefer a well-structured rhyme scheme, which cannot fail to please the composer, the singers, and the audience. All that which is consonance and harmony contributes considerably to heightening music.

There now remains to discuss the style that best suits opera. I believe that a moderate and lovely style befits any opera more than a style that is serious and magnificent, for the art of music, having been invented to delight and uplift the soul, needs to be accompanied by words and emotions expressing all that is delightful. It is not that from time to time the grand style cannot be used, if for nothing else but to underline further what is beautiful, in the same way that sweet and sour spicily mixed greatly excite the palate. However, if the sour prevails, then delight becomes disgust, and any fastidious damsel will spit it out. That is why I insist on reminding you that verse structure must be smooth, the sentences clear and not long, the words easy to understand and charming, the rhymes not rough, and the verses flowing and tenderly sonorous. In the arias, I urge you to imitate at times the fluttering of butterflies, the warbling of birds, or the babbling of brooks. Such sounds dispose the mind to gaiety and restore the soul; and as these are all beautiful things, so are the words that recall and recreate them in our imagination, and the composer always ranges widely with an abundance of notes. Also, you will have noticed, even in the worst operas, that a singer draws warm applause when performing one of those arias in which elegance is added by the use of diminutives, which are so alien to both the French taste and language. Also bear in mind that, in arias, the more general the concepts, the more the audience enjoys them. Finding them either lifelike or true, a man can profit by them honestly with his woman, by singing them in the many instances of jealousy, disdain, mutual promises, absences, and other such situations that arise from day to day among lovers. These, in fact, can prove very useful to you, and the poet will find it much easier to treat general matters, filling his poetic wardrobe, as it were, with such observations, and later using them to clothe the recitatives of his operas. However, in action arias you should avoid the general, and rely only on the particular, for if action is to be spirited, words should so animate it that they suit one particular action and not another. If you, who do not belong to the flock of servile versifiers, want those who read your opera to acknowledge you as a poet, distinguish yourself in the recitative and in at least one aria each act. Entreat the composer, the male and female singers, and even the impresario to allow these arias to be performed in your opera, to further your honor and that of the sacred muses. Perhaps your laments will soften their otherwise unyielding hearts. But if you want more from them, do not expect to obtain it without opposition, hostility, and rejection. Be content that your other arias are not found wanting in purity and spirit. Nor must your forbearance end here.

The profession of composing operas, my dear Martello, is a lesson in ethics for you, one which more than any other teaches poets to master themselves and to forgo their own desires. Be prepared to turn acceptable arias into bad ones. If a singer, whether male or female, wants to follow one of your recitatives with an aria that has won him or her applause in Milan, Venice, Genoa, or elsewhere, even if it is alien to the emotion you wish to convey, who cares? Let it be included, lest your ears be assailed by all sorts of reproaches from sopranos and contraltos. The most you can hope to obtain is that he or she condescends to allow you to stretch out the words less jarring to your concept, in which case you will be undertaking no mean task. It does not matter whether you preserve the correct number of verses or syllables; what matters is that in the words themselves you keep those vowels on which the singer is to perform passagework. An *a* can become an *e*, but not an *i*, which would have a neighing effect, and a howling effect on a *u*. You must also preserve the stress; otherwise short syllables will be pronounced as long, and vice versa. Pray tell me, how will you manage if, instead of a disdainful aria, which was originally in your opera, you are obliged to substitute one that deals with love, and has now to be clothed in words of scorn? If the composer of the music is not an oaf, he will have adapted his notes to the former expression in such a way that it cannot be suited to the latter. Thus, I always deem it better to allow the singers to produce the arias when and as they please, rather than to make myself an accomplice to their defects by adding them myself. It suffices that they not be discordant with the musical texture, which I leave completely in the care of the *maestro di cappella*. If the impresario, who is to pay you for your effort (do not blush, as this is the only kind of poetry that is destined to be rewarded financially), then wants you to change your arias, do so, and offer up to the heavens your heroic patience in atonement for having violated the edict of some muse, or for some other error you may have committed. You wanted Aristotle's poetics on opera, and now you have them. Are you satisfied?"

"From what I hear," I answered, utterly bewildered, "it is more burdensome to do things poorly than to do them well. It takes less effort to write a good tragedy than a bad one, since, from what you say, I deduce that opera is an imperfect imitation of better dramas, and is hence an imperfect sort of tragedy that cannot win applause unless accompanied by music and singing." . . .

"Musical composition is the essence of opera; all other components are incidental, even including poetry. Or if poetry *is* essential, it is like color, which is but an essence of light (to borrow someone else's opinion) that adapts to the surface it illuminates. Thus, as it is variously reflected, so does it take on various colors. Light, in its true form, is colorless, but when it is debased in applying itself to solid bodies, its nature appears different, depending on the greater or lesser roughness of their surface. Thus deformed, it continues to please, but it does so only because, in such circumstances, its color is not thought of as a substance, that is, when it does not behave as it naturally should, but is conditioned by other agents. In this way, let it not displease you more than it should that poetry for opera be demoted from the rank of a principal ingredient to that of an accessory. Such an accessory can nevertheless prove most pleasing. Poetry is like a rich man who, having come down in station, is constrained to earn his way through servitude. Not having forgotten the pride that goes with command, he ill adjusts to his new lot. But when he serves, he is a servant. It is in this fashion that poetry acts honorably, that is, without commanding and only by obeying music, which in theater is the mistress.

Music, furthermore, is one of the most marvelous and perfect arts in the universe. Neither posterity, nor composers, nor singers, nor the instruments can cause it to perish. Music's traits render it eternal in the eyes and minds of men. And no less deserving of fame than the most illustrious poets and philosophers are these venerable and amiable musical craftsmen: Pasquini, Colonna, the two Scarlattis, Perti, Bononcini, Albergati, Ariosti, Zanettini, Benati, Pollaroli, Pistocco, and many more than I could mention will live through the centuries in their compositions.[3] They attained heights in structuring notes

---

3. Martello passes in review the famous opera composers of his day: Bernardo Pasquini (1637–1710); Pirro Albergati (1663–1735); Attilio Ariosti (1666–?1729); Zanettini (Antonio Giannettini,

that had never been reached before by the subtlest tastes. I compare them with our ancient Greek sculptors, who distinguished themselves from their modern followers not so much in the correct contour and in the sure and moving features of the human face as in the subtle undulations of the hair, of the beard and eyebrows, and in the intricate ramifications of the veins and nerves of both the arms and legs, in their fine and delicate extremities, as well as in the representation of the muscles and the definition of the bone structure, exactly as all these parts appear clearly through the skin of human torsos. Neither have I flattered these composers in comparing their merits with those of philosophers and poets, which are no less useful to the public good. The former teach the movements of nature with rather uncertain methods, and the disciplining of the human soul with somewhat greater systematic precision. The latter achieve both aims of philosophy, divesting them of obscure and odious academic terms and rendering them acceptable and accessible even to the common folk and to women, by coloring and painting them in their compositions and letting them insinuate themselves into the intellect by way of the ear through gratifying and harmonious meters. But neither of the two aforementioned faculties, whether intellectual or moral beatitude is sought, can ever lead man to the good fortune of possessing them. Only music that has been adapted to dramatic action has the secret power of distancing the soul from all human cares, at least for that span of time in which the notes can produce their effect, artfully regulating the consonance of both voices and instruments. In fact, if sleep is so highly praised, because for a few hours it has the power to free the senses from the human miseries that oppress them, how much more praiseworthy is an art that, without temporarily interrupting life itself, as sleep does (and is therefore called death's brother), lets us live ecstatically in delightful and contented peace, with our senses wide awake and truly happy?

This art, therefore, which in Italy has attained such exquisite perfection, deserves to be Italy's most cherished and most magnificent spectacle, to be considered most favorably even by the most sophisticated and demanding, and it also deserves to be enjoyed by people living in other countries. It should be courted and obeyed by voices, instruments, poetry, painting, architecture, machinery, mime, and every other art. Finally, it deserves that you not convey the impression in your treatise on theater that there is poetry for opera, because you would be doing an injustice to music, to which it is merely subsidiary, by disjoining the two. The readers' derision would chastise you for such an injustice."

After having spoken at great length, the old man rose; and I, swearing by

---

1648–1721). If "Benati" is Carlo Antonio Benati, a Bolognese living in 1718 mentioned in the third volume of Gaetano Gaspari's catalogue of the Bologna library, he did not achieve sufficient fame to be listed in any music dictionary. For the others, see the Biographical Dictionary. [BJB]

Apollo's tripod, indeed, as an Arcadian by the Stygian marsh, not to concern myself with such matters, got up.

From *Della tragedia antica e moderna* (Rome, 1715), Sessione quinta, pp. 115–53; modern edition in *Scritti critici e satirici,* ed. Hannibal S. Noce (Bari: Laterza, 1963), 275–81, 284–92, 294–96. The complete Fifth Session has been translated by Piero Weiss in "Pier Jacopo Martello on Opera (1715): An Annotated Translation," *Musical Quarterly* 66 (1980): 378–403.

BENEDETTO MARCELLO
from *Theater à la Mode* (1720)[1]

To the Composers of Music

The modern composer need not take account of any rules pertaining to correct composition, except for a few universal principles concerning execution.

He need understand nothing of metrical proportions in music, or of the excellent effect of contrary motion, or of the ugly dissonance of tritones and major sixths. He need not know what or how many modes or tones there are, or how they are divided, or their properties. Indeed, concerning this matter, he might say there are only two modes: major and minor, that is, the major is the one that has a major third, the minor the one that has a minor third. Nor need he have the least idea what the ancients meant by major and minor mode.

He is to make no distinction whatever between the three genera (diatonic, chromatic, and enharmonic), but he should confuse all their notes (*chorde*) haphazardly in one canzonetta, in order with such modern confusion to divorce himself completely from the ancient authors.

He should use greater and lesser accidentals as he sees fit, confusing their signatures in a disorderly way. He should also make use of the enharmonic instead of the chromatic sign, saying that they are the same thing since either one raises by a minor semitone. Thus, he will be totally unaware of the fact that there must always be a chromatic sign between tones in order to divide them,

---

1. The full title reads in translation: Theater à la mode, that is, a sure and easy method to compose and perform Italian operas correctly according to the modern style. This work contains useful and necessary advice for poets, composers, singers of both sexes, impresarios, instrumentalists, stage mechanics and scene painters, comic singers, tailors, pages, extras, prompters, copyists, guardians and mothers of the virtuose, and other people belonging to the theater. Dedicated by the author of the book to its composer.

and an enharmonic only between semitones, as the enharmonic's special function is that of dividing greater semitones, and nothing more. It follows, as we have already said, that a modern *maestro di cappella* must be utterly in the dark concerning these and other such things.

To this end, therefore, he should have scant reading and writing abilities, and consequently need not understand Latin, even though he might have to compose for the Church, where he can introduce sarabands, gigues, courantes, etc., which he will then call fugues, canons, double counterpoint, etc.

Turning now to the theater, the modern composer need know nothing of poetry. He need not be able to understand the sense of a speech, or the difference between long and short syllables, or the exigencies of the dramatic situation, etc. Similarly, he need not notice the difference between wind and string instruments, if he himself is a harpsichordist. If, on the other hand, he is a string player, he need not bother to learn anything about the harpsichord, persuading himself that he can compose well in the modern style without any familiarity with that instrument.

It will therefore not be a bad thing if the modern composer has been a violin or viola player for many years, or a copyist for some famous composer, of whose operas, serenatas, etc., he still keeps the original scores, stealing material from these and from others for ritornellos, sinfonias, arias, recitatives, *follie,* choruses, etc.

Before receiving the poet's work, he should prescribe to him the meters and quantities of the arias' verses, requesting that the poet write it all out in a legible hand, and that it contain the necessary periods, commas, question marks, etc., although when setting the text to music, he need have no regard whatever either for periods, or question marks, or commas.

Before starting to work on the opera, he should call on all the leading female singers, and declare himself willing to serve their genius, that is, provide them with arias without bass, furlanettas, rigadoons, etc., all to the accompaniment of violins, a bear, and extras in unison.

He is to avoid reading the entire opera in order not to become confused. Instead, he should compose line by line, taking care furthermore to have all the arias immediately changed, making use of themes written years before. If the new words of these arias should not fit the notes properly (which is usually the case), he ought again to besiege the poet until he is completely satisfied.

He should compose all the arias with orchestral accompaniment, insuring that every part proceed with notes or figures of equal value, whether these be quarters, eighths, or sixteenths. To compose well in the modern style, he ought to prefer noise over harmony, which latter consists mainly in different values of figures, some tied over, some not, etc. Indeed, to avoid such harmony, the modern composer must use no other suspension than the usual fourth and third at the cadence. If it seems to him that his music is verging on the antiquated, he can close the arias with all the instruments playing in unison.

Let him also be sure that the arias, up to the very end of the opera, alternate between the lively and the pathetic, without paying any attention to the words, modes, or theatrical conventions. If the arias contain substantive nouns such as *padre, impero, amore, arena, regno, beltà, lena, core*, etc., or *no, senza, già*, and other adverbs, the modern composer must set them with long melismas, e.g. *Paaaa . . . Impeeee . . . Amoooo . . . Areeee . . . Reeee . . . Beltàaaa . . . Lenaaaa . . . Coooo . . .* etc., *Noooo . . . Seeen . . . Giàaaa . . .* etc. This will enable him to move beyond the ancient style, which did not employ passage-work on substantive nouns or adverbs, but only in words signifying some emotion or movement, such as *tormento, affanno, canto, volar, cader*, etc., etc., etc.

In the recitatives, modulation may be at will, with the bass moving as frequently as possible. After having composed each scene, if he is married to a virtuosa, he should let his wife listen to it; if not, he should play it to his servant or copyist, etc.

All the ariettas are to be preceded by very long ritornellos with violins in unison, and usually made up of sixteenth and thirty-second notes. These are to be performed mezzo piano in order to render them newer and less tedious, making it clear that the arias that follow have nothing to do with these ritornellos.

The ariettas, then, must proceed without the bass, and in order to keep the singer in tune, he is to be accompanied by violins playing in unison, in which case the violas can play some bass notes, though this is not essential.

When the singer reaches the cadenza, the *maestro di cappella* should have all the instruments stop, leaving it completely up to the virtuoso or virtuosa to go on as long as he or she wishes.

He need not exert much effort on duets or choruses, which he should attempt to eliminate from the opera.

The modern *maestro di cappella* should add that he composes with little care and with very many errors so as to please the audience. In this way, he can condemn the public's taste, which indeed is satisfied at times with the poor music it hears only because it has not had the opportunity of hearing anything better.

He should satisfy the impresario at very little expense, thinking of the many thousands of scudi that the virtuosi of the opera cost him. However, he should be content with a fee that is much lower than what the worst virtuoso earns, so long as he is no worse off than the bear or the extras.

When strolling with the virtuosi, especially with castratos, the composer should always let them walk on his right; he should always hold his hat in his hand, and keep one step behind, bearing in mind that the lowest of these, when performing in the operas, is at least a general, a captain to a king or queen, etc.

He should quicken or slow the tempo of the arias to please the virtuosi, covering up any mistakes they might make in the knowledge that his own reputation, credit, and recompense are in their hands. Consequently, when necessary, he should modify for them arias, recitatives, sharps, flats, naturals, etc.

All canzonettas must be made up of the same things, that is, very extended passagework, syncopations, chromatic progressions, syllable alterations, meaningless repetitions of words (for example: *amore amore, impero impero, Europa Europa, furori furori, orgoglio orgoglio,* etc.). However, when composing an opera, the modern composer must always have before him a list or inventory of all the aforementioned things, without one of which he is never to end any arietta. This he should do to avoid variety as much as possible, since it is no longer in fashion.

Once having ended a recitative in a flat key, he should immediately follow with an aria with three or four sharps in the key signature, again using flats in the following recitative. This he is to do for novelty's sake.

Similarly, the modern composer should divide the sentiment or meaning of the words, especially in the arias, having the performer sing the first line (even though it means nothing in itself), and then introducing a long ritornello with violins, violas, etc.

The modern composer should also remember, when giving a lesson to some opera virtuosa, to instruct her in bad diction. To this end, he should teach her an abundance of divisions and passagework, so that not a word is understood. In this way, the music will stand out all the more and will be better perceived. When the violins play the bass without harpsichord or double bass, it does not matter at all whether the notes of this bass (with respect to the voices or string instruments) cover the singing part, which usually happens in arias for contraltos, tenors, and basses.

Furthermore, the *maestro di cappella* ought to compose canzonettas especially for a contralto or mezzo-soprano, in which the basses accompany by playing the same notes an octave lower and the violins an octave higher, writing out all the parts in the score. This is to be regarded as composing in three parts, although the arietta consists essentially of one part only, doubled an octave lower and an octave higher.

If the composer wishes to compose in four parts, it is indispensable that he have two parts proceed in unison, or at the octave; he can then vary the progress of the theme. For example, if one part moves in quarter notes or eighth notes, the other should proceed in sixteenth or thirty-second notes, etc.

The modern *maestro di cappella* should call the bass moving in eighth notes [*crome*] the "chromatic" bass, even though the meaning of the term *chromatic* escapes him. Furthermore, as we said above, he must deny any knowledge of poetry, as such knowledge belonged to the ancient musicians, that is, Pindar, Arion, Orpheus, Hesiod, etc., who, according to Pausanias, were both excellent poets and musicians. The modern composer should strive his utmost to avoid their example, etc.

He should entice his listeners with ariettas accompanied by pizzicato or muted strings, trombe marine, cymbals, etc.

Besides his honorarium, the modern composer must demand of the impresario the gift of a poet whom he will use as he sees fit. Immediately after having composed the opera, he should have his friends, who understand nothing, listen to it. With their opinion in mind, he should adjust the ritornellos, passagework, appoggiaturas, enharmonic sharps, chromatic flats, etc.

Let the modern composer also be advised that he must not neglect the usual chromatic or accompanied recitative, thereby obliging the poet (who, as we have seen, has been given to him by the impresario) to write him a sacrificial scene, a mad scene, or a prison scene, etc.

He ought never compose arias accompanied only by the continuo bass (*basso solo obbligato*), bearing in mind that, besides being out of fashion, in the time it would take him he could compose a dozen with orchestra.

Should he then want to compose some arias with bass, the latter should at most be made up of two or three notes, repeated or tied together to form a pedal point, making sure especially that all the middle sections consist of old material.

If the impresario then complains about the music, the composer should counter by saying that this is unjust, that he put a third more notes than usual into the opera, which took him almost fifty hours to compose.

If the virtuose or their patrons should not like some aria, the composer should advise them to listen to it in the theater, with the instrumental accompaniment, the costumes, the lights, the extras, etc.

At the end of each ritornello, the *maestro di cappella* should beckon with his head to the virtuosi, so that they will enter on time. This is necessary, as they themselves would never know when to do so because of the usual length and variation of the ritornello itself.

Some arias should be composed in bass style, even though they will be assigned to contraltos and sopranos.

The modern maestro must compel the impresario to put together for him a large orchestra of violins, oboes, horns, etc.; he can save on the double basses, as they are necessary only for the initial tuning up.

The sinfonia will consist of a movement in French overture style (*tempo francese*) or a prestissimo of sixteenth notes in the major mode. This usually is to be followed by a *piano,* in the same key, but in minor. It should end with a minuet, gavotte, or gigue, again in major, thus avoiding, as obsolete and alien to modern fashion, fugues, suspensions, subjects, etc.

The *maestro di cappella* must always make sure that the prima donna gets the best arias. If he has to shorten the opera, he should not allow arias or ritornellos to be taken out, but rather entire scenes of recitative, or the bear, or the earthquake, etc.

If the seconda donna complains that her part has fewer notes than the prima donna's, he must try to console her, evening up the number by adding passagework in the arias, appoggiaturas, tasteful ornaments, etc.

The modern *maestro di cappella* ought to make use of old arias written in other cities, and should bow most reverently to the patrons of the virtuose, to the musical dilettantes, to those who rent seats in the stalls, the extras, the stagehands, etc., entreating them to cater to his needs.

When having to change the canzonettas, he should never change them for the better. When an arietta proves unsuccessful, he must say that it is the aria of a maestro, but that it has been ruined by the singers, that the audience did not understand it, etc. In arias without basso continuo, he must remember to put out the candles at the harpsichord in order to keep his head cool, and should light them up again during the recitatives.

The modern composer should be particularly careful with all the virtuose in the opera, regaling them with old cantatas transposed to fit their voices. He should tell each one of them that the opera is a success uniquely because of her talent; he should say the same thing to every singer, player, extra, bear, earthquake, etc.

Every evening he should allow masked visitors free access to the theater; some he should have sit in the orchestra; for their greater comfort he may at times dismiss the cello or the double bass players.

All modern *maestri di cappella* should see to it that the following words are included under the cast list: "The music is by the ever highly celebrated Signor N.N., *maestro di cappella,* master of concerts, of chamber music, of balls, of fencing," etc., etc., etc.

From *Il teatro alla moda o sia metodo sicuro e facile per ben comporre, ed eseguire l' opere italiane in musica all'uso moderno. Nel quale si danno avvertimenti utili, e necessari a poeti, compositori di musica, musici dell'uno, e dell'altro sesso, impresari, suonatori, ingegneri, e pittori di scene, parti buffe, sarti, paggi, comparse, suggeritori, copisti, protettori, e madri di virtuose, ed altre persone appartenenti al teatro. Dedicato dall'autore del libro al compositore di esso* (Venice, 1720), 14–22; modern edition by A. Marianni (Milan: Rizzoli, 1959), 30–38. There is a complete English translation by Reinhard G. Pauly in *Musical Quarterly* 34 (1948): 371–403, and 35 (1949): 85–105.

Chapter Two

The Italians and the French:
The Great "Querelle"

THE FIRST SIGNS OF THE great *querelle* between supporters of Italian music and those who favored French music date back to the seventeenth century. But only in 1702, with the publication of the Abbé François Raguenet's first pamphlet, does the polemic (which was to last for over half a century) officially begin. The pamphlet was written after Raguenet returned from a journey to Rome. A reaction to his brief and incisive argumentation, which will remain typical of all the defenders of Italian music (it is more pleasant, more varied, more melodious; it touches the heart, it is never boring, etc.), is found in Lecerf de la Viéville's *Comparaison de la musique italienne et de la musique française* (1704), which was followed by a *Traité du bon goût en musique*. Here, Lecerf set down the canons for a rational and classicist taste that tended to reduce music to a minimal status, seeing it as a disquieting and irrational phenomenon outside the realm of reason. Moving from this basic initial approach, the polemic progressively focused on different issues, while its parameters of judgment remained virtually the same. It first centered on the battle between the supporters of Lully and those of Rameau, wherein the former accused Rameau of writing "baroque and barbarous" music—in other words, of being Italianate. Then it centered on the livelier and more complex controversy between the *buffonistes* and the anti-*buffonistes*. Rameau, the unwitting object of such inflammatory diatribes, became the standard-bearer for conservatism and classicizing aristocratic taste, in opposition to the free and easy vivacity of Italian comic intermezzos.

During the first half of the eighteenth century in France there were numerous writings devoted entirely or in part to music, and they all contain references to the *querelle*. All the philosophers who wrote treatises on the arts (Batteux, André, Dubos, etc.) dedicated at least one chapter to music, especially to opera. In this respect, Noël-Antoine Pluche's discussion of music, taken from his great encyclopedic work *Le Spectacle de la nature* (1732–50), is particularly significant. It synthesizes both the modern and the classicizing position effectively and precisely, while underscoring one of the mainsprings of Enlightenment aesthetic thinking: the aspiration to achieve a "significant" art and the rejection of pure ornamentation. This is why instrumental music is rejected as meaningless arabesque.

Numerous references to music are also found in Voltaire's writings; we have chosen a brief excerpt in which Voltaire ironically sums up his position as a staunch classicist and follower of Lully's French tradition.

Among the Encyclopedists, d'Alembert represents a mediating position between Voltaire's classicism and the demands for renewal expressed by Rousseau and Diderot. In the *querelle* between the supporters of Italian taste and those of the French, d'Alembert favored a moderate eclecticism: he advocated taking the music of Italian opera and the poetry of French opera and combining them, thus creating an opera that embodies the best of both. As a popularizer of Rameau's work, and a mathematician and student of harmony, in his *Discours préliminaire* to the *Encyclopédie* d'Alembert delineated a hierarchy of all the fine arts, in which he entrusted the great figures of his time, and progress in general, with the task of raising music from its lowly position on the ladder of the fine arts.

Rousseau occupies a central position in all eighteenth-century musical thought. He was the author of most of the musical entries in the *Encyclopédie,* which were later collected in his *Dictionnaire de musique,* and he wrote numerous pamphlets, among which is the famous *Lettre sur la musique française* (1753). He was even a musician and the author of a one-act opera, *Le Devin du village* (1752), which was very popular in his day and was intended to exemplify Italian style. The excerpts here, from his *Essai sur l'origine des langues,* are a compendium of the basic concepts underlying his ideas on music.

Diderot, who conceived and directed the *Encyclopédie,* was perhaps the most eclectic and gifted of the Encyclopedists. He was also the least directly involved in the *querelle des Bouffons.* Except for his *Leçons de clavecin,* undertaken with his daughter's teacher, Anton Bemetzrieder, he devoted no publications specifically to music, although a number of different viewpoints on music often appear in his works, from the *Lettre sur les sourds et les muets* to the *Entretiens sur le fils naturel,* from the celebrated *Neveu de Rameau* to the *Salons.* It is difficult to select the most significant passages, as the author's viewpoint on music changed according to the different context in which he wrote. The section from the *Neveu de Rameau* is among the few in which he took a position in favor of Italian opera; in his opinion, it embodied primitive vitality, the "cri animal" proper to music.

Friedrich Melchior Grimm, who was born in Germany but moved to Paris, became one of the leading spirits of the *querelle des Bouffons,* with numerous writings of great literary power. His *Le Petit Prophète de Boehmisch-Broda* (1753) has remained a model of satire directed at French opera and music. The article "Poème lyrique" that he contributed to the *Encyclopédie* is more carefully thought out and therefore conceptually more significant. According to Grimm, opera constitutes one of the most powerful means to express feelings and human emotions, far more powerful than either tragedy or comedy.

FRANÇOIS RAGUENET

from *A Comparison between the French and Italian Music and Operas* (1702)

The *Italians* are more bold and hardy in their Airs, than the *French;* they carry their Point farther, both in their tender Songs, and those that are more sprightly, as well as in their other Compositions: Nay, they often unite Stiles, which the *French* think incompatible. The *French,* in those Compositions that consist of many Parts, seldom regard more than that which is principal;[1] whereas the *Italians* usually study to make all the Parts equally shining, and beautiful. In short, the Invention of the one is inexhaustible; but the Genius of the other is narrow and constrain'd: This the Reader will fully understand when we descend to Particulars.

It is not to be wonder'd that the *Italians* think our Musick dull and stupifying, that, according to their Taste, it appears flat and insipid, if we consider the nature of the *French* Airs compar'd to those of the *Italian.* The *French* in their airs aim at the Soft, the Easie, the Flowing, and Coherent; the whole Air is of the same Tone, or if sometimes they venture to vary it, they do it with so many Preparations, they so qualifie it, that still the Air seems to be as natural and consistent as if they had attempted no change at all; there is nothing bold and adventurous in it, it's all equal, and of a Piece.[2] But the *Italians* pass boldly,

---

1. The *Italians,* in their Compositions of three or four Parts, take care, as the Author well observes, to have all the Parts equally beautiful; unlike the *French,* who think they have done their Business if the upper-part and the Base prove good; whilst the other Parts are crowded in without any Design or Fore-sight, and must consequently be very insipid, and ineffectual; whereas the *Italian* Composer suffers nothing to pass without being first well consider'd, and digested: So that besides the Beauty and Sprightliness that attends ev'ry Air, a regular Judgment and Conduct appears through the whole, which never fails of Applause.

2. An instance of this change of the Key in the *Italian* Airs, is particularly to be found in an Air of *Gasparini*'s, in the Opera of *Clotilda,* viz. (*del' fallo sul' camin*) but we must observe, that the most beautiful Part of that Song was omitted by the Singer, which call'd his Judgment into ques-

and in an Instant from *b* Sharp to *b* Flat, and from *b* Flat to *b* Sharp; they venture the boldest Cadences, and the most irregular Dissonance; and their Airs are so out of the way that they resemble the Compositions of no other Nation in the World.

The *French* wou'd think themselves undone, if they offended in the least against the Rules; they Flatter, Tickle, and court the Ear, and are still doubtful of Success, tho' ev'ry thing be done with an exact Regularity. The more hardy *Italian* changes the Tone and the Mode without any Awe or Hesitation, he makes double or treble Cadences of seven or eight Bars together, upon Tones we shou'd think incapable of the least Division. He'll make a *Swelling*[3] of so prodigious a Length, that they who are unacquainted with it can't chuse but be offended at first to see him so adventurous; but before he has done, they'll think they can't sufficiently admire him: He'll have Passages of such an Extent, as will perfectly confound his Auditors at first; and upon such irregular Tones as shall instill a Terror as well as Surprize into the Audience, who will immediately conclude, that the whole Concert is degenerating into a dreadful Dissonance, and betraying 'em by that means into a concern for the Musick, which seems to be upon the brink of Ruin, he immediately reconciles 'em by such regular Cadences that ev'ry one is surpriz'd to see Harmony rising again in a manner out of Discord it self, and owing its greatest Beauties to those Irregularities which seem'd to threaten it with Destruction.

The *Italians* venture at ev'ry thing that is harsh, and out of the way, but then they do it like People that have right to venture, and are sure of Success. Under a

---

tion, and blemish'd his Reputation; nay, he wou'd willingly have left out the whole Air, alledging it to be a Composition not proper for the Theatre, and consequently not like to please the Audience, tho', contrary to his Opinion, it met with a general Applause; for which Reason, we are to consult the Original, and not the Copy Printed here in *London*, where, as we observ'd before, the most beautiful of all the Musick is wanting in the second Part; upon these Words (*d'Eccesso in altro Eccesso*) where, with an inexpressible Boldness, and an extraordinary Judgment, the Composer has hit upon the sense of the Words; and the Vocal Musick rolls with a perpetual Harshness, whilst the Violins without any interruption continue the first Subject, and introduce the former part of the Air again with an admirable Judgment, which shows him to be a great Artist.

Two Songs in *Pyrrhus* and *Demetrius* bear a near Resemblance to the Composition before mention'd, *viz. Veder parmi un ombra nera*, &c. and *Germana addio;* both of 'em Compos'd by the Famous [Alessandro] *Scarlatti;* where, besides the great Harmony there is between the Instruments and the Vocal Part, you will find an inimitable Modulation, and I believe they are two of the most Masterly Airs that ever were Compos'd for the Theatre. Of the same kind are two Airs of *Bononcini* in *Camilla*, viz. (*Consiglio ed Aita*) and (*Amo per servir*) but they are not an equal strength with the two before-mention'd.

One can't comprehend the Meaning of this Artful Harshness in Musick better, than by observing some of the Recitative in *Scarlatti's Cantata's*, where he makes use of all sorts of Dissonance to express the force of the Words, and afterwards Resolves 'em so well that indeed the most beautiful Concords are hardly so sweet and harmonious as his Discords.

3. *By the* Italians *call'd* Messe di Voce.

Notion of being the greatest and most absolute Masters of Musick in the World, like Despotick Soveraigns, they dispense with its Rules in hardy but fortunate Sallies; they exert themselves above the Art, but like Masters of that Art, whose Laws they follow, or transgress at Pleasure: they insult the niceness of the Ear which others court, they defy and compel it; they master and Conquer it with Charms, which owe their irresistible force to the Boldness of the adventurous Composer. . . .

As the *Italians* are naturally much more brisk than the *French,* so are they more sensible of the Passions, and consequently express 'em more lively in all their productions.[4] If a Storm, or Rage, is to be describ'd in a Symphony, their Notes give us so natural an Idea of it, that our Souls can hardly receive a stronger Impression from the Reality than they do from the Description; every thing is so brisk and piercing, so impetuous and affecting, that the Imagination, the Senses, the Soul, and the Body itself are all betray'd into a general Transport; 'tis impossible not to be born down with the Rapidity of these Movements: A Symphony of Furies shakes the Soul; it undermines and overthrows it in spite of all its Care; the[5] Artist himself, whilst he is performing it, is seiz'd with an unavoidable Agony, he tortures his Violin, he racks his Body; he is no longer Master of himself, but is agitated like one possessed with an irresistable Motion.

If, on the other side, the Symphony is to express a Calm and Tranquility, which requires a quite different Style, they however execute it with an equal Success: Here the Notes descend so low, that the Soul is swallow'd with 'em in the profound Abyss. Every String of the Bow is of an infinite Length, ling'ring on a dying Sound, which decays gradually 'till at last it absolutely expires. Their Symphonies of Sleep insensibly steal the Soul from the Body, and so suspend its Faculties, and Operations, that being bound up as it were in the Harmony, that entirely possesses and enchants it, it's as dead to every thing else, as if all its Powers were captivated by a real Sleep.

In short, as for the Conformity of the Air with the Sense of the Words, I

---

4. Of this kind is the Scene which *Nicolini* added to *Pyrrhus* and *Demetrius,* the last Time it was perform'd, and afterward sung in his own Consort. This Scene was compos'd by [Alessandro] *Scarlatti,* in an Opera call'd *Rosaura,* perform'd at *Rome* on [*sic*] *Capranica's* Theatre, where *Nicolini* perform'd *Rosaura's* Part to the Admiration of all that saw him. This Scene, notwithstanding its Excellent Musick, wou'd have been esteem'd as nothing, had it not been perform'd by one so perfect in the Art of Acting, as *Nicolini* is. By this we may make an Estimate of the Composer's Judgment, in fitting the Part for his Performer; and the Performer is no less to be admired in forcing an Applause for that, which, had another perform'd it, would probably have fallen far short of it.

5. I never met with any Man that suffer'd his Passions to hurry him away so much, whilst he was playing on the Violin, as the famous *Arcangelo Corelli;* whose Eyes will sometimes turn as red as Fire; his Countenance will be distorted, his Eye-Balls roll as in an Agony, and he gives in so much to what he is doing that he doth not look like the same Man.

never heard any Symphony comparable to that which was perform'd at *Rome* in[6] the Oratory of St. *Jerome* of Charity, on St. *Martin's* Day in the year 1697, upon these two words *Mille Saette* [a thousand arrows]. The Air consisted of dis-jointed Notes, like those in a Jigg, which gave the Soul a lively Impression of an Arrow; and that wrought so effectually upon the Imagination, that every Violin appear'd to be a Bow, and their Bows were like so many flying Arrows, darting their pointed Heads upon every part of the Symphony. Nothing can be more masterly, or more happily express'd.[7] So that be their Airs either of a sprightly or gentle Style, let 'em be impetuous or languishing; in all these the *Italians* are equally preferrable to the *French:* But there is one thing beyond all this, which neither the *French,* nor any other Nation, besides themselves, in the World, ever attempted; for they will sometimes unite in a most surprizing Manner, the Tender with the Sprightly, as may be instanced in that celebrated Air, *Mai non si vidde ancor piu bella fedelta,* etc.,[8] which is the softest and most tender of any in the World, and yet its Symphony is as lively, and piercing as ever was composed: These different Characters are they able to unite so artfully, that, far from destroying a Contrary by its Contrary, they make the one serve to embellish the other. . . .

The *Italians* are inexhaustible in their Productions of such Pieces as are Composed of several Parts, in which on the other side the *French* are extreamly limited. In *France* the Composer thinks he has done his Business, if he can diversifie the Subject; as for the Accompaniments, you find nothing like it in them; they are all upon the same Chords, the same Cadence, where you see all at once, without any Variety or Surprize. The *French* Composers steal from one another, or Copy from their own Works, so that all their Compositions are much alike. Whereas the *Italian* Invention is infinite, both for the Quantity, and Diversity of their Airs; the number of 'em may modestly be said to be without Number; and yet it will be very difficult to find two among 'em all that are alike. We are daily admiring *Lully's* fertile Genius in the Composition of so

6. And yet the best Entertainments are not to be met with in this place, in respect either of the Musick or the Singers. Here some Scripture Stories, set to Musick, are perform'd every Holy-Day-night, from *All-Saints* to *Easter:* A laudable Institution, design'd to restrain the Populace from more guilty Diversions.

7. It will not be improper to insert in this Place some Examples of the several different Sorts of *Italian* Airs, as they are distinguish'd by the Author; that is, into Brisk lively Airs, Tender Airs, Impetuous Airs, Languishing Airs, and such as are tender and lively at the same time, as that by him mentioned, *Mai non si vedde ancor.* But that the Reader may have a more familiar View of 'em, I'll make Choice only of the Airs in *Camilla,* and *Pyrrhus* and *Demetrius.* [Follows a list of the arias, divided by category.]

8. From Giovanni Bononcini's *Camilla,* first performed in Naples in 1696; the translator saw one of the English productions and was much taken with it (cf. the previous note; "Mai non si vidde" is listed there among the "Airs that are Tender and Lively at the same time"). [BJB]

many beautiful different Airs. *France* never produced a Master that had a Talent like him; this I'm sure no one will contradict, and this is all I desire, to make it appear how much the *Italians* are superior to the *French*, both for the Invention, and Composition; for, in short, this great Man, whose Works we set in Competition with those of the greatest Masters in *Italy*, was himself an *Italian*. He has excell'd all our Musicians in the Opinion of the *French* themselves. To establish therefore an Equality between the two Nations, we ought to produce some *Frenchman*, who has in the same manner excell'd the greatest masters in *Italy*, and that by the Confession of the *Italians* themselves; but this is an Instance we have not yet been able to produce. Besides, *Lully* is the only Man ever appear'd in *France* with a Genius so superior for Musick, whereas[9] *Italy* abounds in Masters, the worst of which may be compar'd to him; they are to be found at *Rome*, *Naples*, *Florence*, *Venice*, *Bolognia*, *Milan*, and *Turin*, in which places there has been a long Succession of them. They have had their *Luigi* [Rossi], their *Carissimi*, their *Melani*, and their *Legrenzi;* to these Succeeded their *Buononcini*, their *Corelli*, and their *Bassani*, who are still Living, and Charm all *Europe* with their Excellent Productions. The first seem'd to have rob'd the art of all her Beauties; and yet those that follow'd have at least Rival'd 'em in an infinite number of Works of a Stamp perfectly New; they grow up there ev'ry Day, and seem

9. Among the ancient Composers of Church Musick, besides *Carissimi*, we may add, *Oratio Benevoli*, and *Francisco Foggia*, and one more ancient than either, *Palestrina*, who was the Inventor of a Style in Musick, call'd from his own Name, *alla Palestrina*, or rather *à Capella*, being the only Style suffer'd to be perform'd in the Pope's Chappel, a Style which none but *Palestrina* cou'd Invent, so none but *Foggia* has been ever able to Copy after him. These Compositions consist of four or five Parts. *Oratio Benevoli* was the Author of four Chorus's, or sixteen real Parts, every Chorus consisting of four Parts each. This *Benevoli* has been so far from being excell'd by any Masters since, that no one hitherto has been able to Rival him. *Carissimi's* Excellence lay in Compositions of two Chorus's, or eight Parts, as likewise for Chamber Songs accommodated to the gust of the Age he lived in.

Francisco Foggia has moreover Compos'd Excellent Church Musick of four or five Parts, in the same Style with *Palestrina*, and has even excell'd him. Among the Moderns, we find *Colonna*, and *Perti* at *Bologna*, *Legrenzi* at *Venice*, *Francisco Grassi*, call'd *Bassetto*, *Ottavio Pitoni*, and *Melani* at *Rome*, *Bassani* at *Ferrara*, with several others.

For the Opera and Cantata's, the first were *Luigi Rossi*, *Cesti*, and *Carissimi;* after them *Celano*, *Stradella*, and *Pier' Simone Augustini*, who have been Excellent in their Style, and something more Modern than the first, and whose Works abound with many things worthily to be admir'd.

After them, and to give the last Hand to the Perfection of *Italian* Musick for Opera's and Cantata's, succeeded the abovemention'd *Scarlatti*, the first Inventor of the Songs accompanied by the Violin alone, and other Compositions very much to be commended. *Pollaroli* the *Venetian* invented the Unison Arietto's, which Invention has been follow'd by the most celebrated Composers, and is at present one of the greatest Beauties in the *Italian* Opera's. To those may be added *Perti, Bononcini, Gasparini*, and many more who are much in Vogue in *Italy*.

For the Symphonies, we may boldly say *Corelli* has set a Pattern to all the World, there being not one of his that is Printed but what is Excellent in its kind. After him may be mention'd *Baldassini, Torelli, Bassani* and *Albinoni*, &c.

to claim the Laurel from their Predecessors; they are Flourishing in all Parts of *Italy*, whereas in *France*, a master like one of them, is lookt on as a *Phoenix;* the whole Realm has been able to produce but one in an Age, and 'tis to be fear'd, no Age hereafter will ever be able to supply the Loss of *Lully.* 'Tis therefore undeniably evident, that the *Italian* Genius for Musick is incomparably preferable to that of the *French.*

We have had no Masterly Compositions in *France* since *Lully*'s Death, so that all true Lovers of Musick must despair of any New Entertainments among us; but if they take the Pains to go to *Italy*, I'll answer for 'em, let their Heads be never so full of the *French* Compositions they'll renounce 'em all that they may have room enough for the *Italian* Airs, which bear not the least resemblance to those in *France*, tho' this is an Assertion no one can rightly comprehend, that has not been in *Italy;* for the *French* have no Notion of anything fine in Musick that doth not resemble some of their Favorite Airs.

From *A Comparison between the French and Italian Musick and Opera's. Translated from the French; With some Remarks* (London, 1709; repr. Farnborough: Gregg, 1968), 13–18, 19–26, 29–34. According to John Hawkins (1776), the translation is by J. E. Galliard; all the footnotes are the translator's. This translation has been reprinted in *Musical Quarterly* 32 (1946): 411–36 and also appears in Strunk, *Source Readings,* 473–88. Original edition: *Paralèle des italiens et des français, en ce qui regarde la musique et les opéras* (Paris, 1702; repr. Graz: Akademische Druck- und Verlagsanstalt, 1966; Geneva: Minkoff, 1976), 28–70.

JEAN-LAURENT LECERF DE LA VIÉVILLE
from *Comparison of French and Italian Music* (1704)

Count: "And so let us talk about Italian."

"Very well then," the Chevalier resumed. "Italian warbles in a pretty fashion on the subject of love: this language has sweet and flattering words that express it perfectly. Yes, young love, hopeful love, happy love, or at least love that knows only pleasant suffering. That is all well and good. But are ladies, and especially opera heroines, always well-behaved? When it pleases them to consign their stage lovers to frustration, envy, and anger, or rather to despair, rage, and fury, how can this be done in Italian, if the language supplies no terms appropriate to these violent passions? One is also very much hindered when it is necessary to draw words of modest and grave expression from Italian—and when magic and sorcery are brought into the discussion, how is the musician to set loud tones that strike fear and horror in the listeners' souls to playful, honey-sweet words?

It is nonetheless true, if the Abbé [Raguenet] will pardon me, that the Italian language has the disadvantage of insipid and excessive sweetness, an effeminate puerility. Its frequent *z*, its perpetual endings in *e*, in *i*, in *o*, etc., divest it of gravity, noble vivacity, and spirited expressions. But, my dear Count, let us proceed and extract ourselves from these trifling details. For, the Abbé R[aguenet] says, '*this is strictly but the material aspect of music*' (p. 27).

You will not be surprised, he says on page 30, that '*the Italians find that our music lulls them*' and that it '*puts them to sleep; that it is even, for their taste, very flat and insipid,*' when '*you consider the nature of French arias and that of Italian arias.*' What he says is true. It is in no way surprising that Italians find our music to be flat and insipid, and the Abbé gives a very sensible reason for this. It's that in our music everything is '*sweet, easy, flowing, connected, natural, coherent, unified, and equal,*' completely opposite to the Italian."

"At least, Sir," said the Countess, "you will not complain that the Abbé is not putting his cards on the table."

"No, I assure you, Madam: his sincerity in this instance is most praiseworthy. But, Madam, based on this description, which of the two, the Italians or ourselves, seems to you to be most in keeping with good taste and on the right path? And you, Count, who are so knowledgeable and so particular when it comes to good eating, with whom would you rather live, a man who would have you eat only casseroles, pastries, stews, and jams, and who would have you drink only muscatel, *eau de Sète,* and *Pitrepite;* or with another who would serve only wine from Tonnerre or Silleri, excellent soups, but scarcely any consommés and white meats, each admirable in its own way, few sweets, and the finest fruits and compotes?"

"Oh," said the Countess, "I'll choose for him. He'll reserve a lifelong place at the latter table."

"There you have it, Madam. We are people who nourish ourselves with all the most delicious and exquisite things nature has given us, and who sometimes even eat morels and truffles, but who don't care for liqueurs, sauces, or spices. And the Italians are people who like pastries, stews, and amber-colored jams, and eat nothing else."

"What is certain," said the young Countess, laughing, "is that you will live longer than they."

"I believe so, Madam, and that our music will be appreciated and highly regarded longer than theirs."

"But," the Count resumed, "to keep to your comparison, as favorable as it may seem to you, you must still confess that stews, and what you call sauces, have something that flatters and excites our sense of taste more than plain white meat, and—more important for the Italians, and more troublesome for you— you cannot help agreeing that there is greater honor and skill for a cook in making stews and delicate sauces than in making healthy soups, or in cooking a rabbit just right."

"Aha," the Countess cried out, "he has you there, Chevalier! Get yourself out of this one if you can."

"He will have a difficult time doing so," the Count added. "For if sauces tantalize the palate more than the best trussed and the best cooked partridge, he must admit that Italian music, perhaps not as good as French music when you come right down to it, still produces a more intense and piquant pleasure; and by the skill of the cook who makes the stews, I have proved to him the advantage in knowledge and distinction that Italian masters have over our own. Speak, speak, my friend. I am grateful to you for having brought this comparison to our attention. It brings to mind so many things in which I take pleasure—and I will gladly stop there."

"So you think you have really tripped me up!" the Chevalier replied. "Well then, listen. First of all, I do not for one moment concede that stews are more pleasing to a discriminating palate than a partridge, or a snipe with the most exquisite aroma. They are more exciting, but less agreeable to us. They do not so much tease as set our mouths on fire, and it's only after our sense of taste has been ruined, and we've worked ourselves up getting used to these dishes, that we find them to be so delicious. At most, a man like yourself, who knows how to eat well, tries five or six of them during a meal, to stimulate his appetite when it begins to fail. But to eat nothing but this, and to eat it all the time—one entrée, then another, then some of this stew, and some of that, while waiting for the sweets and jams, wanting neither partridges, nor fatted chickens, nor Normandy veal—neither the Count nor any of the people as discriminating as he in fine food would put up with it. Now for the application of this comparison. French music, then, is prudent, unified, and natural, and only tolerates from time to time, and at distant intervals, extraordinary harmonies and very unusual ornaments. Italian music, on the contrary, being always forced, always outside the limits of nature, without continuity or progression, rejects our sweet and easy graces. It is not surprising that the Italians find our music dull and insipid, but so much the worse for them, and so much the better for us. They have ruined their taste by the constant use of their piquant and refined harmonies. As for the rest, one may like Italian music, or rather some piece of Italian music, from time to time, but very rarely. Whereas ours is always ready to please. It is everyday fare, simple and excellent, that never tires or repels us. And for constant use, for pieces as extensive as an opera, you must prefer French music to Italian, as you prefer an Avenai wine to a Rossoli, and white meat to stews."

"I will confess, with the same sincerity that the Abbé R[aguenet], who apparently writes in good faith, affects, that in general Italian composers possess more knowledge and depth than ours. But that *all* of them have more than all of ours, no. I have no doubt that Lully was at least as learned as Luigi [Rossi] and Carissimi, and I am convinced that Charpentier at the Sainte Chapelle and Collasse are as much so as Bassani and Corelli. The Italian masters shape, turn, and carve their pieces more finely than our opera composers do. But we must consider whether the Italians do not shape and carve them too much. I have already begun to demonstrate that this is so, and I will show you further: even if our composers were to work their music too little, it would still remain to be seen whether this was due to ignorance or laziness. As for fame, Sir, it is not the trouble one takes but the outcome that decides the matter: it is the quality of the things one has made and not the skill that has been put into making them. What does it matter if our composers are lazy or even ignorant, if with their ignorance and laziness they produce better things, and music that has more true and solid beauty, than the Italians do with all of their depth and application?" . . .

"'*Italian arias are of such an unusual melody that they do not at all resemble those composed by the other nations of the world,*' the Abbé goes on to say (*Paralèle,* p. 32). Fine praise indeed!"

"But, Chevalier," said the Countess, "ought not each nation have its own character in all things, and in music as in anything else?"

"Assuredly, Madam," replied the latter, "this is perfectly so, and I do not doubt that you have noticed that beautiful Italian arias are those in which one senses on occasion something particular, something somehow Italian. But when it is taken to excess, it becomes a very great flaw. Nature is the common mother of all peoples and of all that they produce: she inspires them all, and to achieve excellence, they must express nature according to her inspiration. Nature well expressed is indeed the source and the mark of all beauty. Now then, Madam, although nature may be different among all peoples, it is not so very different that they bear no resemblance to one another when they listen to it and express it, and I think it is not a good sign for Italian music to resemble no other. It would seem that it is less natural, and as countless things that the Abbé says below will demonstrate that it is not, and he cannot deny it, I tell you right now that his very praises give rise to the notion that Italian music is worthless. What does it mean to make music? It is to have a man who praises God, who invokes him, speak in song; likewise a man who feels love, hate, anger, etc.; or a man who complains, prays, threatens, etc. I leave aside church music: that is not what the *Parallèle* deals with. But as for the rest, these are natural passions. Will your music portray them well, if it does not portray them naturally? And will it portray them naturally with such 'an unusual melody'?" . . .

"As for unusual melodies, I beg Madam to make one observation. That is, if this were such an excellent thing, most of the operas that have appeared since

Lully would be far superior to his. As Lully, a productive and original man, has exhausted a great number of the natural harmonies in the twenty or so operas he has given us, the composers who came after him, and who did not wish to be reproached with imitating or plagiarizing him, have often been reduced to searching for strange and peculiar harmonies for those unusual melodies that the Abbé R. praises, and that Lully had scarcely touched. Charpentier, Collasse, Campra, and Destouches, in *Hercule et Omphale,*[1] threw themselves into the effort and expended a great deal of cleverness and skill preparing and embellishing them. Did they produce wonders in so doing? Nothing could have been more detrimental to their works, and these successors to Lully, who were most unfortunate in that he left us so many beautiful things, failed when they had recourse to these elaborations and refinements. Their research and study worked to their disadvantage, and they only made us better appreciate the value and the naturalness of the operas by their teacher, who carried off, so to speak, nearly the whole flower of French music. I do not, however, conclude that Italian music is bad because it is full of 'unusual melodies that do not at all resemble those composed by all the nations of the world.' I have only said that it is a bad sign and a mark that Italian music is hardly natural; and when I have added to this what I infer from other praises of the same caliber that the Abbé R. bestows on Italian music, you will see what I shall conclude."

"But beforehand, Count, we must clear our musicians of his charge that they are too strongly tied to the rules, and '*tease, delight, and flatter our ears too much.*'"

"Oh! as for that reproach," said M. du B., "I can't agree with him by half. What is music made for, if not for '*delighting and teasing our ears*'?"

"And what purpose would the rules serve," the Countess added, "if one did not follow them?"

"They were conceived with felicity and the utmost skill," the Chevalier resumed, "and there is nothing wrong with that. Poets, mathematicians, etc. have sometimes cried out against the rules of their craft, and have attacked them. Musicians never have. All agree that they are very good, and I find it very hard to imagine how it can be a fault to follow them generally. They lead to a precision and sweetness too precious to deviate from them. Not that one should adhere to them blindly and slavishly. Lully placed himself above them from time to time. He was reproached for it, and he merely laughed; and when there were points at which the common rules of composition hindered or imprisoned his genius, he left them behind, to pursue certain great beauties that they would have prevented him from capturing. But he did so with restraint, with the good

---

1. An alternative title for Destouches' *Omphale,* first performed at the Opéra on 10 November 1701. [BJB]

sense worthy of a true musician, and with a selectiveness and taste worthy of a man of wit, rarely and sparingly. For, let it be said in passing, practice, application, and study make craftsmen; but only inspiration, governed by taste, makes excellent craftsmen.

The Abbé R., on the contrary, derives the praise and the glory of Italian musicians from '*the fact that they often make cadences that are extended and re-extended for seven or eight measures*' (*p. 33*); '*from sustained notes of an incredible length*' (*p. 34*); '*from passages with a range to astonish those hearing them for the first time, in frightening keys*' (*p. 36*); '*from the fact that they attempt what is most difficult and most extraordinary*' (*p. 36*), '*and that they offend the delicacy of the ear where others seek only to flatter it. They do so in their conviction,*' according to the Abbé, '*that they are the best in the world at music, that they are its sovereigns and despotic masters, and as people always assured of success*' (*p. 36*)."

"Now then, Chevalier," said M. du B., "be a good fellow: acknowledge that all of that may become quite beautiful when it is well conceived."

"Yes, my friend, just as a well-devised little frown can be most charming and provocative. But what would you say of a woman who frowned incessantly, in the most extravagant fashion? In a word, my dear Count, all of these bold ornamentations, faulty in themselves and contrary to the rules, must be prepared and carried out with great skill; and I believe they are, convinced as I am of the skill and cleverness of the Italian masters with whom I myself am familiar. But this kind of beauty must not be used too lavishly, and in overusing them, like the Italians who violate the rules at every turn, you deprive them of their value, and restore their original defects to them. The first time you hear them in the works of Italian composers, they are enchanting; the second time, they are tolerable; the third time, they are displeasing; the fourth, revolting. They carry everything to excess. 'And what is most noble is often spoiled / By exaggeration and an excess of zeal' ([Molière], *Tartuffe*, Act I). One might say to the Italian masters concerning all these unrestrained embellishments what Voiture[2] said jestingly of new words: 'You will use them three times a week.'"

From *Comparaison de la musique italienne et de la musique française* (Brussels, 1704–6); 2d ed. (Brussels, 1705–6; repr. Geneva: Minkoff, 1972), 21–30, 34–38. It was republished, together with Raguenet's critique and a response by Lecerf, in Jacques Bonnet, *Histoire de la musique* (Amsterdam, 1721 and later editions). Part of the sixth dialogue is translated in Strunk, *Source Readings*, 489–507.

2. The poet Vincent Voiture (1597–1648), renowned for his wit. [BJB]

NOËL-ANTOINE PLUCHE
from *The Spectacle of Nature* (1746)

As speech is the sign of our thoughts, so is writing the sign of speech. The first and foremost goal of each therefore is instruction.

Much the same is true in music and in painting, which hold so prominent a rank among the arts. Music is a type of speaking, and painting a way of writing. If they bring satisfaction to the eye and ear, they do so in order to make their lessons more effective by means of the pleasure that accompanies them; but as soon as they attempt to please without instructing, do they not begin from that very moment to degenerate? Do they not miss the goal toward which they have been leading since their inception? This is a fine question, and it is the only point that we shall treat here, leaving to the great masters the task of teaching the substance and practice of such widespread arts.

There is no one who may not take some liking to the arts; and just as one need not be a poet to appreciate the difference between Virgil, who paints nature, and Lucan, who displays wit, one need not be a musician to sense the true beauties of music and to judge soundly the merit of musicians. But let us risk neither attributing error to them, nor wishing to give any one of them preference over another, except with the aid of a perfectly lucid rule that is acknowledged by musicians themselves and that determines the true worth of their method. We can search for this rule either in the claims of the greatest masters, or in universally accepted ideas, but above all in the needs of society. The judgment of the great masters would seem ill suited to instructing us in our search. They are too divided in their sentiments. The Italians and the French would seem to be those who have the greatest claim to authority, by virtue of their progress in this genre. But jealous as they are of their own methods, neither would seem disposed to profit from the wisdom of the other.

This quarrel, I confess, is very different today from what it once was. It is as if the two nations had drawn closer together. Though they are lovers of melody, the French have for quite some time been putting more energy and harmony into composition than they had in the last century. Italian music, though elaborate and learned, becomes daily more graceful and more lilting. We no longer admire our own music exclusively: there was a pettiness in doing so that disgraced us while impoverishing us. We believe that one can be French, and a good musician; but we adopt gratefully whatever good things clever Italy sends us, and we are not unaware that in every genre beauty has often come to us from beyond the Alps. This reconciliation could have led us to the point we are seeking, if a much livelier dispute had not arisen between our great composers. Sub-ordinates, all performers, and many amateurs take part in this quarrel and often make more noise than the maestros themselves. The quick favor that one of the two parties has won has introduced a completely new style of music among us. According to some, we have at last achieved perfection, and we have found the rule that governs beauty. According to others, we have moved farther away from it than before.

Rameau, having completed a profound study of harmony and of the means of perfecting it, has brought this area of music to a boldness of composition and a freedom of execution to which even the Italians seem not to have taken it. The acclaim justly accorded this famous man has produced many rivals, many imi-tators, and consequently many bad copyists.

On the other hand, Lalande, Mouret, Bousset, Couperin, Dagincour, Leclair, and other composers of the first rank, several of whom are still living, have al-ways claimed that the first merit of music was beautiful melody, because it is melody that provides the style and character of the piece; but [they claimed] that melody was either unrecognizable or incompatible with extreme speed or with too great a burden of chords and ornamentation. Melody being drowned, as it were, at these modern speeds, or totally banished from the new music, the latter ceased to be reasonable; the contempt with which melody was treated in the new music was carried to the point of choosing indifferently the one that least conformed to the character of the subject. But it was a curious error to think that energy and harmony could suffice to make music completely beauti-ful whatever the melody might be; one might just as well set the tune of *Nicolas Gardien* to four parts and pray for peace in full concert to the tune of *Les Niais de Sologne*.[1] What they add seems even more pressing. They say that since we are all born with a little of the geometer in us, or as lovers of symmetry and measures, we are all born musicians to a greater or lesser degree, and that the first step in our music and in that of all more or less civilized peoples was to fashion a melody consistent with the thought or feeling within the soul, and the second step to nourish and bring out this melody through pleasing conso-nances; that harmony is thus a beauty of the second order and necessarily sub-ordinate to the first; that it is a lady-in-waiting who must be careful to aid, present, and show her mistress to best advantage, not to hide her, still less to

---

1. While the expression "Les niais de Sologne" has become proverbial for a feigned simpleton, it may derive from an old chanson. Rameau's *Pièces de Clavecin* of 1724 contains a piece entitled *Les Niais de Sologne*, which might incorporate the tune. The English translation of 1739–48 identifies it as "A fine Piece of Music for the Harpsichord but all in the gay Strain"; *Nicolas Gardien* is called "A Burlesque French Song." [BJB]

destroy her. All of our great melodists acknowledge Rameau's rare talent for harmony; but they claim that a novelty, a procedure that works for a great genius, often inundates us with bad imitators and can suddenly introduce a ridiculous fashion, or a manner full of affectation; that confusion in music is like that in fine wit; that these are the two maladies of the age, both caused by the contagion of example; that the brilliance of this lighthearted music has filled most of our composers with the desire to emulate it, and they now take themselves for so many eagles, rapid in flight and difficult to follow; all this is the reason for the new music, the difficult music, and the music that they themselves call diabolical. But all the newly introduced lively elements, even if they were to run along forever in four parts, to crackle like a torrent of sparks, are in the end—if the melody is lacking—nothing more than little flashes of light, a variety of violent flame, harmonious trifles. They explain their thoughts also in another fashion. Melody, they say, is to the subject one is treating as clothes are to the body one wishes to adorn; and harmony is to the song or melody what the lining and the decoration are to clothing. Decoration can bring out the cut and style of a fine suit of clothes if it is placed with care; if it is too lavish, it will hide the clothing. Four lively and light parts, devoid of melody, are as four rows of *fanfioles*,[2] sewn together and attached to a sack. No fine clothing can result from it, nor any beautiful music. Such is the quarrel of the leading masters of the art. . . .

The first sign of disorder in this fine art was amusing the ear with empty words, or seeking to please it without having it learn anything, and often teaching it something criminal. Having separated two things that were meant to be forever inseparable—that is, the instruction of the mind and the pleasure of the ear—music fell easily into a new aberration, but a lesser one than the first. It is a custom that has become extremely widespread for some centuries to do without vocal music and to endeavor solely to amuse the ear, without presenting any thoughts to the mind; in a word, to claim to satisfy men with a long series of sounds devoid of meaning, which is directly contrary to the very nature of music, which is to imitate, as do all the fine arts, the image and feeling that fill the mind.

Music had invented various instruments, of which some served to set the step of a march or a dance by clearly marked beats; others, by virtue of their brightness, were able to convey certain pronouncements and even the joy of celebrations, when the human voice alone could not; others were found to be more suited to supporting the voice as accompaniment, since they masked it less. They also served in turn to relieve the voice by following after it; to give it

2. Fashionable decorations.

the pitch by preceding it; and to train it in all sorts of tunes by rehearsing them for it.

The success of these different means of exciting pleasure charmed the musician; and as it was easier for him to have a docile instrument than a beautiful voice always at his disposal, he thought he could replace the human voice by the sound of the instrument, which is only an imperfect copy of it. The charm increased when he had brought the range of the instrument and the flexibility of the fingers to the point of producing more than the throat could in certain respects. He abandoned himself entirely to the practice of sounds and dared for a long time to speak to the ear without saying anything to the mind. This showed little understanding of men. A sound devoid of meaning will always be a body without a soul, which can be pleasing at first impression, but cannot be sustained. The emotion of the first bow stroke has never been long-lasting.

Let us proceed to the true cause of the error of so many musicians. Sound is the concern of the ear, as color is of the eye. Beautiful sounds are pleasing to the ear, and beautiful colors are pleasing to the eye. But as colors are intended to distinguish objects, they do not please one for long if they are not attached to some figure, for then they are out of place. Fine marbled paper and beautiful Hungarian embroidery are pleasing colors and nothing more. The first glance is not displeasing: one can even look for useful nuances and nice combinations in them. But these are not paintings; and if you wished to prolong this inanimate spectacle, even by varying it for fifteen minutes at a time, you would not care to: the mind does not search for colors, but for colored objects. In the same way sounds, in their variety, help us to designate an infinite number of thoughts and things. But if the sounds come one after the other without being attached to an object or a thought, they make us weary without our knowing why. Sounds attract us naturally and occupy us with the things of which they are the imitation, or at least the sign. They mark a departure, a movement, a piece of news, a celebration, an opinion, an expression of joy, of sadness, of need, or of some other situation. But they begin to irritate us when they are no longer the signs of anything. Bells and trumpets delight us with their announcements; but once we have heard what they have to say to us, we would like the announcement to end. Similarly, we listen with pleasure to the prelude that prepares the ear for the melody that will follow, or the interlude that allows the voices to rest and forms a pleasant link between two songs, instead of breaking the sequence with a long silence. Even sounds that prolong the expression of the preceding speech or song somewhat are still well received. But there is a kind of absurdity and an inevitable distaste in a long sequence of sounds that are not in themselves significant, or that cease to be so after having alerted us sufficiently.

Thus the musician who wished to have only inanimate sounds heard, or who thought he could dispense with vocal music for long periods of time, experienced how difficult it was to keep our attention when there was no thought to fix it. Being neither accustomed to occupying the mind, nor willing to do so, he redoubled his efforts in favor of the ear. He tried to enchant it with a multitude of ornaments, and as he thought he had no more formidable enemy than drowsiness or boredom, he put all his energy into keeping the ear constantly alert by jiggling and shaking. In instrumental music he increased the various styles that are displayed discreetly in fine singing, and juxtaposed fast and slow passages, great noise and silence, then a long line of crackling sounds, jolts, and sudden bursts of fire.

The most beautiful melody, when only instrumental, almost inevitably becomes cold, and then boring, because it expresses nothing. It is a fine suit of clothes separated from the body and hung on a peg: or if it has an air of life about it, it is at most like a marionette or a mechanical doll, which may astonish us for a moment with its imitation of human movements and even far surpass natural agility. But all of this artificial vivacity cannot compare to the beauty of nature itself, and to the nobility of a graceful bearing. There may still be a semblance of meaning in what a marionette does. When a mime makes his gestures, silent though they may be, we understand them plainly. We guess why he is laughing or lamenting. We know what is upsetting him, what makes him slow down or hasten his steps. He is drawn by an object; he flees before danger. We see a motive, and no one calls him a fool, since there is purpose, soundness, and consequence in all his actions: they are the representation of his thoughts. But we never think well of a mind that passes from sadness to great bursts of laughter, and from banter to seriousness, to tenderness, to anger, and to rage without having any cause to laugh or to become angry. Now, sonatas and many other types of music—are they anything but what we have just described? They are to music what marbled paper is to painting. It even seems that the more impassioned they are, the less reasonable they appear. I am, however, very far from attributing to them all the disadvantage and opprobrium of this comparison. They are rather like the studies that young painters make of the different postures and expressions of man. They are suited to the training of the artist, but not very enjoyable for the public.

From *Le Spectacle de la nature, ou Entretiens sur les particularités de l'histoire naturelle, qui ont paru les plus propres à rendre les jeunes-gens curieux, et à leur former l'esprit* (Paris, 1732–50), vol. 7 (1746), Entretien Dix-huitième, "Suite des professions instructives," pp. 96–102, 111–16. There is an early English translation, *Spectacle de la nature: or, Nature display'd, being Discourses on such Particulars of Natural History* (London, 1739–48).

VOLTAIRE
from *The Temple of Taste* (1733)

There was a concert being given in a country house, bizarrely situated and built the same. The master of the house, seeing the cardinal's carriage at a distance and knowing that His Eminence was from Italy, invited him to the concert. He spoke, in few words, most slightingly of Lully, Destouches, and Campra, and assured the cardinal that at his concert there would be no French music. The cardinal pointed out to him in vain that Italian, French, and Latin music were all very good, each in its own way; that there is nothing so ridiculous as Italian sung in the French manner, unless it is French sung in the Italian manner; for, he told him, in that agreeable tone of voice made for the adornment of reason:

> Fertile nature, ingenious and wise,
> Adorning the universe with its various gifts,
> Speaks to all mankind, but in diverse tones.
> Each people has its own language, as well as its own spirit,
> With sounds and accents adjusted to its voice,
> All precisely noted in Nature's hand:
> The fine and fortunate ear can tell the difference.
> In France one must sing to the Frenchman's tune.
> Lully was able to observe our taste;
> He embellished our art rather than changing it.

To these judicious words my man responded shaking his head: "Come, come," he said, "we will show you something new." So they went inside, and there his concert began.

> Twenty fanatic rivals of the great Lully,
> More the enemies of art and good sense,
> Were disfiguring, in squealing tones,
> French verses with Italic flourishes.
> A prude was overcome with ogling;
> And a certain fop, beside himself with his finery,
> Was humming and quavering, while preening himself;
> And beating false time with his index finger,
> He cried out "Bravo" as they went out of tune.

We left as quickly as we could. It was only after many adventures of this sort that we finally arrived at the Temple of Taste.

From *Le Temple du goût* (Paris, 1733); modern edition by F. Carcassonne, 2d ed. (Geneva: Droz, 1953), 68–69. There are two early English translations (London, 1734 and Glasgow, 1751).

JEAN LE ROND D'ALEMBERT
from *On the Freedom of Music* (1759)

IX

I am astonished first of all that in a century in which so many pens have been brought to bear on the freedom of commerce, the freedom of marriage, the freedom of the press, the freedom of the painted canvas, no one has yet written on the freedom of music. To be a slave to our amusements would be, to use the expression of a philosophical writer, to degenerate not only from freedom, but from servitude itself. You are very shortsighted, our great politicians reply; all freedoms are linked together and are equally dangerous. Freedom of music presupposes that of feeling; freedom of feeling leads to that of thought, freedom of thought to that of action, and freedom of action is the ruin of nations. Let us therefore preserve opera as it is, if we wish to preserve the kingdom, and let us curb the license to sing, if we don't want the license to speak to follow soon after. "That," as Pascal used to say of I don't know which argument of Escobar's, "is what is called arguing according to form. It is not arguing, it's proving."[1]

It is hard to believe, but it is nonetheless true that in certain people's idiom, "*bouffoniste*," "republican," "frondeur," "atheist"—I was about to forget "materialist"—are so many synonymous terms. Their profound logic reminds me of a certain lesson given by a professor of philosophy: "Dioptrics is a science of the properties of lenses; lenses presuppose eyes; eyes are one of our sense organs; the existence of our senses presupposes the existence of God, since God gave them to us; the existence of God is the foundation of the Christian religion; we shall therefore prove the truth of religion as our first lesson in dioptrics."

X

The majesty of the Opéra, say people of taste, would be gravely offended if street entertainers were to be admitted there. Yet if this *majesty* bores us, I don't see what forces us to hold it in reverence. Moreover, why should the majesty of *Armide* be offended by *La serva padrona*, if that of *Cinna* is not offended by *Le Bourgeois gentilhomme?*[2] Why are these connoisseurs, so hard to please, who

---

1. Antonio Escobar y Mendoza (1598–1669), a Spanish Jesuit, cited by Pascal in the seventh of the *Lettres provinciales* as an example of captious reasoning. [EF]

2. D'Alembert contrasts Lully's *Armide*, a *tragédie lyrique*, with Pergolesi's comic intermezzo *La serva padrona*, Corneille's tragedy *Cinna* with Molière's comedy *Le Bourgeois gentilhomme*. [BJB]

would think themselves degraded to see *Bertholde à la cour* following *Roland,* not ashamed to laugh at *Pourceaugnac* after having wept at *Zaïre?*[3] And finally, why are their ears offended by the comic arias of an Italian intermezzo, when their eyes are not offended by the *bambochade*[4] paintings by Téniers or the crippled Chinese figures and the porcelain magots [grotesque figurines] with which their homes are furnished?

XI

Italian music, they say further, would put us off French. What harm can there be, if Italian music is preferable? It is as if Corneille had been forbidden to write his plays on the pretext that they would make people forget those of Hardy and Jodelle.[5] But Italian music is given more credit than it deserves; after hearing it for more than a year, we are very far from having cast aside our own. We run to the Opéra as usual, and the *bouffonistes* who had announced our desertion of it were mistaken in their prophecies. These enthusiasts judged the impression of the crowd by the one that they experienced. They were under the same misapprehension as certain contemporary writers who speak to us incessantly of the progress of the nation in what they call the philosophical spirit and who imagine they have contributed, through their works, to extending this spirit even among the common people. But let there be some miracle worker who sets up shop on the outskirts of the city, and the crowds come running. And the philosophical spirit is taken in like a fool. I picture the true or so-called philosophers, who have some reform to make or to preach, on the banks of a very swift river that they propose to cross; they assemble their contemporaries on the riverbank, harangue them, and exhort them to imitate them. Then they throw themselves into the river, and through a shower of arrows, they swim across it, having no doubt that their entire age is following. They have scarcely crossed when they turn around and see their followers still on the other bank, staring at them, mocking them, and departing; it is the fable of the shepherd and his flock (La Fontaine, Book IX, fable 19). Let us not then judge the effect of Italian music on the average spectator by the effect it has produced on a small number. Its future reign, were it as inevitable as it is doubtful, would need time to become established. Any music, all the more so if it is new, requires some getting used to

3. *Bertholde à la cour* is Vincenzo Ciampi's *Bertoldo, Bertoldino e Cacasenno* (1748), on a libretto by Goldoni; it was performed in Paris in 1753 as *Bertoldo in corte. Roland* is another *tragédie lyrique* by Lully; *Monsieur de Pourceaugnac* is a farcical *comédie-ballet* by Molière, *Zaïre* a tragedy by Voltaire. [BJB]

4. A seventeenth-century term for certain paintings or drawings of pastoral scenes of a rustic or burlesque nature, in the style of the painter David Téniers (1582–1659). [EF]

5. Alexandre Hardy (1570–1632), author of tragicomedies and pastorals; Etienne Jodelle (1532–73), tragic poet, follower of Ronsard, one of the seven poets of the Pléiade. [EF]

in order to be appreciated by the common crowd; this is why, if French opera need fear some decline, it will happen only gradually, and it will be able to outlive the generation that now deplores it. Let this generation enjoy its tranquil pleasures undisturbed, but let it not lay claim to determine those of the next.

XII

There is a more reasonable objection made against Italian music than the preceding: that it will force us to substitute Italian opera for our own, that the former is cold and languid, that we would soon be bored by it, and thus we would lose on the one hand without gaining on the other. Before responding, let us first observe that the other nations of Europe do not seem to have been struck by this objection as we have. They have all without exception rejected our opera and our music, preferring the opera and music of the Italians, either because French opera has not seemed as superior to that of Italy as we imagine, or because their distaste for our music has outweighed the advantages we may have with respect to the librettos or the genre of spectacle. This general decision on the part of Europe is all the less suspect in that, while proscribing our opera, it has universally adopted our spoken theater, which is indeed the best example there has been as yet of the dramatic genre. Foreigners have gone further: despite their preference for Italian music over ours, they have not for all that relinquished our language in favor of Italian, though the latter is perhaps not inferior to French and many men of letters even dare to prefer to it. It would be pointless to say that foreigners are biased against our opera only for want of knowing or hearing it. Among this crowd of Englishmen, Spaniards, Germans, and Russians who come running to Paris from every direction, there is scarcely one whom our operas have not bored to distraction. They perceive it either as a deafening racket or as a plainsong that puts them to sleep with its languor, when they are not outraged by its pretension; if they take pleasure in any part of the performance, it is in our dances; but these are not sufficient compensation for three hours of noise and boredom; they leave stopping up their ears, and one will scarcely see them return. Some, it is true, less difficult to please or less sincere, seem to approve and share our pleasure. They go further; they contend that for the past two years French music has begun to be successful in Vienna, where it was once detested; but I fear that this sudden eagerness for our music among the Austrians may be simply a polite and grateful reception on the part of our new allies.[6]

6. The French troupe had been founded in Vienna in 1752 with the encouragement of the Empress Maria Theresa; d'Alembert is probably referring to the success of Gluck's *La Fausse Esclave*, a *comédie mêlée d'ariettes* (January 1758), soon followed by other French operas by Gluck. [BJB]

XIII

Yet would it be right to determine our taste, as to musical spectacles, according to the opinion and example of foreigners, those who in all else are accustomed to adopting French taste as a model for their own? However general their approval of Italian opera may be, does it follow that we would do well to imitate them? The form of this opera, it must be admitted, makes it uniform and boring; ours is incomparably more varied and more pleasing. We have, it seems to me, understood better than any other nation the true nature of each type of theater; comedy for us is the entertainment of the mind, tragedy that of the soul, and opera that of the senses; that is all it is and all that it can be. Where there is no verisimilitude, there can be no interest, at least not sustained interest; for the interest in a scene is founded on illusion, and illusion is banished from a type of theater in which a wave of the wand transports the audience in a moment from one end of the earth to the other, and in which the actors sing instead of speaking. It is not that good music in a touching scene does not draw a few tears from us on occasion, nor that I wish to renew the trivial objection to tragedies in music, that the *heroes die singing;* let us leave to the common crowd the ridiculous prejudice of believing that music is suited only to the expression of gaiety; experience teaches us daily that it is no less susceptible to expressions of tenderness and grief. But if touching music makes our tears flow, it does so invariably by proceeding to the heart through the senses; it differs in this from tragedy that is declaimed, or, to speak more precisely, *spoken* tragedy, which proceeds to the heart through the depiction and development of the passions. Opera is in the entertainment of the senses, and could not be otherwise. But if the pleasures of the senses, as we experience daily, are dulled when they are too constant, if they require variety and interruption to be enjoyed without weariness, it follows that in this type of performance it is not possible for pleasure to enter our soul through too many senses at once; we cannot leave, so to speak, too many doors open, allowing too much diversity; and opera like ours, which assembles machines, choruses, song, and dance, is preferable to Italian opera, which is limited to staging and singing. It is claimed, I know, that Italian operas have the advantage in that they can be declaimed as well as sung, which is not the case in ours. Supposing this is true, all that one may conclude thereby is that our operas must be sung and our tragedies declaimed.[7] But this supposed advantage of Italian tragedies, that they are equally suited to singing or declamation, makes their merit quite suspect in my eyes. To be able to change character so easily is to have no character at all; and I do not know what one is to think of

---

7. I use here the word *declaim,* inappropriate as it is, because we have no other to contrast spoken tragedy with tragedy that is sung.

a type of play in which the form of performance is arbitrary or indifferent. I will grant, however, if you wish, that if Quinault's best opera were declaimed, it would be less pleasing than Metastasio's best opera likewise declaimed; I will grant further that the best tragedy by Racine, were it set to music, would please us less than the best tragedy in song by Metastasio; but play a tragedy by Racine and one by Metastasio in sequence, and similarly an opera by Metastasio and an opera by Quinault *set to good music,* and despite all the esteem that the Italian poet deserves, I do not doubt that the advantage of the comparison would remain with the two French poets. . . .

XXXVII

It remains for us to consider whether the beauties of Italian vocal music can be transferred to the French language. Foreigners deny it, but we may challenge their ability to judge; several Frenchmen doubt it, and we must admit to them at least that the Italian language will always be infinitely more suited to singing than ours. But after all, must we despair so easily of being able to reconcile Italian singing to our language? It may only be a matter of accustoming our ears to it. If we can manage to do so, it will be by the route we have only recently taken, by fitting French words to excellent Italian tunes, and beginning this effort in comedy, where the audience is always less critical of innovation. This little trick has worked very well in the Théâtre Italien; no precautions were taken against pleasure, and pleasure was had; people thought they were hearing French music because they were no longer hearing Italian words. We must also begin with this same comic genre, to test whether we are correct in judging suitable the new kind of recitative that we have proposed. The *Devin du village,*[8] in which the recitative is well done and very well suited to delivery, would be appropriate, unless I am much mistaken, to the test in question; and there is reason to believe that it would pass. Thus, by gaining ground little by little, by not making sudden innovations that are too bold, by only risking one effort at a time, we shall place ourselves in a position to speak without prejudice or haste on one of the three propositions advanced by Rousseau; namely, that "we can have no music"; for, as for the two others, they seem to me already decided. I believe most firmly with him that "we have no music," or at least that we have too little to be able to take great pride in it; but I cannot agree with him when he adds, "that if ever we have one, it will be so much the worse for us,"[9] since we

8. Rousseau's *intermède,* modeled on the Italian intermezzo, was first given at Fontainebleau on 18 October 1752; public performances began in the next year and continued for more than half a century, spawning numerous imitations. [BJB]

9. From his *Lettre sur la musique françoise* (1753); *Œuvres complètes* 15 (Paris, 1827), 231. [BJB]

will have it, according to him, only when we have changed our own. I owe on this occasion a sort of apology to the reader for the language I have used throughout this piece of writing. I have spoken of Italian and French music as if there were two musics, and as if the first were not indeed the only one that deserved this name. It is solely to conform to usage that I have expressed myself in another fashion; and I confess that instead of using the term *French music,* I should have said "that which we call music and which is not."

XXXVIII

We have much less to reform in our *symphonies*[10] than in our songs. Many of Rameau's leave nothing to be desired. Among a great number of examples that I could mention here, I limit myself to the *Ballet des fleurs* in *Les Indes galantes,*[11] where the dance airs, so well enacted as if in dialogue and so picturesque, form the most expressive mute scene. In this regard, not even the Italians can match our wealth. I completely discount the prodigious amount of sonatas they have given us. All this purely instrumental music, without design, without purpose, speaks neither to the mind nor to the soul; one might as well ask with Fontenelle, "Sonata, what do you wish of me?"[12] The composers of instrumental music will make nothing but an empty noise as long as they do not have in their heads, like the celebrated Tartini,[13] as they say, an action or an expression to be represented. Some sonatas, but a rather small number, have this quality, so desirable and so necessary to commend them to persons of taste. Let us take one entitled *Didone abbandonata.*[14] It is a charming monologue; sorrow, hope, and despair appear in rapid succession and very distinctly, in varying degrees and in different nuances; and one could easily make a very lively and very touching scene of this sonata. But such pieces are rare. Indeed, it has to be admitted that in general one can only grasp all the expressive quality of music when it is joined to words or to dance. Music is a language without vowels; it is up to dramatic action to supply them. It would therefore be desirable that in our operas all *symphonies* be expressive, that is, their meaning always be represented in detail, whether by the scene, or by the action, or by the spectacle; that dance airs, al-

10. *Symphonie,* in this context, means instrumental music, not symphony. [BJB]

11. *Les Indes galantes* is an opéra-ballet by Rameau composed in 1735. [EF]

12. This famous remark, expressing puzzlement in the face of music without words, to which no meaning could therefore be attached, was frequently quoted throughout the century.[BJB]

13. Tartini often sought inspiration for his instrumental music in literary passages, and many of his sonatas and quartets carry verses of Petrarch or Metastasio on the front. [EF]

14. Metastasio's libretto was set by many composers. D'Alembert may be referring to Tartini's G minor chamber sonata, published in 1734, that later acquired the nickname *Didone abbandonata.* [BJB]

ways related to the subject, always representing characters, and consequently always pantomimic, be designed by the composer, so that he be in a position to translate them, so to speak, from beginning to end, and that the dance exactly match this translation; that a *symphonie* required to paint some grand subject, for example the fusion and the separation of the elements, be explained and displayed to the spectator through suitable decor, in which the effects and the movements correspond to the analogous movements in the *symphonie*—in a word, that our eyes, always in concord with our ears, serve continually to interpret the instrumental music.

From *De la liberté de la musique* (Amsterdam, 1759), sections 9–13, 37–38; repr. in Denise Launay, *La Querelle des Bouffons: Texte des Pamphlets avec introduction, commentaires et index,* 3 vols. (Geneva: Minkoff Reprint, 1973), 3:2199–2282.

JEAN-JACQUES ROUSSEAU
from *Essay on the Origins of Language* (1781)

XI
REFLECTIONS ON THESE DIFFERENCES

These are, in my opinion, the most general physical causes of the characteristic differences of primitive languages. Southern ones had to be lively, resonant, accentuated, eloquent, and often obscure by virtue of their energy; northern ones had to be muted, harsh, articulated, piercing, monotone, and clear by virtue of words rather than good construction. Modern languages, mixed and re-formed a hundred times, still retain some of these differences: French, English, and German are the private languages of men who come to each other's aid, who reason calmly among themselves, or of hot-tempered individuals who are quick to anger; but ministers of the gods announcing the sacred mysteries, wise men giving laws to the people, and leaders inspiring the multitudes must speak Arabic or Persian.[1] Our languages are more effective when written than when spoken, and people find us more pleasing to read than to listen to. Oriental languages, on the contrary, lose their vitality and warmth when written: the meaning is only half in the words, and all of its force is in speech; to judge the genius of the Orientals by their books is like trying to paint a man's likeness from his cadaver.

1. Turkish is a northern language.

To examine the actions of men well, one must consider them in all of their relations, and we are not taught to do this. When we put ourselves in the place of others, we always do so such as we have become, not as they ought to be; and when we think we are judging them on the basis of reason, we are doing no more than comparing their prejudices to our own. A man, for example, who can read a little Arabic smiles while leafing through the Koran; if he had heard Mohammed pronounce it, in person, in that eloquent and rhythmic language, with that resonant and persuasive voice that charmed first the ear and then the heart, constantly animating his pronouncements with the tone of enthusiasm, this same man would have prostrated himself upon the ground, crying: "Great prophet, sent from God, lead us to glory and to martyrdom: we wish to conquer or die for you." Fanaticism always seems silly to us, because it has no voice among us with which to make itself heard. Even our fanatics are not true fanatics: they are only scoundrels or madmen. Our languages offer only cries for those possessed by the devil, rather than inflections for those who are inspired.

XII
The Origin of Music and Its Relationships

Along with the first voices, the first articulations or the first sounds were formed according to the type of passion that dictated one or the other. Anger wrests threatening cries, which the tongue and palate articulate. The voice of tenderness is softer; the glottis modifies it, and this voice becomes a sound. But the accents of these passions are more frequent or rare, and the inflections more or less high-pitched, according to the sentiment that accompanies them. Thus the cadence and the sounds originate with the syllables: passion brings all the organs into play and adorns the voice with all of their brilliance; thus poetry, songs, and speech have a common origin. Around the fountains of which I have spoken earlier, the first speeches were the first songs: the periodic, measured recurrences of rhythm and the melodious inflections of accents gave birth to poetry and music along with language; or rather all of this was but language itself for these happy climates and fortunate times, where the only pressing needs calling for the assistance of others were those to which the heart gave rise.

The first stories, the first speeches, the first laws were in verse: poetry was discovered before prose. This had to be so, since passion spoke before reason. The same was true for music: there was at first no music other than melody, nor any melody other than the varied sound of speech; the accents formed the song, the quantities formed the meter, and people spoke as much through sound and rhythm as through articulation and the voice. Talking and singing were once the same thing, says Strabo, which shows, he adds, that poetry is the source of eloquence.[2] He should have said that both came from the same source and were at first but one and the same thing. As for the manner in which the first societies were formed, is it surprising that the first stories were in verse, and that the first laws were sung? Is it surprising that the first grammarians subordinated their art to music, and were professors of one and the other at the same time?[3]

A language with only articulations and voices thus possesses only half of its riches: it conveys ideas, it is true; but to render sentiments and images, it must also have rhythm and sounds, which is to say melody: this is what the Greek language had and what ours is lacking.

We are still astonished at the prodigious effects of eloquence, poetry, and music among the Greeks: these effects do not take hold in our minds, because we no longer experience similar ones; and all we can manage, seeing them so well attested to, is to pretend to believe in them out of kindness for our scholars.[4] Having translated, as best he could, certain pieces of Greek music into our notation, Burette[5] was naive enough to have these pieces performed at the Académie des Belles-lettres, and the academicians were patient enough to

---

2. *Geography,* bk. i.

3. "Archytas atque Aristoxenus etiam subjectam grammaticen musicae putaverunt, et eosdem utriusque rei praeceptores fuisse . . . Tum Eupolis, apud quem Prodamus et musicen et litteras docet. Et Maricas, qui est Hyperbolus, nihil se ex musicis scire nisi litteras confitetur" ("Archytas and Aristoxenus even thought that grammar was a branch of music, and that both were taught by the same teachers [is shown both by Sophron . . . and] by Eupolis, in whom Prodamus teaches both music and letters. And Maricas, who stands for Hyperbolus, admits that he has learned nothing from the musicians except the alphabet"); Quintilian, [*Institutio oratoria*], 1.10.[17]. [Archytas was a philosopher of the early fourth century (this and all dates in this note B.C.). "Aristoxenus" is an early conjecture; the transmitted reading is "Euenus," fifth-century poet and rhetorical theorist; Sophron (fifth century) was a composer of mimes, Eupolis an Athenian comic poet of the late fifth century, Prodamus and Maricas characters in his plays; Hyperbolus was a leading Athenian politician of the time (the play concerned was performed in 421 B.C.). For "musicis" the better reading is "musice"; Maricas admits that he knows nothing of music apart from the alphabet. In classical Greek *mousike* is often used for culture and the arts in general. LAH-S]

4. Undoubtedly one must allow for Greek exaggeration in everything, but to push these allowances to the point of making all differences evaporate is to grant too much to modern prejudice. "When the music of the Greeks," says the Abbé Terrasson, "from the time of Amphion and Orpheus, was at the point where it is today in the cities furthest from the capital, it was then that it halted the flow of rivers, drew oak trees [to it], and caused rocks to move. Now that it has achieved a very high degree of perfection, it is much loved and its beauties are perceived, but it leaves everything in place. And so it was with the verses of Homer, a poet born in a time that still felt the effects of the childhood of the human spirit, in contrast to those that followed it. People were enraptured by his poetry, and they are content today merely to appreciate and esteem that of the good poets." It cannot be denied that the Abbé Terrasson had occasional wisdom, but he certainly did not show it in this passage.

5. Pierre-Jean Burette (1665–1747) left an important work on ancient music entitled *Dissertation sur la mélopée de l'ancienne musique* (1720), in which he transcribed some pieces of Greek music (Hymn to Nemesis, Hymn to Apollo, Dithyramb to Calliope). [EF]

listen to them. I marvel at this experiment in a country whose music is inde-
cipherable to all other nations. Have a monologue from a French opera performed by any foreign musicians you please, and I challenge you to recognize
anything in it: and yet it is these same Frenchmen who claimed the right to
judge the melody of an ode by Pindar set to music two thousand years ago!

I have read that once in America the Indians, upon seeing the surprising
effect of firearms, would pick up musket balls from the ground; then, throwing
them while making a loud noise with their mouths, they were astonished at not
having killed anyone. Our orators, our musicians, and our scholars are like
these Indians. The wonder is not that with our music we no longer do what the
Greeks did with theirs; on the contrary, it would be that one might produce the
same effects with such different instruments.

XIII
ON MELODY

No one doubts that man is affected by his senses; but, for want of distinguishing
the effects, we confuse their causes; we grant too much and too little authority
to sensations; we fail to see that often they affect us not only as sensations, but as
signs or images, and their moral effects also have moral causes. Just as the feelings that painting arouses in us do not originate in the colors, so the influence
that music has over our souls is not the work of sounds. Beautiful colors subtly
shaded are pleasing to the eye, but this pleasure is purely one of sensation. It is
the drawing, the imitation that gives these colors life and soul: the passions they
express stir our own; the objects they represent affect us. Interest and feeling do
not stem from colors; the lines of a touching painting are still touching in an
engraving or print: remove these lines from the picture, and the colors will no
longer have any effect.

Melody does in music precisely what drawing does in painting; it marks the
lines and the figures, of which the chords and the sounds are but the colors. But,
you will say, melody is only a succession of sounds. No doubt; but drawing is
also only an arrangement of colors. An orator uses ink to trace his writings: is
this to say that ink is a most eloquent liquid?

Imagine a country in which the people had no idea of drawing, but where
many, spending their lives combining, mixing, and matching colors, thought
that they excelled in painting. These people would argue about our music precisely as we argue about the music of the Greeks. If you spoke to them of the
emotion that beautiful paintings cause in us, and of the charm of being moved
by a touching subject, their scholars would immediately look deeper into the
matter, compare their colors to ours, consider whether our green is more delicate, or our red more brilliant; they would search for those combinations of

colors that make us cry, others that make us angry; the Burettes of this country would bring together a few distorted shreds of our paintings; then they would ask themselves in amazement what was so marvelous about the coloring.

And if, in some neighboring country, one began to develop some line, some rudimentary sketch, some figure as yet imperfect, all of it would pass for scribbling, for a capricious and baroque style of painting; and in order to preserve taste, they would confine themselves to this simple beauty, which in truth expresses nothing, but which brings out beautiful shades, large patches of color, and gradual variations of hues with no line.

Finally perhaps, progressing slowly, they would arrive at the experiment of the prism. Immediately some famous artist would establish a fine system based on it. "Gentlemen," he would tell them, "to reason well, we must return to physical causes. This is the refraction of light; these are all the primary colors; these are their relationships, their proportions; such are the true principles of the pleasure that painting gives you. All of these mysterious words—drawing, representation, figure—are pure charlatanism on the part of French painters, who think that, through their imitations, they are causing some sorts of emotions in the soul, whereas we know that there are only sensations. They speak wonders to you of their paintings; but just look at my hues."

"French painters," he would continue, "have perhaps observed the rainbow; they have been able to receive from nature some appreciation for shading and some instinct for color. But I have shown you the great, the true principles of this art. What do I mean of 'this art'—of all the arts, gentlemen, of all the sciences! The analysis of colors and the calculation of refractions of the prism provide you with the only precise relationships existing in nature, the rule for all relationships. Now, everything in the universe is merely a question of relationship. So you know everything if you know how to paint; you know everything if you are able to match colors."

What would we say of a painter so deprived of feeling and taste as to reason in this manner and limit stupidly the pleasure that painting gives us to the physics of his art? What would we say of a musician full of similar prejudices, who thought that he saw in harmony alone the source of the great effects of music? We would send the first to paint wainscoting, and we would condemn the second to writing French operas.

Just as painting is not the art of combining colors in a manner pleasing to the eye, neither is music the art of combining sounds in a manner pleasing to the ear. If it only came to that, both would be counted among the natural sciences and not the fine arts. Imitation alone is what raises them to the rank of arts. And what makes painting an imitative art? Drawing. What makes music another such art? Melody.

XIV
ON HARMONY

The beauty of sounds comes from nature. Their effect is purely physical; it results from the convergence of several particles of air set in motion by the sounding body, and by all of its aliquot parts, perhaps to infinity—the whole together produces an agreeable sensation.[6] All men in the universe take pleasure in listening to beautiful sounds; but if this pleasure is not animated by melodious inflections that are familiar to them, it will not delight them, it will not be transformed into exquisite pleasure. The most beautiful songs, in our view, will always leave unmoved an ear that is not accustomed to them; it is a language for which one must have the dictionary.

Harmony itself is in an even less favorable situation. Possessing only conventional beauty, it cannot in any way delight an untrained ear; one must have a long acquaintance with it to sense and appreciate it. An unsophisticated ear hears only noise in what we call consonances. When natural proportions are altered, it is not surprising that natural pleasure no longer exists.

A tone carries with it all of its concomitant overtones, with the relationships of intensity and of intervals that they must have among them in order to produce the most perfect harmony of this same tone. Add to it the third or the fifth, or another consonance, and you are not adding, you are doubling it; you keep the intervallic relationship, but you alter the relationship with respect to intensity.[7] In emphasizing one consonance and not the others, you disrupt the proportion; in attempting to improve upon nature, you make it worse. Your ears and taste are spoiled by an art that is misunderstood. There is no natural harmony other than the unison.

Rameau claims that treble parts of a certain simplicity naturally imply their bass,[8] and that a man with a good but untrained ear will intone this bass naturally. This is a musician's prejudice, negated by all experience. Not only will someone who has never heard either harmony or bass *not* find this harmony or bass on his own, but he will even find them displeasing if he is made to hear them, and he will much prefer the simple unison.

6. A column of air set in vibration, just like a string, emits not only a fundamental tone but divides itself at a central point, called a node, into two equal parts, which give the same sound at the upper octave, and then in still other parts, and so on to infinity, producing, with decreasing intensity, the infinite series of harmonics. [EF]

7. The third and the fifth in fact appear in the harmonic series, for which reason adding a third or a fifth to any tone only duplicates frequencies already contained in the harmonics of that same tone, increasing their intensity. [EF]

8. This means that the melody would be generated by its fundamental bass, to the point that in any given melody the bass that generated it is already implicitly contained in it. [EF]

If you were to spend a thousand years calculating the relationships of sounds and the laws of harmony, how could you make this an imitative art? What is the principle of this supposed imitation? Of what is harmony the sign? And what do chords and our passions have in common?

If you ask the same question about melody, the answer comes by itself: it is already in the reader's mind. By imitating the inflections of the voice, melody expresses laments, cries of sorrow or of joy, threats, moans; all the vocal signs of passion are within its jurisdiction. It imitates the accents of languages and the turns of phrase allotted in each idiom to certain emotions of the soul. Melody does not merely imitate, it speaks; and its inarticulate but lively, ardent, passionate language has a hundred times more energy than speech itself. This is the source of the power of musical imitation; this is how melody holds sway over sensitive hearts. Harmony may cooperate in certain systems by linking the succession of sounds according to a few laws of modulation, by making the intonations more precise, by bringing the ear a guaranteed proof of this precision, and by drawing closer and fixing imperceptible inflections to consonant and linked intervals. But by also providing obstacles to melody, harmony takes energy and expression away from it; it eliminates the passionate accent, for which it substitutes the harmonic interval; it subjugates to two single modes[9] melodies that should have as many modes as there are tones of oratory; it effaces and destroys the multitude of tones or intervals that do not belong to its system; in a word, it separates singing from speech to such an extent that these two languages combat each other, thwart one another, mutually rob each other of any lifelike quality, and cannot unite in any affecting subject without absurdity. This is why people always find it ridiculous to express powerful and genuine passions in song, for they know that in our languages these passions have no musical inflections, and that northerners no more die singing than do swans.

Harmony alone is insufficient even for the expressions that seem to depend solely upon it. Thunder, the murmur of water, winds, and storms are poorly rendered by simple chords. Whatever one may do, noise alone says nothing to the mind: objects must speak in order to make themselves understood; in any imitation, a type of discourse must always supplement the voice of nature. The composer who wishes to portray noise with noise is mistaken; he knows neither the weakness nor the strength of his art, and his judgment is without taste, without knowledge or wisdom.

Teach him that he must portray noise with songs; and that, if he were attempting to make frogs croak, he would have to make them sing: for it is

---

9. The major and the minor mode, that is, those on which the system of tonal harmony is based. [EF]

not enough to imitate, he must move and please; without this his gloomy imitation is nothing; and holding no interest for anyone, it makes no impression.

XV
THAT OUR MOST VIVID SENSATIONS OFTEN ACT
THROUGH MORAL IMPRESSIONS

As long as we wish to consider sounds only according to the disturbance that they excite in our nerves, we shall not possess the true principles of music and of its power over our hearts. Sounds in a melody act upon us not only as sounds, but as signs of our affections, of our feelings; in this way they excite in us the emotions they express, the image of which we recognize in them. Something of this moral effect can be perceived even in animals. The barking of one dog attracts another. If my cat hears me imitate a meow, he is immediately attentive, concerned, and agitated. Should he realize that it is I who am imitating the voice of his fellow creature, he sits back down again and relaxes. Why this difference of impression, since there is none in the disturbance of the nerve fibers and he himself was taken in at first?

If the greatest authority our sensations have over us is not due to moral causes, why then are we so sensitive to impressions that mean nothing to primitive people? Why is our most touching music only an empty sound to the ear of a Caribbean native? Are his nerves of a different nature from ours? Why are they not excited in the same way? Or why do these same disturbances affect some so much and others so little?

As proof of the physical power of sounds the healing of tarantula bites is cited. This example proves just the opposite. Neither specific tones nor the same tunes are necessary to cure all those who have been bitten by this insect; each one of them must have tunes of a song that is known to him and phrases that he understands. An Italian must have Italian tunes; a Turk, Turkish ones. Each is affected only by accents that are familiar to him; his nerves enter into it only insofar as his mind disposes them to do so; he must understand the language that is spoken to him, so that what is said may move him. . . .

XIX
HOW MUSIC HAS DEGENERATED

As language developed, melody gradually lost its former energy by imposing new rules upon itself, and the calculation of intervals was substituted for the subtlety of inflections. In this way, for example, the practice of the enharmonic genus was abolished little by little.[10] Once theaters had adopted a regular form, there was no longer any singing in them except according to the prescribed modes; and as the rules for imitation multiplied, imitative language became weaker.

The study of philosophy and the progress of reason, having perfected grammar, took away from language that lively and passionate tone that had first made it so melodious. From the time of Menalippides [Melanippides] and Philoxenus, musicians, who were at first in the employ of poets and performed only under their direction, and, so to speak, at their command, became independent; and it was this freedom about which Music complained so bitterly in a comedy by Pherecrates, in a passage presented by Plutarch.[11] Thus melody, no longer so dependent on discourse, gradually took on a separate existence, and music became more independent of words. Then, too, little by little, there was an end to those wonders it had produced when it was solely the accent and harmony of poetry, and when it gave the latter that authority over the passions that speech exercised subsequently only over reason. Furthermore, as soon as Greece was full of sophists and philosophers, famous poets and musicians were no longer to be seen. In cultivating the art of persuasion they lost the art of moving. Plato himself, jealous of Homer and Euripides, disparaged the one and was unable to imitate the other.

Soon slavery added its influence to that of philosophy. Greece in chains lost the fire that only warms free hearts; and to praise its tyrants, it could no longer find the tone with which it had celebrated its heroes. The mingling with Romans further weakened what remained of the language of harmony and accent. Latin, a more muted and less musical language, did harm to music in adopting it. The singing practiced in the capital gradually altered that of the provinces; the theaters of Rome harmed those of Athens. When Nero was winning prizes, Greece had ceased to deserve them; and the same melody, shared between two languages, became less suited to them both.

Finally came the catastrophe that destroyed the progress of the human spirit, without removing the vices that were its creation. Inundated by barbarians and enslaved by the ignorant, Europe lost all at once its sciences, its arts, and the universal instrument of both, to wit, perfected harmonious language. These crude men, whom the North had spawned, gradually accustomed all ears to the

10. In Greek music, the enharmonic genus was distinguished from the diatonic by the fact that it contained intervals of quarter tones. [EF]

11. Melanippides and Philoxenus (both fifth century B.C.), poet-composers whose musical reforms—for which they were attacked in contemporary comedy—altered the balance between music and text; see Pseudo-Plutarch, *De musica* 30 (1141C–1142A), who also states that up till Melanippides aulos players were paid by the poets whose words they accompanied. [LAH-S]

harshness of their voices, which were devoid of accent and loud without being resonant. The emperor Julian compared the Gauls' manner of speaking to the sound of frogs croaking.[12] All their articulations were so harsh that their voices were nasal and muted, and they could lend only one sort of brilliance to their singing, which was to emphasize the sound of the vowels in order to cover the harshness and abundance of the consonants.

This noisy singing, together with the inflexibility of voice, obliged the newcomers and the subjugated peoples who imitated them to slow down all of the sounds in order to make them heard. Painful articulation and intensified sounds worked together to chase all feeling of measure and rhythm from the melody. As the passage from one sound to another was always hardest to pronounce, they could do no better than to pause over each one as much as possible, inflate it, and make it burst forth as much as they could. Singing was soon no more than an annoying, slow sequence of sounds that were shouted and drawn out, with no sweetness, measure, or grace; and if some scholars said it was necessary to observe the pronunciation of long and short syllables in singing Latin, it is certain at least that poetry was sung like prose, and that it was no longer a question of feet and rhythm, nor of any sort of measured singing.[13]

Singing, thus stripped of all melody and consisting solely of the strength and duration of sounds, must finally have suggested a way of increasing its resonance with the help of consonances. Several voices, constantly drawling in unison sounds of indefinite duration, happened upon some chords which, in intensifying the noise, made it seem agreeable to them; and so began the practice of discant and of counterpoint.

I do not know how many centuries musicians debated the futile questions that the known effect of an unknown principle caused them to raise. The most indefatigable reader could not bear the verbiage of eight or ten long chapters in Jean de Muris[14] in order to find out whether, in the interval of the octave divided into two consonances, it is the fifth or the fourth that should be the lower;

12. A conflation of two passages in Julian's *Misopogon:* "I have observed even the barbarians beyond the Rhine singing and enjoying savage songs in a language resembling the croakings of birds that utter harsh cries" (337C) and "Everyone (in Antioch) hates me on behalf of dancers and theaters, not because I deprive other people of them, but because I am less interested by such things than by the frogs in the ponds" (357D). [LAH-S]

13. The allusion is evidently to Gregorian chant, considered before Romanticism a kind of music that was both primitive and barbaric, in the pejorative sense of the term. [EF]

14. Johannes de Muris (ca. 1300–ca. 1350), theorist of the Ars Nova, author of numerous treatises on music theory, mathematics, and astronomy. The treatise referred to by Rousseau, however, must have been Jacques de Liège's *Speculum musicae,* wrongly attributed to Johannes de Muris in the manuscript in the Bibliothèque nationale that Rousseau claims he had read "presque entier" (*Dictionnaire de musique,* 1768, p. 318). [BJB]

and four hundred years later one still finds in Bontempi[15] no less boring enumerations of all the basses that must carry the sixth rather than the fifth. Yet harmony gradually took the route that analysis prescribed for it, until finally the invention of the minor mode and of dissonance gave it that arbitrary quality with which it is now replete and that prejudice alone prevents us from seeing.[16]

Melody having been forgotten, and the attention of the musician having turned entirely toward harmony, everything gradually converged on this new object; the genera, the modes, the scale, everything was transformed: harmonic progressions regulated the movement of the parts. As this movement had usurped the name of melody, one could not indeed fail to recognize in the new melody the features of its mother; and our musical system having thus become, by degrees, purely harmonic, it is not surprising that spoken accent has suffered as a result, and that music, for us, has lost nearly all its energy.

That is how singing gradually became an art entirely separated from speech, in which it originates; how the harmonics of sounds obscured the inflections of the voice; and how finally, limited to the purely physical effects of the convergence of vibrations, music found itself deprived of the moral effects that it had produced when it was doubly the voice of nature.

---

15. Giovanni Andrea Angelini Bontempi (ca. 1624–1705), musician and theorist, author, among other works, of an early history of music, *Historia musica nella quale si ha cognizione della teoria e della pratica antica della musica harmonica secondo la dottrina de' Greci* (Perugia, 1695; repr. Bologna: Forni, 1971). [EF]

16. Relating all harmony to this most simple principle of the resonance of strings in their aliquot parts, Rameau bases the minor mode and dissonance on his supposed observation that a sounding string in movement causes other longer strings to vibrate at a twelfth and a major seventeenth lower. These strings, according to him, vibrate and pulsate along their whole length, but they do not resonate. This, it seems to me, is curious physics; it is as if one were to say that the sun is shining and yet one sees nothing.

These longer strings, reproducing only the sound of the highest string, because they subdivide, vibrate, and resonate in unison with it, mix their sound with its sound, and seem not to produce any sound at all. The error is in thinking that they vibrate along their whole length, and in having observed the nodes poorly. Two sounding strings forming some harmonic interval can sound their low fundamental even without a third string: this fact was known and confirmed by Tartini; but a single string has no fundamental other than its own, and it cannot make its harmonics either resonate or vibrate, but only its unison and its aliquot parts. As sound has no cause other than the vibrations of the sounding body, and where the cause acts freely the effect always follows, then to separate vibrations from resonance is to formulate an absurdity. [The allusion is to the theory of lower harmonics, which ought to account for the intervals of the minor triad. In reality, the existence of lower harmonics has never been ascertained; it would require in fact that a sounding body, in addition to its secondary higher sounds (higher harmonics), would also produce lower ones, which, as Rousseau explains, is not possible. The minor chord, therefore, can be justified only mathematically and not acoustically or naturally, as Rameau would have it. A lower string can be caused to sound indirectly only by setting in motion two strings that form a perfect chord of which it is the fundamental; this is the famous third tone of Tartini's experiment. EF]

XX
THE RELATIONSHIP OF LANGUAGES TO GOVERNMENT

These developments are neither fortuitous nor arbitrary; they stem from the unstable nature of things. Languages are formed naturally according to the needs of men; they change and alter according to changes in these same needs. In ancient times, when persuasion took the place of a police force, eloquence was necessary. What purpose would it serve today, when the police force has replaced persuasion? One needs neither art nor image to say "such is my pleasure." What sort of speech remains to be made to the people assembled? Sermons. And why should those who make them care to persuade the people, since it is not the people who name them to profitable offices? Popular languages have become as perfectly useless to us as eloquence. Societies have assumed their final form: nothing more can be changed except with cannons and coins; and as there is nothing more to say to the people, except "give money," it said with signs at street corners, or with soldiers in their houses. There is no need to assemble anyone for that. On the contrary, you must keep subjects apart: that is the first rule of modern politics.

There are languages favorable to liberty; these are the sonorous, prosodic, harmonious languages, whose discourse may be recognized from a great distance. Our languages are suited to the buzzing voices of drawing-room society. Our preachers torment themselves, work themselves into a sweat in their churches, without anyone understanding a word of what they say. After exhausting themselves by shouting for an hour, they come down from the pulpit half dead. It certainly was not worth the effort to have bothered.

Among the ancients, it was easy to make oneself heard by the people on the public square; all day long one could speak there without tiring. Generals harangued their troops; they were heard and were not in the least exhausted. Modern historians who have tried to write harangues into their histories have been mocked for their efforts. Let us imagine a man haranguing the people of Paris in French at the Place Vendôme: let him cry out at the top of his lungs; they will hear him shout, but they will not make out a single word. Herodotus used to read his history to the peoples of Greece assembled in the open air, and applause echoed from everywhere. Today, an academician who reads a paper on the day of a public assembly is scarcely heard at the far end of the hall. If the charlatans of public squares are less numerous in France than in Italy, it is not because they are any less heeded in France, it is only that they are not heard as well. D'Alembert believes we could deliver a French recitative in the Italian manner;[17] it would have to be uttered directly into the ear then—otherwise one

---

17. See chs. 30 and 31 of d'Alembert's essay *De la liberté de la musique*. [EF]

would hear nothing at all. Therefore, I say that any language in which you cannot make yourself heard in a public gathering is a servile language; it is impossible for a people to speak that language and remain free.

I shall conclude these reflections, which are superficial but which may lead to others more profound, with the passage that suggested them to me:

> It would be a matter for philosophical consideration to observe in fact and to show by example to what extent the character, customs, and interests of a people influence its language.[18]

From *Essai sur l'origine des langues,* in *Traités sur la musique* (Geneva, 1781), chs. 9–15, pp. 283–302, and chs. 19–20, pp. 319–25; modern edition by Angèle Kremer-Marietti (Paris: Aubier Montaigne, 1974), 142–57, 168–75. There is also an English translation, *On the Origin of Language,* trans. John H. Moran and Alexander Gode (New York: F. Ungar, 1966). Chapters 12–19 are translated in Edward A. Lippman, ed., *Musical Aesthetics: A Historical Reader,* vol. 1: *From Antiquity to the Eighteenth Century* (New York: Pendragon Press, 1986), 323–37.

DENIS DIDEROT
from *Additions to the Letter on the Deaf and Dumb* (1751)

In music, the pleasure of sensation depends on a particular disposition not only of the ear, but of the whole nervous system. If there are heads that resonate, there are also bodies that I would readily call harmonic: men in whom all the fibers oscillate with so much quickness and energy that upon experiencing the violent movements that harmony provokes in them, they sense the possibility of even more violent movements and conceive the idea of a sort of music that could make them die of pleasure. They imagine their existence to be attached to a single taut fiber that too strong a vibration might break. Do not think, mademoiselle, that these beings who are so sensitive to harmony are the best judges of expression. They are almost always incapable of that sweet emotion in which sentiment does not prejudice comparison. They are like those delicate souls who cannot hear the story of some unfortunate man without shedding a tear, and for whom there are no bad tragedies.

Music, moreover, is in greater need of finding in us these favorable dispositions of the senses than either painting or poetry. Its hieroglyphic is so light and

18. Charles Pinot Duclos, *Remarques sur la grammaire générale et raisonnée,* p. 2 [*Œuvres complètes de Duclos,* 10 vols. (Paris, [1806]), 9:9].

so fleeting, it is so easy to lose or to misinterpret it, that the most beautiful instrumental passage would have no great effect if the unfailing, sudden pleasure of pure and simple sensation were not infinitely superior to that of expression, which is often ambiguous. Painting shows the very object, poetry describes it, but music barely awakens a notion of it. Its only resource is in intervals and the length of sounds; and what analogy can be drawn between drawing pencils of this sort and spring, darkness, solitude, etc., and most objects? How is it then that of the three arts that imitate nature, the one in which expression is the most arbitrary and the least precise speaks the most forcefully to the soul? Could it be that by revealing objects less it leaves freer rein to our imagination, or that music is more suited than painting and poetry to producing this tumultuous effect in us because we must be shaken to be moved?

These phenomena would surprise me much less if our education were more like that of the Greeks. In Athens, nearly all young men devoted ten or twelve years to the study of music; and as a musician had only musicians for judges and listeners, a sublime piece would naturally cast a whole gathering into the same frenzy that excites those who perform their works at our concerts. But it is the nature of any enthusiasm to spread and to grow according to the number of enthusiasts. Men have then a reciprocal effect on each other, through the energetic and living image they present of the passion by which each one of them is moved; hence this mad joy at our public celebrations, the fury of our popular riots, and the surprising effects of music on the ancients, effects which the fourth act of *Zoroastre*[1] would have revived among us, if our pit had been filled with people as well trained in music and as sensitive as the youth of Athens.

From *Additions à la Lettre sur les sourds et les muets à l'usage de ceux qui entendent et qui parlent* (Paris, 1751), 107–9; modern edition by Jacques Chouillet in *Œuvres complètes, édition critique et annotée,* ed. H. Dieckmann and J. Varloot, vol. 4 (Paris: Hermann, 1978), 206–8.

DENIS DIDEROT
from *Rameau's Nephew* (1760)

He: Song is an imitation of physical noises or of the accents of passion, through the sounds of a scale invented by art or inspired by nature, whichever

1. Opera in five acts by Rameau, first performed on 5 December 1749. [BJB]

you please, either with the voice or with an instrument; and you see that with the necessary changes, the definition would exactly fit painting, eloquence, sculpture, and poetry. Now, to come to your question: what is the model for the musician or the song? Declamation, if the model is living and thinking; sound, if the model is inanimate. You must think of declamation as a line, and song another line that snakes its way above the first. The more this declamation, a type of song, is strong and realistic, the more the song that conforms to it will divide it up into a greater number of points; the more realistic the song, the more beautiful it will be. And this is what our young musicians have understood very well. When you hear *Je suis un pauvre diable,* you believe you recognize the lament of a miser; if he weren't singing, he would speak in the same tones to the earth when he entrusts his gold to it, saying, *O terre, reçois mon trésor.*[1] And would the young girl, who feels her heart tremble, who blushes, who is troubled and begs the gentleman to let her leave, express herself otherwise? There are all sorts of characters in these works, an infinite variety of declamations. That, I tell you, is sublime. Go, go hear the passage in which the young man, who senses that he is dying, cries out: *Mon coeur s'en va.*[2] Listen to the singing, listen to the orchestra, and you will tell me afterwards what difference there is between the true expression of a dying man and the movement of this song. You will see whether the line of the melody doesn't correspond exactly to the line of declamation. I am not talking about meter, which is another of the conditions of melody; I confine myself to expression; and there is nothing more obvious than the following passage that I read somewhere, *Musices seminarium accentus.*[3] Accent is the breeding-ground of melody. Consider then how difficult and how important it is, to know how to write recitative well. There is no beautiful air from which one cannot make a beautiful recitative, and no recitative from which in turn a clever man cannot draw out a beautiful air. I should not claim that someone who recites well will sing well, but I should be surprised if someone who sings well was not also able to recite. Believe everything I'm telling you now, for it's true.

I: I would wish for nothing better than to believe you, if I were not held back by one small obstacle.

He: And this obstacle is?

I: That if this music is sublime, then that of the divine Lully, of Campra, Destouches, Mouret, and even—just between you and me—that of your dear uncle, must be a bit dull.

1. Arietta sung by the miser Sordide, in the first act of Duni's *L'Isle des fous,* first performed on 29 December 1760 at the Comédie-Italienne. [BJB]

2. From François-André Danican Philidor's *Le Jardinier et son seigneur,* first performed by the Opéra-Comique at the Foire Saint-Germain, 18 February 1761. [BJB]

3. Martianus Capella, *De nuptiis Philologiae et Mercurii* 3.268. [BJB]

He, *coming closer to my ear, replied:* I wouldn't want to be overheard, for there are many people here who know me. It *is* dull. It's not that I care about my dear uncle, dear as he is. He's as hard as stone. He could see me at my last gasp, and he wouldn't lift a finger to help me. Do what he will in octaves, in sevenths, oo, oo, ah, ah, doo, doo, doodle-oodle-loo, with the devil of a din; those who are beginning to know better, and who no longer take that racket for music, will never put up with it. It should be forbidden by order of the police for any person, of any quality or rank, to have Pergolesi's *Stabat* sung. This *Stabat* should have been burned at the hand of the executioner. My God, these damned *Bouffons*, with their *Servant Mistress*, their *Tracollo*,[4] have really given us a few swift ones in the behind. It used to be that *Tancrède, Issé, L'Europe galante, Les Indes*, and *Castor, Les Talents lyriques*,[5] would run for four, five, six months. The performances of *Armide* went on forever.[6] Nowadays they all come crashing down on you one after another, like a house of cards. And so Rebel and Francoeur spurt and sputter with rage.[7] They say that all is lost, that they are ruined; and if this singing rabble from the fairs is tolerated much longer, our national music will go to the devil, and the Royal Academy of the Dead-End[8] has only to close up shop. There is certainly some truth in what they say. The old fogeys who've been coming here for thirty or forty years, every Friday, instead of enjoying themselves as they used to, are bored, and they yawn without really knowing why. They wonder at it and don't know what to say. Why don't they come to me? Duni's prediction will come true; and at the rate it's going, I swear I'll die if in four to five years, dating from the *Peintre amoureux de son modèle*,[9] there's a living soul in the famous Dead-End. These

4. Pergolesi's intermezzi *La serva padrona* and *Tracollo* (the name of the main character; the work goes under various titles but is usually known as *La contadina astuta* or *Livietta e Tracollo*). Both were performed at the Opéra, the former on 1 August 1752, the latter on 1 May 1753. [BJB]

5. *Tancrède* (1702) and *L'Europe galante* (1697) are by Campra, *Issé* (1697) by Destouches, and *Les Indes galantes* (1735), *Castor et Pollux* (1737), and *Fêtes d'Hébé ou les Talents lyriques* (1739) by Rameau. [BJB]

6. Lully's *Armide*, first performed on 15 February 1686, continued to be staged as late as 1764. [BJB]

7. François Rebel (1701–75) and François Francoeur (1698–1784). Friends from youth and both violinists, they functioned as co-directors of the Académie Royale de Musique from 1757 to 1767, a term beset with problems, among them the repercussions of the *querelle des Bouffons* and the fire at the Opéra in 1763. [BJB]

8. "Académie Royale du cul de sac," so called because it was reached from the Palais-Royal by a cul-de-sac called Cour Orry; below, it is called "Impasse," a name preferred by the fastidious Voltaire to one that includes "cul." [BJB]

9. Opera by Duni, first performed at the Foire Saint-Laurent on 26 July 1757. Egidio Duni (1708–75), an Italian composer at the French-influenced court of Parma, wrote the opera for Paris, where he settled in 1758. His *opéras comiques*, disproving Rousseau's assertion that the French language was inimical to music, were highly successful. He was a friend of Diderot's, which may account in part for the prominent mention he receives in *Le Neveu de Rameau*. [BJB]

good people have renounced their *symphonies* in order to play Italian ones. They thought they could accustom their ears to the latter, without its having some effect on their vocal music, as if the *symphonie* weren't to song, except for a bit of license inspired by the range of the instrument and the agility of the fingers, what song is to true declamation. As if the violin didn't ape the singer, who will one day, when difficulty has taken the place of beauty, ape the violin. The first to play Locatelli was the apostle of the new music. Nonsense! We shall grow used to the imitation of the accents of passion or of natural phenomena through song, and the voice, and with instruments, for this is the whole extent of music's concern, and yet shall we preserve our appreciation for the flights, lances, glories, triumphs, and victories? *Va-t'en voir, s'ils viennent, Jean.*[10] They imagined that they could cry or laugh at scenes of tragedy or comedy set to music, that the accents of rage, hatred, jealousy, the true laments of love, the ironies, and the pleasantries of the Italian or French theater could be brought to their ears, and that they would remain admirers of *Ragonde* and *Platée*.[11] Mark my words: stuff and nonsense! They imagined that they could experience time and again how easily and with what flexibility and gentleness the harmony, prosody, ellipses, and inversions of the Italian language lent themselves to art, movement, expression, turns of melody, and the measured value of sounds, and that they would continue to ignore how much their own is stiff, muted, heavy, weighty, pedantic, and dreary. Really! They have convinced themselves that having mixed their tears with the sobbing of a mother who is grieving over the death of her son, having trembled at the will of a tyrant who commands a murder, they would not be bored by their fairy tales, their insipid mythology, their sugary little madrigals that are no less the mark of the poet's bad taste than of the poverty of the art that puts up with them. These good folk! This is not and cannot be. The true, the good, and the beautiful have their rights. We dispute them, but admire them in the end. Anything marked in a different stamp is admired for a time; but we end up yawning. Yawn then, gentlemen; yawn at your leisure. Don't be shy. The rule of nature, and of my trinity, against which the gates of hell will never prevail, is quietly coming: the true, which is the father, engenders the good, which is the son, from whom the beautiful, which is the holy spirit, proceeds. The foreign god places himself humbly beside the local idol; little by little, he strengthens his position; one fine day, he nudges his comrade aside; and ta-da, the idol is down. They say that's how the Jesuits founded Christianity in China and India. And whatever the Jansenists say, this politic method

10. The refrain of a chanson that became proverbial, with the meaning "Tell me another!" [BJB]

11. *Le Mariage de Ragonde*, an opera by Mouret (1714), revised as *Les Amours de Ragonde* in 1742, and *Platée*, a *comédie lyrique* by Rameau (1745). [BJB]

proceeding to its goal, silently, without bloodshed, without martyrs, without even a hair out of place, seems the best to me.

I: Everything you've just said makes some sense, more or less.

He: Some sense! So much the better. I'll be damned if I try. It just comes out that way. I'm like the Dead-End musicians, when my uncle appeared; if I make sense, it's because a coalman will always know more about his trade than an entire academy, and than all the Duhamels in the world.[12]

And then he began to walk about, humming in a low voice some of the arias from *L'Isle des fous*, from *Le Peintre amoureux de son modèle*, *Le Maréchal ferrant*, *La Plaideuse*,[13] and from time to time he cried out, raising his hands and face to the sky: "Is that beautiful, my God! Is it beautiful! How can you have a pair of ears in your head and ask such a question?" He was getting carried away and began to sing very softly. He raised his voice as he grew more impassioned; then came the gestures, the grimaces, and the contortions; and I said, that's it, he's losing his mind, some new scene is about to take place; and indeed, he burst out in a loud voice, "Je suis un pauvre misérable . . . Monseigneur, monseigneur, laissez-moi partir . . . O terre, reçois mon or; conserve bien mon trésor . . . Mon âme, mon âme, ma vie! O terre! . . . Le voilà le petit ami; le voilà le petit ami!—Aspettare e non venire . . . A Zerbina penserete . . . Sempre in contrasti con te si sta."[14] He was piling up and mixing together some thirty arias, Italian, French, tragic, comic, of every sort; sometimes, in a baritone voice, he descended into hell; sometimes, singing at the top of his lungs and mimicking a falsetto, he tore into the upper part of the arias, imitating in movement, gesture, and demeanor the different characters who sang, alternately furious, calm again, imperious, or derisive. In one moment he was a young girl crying and he portrayed all of her simpering manners; in the next, he was a priest, a king, a tyrant, he threatened, he commanded, he lost his temper; he was a slave, he obeyed. He relented, he sorrowed, he lamented, he laughed, never out of tune, off tempo, or missing the meaning of the words, or the character of the tune. All the chess players had left their games and gathered around him. The café windows were thronged with passers-by who had stopped at the noise. Howls of laughter threatened to bring down the ceiling. He noticed nothing; he continued, overcome with delirium, with an enthusiasm so close to madness that it

12. Henri-Louis Duhamel du Monceau (1700–82), agronomist and botanist, author, among other things, of *Art du charbonnier* (1760). [BJB]

13. *Le Maréchal ferrant*, by François-André Danican Philidor (1761); *Le Procès, ou La Plaideuse*, by Duni (1762). [BJB]

14. A melange of arias drawn from French operas mentioned earlier, and three arias from *La serva padrona*. [BJB]

wasn't clear that he would come out of it, that it wouldn't be necessary to throw him into a coach and take him straight to the asylum. Singing a scrap of the *Lamentations* of Jommelli,[15] he repeated with precision, sincerity, and incredible warmth the loveliest passages of each piece. He shed a torrent of tears over that beautiful recitative in which the prophet depicts the desolation of Jerusalem, and he drew tears in turn from everyone present. It was all there, the delicacy of song, the forcefulness of expression, and the sorrow. He stressed in particular the places where the composer had demonstrated his great mastery; if he left off singing, it was to take the instrumental parts, which he abandoned quickly to return to the vocal ones, linking one to the other so as to preserve the connections and the unity of the whole. He grabbed hold of our souls and held them suspended in the most curious situation I have ever experienced. Was I in awe? Yes, I was in awe! Was I moved to pity? I was moved to pity; but a tint of ridicule had blended into these sentiments and was distorting them.

But you would have burst out laughing at the way in which he imitated the different instruments. With his cheeks bulging and puffed up, in a low, husky voice, he portrayed the horns and bassoons; he took on a bright nasal sound for the oboes; quickening his voice to an incredible speed for the string instruments, for which he sought the truest sounds; he whistled for the piccolos, he warbled for the flutes, shouting, singing, thrashing about like a madman, playing all the dancers, all the singers, an entire orchestra, a whole opera house, dividing himself up into twenty different roles, running, stopping, with the look of a fanatic about him, his eyes sparkling, his mouth foaming. It was deadly hot; and the sweat that ran down the creases of his forehead and the length of his cheeks mixed with the powder from his hair, flowing down and streaking the top of his clothing. What did I not see him do? He cried, he laughed, he sighed; he gazed with tenderness, calm, or fury; he was a woman fainting with grief; he was an unfortunate soul abandoned to the depths of his despair; a temple rising; birds growing quiet at sunset; water murmuring in a cool and lonely place, or descending in torrents from the mountaintops; a storm, a tempest, the lament of those who are about to perish, mingled with the whistling of the winds and the roar of thunder; he was the night with its darkness; he was shadow and silence; for silence itself is depicted in sounds. He had lost his head completely. Worn out with fatigue, like a man coming out of a deep sleep or a long lapse into abstraction, he stood immobile, dazed, astonished. He looked around him like a lost man who is trying to remember where

15. Niccolò Jommelli's Lamentations were regularly performed at the Concert Spirituel during Lent, together with Pergolesi's *Stabat mater*. [BJB]

he is. He was waiting for his strength and reason to return; he wiped off his face mechanically. Similar to one who might wake to see his bed surrounded by a great number of people, in complete oblivion or in a profound ignorance of what he had done, he cried out in the first moment: "Well, gentlemen, what is it? Why are you laughing and looking surprised? What is the matter?" Then he added, "*That* is what you must call music and a musician. Yet, gentlemen, you mustn't despise certain passages of Lully. I challenge anyone to improve the scene *Ah! j'attendrai* without changing the words.[16] You must not despise certain passages of Campra, airs for the violin by my uncle, his gavottes, his *entrées* for soldiers, priests, sacrificers . . . *Pales flambeaux, nuit plus affreuse que les ténèbres . . . Dieux du Tartare, Dieu de l'Oubli.*"[17] Thereupon he raised his voice to the fullest; he held out the sound; those nearby ran to the windows; we put our fingers in our ears. He added: You need lungs for this; a big voice, a volume of air. But before long, the feast of the Assumption will pass, as have Lent and Epiphany.[18] They don't yet know what should be set to music, nor consequently what is suited to a musician. Lyric poetry has yet to be born. But they will get there; from hearing Pergolesi, the Saxon [Hasse], Terradellas, Traetta, and the others; from reading Metastasio, they will have to get there.

I: What then, have Quinault, Lamotte, and Fontenelle understood nothing?

He: Nothing of the new style. There aren't six consecutive lines in their charming poems that can be set to music. There are clever maxims; there are light, tender, and delicate madrigals; but if you want to see how much all of that is devoid of possibilities for our art, which is the most violent of all, without excepting that of Demosthenes, recite these passages to yourself. How cold, languid, and monotonous they will seem! That's because there is nothing in them that can serve as a model for a song. I would sooner have La Rochefoucauld's *Maximes* or Pascal's *Pensées* to set to music.[19] The animal cry of passion must dictate the appropriate line. These expressions must be compressed; the sentence short, the meaning abrupt, suspended, and the musician able to have the whole and each of its parts at his disposal; [he must be able to] omit a word, or

16. Monologue of Roland in *Roland,* Act IV, sc. 2. [BJB]

17. Aria sung by Télaïre in the second act of Rameau's *Castor et Pollux* and aria from Rameau's *Le Temple de la gloire.* [BJB]

18. Meaning that French music has had its day. [BJB]

19. François, duc de La Rochefoucauld (1613–80). His *Réflexions ou Sentences et Maximes morales* (1665) went through four editions during his lifetime; written in a pessimistic vein and exposing common illusions, they shocked his contemporaries. The *Pensées* of Blaise Pascal (1623–62), a collection of fragments intended to reconcile man with faith in God, published after his death, were condemned by philosophers of the Enlightenment. [BJB]

repeat it, add to it one that is missing, turn the phrase this way and that like a polyp, without destroying it—which makes poetry for music much more difficult in French than in languages with inversions that offer all of these advantages automatically: "Barbare, cruel, Plonge ton poignard dans mon sein. Me voilà prête à recevoir le coup fatal. Frappe. Ose . . . Ah, je languis, je meurs . . . Un feu secret s'allume dans mes sens . . . Cruel amour, que veux-tu de moi . . . Laisse-moi la douce paix dont j'ai joui . . . Rends-moi la raison."[20] The passions must be strong; the tenderness of the musician and the lyric poet must be extreme. The air is nearly always the peroration of the scene. We must have exclamations, interjections, suspensions, interruptions, affirmations, negations; we appeal, we invoke, we cry out, we moan, we weep, we laugh out loud. No wit, no epigrams; none of these fine thoughts. That's all too far removed from simple nature. Now don't go thinking that the style of actors and their declamation can serve as a model for us. Bah! It must be more energetic, less stylized, more genuine. Simple speeches, the common voices of passion are the more essential to us the more the language is monotone and less accented. The cry of an animal or of an impassioned man gives them tone and accent.

While he spoke to me in this way, the crowd surrounding us had withdrawn, either hearing nothing or taking little interest in what he was saying, because in general men, like children, prefer amusement to instruction; each one had returned to his game, and we had remained alone in our corner. Seated on the bench, his head leaning against the wall, his arms hanging down, his eyes half closed, he said to me: "I don't know what's wrong with me; when I came here I was fresh and full of energy, and here I am crushed and broken as if I had walked ten leagues. It came over me all at once."

From *Le Neveu de Rameau, satire, publiée pour la première fois sur le manuscrit original autographe,* ed. Georges Monval (Paris, 1891), 78–88; some of the notes are drawn from this edition. Written by Diderot ca. 1760 but not published during his lifetime, it was first published in a German translation by Goethe (Leipzig, 1805). Modern edition by Henri Coulet in *Œuvres complètes, édition critique et annotée,* ed. H. Dieckmann and J. Varloot, vol. 12 (Paris: Hermann, 1989), 158–70. English translations: *Rameau's Nephew and Other Works,* trans. Jacques Barzun and Ralph H. Bowen (Indianapolis: Bobbs-Merrill, 1964) and *Rameau's Nephew and D'Alembert's Dream,* trans. L. W. Tancock (Harmondsworth: Penguin, 1966). The same excerpt is also given in Lippman, ed., *Musical Aesthetics* 1:367–74.

20. Evidently an improvised adaptation of two scenes from Racine's *Phèdre* (II, 5 and I, 3) to operatic language. [BJB]

FRIEDRICH MELCHIOR GRIMM
from *The Little Prophet of Boehmischbroda* (1753)

VIII
THE COLLECTION

And I was bored in this fashion for two and a half hours, listening to a collection of minuets and airs they call gavottes, and others they call rigadoons, tambourins, and contredanses; the whole interspersed with a few scenes in plainsong, such as we sing at Vespers to this day, and with a few songs I heard played in the outskirts of Prague, notably at the sign of the White Cross and that of the Archduke Joseph.

And I saw that in France they called this an opera, and I wrote that down in my notebook in order to remember it.

IX
THE HIGH TENOR

And I was very pleased to see the curtain fall, and I said: Ah! may I never see it rise again!

And the voice that was my guide began to laugh, and I realized that it was making fun of me, though this distressed me, for it is not in my nature to appreciate mockery.

And the voice said to me: You will not go off to the ballroom at Prague, and you will not go; for that is not my intention.

And you will spend the night here writing down my wishes, which I shall dictate to you: and you will announce them to this people whom I cherished in the past, and who have become hateful to me by their frequent desertions.

And you will have them printed, if you can find a printer: for lying has taken hold of their printing houses, and the truth is no longer printed with approval and privilege.

And I heeded the voice, because my mother told me: be obedient. And I said to the voice that spoke to me: I am subject to your will; but if you take pity on me and do not wish to punish me too harshly, keep them from singing while I write down your wishes, and deliver me from the fear of seeing the thing they call opera start up again: for their songs have afflicted me, their games have distressed me, their sadness is sullen, and when they are happy, they bore me.

And the voice said to me in its kindness: Take heart, for you are my son, and you were dear to me before you had written the three minuets for the carnival of Prague, of which the second is in a minor key.

And they will sing no more, and your ears will be at peace, for they are in a state of great exhaustion, and their actors, and the woodchopper,[1] and the violinists of their orchestra are in need of rest, for the next performance is at hand.

And I determined that for the health of the lungs to it was better to play the horn in the forest of Boehmischbroda from sunrise to sunset than to sing high tenor three times a week in their wretched Opéra.

X
THE CORNER

And in this fashion the voice soothed me, and it ordered me to place myself in a corner that is called the corner on the Queen's side,[2] because it is beneath the Queen's box to this very day.

And even though it was dark, luminous people were present there. And there the philosophers, the great wits, and the chosen few of the nation assemble to this day; and the outcasts do not enter, for they are excluded.

And good and evil are spoken there, and the word and the thing. And it is there one hears the word that saddens bad poets, and the thing that makes bad musicians tremble.

And people are seldom bored, because they scarcely listen, and they talk a great deal, even though the attendant says: Gentlemen, please be good enough to lower your voices; gentlemen, please lower your voices!

And they pay no attention to what the attendant says, for they prefer to converse than to hear what they call singing.

And when everyone had left and they had said a great many bad things about what they call opera, I drew my notebook from my pocket and I said to the voice: Make yourself heard that I may write down your wishes, and that I may announce them to the people, whom you call frivolous, even though their singing is ponderous, and whom you call lively and playful, even though their opera is sad and gloomy.

And the voice that had spoken to me grew loud, insistent, and full of pathos, and I wrote.

---

1. The time-beater; Grimm had devoted an earlier chapter to "the woodchopper," in which he noted that although his duty was called "beating the time," the musicians were never together; see Strunk, *Source Readings*, 622–23. [BJB]

2. The partisans of Italian opera gathered in the corner under the Queen's box. [BJB]

XI
Here Begins the Revelation

O walls that I have raised with my own hands as monument to my glory, O walls once inhabited by a people I called my own, because I had chosen them from the beginning to make them the foremost people of Europe and to carry their glory and fame beyond the boundaries I set for the universe.

O city who call yourself great because you are vast, and glorious because I have covered you with my wings: hear me, for I am about to speak.

And you, O square where they have erected the theater of the Comédie Française, to which I bequeathed genius and taste, and to which I said: You will have no equal in the universe, and your glory will be carried from east to west, and from south to north: hear me, for I am about to speak.

And you, frivolous and haughty theater who have falsely claimed the title of Academy of Music though you are not one,[3] and even though I have not allowed you to do so: hear me, for I am about to speak.

O frivolous and flighty people, O people inclined to desertion and abandoned to the madness of your pride and vanity:

Come that I may reckon with you, I who may, if I wish, reckon you for nothing: come let me confound you in your own sight, and let me write your cowardice on your proud forehead in my own hand in all the languages of Europe! . . .

XIV
The Florentine

And just as I had brought the other arts from Italy to give them all to you, I wished also to bring music into your hearts and to adapt it myself to the spirit of your language.

And I wished to create your musicians, and to form them, and to teach them to compose music according to my ear and my heart.

And you have scorned my favors, because I showered them over you in abundance.

And in your stubbornness you fashioned for yourselves an Opéra that has bored me for twenty-four years, and which is to this day the laughingstock of Europe.

And in the obstinacy of your extravagance, you have made it into an Acad-

---

3. Académie Royale de Musique was the official title of the Paris Opéra, by which it was commonly known from the seventeenth century; the location varied. [BJB]

emy of Music, even though it is not one and I have never recognized it as such.

And you chose the Florentine as your idol without consulting me, even though I had not sent him.[4]

And because he had received the light of genius, you dared to set him against me, because I had given you my servant Quinault in my mercy.

And you believed that his monotony would make me impatient and force me to abandon you because I act swiftly, and you sought to wear me down with the multitude of your offenses.

And you cried out in your great ignorance: Ah, here is the creator of Song, ah here he is!

And because he did what he was able, despite the poverty of his ideas, you call him creator to this day when he has created nothing, and the Germans have been exhausting my ears and vexing me for the past two hundred years, in their churches and vespers, with a singing that you call *your* recitative, when it is actually theirs (even though they do not boast about it, because they think it is bad), and which, in your foolishness, you believe to this day to have been invented by the Florentine whom you call Monsieur de Lully.

XV
THE PRECURSOR

And the stubbornness and obstinacy of your madness notwithstanding, I have not rejected you in my anger as you deserve, and I have not abandoned you to the scorn of your neighbors.

And I took pity on your still childlike judgment and your hardness of hearing, and I set about to bring you back onto the right road by those very paths upon which you had gone astray in the folly of your heart.

And I set about provoking distaste in you for the monotony of the Florentine and the insipidity of those who have followed him for more than forty years.

And I formed a man deliberately, and I organized his mind, and I brought him to life, and I said to him: Have genius, and he did.[5]

And when it was time, I sent for him and I said to him: Take over the theater they have called the Academy of Music even though it is not one, and purge it of all this bad music that they have had made by people whom I never acknowledged, beginning with the Florentine whom they call great, down to little Mouret whom they call kind and gay.

4. Jean-Baptiste Lully. [BJB]
5. In his annotated copy of Grimm's pamphlet, Rousseau identified him as Rameau. [BJB]

And you will astonish them with the fire and force of the harmony I have placed in your mind and with the abundance of ideas with which I have supplied you.

And they will call that which is harmonious baroque, as they call that which is insipid simple. And when they will have spent fifteen years calling you a barbarian, they will no longer be able to do without your music because it will have opened up their ears.

And you will have prepared the way that I have imagined, to give music to this nation that is not worthy of my blessings; for you are my servant.

XVI
THE SINGER

And I never grew weary of showering you with my favors. And I sent to you my servant Fel[6] whom I drew from the depths of her province, which I call my own province because I love it.

And I said to her: You are my daughter, for I have formed you according to my heart and my desires, and I have given you a great and beautiful voice as I have never given to anyone among this people, for it is light, and I have given your soul taste, and I have adorned you with a great talent.

And I send you into this theater which they call an Academy of Music though it is not one. And you will teach this people to sing, for they do not know what singing is, and you will not shout, and you will not make long and drawn-out sounds.

And you will take no account of the roar they make in the ignorance of their hearts, at the bursting forth of voices and the humming of cadences and the heavy sounds they have their actors bring forth from their very entrails.

And you will do without this applause, for I have given you a brave heart that you may do good, which is not applauded, in preference to evil, which is.

And you will sing the music of my servant Rameau in your fashion, which is not theirs, and because you will not shout (for I forbid you to do so) they will say: Ah what a lovely throat! Whereas I say: Ah what a great and beautiful voice I have given my servant Fel, whom I have created according to my heart and my desires.

And foreign peoples will come to this theater called the Academy of Music without my consent and even though it is not one, and they will go there because of you.

---

6. Marie Fel (1713–94); French soprano at the Opéra 1734–58. In addition to singing in many of Rameau's operas, she created the role of Colette in Rousseau's *Le Devin du village*. [BJB]

And they will admire you, even as they make fun of the tediousness of your Opéra, and they will shout: Ah, here is the Singer, here is the Singer! . . .

XVIII
The Messenger

This is why the vanity and insolence of your recalcitrance have reached their height and I am weary of tolerating them.

One moment longer, and I shall sweep you away, as the southern wind sweeps dust from the fields, and I shall plunge you once again into the mire of barbarism out of which I had drawn your fathers in my mercy.

And here is the last miracle that I have resolved to perform, and I shall perform one such as I have never done: for I am beginning to despise you because I no longer find you worthy.

And I swear and say: Here is the last! And I choose for my messenger my servant Manelli,[7] and I pull him out of the mud and I give him shoes and I say to him: Leave your wooden clogs behind, and when you have roamed the provinces of Germany in order to have bread to eat and water to drink, I shall send you where praise awaits you and where you will do my will.

And I shall place Bourbons to your right and Bourbons to your left, and they will protect you, because I love them and I have given them a taste for beautiful things.

And you will sing in this theater they call the Academy of Music without my consent and even though it is not one, and you will force them to applaud you in exaltation, whether they wish to or not.

And you will not know what to make of your fame, and you will cry out in the modesty of your heart: No, not unto me, not unto me, for in my country there are five hundred who are more worthy than I, and I am the least of the family.

But I have chosen you deliberately, despite your heart's modesty, from among the five hundred who are above you, to humiliate this vain and proud people whom I begin to despise because I no longer find them worthy.

And you will bring them the music of my servant Pergolesi who to this day is called divine, because I caused him to spring forth fully grown from my forehead.

And this will be the time of signs and of miracles.

And the philosopher will leave his study, and the geometer his calculations, and the astronomer his telescope, and the chemist his vial, and the witty man

7. Pietro Manelli, leading singer of the Italian troupe. [BJB]

his acquaintances, and the painter his brush, and the sculptor his chisel; and only their wives will not want to go, for they will have no ear for it; and the boxes at the theater will be filled with men.

And they will all come to applaud you, and they will await your companion as the lover awaits his beloved in the impatience of his heart; and they will be overcome with rejoicing; and they will raise their hands to heaven in their souls' ecstasy.

And they will embrace each other joyously; and the stranger will hold a stranger in his arms; and they will offer each other congratulations for knowing such pleasure.

For I shall have opened their ears, and they will cry out: Oh! oh! what music! Oh! what music!

And when they will have listened to it for three months, they will no longer be able to tolerate the slowness and monotony of the singing they call recitative, and which I call plainsong.

And the monologues they call touching will make them yawn; the scenes they call interesting will bore them; and they will fall asleep during the scenes they call gay.

And a feeling of vertigo will seize them, and they will no longer know what they want or what they do not want.

XIX
The Marvelous

O people caught up in the ecstasy of your distraction, o people of little understanding, listen to my voice which speaks to you for the last time, and be receptive to the constancy of my warnings.

Spare me the tediousness of your Opéra that keeps me from attending it. Renounce the prejudices that nourished you at your mother's breast and with which you still quench your thirst daily.

Deliver me from the puerile genre you call the marvelous,[8] when it is so only for you and for children; be sincere in your repentance and I shall open my arms to you and I shall forget your iniquities and those of your fathers.

And I shall make you an Opéra according to my heart and my desires, and I shall call it the Academy of Music, because it will be one.

And I shall be its inspector, and there will no longer be a woodchopper at the head of your orchestra, and no longer carpenters running your chorus.

And I shall be in your orchestra, and I shall bring it to life, and I shall teach it

8. "Le merveilleux": the wondrous effects of stage design, ballet, and machinery, designed to underline the splendor and magnificence of the operas of gods and heroes. [BJB]

to sense genius so that it may render it with taste, and I shall chase away the bad violinists, and I shall give you others like Canavas in their place.[9]

And I shall give you actors who will sing like my servant Jélyotte[10] and my servant Fel, and you will no longer hear howling on the stage of your theater.

And I shall banish from your theater the demons and the ghosts and the fairies and the genies and all the monsters with which your poets have infected it by the power they have given to magic wands in their fit of madness, and without my consent.

And I shall devote your Opéra, like that of the Italians, to great scenes and to passions, and to expression of all sorts, from the pathetic to the comic.

And you will no longer enjoy playing at making storms and thunder and lightning, for I shall teach you how to make Merope, Andromache, and Dido speak.

And I shall be with your poets and your musicians: and I shall teach your poets to write words, and your musicians to compose music.

And I shall give your poets invention and imagination, so that they will no longer need a wand or spells.

And just as your musicians have composed mere notes until now, so they will compose music that is truly music, and I shall place genius in their scores and taste in their accompaniments, and I shall deliver them from the weight of the notes with which they burden them, and I myself shall select them.

And I shall teach them to be simple without being dull, and they will no longer call what is monotonous lovely simplicity. And I shall create your recitative, and I shall teach them to compose music that has character and a precise, distinct pace, and which is not devoid of expression.

And I shall work with them and my spirit will guide them, and I shall assign to each genre its limitations and its distinctive character, from tragedy down to the intermezzo.

And as I had one performed by my servant Jélyotte and my servant Fel, which pleased you greatly, because I had it done according to my wishes, by a man with whom I do as I please, even though he grumbles at me; for I rule over him, whether he likes it or not, and I called his intermezzo *Le Devin du village*.[11]

In the same way I shall teach your musicians to compose pastorales and comedies and tragedies, and they will no longer need to say: this is comic and that

9. Probably Joseph Canavas (ca. 1714–76), an Italian violinist who made his career in France and was then at the height of his fame, especially as a soloist in the Concert Spirituel. [BJB]

10. Pierre de Jélyotte (1713–97), leading singer of the Opéra, for whom Rousseau wrote Colin in *Le Devin du village*. [BJB]

11. Jean-Jacques Rousseau's *Le Devin du village*, a one-act opera first performed at Fontainebleau on 18 October 1752, then at the Paris Opéra on 1 March 1753. [BJB]

is tragic, for it will be evident without their saying so, even though they do well to say so today.

And your glory will shine forth in every direction, and I myself shall spread it to all nations, and you will be called the People par excellence, and you will have no equal, and I shall not grow weary of looking at you because it will give me pleasure to see you.

And your genius, your wit, your taste, your grace, your charm, and your kindness will make my heart tremble with joy, for you will be my people, and there will be no other like you.

From *Le Petit Prophète de Boehmisch-Broda* (Paris, 1753), chs. 8–11, 14–16, 18–19; repr. in Launay, *La Querelle des bouffons* 1:154–61, 167–73, 176–84. A selection of excerpts is translated in Strunk, *Source Readings*, 619–35.

FRIEDRICH MELCHIOR GRIMM
from the article "Poème lyrique" in the *Encyclopédie* (1765)

The Italians have called the lyric poem or the musical spectacle *opera,* and this word has been adopted in French.[1]

All imitative art is founded on a falsehood: this falsehood is a type of assumption established and admitted by virtue of a tacit agreement between the artist and his judges. Allow me this first falsehood, the artist has said, and I shall lie to you with so much truth that you will be deceived by it, whether you like it or not. The dramatic poet, the painter, the sculptor, the dancer or mime, the actor—all have a particular assumption according to which they undertake to deceive, and which they cannot lose sight of for a single moment without removing us from this illusion that makes our imagination party to their trickery; for it is not truth, but the image of truth that they promise us, and what makes their productions charming is not nature, but the imitation of nature. The closer an artist comes to achieving this in the assumption he has chosen, the more talent and genius we attribute to him.

The imitation of nature through singing was surely one of the first that presented itself to the imagination. Every living creature is prompted by the feeling of his existence to utter in certain moments sounds that are more or less melo-

1. Throughout this extract "poème lyrique" and "poète lyrique" have been translated literally; it should be kept in mind, however, that Grimm is speaking about the opera libretto, verse specifically written for music, and the opera librettist. [BJB]

dious, according to the nature of his organs: how could man have remained silent among so many singers? Joy, in all likelihood, inspired the first songs; we sang at first without words, then sought to adapt to singing a few words consistent with the feeling it was supposed to express; the first music thus consisted of the couplet and the song.

But the man of genius did not limit himself for very long to these songs, the simple children of nature; he conceived a bolder, more noble plan, that of making singing an instrument of imitation. He soon realized that to the degree that our soul takes leave of its normal balance, we raise our voices and our discourse becomes more forceful and melodious. By studying men in different circumstances, he heard them sing truly on all of life's important occasions; he saw further that each passion, each of the soul's affections, had its accent, its inflections, its own melody and song.

From this discovery imitative music was born and along with it the art of singing, which became a kind of poetry, a language, an art of imitation, whose assumption was to express through melody and with the aid of harmony all types of speech, accent, and passion, and sometimes even to imitate physical effects. The uniting of this art, as sublime as it is close to nature, with dramatic art gave birth to the spectacle of *opera,* the most noble and brilliant of modern entertainments. . . .

Music is a language. Imagine a nation of visionaries and fanatics whose minds were always exalted, whose souls were always in a state of ecstasy and intoxication; who, despite our passions and principles, surpassed us in their subtlety, the purity and delicacy of their senses, in the mobility, refinement, and perfection of their voices—such a people would sing instead of speaking; their natural language would be music. The lyric poem does not represent beings of a constitution different from ours, but only of one that is more highly developed. They express themselves in a language that one cannot speak without genius, but that one cannot hear either without a delicate sensibility, without a refined and trained ear. Thus those who have called singing the most fantastic of all languages, and who have mocked a spectacle in which the heroes die singing, were not as correct in their judgment as was initially thought; but as they perceive in music at most a harmonious and pleasing noise, a succession of chords and cadences, they must consider it a language that is foreign to them; it is not for them to assess the talent of the composer; one must have an Attic ear to judge the eloquence of Demosthenes.

The musician's language has the same advantage over the poet's that a universal language has over a particular idiom; the latter speaks only the language of its time and place, the former speaks the language of all nations and all ages.

Every universal language is vague by its very nature; thus the musician, in attempting to embellish theatrical representation through his art, has been obliged to have recourse to the poet. Not only does he need him to create the overall design of the lyric drama, but he cannot do without an interpreter on all the occasions in which precision of speech becomes indispensable, in which the vagueness of musical language would lead the spectator into uncertainty. The musician needs no help in expressing grief, despair, the delirium of a woman threatened by a great misfortune; but his poet says to us: this weeping woman whom you see is a mother who fears some mortal catastrophe for her only son; this mother is Sarah, who, upon not seeing her son return from the sacrifice, recalls the mystery with which this sacrifice was prepared, and the care that was taken to keep her away from it . . .

Having thus named the subject and created the situation, having prepared and established it through his speeches, the poet furnishes no more than the raw material, which he abandons to the genius of the composer; it is up to the latter to give it expression and to develop all the subtlety of detail that it may furnish.

A universal language that strikes our senses and our imagination immediately is also by its very nature the language of passion and feeling. Its expressions, going straight to the heart without passing, so to speak, through the mind, must produce effects known in no other idiom, and this very vagueness, which prevents it from granting its accents the precision of speech, leaves to our imagination the task of interpretation, and gives it an authority that no language could exert over it. Music shares this power with that other universal language, gesture. Experience teaches us that nothing commands the soul more imperiously, nor moves it more powerfully, than these two ways of speaking to it.

The drama in music must therefore make an impression far deeper than ordinary tragedy and comedy. It would be pointless to employ the most powerful instrument to produce only mediocre effects. If the tragedy of Merope moves me, touches me, causes me to shed tears, then in opera the anguish, the mortal fears of this unfortunate mother must all penetrate my soul; I must be frightened by all of the phantoms that obsess her, and her grief and madness must shatter me and tear out my heart. The musician who would settle for a few tears, for a passing emotion, would be well beneath his art. The same is so for comedy. If the comedy of Terence or Molière is enchanting, then comedy in music must be dazzling. The one represents men as they are, the other gives them an extra touch of verve and genius; they are very close to madness. To recognize the merit of the former, one needs only ears and common sense; but comedy that is sung seems to be made for the elite among people of wit and taste; music lends an original character to absurdity and manners, a subtlety of expression that demands a quick and delicate touch, and well-trained ears, in order to be understood.

But passion has its rests and intervals, and the art of the theater demands that the course of nature be followed in this. One cannot always be bursting with laughter at a performance, or melting in tears. Orestes is not always tormented by the Eumenides; Andromache in the midst of her fears perceives some ray of hope that calms her; it is only a short distance from this certainty to the dreadful moment in which she will see her son perish. But these two moments are different, and the latter only becomes more tragic in contrast to the tranquillity of the former. Secondary characters, whatever interest they may take in the action, cannot share the passionate accents of their heroes. In the end, the most moving situation only becomes touching and terrible by degrees; it must be prepared, and its effect depends in large part on what has preceded and occasioned it.

These are, then, two quite distinct moments of the lyric drama, the quiet moment and the passionate moment; and the primary concern of the composer must be to find two sorts of declamation that are essentially different and specific, the one to convey quiet discourse, the other to express the language of passion in all its force, variety, and disorder. This latter type of declamation bears the name of air or *aria;* the former has been called *recitative.* . . .

Recitative functions without the help of the orchestra, and differs from ordinary declamation only in that it marks the inflections of speech with intervals that are more perceptible and suited to notation. It is no less worthy of the attention of a great composer, who will know how to put a great deal of spirit, subtlety, and variety into it. He may even accompany it with the orchestra, and interrupt it in the pauses with different musical ideas whenever the actor's declamation, without becoming singing, is more animated and approaches the moment in which the force of passion transforms it into an aria.

This internal economy of musical drama, founded on the one hand on the truth of imitation, and on the other on the nature of our senses, must serve as an elementary poetics for the lyric poet. He must, in fact, subordinate himself in all things to the musician; he can claim only a secondary role; but there are still appreciable means for him to share in the glory of his partner. . . .

The result of these observations is that the poet, whatever talent he may have, can scarcely claim to have succeeded in this genre if he himself does not understand music. He is too dependent on it at every turn to remain unaware of its elements, style, and subtleties. He must take as much care as the composer to distinguish the recitative from the aria in his poem; if this fundamental distinction were not made, the most beautiful poem in the world would be the least lyrical and the least suited to music. In arias, the musician is within his rights to demand of his poet a style that is simple, separable, and easy to break into parts; for the disorder of the passions necessarily leads to the breaking up of speech, which too elaborate a structure of verses renders impracticable. Alexandrine verse would be ill suited to the scene or the recitative, because the rhythm is much too long, and it generates long and rounded sentences, which musical declamation abhors. It is conceivable that harmonious, rhythmic verse could nevertheless be ill suited to music, and that there could be a language in which, by a rather strange misuse of terms, what might have been called lyric is least suited to singing.

Three qualities are essential to the language in which the lyric poem is to be written.

It must be simple, and while preferring ordinary language, it must not therefore fail to be noble and touching.

It must be graceful and harmonious. A language in which the harmony of the poetry consists principally in rounding out the line, or in which the poet achieves harmony only through a richness of meter, would scarcely be suited to music.

And finally, the language of the lyric poem must, without losing its natural quality or its grace, lend itself to the inversions of word order[2] that expression, warmth, and the disorder of the passions make indispensable at every instant.

There are few languages that unite three qualities as rare as these; but there is none in which the lyric poet may not successfully speak, if he truly knows the nature of the drama and the spirit of the music. . . .

On French Opera

According to the definition of a famous writer, French opera is epic transformed into action and put on stage. What the discretion of the epic poet reveals only to our imagination, the lyric poet in France has undertaken to bring before our eyes. The tragic poet takes his subjects from history; the lyric poet seeks his in epic, and having exhausted ancient mythology and modern sorcery, having placed on the stage every possible divinity, and having recast everything in form and figure, he has now created fantastic beings. Endowing them with supernatural and magic powers, he has made them the principal device of his poem.

It is therefore the *merveilleux,* the marvelous made visible, that is the soul of French opera; the gods, goddesses, demigods, shades, genies, fairies, magicians, virtues, passions, abstract ideas, and allegorical beings are its actors. This visual fantasy has been thought so essential to the drama that poets would think it impossible to treat a historic subject without mixing in some supernatural incidents and fantastic beings of their own creation.

2. The problem of inversions was a prime topic of discussion among linguists and philosophers. See in particular Diderot's *Lettre sur les sourds et les muets* (Paris, 1751), which places it at the center of a complex aesthetic problem. [EF]

In order to judge whether this genre merits the approval of an enlightened nation, critics and people of taste should consider and decide the following questions.

Would it not be contrary to common sense, which genius has always piously respected in the imitative arts, to attempt to make the marvelous suitable to theatrical representation? Does what was great and noble in the imagination of the poet and his readers not become puerile and petty, when it is thus made visible? . . .

If this genre has produced only dramas devoid of all interest and truth, would it not therefore have impeded the progress of music in France, while this art has been carried to the highest degree of perfection in the other parts of Europe? How could musical style have taken form in a country in which only imaginary beings, whose accents have no model in nature, are made to sing? As their declamation is arbitrary and indeterminate, would it not have produced a cold and soporific type of singing, an unbearable monotony that no one could have tolerated were it not for the ballets? Would not musical expression thus have been reduced to playing on words, so that a singer could not utter the word *tears* without the composer making him cry even though he had no cause for affliction, and that in the saddest circumstance he could not mention a bright mood without the composer assuming the right to have him display the brilliance of his voice at the expense of his soul's disposition? Would there not have resulted from this method a dictionary of words reputed to be lyrical, a dictionary that a clever composer would not fail to present to his poet, so that he would have, in a single collection, all the words that are of no use to music and must never be used in the lyric poem?

Would not this false genre, in which nothing is reminiscent of nature, have prevented the French musician from knowing and feeling the fundamental distinction between aria and recitative? Operatic recitative would have become a heavy, drawn-out chant, similar to the Gothic chant of our churches. In order to lend it expression, it would have been overburdened with *ports de voix*, trills, tremolos, and despite these laborious efforts, the art of punctuating the song, of asking a question, of making an exclamation while singing would not have even been imagined. The unbearable slowness of this recitative and its character, contrary to every sort of declamation, would, moreover, have made the performance of a true scene impossible on stage. The aria, that other principal part of musical drama, would still be so rare that the word air itself would be heard only in reference to pieces that the musician writes for dancing, or to couplets containing maxims that the poet uses in the dialogue of a scene, and from which the composer writes songs that the actor sings with some kind of movement. They could have added a few ariettas to enliven the performance, but they are never appropriate or relevant to the subject, and their very name is an indication of their poverty and puerility. These "little airs" would have contributed marvelously to delaying the progress of music; for it is no doubt better for music to express nothing than to see it torment itself over a *lance*, a *murmur*, a *fluttering*, a *chain*, a *triumph*, etc. . . .

ON ITALIAN OPERA

In Italy, they fairly quickly did away with this false genre called the marvelous, which the barbaric taste of the previous century had introduced on all the stages of Europe; and as soon as they began to sing on stage, they felt that only tragedy and comedy could be set to music. A fortunate coincidence having given rise to the simplest, most touching, most energetic, most effortless of lyric poets—the illustrious Metastasio—and at the same time to a great number of musicians of genius whom Italy and Germany have produced, foremost among whom posterity will read in indelible letters the names of Vinci, Hasse, and Pergolesi, the musical drama has been brought in this century to the highest degree of perfection. All the great scenes, the most interesting plots, the most touching, the most terrible—whatever falls within the domain of tragedy or of true comedy has been subjugated to the art of music and received from it in return a degree of expression and enthusiasm that has swept along people of wit and taste everywhere, as well as common people. Music having been dedicated in Italy from its birth to its true purpose, namely, to the expression of sentiment and of the passions, the lyric poet could not have mistaken what the composer expected of him; nor could he in turn have led the latter astray, and made him leave the path of nature and of truth. . . .

Why then, given such powerful means, has Italian opera not revived in our day the awe-inspiring effects of ancient tragedy, as history has recorded them? How have we been able to witness the performance of certain scenes without fear of having our hearts too grievously wounded, and of falling into a state too painful and too close to the wretched circumstances of the heroes of the drama? On these occasions an enlightened critic will accuse neither the poet nor the composer of being unequal to the subject: we must then consider by what means so many sublime efforts of genius have either been made useless, or reduced to very little effect.

When a spectacle serves only as an amusement for an idle people—that is to say, for that elite of a nation who are said to be well-bred—it cannot ever achieve real importance; whatever genius you grant the poet, the theatrical performance along with a thousand details of his poem must inevitably reflect the frivolity of its purpose. In writing tragedies Sophocles worked for the nation, for religion, and for the most august solemnities of the republic. Among the modern poets, Metastasio has perhaps enjoyed the sweetest and happiest destiny; sheltered from envy and persecution, which are today, as they sometimes were among the ancients, all too readily the reward accorded to genius for virtues and services rendered to the state, the talents of the foremost poet of Italy have been continually honored by the protection of the House of Austria: yet how different is his role in Vienna from that of Sophocles in Athens! For the ancients, theater was an affair of state; for us, if the police take an interest in it, it is in order to pick a thousand little quarrels with it, to make it conform to countless strange properties. The audience, singers, and impresarios have all usurped a ridiculous authority over the lyric poem, and its creators, the poet and the composer, themselves victims of this tyranny, have been the least consulted in its performance.

Everyone knows that in Italy people do not assemble in the theaters only to see the show; the boxes have become so many conversation circles that start, and stop, and start up again many times during the performance. The custom is to spend five or six hours at the opera, but not in order to give it five or six hours of attention. They require of the poet only a few touching situations, a few very fine scenes, and they do not expect much for the rest. When the composer has managed to set those famous passages that everyone knows by heart in a manner both new and worthy of his art, they are delighted, they are ecstatic, they abandon themselves to enthusiasm; but once the scene is over, they no longer listen. So two or three arias, a lovely duet, or a very beautiful scene suffice for the success of an opera, and they are indifferent to the drama as a whole, provided it has produced three or four delightful moments, and that it lasts the amount of time they had intended to spend at the opera house.

In a nation impassioned by singing, which makes the greatest sacrifices to the charm of the voice and where singing has become an art that demands, besides the most favorable disposition of the organs, the longest and most persistent study, the singer usurped early on an illegitimate authority over the composer and the poet. Everything is sacrificed to his talents and his whims. People are not shocked by the imperfections of the dramatic action, provided the singing is excellent, delightful, and enchanting. Concerning himself with neither the circumstances of the plot nor the nature of his role, the singer limits all his attention to vocal expression; the scene is recited and acted with a shameful neglect. Though they should be spectators, the public remains merely auditors. They close their eyes and open their ears; and leaving to the imagination the task of showing the true carriage, gestures, features, and face of Hector's widow, or of the founder of Carthage, they content themselves with listening to the true sounds of the same. . . .

The comic opera or *opera buffa* has not been subject, in truth, to all of these abuses; but on the other hand, it has been practiced only by mediocre poets and clowns who sacrifice everything to the passing jest. These plays are generally full of comic situations, because the need to place the aria produces the need to create the situation; but as long as it is original and pleasing, the poet is forgiven the extravagance of the design and of the whole, as well as the pitiful means he has used to create the situations.

One must admit, to the glory of the poet and the composer, that they were never for an instant mistaken in their vocation or in the purpose of their art; and if Italian opera is full of flaws that weaken its impression and effect, there is fortunately not a single one that cannot be removed without affecting the substance and essence of the lyric poem.

From the article "Poème lyrique" in the *Encyclopédie,* vol. 12 (Paris, 1765), 823–36.

Chapter Three

European Rationalism and Theories of Harmony

THERE EXISTS A LONG TRADITION of theoretical studies on music, going back to Descartes, Mersenne, and Kircher, or, going back still further, to Zarlino, Vicentino, etc., according to which music is a science, and is to be studied as such, identifying its rules and laws, which essentially remain immutable throughout history. This tradition was taken up again in the eighteenth century; obviously, as in the past, such studies focused on harmony, the aspect of music that lends itself best to scientific investigation. Since the time of Pythagoras music has always been viewed from a double perspective. On one hand, it has a transitory aspect, which appeals to feelings, to the ear, and produces auditory pleasure; on the other, it has a rational, speculative, and permanent aspect, which is closer to mathematics and philosophy than to everyday instrumental practice. The invention (or the discovery) of harmony afforded the theoretician the opportunity of uniting both the rational and the perceptible aspects. The eternal laws of harmony are founded on physical phenomena and the ear perceives them as pleasant on the strength of their fundamental nature. Reason only recognizes and identifies them as such and explains their laws. The new discoveries in acoustics, the study of the phenomenon of harmonics, the discovery of the difference tone (Tartini), and logarithmic calculation applied to acoustics (Euler, Sauveur) broadened the horizons of knowledge and above all laid the foundations for a study of instrumental music as an autonomous language.

In his famous *Gradus ad Parnassum* (1725), Johann Joseph Fux was still partly bound to an abstract vision of music. In this treatise on composition, in the form of a dialogue between teacher and pupil mainly devoted to counterpoint, Fux, following a very ancient tradition, distinguishes between speculative and practical music. In the process, he loses himself in subtle numerical contemplation of a rather medieval stamp. Yet in the practical part, in which he examines the various musical styles, his reasoning becomes more concrete; while keeping faith with the principle that counterpoint and harmony represent the foundations of music, he does not disdain to give advice to composers who have to write arias subject to the vagaries of fashion, "arbitrary music" that changes "every five years."

Quite a different conceptual rigor and density of thought mark the works of Jean-Philippe Rameau, perhaps the greatest theorist of the eighteenth century. He developed his harmonic theory in numerous treatises on harmony and in his disputes with the Encyclopedists, especially with Rousseau. All chords and their inversions originate from a single sound—the harmonic center or fundamental sound—through the first harmonics in the overtone series. In his treatise *Observations sur notre instinct pour la musique et sur son principe* (1754), which is obviously a polemic against the Encyclopedists and all aesthetic theories that tended to attribute the sphere of art exclusively to taste and feeling, Rameau attempted to restore the unity of perception and reason. He did so by showing how anyone, even those lacking any kind of theoretical knowledge, can grasp the basic elements of harmony by means of instinct. Similarly, melody too is not the product of a particular inventiveness, but is already contained and implied in harmony.

The work of Giuseppe Tartini followed along the same lines as that of Rameau. In his studies *Trattato di musica secondo la vera scienza dell'armonia* (1754), *De' principi dell'armonia musicale contenuta nel diatonico genere* (1767), and *Traité des agréments de la musique* (1771), he investigated the laws governing harmony, convinced of their scientific and natural basis.

We have preferred to close this chapter with yet another passage from Diderot, which could have been included elsewhere. His *Principes généraux de la science du son* are part of the *Mémoires sur différens sujets de mathématiques,* published in 1748. These are youthful works that, in content, are very close to what he would write not long thereafter for the *Encyclopédie* in the article on the *Beautiful.* According to Diderot, the pleasure produced by harmony consists in the perception, even though unconscious, of the relationships between sounds: between the perception of the harmonic relationships among sounds and the science of sounds there is only a difference of degree, not of quality.

JOHANN JOSEPH FUX
from *Steps to Parnassus* (1725)

I

Music is a generic and far-reaching term, which contains many species, such as the music of the spheres, earthly music, natural, artificial, historic music, etc. Having in view brevity and utility rather than curiosity, I intend only to treat artificial music. Artificial music is twofold: speculative and practical. It is the former, speculative music, that will be treated in this book; I shall briefly present only those things that seem necessary to practice. The second, practical part, I shall put off for expanded treatment in Book 2. Since our music has to do with sound as its object, the latter will be the first topic.

II
On Sound

Following Aristotle's definition, Mersenne states in the first book of his *Harmonie universelle*, prop. 2, that sound is a movement of air;[1] this surely cannot mean any kind of air, since air in its natural state is undoubtedly moving, but according to the aforementioned Aristotle—cited in the same place by Mersenne—"aër est expers soni" (air by itself does not produce sound). Hence it follows that not any movement of air whatsoever constitutes sound, but air that is affected by something external that encloses and compresses it and thus is the effective cause of sound. This is, however, the subject of physics, for the musician does not consider sound abstractly but relatively and comparatively, namely, how one sound differs from another by reason of its height or lowness. Since this comparison is mainly done with the help of numbers, these are explained in the following chapter.

III
On Numbers, their Proportions, and their Differences

By numbers, I mean the elements of arithmetic: 1, 2, 3, 4, 5, 6, 7, 8, 9. The musician uses these in order to identify intervals by comparing one number to another, and by seeking their distances, differences, excesses, and shortfalls.

---

1. Marin Mersenne, *Harmonie universelle* (Paris, 1636; repr. Paris: Centre National de la Recherche Scientifique, 1963), bk. 1, prop. 2 [BJB]

There are many species of numbers. However, we shall pass over those that are not helpful to our purpose, and we shall mention only the following, namely, rationals and irrationals, radicals and irradicals. Rational numbers are those that can be divided by a number without a remainder, as 6 can be divided by 2 and 3, and 12 by 2, 3, 4, and 6. Irrational numbers are those that cannot be measured or divided in this manner, just as 3, 5, 7, and 9 cannot be divided by 2. Radical numbers are those that cannot be reduced to smaller numbers while preserving that proportion which they determine; irradical numbers are their opposite.

Moreover, it is known that various ratios and differences originate from proportions or the comparison of one quantity to another. The question is what this proportion is. Euclid and others defined it as follows: "duarum quantitatum unius ad alteram habitudo in eodem genere propinquo" ("the relationship one to the other of two quantities of the same narrow kind").[2] The quantity mentioned here is twofold: continuous, within a certain body, as a line, beam, surface, etc., and discrete, and it is found in a certain plurality, such as a people, or numbers, etc. By relationship is meant the relation of one quantity to another "of the same narrow kind," to ensure that the proportion not be taken from a continuous to a discrete quantity, such as from a line to a number, but only from line to line and from number to number.

The musician is able to achieve his purpose with the help of a continuous quantity by measuring lines, strings, etc.; however, this measurement ultimately must be reduced to numbers—namely, by how many parts one line exceeds another in length, and by how many the latter is shorter. In this place I have thought it right to speak only about the proportion generated by discrete quantity, in other words, from a comparison of one number to another.

It is clear that the definition of proportion adduced above is general and extends to any proportion. Hence a special definition must be devised appropriate for no other discipline than music, and this is: musical proportion is the relationship or relation of one sounding number to another. This definition is self-evident from what has been said above, and does not require further explanation.

This proportion can be twofold, that is, equal and unequal. An equal proportion arises from comparing numbers of equal value, such as 1 to 1, 2 to 2, 3 to 3, etc. An unequal proportion is produced by comparing numbers of unequal value, for example, 1 to 2, 3 to 4, 5 to 8, etc.

It is well known that musical intervals, or consonances and dissonances, are produced by a divergence of sounds; from this can be gathered that neither are those proportions whose quantities are of equal value capable of producing in-

2. Euclid, *Elements*, bk. 5, def. 3. [LAH-S]

tervals, nor, for this very reason, can a unison be understood as an interval. In practice, another judgment should be made concerning the unison, which I shall demonstrate when I discuss consonances and dissonances one by one. Furthermore, from the comparison of numbers of unequal value result many genera of proportions, which the musician commonly limits to five: the multiple genus (*genus multiplex*), the superparticular (*superparticulare*), the superpartient (*superpartiens*), the multiple superparticular (*multiplex superparticulare*), and the multiple superpartient (*multiplex superpartiens*). That each of these contains nearly innumerable species will be demonstrated in the following chapters. . . .

On Mixed Style

By mixed style, I mean a composition performed now with one, two, three, or more voices together with instruments and now with a full chorus, the style most often found in churches today. Since this is common and heard frequently, I do not think it worthwhile to discuss it at length and give examples. I shall only remind you, Joseph, never to forget the purpose and goal of church music, which is to stimulate devotion and the Divine Service, and not to confuse this style with those of the theater and dance, as many do. On the other hand, one should not adopt sterile ideas, which have no sap, thinking sacred music to be like that, and thus fall into an unpleasing surliness that will breed more disgust than devotion. Instead, one should seek agreeable harmony that fills the mind of the listener with delight. Thus remember all you have been taught so far in this long discourse for your instruction, and arrange your composition accordingly, so that it may be worthy in the sight of God and praiseworthy in the eyes of men.

On Recitative Style

Recitative style is nothing else than a speech expressed in music or oratorical delivery. Just as the declaimer varies his voice in different ways according to the particular kind of speech—so that it is now agitated, now relaxed, now raised, now lowered—and just as he tries to put on the appearance of an affect that he has it in mind to express, so must a composer vary the setting of a text. In recitative that borders on ordinary speech the music must be set in a more relaxed voice. In a dispute a sharp voice, like one crying out loud, should be used with a continuously changing bass. Music full of solemnity—with a bass changing rarely—should be added to a text expressing dignity. This is especially appropriate in the church style, which is often accompanied by instruments. . . .

Aloysius: As far as secular music is concerned, that is, chamber and theater music, it is reasonable to arrange it differently, since it has a different purpose. The purpose of secular music is to refresh the minds of the listeners and to

move them to various passions. The passions occurring in recitative are generally the following: anger, compassion, fear, violence, vexation, desire, and love.

Anger should be expressed by a kind of agitated voice rising in pitch, and
if very vehement with a kind of shout, the voice breaking off. This can be
achieved with small note values persistently rushing upwards and a bass changing often. It is very important to observe the condition of the angered person. If
he is a king, he will not go so far as to shout like a woman, but, preserving the
dignity of his majesty, he will manifest his indignation with regal earnestness.
This must be taken into account in all other passions also.

Compassion demands a lamenting, sometimes interrupted melody, which
should employ long note values that form dissonances, with the bass remaining
stationary for long periods. Fear calls for a low and hesitant voice. Violence is
expressed by a forceful, intense voice, and one to be taken seriously. Desire uses
an exuberant melody, but, however, is gentle and relaxed. The passion of love is
expressed by a coaxing, tender, and agile melody. However, since love is often
accompanied by other passions, these also must be carefully considered. . . .

Joseph: This, then, is the recitative. What rule do you give for the composition of arias, as they are commonly called?

Aloysius: What can I say about arbitrary music, which is subject to change
every five years or so? I do not disapprove of this eagerness for novelty, but
highly praise it. If a middle-aged man appeared today dressed in the clothes
worn fifty or sixty years ago, he would certainly run the risk of ridicule. Thus
music must be accommodated to the times, too. However, I have never seen or
heard of a tailor, however addicted to fashion, who had sewn the sleeves of a
shirt to the thigh or knee; neither has there been an architect so foolish as to
have built the foundation of a building on top of the roof. This we see and hear
all the time in music—to the dismay of many a skilled musician, and the disgrace of music—where the rules of nature and art are turned upside down, the
foundation is torn from its proper place and put on top, and the remaining
parts are placed beneath, without regard to the foundation. Therefore, Joseph,
you will strive in time with all your might for novelty and invention; but by no
means overturn the rules of art, which imitates and perfects nature, but never
destroys it. If you master all this through continuous practice and if you acquire
skill, Joseph, I trust you will have all you need to become famous as an exceptional composer.

From *Gradus ad Parnassum, sive manuductio ad compositionem musicae regularem, methodo
nova, ac certa* (Vienna, 1725; repr. New York: Broude Bros., 1966), 1–3, 273, 276–77, 278–79.
The Leipzig, 1742 edition has been reprinted by Olms (Hildesheim, 1974). The English
translation by Alfred Mann, *Steps to Parnassus* (New York: W. W. Norton, 1943; repr. 1965
with the title *The Study of Counterpoint*), includes only the sections on counterpoint (preface
and pp. 41–139 and 279 of the original edition).

JEAN-PHILIPPE RAMEAU
from *Treatise on Harmony* (1722)

I
ON MUSIC AND SOUND

Music is the science of sounds; consequently, sound is the principal subject of music.

Music is ordinarily divided into harmony and melody, although the latter is only a part of the former, and one need only know harmony to be perfectly schooled in all the properties of music, as will be proven by what follows.

We shall leave to physics the task of defining sound; in harmony we distinguish only low and high, without pausing to consider its strength or its duration. All knowledge of harmony must be based on the relationship between low and high sounds.

Low sounds are the deepest, like those produced by male voices, and high sounds are the highest, like those produced by female voices.

We call the distance from a low sound to a high sound an *interval;* and from the different distances that may be found between one sound and another, different intervals are formed, the degrees of which take their names from arithmetical numbers; thus the first degree can be denoted only by *unity,* whereby we call two sounds on the same degree a *unison;* consequently, the second degree is called a *second,* the third a *third,* the fourth a *fourth,* the fifth a *fifth,* the sixth a *sixth,* the seventh a *seventh,* and the eighth an *octave,* and so on, assuming that the first degree is always the lowest and that the others are formed by raising the voice successively according to its natural degrees.

II
ON THE DIFFERENT WAYS IN WHICH THE RELATIONSHIP BETWEEN SOUNDS CAN BE KNOWN TO US

In order to understand the relationship between sounds, we have chosen a string stretched in such a way that it can produce a sound; we have then divided the string into several parts with movable bridges, and have found that all the sounds or the intervals that could harmonize were contained within the first five divisions of this string, by comparing each length that resulted from this division with the whole.

Some have sought this relationship in the relations between the numbers marking the divisions; others, having observed the lengths resulting from these divisions, have sought this same relationship between the numbers marking the different lengths; still others, having noted that the communication of sound to the ear could not occur without the participation of air, have sought this relationship in the relations between the numbers that mark the vibrations of these different lengths. We shall not stop to consider several other ways in which this relationship can be known to us, as in the varying thicknesses of the string, in the different tensions produced by weights, or in wind instruments, etc. We have found, in short, that all the consonances are contained within the first six numbers, with the exception of thicknesses and weights, for which one must use the squares of these basic numbers; this has resulted in attributing all the power of harmony to that of numbers, after which it is merely a question of making their correct application to the method upon which one wishes to base one's system.

It must now be noted that the numbers marking the divisions of the string or its vibrations follow their natural progression, and everything is based on the rules of arithmetic; however, the numbers that mark the lengths of the string follow an inverse progression, which undermines in part the rules of arithmetic, or rather obliges us to reverse them, as we shall see later on. But if the choice of these operations is indifferent with regard to harmony, we shall adhere only to those in which the numbers follow their natural progression, because everything is much more intelligible. . . .

XIX
Continuation of the Preceding Chapter, in which It Seems that Melody Derives from Harmony

It seems at first that harmony derives from melody, in that the melody produced in each voice becomes harmony through their union; but it was necessary to determine beforehand a path for each of these voices, so that they might harmonize together. Now whatever order of melody one observes in each individual part, the whole will produce good harmony only with difficulty, if at all, if this order is not dictated by the rules of harmony. Therefore, to make this harmonic whole more intelligible, we begin by teaching how to form a melodic line; and assuming we make some progress here, any ideas we may have about it vanish as soon as another part has to be joined to it; we are no longer masters of the melodic line, and while we strive to find the path that one part must follow in relation to the other, we often lose sight of the one that had first been proposed, or at least we are obliged to change it; otherwise, the constraint this first part imposes on us does not always allow us to give the others as perfect a melodic line as we might wish. Thus it is harmony that guides us, and not melody. It is true that a learned musician may devise a beautiful melody suitable for harmony; but how does he acquire this happy faculty? Might not nature have made a contribution? No doubt. And if, on the contrary, nature has refused him this gift, how can he succeed? Only by the rules. And whence do we derive these rules? This is what we must examine further.

Does the first division of the string offer us initially two sounds from which we can form a melody? Surely not, for a man who sings only octaves would not produce a very beautiful melodic line. The second and third divisions of this string, from which all harmony proceeds, do not furnish sounds more suitable for a melody, since a melodic line composed only of thirds, fourths, fifths, sixths, and octaves would still not be perfect. Harmony, then, is created first, and so it is from harmony that the rules of melody must inevitably be derived, which is also what we are doing when we take those harmonic intervals of which we have just spoken separately, in order to form a fundamental progression. This is not yet melody, but when these intervals are combined above one of their component sounds, following naturally a diatonic path determined by their progression itself, when they serve mutually as a foundation, we then draw from these consonant and diatonic progressions all the melody necessary. Thus we had to know the harmonic intervals before the melodic, and the only melodic line that one can teach a beginner consists of these consonant intervals, if this can be called melodic. We shall see in Chapter XXI that the ancients derived what they called *modulation* solely from melody, whereas it comes from harmony.

Once we have an understanding of this consonant progression, it is no more difficult to add three sounds above one of those which serve as our bass than it is to add one. Here is what may be understood in either case: you can place the third, the fifth, or the octave above the bass; or rather, above the bass you must place the third, the fifth, *and* the octave. In order to use one or the other, you must know them, and if you know them, it is no more difficult to use them together than to use them separately. Then, if the bass descends a third, the part that formed the third becomes the fifth; we cannot explain it otherwise. But if in these different progressions of a bass you find the third here, the octave there, and the fifth elsewhere, you must always know what has to follow them according to the different progressions of the bass. And so, without thinking about it, we teach composition in four parts, while we explain it only in two. Therefore, since I must know what follows each consonance, according to the different progressions of the bass, each one of these consonances coming alternately upon the other, it is no more difficult to use them together than individually, all the more so since if I am unable to distinguish them all together, I only follow each one separately. Thus, from one to the other, I find a way of composing a perfect harmony in four parts, from which I derive all the knowledge necessary to achieve perfection. Moreover, the explanation that we add to this keeps us from going wrong. If we may rely on the experience that several people have had, people who knew only the value of the notes, after having read our rules twice, composed as perfect a harmony as one might wish. Furthermore, if one of these composers allows himself the satisfaction of hearing what he has produced,[1] his ear will be trained little by little; and if he becomes sensitive to perfect harmony, to which these beginnings lead him, he can be certain of success, which depends entirely on these first principles.

After this, there is no doubt that once these four parts are familiar to us, we can reduce them to three or two. But what knowledge can a composition in two parts give us, even if we were to grasp it completely, which is nearly impossible, since we are not guided by any fundamental? Anything we may teach in this fashion is always sterile, either because our memory is insufficient, or because we can only retain everything with difficulty; and in the end we are obliged to add these words: *Caetera docebit usus* (practice will teach the rest). Do we wish to go on to three and four parts? So little is said about it that one must have genius and taste equivalent to those of the great masters in order to understand what they wish to teach us. Zarlino[2] says of four parts that they can scarcely be taught on paper, and that he leaves them to the discretion of composers, who can base themselves on his previous rules for two and three parts. Our opinion is exactly the opposite, for we have just said that harmony can only be taught in four parts, in which everything relating to it can be found in only two chords (as we have noted throughout), and that it was very easy to reduce these four parts to three or to two; whereas Zarlino, who does not define either these two or three parts precisely, admits that he cannot define four, after having agreed that perfect harmony consists of four parts, which he compares to the four elements.[3] We shall say in conclusion that if up to now it has not been possible to derive a perfect knowledge of harmony from the rules transmitted, the principle that we have set out is a certain goal to achieve this knowledge, which excludes nothing.

XX
On the Properties of Chords

It is certain that harmony can stir different passions in us, according to the chords used. There are sad, languishing, tender, agreeable, gay, and surprising chords. There are also certain progressions of chords that express the same pas-

---

1. It is partly for this reason that we give rules for accompaniment.
2. *Istitutioni harmoniche* (Venice, 1573), pt. 3, ch. 65, p. 320.
3. Ibid., ch. 58, p. 281.

sions, and although it may be well beyond my reach, I am going to offer as much explanation as my experience allows me.

Consonant chords can be found everywhere, but they must be used most often in songs of rejoicing and magnificence; and, as one cannot avoid including dissonant chords, one must arrange it so that the dissonances arise naturally, that they are prepared as much as possible, and that the most audible parts, such as the upper part and the bass, are always consonant with each other.

Sweetness and tenderness are sometimes rather well expressed by prepared minor dissonances.

Tender laments sometimes require dissonances by borrowing and by supposition,[4] minor rather than major, placing the major dissonances that may occur in the middle parts, rather than in the outer parts.

Languor and suffering are expressed very well with dissonances by borrowing, and especially with chromaticism, about which we shall speak in the following book.

Despair and all the passions that lead to rage or have some element of surprise require unprepared dissonances of all kinds, especially major dissonances in the upper part. It is even effective in certain expressions of this nature to go from one key to another by means of an unprepared major dissonance, without offending the ear through too great a disproportion between these two keys. This is why it can only be done prudently, much the same as all the rest: if one simply piled dissonance upon dissonance, anywhere they might occur, it would be a much greater flaw than allowing only consonances to be heard. Dissonance must be used, then, only with a great deal of discretion, even allowing it to remain unheard in chords from which it cannot be separated, by suppressing it deftly when its harshness does not suit the expression, distributing the consonances that compose the rest of the chord among all the parts. For one must remember that the seventh, from which all dissonances arise, is only a sound added to the perfect chord,[5] that this sound does not destroy the foundation of this chord, and that it can always be suppressed when you consider it appropriate to do so.

Melody has no less force in expression than harmony, but it is almost impossible to give certain rules for it, since good taste plays a larger role here than the rest. So we shall leave to those happy talented few the pleasure of distinguishing

4. ". . . Dissonances par emprunt, & par supposition." In Rameau's terminology, "borrowing" refers to chords in which the root is missing, e.g. diminished seventh chords acting as dominants, in which the root is presupposed. "Supposition" normally refers to downward-resolving appoggiaturas, but Rameau gives it a specific meaning, restricting it to chords that exceed an octave, that is, ninth and eleventh chords. [BJB]

5. The "perfect chord" is Rameau's term for a triad. [BJB]

themselves in this genre, on which nearly all the power of feeling depends. We hope that skilled persons, to whom we have said nothing new, will not begrudge our having revealed secrets of which they had perhaps hoped to be the sole possessors, since our limited wisdom does not allow us to contend with them for that last measure of perfection, without which the most beautiful harmony sometimes becomes insipid, and through which they are always capable of surpassing all others. It is not that, once we know how to arrange a succession of chords appropriately, we cannot derive from it a melody suited to the subject, as we shall see in what follows; but taste is always the prime mover.

It is here that the ancients had the better of us, if we may believe them; with his melody one made Ulysses weep; another made Alexander take up arms; another made a furious young man sweet-tempered and humane. In short, the surprising effects of their music may be seen at every turn. On this question Zarlino's judgment is quite reasonable: he says first that to them the word harmony often meant only a simple melody, and that all these effects stemmed more from spirited discourse, whose force increased through the manner in which they recited it while singing, than from their melody alone, which certainly could not take advantage of all the diversity that perfect harmony, which they did not know, procures for us today. Their harmony, he says further,[6] consisted of a perfect chord above which they sang all sorts of airs indifferently, a bit like what we hear on our bagpipes or our hurdy-gurdies, which he calls *sinfonia*.

For the rest, a good composer must give himself over to the characters he wishes to portray; like a talented actor, he must put himself in the place of the one who is speaking, believe himself to be in the places where the different events that he wishes to represent take place, and take the same part as those who are most concerned; he must be good at declamation, at least within himself, and sense when the voice must rise or fall more or less, in order to make his melody, harmony, modulation, and movement conform to it.

From *Traité de l'harmonie réduite à ses principes naturels* (Paris, 1722; repr. New York: Broude Bros., 1965, and in Rameau, *Complete Theoretical Works,* vol. 1, ed. Erwin R. Jacobi [American Institute of Musicology, 1967]), Bk. 1, chs. 1–2, pp. 1–3, and Bk. 2, chs. 19–20, pp. 138–43. An English translation is also available: *Treatise on Harmony,* transl. Philip Gossett (Mineola, N.Y.: Dover, 1971).

6. *Istitutioni harmoniche,* pt. 3, ch. 79, p. 356.

JEAN-PHILIPPE RAMEAU
from *Observations on Our Musical Instinct and on Its Principle* (1754)

PREFACE

To enjoy fully the effects of music, one must be in a state of pure self-abandonment, and to judge it, one must rely on the principle by which one is affected. This principle is Nature herself, from whom we receive that feeling that moves us in all our musical works. She has made us a gift of what one might call *Instinct*. Let us then consult Nature in our judgments, let us see how she displays her mysteries to us before we decide; and if there are still men so full of themselves as to dare to decide on their own authority, there is reason to hope that there are no longer any so credulous as to listen to them.

A man whose mind is preoccupied while hearing music is never in a situation free enough to judge it. If in his opinion, for example, he attributes the essential beauty of this art to the transitions from low to high, soft to loud, or quick to slow—means that are used to vary sounds—he will judge everything according to this prejudice, without reflecting upon the fragility of these means, on how little merit there is in using them, and without realizing that they are foreign to harmony, which is the sole principle of music and the source of its greatest effects.

How differently a truly sensitive soul will judge! If it is not fully convinced by the force of expression, by those vivid images of which harmony alone is capable, the soul is not completely satisfied; not that it is not able to accept everything that may amuse it, but at least it appreciates things only in proportion to the effects it experiences from them.

It is for harmony alone to stir the passions; melody draws its strength solely from this source, from which it emanates directly. And as for the differences between low and high, etc., which are but superficial modifications of melody, they contribute almost nothing here, as will be demonstrated in the course of the present work by some striking examples, in which the principle is verified by our instinct, and this instinct by its principle; that is to say, in which the cause is verified by the effect one experiences, and this effect by its cause.

If the imitation of sounds and movements is less frequently used in our music than in Italian music, it is because the chief element in ours is feeling, which has no regular motion and may not therefore lend itself in every instance to a regular measure without losing the lifelike quality that makes it so appealing.

The physical is expressed in measure and movement; the pathetic, on the contrary, is expressed in harmony and inflections, something that one must weigh carefully before deciding which should tip the balance.

As the comic genre is almost never devoted to the expression of feeling, it is consequently the only one that is always susceptible to the rhythmical movements with which we credit Italian music, without acknowledging, however, that our composers have used them rather well in the small number of attempts that the delicacy of French taste has allowed them to make—attempts in which it has been demonstrated, by venturing it, how easily we were able to excel in this genre.[1] . . .

OBSERVATIONS ON OUR MUSICAL INSTINCT AND ON ITS PRINCIPLE

Music is natural to us. We owe to pure instinct alone the pleasant feeling it inspires in us. This same instinct is activated in us by several other things that may well have some relationship to music. This is why it cannot be indifferent to persons who cultivate the sciences and the arts to know the principle upon which such an instinct is based.

This principle is now known: it exists, as we cannot fail to know, in harmony, which results from the resonance of any sounding body, such as the sound of our voice, of a string, a pipe, a bell, etc. And to be convinced still further, we need only examine ourselves in all the steps we take in music.

For example, a man without experience in music, as well as one who is an expert, ordinarily takes the first sound he makes from the middle of his vocal range when he sings freely, and always ascends thereafter, even though the range of his voice may extend almost as far below as above this first sound. This is absolutely consistent with the resonance of the sounding body, from which the emanating sounds are all above that of its fundamental tone, which we believe to be the only one we hear.

On the other hand, however little experience we may have, we never fail, when improvising on our own, to sing in succession, always ascending, the perfect chord composed of the harmony of a sounding body, of which the major is always preferred to the minor, unless the latter is suggested to us by some reminiscence.

---

1. *Les Troqueurs,* performed at the most recent Saint-Laurent and Saint-Germain fairs, and *La Coquette trompée,* performed at Fontainebleau in 1753. [Both are by Antoine Dauvergne; the first, an *intermède,* was given on 30 July, the second, a *comédie lyrique,* on 13 November; it was a great success and enjoyed many revivals. BJB]

If we normally sing the third first in the perfect chord in ascending, although a sounding body only produces it at the double octave, which is the seventeenth, and then the fifth above the octave, which is the twelfth, it is because we naturally reduce all the intervals to their smallest degrees because the ear determines them more readily and the voice reaches them more easily.[2] But the same will not hold true for a man without experience, who has never heard music or who has never listened to it, for there is a difference between hearing and listening. If this man sings a somewhat low sound, very clear and very distinct, and if he then lets his voice continue quickly, without anything particular in mind, not even the interval he would like to reach, then the process being purely mechanical, he will certainly sing the fifth first, in preference to all other intervals, according to an experiment we have done more than once.[3]

It is well known that the fifth is the most perfect of all consonances; the rest of these observations will only serve to confirm it.

The smallest natural intervals, called *diatonic*,—those, in a word, of the scale C D E F, etc.—are suggested only by way of the consonances through which they pass and which they form in succession, so that these consonances will always occur first to any person without experience. Moreover, as soon as we wish to follow the order of these smallest intervals, without having recourse to any prior knowledge, we will always ascend by a whole tone and descend by a semitone, especially if we wish to return immediately afterwards to the first sound that was the point of departure. For example, if you call this first sound that represents a sounding body C, its fifth G,[4] which resonates with it, will take hold of the ear at once, and attempting to progress from C to its nearest degree, this G will appear then as a new sounding body with all its harmony, which consists of its major third B and its fifth D, so that we are forced thereby to ascend by a whole tone from C to D, and to descend by a semitone from C to B.

On the other hand, after ascending a tone, we are naturally inclined to sing another: the semitone will come to mind only through prior knowledge, because two whole tones form a major third, which resonates in the sounding

---

2. See my reply to Euler on the identity of octaves, p. 13. [*Extrait d'une réponse de M. Rameau à M. Euler sur l'identité des octaves, d'où résultent des vérités d'autant plus curieuses qu'elles n'ont pas encore été soupçonnées* (Paris, 1753; repr. in Rameau, *Complete Theoretical Works*, ed. Jacobi, vol. 5). BJB]

3. The Reverend Father Castel discussed this experiment in the *Journal de Trévoux*. [The Jesuit mathematician Louis-Bertrand Castel (1688–1757). His correspondence with Rameau was published by Jacobi in Rameau, *Complete Theoretical Works*, vol. 6. BJB]

4. We say *fifth* instead of twelfth, and *third* instead of seventeenth because of their identity or "equisonance," caused by the octave.

body, while the tone and semitone form only a minor third, which does not resonate; moreover, after these two tones, we will feel compelled to sing a semitone in order to go on to a fourth, since the third whole tone is resisted because it makes a dissonance. For this reason it has always been said, because it has been experienced, that three whole tones in sequence are not natural. After this last semitone then another one will never come to mind; the whole tone will prevail in every ear in order to achieve the consonance of the fifth.

Such is the authority of consonances over the ear, which is concerned at that moment only with the degrees that form them or lead to them. These consonances are, moreover, only the product of the resonance of the sounding body; this should be emphasized, since we can only infer that the principle demonstrated is the instrument of all these faculties that we have just acknowledged are natural to us.

There is more; however little experience we may have, we can find unassisted the fundamental bass in all the points of repose in a song, according to the explanation given in our *Nouveau système*, page 54,[5] which proves yet again the authority of the principle over all its effects, since in this case the progression of these effects reminds the ear of the progression of the principle that determined it, and consequently suggested it to the composer.

This last experiment, in which instinct alone is at work, as in the preceding ones, proves clearly that melody has no principle other than the harmony produced by the sounding body, a principle in which the ear is so engaged that, without our even thinking about it, it alone suffices to locate immediately the harmonic foundation on which this melody depends. This happens not only to the composer who conceived it, but also to any person of ordinary experience. Thus we find any number of musicians able to accompany by ear a song that they are hearing for the first time.

From *Observations sur notre instinct pour la musique et sur son principe où les moyens de reconnoître l'un par l'autre conduisent à pouvoir se rendre raison avec certitude des différens effets de cet art* (Paris, 1754; repr. New York: Broude Bros., 1967; Geneva: Slatkine Reprints, 1971, and in Rameau, *Complete Theoretical Works*, vol. 3, ed. Erwin R. Jacobi [American Institute of Musicology, 1968]), pp. iii–ix, 1–11. A larger excerpt is included in Lippman, ed., *Musical Aesthetics* 1:339–59.

5. *Nouveau système de musique théorique, où l'on découvre le principe de toutes les règles nécessaires à la pratique, pour servir d'introduction au traité de l'harmonie* (Paris, 1726; repr. in Rameau, *Complete Theoretical Works*, 2). [BJB]

GIUSEPPE TARTINI

from *On the Principles of Musical Harmony Contained in the Diatonic Genus* (1767)

The author of the *Treatise on Music according to the True Science of Harmony*,[1] after publishing his work, thought it would be to his advantage to gain the opinion of the learned. To this effect, he sought to establish a correspondence with the most famous of them (most of whom were still living), exhorting them to inform him of the difficulties they had met and objections they had raised when examining his work. These learned gentlemen proved most compliant in providing him with all he sought to know and needed. That is why he publicly reiterates here his gratitude to those whom privately he has already thanked, and redoubles it, as he hopes and desires that this public testimony, together with the present dissertation, will come into their hands. If this happens, and they find the things therein contained to be true, let them consider this dissertation a public benefit, deriving from their kindness and consideration toward the author, who would never have realized what was truly needed to advance musical theory had it not been for this private correspondence.

The author is convinced that the lack of a true understanding of the diatonic genus prevents, and would always prevent, an understanding of the true principles of harmony. He is also convinced that the learned, either those who privately have helped the author, or those who publicly have produced writings and musical works, are totally lacking in this essential understanding. They believe that the diatonic genus consists only of the natural musical scale as expressed and contained in the usual Italian solfeggio, *ut, re, mi, fa, sol, re, mi, fa;* and that this is the first and only principle of that genus which the ancient Greek teachers called diatonic, and which truly constitutes the real essence of ancient and modern music. They deceive themselves, but they cannot be blamed, as it was impossible for them to know more about this subject. And how were they to know? Certainly not from the books by authors in the profession, as not even one treats this genus soundly in its first principles. Not even the Greeks did so, although they established it. The first two, Pythagoras and Plato, set out to reveal the surface of diatonic music, conceived as a part of that universal harmony which for them was the law of the universe. But at the same time they strove with extreme jealousy to conceal its substance, which they sur-

---

1. Tartini refers to his *Trattato di musica secondo la vera scienza dell'armonia* (Padua, 1754). [BJB]

rounded in mystery. Later Greeks, such as Didymus, Aristoxenus, and Ptolemy, only brushed the surface of what had been discovered and established by the first two; they added nothing substantial, which was not their object. It was equally impossible for the learned to know it by themselves, not because they lacked talent, culture, and perceptiveness, but rather because of a lack of commitment and the present state of their studies. It is true that music is a part of their physical and mathematical concerns, but not the part that has much interested them. Very few deemed it worthy of their efforts, in contrast to many who treated it superficially, perhaps more as a pastime than as a true occupation. Furthermore, the present basis of their studies is the physical and mathematical genus, which has completely changed direction from ancient Greek teachings. In fact, research on musical harmony conducted by the learned of modern times has continued to be in the physical genus, in which (it must be confessed, to their credit) they have made marvelously interesting discoveries of physical and acoustic phenomena that were totally unknown to the ancients, who, by a completely different method, the demonstrative basis, undertook to establish musical principles. The learned men of our day have based their studies on these discoveries in the certainty of not being mistaken, as the foundations are grounded in nature itself. Consequently, they have no longer given serious thought to the original Greek teachings. Nevertheless, the latter are still valid after thousands of years. What is more, the learned of our day have sought and continue to seek to adapt their discoveries not to a different musical genus, but precisely to that of the Greeks, the diatonic. In fact, if someone presumes to change or alter it, he is ridiculed by these same learned men and rejected by the musical profession. This is an infallible sign that although that genus was deductively established by the most famous Greeks, Pythagoras and Plato, nevertheless it possesses natural truth to such an eminent degree as to act as proof and law of the agreement or disagreement with discoveries in physics, whenever it is wished to apply them to that genus. However, it is impossible that there not be an equal source of truth in those many physical and acoustic phenomena, the discovery of which is all to the credit of our present-day scholars. They are physical laws of the same nature to which the diatonic genus eminently belongs. Thus it is not possible for nature to contradict itself in its first universal impressions, such as music in the diatonic genus constitutes for mankind. Thus it follows of necessity that the Greek teachings, deriving from the same natural basis, must be as true as the physical discoveries by the learned men of our day: the former, because for thousands of years they have held their own both with respect to the common understanding of nature and the test of physical discoveries; the latter, because they are real and positive laws of nature itself.

The author considers it a manifest absurdity that anyone could believe that there can be a contradiction between two truths confirmed by the same natural principle and belonging to the same category. It is also a fact that it is not easy to join them together in one and the same conceptual point of nature wherein between them they form a perfect unity. This is because, after so much ancient and modern research, this point of agreement has not yet been discovered or seen. This is that point which the present author claims to have discovered, and which he presents to the public in this dissertation, so that the community of the learned may examine and decide whether anyone who equates the diatonic genus with the so-called natural scale is mistaken, and whether it consists in the principles set down in this dissertation, without previous knowledge of which it is impossible to define the diatonic genus and to know exactly what it is. Let them also examine and decide whether, in the face of the Greek teachings deduced by the demonstrative genus, of the modern discoveries based on the physical genus, and of their close agreement in that point, from which (as from a first principle) it necessarily results that ancient and modern music are in the diatonic genus—as confirmed by the opinion of all mankind—the view of those who admit no other principle of music than the ear and experience can ever stand up.

Lastly, let them examine and decide if this truly and necessarily is that first principle according to which all particular musical systems that are deduced rationally from either a physical or a demonstrative genus have to be resolved, and if any system independent of these two genera is necessarily false or purely ideal. So that the word genus, which the present author uses in connection with demonstrative entities (in his dissertation these are sometimes referred to as principles), not be accused of being obscure, we wish to make clear that by the two terms, genus and principle, are meant the foundation of ratios and proportions as a real and positive science, both as an abstraction and as applied to a physical subject. The reasons for this will be given in due course. Besides, it does no harm if the scheme of this science is understood in the usual way instead of in that of the present author; it is enough to bear in mind that by these terms are meant the foundation of the ratios and the proportions. Similarly, it should not be considered superfluous if the author has repeated here many concepts that have already been expounded in his *Treatise on Music*. Not only will they be treated differently here, if truth is invariable, the author cannot but repeat the truth itself of what he has written. The ability to reproduce it after private discussions and debates accrues to his advantage, as it is a manifest sign that it has withstood every test.

Lastly, no attention is to be paid to his plain style, nor to the unscientific terms he sometimes uses; they will be intelligible because they are explained. Neither is the reader to pay any mind to any accidental mistake (not of method, however) that may appear in this dissertation, put together and completed in spare moments, nor to any disordered presentation of material that could have been improved. It would have been quite easy for the author to avail himself of the generous help of the learned, who would have given our subject matter a different appearance. The present author, however, is not ashamed to show himself as he is, rough and uncultured; indeed, it works to his advantage, as he is both pleased and anxious that the naked truth be seen. On the other hand, he is sorry if he appears arrogant when, in order to contradict them, he names and refers to those of whom he is unworthy of being either a disciple or a servant. He is fortunate that his character is sufficiently well known that that which is a necessity of his enterprise and of his most disagreeable circumstances should not be taken for arrogance. It is his duty to truth and to his musical profession, which lacks it, to expound it with all his strength in order to contrast it with what is false. Receiving authority from the name and fame of those who profess its falsehood can seriously harm anyone who is unable to distinguish for himself between what is true and what is false, and consequently sets store by illustrious names. Having learned at his own expense that the modesty of his expression can be construed as weakness in reasoning, the author has been compelled here to change his language in order not to jeopardize the strength of his arguments, but never his conduct, in order to maintain inviolable the due respect owed each man. Therefore, the author declares that, to the same degree that he desires to be reserved in manner, he wants to be free and candid as he regards his subject matter, and he forthwith gives evidence of this by openly declaring that he who does not possess the two basic requisites of the common knowledge of ratios and proportions and of the art of music in more than a superficial manner should not bother to read this dissertation. A fine thing! The author's *Treatise on Music* has been accused of being supremely obscure. Is the author then free to change the disposition of things so that, if they are by their own intrinsic nature difficult and obscure, he can and should render them simple and plain? It is his obligation to find and uncover them where and as they are. The obligation of those who long for knowledge is to examine whether the author has told the truth; and when he has, both the author and he who loves knowledge must adjust to the truth, whether it be by nature easy or difficult. Have not the most illustrious modern philosophers been seeking the true principles of musical harmony for some two centuries? Have these principles yet been ascertained, or are they not at present more than ever a subject of debate? This being so, it is sure proof that their nature is most difficult to penetrate. Whatever the present author has been able to do to make these concepts more intelligible he has done by bringing together the relevant principal concepts of both ancient and modern music with the respective physical discoveries of the moderns and with the demonstrative teachings of the ancients. But together with this positive aspect comes the difficult one of having to examine, at the same time and in the same place, three different foundations: that is, physics, logic, and practical music. In this, the author has not been able to apply a rigorous method of investigation; rather, he must oblige his readers to be particularly attentive.

This, however, may very well be the true task, as any musical system that does not stand the test of these three combined foundations is certainly false. An argument for the infallible truth of what the present author sets forth here will be seeing it not only supported by these foundations, but so intrinsic to them as to form a perfect unity with them. In keeping with these three foundations, then, which the author calls genera and principles, he will divide the present dissertation into four chapters. In the first, he will discourse mainly upon the physical foundation, selecting as needed those physical and acoustic phenomena that are both the most explicit and most similar to the physical and harmonic laws imposed upon them by nature, as the sonority of a taut string is related to the number of sounds that it produces simultaneously. This phenomenon is so well known that it has been chosen by the most celebrated theorists as the foundation of a system, as is also the third sound that results from the two given sounds played together.[2] This phenomenon is of recent discovery, but is particularly significant. The tromba marina is also a good example of a true and natural physical and harmonic monochord, but it will be discussed in its appropriate chapter, which is the third. In the second chapter the author will mainly discuss the demonstrative basis, where he will expound and explain the necessary concepts that the common mode of thinking lacks when applying this foundation to musical considerations. This is the prime reason why, up to now, it has been impossible to discover the true principles governing harmony. In the third chapter he will essentially deal with the basis of practical music, explaining those fundamental and integral parts of present-day music without which it is impossible to understand the diatonic genus in music; and those who venture to propose systems cannot fail to fall into perpetual falsehood or be victims of serious errors.

Finally, in the fourth and last chapter, the author will show the conjunction of these three foundations, reducing them to that perspective which will of necessity lead to the most intimate understanding of the diatonic genus. In this the author's contention will be confirmed in the full light of day, namely that an intimate knowledge of this genus is totally absent both among scholars of music (with one exception), as well as among scholars of physics and mathematics, who, lacking this knowledge, uselessly and indeed harmfully pursue their search for the true principles of musical harmony. The author believes that, for such a complex subject, this is the best order that can be offered to facilitate

2. The "third sound" is Tartini's term for the difference tone, which results when two tones are played loudly. Tartini considered it the fundamental bass of the given interval and proof of the physical basis of the harmonic system. See Alejandro Enrique Planchart, "A Study of the Theories of Giuseppe Tartini," *Journal of Music Theory* 4 (1960): 32–61, esp. 36–40. [BJB]

understanding, provided that it is clear that each of the three first chapters also includes some part that by its nature also pertains to the other chapters. Therefore, in each of the three, the author has had to add the word "principally," in order to make it clear that although the main subject of each chapter is the foundation therein proposed, inevitably what is dealt with in one chapter will present elements in common with others, being common to the other foundations or fundamentals. Each chapter will be divided into paragraphs, which will be numbered according to the chapter to which they belong and in which they are contained. Thus the division into the various paragraphs will make it easier to distinguish those parts that refer to more than one foundation. In other words, the author has done everything in his power, following his own judgment and that of others, to facilitate understanding of the concepts set down in this dissertation. Yet he feels obliged to repeat, in conclusion, that this in no way alters the nature of the concepts herein contained. The latter are difficult in themselves, and not through any fault of whoever deals with them and attempts to show what they are. The reader may indeed wish to ascertain their truth, but he should do so bearing in mind their nature, which means that he must avoid a superficial reading (which the present author would venture to call a rash pretension), but must apply himself with that zeal and attention which are required in order to comprehend many uncommon things, which are dependent on principles that hitherto have been imperfectly understood. The author compels no one to undertake such an onerous task, yet without effort no one can hope to arrive at a correct understanding of this dissertation. It remains to be seen who wishes to undertake this labor, to discover in the end who the lovers and seekers of truth really are.

From *De' principi dell'armonia musicale contenuta nel diatonico genere* (Padua, 1767; repr. Hildesheim: Olms, 1970; Padua: Cedam, 1974), Preface.

DENIS DIDEROT
from *General Principles of the Science of Sound* (1748)

In any conjecture where our senses are involved, we must take into account the object, the state of the sense, the image or impression transmitted to the mind, the condition of the mind at the moment at which it receives the impression, and the judgment that it passes on it.

The state of the object is sometimes independent of me, but I will always know whether this state is good or bad by the use for which the object is intended. The organ of perception may be pure or tainted. The image or the impression is affected by the condition of the organ. The mind is subject to reversals; hence a host of varying judgments arise.

Whom shall I take as a guide? Upon whom should I rely? On you? On me? It is the one who, well informed of the purpose of the object, does not risk being mistaken as to its condition; whose perception is pure; who possesses a healthy mind, and in whom the images of the objects have not been distorted by the senses.

I shall not linger over the application of these principles to the science of sounds; that is too easy a task. I shall only observe in general that an object is more or less complex according to whether it offers the mind greater or fewer relationships to grasp and combine at the same time, and according to whether these relationships are more or less distant.

We shall demonstrate in what follows that musical pleasure consists in the perception of the relationships of sounds. From which it follows clearly that it will be the more difficult to judge a piece of music the more it is laden with these relationships and the farther they are apart.

Once we know how the ear assesses intervals of sounds, we shall not hesitate to declare that it will more easily perceive the relationship of two sounds that are related to each other as one is to two, than if they were related to each other as eighteen is to nineteen. Supposing that is the case, the relationships of a series of tones would require more talent, training, and attention to be perceived and consequently heard with pleasure than would be necessary for each of these relationships taken separately. It is one thing to assess the relationships of sounds that succeed each other in a piece, yet another to combine these relationships among themselves, compare them, distinguish them when they are presented all at once in harmony, and compare the successive parts of this harmony one with another. One person takes in the whole of an immense edifice; another barely grasps the relationship of a column to its pedestal.

If then melody and harmony increase the relationships in a work, so that only the best-trained ears can perceive them all, this work will only be appreciated by a small number of those who have a certain aptitude, a discernment proportionate to the multitude of these relationships; and so it happens that the songs of primitive peoples will be too simple for us, and ours too complex for them.

Experience supports my ideas. We know that a peasant, endowed with a sensitive ear, could not bear to hear an excellent flute duo playing together, although their separate parts had delighted him in turn.

Music has thus invariable principles and a theory. This is a truth the ancients knew. Pythagoras posited the first foundations of the science of sounds. He did not know how the ear perceives relationships; he was even mistaken about their limits, but he discovered that perception of them was the source of musical pleasure. . . .

REMARK

But this origin is not peculiar to musical pleasure. Pleasure, in general, consists in the perception of relationships: this principle obtains in poetry, in painting, in architecture, in moral philosophy, in all of the arts and all of the sciences. A beautiful machine, a beautiful painting, a beautiful portico are pleasing to us only through the relationships we observe in them: could it not even be said that this is as true of a good life as it is of a good concert? The perception of relationships is the unique foundation of our admiration and pleasure; and this must be the point of departure for explaining the most subtle phenomena that are offered to us by the sciences and the arts. Things that seem most arbitrary to us have been suggested by relationships, and this principle must serve as the basis for a philosophical essay on taste, if there is ever anyone with sufficient knowledge to apply it generally to all that it encompasses.[1]

But once you have acknowledged that pleasure consists in the perception of relationships, you will be obliged to go one step further and agree that pleasure must vary with the relationships, and that the simplest relationships, more easily grasped than the others, must also be more generally pleasing. Now of all relationships the simplest is that of equality; it was thus natural for the human mind to seek to introduce it everywhere that it might occur. And that is what happened. For this reason the wings of a building are made equal, and the sides of a window parallel. If utilitarian reasons require that we stray from it, we obey them; but we do so regretfully, and the artist never fails to return to the relationship of equality from which he has strayed. This return, which is commonly attributed to instinct, to caprice, to imagination, is nothing other than homage rendered to the natural appeal of harmony and of relationships; to this we owe an infinite number of minute ornamentations that are always called arbitrary and are nothing of the kind. Architecture alone could furnish me with countless examples, but they would be out of place here.

I shall content myself with applying my ideas to an observation that those who have some experience in hearing and reading music will have made: it is that high sounds do not normally last as long as low ones. The upper parts move quickly, while the basses move slowly, unless the subject requires that they quicken their pace. Can we truly believe that composers have worked in this manner for no reason, and that their fancy is the only rule they followed? If we do, we are mistaken.

They were secretly guided by the perception of relationships: if they have allowed the high sounds to move quickly, and if they have slowed down the low

---

1. Diderot himself was to do so three years later, in his article on the Beautiful in the *Encyclopédie*. [EF]

ones, it is because the relationships that the latter have among themselves are more difficult to grasp than those of the former, all else being equal, since the string that produces high sounds makes many more vibrations in a given time than the one that produces low sounds. So much for the use of simple relationships, and now for the return from composite relationships to simple ones.

If the mind, which is naturally lazy, adjusts willingly to simple relationships, as it favors variety no less than it fears weariness, we are occasionally forced to use composite relationships, sometimes to highlight the simple ones, sometimes to avoid monotony, sometimes to increase expression; that is the source of the use we make of dissonance in music, a use more or less frequent, but almost always necessary. But dissonance, according to musicians, usually must be prepared and resolved, which, of course, simply means that if you have good reason to abandon simple relationships in order to present composite ones to the ear, you must return immediately to the use of the former.

OBJECTION

But how can it be, you will say, that the pleasure of chords consists in the perception of relationships of sounds? Does an awareness of these relationships, then, always accompany the sensation? This would seem difficult to accept; for how many people with sensitive ears are unaware of the relationship of the vibrations that form the fifth or the octave to those that produce the fundamental! Does the mind have this knowledge without realizing it, much as it judges the size and distance of objects without the least notion of geometry, although a kind of natural and secret trigonometry seems to play a large role in the judgment it makes?

REPLY

We shall come to no decision in the matter; we shall content ourselves with observing that experience has shown that the most perfect chords are formed by sounds with the simplest relationships between them, that these relationships can affect our mind in two ways, through feeling or perception, and that they affect most men in the first way only.

From *Principes généraux de la science du son*, in *Mémoires sur différens sujets de mathématiques* (Paris, 1748), §2. Fondement de la théorie de la science des sons (pp. 3–7) and §6. Du son considéré comme fort ou faible (pp. 52–58). Modern edition by Jean Mayer in *Œuvres complètes, édition critique et annotée*, ed. H. Dieckmann and J. Varloot, vol. 2 (Paris: Hermann, 1975), 231–81.

Chapter Four

The Birth of Historiography and the Reports of Foreign Travelers in Italy

T HE FIRST TRUE HISTORIES of music were preceded by numerous observations on the subject. From the very beginning of the eighteenth century, almost all writings on music contain reflections of a historical nature, though often fanciful and of scant reliability. The first treatise to present a minimum of systematic historical organization is Jacques Bonnet's *Histoire de la musique et de ses effets depuis son origine jusqu'à présent* (1715), though he was primarily interested in amassing scraps of information, curiosities, and anecdotes on music and musicians, without providing a cohesive picture of his subject. In his preface, included in this chapter, he delineates the aims of his research, in which disquisitions on the origin of music occupy a position of prime importance, bolstered, as usual, with quotations from the authors of classical antiquity. This history of sorts ends with a treatise on good taste, after the example of Lecerf de la Viéville, in which he takes up the *querelle* between the Italians and the French, siding with the latter.

Another treatise belonging to the prehistory of historical research true and proper is John Brown's lengthy *A Dissertation on the Rise, Union, and Power, the Progressions, Separations, and Corruptions, of Poetry and Music* (1763). This work immediately enjoyed great fame in Europe, as witnessed by its translations into German (1769) and Italian (1772). It too is a hybrid, combining elements of both a historical and a theoretical approach. In fact, the historical framework serves not so much to illustrate the development or evolution of music as seen through its major figures as to demonstrate his theses regarding the "progress" and "corruption" of music. This is borne out by the pages included here on the origin of music in "uncivilized" societies, which was a favorite theme of eighteenth-century theorists. Similarly, in addition to reiterating the usual eighteenth-century platitudes regarding the absurdity of operatic performances, the passage in which Brown rather fancifully traces a general outline of the history of opera reveals no true interest in historical research.

The Bolognese musician Giovanni Battista Martini undertook one of the first significant historiographic works, which, however, focused exclusively on antiquity, the period that most interested him. As virtually no music of antiquity has come down to us, Padre Martini's *Storia della musica* (1757–81) is in fact an antiquarian investigation based on the sources, on the theorists of antiquity, and on the documents and evidence he had succeeded in obtaining. Like all the others, Padre Martini was also interested in the problem of the origin of music, but his historiographic awareness, far more conscientious than Bonnet's, imposed a much more scientific approach to these themes, which in themselves are so vague and apt to veer toward the fabulous and the mythological.

The histories written by Charles Burney and John Hawkins, which appeared about twenty years later, take us into a completely different climate. Their research can be included in the category of authentic histories of music, although allowances must be made for the limited knowledge of the era, the few technical means available for research, the difficulties of listening, etc. Burney's preface to *A General History of Music from the Earliest Ages to the Present Period* (1776–89) and Hawkins's conclusion to *A General History of the Science and Practice of Music* (1776) clearly outline the methodology that informed their research, together with the two authors' ideas on music. Although the two works follow different approaches, they are nevertheless closer than would appear at first glance because of the rigor of their research and, above all, because of the effort to succeed, perhaps for the first time, in tracing a true and proper history, not just a collection of anecdotes or citations from classical authors. Music, with its historical development, however such development would come to be conceived later, becomes the true protagonist of these works. The focus of interest is no longer the mythical accounts of the origin of music but the musicians and their works.

The numerous reports, diaries, and letters by foreign travelers, though not systematic works of history, are nevertheless significant and indispensable documents and sources of information on both the present and the recent past. This chapter includes a letter by Charles de Brosses, a French magistrate and scholar who traveled to Italy in 1739–40, where he had the opportunity of meeting many musicians of the time, including Marcello, Tartini, and Vivaldi. The letter included here offers precious testimony to both the dark and bright side of Italian theater life. Twenty-six years later the English physician Samuel Sharp tallies some of the same criticisms, adding valuable information on the salaries of singers and dancers and the increasing role of dance in Italian opera. A sharp retort by the "literary scourge" Giuseppe Baretti, who was familiar with English and Italian customs, though not a devotee of opera, dismisses singing as "only a diversion, and attended to with no more seriousness than a diversion deserves."

The last passage included in this chapter, taken from Johann Nikolaus

Forkel's introduction to his *Allgemeine Geschichte der Musik* (1788–1801), brings us to the threshold of Romanticism. His greatest concern was to formulate interpretive and historical categories capable of sustaining a complete history of music in a rigorously consistent framework, in which creative figures play a significant role in the evolution of music according to a precise line of development.

JACQUES BONNET
from *History of Music and of Its Effects, from Its Origins to the Present* (1715)

PREFACE

I should never have conceived of writing the history of music from its origins to the present day, I should not even have dared to undertake it, were it not for some rather curious papers on the subject that I found among the manuscripts of my uncle, the Abbé Bourdelot, as well known among scholars for his works as for his Academy of Sciences, and in the manuscripts of my brother, Bonnet Bourdelot, physician to the king, and first physician to the duchess of Burgundy.[1]

To these papers I have added, with the assistance of public and private libraries, whatever useful and agreeable things I have been able to gather from a portion of the authors who have dealt creditably with music, in an attempt to conform to current standards of taste.

But although more than twelve hundred authors have treated this field of knowledge, not one has ventured to write the history of it, at least in our language, either because of the uncertainty of success, or for want of having thought to do so, which has reduced me to writing it solely according to the rules of common sense. Thus it will not be surprising if I have occasionally made mistakes in the terminology of the art and in the presentation of facts, which are difficult to set out in chronological order because of their antiquity, and of which one cannot speak with certainty. But I shall present only what

1. Pierre Bourdelot (1610–1685), physician to Louis XIII, and Pierre Bonnet-Bourdelot (1638–1708). [BJB]

history has preserved for us of the most famous musicians who have distinguished themselves in their art. Moreover, it is truly difficult to perfect a work to the point necessary nowadays to earn the approval of connoisseurs and to preserve it from the censure of the critics who hold forth today in certain public places as if they sat beneath the porticos of the Greeks.[2]

In any case, I have tried through my studies to discover the origin of music. It passes for the first of the sciences in the view of Timagenes and Quintilian, who even say that it is pleasing to the Immaterial Essences.[3]

Thales,[4] Pythagoras, and Plato claimed that music was a convergence of all imaginable perfections; they wrote very searching treatises about it, known to us only by tradition; but some rather excellent ones still remain, like those of St. Augustine,[5] Aristoxenus,[6] Euphranor,[7] Archytas,[8] Aristotle,[9] Plutarch,[10] and Ptolemy,[11] not to mention modern authors such as St. Gregory, Guido of Arezzo, Glareanus, Zarlino, and Père Mersenne of the Friars Minim. It is partly in the works of these great musicians that I have sought information for the compilation of this history, as well as in a number of others that I needed and found in the Royal Library, with the help of the assistant librarian, M. Clement, who had a thorough knowledge of authors who have dealt with music. I have written fourteen chapters, as succinct and well organized as possible for the better understanding of the reader. I dare flatter myself that the reading of them will not prove useless, at least to those who have a taste for music and whose occupations do not allow them to dedicate themselves to such research. I hope also that musicians will be grateful to me for having given them a complete account of their art, being persuaded that both the former and the latter will find here

2. A reference to the Porch or Stoa, i.e. the Stoic school of philosophy. [BJB]

3. Quintilian, *Institutio oratoria* 1.10.10. Bonnet misread the continuation; it is Virgil who speaks about music's importance to the understanding of "divine matters," i.e. the gods. [LAH-S]

4. Possibly Thaletas of Crete, who, according to Pseudo-Plutarch, *De musica* 1146C, cured the plague by means of music. Pythagoras is said to have admired and played his compositions. (Thales the scientist is not known to have concerned himself with music.) [LAH-S]

5. Augustine, the bishop of Hippo, wrote a six-book work *De musica*. [LAH-S]

6. Aristoxenus of Tarentum (late fourth century B.C.), pupil of Aristotle, best known in antiquity and in modern times for his writings on music, especially the *Harmonic Elements*. [LAH-S]

7. Euphranor (fourth century B.C.), a mathematician of the Pythagorean school, is said to have written on the aulos and on auletes. His works have not survived. [LAH-S]

8. Archytas (early fourth century B.C.), mathematician and inventor, Pythagorean. Of his writings on music only a few fragments survive [LAH-S]

9. The reference is to the musical questions discussed in bk. 19 of the *Problems* attributed to him, but probably written by later philosophers of his school. [LAH-S]

10. The reference is to the short essay on music preserved among his works but no longer thought genuine. [LAH-S]

11. Ptolemy (mid second century A.D.), astronomer, astrologer, geographer, and music theorist. [LAH-S]

unusual facts that would be completely unknown to them were it not for the care I have taken to bring them once again to light. . . .

XII
DISSERTATION ON GOOD TASTE IN ITALIAN AND FRENCH MUSIC, AND ON OPERAS

In a preceding chapter I reported on the origin of the antipathy between Italian and French musicians that has existed since the time of the emperor Charlemagne, concerning a high Mass.[12] It might be surprising that this quarrel could have lasted so many centuries, were Italians not known to be an uncompromising nation. It seems that people try in vain to bring them into agreement on the perfection of their art, with treatises that draw parallels between the music and opera of Italy and the music and opera of France. I cannot refrain, nonetheless, from reporting yet another in the form of letters sent to me in 1712 by one of my friends, to which I have made those additions I thought necessary to the subject in order to insert it within the body of this *History,* and which might find as many partisans of French music as the one written in 1702 in favor of Italian music;[13] we are obliged, moreover, to change our opinions from time to time in order to yield to sound experience, which is more forceful and convincing than all the argumentation.

It is apparently, Sir, to learn what I might know of music that you ask my opinion concerning the Italian style that now reigns in Paris, since there is no one who can decide the matter more justly than you; I obey you nonetheless, but not as a musician predisposed in favor of one style or the other. Rather, I shall tell you what I think according to the natural inclination for this science I received at birth. I shall not make use of the terms of the art with which musicians are obliged to burden their treatises on music and which often serve only to confuse the reader rather than instruct him. I shall try to be mindful of those who will read my work, so that they will understand me even without knowing music.

You know as I do, Sir, that there are at present two factions that have formed here in music: the one outspoken admirers of Italian music, supported by a small sect of those who are semi-learned in the art—people, nevertheless, of

12. Bonnet retails an anecdote concerning a dispute between the emperor's and the pope's choirmasters, in which the latter wished to sing Gregorian chant, the former Ambrosian or Gallican chant. Burney quotes a somewhat different version from an early chronicle; see *A General History of Music,* ed. Frank Mercer, 2 vols. (New York, 1957), 1:449–51. [BJB]

13. François Raguenet, *Paralèle des Italiens et des Français, en ce qui regarde la musique et les opéras* (Paris, 1702); see the excerpt in Ch. 2 above. [BJB]

rather high station who judge supremely and proscribe French music absolutely as dull and tasteless, or completely insipid; the other faction, faithful to its country's tastes and with a deeper knowledge of the art of music, cannot suffer without indignation the fact that in the capital city of the kingdom the good taste of French music is despised, and they consider Italian music bizarre, capricious, and a rebel against the rules of the art. There is nonetheless, in the midst of all this, an attitude that may be adopted in order to reconcile the factions, which is to do justice to both styles by considering each according to its nature.

One would have to be lacking in knowledge and good taste not to admit that good Italian music contains in general what is most learned and refined in the art, and that we owe it a large part of what is pleasing in our own; that the Italians are our masters in the cantata and sonata, although those of Bernier and Morin may well be compared with theirs.[14] I admire in their works the novel designs of their figures, so well conceived and so successfully executed; the sparkling vivacity of their repeated imitations, the variety of their melodies, the diversity of their keys and modes, so well linked one to the other, and their harmony, as exquisite as it is learned.

But if we grant them knowledge and invention, must they not grant us, with the same fairness, the natural good taste that we possess, and the tender and noble execution at which we excel, especially in instrumental music? Must not the enrichments we have added from our own wealth prevail? And are we not like schoolboys who, having profited from our teachers' lessons, have at last become more knowledgeable than they? Might it not be said, without offending the partisans of Italian music, that their ornaments, which are too frequent and misplaced, stifle expression, and that they do not give their works enough character? They are like Gothic architecture, which, overburdened with decoration, is obscured by it, and one can no longer distinguish the body of the work.

It could be said further that Italian music is like an amiable coquette who, though heavily made up, is still full of life and kicks up her heels, seeking to dazzle everywhere indiscriminately and without knowing why, like a featherbrained woman who displays her excess of feeling in whatever subject she may be dealing with. When it is a tender love, more often than not she makes it dance a gavotte or a jig. Could it not be said that what is serious becomes comi-

---

14. Nicolas Bernier (1665–1734) and Jean-Baptiste Morin (1677–1754); Morin deliberately set out to "retain the sweetness of our French style of melody, but with greater variety in the accompaniments and employing those rhythms and modulations characteristic of the Italian cantata" (preface to his first volume of *cantates françaises*, 1706, cited in *New Grove*). [BJB]

cal in her hands, and that she is more suited to light-hearted little songs than to treating noble subjects? Or like actors with a talent only for comedy, who fail miserably and turn the tragic into the ridiculous when they attempt it? It must be acknowledged that the majesty of French music treats heroic subjects with more nobility and is much better suited to ancient tragedy and to drama, whereas all passions seem uniform in Italian music. Joy, anger, grief, requited love, the lover who fears or hopes: everything seems to be portrayed with the same features and the same character. It is a constant jig, always bubbling or leaping about. If the singer starts alone, the instrument echoes the melody; this design, often based on a strange melody, not only touches on all the notes of the mode, but even on those that are foreign to it; these may fit well or ill, to such an extent that their works pass through all the keys and change modes at every moment, so that one cannot say in the end to which they belong. After this long procession, repeating the same melody twenty times, the voice as well as the instrument, a repeat must be made da capo; this transition is sometimes very hard on the ear, as it is often a matter of two neighboring tonics. But it usually happens that they skip it in order to avoid prolixity and minimize boredom. It is a great defect in all intellectual works, and especially in music, to be incapable of ending: one must learn to exercise restraint; a good work loses half its merit when it is too diffuse. . . .

But if this elaborate music is suited to Italian and Latin words, why subject the French language to it? Does an Italian behave like a Frenchman? Their tastes, clothes, customs, manners, pleasures—are they not all different? Why should their songs and playing styles not be different also? Does an Italian sing like a Frenchman? Why insist that a Frenchman sing and play like an Italian? Each nation has different customs. Why insist on disguising French music and making it extravagant? French music, whose language is so unaffected and cannot suffer the least violence, is enemy to the frequent repetitions of those long sustained passages that are tolerated in Latin or Italian music, but are not at all suited to ours.

French music may be compared to a beautiful woman, whose simple, natural, artless beauty wins the hearts of all those who gaze upon her, who has only to appear in order to be pleasing, and who need not fear being overcome by the affected, mincing manner of the extravagant coquette, who seeks to win people over at any price, and to whom we have already compared Italian music.

From *Histoire de la musique et de ses effets depuis son origine jusqu'à présent* (Paris, 1715; repr. Graz: Akademische Druck- und Verlagsanstalt, 1966; Geneva: Slatkine Reprints, 1971), Preface; pp. 291–96, 299–300.

JOHN BROWN
from *A Dissertation on the Rise, Union, and Power,*
the Progressions, Separations, and Corruptions,
of Poetry and Music (1763)

> BLEST Pair of Syrens, *Pledges of Heaven's Joy,*
> *Sphere-born harmonious* Sisters, VOICE *and* VERSE,
> Wed *your divine Sounds, and mix'd Pow'r employ!*

So said the sublime MILTON,[1] who knew and felt their Force: But Those whom *Nature* had thus *joined* together, *Man,* by his false Refinements, hath most *unnaturally* put *asunder.*

The Purpose of the following Dissertation, therefore, is to trace the *Rise, Union,* and *Progression* of *Poetry* and *Music,* as they are found to exist in their several Kinds and Gradations among Mankind; thence to consider the Causes which have produced that *Separation* under which they now lie, and have often lain, among the more polished Nations; and in Conclusion, to point out the *Circumstances* in which, and the *Means* by which, they may possibly be *again united.*

II
THE PROPOSED METHOD OF INQUIRY

Whatever is founded in such *Passions* and *Principles* of Action, as are *common* to the whole *Race* of *Man,* will be most effectually investigated, as to its *Origin* and *Progress,* by viewing Man in his *savage* or *uncultivated* State. Here, before Education and Art have cast their Veil over the human Mind, its various Powers throw themselves out, and all its Workings present themselves instantly, and without Disguise.

It may be affirmed with Truth, that, for Want of beginning our Inquiries at this early and neglected Period, and by viewing Man under his State of *Civilization* only, many curious and interesting Questions have been left involved in Darkness, which might have been clearly unfolded by a free and full Research into the Passions, Propensities, and Qualities of *savage* Man.

This the Writer hopes to make appear in a more *extensive Degree,* and on

1. *At a Solemn Musick,* ll. 103. [BJB]

Subjects of *higher Importance*, through the Course of a future Work;[2] of which, some of the Principles here delivered will make an incidental Part. In the mean Time, he intends to treat the present Subject in the Way now proposed, by deducing his Argument from the first great and original Fountain of *savage Life* and *Manners.*

III
Of Music, Dance, and Poem, in the Savage State

By examining savage Life, where untaught Nature rules, we find that the *agreeable Passions* of Love, Pity, Hope, Joy, and Exultation, no less than their *Contraries* of Hate, Revenge, Fear, Sorrow, and Despair, oppressing the human Heart by their mighty Force, are thrown out by the three Powers of *Action, Voice,* and *articulate Sounds.* The *Brute* Creatures express their Passions by the two first of These; some by *Action,* some by *Voice,* and some by *both* united: Beyond these, *Man* has the added Power of *articulate Speech:* The same Force of *Association* and *Fancy* which gives him *higher Degrees* and a *wider Variety* of *Passion,* gives rise to this *additional Power* of expressing those Passions which he feels.

Among the *Savages* who are in the *lowest Scale* of the human Kind, these several Modes of expressing their Passions are found altogether suited to their wretched State. Their *Gestures* are *uncouth* and *horrid:* Their *Voice* is thrown out in *Howls* and *Roarings:* Their *Language* is like the *Gabbling of Geese.*

But if we ascend a Step or two higher in the Scale of savage Life, we shall find this *Chaos* of *Gesture, Voice,* and *Speech,* rising into an agreeable *Order* and *Proportion.* The natural Love of a *measured Melody,* which Time and Experience produce, throws the *Voice* into *Song,* the *Gesture* into *Dance,* the *Speech* into *Verse* or *Numbers.* The addition of musical *Instruments* comes of Course: They are but *Imitations* of the human Voice, or of other natural Sounds, produced gradually by frequent Trial and Experiment.

Such is the Generation and natural Alliance of these three *Sister-Graces, Music, Dance,* and *Poem,* which we find moving Hand in Hand among the savage Tribes of every Climate.

For the Truth of the Fact, we may appeal to most of the Travellers who describe the Scenes of uncultivated Nature: All these agree in telling us, that *Melody, Dance,* and *Song,* make up the ruling Pastime, adorn the Feasts, compose

---

2. The Work advertised at the End of this Dissertation. [*Principles of Christian Legislation, in Eight Books, being An Analysis of the various Religions, Manners, and Politics of Mankind, in their Several Gradations: of the Obstructions thence arising to the general Progress and proper Effects of Christianity: and of the most practicable Remedies to these Obstructions.* BJB]

the Religion, fix the Manners, strengthen the Policy, and even form the future Paradise, of savage Man. That having few Wants, and consequently much Leisure, the barbarous Tribes addict themselves to these alluring Arts with a wonderful Degree of Passion, unless where their Manners are corrupted by an incidental Commerce with the Off-scum of civilized Nations. By these attractive and powerful Arts they celebrate their public Solemnities; by these they lament their private and public Calamities, the Death of Friends, or the Loss of Warriors: By these united, they express their Joy in their Marriages, Harvests, Huntings, Victories; praise the great Actions of their Gods and Heroes; excite each other to War and brave Exploits, or to suffer Death and Torments with unshaken Constancy.

These are the Circumstances most *common* to the savage Tribes: Besides these, there are many *peculiar* Modes which arise from their different Climates, Situations, Opinions, Manners. Among some Tribes the *joyous* Passions, among some the *gentle*, among others the *ferocious*, predominate and take Place. To give all the Varieties of these savage and festal Solemnities, were an endless Labour. Let the following Account suffice, as a general Image of the rest; which is singled out, not only because it is the most circumstantial; but likewise for the particular Relation which it will be found to bear to a following Part of this Inquiry.

The IROQUOIS, HURONS, and some less considerable Tribes, are free and independent Savages, who inhabit the northern Continent of AMERICA; and extend their Settlements from the Back of the *British Colonies* to the Borders of the *Great Lakes,* along the Skirts of LOUISIANA, and down the River OHIO, towards the MISSISIPI [*sic*], and the Gulph of FLORIDA. Father LAFITAU[3] gives the following Description of their festal Solemnities; which it is necessary to transcribe at large in order to give an adequate Idea of their Manners and Character. . . .

IV
OF THE NATURAL CONSEQUENCES OF A SUPPOSED CIVILIZATION

While these free and warlike Savages continue in their present *unlettered* State of Ignorance and Simplicity, no material Improvements in their *Song-Feasts* can arise. But let us suppose that the Use of *Letters* should come among them, and, as a Cause or Consequence of *Civilization*, be cultivated with that Spirit which is natural to a free and active People; and many notable Consequences would

---

3. *Moeurs des Sauvages ameriquains, comparées aux moeurs des premiers temps,* 2 vols. (Paris, 1724), 2:213ff. [There follows a long extract describing the ceremonies of some North American Indian tribes. BJB]

appear. Let us consider the most probable and striking among these natural Effects.

1. Their Idea of *Music,* in its most *inlarged* Sense, would comprehend the three Circumstances of *Melody, Dance,* and *Song.* For these three, as we have seen, being naturally conjoined, because naturally producing each other, would not *separately* command the Attention of such a People at their public Festivals. Therefore *Instrumental Melody,* without *Song,* would be little attended to, and of *no Esteem;* because it would want all those Attractions which must arise from the correspondent *Dance* and *Song.*

2. In the early Periods of such a Commonwealth, the *Chiefs* or *Legislators* would often be the *principal Musicians.* The two Characters would commonly coalesce; for we find, that, among the savage Tribes, the *Chiefs* are they who most signalize themselves by *Dance* and *Song;* and that their *Songs* rowl principally on the *great Actions* and *Events* which concern their *own Nation.*

3. Hence, their most ancient *Gods* would naturally be styled *Singers* and *Dancers.* For the most ancient *Gods* of civilized Pagan Countries, are generally their early *Legislators,* who taught their People the first Arts of Life. These deceased Legislators, therefore, when advanced to the Rank of Gods, would naturally be delivered down to Posterity with the same Attributes and Qualities by which they had distinguished themselves in Life: And it appears, from the last Article, that these Qualities would naturally be those of *Dance* and *Song.*

4. Measured Periods, or in other Words, *Rythm, Numbers,* and *Verse,* would naturally arise. For measured Cadence, or *Time,* is an essential Part of Melody, into which the human Ear naturally falls. And as the same Force of Ear would lead the Action or Dance to correspond with the Melody, so the Words or Song must, on a like Principle, keep Pace with *Both.* Among the *savage Americans* we see the first Rudiments of poetic Numbers, emerging from this Source. For "as the Means of adjusting the Words to the Air or Melody, they sometimes strike off Syllables from their Words." And such is the natural Generation of *Rythm* and *Verse.*

5. Their earliest *Histories* would be written in *Verse.* For we see, that among the savage Tribes, the Actions of their Heroes and Gods, and the great Events of their Nation, make a principal Part of their Songs. Whenever, therefore, the Use of Letters should come among such a People, these *ancient Songs* would naturally be *first recorded,* for the Information and Use of future Times.

6. Their most ancient *Maxims, Exhortations, Proverbs,* or *Laws,* would probably be written in Verse. For these would naturally make a Part of their *Songs* of Celebration, and would by Degrees be *selected* from thence, would in Time become the *Standard* of *Right* and *Wrong,* and as such, be treasured up and appealed to by the improving Tribe.

7. Their *religious Rites* would naturally be performed or accompany'd by

Dance and *Song*. For it appears from Fact that the great Actions of their Gods and Heroes are the most general Subject of the savage Dance and Song; and the common End of Pagan Rites hath ever been, to praise the Gods of the Country, and by these Means (as well as by Sacrifice) to appease their Wrath, or secure their Favour.

8. Their *earliest Oracles* would probably be delivered in *Verse*, and *sung* by the Priest or Priestess of the supposed God. For these *Oracles*, being supposed to be *inspired* by a deceased *Chief* (now a *Deity*) who had himself delivered his Exhortations in this *enthusiastic Manner*; and being addressed to a Tribe among whom this Mode of Instruction universally prevailed, no other Vehicle but that of *Verse* and *Song* could at first gain these *Oracles* either *Credit* or *Reception*.

9. Their *Melody* would be *simple*; and derive a considerable Part of its Power from its *Rythm* or *Measure*, without any Mixture of *artificial Composition*. First, because this Kind would be most suited to the *Powers* of the barbarous *Legislators* or *Bards*, at once *Composers* and *Performers*, among whom nothing artificial or refined could as yet take Place. Secondly, because this *Simplicity* of Manner would be best adapted to the Capacity of the surrounding People, incapable, in this early Period, to be attracted or moved by any thing but what *Nature* dictates.

10. The Force of this simple Melody would be much increased by the Power of early *Association* and continued *Habit*. For this, by *appropriating* certain *Sounds* to certain *Subjects*, would raise their Melody into a Kind of natural and expressive Language of the Passions.

11. Their *Songs* would be of a *legislative* Cast; and being drawn chiefly from the Fables or History of their own Country, would contain the essential Parts of their *religious, moral,* and *political* Systems. For we have seen above, that the *Celebration* of their deceased Heroes would of Course grow into a *religious* Act: That the *Exhortations* and *Maxims* intermixed with these *Celebrations*, and founded on the *Example* of their *Heroe-Gods*, would naturally become the *Standard* of *Right* and *Wrong*; that is, the Foundation of *private Morals* and *public Law*: And thus, the whole Fabric of their *Religion, Morals,* and *Polity*, would naturally arise from, and be included in their *Songs*, during their Progress from savage to civilized Life.

12. MUSIC, in the extended Sense of the Word (that is, including Melody, Dance, and Song) would make an essential and principal Part in the *Education* of their Children. For the important Principles of their *Religion, Morals,* and *Polity*, being delivered and inculcated in their *Songs*, no other Method could be devised, which would so strongly impress the youthful Mind with the *approved Principles* of *Life* and *Action*.

13. MUSIC therefore (in this extended Sense) must gain a great and *universal Power* over the minds and Actions of such a People. For through the Force of

early and continued *Habit*, together with the irresistible Contagion of general *Example*, while every thing pleasing, great, and important, was conveyed through this Medium, and through this only, such strong Impressions would strike themselves into the growing Mind, as would give it its ruling Colour through Life, and such as no future Incidents could easily weaken or efface.

14. In the Course of Time, and the Progress of Polity and Arts, a *Separation* of the several Parts or Branches of Music (in its extended Sense) would naturally arise. Till a certain Period of Civilization, Letters, and Art, the several Kinds would of course lie confused, in a Sort of undistinguished Mass, and be mingled in the same Composition, as Inclination, Enthusiasm, or other Incidents might impel. But repeated Trial and Experiment would naturally produce a more artificial Manner; and thus, by Degrees, the several Kinds of Poem would assume their legitimate Forms.

15. If their warlike Character continued, the *Dance* would naturally *separate* from the *Song;* and would itself become a *distinct Exercise* or *Art*, for the sake of increasing their Strength and Agility of Body, as the Means of rendering them invincible in War. For the Dance or Action of their Song-Feasts, being only secondary, and merely an Appendage to the Song, would not be of a Character sufficiently severe for the fierce and stubborn Contention of those who were destined to the immediate Toils of warlike Service.

16. After a certain Period of Civilization, the complex Character of *Legislator* and *Bard* would *separate*, or be seldom united. For as the Society grew more populous, and the increasing Arts of Life increased the Labours and Cares of Government, the *musical Art* (in its extended Sense) would of course be delegated by the civil Magistrate, to such Men of Genius and Worth, as might apply it to its proper Ends, the Instruction and Welfare of Mankind.

17. *Hymns* or *Odes* would be composed, and *Sung* by their Composers at their festal Solemnities. For these, in their simple State, are but a Kind of rapturous Exclamations of Joy, Grief, Triumph, or Exultation, in Consequence of some great or disastrous Action, known, alluded to, or expressed: A Species of Composition which naturally ariseth from the savage Song-Feast.

18. The *Epic Poem* would naturally arise, and be sung by its Composers at their public Solemnities. For it appears above,[4] that their earliest Histories would be written in Verse, and make a Part of their public Song-Feasts. Now the *Epic Poem* is but a Kind of *fabulous History*, rowling chiefly on the great Actions of ancient Gods and Heroes, and artificially composed under certain Limitations with Respect to its *Manner*, for the Ends of Pleasure, Admiration, and Instruction.

19. From an *Union* of these two, a certain rude Outline of *Tragedy* would

---

4. Article 5.

naturally arise. We may see the first Seeds or Principles of this Poem, in the Conduct of the savage *Song-Feast.* A *Chief sings* some great Action of a God or Heroe: The surrounding *Choir answer* him at Intervals, by Shouts of Sympathy or concurrent Approbation.

20. In Process of Time, this barbarous Scene would improve into a more perfect Form: Instead of *relating,* they would probably represent, by Action and Song united, those great or terrible Atchievements which their Heroes had performed. For of this, too, we find the Seeds or Principles in the savage State. "After a Chief of War hath recounted the Battles he had fought, they who are present will often rise up to dance, and represent those Actions with great Vivacity." If to this we add the usual Exclamations of the surrounding Choir, we here behold the first *rude Form of savage Tragedy.*

21. If the *Choir* should be *established* by general Use, and should animate the Solemnity by *Dance* as well as *Song;* the *Melody, Dance,* and *Song* would of course *regulate* each other, and the *Ode* or *Song* would fall into *Stanzas* of some *particular Kind.* This appears from the third Article.

22. Another Consequence of an *established Choir* would be an unvaried Adherence to the *Unities* of *Place* and *Time.* For a numerous Choir, maintaining their Station through the whole Performance, must give so forcible a Conviction to the Senses, of the *Sameness* of *Place,* and *Shortness* of *Time,* that any Deviation from this apparent Unity must shock the Imagination with an Improbability too gross to be endured.

23. Not only the Part of the tragic *Choir,* but the *Episode* or *interlocutory* Part would be also *sung.* For as the *Ode* and *Epic* would be *sung* from the earliest Periods; so when they became *united,* and by that Union formed the tragic Species, they of Course maintained the same Appendage of *Melody,* which Nature and Custom had already given them.

24. While the Nation held its *fierce* and *warlike* Character, the *tragic* Representations would chiefly turn on Subjects *distressful* or *terrible.* For thus they would animate each other to *Victory* and *Revenge,* by a Representation of what their *Friends* had *done* and *suffered.* These Subjects would likewise be most accommodated to the natural Taste of the poetic Chiefs of such a People; whose Atchievements must produce and abound with Events of Distress and Terror. They also would be best suited to the Genius and Ends of their State and Polity: For as the leading View of such a fierce and warlike People must be to destroy Pity and Fear; so this would most effectually be done, by making themselves familiar with distressful and terrible Representations. The gentle Passions, and less affecting Actions, which might fill the Spectacles of a mild and peaceful Nation, would be insipid to the Taste, and incompatible with the Character, of such a warlike People.

25. As their Tragedy would be intended as a *visible Representation* of their

ancient Gods and Heroes, so it would be natural for them to invent some Means of *strengthening* the *Voice,* and *aggrandising* the *Visage* and *Person,* as the means of compleating the Resemblance: For in all Savage Countries, the *tallest* and *strongest* Men are generally selected as their *Chiefs.*

26. As their Tragic *Poets* would be *Singers,* so they would be *Actors,* and perform some capital Part in their own Pieces for the Stage. For we see these different Characters are naturally united in the savage State: Therefore, till some extraordinary Change in Manners and Principles should ensue, this *Union* would of Course continue.

27. *Musical Contests* would be admitted as *public Exercises* in such a State. For we have seen, that the important Articles of Religion, Morals, and Polity, would naturally make a Part of their public Songs: therefore public Contests of this Kind would be regarded as the best and surest Means of raising an Emulation of a most useful Nature; and of strengthening the State, by inforcing all the fundamental Principles of Society in the most striking and effectual Manner.

28. The Profession of *Bard* or *Musician* would be held as very honourable, and of high Esteem. For he would be vested with a Kind of *public Character:* and if not an original Legislator, yet still he would be regarded as a *subordinate* and *useful Servant* of the *State.*

29. *Odes,* or *Hymns,* would naturally make a Part of their *domestic Entertainments:* and the *Chiefs* would be proud to signalize themselves by their Skill in *Melody* and *Song.* For their Songs being enriched with all the great and important Subjects relative to the public State; nothing could be more suitable to a high Station in the Commonwealth, than a Proficiency in this sublime and legislative Art.

30. When *Music* had attained to this State of relative Perfection, it would be regarded as a *necessary Accomplishment.* And if any Man, or Society of Men, were unacquainted with the Practice and Power of Music, their Ignorance in this Art would be regarded as a capital Defect: For it would imply a Deficiency in the three great leading Articles of Education, *Religion, Morals,* and *Polity.*

31. The Genius of their *Music* would *vary* along with their *Manners:* For Manners being the leading and most essential Quality of Man; All his other Tastes and Acquirements naturally correspond with *These;* and accommodate themselves to his Manners, as to their chief and original Cause.

32. As a Change of Manners must influence their Music, so, by reciprocal Action, a Change in their Music must influence Manners: For we have seen, that Music was the *established Vehicle* of all the great Principles of Education: Therefore a Change in Music must tend to bring on a Change in *These.*

33. A Provident Community of Principles, uncommonly severe, would probably fix both the Subjects and Movements of Song and Dance, by Law:

This would arise from their Knowledge of the mutual Influence of Manners and Music on each other.

34. In a Society of more libertine and relaxed Principles, the Corruption of Music would naturally arise, along with the Corruption of Manners; for the Reasons now assigned: and the Musicians, Bards, or Poets, would be the immediate Instruments of this Corruption. For being educated in a corrupt State they would be apt to debase their Art to vile and immoral Purposes, as the means of gaining that Applause which would be the natural Object of their Ambition.

35. In Consequence of this Corruption, a gradual and total *Separation* of the *Bard's* or *Musician's* complex Character would ensue. For the *Chief* would now no longer pride himself on the Character of *Poet* or Performer; nor the *Man* of *Genius* and *Worth* descend to the Profession of *Lyrist, Singer*, or *Actor:* Because these Professions, which had formerly been the Means of inculcating every thing laudable and great, would now (when perverted to the contrary Purposes) be disdained by the Wise and Virtuous.

36. Hence the Power, the Utility and Dignity of *Music* would sink into a general Corruption and Contempt. This Consequence is so plain, as to need no Illustration. . . .

XII

Of the State and Separation of Music and Poetry
among the Polished Nations of Europe
through the Succeeding Ages

. . . The State of the *Opera* will deserve a more particular Elucidation: And to this End we must endeavour to trace it to its Origin, which lies in great Measure hid in Darkness. Riccoboni is of Opinion that the first ever represented, was that which the *Doge* and *Senate* of Venice exhibited for the Entertainment of Henry the third of France, in the Year 1574.[5] But this Account is by no means satisfactory: For Sulpitius, an Italian, speaks of the *musical Drama,* as an Entertainment known in Italy in the Year 1490.[6]

History traces the Rise of the *Opera* no farther: But a Circumstance men-

5. *Theat.* etc. [Louis Riccoboni, dit Lelio, *Histoire du Théâtre Italien depuis la decadence de la Comédie Latine,* 2 vols. (Paris, 1731). The work was Cornelio Frangipane's *Proteo,* with music (now lost) by Claudio Merulo. BJB]

6. Charles Ménestrier, *Des Représentations en musique anciennes et modernes* (Paris, 1681; repr. Geneva, 1972 and 1992) [p. 155, quoting the dedication of Giovanni Sulpizio's edition of Vitruvius (Rome, 1486) to Cardinal Raffaele Riario, in which he praises him for having organized theatrical events that included singing. BJB]

tioned by SULPITIUS, who was a Man of Letters, may seem to lead us up to its true Origin. He is by some supposed to have been the Inventor of this *musical Drama;* but he ingenuously tells us himself, that he only *revived* it.[7] We have seen above, that the *Tragedy* of the ancient *Greeks* was accompanied with Music; that the same Union was borrowed and maintained through the several Periods of the *Roman* Empire: If therefore we suppose, what is altogether probable, that the Form of the ancient Tragedy had been still kept up in some retired Part of ITALY, which the Barbarians never conquered; we then obtain a fair Account of the Rise of the modern *Opera,* which hath so much confounded all Inquiry.

As VENICE was the Place where the *Opera* first appeared in Splendor, so it is highly probable, that *there* the *ancient Tragedy* had slept in Obscurity, during the Darkness of the Barbarous Ages. For while the rest of ITALY was over-run by the Nations from the North, the Seas and Morasses of VENICE preserved *Her* alone from their Incursions: Hence, History tells us, the People flocked to VE-NICE from every Part of ITALY: Hence the very Form of her Republic hath been maintained for thirteen hundred Years: And from these Views of *Security,* it was natural for the helpless Arts to seek an Asylum within her Canals, from the Fury and Ignorance of a barbarous Conqueror.

Other Circumstances concur, to strengthen this Opinion. The *Carnaval* first appeared in Splendor, and still wears it at VENICE, beyond every other Part of ITALY: Now the *Carnaval* is, in many Circumstances, almost a Transcript of the ancient *Saturnalia* of ROME.

In the *Venetian Comedy,* the *Actor* wears a *Masque:* A palpable *Imitation,* or rather *Continuance,* of the old *Roman* Custom.

That the modern *Opera* is no more than a Revival of the old *Roman Tragedy,* and not a new-invented Species, will appear still more evident, if we consider, that it is an Exhibition altogether out of Nature, and repugnant to the universal Genius of Modern Customs and Manners. We have seen the natural Union of Poetry and Music, as they rise in the savage State; and how this Union forms the tragic Species in the natural Progression of Things. Hence we have deduced the musical Tragedies of ancient GREECE: But in ancient ROME, it appears, they arose merely from *Imitation* and *Adoption.* Nor could it be otherwise; because the *Romans* wanted the first seeds or Principles from whence the musical Trage-dies of the *Greeks* arose. The same Reasoning takes Place, with Respect to the modern *Opera:* It emerged at a Time, when the general State of Manners in EUROPE could not naturally produce it. Had it been the Result from *Nature,* its Production would have been more *general.* It emerged in that very City, where most probably it must have lain hid: In a City, whose other Entertainments are evidently borrowed from those of ancient ROME. And if to these Arguments we

7. Ibid.

add this farther Consideration, that the Subjects of the very first *Operas* were drawn from the Fables of ancient GREECE and ROME,[8] and not from the Events or Atchievements of the Times; and farther, that in their *Form,* they were exact Copies of the *ancient Drama;* these accumulated Proofs amount to near a Demonstration, that the *Italian Opera* is but the *Revival* of the old *Roman Tragedy.*[9]

Such being the *Birth* of the modern *Opera,* no Wonder it inherits the *Weakness* of its *Parent:* For we have seen, that the *Roman Tragedy* never had its proper Effects, considered in a *legislative* View; having been separated from its important Ends before its Arrival from GREECE. As therefore it had declined into a mere *Amusement* when it was first adopted by ROME; and as we have seen, that in Proportion as the Roman Manners grew more dissolute, Tragedy sunk still lower in its Character, till at length it became no more than a Kind of mere *Substratum* or *Groundwork,* on which the Actors displayed their Abilities in *Singing* and *Gesticulation;* it was altogether natural that it should rise again in the same unnerved and effeminate Form.

From these Causes, therefore, we may trace all the Features of the modern *Opera,* however *unnatural* and *distorted* they may appear. The *Poem,* the *Music* and the *Performance,* as they now exist in *Union,* are the manifest Effects of this spurious Origin.

First, That the *Subject* of the *Poem* should, even on its first Appearance, be drawn from Times and Countries little interesting, and *Gods* and *Wonders* and *celestial Machinery* introduced, which neither the Poet nor his Audience *believed* in, could only be the Effect of a *blind* Principle of *Imitation,* tending to mere *Amusement.*—The established Separation of the Poet's from the Musician's Art was productive of parallel Effects: For the Poet, ambitious only of shining in his particular Sphere, became generally more Intent on Imagery than Pathos: Or else, instead of being *principal,* he became *subservient* to the Composer's Views; from whence arose a Motley kind of Poem (calculated only for a Display of the Musician's Art) which degenerated by Degrees into a mere *Pasticio.*

Secondly; the same Causes account for all the Absurdities of the *Music.*—The *Recitative,* or perpetual musical Accompanyment in the declamatory Parts, is a Practice so much at Variance with modern Manners, that it extorted the following Censure from a candid Critic: "I beg Pardon of the Inventors of the *musical Tragedy,* a Kind of Poem, as *ridiculous* as it is *new."*—"If there be any

8. The Subjects of the first *Operas* were APOLLO and DAPHNE, ORPHEUS and EURIDICE, ALCESTES and ATYS; which last, in the Title Page of the oldest extant Edition [i.e., the setting by Lully], is called *a musical Tragedy.*

9. As these Circumstances prove that the *modern Opera* is a *Revival* of the *old Roman Tragedy;* so, we are led from hence to a probable Conjecture concerning the *measured Recitation* of the *Roman Tragedians:* And that it was something of the Nature of modern *Recitative.*

thing in the World that is at Variance with *tragic Action*, it is *Song*." "The *Opera* is the *Grotesque* of Poetry; and so much the more intolerable, as it pretends to pass for a regular Work."[10] Now if, along with DACIER, we regard the *Opera* as a modern *Invention*, this Circumstance of the perpetual musical Accompanyment is indeed *unaccountable*: But if we regard it as a mere *Imitation* or *Continuance* of the old *Roman Tragedy*, and trace *this* upwards to its true Fountain, the *Greek Drama*; and again follow *this* to its original Source, the *Savage Song-Feast*; we then see how naturally these *extremes unite*; and discern the rude *Melody* and *Song* of the *barbarous Greek* Tribes gradually melted into the *Refinements* of the *modern Opera*. —Again, as the Separation of the Poet's from the Musician's Art produced an *improper Poetry*; so the Separation of the Musician's from the Poet's Character was productive of improper and *unaffecting Music*: For the Composer, in his Turn, intent only on *shining*, commonly wanders into unmeaning Division, and adopts either a delicate and refined, or a merely popular Music, to the Neglect of true musical Expression: Hence, too, the *Da Capo* had its natural Origin: A Practice which tends only to tire and disgust the Hearer, if he comes with an Intent of being *affected* by the *tragic Action*, or with any other View than that of *listening* to a *Song*.[11]

Thirdly, with Regard to the *Performance* of the *Opera*.—The theatrical Representation is of a Piece with the Poetry and Music: For, having been regarded, from its first Rise, more as an Affair of astonishing Shew than of affecting Resemblance, it is gaudy, flaunting, and unnatural. The Singers (like the *Poet* and the *Musician*) being considered merely as Objects of Amusement, no Wonder if their Ambition seldom reacheth higher than to the Display of an artificial Execution.—As a Consequence of these Principles, the *Castrati* were introduced into all Sorts of Characters, in spite of Nature and Probability; and still continue to represent Heroes and Statesmen, Warriors and Women.—The flourished Close or Cadence arose naturally from the same Sources: From a total Neglect of the Subject and Expression, and an Attention to the mere Circumstance of Execution only.—The frequent *Encore*, or Demand of the repeated Performance of particular Songs was the natural Effect of the same Causes. No Audience demands the *Repetition* of a pathetic Speech in *Tragedy*,

10. Alexandre Dacier, *La Poetique d'Aristote . . . traduite en françois, avec des remarques critiques* (Paris, 1692), 85.

11. The *Da Capo*, which is so striking an Absurdity in the more modern Operas, was not used in those of older Date. Even [Giovanni Paolo] COLONNA, who lived about the middle of the sixteenth [*sic*] century, employed it not; as appears by one of his Operas performed at the Academy in BOLOGNA, A.D. 1688. But in an Opera of *Old* [Alessandro] SCARLATTI (entitled *La Teodora*) composed in 1693, the *Da Capo* is found, though not in all his Songs. After that Period, the Use of it seems to have become *general*: for in an Opera of [Francesco] GASPARINI (intitled *Il Tartaro nella China*) composed in 1715, the *Da Capo* is found in every Song.

though performed in the finest Manner, because their Attention is turned on the Subject of the Drama: Thus if the Audience were *warmed* by the *Subject* of an *Opera,* and *took Part* in the main *Action* of the Poem, the *Encore,* instead of being *desireable,* would generally *disgust:* But the whole being considered as a mere *musical Entertainment,* and the tragic *Action* commonly *forgot,* the artificial Performance of a *Song* became naturally a chief Object of Admiration, and the Repetition of it a chief *Object* of Request.

From *A Dissertation on the Rise, Union, and Power, the Progressions, Separations, and Corruptions, of Poetry and Music* (London, 1763; 2d ed., London, 1772; repr. New York: Garland, 1971), sections 1–4, pp. 25–29, 36–46, and sec. 12, pp. 200–206.

GIOVANNI BATTISTA MARTINI
from *History of Music* (1757)

PREFACE

Man is prompted to fulfill his innate desires through a powerful natural inclination. As he is solicitous in pursuing truth in order to please his intellect, so is he likewise unremitting in his search for pleasure in order to appease, along with his other senses, that of hearing, to the delight of which Nature has ordained singing and sound. Similarly, through experience Nature has conveyed her enduring laws, upon which the distinguished scientific art, which we call harmonic music, has in the end been based and established.

What wonder, then, if in every age this has been highly revered by all countries and peoples. What is strange, however, is that this art, as far as I know, has never been able to take pride in seeing its most glorious achievements resplendently set forth in a complete historical account.

During Hadrian's reign, Greek music was enriched by Dionysius of Halicarnassus the younger, who sought to restore esteem to the ancient recollections of it; it would have been both fortunate and distinguished among others, if the wickedness of time had left us his twenty-six books, which we today desire in vain.[1] Fortunately, Greek music can console itself with the few but

---

1. Gerardus Johannes Vossius, *De quatuor artibus popularibus, de philologia, et scientiis mathematicis* (Amsterdam, 1650), bk. 3, ch. 15: "In the reign of the Emperor Hadrian Dionysius of Halicarnassus flourished: not the author of the *Roman Antiquities* and outstanding critic, who lived under Augustus, but a later one, called sophist and musician, since he practiced music above all."

well-planned monumental works that Vossius[2] and Bontempi[3] devoted to it with extreme diligence and elegance of form.

More favorable has been the fortune of music, especially modern music— and not only French music, which has been described in such a scholarly manner by M. Bonnet[4]—through the lustrous glory so advantageously brought to it by the luminous writings of Gafurio,[5] Zarlino,[6] Vincenzo Galilei,[7] Doni,[8] and many others. Yet music cannot be utterly satisfied, as it still lacks the full light of a complete history, wherein its origin, progress, development, establishment, and perfection are brought to high regard in the public eye.

It is hardly to be believed that, having been examined by so many learned men from its origins down to the present, and especially by the most erudite Greeks, music has never been sufficiently honored by their considerations as to have been deemed worthy of such a lofty undertaking. Undoubtedly, many must have attempted it, but failed because of the many obstacles they came up against. Among these there are two that have long seemed to me to be particularly unsurmountable.

The first ages of the world are so poor in the monuments that have come down to us, and so remote in time even from each other, that when brought together they can take no other form than of a chance collection. Holy Writ, mainly intended as a history of God's people, touches on the subject of music only in passing, mentioning rather than describing the songs, the sounds, and some instruments, in the circumstances in which they arose. Hebrew writers are not very helpful in this respect, both because of the scant information they provide and the little trust one can put in them. After them, the Egyptians, the

---

He set out to perpetuate his name with twenty-four books of *Notes on Rhythm* and twenty-six books of *Musical History,* in which he mentioned auletes, citharodes, and poets of all kinds; in addition twenty-two books of *Musical Discourses,* etc." [All these are lost. The information comes from the entry in the *Suda* (formerly supposed the work of one Suidas), δ 1171 (2:109 in Ada Adler's edition); "twenty-six" is an error for "thirty-six." LAH-S]

2. Gerardus Johannes Vossius, the work cited [n. 1] and elsewhere.

3. Giovanni Andrea Angelini Bontempi, *Historia musica* (Perugia, 1695).

4. *Histoire de la musique et de ses effets, depuis son origine jusqu'à présent* (Paris, 1715; Amsterdam, 1721, 1725, and 1726).

5. Franchino Gaffurio, *Theoricum opus musice discipline* (Naples, 1480); *Theorica musice* (Milan, 1492); *Practica musice* (Milan, 1496); *Angelicum ac divinum opus musice* (Milan, 1508); *De harmonia musicorum instrumentorum opus* (Milan, 1518).

6. Gioseffo Zarlino, *Istitutioni harmoniche* (Venice, 1558, 1562, 1573, 1589); *Dimostrationi harmoniche* (Venice, 1571, 1589); *Sopplimenti musicali* (Venice, 1588).

7. *Dialogo di Vincentio Galilei nobile fiorentino della musica antica, et della moderna* (Florence, 1581); *Discorso di Vincentio Galilei nobile fiorentino, intorno all'opere di messer Gioseffo Zarlino* (Florence, 1589).

8. Giovanni Battista Doni, *Compendio del trattato de' generi, e de' modi* (Rome, 1635); *Annotazioni sopra il compendio de' generi e de' modi* (Rome, 1640); *De praestantia musicae veteris libri tres* (Florence, 1647).

Assyrians, the Chaldeans, and other ancient Oriental peoples have the misfortune that no more than the names of some of their kings are known to us; for the rest, not just their music, but almost all of their important activities are enveloped in a dense cloud of obscurity. Greece is beginning to be described, and that rather extensively; indeed, its music is sometimes given excessive attention. However, the many fables in which they enveloped their truth make us progressively more suspicious and uncertain as to the worth of their narratives.[9] Thus from the beginning of the world, up to approximately the time when Pythagoras flourished, one either has to be content with a rather defective series of narrative events, or else not search for a history.

This is the first insuperable obstacle that presents itself to him who, during the long span of the first thirty-five centuries, seeks an uninterrupted course of certain facts and events that are not mythical. Such difficulty, however, although insurmountable, need not frighten anyone, nor make the compiling of our history an impossible task, since this obstacle has not prevented others from compiling histories of the other sciences and arts that are by far more necessary to human society.

As regards the other difficulty, which at first glance is no less formidable, I should like to think, or at least hope, that I have sufficiently dispensed with it. When I took to considering music, together with its immense procession of the most varied and strange events, I also pondered the prerogatives and faculties required to fashion this matter into a history. These were both numerous and arduous, and were all to be concentrated in whomever undertook to provide them with a historic cast worthy of attention. Each event associated with either sacred or secular matters had to be reported in sufficient detail. Great expertise was necessary in treating the natural sciences, and a complete knowledge of geometric proportions. A huge number of texts by theoretical and practical authors were similarly necessary, along with the time to read them, the ability to understand them, and the discernment to evaluate them properly. It was necessary to go deeply into what is commonly referred to as the musical taste of every age, region, and nation. It was essential to be skilled in poetry, the inseparable companion of music.[10] It was likewise indispensable to be highly knowledgeable in both dialectics and moral philosophy. Furthermore, a practical knowledge of the many difficult and different languages, but especially Greek, was imperative. Finally, I leave it to anyone to ponder whether natural inclination,

---

9. Quintilian, *Institutio oratoria*, bk. 2, ch. 4. Flavius Josephus, *Contra Appionem*, bk. 1.

10. Calcidius, *Luculenta Thimaei Platonis traductio, et eiusdem argutissima explanatio*, fol. 54v: "That poetry is blood sister to music is obvious to all." Plutarch, *Symposiacae quaestiones* 9.14.2 [*Moralia* 744F] in the version of Guillaume Xylander (Paris, 1570): "that poetry is associated with music."

coupled with a long preparation—without which nothing perfect can be achieved—need be concentrated in the historian if he is to set himself to such a demanding endeavor.

In the light of difficulties so numerous and so considerable, I was neither so bold as to be presumptuous, nor so weak as not to want to try anything. My inadequate ability to overcome the arduous things and grasp the inner significance of difficult matters, without both sufficient intelligence and erudition in the required sciences and arts; with scant documents and information necessary to approach such a lofty labor, and with but a smattering of theory and almost with the sole help of practical knowledge—all this ill prepared me to set sail on such treacherous waters. I had no alternative but to resort to others for guidance, in order to draw the necessary enlightenment to dissipate all obscurity and avoid misunderstandings; in a word, to gain all the learning I lacked so as to avoid errors and to overcome those obstacles which, without the help of others, I would not have been competent enough to surmount. Thus, I believe I can complete my history as I had desired, and that my abilities had allowed me no more than to hope.

However, if despite all my diligence and toil I should not have succeeded in bringing it to that final desired perfection, I should greatly appreciate it if others, following in my footsteps, would reach the goal to which I aspired, taking solace in the thought that I had at least inspired them in such a praiseworthy undertaking. Lastly, I am more than willing to acknowledge frankly any shortcoming my work may contain, and also to explain, on request, anything not clearly expressed.

I am animated by a sincere sense of what is right and true, which makes me ignore whatever might cause me to deviate from it. Consequently, whosoever is similarly disposed will readily find me filled with the esteem and respect due to any critic who seeks no more of me than to combat imposture and falsehood.

However, before the kind reader sets out on the lengthy journey on which we are about to embark, I deem it beneficial to summarize the entire work.

Our history begins with the creation of the world, after which will follow the little we know of the music of the Jews up to the birth of our Savior. The Bible will indeed be a safe guide for us, yet not such a clear one that it will not often be necessary to resort to reasonable conjecture, if we do not wish to act more as a writer, narrating facts, than as a historian, seeking connections. The basic principles of music themselves must lead us to the real meaning of the interpretations, for if these principles are lacking, such interpretations can easily prove fallacious. Such moderation, however, is to be exercised in this process as in no way to diminish the merit of music. Nor should too much be assigned to music by going beyond its appropriate limits.

We shall then examine the music of the Chaldeans and the Egyptians, which, being very ancient, would merit extraordinary esteem, if a commensurate amount of light clarified it.

We shall then go on to consider the music of the Greeks, who were masters in all the arts and sciences that have come down to us, and whose teachings were ever more respected as oracles. However, had the Greeks loved poetry less, their musical teachings would have seemed more sincere to us, without the inconvenient mingling of so many fables for which Greece has had to suffer the notorious epithet mendacious.[11] Therefore, he who wishes to follow me must of necessity bear equally with music, still fabulous and metaphorical, even when it is divided into moral, theoretical, and practical categories. The poets are largely to blame for such inconvenience, for in order to impress ideas more easily on the minds of men, and especially upon the young, they deemed it wise to resort to fables, not only to extol the deeds of gods and heroes, but also to provide instruction in the arts and sciences.[12] I do not flatter myself that I have succeeded in presenting what is certain and true in the clearest possible way, but I promise all diligence and industriousness possible to achieve it.

The Greeks are followed by the Tyrrhenians [Etruscans], today called Tuscans, the ancient inhabitants of Latium, and then the ancient Romans. The music of these peoples is quite similar to that of the Greeks, as a stream to its source, from which the same principles and precepts both derive and are acknowledged.

The final place, but the first in order of dignity and distinction, is held by the music of the Latins, who practiced it from the time of the Redeemer up to the present. This last section will have all the necessary breadth, thus enabling us to explain in full its principles, and describe and examine its development up to our time. There are, however, some centuries that are poor in historical facts and almost completely lacking in information: the persecutions of Christians in the first three centuries, the division and decadence of the Roman Empire, and the invasions of the barbarians are responsible for the loss, no less of music than of the other arts and sciences. However, at the beginning of the ninth century Charlemagne revived the arts, partly through the painstaking diligence of monks who, through practical application and their learned writings, preserved them intact, and particularly music, amidst the ravages of war, and partly through Guido of Arezzo who, in the eleventh century, made all types of music,

11. ". . . Et quidquid Graecia mendax / Audet in historia . . ." ["and all the lying tales of Greek history"]; Juvenal, *Satires,* 10.174–75. "Portentosa Graeciae mendacia" ["the monstrous lies of Greece"]; Pliny, *Natural History,* 5.4.

12. "Poetry, deriving its precepts from philosophy and combining them with fiction, makes learning easy and pleasant for the young." Plutarch, *De audiendis Poetis.*

but especially singing, both clearer and easier. Such was their collective contribution that there has been no century up to the present that is not rich in materials, or in which music was not embellished and greatly enhanced.

While the order I have proposed to follow obviously compels me to observe the course of events, I am under no such obligation where uncertain chronologies are concerned, those that could bog us down in discussions far removed from our objectives. This is especially so as the historical events that are related to music are neither so frequent nor so interwoven as to allow me to follow them with any precision. Therefore, I believe that it will better suit our purposes if we view historic events in terms of successive periods rather than as a sequence of years.

If, in following this procedure, we should come across events that, in order to be better understood, are deserving of more detailed explanation, I deem it more fitting, so that our treatise not suffer undue delay, simply to treat them in passing, leaving a fuller discussion to various dissertations, where they will receive all due attention. In this way, they will neither lack the necessary completeness, nor will their subject matter be insufficiently expounded, thus granting both aspects perfect intelligibility. . . .

FIRST DISSERTATION:
WHAT FORM OF SINGING IS NATURAL TO MAN

I have often sought to understand why it is that so many who are naturally predisposed to song, who indeed are enamored of it, are also just as naturally inept and unable to perform one: thus, however much delight and pleasure they have in hearing it, equally do they find themselves entangled in an insuperable inability to do it themselves. It is a fact that the Creator linked body and mind together, so that one could be in support of the other, not only as regards external actions but also in expressing inner desires. Thus, I mused, it is either the body's or the mind's fault, if someone who so much likes singing is incapable of producing pleasurable song. As for the mind, it is certain that being one for every man, unable either to desire or not desire what truly pleases it, when resolving to produce song, it will make every effort to resort to music which has previously pleased it greatly. As for the body, however, if it used the same instruments to produce song as it does to listen to it, then the singing thus produced would undoubtedly be as perfect and delightful as the singing perceived by the ear. Nor perhaps would there be anyone who, delighted by song and wishing it to be sweet-sounding, would render it unpleasant. But the body's structure is made up of various organs; those that cater to the senses and those to movement are extremely different both in structure and in the way they function. Hearing is the function of the ears, which relay song and other sounds to the place where the mind hears and comprehends them. What creates song are the vocal organs, distant from the ears, and structurally different, so much so that they can be ill suited to obey when the mind commands them to sing, even though the ears may be perfectly structured and capable of conveying song to the mind. Or, the ear can at least be disposed so as to enable the mind to perceive the pleasure of song, though the vocal organs themselves are not able to produce it pleasurably. Yet however they produce it, Nature when creating song took special care expressly to predispose the vocal organs to produce a certain form of song that is easy and common to everyone, and proportionate to that inclination it wished to impress on everyone's mind.

In fact, if we take into account evidence from whatever historical period and people, and if we notice the singing that artlessly and effortlessly issues from anybody, it sounds similar in form, or not much different. The universal uniformity and constancy of spontaneous song bears evidence to a precise design on the part of Nature, or to a law founded in our own constitution, which makes us adopt a certain method or form of singing, which we may, indeed must, call natural.

In accordance with this law, Nature provided us with two faculties or dispositions toward song, the difference between the two being that one tends to form natural song, the other to perfect it through art.

The exercise of both is perfectly free, but not the kind of song. When they so wish, the unlearned can certainly start singing; but, constrained by Nature, they can only produce natural song, which they do with ease and without effort. This is not so with the other category of singing, which cannot be acquired without hard work and study. Yet we must want to acquire it, and to do so we have to resort to art, which gives this type of singing its quality and its artfulness, whereby it is perfected and made elegant.

Here it should be pointed out that by "art" we do not merely mean precepts, nor simply a method of training whomever desires to improve his singing. If someone has an excellent and natural disposition for singing, this person, as we see all the time, by listening at length to fine singers and by training himself in imitating them can achieve the goal he desires, even to equal them. The reason for this seems to be that precepts and method make the acquisition of skill easier and surer, but practice alone enables one to acquire true mastery, wherein lies art's stated objective. Thus for the practical possession of any knowledge it should be of little importance whether this training occurs by following the stated precepts, or by imitating those who practice it. However it is exercised, it always depends on art, and the help of study and hard work, which refine one's natural inclination. Furthermore, it classifies this mode of singing as artful (*artifiziale*), as it is achieved without teaching, and only through successful imitation.

This last aspect of singing will not be treated here, as the plan of our work compels us to consider it elsewhere. Lastly, we shall now investigate what natural singing is, that which Nature has given everyone.

Up to now, we have had no difficulty using the term "natural," but the meaning of the word "song" is not so simple. In fact, it is easier to understand than to explain. Countless authors have spoken about song, but few have explained what it means, and fewer still have defined it satisfactorily.

Rather, they have described it in so many ways, and with such a variety of additions, that I deem it better to extrapolate that which will enable us to formulate a more clearly representative idea of our subject. Thus one could say that song is nothing other than a series of high and low utterances (*voci*), the purpose of which is to delight the ear.[13] In this respect, song is distinct from the sweetness of prose and poetry, which derive their sweetness from the words, and not from utterances. It will further distinguish itself from the sweetness of sounds, which have no utterance except high and low. Lastly, it distinguishes itself from the sweetness of speech which, though utterance, is yet lacking in either high or low tones. Not that it does not pass through either of the two, but it does so with such speed and momentary vibration that the ear cannot sensibly determine its precise value and discern it; since it cannot judge it, it is as if it lacked both high and low tones.[14]

As for utterance, properly speaking it is no more than the sound produced by the body's organs, which, as we said, were given to us by Nature for speech,[15] that is to say, to provide us with a means whereby to express our inner emotions. As the latter are many and varied, they could not be expressed through just one utterance. Utterance must therefore be varied; as it is an entity that can vary only by degree, it follows that its variations are discernible not in terms of differ-

13. "A song or air is a progression of the voice or other sounds through certain natural or artificial intervals that are pleasing to the ear or the mind, and which signify joy, sadness, or some other passion by their various movements"; Marin Mersenne, *Harmonie universelle* (Paris, 1636), bk. 6 ("Traitez de la voix et des chants. Livre second des chants"), prop. 1, p. 89.

14. Aristoxenus, *Elements of Harmony*, bk. 1, p. 18 [Meibom]: "We must try to outline the nature of melody. It has already been stated that the movement of the voice in it must be by intervals, so that musical melody is thus distinct from that of speech; for one also speaks of a kind of melody in speech, composed of the accents in the words; for it is natural to raise and lower the pitch in conversation." [In classical Greek, the basis of accent in individual words was not stress but pitch; hence the reference is to word-accent, not to sentence intonation. LAH-S]. Aristides Quintilianus, *De musica,* bk. 1, p. 7 [Meibom]. Boethius, *De musica,* bk. 1, ch. 12.

15. Franciscus Salinas, *De musica* (Salamanca, 1577), bk. 2, ch. 3, p. 48: "For in artificial instruments singing voices [*voces canorae*] similar to the human voices with which we sing may be found in strings or reeds; so that [in Latin] we speak of the songs [*cantus*] not only of human beings, but also of flutes; and Horace said 'singing with the lyre' [*cithara canentem:* a misquotation of *Odes* 1.31.1 *cithara carentem,* "without a lyre"; but cf. Tacitus, *Annals* 14.14.1 *cithara . . . canere*], and Ovid [*Tristia* 4.1.12], 'The shepherd soothes the sheep with song from the reed.' Therefore we call the strings of instruments voices also, since they perform the melody like human voices."

ent kinds, but only of different degrees. These degrees, as they rise and fall, give utterance its high and low sounds.

From *Storia della musica* (Bologna, 1757–81; repr. Graz: Akademische Druck- und Verlagsanstalt, 1967), vol. 1, Prefazione, pp. 1–7; Dissertazione prima, pp. 83–87.

CHARLES BURNEY
from *A General History of Music* (1776)

The feeble beginnings of whatever afterwards becomes great or eminent, are interesting to mankind. To artists, therefore, and to real lovers of art, nothing relative to the object of their employment or pleasure is indifferent.

Sir Francis Bacon recommends histories of art upon the principle of utility, as well as amusement; and collecting into one view the progress of an art seems likely to enlarge the knowledge, and stimulate the emulation of artists, who may, by this means, be taken out of the beaten track of habit and common practice, to which their ideas are usually confined.

The love of lengthened tones and modulated sounds, different from those of speech, and regulated by a stated measure, seems a passion implanted in human nature throughout the globe; for we hear of no people, however wild and savage in other particulars, who have not music of some kind or other, with which we may suppose them to be greatly delighted, by their constant use of it upon occasions the most opposite: in the temple, and the theatre; at funerals, and at weddings; to give dignity and solemnity to festivals, and to excite mirth, chearfulness, and activity, in the frolicsome dance. Music, indeed, like vegetation, flourishes differently in different climates; and in proportion to the culture and encouragement it receives; yet, to love such music as our ears are accustomed to, is an instinct so generally subsisting in our nature, that it appears less wonderful it should have been in the highest estimation at all times, and in every place, than that it should hitherto never have had its progressive improvements and revolutions deduced through a regular history, by any English writer.

Indeed, though time has spared us a few ancient histories of empires, republics, and individuals, yet no models of a *History,* either *of Music,* or of any other *art* or *science,* are come down to us, out of the many that antiquity produced. Plutarch's Dialogue on Music approaches the nearest to history; but, though it abounds with particulars relative to the subject, it is so short and defective, that it rather excites than gratifies curiosity.

Some of the writings of Aristotle and Aristoxenus that are lost, though they were not express histories of music, would, nevertheless, had they been preserved, have satisfied our doubts concerning several parts of ancient music, which are now left to conjecture.

"Aristotle, the disciple of Plato," says Plutarch, "regarded melody as something noble, great, and divine." Now, as this passage is not to be found in the remaining works of Aristotle, it is imagined that Plutarch took it either from his *Treatise on Music*[1] or the second book of his Poetics, where he treated of the Flute and Cithara, both which works are lost. And yet Kircher, in his *Musurgia*,[2] speaking of the ancient writers on Music, whose works he had consulted among the manuscripts in the Jesuit's College Library at Rome, names Aristotle;[3] but I sought in vain for the Treatise which he had written expressly on Music, nor could I find there any work by that philosopher relative to the subject, except his Acoustics.[4]

Almost all the ancient philosophers, especially the Pythagoreans, Platonists, and Peripatetics, wrote treatises on Music, which are now lost. Meursius, in his notes on Aristoxenus, enumerates, among others, the following ancient writers on music, of whom we have nothing left but the name: Agenor, of Mytilene, mentioned by Aristoxenus,[5] from whom sprung a sect of musicians called *Agenorians;* as from Eratocles, the *Eratocleans;* from Epigonus, the *Epigonians,* and from Damon, who taught Socrates music, the *Damonians.*[6]

But of all the ancient musical writers, the name of no one is come down to us, of whose works I was in greater want than those of the younger Dionysius Halicarnassensis, who flourished, according to Suidas, under the emperor Adrian, and who wrote twenty-six books of the *History of Musicians,* in which he celebrated not only the great performers on the Flute and Cithara, but those who had risen to eminence by every species of poetry. He was, likewise, author

---

1. Ὑπὲρ μουσικῆς. [The quotation comes from pseudo-Plutarch, *De musica* 23 (*Moralia* 1139B) = Aristotle fr. 47 Rose. LAH-S]

2. *Musurgia universalis sive ars magna consoni et dissoni* (Rome, 1650), 1:545.

3. [Aristotle makes several references to music, but the treatise on the subject ascribed to him by Diogenes Laertius (*Lives of the Philosophers* 5.26) does not survive; the reference will be to bk. 19 of the *Problems* compiled by later members of his school. Kircher does not claim to have seen a manuscript of Aristotle, but a collection of Greek musical writers; this appears to be Cod. Vaticanus Graecus 2365, which contains Aristides Quintilianus, Ptolemy, Porphyry, Bryennius, Pseudo-Plutarch, Cleonides (called "Euclid"), Euclid, Aristoxenus, Alypius, Gaudentius, and Nicomachus (Thomas J. Mathiesen, *Ancient Greek Music Theory: A Catalogue Raisonné of Manuscripts* [RISM Bxi: Munich: G. Henle Verlag, 1988], 611–16). LAH-S]

4. Περὶ ἀκουστῶν.

5. Bk. 2, p. 36. [Joannes Meursius's edition of Aristoxenus was published in Leiden in 1616. BJB]

6. The list of Greek writers on the subject of music, whose works are lost, amounts, in Fabricius to near thirty. [Johann Albert Fabricius, *Biblioteca Graeca* (Hamburg, 1705–28 and subsequent editions). BJB]

of five books, written in defence of Music, and chiefly in refutation of what is alledged against it in Plato's Republic.[7] Aristides Quintilianus[8] has, also, endeavoured to soften the severity of some animadversions against Music in the writings of Cicero;[9] but though time has spared the defence of this author, yet it does not indemnify us for the loss of that which Dionysius junior left behind him; as testimonies are still remaining of his having been a much more able writer than Arist. Quintilianus.[10]

But though all the musical histories of the ancients are lost, yet almost every country in Europe that has cultivated the polite arts, has, since the revival of learning, produced a history of Music, except our own. Italy can boast of two works under that title; one written in the latter end of the last century by Bontempi,[11] and that of Padre Martini, in this.[12] France has likewise two, one by Bonnet,[13] and one by M. de Blainville;[14] and Germany has not only produced two histories of Music in its own language, by Gaspar Printz,[15] and M. Marpurg,[16] but one in Latin, lately published in two volumes, 4to. by the prince abbot of St. Blasius.[17] Unluckily, those of P. Martini, and M. Marpurg, are not yet finished; and that of the learned abbot only concerns church music; so that though much has been done, much is still left for diligence to do;[18] and how-

---

7. [On Dionysius Halicarnassus the younger, see above, n. 1 to the excerpt from Martini. BJB]

8. Pp. 69ff. [Aristides, *De musica;* Burney used Meibom's edition of 1652. BJB]

9. *In Politic.* [Aristides, *De musica,* bk. 2, ch. 6 (Winnington-Ingram p. 61), refers to a lost passage from Cicero's *Republic.* LAH-S]

10. See Fabricius, *Bibliotheca Graeca,* bk. 3, ch. 10.

11. Giovanni Andrea Angelini Bontempi, *Historia musica* (Perugia, 1695).

12. Giambattista Martini, *Storia della musica* (Bologna, 1757 and 1770). [The third volume was published in 1781. See the excerpts above. BJB]

13. Jacques Bonnet, *Histoire de la musique, et de ses effets* (Paris, 1715; Amsterdam, 1726). [See the excerpts above. BJB]

14. Charles-Henri Blainville, *Histoire générale, critique et philologique de la musique* (Paris, 1767).

15. Wolfgang Caspar Printz, *Historische Beschreibung der edelen Sing- und Kling-Kunst* (Dresden, 1690).

16. Friedrich Wilhelm Marpurg, *Kritische Einleitung in die Geschichte und Lehrsätze der alten und neuen Musik* (Berlin, 1759).

17. Martin Gerbert, *De cantu et musica sacra a prima ecclesiae aetate usque ad praesens tempus* (Saint-Blaise, 1774).

18. The history of Music by M. Bonnet is written upon a very narrow plan; for the second volume contains nothing more than exclusive eulogiums of Lully, and illiberal censures of every species of Italian music. And though the work of M. de Blainville is nominally a *General History of Music,* yet, notwithstanding the splendid promises in the title, the whole *historical, critical,* and *philosophical* parts of this work are comprised in less than half a thin quarto; the rest of the volume being filled with a treatise of composition. The Musical Dictionary of M. Rousseau, without promising any thing more than an explanation of terms peculiar to the repertory and practice of Music, affords not only more amusement, but more *historical information* relative to the art, than perhaps any book of the size that is extant. [Jean-Jacques Rousseau's *Dictionnaire de musique* was first published in 1768; there are many later editions. BJB]

ever I may respect the learning, and admire the industry and abilities of some of these writers, yet I saw the wants of English musical readers through such a different medium, that I have seldom imitated their arrangements, and never servilely copied their opinions. Printed materials lie open to us all; and as I spared no expense or pains either in acquiring or consulting them, the merely citing the same passages from them, cannot convict me of plagiarism. With respect likewise to manuscript information, and inedited materials from foreign countries, few modern writers have perhaps expended more money and time, undergone greater fatigue, or more impaired their health in the search of them, than myself.

And yet, though all will readily allow, *in general,* that perfection is not to be expected in the works of man; it is evident that, in *particular cases,* little tenderness is shewn to imperfection in the most difficult and laborious undertakings.

If I might presume to hope, however, for any unusual indulgence from the public with respect to this work, it must be from the peculiarity of my circumstances during the time it was in hand; for it may with the utmost truth be said, that it was composed in moments stolen from sleep, from reflection, and from an occupation which required all my attention, during more than twelve hours a day, for a great part of the year.

If it be asked, why I entered on so arduous a task, knowing the disadvantages I must labour under, my answer is, that it was neither with a view to rival others, nor to expose the defects of former attempts, but merely to fill up, as well as I was able, a chasm in English literature. I knew that a history of Music was wanted by my countrymen, and was utterly ignorant that any one else had undertaken to supply it; yet, to confess the truth, I did, at first imagine, though I have been long convinced of my mistake, that, with many years practice and experience in musical matters, some reading, and the possession of a great number of books on the subject, I should have been able to compile such a history as was wanted, at my leisure hours, without great labour or expence.

But, after I had embarked, the further I sailed, the greater seemed my distance from the port: doubts of my own abilities, and respect for the public, abated my confidence; my ideas of what would be required at my hands were enlarged beyond my powers of fulfilling them, especially in the narrow limits of two volumes, and in the little time I had allowed myself, which was made still less by sickness.

A work like this, in which it is necessary to give authorities for every fact that is asserted, advances infinitely slower, with all the diligence that can be bestowed upon it, than one of mere imagination, or one consisting of recent circumstances, within the knowledge and memory of the writer. The difference in point of time and labour is as great as in building a house with scarce materials produced in remote regions of the world, or with bricks made upon the spot, and timber from a neighbouring wood; and I have frequently spent more time in ascertaining a date, or seeking a short, and, in itself, a trivial passage, than would have been requisite to fill many pages with conjecture and declamation.

However, after reading, or at least consulting, an almost innumerable quantity of old and scarce books on the subject, of which the dulness and pedantry were almost petrific, and among which, where I hoped to find the most information, I found but little, and where I expected but little, I was seldom disappointed; at length, wearied and disgusted at the small success of my researches, I shut my books, and began to examine myself as to my musical principles; hoping that the good I had met with in the course of my reading was by this time digested, and incorporated in my own ideas; and that the many years I had spent in practice, theory, and meditation, might entitle me to some freedom of thought, unshackled by the trammels of authority.

Concerning the music of the Greeks and Romans, about which the learned talk so much, it is impossible to speak with certainty; however, the chief part of what I have to say with respect to its theory and practice, is thrown into a *Preliminary Dissertation,* in order that the narrative might not be interrupted by discussions concerning dark and disputable points, which will be generally uninteresting even to musical readers; and in which it is very doubtful, whether I shall be able either to amuse or satisfy the learned.

It is, indeed, with great and almost hopeless diffidence, that I enter upon this part of my work; as I can hardly animate myself with the expectation of succeeding in enquiries which have foiled the most learned men of the two or three last centuries. But it has been remarked by Tartini, in speaking of ancient music, that doubt, difficulty, and obscurity, should not be imputed to the author, but to the subject, since they are in its very essence:[19] for what, besides conjecture, is now left us, concerning things so transient as sound, and so evanescent as taste?

The land of conjecture, however, is so extensive and unappropriated, that every new cultivator has a right to break up fresh ground, or to seize upon any spot that has long lain fallow, without the sanction of a grant from anyone who may arrogate to himself the sovereignty of the whole, or of any neglected part of it. But though no one has an exclusive right to these imaginary regions, yet the public has a just power of censuring the methods of improvement adopted by any new inhabitant, and of condemning such productions as may be deemed unfit for use.

The opinions of mankind seldom agree, concerning the most common and obvious things; and consequently will be still less likely to coincide about

---

19. See the Preface to his *De' principi dell'armonia musicale contenuta nel diatonico genere* (1767), above, Ch. 3. [BJB]

others, that are reducible to no standard of truth or excellence, but are subject to the lawless controul of every individual who shall think fit to condemn them, either with, or without understanding them.

Dr. Johnson has well said, that "those who think they have done much, see but little to do;" and with respect to ancient music, I believe those who have taken the greatest pains to investigate the subject, are least satisfied with the success of their labours.

What the ancient music really was, it is not easy to determine; the whole is now become a matter of faith; but of this we are certain, that it was something with which mankind was extremely delighted: for not only the poets, but the historians and philosophers of the best ages of Greece and Rome, are as diffuse in its praises, as of those arts concerning which sufficient remains are come down to us, to evince the truth of their panegyrics. And so great was the sensibility of the ancient Greeks, and so accentuated and refined their language, that they seem to have been, in both respects, to the rest of the world, what the modern Italians are at present; for of these last, the language itself is music, and their ears are so polished and accustomed to sweet sounds, that they are rendered fastidious judges of melody, both by habit and education.

But as to the superior or inferior degree of excellence in the ancient music, compared with the modern, it is now as impossible to determine, as it is *to hear both sides.*

Indeed it is so entirely lost, that the study of it is become as unprofitable as learning a dead language, in which there are no books; and yet this study has given rise to so much pedantry, and to such an ambition in modern musical authors, to be thought well versed in the writings of the ancients upon music, that their treatises are rendered both disgusting and unintelligible by it. *Words* only are come down to us without *things.* We have so few remains of ancient Music by which to illustrate its rules, that we cannot, as in Painting, Poetry, Sculpture, or Architecture, judge of it, or profit by examples; and to several of these terms which are crammed into our books, we are utterly unable to affix any precise or useful meaning. To write, therefore, in favour of ancient music now, is like the emperor Julian's defending paganism, when mankind had given it up as indefensible, and had attached themselves to another religion.

However, it is, perhaps, a fortunate circumstance for modern music that the ancient is lost, as it might not have suited the genius of our language, and might have tied us down to precedent; as the writers of modern Latin never dare hazard a single thought or expression without classical authority.

The subject itself of ancient music is so dark, and writers concerning it are so discordant in their opinions, that every intelligent reader who finds *how little there is to be known,* has reason to lament that there still remains so much to be said. Indeed, I should have been glad to have waived all discussion about it: for, to say the truth, the study of ancient music is now become the business of an Antiquary more than of a Musician. But in every history of music extant, in other languages, the practice had been so constant for the author to make a display of what he knew, and what he did *not* know concerning ancient music, that it seemed absolutely necessary for me to say something about it, if it were only to prove, that if I have not been more successful in my enquiries than my predecessors, I have not been less diligent. And it appeared likewise necessary, before I attempted a history of ancient Greek music, to endeavour to investigate its properties, or at least to tell the little I knew of it, and ingenuously to confess my ignorance and doubts about the rest.

Indeed it was once my intention to begin my history with the invention of the *present musical scale* and counterpoint; for

What can we reason, but from what we know?[20]

But it was impossible to read a great number of books upon the subject, without meeting with conjectures, and it was not easy to peruse these, without forming others of my own. If those which I have hazarded should throw any light upon the subject, it will enable my readers to travel through the dark maze of enquiry with more facility, and consequently less disgust; and if I fail in my researches, and leave both the subject and them where I found them, as the expectation which I encourage is but small, so it is hoped will be their disappointment. For with respect to all I have to say, I must confess that the Spanish motto, adopted by Francis le Vayer, is wholly applicable.

De las cosas mas seguras
La mas segura es dudar[21]

In wading through innumerable volumes, with promising titles, and submitting to the drudgery *of all such reading as was never read,* I frequently found that those who were most diffuse upon the subject, knew least of the matter; and that technical jargon, and unintelligible pedantry so loaded each page, that not an eligible thought could be found, in exploring thousands of them. Indeed my researches were sometimes so unsuccessful, that I seemed to resemble a wretch in the street, raking the kennels for an old rusty nail. However, the ardour of enquiry was now and then revived by congenial ideas, and by gleams of light emitted from penetration and intelligence; and these will be gratefully acknowledged, whenever they afford assistance.

20. Alexander Pope, *An Essay on Man,* Epistle 1 (1733), 1. 13. [BJB]
21. The most secure of all secure things, is to doubt. [This proverb is quoted at the end of the *Cincq dialogues* of François de La Mothe Le Vayer (1588–1672), a treatise on Christian skepticism. BJB]

There are already more profound books on the subject of ancient, as well as modern Music, than have ever been read; it was time to try to treat it in such a manner as was likely to engage the attention of those that are unable, or unwilling, to read treatises written, for the most part, by persons who were more ambitious of appearing learned themselves, than of making others so. Indeed, I have long since found it necessary to read with caution the splendid assertions of writers concerning music, till I was convinced of their knowledge of the subject; for I have frequently detected ancients as well as moderns, whose fame sets them almost above censure, of utter ignorance in this particular, while they have thought it necessary to *talk about it.* Apuleius, Pausanias, and Athenaeus, among the ancients, were certainly musicians; but it is not so evident that Cicero, Horace, and others, who have interspersed many passages concerning Music in their works, understood the subject any more than our Addison, Pope, and Swift. Among these, the two first have written odes on St. Cecilia's day, in which they manifest the *entire separation* of Music and Poetry, and shew the possibility of writing well on what is neither felt nor understood. For Pope, who received not the least pleasure from Music himself, by the help of his friends, was enabled to describe its power with all the rapture and sublimity of a great genius, *music-mad.* This appears not only in his Ode of St. Cecilia, but in speaking of Handel, in the Dunciad.

Music and its admirers were ever contemned by him and Swift; but, having neither taste nor judgment in this art, they were surely unqualified to censure it. Few conquerors ever aimed at *universal monarchy,* compared with the number of authors who have wished to be thought possessed of *universal knowledge;* and yet these great writers, who discover, in what is within their competence, a vigour of mind, and elevation of genius, which inclines mankind to regard them as beings of a superior order, whenever they hope by the power of thinking to supply the place of knowledge, discover an imbecillity, which degrades them into common characters.

I will not, however, over-rate musical sensations so far as to say, with the poet, that the man who cannot enjoy them "*is fit for treasons, stratagems, and spoils*",[22] there being, perhaps, among mankind, as many persons of bad hearts that are possessed of a love and genius for music, as there are of good, that have neither talents nor feeling for it: but I will venture to say, that it has been admired and cultivated by great and eminent persons at all times and in every country, where arts have been cherished; and though there may be no particular connection between correctness of ear, and rectitude of mind, yet, without the least hyperbole it may be said, that, *caeteris paribus,* the man who is capable of

---

22. Shakespeare, *Merchant of Venice,* V.i.81. [BJB]

being affected by sweet sounds, is a being *more perfectly organized,* than he who is insensible to, or offended by them.

But, as the Constable in Much ado about Nothing says, "these are gifts which God gives,"[23] and lovers of music should be content with their own superior happiness, and not take offence at others for enjoying less pleasure than themselves. However, it is no uncommon thing for the rich to treat the poor with as much insolence, as if it were a crime not to be born to a great estate; yet, on the other hand, to be proud of beggary and want, is too ridiculous for censure.

With respect to the present work, there may, perhaps, be many readers who wish and expect to find in it a deep and well digested treatise on the theory and practice of music: whilst others, less eager after such information, will be seeking for mere amusement in the narrative. I wish it had been in my plan and power fully to satisfy either party; but a history is neither a body of laws, nor a novel. I have blended together theory and practice, facts and explanations, incidents, causes, consequences, conjectures, and confessions of ignorance, just as the subject produced them. Many new materials concerning the art of Music in the remote times of which this volume treats, can hardly be expected. The collecting into one point the most interesting circumstances relative to its practice and professors; its connection with religion; with war; with the stage; with public festivals, and private amusements, have principally employed me: and as the historian of a great and powerful empire marks its limits and resources; its acquisitions and losses; its enemies and allies; I have endeavoured to point out the boundaries of music, and its influence on our passions; its early subservience to poetry, its setting up a separate interest, and afterwards aiming at independence; the heroes who have fought its battles, and the victories they have obtained.

If the titles of my chapters should appear too general and miscellaneous, and the divisions and sections of my work too few; if method and minute exactness in the distribution of its several subjects and parts should seem wanting; the whole is, perhaps, the more likely to be read for these deficiences; for a history, of which the contents are symmetrically digested, separated by chapters, and sub-divided into sections, may be easily consulted, but is no more likely to be read throughout, than a dictionary.

My subject has been so often deformed by unskilful writers, that many readers, even among those who love and understand music, are afraid of it. My wish, therefore, is not to be approached with awe and reverence for my depth and erudition, but to bring on a familiar acquaintance with them, by talking in

---

23. Shakespeare, *Much Ado about Nothing,* III.iv. [BJB]

common language of what has hitherto worn the face of gloom and mystery, and been too much "sicklied o'er with the pale cast of thought;"[24] and though the mixing biographical anecdotes, in order to engage attention, may by some be condemned, as below the dignity of science, yet I would rather be pronounced trivial than tiresome; for Music being, at best, but an amusement, its history merits not, in reading, the labour of intense application, which should be reserved for more grave and important concerns.

I have never, from a vain display of erudition, loaded my page with Greek; on the contrary, unless some disputable point seemed to render it necessary, or the passage was both remarkable and short, I have industriously avoided it, by referring my learned readers to the original text. The modesty of citation may, however, be carried to excess; for quotations of remarkable passages are very amusing and satisfactory to learned readers, and often prevent suspicions of misrepresentation. There is no pedantry in a margin; and the ancients are perhaps never so entertaining as in the fragment way of quotation. As I pretend not to such a profound and critical knowledge in the Greek language as to depend entirely upon myself, in obscure and contested passages, I have, when such occurred, generally had recourse to the labours of the best translators and commentators, or the counsel of a learned friend. And here, in order to satisfy the sentiments of friendship, as well as those of gratitude, I must publicly acknowledge my obligations to the zeal, intelligence, taste, and erudition of the reverend Mr. Twining; a gentleman whose least merit is being perfectly acquainted with every branch of theoretical and practical music.[25]

As ancient Greek Music had its *technical terms,* as well as the modern Italian, with which many excellent scholars and translators from that language, for want of an acquaintance with Music, and Greek musical writers, have been utter strangers, I may venture to observe that I have tried, and I hope not always without success, to trace these terms in ancient authors, in order to discover their original acceptation.

It would be a false, and perhaps offensive modesty, if I were here to trouble the reader with apologies for the length and frequency of quotations from the Iliad and Odyssey, and other ancient poets besides Homer; as it will be shewn, that history has no other materials to work upon in times of high antiquity, than those poems, which have always been regarded as historical; prose compo-

---

24. Shakespeare, *Hamlet,* III.i, Hamlet's soliloquy. [BJB]

25. Thomas Twining (1735–1804); he later published *Aristotle's Treatise on Poetry, Translated: With Notes on the Translation, and on the Original; and Two Dissertations, on Poetical and Musical Imitation* (London, 1789). An excerpt from this work is available in *Music and Aesthetics in the Eighteenth and Early-Nineteenth Centuries,* ed. Peter le Huray and James Day (Cambridge, 1981), 197–208. BJB]

sitions having been utterly unknown in Greece for 300 years after most of them were written.[26]

I have never had recourse to conjecture, when facts were to be found. In the historical and biographical parts, I have asserted nothing without vouchers; and I have made the ancients tell their own story as often as was possible, without disputing with them the knowledge of their own history, as many moderns have done; for I cannot help supposing them to have been full as well acquainted with their own affairs 2,000 years ago, as we are at present. An ancient Greek might, with almost equal propriety, have pretended to foretell what we *should be*, at the distance of 2,000 years, as we determine now what they then *were*.

Indeed it was my intention, when I first entered upon this work, to trace the genealogy of Music in a *right line*, without either meddling with the collateral branches of the family, or violating the reverence of antiquity. I wished and determined to proportion my labour to my powers, and I was unawares seduced into a course of reading and conjecture, upon matters beyond the reach of human ken, by the chief subject of my enquiries being so extensively diffused through all the regions of literature, and all the ages of the world. I found ancient Music so intimately connected with Poetry, Mythology, Government, Manners, and Science in general, that wholly to separate it from them, seemed to me like taking a single figure out of a group, in an historical picture; or a single character out of a drama, of which the propriety depends upon the dialogue and the incidents. If, therefore, a number of figures appear in the background, I hope they will give *relief*, and somewhat keep off the dryness and fatigue which a single subject in a long work, or a single figure, if often repeated, though in different points of view, is apt to produce.

DEFINITIONS

Ancient writers upon science usually began with definitions; and as it is possible that this work may fall into the hands of persons wholly unacquainted with the elements of Music, a few preliminary explanations of such difficulties as are most likely to occur to them, may somewhat facilitate the perusal of the technical parts of my enquiries.

Music is an innocent luxury, unnecessary, indeed, to our existence, but a

---

26. Cadmus Milesius, whom antiquity allowed to have been the inventor of history *in prose*, flourished, according to Sir Isaac Newton, 550 years B.C. and Herodotus, the oldest Greek historian whose writings are preserved, died 484 years before the same aera. [There was some doubt, even in antiquity, that Cadmus existed; few would accept it now. LAH-S]

great improvement and gratification of the sense of hearing. It consists, at present, of *Melody, Time, Consonance, and Dissonance.*

By Melody is implied a series of sounds more fixed, and generally more
lengthened, than those of common speech; arranged with grace, and, with respect to Time, of proportional lengths, such as the mind can easily measure,
and the voice express. These sounds are regulated by a scale, consisting of tones
and semitones; but admit a variety of arrangement as unbounded as imagination.

Consonance is derived from a coincidence of two or more sounds, which
being heard together, by their agreement and union, afford to ears capable of
judging and feeling, a delight of a most grateful kind. The combination and
succession of Concords or Sounds in Consonance, constitute Harmony; as the
selection and texture of Single Sounds produce Melody.

Dissonance is the want of that agreeable union between two or more sounds,
which constitutes Consonance: in musical composition it is occasioned by the
suspension or anticipation of some sound before, or after, it becomes a Concord. It is the Dolce piccante of Music, and operates on the ear as a poignant
sauce on the palate: it is a zest, without which the auditory sense would be as
much cloyed as the appetite, if it had nothing to feed on but sweets.

Of musical tones the most grateful to the ear are such as are produced by the
vocal organ. And, next to singing, the most pleasing kinds are those which approach the nearest to vocal; such as can be sustained, swelled, and diminished,
at pleasure. Of these, the first in rank are such as the most excellent performers
produce from the Violin, Flute, and Hautbois. If it were to be asked what instrument is capable of affording the greatest effects? I should answer, the Organ;
which can not only imitate a number of other instruments, but is so comprehensive as to possess the power of a numerous orchestra. It is, however, very
remote from perfection, as it wants expression, and a more perfect intonation.

With respect to excellence of Style and Composition, it may perhaps be said
that to practised ears the most pleasing Music is such as has the merit of novelty,
added to refinement, and ingenious contrivance; and to the ignorant, such as is
most familiar and common.

Other terms used in Modern Music, as well as those peculiar to the Ancient,
are generally defined, the first time they occur, in the course of the work.

From *A General History of Music from the Earliest Ages to the Present Period. To which is Prefixed
a Dissertation on the Music of the Ancients*, 4 vols. (London, 1776–89); ed. in 2 vols. by Frank
Mercer (New York: Dover Publications, 1957), Preface. Mercer used the second edition of
vol. 1 (1789), followed here; it differs from the first mainly in the rearrangement of material:
Burney moved the definitions to the end of the Preface and incorporated the introduction to
the Dissertation on ancient music.

JOHN HAWKINS
from *A General History of the Science and Practice of Music* (1776)

In the original plan of the foregoing work, it was for reasons, which have yet their weight with the author, determined to continue it no farther than to that period at which it is made to end. It nevertheless appears necessary, on a transient view of the present state of music, to remark on the degree of perfection at which it is at this time arrived; and from such appearances as the general manners of the times, and the uniform disposition of mankind in favour of novelty, to point out, as far as effects can be deduced from causes, the probable changes which hereafter it will be made to undergo; as also those improvements which seem to be but the consequence of that skill in the science to which we have attained.

That we are in possession of a more enlarged theory than that of the ancients will hardly be denied, if the arguments contained in this work, and the opinions and testimonies of the gravest authors are allowed to have any weight; and that we should excel them in our practice seems to be but a necessary consequence; at least the order and course of things, which are ever towards perfection, warrant us in thinking so. Whatever checks are given to the progress of science, or the improvement of manual arts, are accidental and temporary; they do but resemble those natural obstacles that impede the course of a rivulet, which for a short time may occasion a small deviation of its current, but at length are made to yield to its force.

In the comparison of the modern with the ancient music it must evidently appear that that of the present day has the advantage, whether we consider it in theory or practice: the system itself as it is founded in nature, will admit of no variation; consonance and dissonance are the subjects of immutable laws, which when investigated become a rule for all succeeding improvements. Whatever difference is to be found between the modern and ancient musical system, has arisen either from the rejection of those parts of it which the ancients themselves were willing enough to give up, and which as it were by universal consent, have been suffered to grow into disuse; or such additions to it as reason and experience have at different periods enabled men to make. To instance in a few particulars; the enarmonic and chromatic genera, with all the species or colours of the latter, are no longer recognized as essential parts of music; but the diatonic, attempered as it is with a mixture of chromatic intervals, is found to answer the purpose of all three; and the extension of the scale beyond the limits of the bisdiapason is no more than the extended compass of the modern instruments of all kinds naturally leads to. As to the philosophy of sound, or the doctrine of phonics, it appears that the ancients were almost strangers to it: this is a branch of speculative music; and as it results from the modern discoveries in physics, the moderns only are entitled to the merit of its investigation.

With respect to the relations of the marvellous effects of the ancient music, this remark should ever be uppermost in the minds of such as are inclined to credit them, viz., that men are ever disposed to speak of that which administers delight to them in the strongest terms of applause. At this day we extol the excellencies of a favourite singer, or a celebrated performer on an instrument, in all the hyperbolical terms that fancy can suggest; and these we often think too weak to express those genuine feelings of our own which we mean to communicate to others.

It has been asserted by a set of fanciful reasoners, that there is in the course of things a general and perpetual declination from that state of perfection in which the author of nature originally constituted the world; and, to instance in a few particulars, that men are neither so virtuous, so wise, so ingenious, so active, so strong, so big in stature, or so long lived, as they were even long after the transgression of our first parents, and the subsequent contraction of the period of human life: but no one has ever yet insinuated that the vocal organs have participated in this general calamity; or that those mechanic arts to which we owe the invention and perfection of the various kinds of musical instruments, are in a less flourishing state than heretofore: till the contrary can be made appear, it may therefore be fairly presumed that in this respect the moderns have sustained no loss.

Farther, if a comparison be made between the instruments of the ancients and those of the moderns, the advantage will be found to be on the side of the latter: the ancient instruments, excepting those of the pulsatile kind, which in strictness are not to be considered as a musical species, as producing no variety of harmonical intervals, are comprehended under two classes, namely, the Lyre and the Tibia; the former, under all its various modifications, appears to have been extremely deficient in many of those circumstances that contribute to the melioration of sound, and which are common to the meanest instruments of the fidicinal kind; and, notwithstanding all that is said by Bartholinus and others, of the ancient tibia,[1] and the extravagant elogies which we so frequently meet with of the ancient tibicines, we know very well that the tibia was a pipe greatly inferior to the flutes of modern times, which are incapable of being constructed so as not to be out of tune in the judgment of a nice and critical ear; and to these no miraculous effects have ever yet been ascribed. To these two classes

---

1. Casparus Bartholinus, *De tibiis veterum et earum antiquo usu libri tres* (Rome, 1677). [BJB]

of instruments of the ancient Greeks, the Romans are said to have added another, viz., the hydraulic organ, for the use whereof we are as much to seek, as we are for a true idea of its structure and constituent parts.

It is true that the instruments in use among the moderns, in the general division of them, like those of the ancients, are comprehended under the tensile and inflatile kinds; but numberless are the species into which these again are severally divided; to which it may be added, that they have been improving for at least these five hundred years. And now to begin the comparison; the instruments of the viol kind are so constructed as to reverberate and prolong that sound, which, when produced from the Lyre, must be supposed to have been wasted in the open air; the modern flutes, as far as can be judged by a comparison of them with the graphical representations of the ancient Tibiae, have greatly the advantage; and as to pipes of other kinds, such as the Hautboy, the Bassoon, the Chalumeau, and others, these, as having the adjunct of a reed, constitute a species new and original, and are an invention unknown to the ancients.

To the hydraulic organ, said to have been invented by Ctesibus of Alexandria,[2] we have to oppose the modern pneumatic organ; not that rude machine of Saxon construction, a representation whereof is given in page 615 of this work,[3] but such as that noble instrument used in divine worship among us, that of St. Paul's or the Temple church for instance.

Upon a view of the ancient and modern practice of music, and a comparison of one with the other, grounded on the above facts, we cannot but wonder at the credulity of those who give the preference to the former, and lament, as Sir William Temple in good earnest does, that the science of music is wholly lost in the world.[4]

But this is not the whole of the argument: as far as we can yet learn, it is to the moderns that we owe the invention of music in consonance; and were it otherwise, and it could be said that we derive it from the Greeks, the multiplication of harmonical combinations must be supposed to be gradual, and is there-

---

2. Ctesibius of Alexandria (fl. third century B.C.); he was well known in antiquity for various inventions involving air or water pressure, including the hydraulis. [BJB]

3. The illustration, said to be of an organ from the time of King Stephen (1135–54), was taken from the Psalter of Eadwine in Trinity College, Cambridge. [BJB]

4. In his *Essay upon the Ancient and Modern Learning*. [" 'Tis agreed by the Learned, that the Science of Musick so admired of the Ancients is wholly lost in the World, and that what we have now is made up out of certain Notes that fell into the Fancy or Observation of a poor Fryar, in chanting his Mattins. So as those two Divine Excellencies of Musick and Poetry are grown, in a manner, to be little more, but the one Fidling, and the other Rhyming; and are indeed very worthy of the Ignorance of the Fryar, and the Barbarousness of the Goths that have introduced them among us." *The Works of Sir William Temple, Baronet*, 2 vols. (London, 1720), vol. 1, Miscellanea, Part 2, Essay 1, p. 162. BJB]

fore to be ascribed to the moderns; a circumstance that must necessarily give to the music of any period an advantage over that of the age preceding it. Nor is this kind of improvement any thing more than what necessarily results from practice and experience. In the sciences the accumulated discoveries of one age are a foundation for improvement in the next: and in the manual arts it may be said, that those who begin to learn them, in their noviciate often attain that degree of perfection at which their teachers stopped.[5]

This is the natural course and order of things: but how far it is liable to be checked and interrupted may deserve consideration. With respect to music it may be observed, that much of its efficacy is by the vulgar admirers of it attributed to mere novelty; and as these are a very numerous party, it becomes the interest of those who administer to their delight to gratify them, even against the conviction of their own judgments, and to the injury of the art. If novelty will ensure approbation, what artist will labour at intrinsic excellence, or submit his most arduous studies to the censure of those who neither regard, or indeed are able to judge of their merits?[6]

To this disposition we may impute the gradual declination from the practice and example of the ablest proficients in harmony, discoverable in the composi-

5. This observation will be found to be true in many and various instances: as it respects music, it may suffice to say that the young women of this age are finer performers on the harpsichord than the masters of the last; and that there are now many better proficients on the violin under twenty, than there were of double their age fifty years ago.

6. That some persons do not love music is a known fact; and Dr. Willis, the great physician and anatomist, has endeavoured to account for it by his observations on the structure of the human ear; and that the majority of those who frequent musical entertainments have no sense of harmony is no less certain. The want of this sense is no ground for reproach, but the affectation of it in those to whom nature has denied it, is a proper subject for ridicule. If it be asked what is the test of a musical ear, the answer is, a general delight in the harmony of sounds. As to those to whom harmony is offensive, and who yet affect a taste for music, their own declarations are often evidence against them, and in general they will be found to be:

—Such as having no defect in their vocal organs, are unable to articulate even a short series of musical sounds.

—Such as at a musical performance express an uneasiness at the variety and seeming intricacy of the harmony, by a wish that all the instruments played the same tune.

—Such as think the quickest music the best, and call that spirit and fire which is but noise and clamour.

—Such as by the delight they take in the music of French horns, clarinets, and other noisy instruments, discover that the associated ideas of hunting, and the pleasures of the chase are uppermost in their minds.

—Such as think a concert a proper concomitant of a feast.

—Such, as having no scruple to it on the score of their religious profession, complain of cathedral music as being dull and heavy.

—And lastly, such as at the hearing an adagio movement, or any composition of the pathetic kind, the eighth concerto of Corelli, for instance, complain of an inclination to sleep.

[Hawkins probably refers to Thomas Willis, *Cerebri anatome: cui accessit, Nervorum descriptio et usus* (London, 1664). BJB]

tions of the present day, which, as they abound in noise and clamour, are totally void of energy. Music of this kind, constructed without art or elegance, awakens no passion: the general uproar of a modern symphony or overture neither engages attention, nor interrupts conversation; and many persons, in the total absence of thought, flatter themselves that they are merry. To assist this propensity, and as much as possible to banish reflection, the composers of music seem now to act against a fundamental precept of their art, which teaches that variety and novelty are ever to be studied, by reprobating, as they uniformly do, the use of all the keys with the minor third, upon a pretence that they tend to excite melancholy ideas;[7] and by rejecting those grave and solemn measures, which, besides that they correspond with the most delightful of our sensations, form a contrast with those of a different kind. Is this to promote variety, or rather is it not contracting the sources of it? Nor is the structure of their compositions such as can admit of any other than an interchange of little frittered passages and common-place phrases, difficult to execute, and for the most part so rapid in the utterance, that they elude the judgment of the ear; and, without affecting any one passion, or exciting the least curiosity concerning the composer, leave us to wonder at the art of the performer, and to contemplate the languid effects of misapplied industry.

There can be no better test of the comparative merits of the music of the present day, and that which it has taken place of, than the different effects of each. The impression of the former was deep and is lasting: the compositions of Corelli, Handel, Geminiani, yet live in our memories; and those of Purcell, though familiarized by the lapse of near a century, still retain their charms; but who now remembers, or rather does not affect to forget the music that pleased him last year? Musical publications no longer find a place in our libraries; and we are as little solicitous for their fate as for the preservation of almanacs or pamphlets.

That music was intended merely to excite that affection of the mind which we understand by the word mirth, is a notion most illiberal, and worthy only of those vulgar hearers who adopt it. On the contrary, that it is an inexhaustible source of entertainment, or, as Milton finely expresses it, "of sacred and home-felt delight,"[8] is known to all that are skilled in its precepts or susceptible of its

---

7. There is nothing more certain than that those who reason in this manner are ignorant of the structure of the human mind, which is never more delighted than with those images that incline us most to contemplation. Else why do the poets so strenuously labour to awaken the tender passions? Why are the ravings of Lear, or the sorrows of Hamlet made the subjects of public speculation? Such as approve only of mirthful music, to be consistent should proclaim aloud their utter aversion to all theatric representations except comedy, farce, and pantomime, and leave the nobler works of genius for the entertainment of better judges.

8. *A Mask* (*Comus*), l. 262. [BJB]

charms. The passions of grief and joy, and every affection of the human mind, are equally subservient to its call; but rational admirers of the science experience its effects in that tranquillity and complacency which it is calculated to superinduce, and in numberless sensations too delicate for expression.

It is obvious to men of understanding and reflection, that at different periods false notions have prevailed, not only in matters of science, where truth can only be investigated by the improved powers of reason, but in those arts wherein that discriminating faculty, that nameless sense, which, for want of a more proper term to define it by, we call taste, is the sole arbiter. In painting, architecture, and gardening, this truth is most apparent: the love of beauty, symmetry, and elegance, has at times given way to a passion for their contraries; fashion has interposed in subjects with which fashion has nothing to do: nevertheless it may be observed, that while opinion has been veering round to every point, the principles of these arts, as they are founded in nature and experience, have ever remained in a state of permanency.

To apply this reasoning to the subject before us: we have seen the time when music of a kind the least intelligible has been the most approved. Our forefathers of the last century were witnesses to the union of elegance with harmony, and we of this day behold their separation: let us enquire into the reason of this change.

The prevalence of a corrupt taste in music seems to be but the necesary result of that state of civil policy which enables, and that disposition which urges men to assume the character of judges of what they do not understand. The love of pleasure is the offspring of affluence, and, in proportion as riches abound, not to be susceptible of fashionable pleasures is to be the subject of reproach; to avoid which men are led to dissemble, and to affect tastes and propensities that they do not possess; and when the ignorant become the majority, what wonder is it that, instead of borrowing from the judgment of others, they set up opinions of their own; or that those artists, who live but by the favour of the public, should accommodate their studies to their interests, and endeavour to gratify the many rather than the judicious few?

But, notwithstanding these evils, it does not appear that the science itself has sustained any loss; on the contrary, it is certain that the art of combining musical sounds is in general better understood at this time than ever. We may therefore indulge a hope that the sober reflection on the nature of harmony, and its immediate reference to those principles on which all our ideas of beauty, symmetry, order and magnificence are founded; on the infinitely various modifications of which it is capable; its influence on the human affections; and, above all, those nameless delights which the imaginative faculty receives from the artful disposition and succession of concordant sounds, will terminate in a thorough conviction of the vanity and emptiness of that music with which we now are pleased, and produce a change in the public taste, that, whenever it takes place, can hardly fail to be for the better.

From *A General History of the Science and Practice of Music*, 5 vols. (London, 1776; repr. from the London, 1853 ed., New York: Dover, 1963), Conclusion, pp. 917–19. The 1875 edition has been reprinted by Akademische Druck- und Verlagsanstalt (Graz, 1969).

CHARLES DE BROSSES
from *Letter to M. de Maleteste* (1739–40)

Music and Theatrical Performances

No matter what you say, my dear Maleteste, you will not persuade me; and, in our current preoccupation concerning which of the two musics we prefer, we could argue for a whole century without convincing each other. I have, first of all, only to challenge your ability to judge, as I would any Frenchman who attempts to make pronouncements on Italian music without having heard it performed in its native land. The French can no better know what effect *Artaserse*[1] produces in the theater than the Italians can appreciate the effects of *Armide*.[2] I have heard the second and the last act of this French opera sung in Rome at Cardinal Ottoboni's.[3] It was the best they could have chosen among Lully's works; the natives yawned, and we shrugged our shoulders.

Nothing could have been more ridiculous; it was obvious that no singer can perform music other than that of his native country well. The Italian music that we sing in France must seem no less ridiculous there than ours does in Rome; one must be wary of judging it on that basis, and certainly, in order to judge it, almost as much as to sing it, one must be perfectly conversant with the language and enter into the feeling that the words express.

I will add further here what I have always maintained, namely, that an operatic scene may not be separated from the dramatic action that produces a large part of its expression and force, and that it is therefore not suited to chamber concerts.

1. By Hasse, Venice, 1730, or by Leonardo Vinci, Rome, 1730. [EF]
2. By Lully, libretto by Quinault, Paris, 1686. [EF]
3. Pietro Ottoboni (1667–1740), grand nephew of Pope Alexander VIII. A passionate lover of music, and author of opera librettos, he became one of the great Roman patrons of music, sponsoring performances of operas and oratorios with the best musicians available, including Corelli and Alessandro Scarlatti (who set a number of his librettos). [BJB]

In Paris we hear pretty Italian minuets, or grand arias laden with roulades; thereupon, having acknowledged the beauty of the harmony and the melody, we claim that Italian music can do no more than play around over the syllables, and that it lacks the expression that characterizes feeling. This is not at all so; it excels as much as ours, according to the spirit of the language, at conveying and truly expressing feelings in a forceful or touching manner. These simple and moving passages are the ones most admired in their operas; but our French female singers never choose to perform these sorts of arias, because they themselves would not know how to sing them, and they do not feel their power; because, as they are simpler and more lacking in melodies than the others, we would not appreciate them; and because the merit of these bits and pieces torn from a tragedy consists in accuracy of expression, which one cannot feel without being familiar with what has preceded it and with the true situation of the actor.

I found here the other day, at Pagliarini the bookseller's, a treatise on the two musics, written by a Frenchman named Bonnet.[4]

Despite the paradoxes to which he is driven by his stubborn insistence on the simplicity of musical declamation and his desire to maintain that music is not meant to be melodious, one discerns in his book a man of wit and taste, a just admirer of Lully, who nearly always reasons well, as long as French music is the issue.

As soon as he comes to Italian music, there can be nothing more absurd than everything he says; there is not the shadow of truth or the appearance of common sense in it; he cannot bear it! He says the absolute worst about it; he reveals himself in an instant as someone who has never been to Italy, does not know a word of the language, and, what is more, has never heard true Italian arias.

He proposes as the masterpiece of Italian music a certain old tune, supposedly Italian, *Io provo nel cuore un lieto ardore,* fabricated in France, as far as I can judge, and repeated for the past fifty years; this is his point of comparison for judging the rest.

The musician Menicuccio[5] found this book on my table, began to read a few pages, and stood stunned by this height of folly. I took the opportunity to remind him to what extent he himself was unjust in his antipathy for our French music, which he knows scarcely better despite his short stay in France, for Italians are still more unjust in our regard than the greatest partisans of French music could be in theirs.

<hr />

4. Jacques Bonnet, *Histoire de la musique et de ses effets depuis son origine jusqu'à présent* (Paris, 1715); see the excerpt at the beginning of this chapter. [BJB]

5. Nickname of Domenico Ricci (ca. 1700–51), Italian soprano castrato who sang both in the Papal Chapel and in Roman theaters. [BJB]

Nothing can make them reverse their obstinacy against our music; they are so infatuated with their own that they cannot imagine it would be tolerable to hear any other mentioned.

The famous composer Hasse, known as *il Sassone,* nearly choked with anger at me in Venice over a few gentle points I wished to make to him concerning his invincible prejudice. "But," I said to him, "have you heard anything of our music? Do you know what our operas by Lully, Campra, and Destouches are like? Have you glanced at *Hippolyte* by our Rameau?"[6]

"I! no," he replied, "God keep me from ever seeing or hearing any music other than Italian, because no other language can sing, and there can be music only in Italian. Your language is full of harsh syllables, inappropriate for singing and detestable in music. Let no one speak to me of any other language." "But Latin," I said to him, "so noble, so resonant a language, what effect has it had on you? What effect have the Psalms of David, so poetic, so full of lyrical images, had on you? You are not aware that we have a certain Lalande, whose church music surpasses all of your composers in this same genre." And with that, I saw my man nearly suffocate with anger against Lalande and his champions: he was starting to turn chromatic; and if his wife Faustina[7] had not put herself between us, he would have hooked me with a sixteenth note and showered me with sharps.

I have found only Tartini reasonable on this point. Though he has never left Padua, he is well aware that each nation must have its own music, true to the spirit of its language and to the type of voices that the country produces; consequently different from others, and appreciated by foreigners only to the extent that they begin to feel at home in the country itself. The same is also true for comedy, which can be truly amusing only for the people among whom it originates, because each people has its own absurdities as well as its own type of singing, and because one and the other can be truly appreciated only by those to whom they are familiar.

The comedies of Aristophanes and Congreve are suited to making only the Greeks or the English laugh, or at least those who have begun to feel truly conversant with the language and customs of these two peoples. But perhaps singing, as natural as it seems to be to mankind, has something of the ridiculous in it, as do accents and any inflection of the voice that strays from simple speech. No one can hear a foreign song for the first time, whatever it may be, without wanting to laugh; little by little one grows accustomed to it and obtains two kinds of pleasure of the same sort, instead of one. It is a true gain.

6. *Hippolyte et Aricie,* first performed in 1733. [BJB]

7. Faustina Bordoni (1700–81). She was one of the most renowned singers of the age. At the time of her marriage to Hasse in 1730 she had been singing regularly in Italy, Germany, and London for fourteen years, and was still performing in Paris in 1750. [BJB]

The courts of Europe, in which the French language is more frequently spoken than Italian, perform only Italian and never French operas; it is an additional pleasure of which they deprive themselves voluntarily. I see people among us who would have our modern composers *italianize* our music. I have countless reasons for not agreeing with them, among others because I prefer that there be two musics instead of only one.

I would only wish to see Italian opera established in Paris if at the same time we let ours continue as it is. I confess that there would be some danger that the foreign one might harm the national one, especially in a city where novelties are taken up almost to the point of frenzy; the virtuosity and beautiful melodies of the one could make the monotonous simplicity of the other seem insipid: people accustomed to champagne are not moved by a wine from Nuits, although both are good wines of their type. But to give you the opportunity to compare them more at your leisure, here is what I can tell you about theatrical performances in Italy.

Italians have a greater taste for theater than any other nation; and, as they have no less a taste for music, they barely distinguish one from the other, so much so that most often tragedy, comedy, and farce, everything for them is opera. Only in Genoa have I seen spoken tragedies. Simple comedies are more common; but I have seen three operas performed concurrently in Naples, two comedies and one tragedy.[8] There are four in Rome this winter: three tragedies, at the Aliberti theater, the Argentina, and the Capranica, and a charming comedy at the Valle, not to mention the Tordinona,[9] which might not have remained vacant if the impresarios were not afraid that the imminent death of the pope would disrupt them.

This abundance of theatrical music comes, no doubt, from the fact that they have many good composers and very few good dramatic poets. I would have difficulty naming any author of tragedies among them comparable to the second rank of ours. I have read some tragedies in the Greek style, by their ancient authors; I believe they are no longer performed: they seemed tiresome to me. *Merope* by Maffei[10] and some other plays by different poets offer, occasionally, some rather fine scenes, of simplicity and of pathos; but they are often

8. The tragedy was *Partenope*, by Domenico Sarri (mentioned in an earlier letter; he saw it on 4 November 1739); *La Frascatana* (*Amor vuol sofferenza*) by Leonardo Leo (seen before 24 November 1739); the third is not mentioned. [BJB]

9. These were Gaetano Latilla's *Siroe*, Jommelli's *Ricimero re de' Goti*, Giuseppe Scarlatti's *Merope*, and Rinaldo di Capua's *La libertà nociva*. A farce was playing at the Tordinona, *La nuova scuola di Cornelia*. [BJB]

10. Scipione Maffei (1675–1755); his *Merope*, written in 1713, had a wide following and was imitated by Voltaire. [BJB]

trivial and never uplifting. Moreover, as I am not truly conversant with what they have on this subject, I must not say too much about it, any more than about the style of their tragic actors, which I did not like. Perhaps the troupe was not good, and I saw only that one; perhaps it was my fault rather than theirs that they bored me, for I understood the language very little then.

For tragedies in the form of opera, they have an excellent author still living, Metastasio, whose plays are full of wit, intrigue, dramatic turns of events, and of interest, and would no doubt work to great effect if they were played as simple spoken tragedies, leaving aside all the little arietta business and operatic devices, which it would be easy to remove. . . .

The number and grandeur of theaters in Italy is a good indication of the nation's taste for this form of entertainment. Even ordinary cities have theaters more beautiful than those in Paris. In the great cities, like Milan, Naples, Rome, etc., they are truly vast and magnificent, built in a beautiful, noble, and very ornate style of architecture.

The Teatro Reale in Naples is tremendous in size. It has seven tiers of boxes, led into by corridors, and a wide and deep stage, equipped for displaying large scenery in perspective. In Rome, the theater called Alle Dame built by Count Alibert, a French nobleman in the service of Queen Christina, is the largest and is considered the finest; it is there that great tragedy is normally played. The second, the Argentina, squared off at one end and round at the other, is not as big as the former but more compact and holds almost as many people in a smaller space. The Tordinona, more or less the same shape, is also very lovely.

In some theaters they were careful to construct the boxes in the same tier each projecting slightly above the next as you move away from the stage, so that the front ones would not interfere with the view of those furthest back. The spectators are never placed on the stage, neither at the theater nor at the opera; it is only in France that we have this silly habit of taking up a space that is meant only for the actor and for the stage decorations; but in France a great many people go to the theater more for the spectators than for the spectacle.

There are theaters in which they have rigged a platform (the Ringhiera) below and all along the first row of boxes, above the main floor. This device seems to me very clever. The men are seated there, and by standing up during the intermissions, they are able to make conversation with the ladies seated in the boxes. The main floor is full of benches like a church, and people sit there. It is no less chaotic for all that; there is a jangle of claques on behalf of the actors, of applause as long as the favorite of one faction is singing, sometimes even before he begins, of echoes rebounding from the highest boxes, poems tossed or shouted in praise of the singer; in a word, a deafening noise so annoying, so indecent that the first row of boxes becomes uninhabitable. It is abandoned to ladies of questionable virtue, since it is too close to the main floor, which is scarcely populated by any but the rabble, above which the first row is barely elevated.

Persons of quality rent the second, third, and even, if it is crowded, the fourth row of boxes; the higher ones are for the people. It is not the custom here, as it is in France, for the nobility to buy a ticket at the entrance and sit where they wish. They give out tickets only for the main floor at the door, at a very reasonable price, and each person must have his box seat rented for the whole season.

Here and in the major cities, operas begin either in the month of November or toward Christmas and Epiphany, and last until Lent. There are none at all during the rest of the year. The musicians either do nothing then, or gather in small troupes to go to Reggio, to the fair at Alessandria, or to other lesser cities, sometimes even to the country during the fall, when many of the nobility have retired to the countryside, in their nearby villas.

As soon as the theaters open here, the gatherings at the Princess Borghese's, at the home of the Bolognetti, etc. have already ended. The general meeting place is at the opera, which is very long, and lasts from eight or nine o'clock until midnight. The ladies hold *conversazione,* so to speak, in their boxes, where their acquaintances in the audience go to pay short visits. I have told you that everyone must have his rented box. As there are four theaters in which there are performances this winter, we have entered society by renting four boxes, at the price of twenty sequins each for the four. When I arrive, it is as if I were at home. People train their lorgnettes on the crowd in order to distinguish their acquaintances and visit with one another if they wish. The appreciation that these people have for the performance and the music is more apparent in their attendance than in the attention they give it. Once past the first performances, in which silence is rather modest, even on the main floor, it is not fashionable to listen, except in the interesting spots. The principal boxes are properly furnished and lit with candelabra. Sometimes people gamble in them, but more often they chat, seated in a circle about the box; for this is how they sit, and not as in France where the ladies embellish the spectacle by sitting in a row at the front of each box, from which you may conclude that, despite the magnificence of the theaters and the decoration of each box, the view of the whole is infinitely less beautiful than in ours.

I once took it upon myself to play chess with Rochemont, when I found myself almost alone in a box at the Teatro della Valle, at the charming comedy called *La Liberté dangereuse,*[11] which is not very popular but which I found

11. *La libertà nociva,* by Rinaldo di Capua, staged 17 January 1740. De Brosses refers to it again below. [BJB]

much more amusing than their great tragedies. Chess is marvelously useful for filling the void of these long recitatives, and music for interrupting too great an attention to chess.

When the Duke of Saint-Aignan goes to the theater, he practices a form of gallantry that is very well conceived and, from what he says, less costly than it appears. He sends his officials to serve ices and refreshments in all the ladies' boxes.

Italian opera differs greatly from French in the choice of subjects, in the structure of the dramas, and in the number and type of actors, as well as in the way they are hired. It is not, like ours, a stable company, composed of the same people who are replaced as need be. Here an impresario who wishes to stage an opera for the winter obtains the permission of the governor, rents a theater, gathers the voices and instruments from various places, bargains with the workers and the stage designer, and often ends up bankrupting them, much like our provincial theater directors. For greater security, the workers have boxes designated as payment to themselves, which they then rent out at a profit. At each theater two operas are performed per winter, sometimes three, so that we expect to have eight or so during our stay. There are new operas and new singers every year. People do not want to see a play, a ballet, a set, or an actor already seen in a previous year, unless it is some excellent opera of Vinci's, or some very famous singer. When the celebrated Senesino[12] appeared in Naples last fall, they cried: "What's this! Here's a singer we've already heard; his singing will be outdated." His voice is a bit worn; but for my taste, he has the best singing style I have heard.

Here is how they are able to provide so many novelties, both in the dramas and in the voices: once a libretto (*poème lyrique*) is composed, it is common property belonging to everyone; composers are not rare; whoever among them wishes to work takes a libretto already set to music by several others, for which he composes new music to the same words. They choose the operas of Metastasio above all; there are scarcely any upon which the most famous maestros have not worked in turn. This method is both practical and useful; we should make use of it in France, where operas often fail because of the poet, as it is not possible to compose good music to bad lyrics. . . .

Here they do not revise, print, or engrave music; thus only the most famous passages are remembered, and the rest is soon forgotten. Italian composers must nonetheless be astonishingly prolific to work in so many workshops on the same libretto without repeating each other too often. Their facility is no less great; a maestro, from whom the impresario requests an opera, composes it in

12. Francesco Bernardi, called il Senesino, a celebrated alto castrato. He was past his prime by 1739, and ceased singing the next year; he died in 1759. [BJB]

its entirety in a month or six weeks. "Is it surprising," Tartini said to me one day, "that most of the time our recitatives are worthless, since the composer pays attention only to the declamation?" As for me, I forgive them, now that the audience is so much in the habit of not listening to recitative. Tartini complained also about another abuse, which is that the composers of instrumental music try to write vocal music and vice versa. "These two types," he said to me, "are so different that what is suited to one can hardly be suited to the other; each one must stick to what he is talented at. I have," he said, "been asked to work for theaters in Venice, and I have never wanted to, knowing full well that a throat is not the same as the neck of a violin. Vivaldi, who tried to compose in both genres, was always booed in the one, while he was very successful in the other."[13] These composers are badly paid; the impresario gives them thirty or forty pistoles. That is all they earn from it, along with the price of the first copy of the arias, which are expensive when new, but they make nothing more from them once they are public and it is easy to make copies.

I told you that in Italy they simply do not engrave or print any music, either vocal or instrumental. There would be too much to do: concertos, orchestral pieces rain down on them from every side. As for voices, they do not need many. Italian opera is ordinarily composed of only a half dozen characters, without the whole apparatus of choruses, or festive songs and dances that you find in ours. . . .

Italian operas are thus true, completely tragic tragedies, in the style of Corneille and Crébillon; Atreus would not seem too strong a subject to them. The dramas are in three very long acts, with the location of the scene changing two or three times per act, so that they can display a greater number of sets. All the scenes are in recitative, and they normally end in a great aria. The singer exits because he has sung his aria; another stays because he has to sing one; in a word, I find that they do not understand the business of establishing links from one scene to another. In these long acts there are neither trios, nor choruses of voices, except for a poor little chorus at the end of the last act. There are no dances: there are only scenes of endless recitatives, followed by an aria. This monotonous structure is undeniably inferior to ours. I confess that our *fêtes*[14] are often poorly contrived, and not at all convincing for the time and place in which they are set; but then that is the fault of the poet, and not of the poem.

13. Antonio Vivaldi (1678–1741), though greatly admired as a violinist, was quite frequently criticized as a composer; Tartini's attitude was not shared by Goldoni, who reported that Vivaldi's operas were mostly well received. [BJB]

14. In his *Dictionnaire de musique* Rousseau defines a *fête* as "an entertainment of song and dance introduced during the act of an opera, which always interrupts or suspends the action"; *fête* applies particularly to tragedies, *divertissement* to ballets. [BJB]

Another and far more considerable defect of our best tragedies in music is that, when the action of a character has most stirred the soul, the latter is distracted from its emotion because the eyes are taken up with a dance and the ears with a song, each of which forms an entertainment of another sort and chills the emotion, which the main action must then rekindle when it returns to the stage. By trying to bring together too much pleasure all at once, opera weakens the enjoyment of it; thus, along with many pleasant moments, opera, for me, has moments of boredom, unlike good French tragedy in which interest produces its effect without diversion, warmth of feeling is increased gradually, and each act finds the heart warmed from the preceding one.

The partisans of opera will say that one does not go out of interest in the subject, but rather for the accessories of music, spectacle, and dance; this is true, and this too is what makes me prefer comedy and tragedy, because the pleasures of the mind are more intense than those of the eyes and ears. If the Italians thought they were avoiding the drawbacks that I note in our opera by the choice of subject in theirs, and by stripping them of those devices that interrupt the main action, they are very much mistaken. Their librettos (I mean those of Metastasio) are truly admirable and engaging; but the arias tacked on at the ends of scenes, and not always sufficiently linked to the subject—these exquisite arias that make Italian music so far superior to our own—produce the same effect of distraction, by letting interest wane even while they enchant the ears. Given that this defect is a vice intrinsic to librettos, I still prefer the variety of ours to the uniform construction of theirs. . . .

If you are shocked to see the intermissions of a solemn tragedy filled by pantomime ballets, you would be even more so to see it interrupted by interludes. They call these *intermezzi,* little farces in two acts, in the low comic style, a bit like those performed on the boards at the Place royale.

Judge whether such pieces make any sense in the intermissions of a tragedy; but, please, forgive them, for they are a delight, provided the music is perfectly lovely and perfectly well performed; what is ordinary in this genre is no more than trivial and low. These little farces have only two or three comic characters; the music is simple, gay, natural, comic in expression, lively, and laughable in the extreme. I wish that you could hear the husband imitating his wife who is losing all her money at faro, the regrets of a poor devil about to be hanged, or some duet depicting a bizarre quarrel, or a reconciliation between a lover and his mistress; nothing in the world could be more amusing. Add to this the realistic manner in which it is treated by the musician and portrayed by the singer, and the singular precision of the performance. These comic characters cry, laugh heartily, exert themselves, and do all sorts of pantomime, without ever straying from the tempo by an eighth of a second. I confess that these sorts of pieces, when they are like *Il maestro di musica* of Scarlatti, *La serva padrona*, and *Livietta e Tracollo* by the charming Pergolesi,[15] give me greater pleasure than all the others. The bluestockings in this country, who admire only serious operas, tease me for having lost my head over them. But I persist in my opinion that the less serious the genre, the more successful Italian music is at it. Indeed, it seems to exude gaiety, and to be in its element. I also like their comic operas in which serious and comic roles are combined. A lovely one by Rinaldo di Capua was performed at the Valle theater,[16] and I saw a charming one by Leonardo Leo in Naples.[17] I do not think we could succeed at making music funny, although we have excellent comedies of a slightly more elevated sort, witness the *Fêtes vénitiennes,*[18] in which the tone is truly comic, and, please God, may there often be ones like it! . . .

To summarize in a word the unprecedented length of this dissertation to which your letter has driven me, well beyond my expectation and yours, Italian music is certainly superior to ours; but our opera is equal to theirs, all things considered, if only because it would be easier for their opera to take on the form of ours than it would be for French singing to take on the brilliant character and the pleasing features of Italian song.

From Charles de Brosses, *Lettres familières,* ed. Giuseppina Cafasso and Letizia Norci Cagiano de Azevedo, 3 vols. (Naples: Centre Jean Bérard, 1991), vol. 2, Letter 51, pp. 979–84, 987–91, 992–93, 997–99, 1012–13, 1018. Some of the notes are taken from this edition. Portions of this and another letter are translated in *Readings in the History of Music in Performance,* ed. Carol MacClintock (Bloomington and London: Indiana University Press, 1979), 268–87, 360–63.

15. *Il maestro di musica,* formerly thought to be by Pergolesi, is listed as spurious in the *New Grove* on the grounds that it is mostly a pasticcio of Pietro Auletta's *Orazio* (Naples, 1737); the first performance was at Paris in 1752; a French version was performed in 1755. *La serva padrona* was first performed in Naples in 1733; *Livietta e Tracollo* (an alternative title for *La contadina astuta*) was given in Rome in 1737. [BJB]

16. The dramma giocoso *La libertà nociva,* performed on 17 January 1740; de Brosses refers to it earlier in the letter. Rinaldo di Capua (ca. 1705–ca. 1780) was at the beginning of his fame in Rome when de Brosses heard him. [BJB]

17. See n. 8. [BJB]

18. An *opéra-ballet* by André Campra, first performed at the Opéra on 17 June 1710 and frequently given thereafter. Part of the humour consisted in the quotations from well-known operas by Marais (the tempest from *Alcione*), Destouches (the *sommeil* from *Issé*), and Lully (two entrées from *Atys*). [BJB]

SAMUEL SHARP
from *Letters from Italy* (1767)

Naples, Nov. 1765

Sir,

A stranger, upon his arrival in so large and celebrated a city as *Naples*, generally makes the publick spectacles his first pursuit. These consist of the King's Theatre, where the serious Opera is performed, and of two smaller theatres, called *Theatro Nuovo*, and the *Theatro dei Fiorentini*, where they exhibit burlettas only. There is also a little dirty kind of a play-house, where they perform a comedy every night, though the Drama has so little encouragement at *Naples*, that their comedies are seldom frequented by any of the gentry, but seem to be chiefly an amusement for the populace, at least, that class of people just above the populace: However, I shall not fail to describe the present state of that stage, after having spoken of their Opera-houses.

The King's Theatre, upon the first view, is, perhaps, almost as remarkable an object as any a man sees in his travels: I not only speak from my own feeling, but the declaration of every foreigner here. The amazing extent of the stage, with the prodigious circumference of the boxes, and height of the cieling, produce a marvellous effect on the mind, for a few moments; but the instant the Opera opens, a spectator laments this striking sight. He immediately perceives this structure does not gratify the ear, how much soever it may the eye. The voices are drowned in this immensity of space, and even the orchestra itself, though a numerous band, lies under a disadvantage: It is true, some of the first singers may be heard, yet, upon the whole, it must be admitted, that the house is better contrived to see, than to hear an Opera.

There are some who contend, that the singers might be very well heard, if the audience were more silent; but it is so much the fashion at *Naples*, and, indeed, through all *Italy*, to consider the Opera as a place of rendezvous and visiting, that they do not seem in the least to attend to the musick, but laugh and talk through the whole performance, without any restraint; and, it may be imagined, that an assembly of so many hundreds conversing together so loudly, must entirely cover the voices of the singers. I was prepossessed of this custom before I left *England*, but had no idea it was carried to such an extreme. I had been informed, that though the *Italians* indulged this humour in some degree, yet, when a favourite song was singing, or the King was present, they observed a deep silence: I must, however, deny the fact in both cases, from what I have seen,[1] though, possibly, they may have paid more regard to some songs, than to those I heard; and, probably, the audience may have shewn to Don *Carlos,* King of *Naples,* more respect than they do to his son, a youth of fifteen. . . .

Sir,   *Naples, Nov. 1765*

Notwithstanding the amazing noisiness of the audience, during the whole performance of the Opera, the moment the dances begin, there is a universal dead silence, which continues so long as the dances continue. Witty people, therefore, never fail to tell me, the *Neapolitans* go to *see,* not to *hear* an Opera. A stranger, who has a little compassion in his breast, feels for the poor singers, who are treated with so much indifference and contempt: He almost wonders that they can submit to so gross an affront; and I find, by their own confession, that however accustomed they be to it, the mortification is always dreadful, and they are eager to declare how happy they are when they sing in a country where more attention is paid to their talents.

One would suppose, from the regard shewn to the dances, that a superior excellence should be expected in this art; but *Naples* does not at present, afford any very capital performers, nor do the dances which have been brought on the stage this season, reflect much honour on their taste. They are, in general, exceedingly tedious, some lasting thirty-five minutes, and others twenty-five, with incidents and characters too vulgar and buffoonish; but it must be confessed that their scenery is extremely fine; their dresses are new and rich; and the musick is well adapted; but, above all, the stage is so large and noble, as to set off the performance to an inexpressible advantage.

The *Neapolitan* quality rarely dine or sup with one another, and many of them hardly ever visit, but at the Opera; on this account they seldom absent themselves, though the Opera be played three nights successively, and it be the same Opera, without any change, during ten or twelve weeks. . . .

Sir,   *Naples, Nov. 1765*

I propose, in this letter, to give you a description of the great Opera-House; and as all the *Italian* theatres are built on the same plan, diff'ring

1. The opera he saw at San Carlo was *Il Creso,* by Antonio Sacchini. [BJB]

only in the number of boxes, I desire you will consider it as a specimen of the others, tho' the Pit is indeed a little particular; for the seats have elbows, which circumstance, I believe, is peculiar to this one Theatre.

The Pit here, as I have already hinted, is very ample; it contains betwixt five and six hundred seats, with arms resembling a large elbow chair, besides an interval all through the middle, and a circuit all round it, under the boxes, both of which I judge, in a crowded house, will hold betwixt one and two hundred people standing. The seat of each chair lifts up like the lid of a box, and has a lock to fasten it. There are, in *Naples,* Gentlemen enough to hire by the year the first four rows next to the orchestra; who take the key of the chair home with them, when the Opera is finished, lifting up the seat, and leaving it locked. By this contrivance, they are always sure of the same place, at whatever hour they please to go to the Opera; nor do they disturb the audience, though it be in the middle of a scene, as the intervals betwixt the rows are wide enough to admit a lusty man to walk to his chair, without obliging any body to rise. The usual payment for the seasons, or the whole year, in which they give four operas, is twenty ducats, about three pounds fifteen shillings; the people who do not hire their seats by the year, pay three carlines, about thirteen pence halfpenny, for their place in the pit.

The boxes are not disposed like ours, into front and side boxes, but into six ranges, one above another, all round the house: The three lower ranges are hired either for the season, or the whole year, by the Ladies of distinction: The price of a box for the whole year, is two hundred and forty ducats, equal to about forty-six or forty-seven pounds sterling. The price of a season is proportioned to the length of the season: The other three ranges are let by the night; but no man or woman can go into the boxes, paying only for one person, as in *France* and *England.* Strangers who come to *Naples* for a short time, if they are either people of figure, or well recommended, are invited into the boxes of the nobility; if they are not, they hire a box for the night, and seldom fail to find one in the second or third range, for, should it happen that they are all taken up for the season by persons of quality, yet some of these persons of quality are not so delicate, but that they order the undertaker of the opera to let out their boxes when they do not go themselves, and often stay at home purposely on *gala* nights, and at the opening of a new opera, when, sometimes, they are hired for the night at an exorbitant price, such as fifteen ducats, and sometimes much more. . . .

Sir,   *Naples, Dec. 1765*

It is the custom in *Italy* to light the stage only, which renders their spectacles frightfully dark and melancholy. They pretend it is an advantage to the performers and the stage; and so far is true, that if there must be only such a small quantity of light in the house, it is much better to place it on the stage, than on any other part, but on *gala* nights, when it is illuminated in every part, the *Italians* seem as much pleased with it as a stranger, so that I imagine it is to save the expence of so many wax tapers, that the custom is continued. These tapers are almost as big as small torches, and are disposed very unartfully against the sides of the boxes, as high as the fourth range; so that the glare, the heat, and the smell of them, are very offensive to those who sit in the boxes, on which account, it is not unusual, on the *gala* nights, when the King is not there, to see the people in the boxes extinguish several of them. When his Majesty is present, they do not take that liberty; but if, instead of these tapers, there were a sufficiency of lustres hanging over the pit, the purpose would be answered without the least annoyance.

Dark as the boxes are, they would be still darker, if those who sit in them did not, at their own expence, put up a couple of candles, without which it would be impossible to read the opera; yet there are some so frugal, as not to light up their box, though the instances are rare. It is not the fashion here, nor to the best of my remembrance, in any part of *Italy,* to take a small wax light to the house, and, therefore, hardly any man has eyes good enough to make use of a book in the pit. . . .

The performers are not paid so liberally at *Naples* as at *London,* but considering the different expence of living in the two places, the proportion is not very short amongst the capital singers, as may be gathered from the salary of *La Gabrieli,*[2] who received for singing the last year eighteen hundred sequins, (nine hundred pounds sterling) and has contracted for the same sum, the ensuing year. *Aprile,*[3] the first man, has

---

2. Francesca Gabrielli (b. ca. 1735), who was probably the sister of the more famous Caterina Gabrielli, sang as seconda donna in the production Sharp saw. However, the Gabrielli to whom he refers is Caterina (1730–96), who had taken the 1765–66 season off to sample private life with a nobleman. The prima donna in *Il Creso* was Antonia Maria Girelli Aguilar. [BJB]

3. Giuseppe Aprile (1732–1813). A soprano castrato, he began singing opera in 1752; from 1756 to 1769 he was at the court of Württemberg in Stuttgart, where Jommelli was Kapellmeister, but he spent the 1765–66 season in Naples and Palermo. After retiring in 1785 he turned to teaching, numbering among his pupils Domenico Cimarosa and Lady Catherine Hamilton; his book of vocal exercises, *The Modern Italian Method of Singing, with a Variety of Progressive Examples and Thirty-six Solfeggi* (London, 1791), was very popular. [BJB]

three thousand five hundred ducats. *Genaro,*[4] the first dancer amongst the men, has two thousand ducats, and *La Morelli,*[5] the first woman dancer, one thousand five hundred ducats. A ducat is worth about three shillings and ten pence.

The impressario, or manager, is bound to very bad terms, so that his profits are inconsiderable, and sometimes he is a loser. The theatre being a part of the palace, the King reserves for himself, his Officers of State, and Train, fifteen boxes; nor does the King (or rather the Regency) pay the manager one farthing, whereas the late King used to present him annually four thousand ducats. The junto deputed by his Majesty to supervise the Opera, reserve to themselves the right of nominating singers and dancers, which obliges the manager sometimes to pay them an exorbitant price. Another disadvantage he lies under is, the frequent delay of payment for the boxes, and a manager must not take the liberty to compel persons of quality to pay their just debts.

You will wonder how I became possessed of these particulars; accident threw them in my way, and you may depend on their authenticity.

The two burletta Opera Houses are not in much request, except when they happen to procure some favourite composition, the grand Opera being the only object of the *Neapolitans,* which, indeed, has such preeminent encouragement, that the others are forbidden, by authority, to bring any dancers on their stage, without a special licence, lest they should divert the attention of the public from the King's Theatre. . . .

From *Letters from Italy, Describing the Customs and Manners of that Country in the Years 1765 and 1766,* 3d ed. (London: Henry and Cave, 1767), Letters 19–22.

4. Gennaro Magri, the famed Neapolitan dancer and choreographer, author of the most important eighteenth-century treatise on dance technique, *Trattato teorico-prattico di ballo* (Naples, 1779). There is an English translation by Mary Skeaping, Annalisa Fox, and Irmgard E. Berry, *Theoretical and Practical Treatise on Dancing* (London: Dance Books, 1988). [BJB]

5. It is not certain which Morelli—a large dancing family—Sharp intends, but the most likely is Margherita, who was prima ballerina at many important Italian theaters during the 1760s and 70s. [KKH]

GIUSEPPE BARETTI
from *An Account of the Manners
and Customs of Italy* (1768)

. . . Mr. Sharp, whose tenderness of bowels is certainly greater than his power of investigation, appears very much concerned at our considering the opera *as a place of rendezvous and visiting,* rather than as a temple sacred to the awful deities of harmony and melody; and he is almost angry with us, because *we do not seem in the least to attend to the music, but laugh and talk through the whole performance without any restraint, so that we cover intirely the voices of the singers by our conversing so loudly together.* . . .

What a deal of wisdom lavished on so trifling a subject as that of an Italian opera! But see how shamefully poor strangers are imposed upon by these naughty writers of travels? Poor Mr. Sharp had been made to believe, that the grave Italians observed *due silence* at an opera when a favourite song was sung, or a king was present; and none of the two facts proves true! Who will ever give credit hereafter to such story-tellers! However, thank our stars, a more accurate observer of Italian customs and manners has at last visited that distant region; is gone to the opera at Naples; has found to his great astonishment that two facts of so infinite importance have been grossly misrepresented; has denied them of course; and has thus rendered Old England much wiser than it was before his great discovery. . . .

But let me not lose sight of Mr. Sharp's account of our opera's and opera-matters. In his usual affecting strain he says, that *a stranger who has a little compassion in his breast, feels for the poor singers, who are treated with so much indifference and contempt by the Italians, as not to be listened to when they sing on the stage.*

The musicians are indeed very unlucky to meet nothing but contempt in a profession, in which they take refuge, and for which they quit trade and manufactures merely to avoid such treatment! But what an abominable people are the gentry of Italy! Oh the barbarians who do not feel for their poor singers! How can they be so utterly deprived of that virtue, which is the characteristic of true Christians, of the English in general, and of Mr. Sharp in particular! And how can the Italian singers *submit to so gross an affront, and to so dreadful a mortification,* as Mr. Sharp expresses it in his usual pathos and true sublime!

But, Sir, you must excuse me for my laughing at these dismal accounts of our customs and manners. If singing was bread and cheese to the Italians, and if they trampled madly upon their bread and cheese, you could not express their madness in more energetic terms. But singing is only a diversion, and attended to with no more seriousness than a diversion deserves. I have told you already, that we have so great a plenty of music in Italy as to have very good reason to hold it cheap; and every sensible Englishman must wonder at your wonderful wonder on such trifling occasions, and at your solemnity of scolding, as if we were committing murder when we are talkative in the pit, or form ourselves into card-parties in our boxes. Our singers then, though we be unwilling to listen, would be very impertinent, if they did not sing their best, since they are very well paid for so doing; and Caffarello was soon taught better manners when he took it into his head not to do his duty upon the stage of Turin on pretence that the audience was not attentive to his singing. He was taken to jail in his Macedonian accoutrements for several nights as soon as the opera was over; and brought from the jail to the stage every evening, until by repeated efforts he deserved universal acclamation.[1]

Mr. Sharp wonders also, that *it is not the fashion in Italy, as it is in England, to take a small wax-light to the opera, in order to read the book.* A very acute remark as usual; to which I have nothing to say, but the Italians are not so good-natured as the English, who have patience enough to run carefully over a stupid piece of nonsense while a silly eunuch is mincing a vowel into a thousand invisible particles. When we are at the opera, we consider those fellows in the lump as one of the many things that induced us to be there; and we pay the same attention to their singing which we pay to other parts of that diversion. We fix our eyes, for instance, a moment or two on the scenes and the dresses, when they happen to be new and superlatively well imagined: and our singers would be very ridiculous indeed, if to their customary impudence they added that of pretending to much more regard than what we pay to the pencil of an ingenious scene-painter, or even to the elegance of a fanciful taylor. Our gentlemen then, as well as those of London, have the ladies to look at; and the ladies, we will suppose, have that of looking at the gentlemen, or at one another's cloaths and head-dresses; and having their hands thus full, besides the affair still more important of laughing and talking, what need have they to look in the book? And then, if the opera is not one of those composed by Metastasio, we know certainly beforehand, that it is some composition full as witty as the *Lavinia's* and *Catarat-taco's* of our famed Bottarelli;[2] or if the opera is Metastasio's, we know likewise for certain beforehand, that it is as perfectly butchered by the opera-poet, as those that are exhibited in the Haymarket. Let any of the two be the case, would

1. Also known as Caffarelli (1710–83; his original name was Gaetano Majorano). He was a mezzo-soprano castrato who enjoyed fame and notoriety throughout Italy and in England, France, Portugal, and Spain. Hot-tempered and at times violent, he once engaged in a duel with the French poet Ballot de Sauvot over the merits of Italian and French music. [BJB]

2. Giovanni Gualberto Bottarelli (fl. 1762–79), an Italian librettist active at the King's Theatre in London. [BJB]

we not be supremely ridiculous to pore for some hours over an opera-book with a small wax-light in our hands?[3]

From *An Account of the Manners and Customs of Italy; with Observations on the Mistakes of some Travellers with Regard to that Country,* 2 vols. (London: T. Davies, 1768), 1:302–4, 309–13 (from Ch. 17, Present State of Music in Italy).

JOHANN NIKOLAUS FORKEL
from *General History of Music* (1788)

INTRODUCTION

§ 1

The different forms in which music appears in its history over several millennia among ancient and modern peoples cannot be correctly surveyed and evaluated without a precise notion of their gradual development, from the first basic elements to the highest and most perfect union of all parts in a complete whole. In its first epochs—among the first peoples on earth—music appeared as if in its childhood: only the first and simplest elements can be observed. During the following periods, among somewhat more civilized nations, to these first few elements some new ones were added, but without any significant advance toward the perfection of the whole. Finally, among yet later and more cultivated peoples the increase in individual parts may be more or less considerable. Still, there may be no one nation that unites the totality of individual elements pertaining to the whole and thus presents a picture of the highest perfection of the art. How should it be possible, then, to judge correctly all these differences, which arise not only from a smaller or larger number of individual parts, but also from the influence of different climates, the social conditions, the manner of living, the moral sense, and other cultural values of the nations, without knowing how the inner nature of art was necessarily constituted, in its childhood as well as in every stage of its development, and without a standard by which its state among these various nations may be at least roughly determined? This standard must consist in the correct conception of music as a whole.

3. In his response to Baretti, *A View of the Customs, Manners, Drama, &c. of Italy, as they are described in the Frusta Letteraria; and in the Account of Italy in English, written by Mr. Baretti: compared with the Letters from Italy, written by Mr. Sharp* (London: W. Nicoll, 1768), Sharp remarks: "This last sentence may serve to justify Mr. Sharp against the reproaches of Mr. Baretti, for his silence with regard to Metastasio in his account of operas and opera-houses" (pp. 55–56). [BJB]

Arts and sciences grow to perfection, like all creations of nature, only step by step. The expanse between the first beginning and highest perfection is filled with such diverse intermediate creations that not only are the progressive steps from simple to complex and from small to large discernible everywhere, but every link in the succession may be observed as a whole as well. Thus sciences and arts resemble polyps, whose hundred severed limbs all live by themselves and appear to be complete polyps, but smaller ones.

Thus a picture that comprehends the gradual progression of music from its first beginning to the highest perfection, faithfully tracing the path the human mind pursues in developing its capabilities in general—and our art in particular—appears to be the best means to enable the reader to assess all the possible differences in which this art appears in all nations known to us, and to determine, at least not entirely without a basis, when and where it had, or was capable of having, true intrinsic worth. For a number of reasons, drawing such a picture is beset with many difficulties. First, the various features are scattered throughout nature and may be assembled only with great effort. Second, even once they have been collected successfully, they are not easily joined in a whole. Finally, it is not enough to discover from ancient and modern historical writers what these individual features were and are; one also has to be a theorist, critic, even a moralist to be able to demonstrate what they must have been. The painter of such a picture is thus compelled to proceed like Apelles, who, in order to paint a perfect Venus, combined the most beautiful features of several beautiful women in a single image. Nature, as in all her works, has scattered only single beauties in music as well. It is the task of man to seek them out and, by an apposite arrangement, to produce new and more perfect creations than Nature herself.

§ 2

The surest guide in this investigation may be offered by the similarity traceable between man's language and his music, which reaches back not only to their origins but extends throughout their complete development from their beginning to their highest perfection. In its origin, music, just like language, is nothing but the vehement tonal expression of a feeling. Both spring from a common source: sensation (*Empfindung*).[1] Although they separated subsequently, each in its own way grew into what it was capable of becoming—one the language of the mind, the other the language of the heart—and yet both retained so many

---

1. *Empfindung*, a term Forkel uses throughout the Introduction, carries two primary meanings, best expressed in different English terms: sensation or sensory perception, and feeling or emotion. When Forkel uses *Empfindung* in the active, physical sense, it has been translated as "sensation"; the response it evokes has usually been translated as "emotion" or "feeling," sometimes as "sensibility." [BJB]

characteristics of their common ancestry that even at their greatest distance they still speak in similar manner to mind and heart. The derivation and multiplication of expressions from the first utterances of sensation, their construction and composition, which are not only designed to awaken emotions or concepts, but also to awaken and communicate them unequivocally: in short, all the attributes that make the one the consummate language of the mind likewise make the other the consummate language of the heart. Thus, whoever discerns the nature of one may easily be led to a correct and complete understanding of the other through recognition of the similarity governing the two. This preliminary statement about likenesses in the structure of our emotional and conceptual language[2] will find greater confirmation in the course of this Introduction, when such similarities will be pointed out at the appropriate time and place, and the reasons and causes of this relation demonstrated.

The First Age of Music

§ 3

Although tone—or rather, in this context, sound—is only the medium through which music becomes audible, it is taken mostly as the thing itself by nations still immature and uncultivated. Each individual sound is assumed to be music. When one considers mere sound in all its modifications (for instance, loud, soft, sharp and rough, gentle, dark, muffled, thick, thin, and so forth) and, furthermore, how it is able through these many different modifications to

---

2. In his *Dell'origine e delle regole della musica colla storia del suo progresso* (Rome, 1774), Eximeno made a similar comparison, but from another viewpoint than the one taken in the present work, as will become clear. True, he assumes that music is a real language, but seeks this resemblance not in the similar derivation and composition of its means of expression, in a word not in the inner nature of the art, but purely in externals, that is to say in prosody. In consequence, he does not advance his comparison beyond the first utterances of sensation, and thinks that from them alone, as they were gradually linked to prosody, music was born and developed. This is of course very shallow; but a man who like Eximeno had studied music for only four years when he published his book was in no position to penetrate more deeply into its true nature. [For Eximeno, see also the excerpt in Ch. 9. BJB]

This relationship was understood far better by a Spaniard, Francisco Salinas, who in the preface to his *De musica* writes: "They [grammar and music] are from their very beginnings so similar that they are thought to have been not merely sisters, but almost twins. For as grammar starts out with letters, from which it takes its name, then strives, by way of the syllables formed from combinations of letters and the words formed from groups of syllables, to attain to achieving a complete act of speech; so music, which is named for the Muses, to whom antiquity ascribed every kind of expertise in performance, completes and composes a melody or song from sounds, and intervals formed from combinations of sounds, and consonances formed from groups of intervals." Salinas was Professor of Music at Salamanca; his work was published in 1577.

affect the ear, and, consequently, human sensibility,[3] then it is less surprising that the pleasure it may occasion by itself alone can come to be regarded as a pleasure that derives from real music. Man, in the first stage of his development, is only a passive being; his soul has not yet been made active. Sensual impressions are the only ones he can receive, and he has not yet developed the capability of being affected by other impressions that require the mind to make comparisons and then to draw pleasure from the observation of a relation or a symmetry. These sensual impressions need to be all the stronger and more overpowering, the less the mind is educated to deal with them.

This explains why we find in all savage and uncivilized nations such great pleasure in the sounds made by noisy instruments such as drums, rattles, and blaring trumpets, as well as very loud and barbaric shouting. Nature has created a direct connection between man's heart and his hearing; all passions communicate themselves through their own peculiar tones, which evoke in the heart of those who perceive them the same passionate sensation that set these tones in motion.[4] This immediate perception between tone, ear, and heart is the same in all peoples, whether the most primitive or the most cultivated, with one difference: the more primitive a people is, and the more it perceives only sensually without being capable of intellectual reflection, the more vivid the sensations are and the means to awaken them. Thus, mere tone, seen by itself only as an expression of passions, has to be, at this stage of development, rough and strong, corresponding in every way to the strength of the means required to awaken the sensation. . . .

§ 5

Before a people reaches this point, that is, learns to associate ideas and concepts with the sensations of the tones, it must first have simply sensed them for centuries. Even then, when it begins to associate ideas and concepts with sensations, for a long time these ideas are so imperfect and limited that their influence on a development of any kind remains unnoticed for almost an equally long time. Long experience and practice are necessary to associate sensations and concepts

---

3. The cause of enjoyment or dislike of sounds made by living beings or inanimate objects is inherent in their relationship to the auditory nerves. Sounds or voices of living beings are expressions of their different states of mind and consequently draw another cause of enjoyment or dislike through sympathy. S. Tiedemann, "Aphorismen über die Empfindnisse," in *Das deutsche Museum* (December 1777).

4. J. G. Sulzer, art. "Musik" in *Allgemeine Theorie der schönen Künste* (Leipzig, 1771–74), and Cicero, *De oratore*, bk. 3 [section 216]: "For every emotion has naturally its own facial expression, and sound, and gesture; and one's whole body, and one's entire expression, and all one's utterances, like the strings of a lyre, sound according as each emotion strikes them."

in the way found among more developed peoples. This can best be observed in the case of all those unfamiliar phenomena that are encountered for the first time. It is thus undeniable, and history proves it, that entire populations have been able to love and practice music for centuries without becoming aware of the elementary differences perceptible between tones. If a man acquires ideas and concepts only through a civic constitution, if the body loses strength and harshness only as the mind gains in ideas, then of necessity not only can one imagine this man only as existing in civic circumstances but as having existed in these circumstances for a considerable time before one can assume that the gently warbling tone of a nightingale will appeal more to him, or rather, will have made a more pleasant impression on his sense of hearing than the loud roaring or shrieking sounds of his own throat or that of his fellow man. Therefore, the very first music of all rude and uncultivated nations was nothing more than sound and noise, without any regard to the infinite variations in sound.

§ 6

However, it might be asked, how could such noise delight whole peoples for centuries? If nothing were added to this noise to render it more enjoyable or even pleasant for the duration, it would indeed be incomprehensible, and insufferably monotonous even for the most rude and uncivilized people. However, in the first stage of his development, man soon noticed that all simple things became more enjoyable through being repeated in a regular manner. Such regular repetition of simple things that in themselves are incapable of variety we call in music "measure," or by its original term, rhythm. A tone in itself is expression of a sensation; and sensation follows the laws of motion, because it itself is a motion. Consequently, the sensation stirred by a simple tone, if it is to be enjoyable, must be renewed through motion or repetition from time to time in accordance with a certain pattern. The degree of enjoyment provided by such rhythmic repetition of simple tones—whose monotony otherwise would soon be tiring—may be judged from the use made, even in more modern times, of our drums. By the variety of rhythmic beats alone, not only is the movement of marching facilitated, determining the speed or slowness of steps, but it may also give rise to feelings of bravery and courage in the heart of those men for whom this martial and solely rhythmic music originally was intended. An exhaustive treatment of the causes of these effects of rhythm will be found in Sulzer's dictionary under "Rhythmus,"[5] to which I refer the reader in order to avoid digression. Thus, one may not only suppose this effect of rhythm to be certain and undeniable, but also be convinced that all half-savage, half-

5. See the work cited in n. 4. [BJB]

cultivated peoples introduced variety and interest into their first music (that is, their simple sounds and noises) only thus, not by modifying the tones themselves. Their instruments—drums, clappers, rattles, etc.—are excellent proof; without the aid of rhythmic movement and variety, only a monotony wearisome and for that very reason unbearable even for the most primitive peoples could have been produced from them. . . .

§ 8

It cannot be determined exactly for how long a people can maintain this crude state of music. Today we find it among many Asian, African, and American peoples; and we know that for centuries they have made no progress in other branches of culture as well.

As ugly as this crude and barbaric music is in itself, it is still useful to those uncivilized peoples for their amusement and entertainment of various sorts. They use it, together with dance, not only for domestic and social pastimes, but also for celebrations, religious ceremonies, and in war. Yet, with all of these different applications, the music is always the same deafening and shattering noise, and the people love it all the more the less their minds engage or are capable of engaging with it.

THE SECOND AGE OF MUSIC
§ 9

The similarity discernible in more than one respect between sensations and thoughts had of necessity to cause man, as his intellect grew, not only to increase the expressions of both his thoughts and his feelings, but also to adapt them, little by little and always more precisely, to the different and particular manner in which both commonly express themselves. Up to this point, his articulations of speech were nothing but interjections and simple words with which he designated the external objects in his immediate surroundings. With repeated experience in observing these objects, he gradually discovered ever newer sides and new characteristics that distinguished them from other objects of the same kind, and for which the simple words he possessed no longer sufficed as description. The exclamations evoked by his sensations were still very simple and consisted of mere simple sounds without connection. The more often the same sensation was re-evoked, the more closely the man who felt it understood it and observed that even among sensations, as among objects and thoughts, there is a difference, that there are principal sensations and secondary ones, some more or less agreeable, others more or less unpleasant, sad, happy, etc., to express, describe, or imitate which the simple sounds he had used up to that point, whether high or low, no longer sufficed, just as the simple speech articulations did not suffice to designate external objects with their distinctions and particular qualities.

§ 10

In language, this observation of various characteristics and relationships of external objects and thoughts led to inflections and multiple alterations of the original speech articulations, giving rise to the invention of what we call parts of speech, while in music, or rather in the language of feeling, it gave origin to a collocation of tones that with respect to their reciprocal relations consist of principal and secondary tones, or, to make an analogy with grammatical terms, of nouns, adjectives, and conjunctions. Through these first attempts and these first steps toward a construction of a true language of tones or feelings the foundation was laid for regulated and coherent rows of tones,[6] which we now call scales, whose simple formation cost the human mind so much effort and toil that it was fully realized only after many centuries. . . .

§ 13

Only from the period in which man sought to construct such rows of tones does music begin to deserve to be called an art, a true language of feeling. As long as it consisted only of tones evoked by sensations it did not merit such a designation. Every animal has in common with human beings these kinds of unconnected tones evoked by sensations, but only man, by means of his intellect, is able to collect and connect these sounds in such a way that they become a means to transmit to others the most delicate and tender emotions of his soul and to describe and communicate to others the most invisible inner feelings. It is easy to imagine that such a refined language could have reached the state of perfection in which it is now only in very slow stages, and that earlier, for many centuries, it had sought to evoke a simple stirring of the emotions before it progressed so far as to evoke a certain feeling, and in such a manner that it could be distinguished from others like or unlike it. To arrive at this point the restricted rows of tones of the ancients no longer sufficed, for in addition to their limited range they also had a number of other serious deficiencies—as we shall see—and even then there were many things in part to be discovered, in part to be extended and developed. . . .

§ 17

In the first age of music, the art was, in a certain sense, still the simple language of needs. Our hearts have necessities as much as our bodies. Thus the expres-

---

6. Forkel's term is "Tonreihe" (translated here as "row of tones"), by which he means the Greek tetrachords; for scale he uses "Tonleiter." [BJB]

sions of music itself characterized the sensation just as it presented itself, namely in a harsh, strong, vehement, and incoherent manner. The art had to proceed in an entirely different manner as soon as it no longer wished to be the product of necessity but a means to invoke both pleasure and delight through memory and the excitement of states of mind full of feeling. It no longer had to describe every sound evoked by sensation as it was commonly articulated by primitive man, but had to give it nobility and, in general, it had to gather and join together only the most beautiful sounds in order to express not just a certain state of mind but to excite pleasure and delight at the same time. For this, the collocation of the small rows of tones already mentioned was not even sufficient, by itself, to produce a little song to express a certain state of mind. However complex the inner expressions can become, by using various transpositions and internal changes, their variety is not yet sufficient, and it is necessary to employ yet other means—if their variation is considered only in itself—to render them much more complex, before they can serve for the best composition, even just the briefest musical statement.

I. Rhythm is one of the first means to enlarge and embellish expressions in this way. The most primitive people used it for their monotonous music, and indeed because of this very monotony it was all the more necessary. At its origin, rhythm was simply the varied repetition of one single and the same thing, but in its further development, once it had gradually been applied to more and more objects, it could assume a much greater importance precisely because, considered as accent, it conveniently separates the principal from the secondary sounds, contributing not only to embellish the number of expressions proper to music, but also to increase them immensely. As soon as man began to perceive the various meanings that the individual components of a series of connected tones had among themselves, he must soon have realized of necessity that by means of accent and by lengthening and shortening the tones those different meanings of sounds could not only be strengthened and altered in very different ways, but also could be enlarged. It is known that the Greeks made excellent use of these means to strengthen and increase the expressions proper to music. Being an inventive people as well as one exceedingly devoted to this art, they were bound to notice quite soon the lack of internal expressions deriving from the redisposition of tones in their rows, and so they were obliged to use external aids whenever possible. For this reason, it seems, the rhythm of the Greeks became so diverse. But as the number of internal expressions[7] gradually increased

---

7. I understand "internal expressions" as those resulting from various displacements and modifications of tones to a higher or lower pitch level, which we commonly call modulation. External expressions are obtained primarily through rhythm, but the physical qualities of sound may be included here as well.

with the discovery of harmony, the extension of these rows of tones, and hundreds of other aids as well, it was no longer so necessary to have such a variety of rhythm, and this on the one hand was gradually limited to the most indispensable and most serviceable forms, and on the other was not regarded with such importance. This is the real reason, based on the nature of the things itself, that rhythm in the modern era seems to have much less variety than that in the age of the Greeks, and not because, as the worthy Isaac Vossius[8] maintains, we have regressed in this art.[9]

II. Besides the improvement and diversification of rhythm that must have been achieved by peoples who had such limited rows of tones to vary or only to embellish or correct the expressions proper to their art, these peoples must soon have felt the need to determine the intervals of their rows of tones with greater exactitude and precision. As soon as a people possessed a row of tones wide enough to contain intervals of a third or a fifth, the purity of these intervals posed no difficulty at all: they were so natural at that point that it was not easy to mistake them. Only the tones in between these larger intervals had to remain without a proper reciprocal relationship for a long time, for in such limited rows of tones there were not enough points of comparison, that is, not every tone could be provided with its own fifth in order to determine its purity. As we know principally from the history of Greek music, this state of affairs remained in effect until not only the rows of tones were extended but also, with the invention of harmony, as many and as accurate means of comparison were achieved as were absolutely necessary for the exact determination of the relationships between sounds. This, too, was the work of the modern age. What the ancients had achieved in this respect was somewhat of an improvement, compared to what their predecessors had done, but far from being sufficient to construct from their limited rows of tones something that, with regard to the significance of the single tones found within them, might have been similar to the varied meaning of the words within a sentence. Their adjectives or conjunctions, to continue the analogy, were always too small or too large with respect to the noun, and thus, so far as its relationships were concerned, never indicated with sufficient precision what they ought or meant to say, but always too much or too little.

III. The modifications of tones, simply in respect of their physical condi-

---

8. See his *De poematum cantu et viribus rhythmi* (Oxford, 1673).

9. Thus, the notion that the rhythm of the Greeks was more diverse than ours is wrong. Strictly speaking, all rhythms used in ancient music exist in modern music as well. But the ancients used them with less mixture, and primarily in songs whose melodies accommodated the words purely syllabically; in any case, rhythm was much more important for them than for us for want of sufficient internal expressions. Under these conditions, rhythm could be much more noticeable, and thus easily give rise to the notion that it had largely been lost in modern times.

tion, are likewise external aids to embellish and increase the expressions proper to music. Their necessity and effect could not remain unknown to a people once its sensitivity to meaning and expression had been awakened. The tones themselves may be harsh, soft, strong, weak, etc., and in each of these modifications they may contribute a very great deal to the variation of expression. Even the most uncivilized child of nature communicates something pleasant or enjoyable to his fellow man, not only through different words but also through a distinctly different tone of voice, rather than something unpleasant. Why then should a man who had already reached a significantly higher stage in his development not also have possessed such an effective means to beautify his music, the true expressions of his feelings?

In its second age, music seems to have reached this point in its development, and it is more than likely that it did not extend any further with many ancient peoples, even with the Greeks, as we shall see at the appropriate place. In a certain sense, this age represents the adolescence of the art, just as the first age represented the stage of its childhood. Both lasted for centuries and perhaps would still continue today—or perhaps would have even regressed, as the music of the Chinese, the modern Greeks, and many Asian nations proves—if culture, reborn in Europe in the Middle Ages, had not extended to this art also, and by the most varied means laid the foundation for a progressive development to the perfection in which we see it now and hope to see it for a long time to come. . . .

The Third Age of Music
§ 18

Our faculties of cognition and perception arise from one and the same fundamental force of the mind, and differ principally only in this, that during thought and cognition, the mind is in an active state, whereas during perception it is in a passive state. This common basic source is a new proof that the external expressions of both forces are subject in their entirety to rules of the same kind. Just as thought is nothing but the representation of an object with its characteristics and relationships, so sensation is nothing but a feeling successively evoked in us by an object with its parts, which are the same as those that, in reference to thought, are designated characteristics and relationships. The more man discovered objects of thought and sensation, the more necessary it became to make exact distinctions among them according to their characteristics and relationships. This necessity naturally had to create not only an impulse for a substantial extension and increase of expressions in language and art, but also to lead, step by step, to the highest possible and most exact determination of these expressions in order to avoid any ambiguity and possible misunderstanding among such a great number of conceptions and sensations that men wanted to communicate to each other or awaken and maintain in themselves.

§ 19

Neither the amount nor the exactness of expressions proper to music in the second age—or the so-called adolescence of art—was adequate for the representation of so great a diversity of sensible objects, considering the differences among all their characteristics and relationships. Even the representation of a sensation with very few characteristics or a little song with few expressions proper to music could be accomplished only very imperfectly, and precisely for that reason during that age music and poetry had to be pressed into that very union to which some modern writers, who have no clear understanding of the true nature of the art, wish to lead us back.[10] That should be no better than if we now were to throw out the largest part of our wealth of language, which we have acquired with so much effort, together with our knowledge of its correct use, and return to the period of that poverty of language in which, for mutual understanding, it was necessary to resort to gestures. From this one may conclude with the highest degree of probability not only from the nature of the thing, but even from the reports of ancient writers, that, precisely because of this intrinsic imperfection, this lack of internal expressions and characteristics, music, poetry, and gestures were completely inseparable in antiquity. Exactly for this reason Plato could see no significance in instrumental music and considered it an abuse of melody.[11] If music in his time had been as rich in expressions and characteristic combinations as it must be in order to be an art effective in itself and a language of feelings, he was connoisseur enough to have felt that even without words music is not without meaning, and that it is able to describe and express passions and feelings in its own way, with all their modifications, just as well as when it is united with poetry.

Thus, if music had to become an art existing on its own and operating entirely by its own forces, if it had not only to arouse an emotion with all its characteristics and relationships, but also be capable of maintaining it, in short, if it had to be for feelings what language is for the mind, then its proper expressions had to be extended and determined in the same measure as those of language.

10. So above all Brown, in his observations on poetry and music according to their origin [*A Dissertation on the Rise, Union, and Power, the Progressions, Separations, and Corruptions of Poetry and Music* (London, 1763)], who sets out to imprison poetry and music in so close a union that neither can appear in its true colors. [An excerpt is given in this chapter. BJB]

11. In the *Republic*, bk. 3, 99C–E Plato condemns the use of unnecessarily complex instruments. In *Laws*, bk. 7, 812D–E he discourages teaching students the complications of instrumental accompaniment. [LAH-S]

For this, the limited rows of tones of the ancients and their imperfect relationships, as we have seen, were completely insufficient.

§ 20

Nothing has contributed more to this extension and to a more exact determination of musical expressions than harmony in its present state. Only through
harmony could music become what it is today, namely a true and proper language of emotion. I wish to speak first of its influence on a more exact determination of musical expressions. It has been mentioned above that only at one
single point is any expression of a sensation precisely that sensation which distinguishes it from all the others, and that all other points and degrees of it, in
one way or another, at greater or lesser distance, border on another principal
emotion, to whose more precise determination they may serve just as well as to
that of the first emotion, as soon as their conditions and relationships to each
other are changed. If, as has already been said, the nature and connection of
musical expressions is to be founded on this connection of emotions, then these
expressions have to contain a means to permit an exact determination of what
kind of emotion they are to suggest. To this end, harmony is one of the most
effective and certain means. Both the limited rows of tones of the ancients and
our modern extended scales have many individual tones in common, which
without an appropriate means of determination may easily be confused with
one another and considered as belonging now to one scale, now to another.
Thus, melodies composed in these scales must always retain a certain ambiguity
and uncertainty if they cannot be clearly distinguished by some means that establishes beyond any doubt to which scale they belong. The following melody
[see Ex. 1] belongs to C and G major of our modern keys as well as to A and E

Ex. 1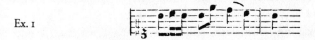

minor. In each of these four relationships, it has unquestionably a different
meaning, but to which is the listener to assign it, if there is no basis of determination connected to it that may serve as a guide? Harmony, when added to the
melody, will provide such a guide for the listener and will clarify the relationship and therefore the meaning of the melody beyond doubt, for instance [see
Ex. 2].
    It is certainly true that each individual relationship in this melody could
have been established even without harmony, by means of the preceding and
succeeding purely melodic tones, but only to a certain extent, by no means so
quickly and unambiguously as it is with the help of harmony. It is therefore
undeniable that any melody by itself will remain uncertain and ambiguous in

Ex. 2

its relationships if a harmonic tone is not added, at least from time to time, as a more exact determinant. The very uncertainty of relationships in pure melody makes it possible to give a song such complexities of meaning, by adding or varying harmony, that one never thinks that one is hearing the same work, although the melody remains the same. From this richness of meaning in pure melodies one may conclude with more probability than from any other reason that the ancients must necessarily have possessed at least some sounds that functioned as harmonic determinants, and that in music of such a limited range, which according to all probability can consist of only little songs, the octave and fifth were the essential and determining notes in every scale. The ancients could not have had any other kind of harmony, that is, one like ours, which itself becomes a kind of melody, and consequently consists of several melodies joined together. Neither the range and composition of their small rows of tones, nor the quality and compass of their musical instruments allowed for such a harmony.

§ 21

The second advantage that the discovery of harmony has given our language of sounds is the remarkable increase in the characteristic expressions of this art that it alone has rendered possible. This increase is intimately connected with the closer and more exact determination of expression, likewise achieved by means of harmony, for the increase arises together with the greater definiteness and is its natural and necessary consequence. Yet these two aspects are not the same thing, even though both always go hand in hand. Harmony determines the relationships of expressions primarily through tones that are already called essential, in the purely melodic sense, in the context of scales, for it is chiefly by means of these tones that one scale is distinguished from another. But harmony serves to increase expressions proper to music only when it is formed into a melody itself, as it were; and, being combined with another, not simply side by side with its individual principal tones, it gives rise to new combinations through mutual interweaving. The determination of relationships thus may be achieved through the principal or basic tones of scales alone. Even in our times, many composers use harmony only in this manner. A composition of this kind is called monodic or homophonic. But the chief contribution of harmony to increasing the characteristic expressions of music is through the artful manner in which several melodies are combined. This kind of composition is called polyodic or polyphonic. To this type of composition belong all the imitations of different voices, the various devices governed by the rules of double counter-point, etc.

To make this quite clear, I shall give an example of each case. The melody given above, which by itself could be assigned to four different keys, required the addition of harmony in order to be definitely ascribed to any one scale and thus lose its ambiguity. Secondly, precisely by means of adding harmony, out of a single characteristic expression many different forms with very different meanings have been obtained. In this case, harmony has contributed both to the definition and to the increase in the expressions proper to this art. In the following short example [see Ex. 3] the harmony does the same. In the next

Ex. 3

example, however, it is quite otherwise; by rearranging the two voices a new expression has been gained, which is closely related and for that very reason finely modified [see Ex. 4]. How manifold this increase of expressions can be-

Ex. 4

come through similar contrapuntal devices in several voices, and in general through polyphonic procedures in composition, is known to anyone who is acquainted with harmony and its true use; and the amateur who has never recognized its necessity from his inner feelings may draw proof from this that double counterpoint with all the related compositional devices is not a useless, empty game; but rather is based no less on the nature of the art and the sensibility of man than are song, dance melody, and all other simpler kinds of composition. Double counterpoint is founded on the multiple modifications of sensations and on the best proper use of the whole wealth of art that nature offers for the appropriate expression of all these diverse emotions.

From *Allgemeine Geschichte der Musik,* 2 vols. (Leipzig, 1788–1801; repr. Hildesheim: Olms, 1962; Graz: Akademische Druck- und Verlagsanstalt, 1967), 1:1–15.

Chapter Five

The Reaction of Italian Humanists
and Literati to Music

THE ROBUST ANTIMUSICAL tradition typical of Italian culture continued throughout the eighteenth century, even though Italy was the homeland of *bel canto,* though foreign travelers flocked there to listen to music in theaters and in the academies, and though the most important instrumental schools flourished in Italy. Numerous writings on music have come down to us from literati and learned men such as Mattei, Algarotti, Planelli, and Milizia, and from poets directly involved in the production of opera librettos such as Apostolo Zeno and Pietro Metastasio. Although their positions differ, they concur in calling for the musician to be subservient to the poet and in affirming, albeit with various subtle distinctions, that music is an art of a lower order, to be regarded with suspicion and kept, as much as possible, in quarantine. Only Gluck's reform succeeded in partially reconciling Italian culture to music, since it satisfied the traditional aspiration of a return to drama based on the ancient model in which the music and trills of the singers did not prevail over the more important literary and dramatic aspects.

Francesco Algarotti's *Saggio sopra l'opera in musica,* written in 1755 and reprinted with some changes in 1763, was a product of this climate of suspicion toward the music that accompanied modern "tragedy." Algarotti's rationalist turn of mind does not go so far as to require that music be banned from theaters, but he does call for the correction of abuses. In essence, he asks that music be treated with greater moderation, in order that it be limited to its proper role of "minister and helpmate of poetry." In Algarotti's writings, albeit with a more rationalist focus, opera is portrayed in a manner that anticipates Gluck's and Calzabigi's reform.

Antonio Planelli's essay *Dell'opera in musica* is more obviously in line with Gluck's reform; however, it was published in 1772, when that reform had already been widely debated all over Europe. Planelli gives up the idea that opera is tragedy accompanied by music, and attempts to identify the expression of "the pathetic" as the specific element of the new type of operatic spectacle. He too calls for the elimination of abuses in the name of a classical or neoclassical ideal. His aim, however, is to bring about a type of opera in which moderation of both musical and dramatic elements enables free expression of the element of pathos, which consists mainly in the "happy mean."

Francesco Milizia's *Trattato completo, formale e materiale del teatro* (1794) belongs to the last years of the eighteenth century, a period in which Italian opera was in steep decline. The part of Milizia's treatise devoted to opera discusses this condition and calls for a return to a simpler and more moving theater: "the great illness of modern Italian music lies in excess." Excessive affectation leaves the heart cold and diverts the musician from imitating nature. In Milizia's writing the ideals of Gluck's reform make themselves felt, even though the kind of opera he sought is undoubtedly closer to the mellow neoclassical ideal of the Italians than to the dramatic forcefulness of Gluck's opera.

Finally, a strange witness to the antimusical attitude of poets and literati that was still to be found in the last years of the century: Alfieri's introduction (1796) to his tragedy *Abele,* reproduced here in its entirety. The author outlines a new type of theatrical representation that he calls *tramelogedy,* which should constitute an honorable compromise between traditional opera, a "nauseating amusement of the ear," and austere classical tragedy. In order to educate the public, by now "accustomed to languishing in theaters . . . without even having a theater," Alfieri plans a type of theatrical performance in which music appears only in some parts, where the "marvelous" prevails; for the rest, "the primacy of tragedy over music" is maintained. Alfieri concludes with the request that tragedy proper return to its origins, that is, that it be freed from the corrupting force of music. Opera is instead to treat "fabulous, playful, and amorous" themes, which are proper to this genre.

Metastasio (Pietro Trapassi) deserves a lengthy chapter to himself. The greatest eighteenth-century librettist, responsible for both the merits and the defects of Italian opera in his day, he can be considered the veritable creator of the model for serious opera, which prevailed for almost a century. With its rigid stereotypes and its historical, mythological, and fantastic plots it served more than a generation of musicians. Because of their perfect operatic suitability, his most famous librettos were set to music more than a hundred times. His rigorous division of an opera into recitatives (to which the action was entrusted) and arias (to which lyrical effusion was entrusted), which Metastasio claimed to have derived directly from Greek tragedy, led to serious opera's becoming stylized and sharply contrasted with comic opera, which was at first more malleable and less rigidly codified. Nonetheless, Metastasio is to be credited with having greatly enhanced the quality of librettos. Bowing to then-current theories, he maintained that poetry's dominion was to go unchallenged, and that literary texts were not to be subjected to the whims of composers and singers. In reality, nothing could be more musical, or rather, more operatic, than his librettos, which already seem to contain and suggest the aria that the musician is to compose. This section contains a well-known letter that Metastasio wrote to Saverio Mattei, a man of letters, in 1770, in which he expounds his ideas on music and theater, drawing the usual obligatory parallels with ancient tragedy: the simplicity of ancient music was linked to its greater effectiveness, compared with the more advanced but more artificial modern music.

FRANCESCO ALGAROTTI
from *Essay on Opera* (1755)

Preface

Of all the ways devised by man of producing delight in noble souls, perhaps the most ingenious and accomplished is opera. Nothing in its formation was neglected; no ingredient or means was overlooked to ensure that opera attain its proposed end. It may well be claimed that the most attractive qualities of poetry, music, mime, dance, and painting all combine happily in opera to delight the emotions, to charm the heart, and sweetly to seduce the mind. However, the same thing happens with operas that happens with mechanical devices, namely, the more complex they are, the more apt they are to break down.

It is therefore small wonder that this ingenious device, being made up of so many parts, does not always achieve its purpose, even though those whose task it is to join together and arrange all its parts do so with the greatest diligence and effort. Yet those who at present sit as arbiters of our pleasures care nothing for what is required to arrange an opera properly. In fact, if we consider what little effort they put into choosing a libretto, or a plot, how little they care if the music will go with the words, or if the manner of singing and reciting is genuine, or if there is a link between the dances and the action, if the set designs and even the theaters themselves are properly constructed, it is very easy to understand how any theatrical presentation, which by nature should be among all the most delightful, turns out to be so insipid and tedious. Because of the confusion created among its various parts, there remains no trace of imitation. Illusion, which is born only of a perfect accord between its parts, vanishes utterly. It follows that opera, one of the most artful contrivances of the human spirit, becomes languid, disconnected, unrealistic, monstrous, grotesque, and deserving of all the blame and censure of those who justly hold pleasure to be the serious and important thing it is.[1]

Now, whoever should set his mind to restoring opera to its former glory and decorum would do well, first of all, to undertake a task that may be very difficult to conclude positively, but which nevertheless is most necessary. I refer to the task of bringing order into the musical world, and of subjecting the virtuosi to discipline and rule as they were in times past. In truth, even if a drama is sensibly written and composed, how will it then be performed if no one listens to the directors? And how can it be sensibly written and composed, if those who should obey are the very ones who set down the law and who command? In short, what good can be expected of a group of people where no one wants to stay in his assigned place, where all sorts of affronts are heaped upon the *maestro di musica,* and even more so upon the poet, who ought to preside over and govern everything? What can one expect of a situation in which disputes and outrageous demands break out daily among the singers over the number of the ariettas, the height of a helmet, or the length of a cloak, all much more difficult to settle than those of protocol at a conference, or of precedence among ambassadors from various kingdoms?

Such abuses should immediately be done away with, so that poets in particular can be given back that control unjustly taken from their hands, and with more energetic measures undertake the task of reordering and correcting everything. For no legislator will set himself to making laws in a state that has been overthrown if the magistrates have not been reinstated in authority. Nor will a military leader approach his enemy until license and disorder have been eliminated from the ranks of his soldiers. But who will initiate such an undertaking? In the past, a theater was presided over by a chorus director or official,[2] and

---

1. Among the many things written against opera that could be put in evidence, an English writer [signed "Philonus"] expresses himself as follows: "as the waters of a certain fountain of Thessaly, from their benumbing quality, could be contained in nothing but the hoof of an ass, so can this languid and disjointed composition [of the Opera] find no admittance but in such heads as are expressly formed to receive it"; *The World,* no. 156 [18 December 1755]. Much earlier, the prudent Addison prefaced his essay in the first volume, no. 5, of *The Spectator,* which concerns Italian opera, with this verse of Horace: "Spectatum admissi risum teneatis amici?" ["If you were let in to see, could you hold your laughter, my friends?" *Ars poetica* 5]. And Dryden has said:

> For what a song, or senseless Opera
> Is to the living labour of a play,
> Or what a play to Virgil's works would be,
> Such is a single piece to history.
>   To Sir Godfrey Kneller [ll. 150–53]

[For Addison's essay, written in 1711, see below, Ch. 8. BJB]

2. By using the terms "coragus" and "aedile" Algarotti alludes to ancient Greek and Roman theater. [BJB]

everything proceeded in the most orderly and appropriate manner when the ancient republics wanted to use theatrical representations to instill virtue in the people, or at least keep them amused for the tranquillity of the state. At present, theaters are in the hands of impresarios who seek only to profit from the curiosity and idleness of a few. Most of the time they do not know what they ought to do, or, because of the myriad obligations they are burdened with, they cannot carry out anything successfully. Unless things change, to speak of such matters is useless and all hope is in vain. And how can they change, if not at the court of some prince who is dear to the Muses, and whose theater is presided over by a competent director, who in his person combines both determination and vigor? Only then will the singers be subject to rule and order, and we shall be able to hope to see in our day what Rome and Athens saw in the times of the Caesars and the Pericleses. . . .

On Music

Another major reason for the present decadence of music is the particular dominion it has taken upon itself to found, and which today has reached such a height. The composer behaves like a despot, doing exactly as he likes, concerned solely with musical matters. There is no way in the world to make him understand that his role has to be subordinate, and that music produces its best effects when it ministers to poetry. Its proper function is to dispose the mind to receive the impressions made by the verses, and so to stir those emotions that are analogous to the precise ideas that the poet is to elicit, in a word, to give the language of the Muses greater vigor and energy.

The criticism already leveled against opera, that people die *singing*, merely stems from a lack of the necessary harmony between the words and the song. If the trilling were stopped when the passions speak, and the music were appropriately written, it would be no more unseemly if a man went to his death singing than if he did so reciting verses. Everyone knows that in ancient times the poets themselves were musicians. Vocal music was therefore what it is supposed to be in accordance with its own basic principles: a more forceful, livelier, and warmer expression of the concepts and emotions of the soul. Now, however, that the two twins, poetry and music, are separated, is it surprising that, one having to paint what the other has drawn, the colors are charming but the contours deformed? Such an enormous difficulty can only be remedied by the composer himself, who should hear from the poet's mouth what his intentions are. Before setting notes to paper, he should come to an understanding with the poet, and subsequently consult him on what he has written. The composer should be dependent on the poet to the same extent that Lully depended on Quinault, or Vinci on Metastasio, as theatrical discipline correctly prescribes.

Among the various unseemly elements of modern music, we must first of all mention what first strikes the ears at the very beginning of the opera, that is, the overture.

These overtures—the noisier the better—are always composed of two fast movements and one slow one; they never vary and always proceed at the same pace and in the same manner. What diversity, furthermore, should there not be between one overture and another? Between one, for example, preceding the death of Dido, abandoned by Aeneas, and one preceding the marriage of Demetrius and Cleonice? Its main purpose is to announce the action in some way, to prepare the audience to receive the overall emotional impression produced by the drama. Therefore, it is from this that it should take its countenance and bearing, as does the exordium from the oration. Today, however, overtures are considered to be totally detached and different from the drama, similar to a resounding fanfare, as it were, with which to fill in the empty spaces and numb the ears of the audience. Although some intend the overture as an exordium, it varies little from the exordia of those writers who, with high-sounding words, are forever discussing the loftiness of their subject and the lowliness of their own genius: they suit any subject and can just as easily precede any oration.

Overtures are followed by recitatives, and if the former are usually the loudest part of the music, the latter are the most muffled. It seems that composers are by now of the opinion that recitatives do not warrant excessive care, as they cannot be expected to produce much delight in the listener. The opinion of ancient composers was quite different. It suffices to read what Jacopo Peri, who is justly said to be the inventor of recitative, has to say on this matter in his *proemio* to *Euridice*.[3] Having set himself to finding the type of musical imitation that best suits dramatic poems, he turned his genius and his diligence to discovering what the ancient Greeks had done in similar cases. He observed which words in our speech have a resounding quality, and which ones do not, that is, which have the capacity to carry consonances, and which do not. He began to study with great care the various ways we express pain, happiness, and the other emotions by which we are affected. This he did in order to have the bass proceed in time with them, now faster, now slower. In all of this, he did not neglect to examine most scrupulously the very nature of our language, nor to consult many gentlemen who were highly experienced in listening to both poetry and music. And, he concluded in the end that the foundation for such imitation had to be a harmony closely patterned on nature, something halfway between ordinary speech and melody: a tempered system between the kind of speech he says the ancients called *diastematic,* as if sustained and suspended, and that which they called *continued.*

3. Peri's Foreword to *Euridice* (1601) is translated in Strunk, *Source Readings,* 373–76. [BJB]

Such were the endeavors of composers of the past, who proceeded with great care and consideration. The results of their efforts clearly proved that they did not pursue vain subtleties. The recitative was varied and drew its form and soul from the quality of the words. At times it ran just as fast as the words; at times it proceeded slowly, and above all it stressed those inflections and those accentuations that forceful emotions have the power to convey to human expression. Properly wrought, the recitative was listened to with delight; and many still recall how some passages of simple recitative touched the audience in a way that no aria, in our present day, has been able to do.

At present, recitative seems to produce some emotion when, as they say, it is *obbligato,* and accompanied by instruments. Perhaps it would not be a bad idea if such a practice were more common than it is. What warmth and life do not accrue to a recitative when the part that extols passion is strengthened by the orchestra, and the heart and imagination are at once assailed by every kind of weapon? In my opinion, no better proof of this could be adduced, by way of example, than most of the last act of Vinci's *Didone,* which is entirely fashioned in this manner.[4] Surely Virgil himself would have been pleased with it, so animated and charged with emotion is it. Such an approach would produce yet another good effect: there would not be such a difference and disproportion between the style of the recitative and that of the arias. Consequently, there would be greater harmony among the various parts of the opera. Many are those, in fact, who more than once must have been offended by the typical rapid transition from a smooth and slow recitative to an extremely ornate arietta, wrought with all the refinements of the art. Would it not amount to the same thing if someone, while walking, suddenly took to jumping and performing somersaults?

It is quite true that, in order to achieve a sweeter accord among the various parts of an opera, it would also be advisable to elaborate less and to reduce the instrumentation of the arias themselves, which is not usually done. They have always constituted the most important part of an opera. And, as theater music has continued to evolve and be refined, arias have achieved even greater prominence. In the beginning they were extremely simple, compared to what they are today. In fact, in terms both of melody and accompaniment, they stood out only slightly from the recitative. The elder [Alessandro] Scarlatti was the first to give them more animation and spirit, adorning them above all with beautiful and abundant accompaniments. Nevertheless, they were employed with moderation; they were open and clear, they bore the touch of mastery, and they were not overpolished and fussy.

4. Leonardo Vinci, *Didone abbandonata,* on a libretto by Metastasio, first performed in Rome 14 January 1726. [BJB]

This is true not just because of the vastness of the theaters themselves, where careful workmanship is lost at a distance, but also because of the voices, to which the arias are subservient. Many things have changed from Scarlatti's time to ours, in which we have gone beyond all limits; arias are overwhelmed and disfigured by the ornaments with which they are increasingly embellished. The ritornellos that precede them are much too long and often superfluous. In arias expressing rage, for example, verisimilitude is stretched to the breaking point: how can a man in a fit of rage wait with his hands in his belt until the aria's ritornello is concluded before venting the passion seething within his heart? Then, when the ritornello is over and the singer comes in, what else do all those violins accompanying him do if not confuse and cover his voice? . . . Currently, one of the most cherished practices, sure to elicit the most enthusiastic applause, is to have a voice and an oboe compete in an aria, or a voice and a trumpet, and by having them engage in quick repartees to create an endless competition between the two that almost turns into a duel to the last breath. If such skirmishes can win over most of the audience, they also prove insufferable to the sanest among the listeners. The delight produced when doing the opposite cannot be sufficiently expressed, that is, by occasionally offering a restrained accompaniment to the arias, with different types of instruments, such as the viola, the harp, the trumpet, the oboe, and perhaps even the organ, as was formerly the custom.[5] But it should be done so that each type of instrument suits the nature of the words it is to serve, and that the instruments enter from time to time where the expression of a given passion most calls for them. In this way, the singer's voice would never be covered, but rather the emotional charge of the aria would be enhanced, and the accompaniment would be similar to beautifully rhythmic prose, which, in the words of the sage himself, should be like the hammering of blacksmiths, a mixture of music and labor.

These, however, though very serious, are not the greatest irregularities that now characterize the composition of arias. We must go further in order to discover the primary root of this evil. The major problem, in the opinion of true composers, lies in the manner in which the very subject matter of arias is chosen and executed. Rarely is any attempt made to have the melody flow naturally or respond to the emotions of the words that it is to clothe. The great variety of ways of treating melody, turning it this way and that, makes it difficult to refer to a common center or a point of unity.

The primary concern of modern composers is to blandish, entice, and surprise the listener, not to move his heart or spark his imagination. The three main ways whereby composers achieve their purpose are: the frequent use of

---

5. An organ can be seen in the orchestra of the theater in the famous Cattaio villa. [The Cattaio is in Battaglia Terme, near Padua. EF]

extremely high or low notes, the proliferation of passagework, and the endless repetition of words, entangling them at will. . . .

How boring and insufferable are those repetitions and jumblings of words, only for the sake of the music, and in themselves senseless! Words should not be repeated except in the order that emotion dictates, and after the complete sense of the aria has been conveyed. Most of the time, the first part should not be repeated da capo either. This newfangled invention runs counter to the natural flow of language and emotion, which do not fall back upon themselves, turning after their height to a lesser state.

Anyone can tell when an aria is emotionally impassioned and frenzied. However, when encountering in an aria the words "father" or "son," the composer never fails to use held notes, sweetening them as much as possible, and suddenly slow the impetus of the music. By so doing, he is persuaded that, besides giving the words their appropriate emotion, he has also provided his composition with variety. We, instead, would say that he has ruined it by producing such dissonance, with regard to expression, as cannot be tolerated by one in full possession of his wits; it is not the sense of the individual words that should be expressed, but only their general meaning. Variety has to result from the various modifications of the same subject, and not from what is pinned onto the subject, or is alien and repugnant to it.

It seems that our composers behave like those writers who, paying no attention to word order or to how speech is organized, aim only at stringing together beautiful words. However harmonious and full-sounding they may be, the ensuing oration will only prove vain and ineffectual. The same is true for music, if the composer does not aim at portraying some image or expressing some emotion.[6] It will also prove vain; and after having perhaps elicited some fleeting sign of approval, it will be laid aside and condemned to eternal silence and oblivion, no matter how much artistry went into the selection of its musical combinations. On the other hand, the so-called *parlante* arias, those that depict and express, and that are more natural, remain etched in the collective memory; true simplicity, which alone can imitate nature, will always be preferred to the most intricate ways of seasoning art.

From *Saggio sopra l'opera in musica* (Livorno, 1755), 7–12, 24–37; modern edition in *Opere di Francesco Algarotti e Saverio Bettinelli,* ed. Ettore Bonora (Illuministi italiani 2; Milan and Naples: Ricciardi, 1970), 435–37, 443–51. The 1755 and 1763 editions have been reprinted by Libreria Musicale Italiana (Lucca, 1989), and the 1763 edition by F.A.R.A.P. (Bologna, 1975). Algarotti's essay received wide circulation in the eighteenth century; it was translated into

6. "Music that portrays nothing is only noise; and without familiarity, which distorts everything, it would cause no more pleasure than a succession of harmonious and sonorous words without order or connection"; [d'Alembert], in the Preface to the *Encyclopédie.*

English (London, 1767, and Glasgow, 1768), German (Kassel, 1769), French (Pisa and Paris, 1773), and Spanish (Madrid, 1787). An excerpt from the 1768 translation, partially overlapping with the present one, appears in Strunk, *Source Readings,* 657–72.

ANTONIO PLANELLI
from *Opera* (1772)

III
On Theater Music

Melodramma thus composed by the poet passes into the hands of the *maestro di cappella.* Following the method of earlier passages, in this section our observations will center on the type of music required by *melodramma,* which I shall call theater music. In order to expound as best I can the subject matter I propose to discuss, I hope my reader will bear with me if I preface my discussion of the generation of sound and the nature of music in general with some remarks that are very simple and can easily be understood by anyone. Such observations will serve as principles governing the stylistic rules of theater music; in other sections they will apply to theater decoration and dance.

1. *On Music in General*
§2. THE DIFFERENCE BETWEEN ANCIENT AND MODERN MUSIC. Modern music (which draws its perfection from the Italians, as did ancient music from the Greeks)[1] is far superior to the ancient; aesthetically it is much richer, more varied, and more complex than the ancient, the aesthetics of which was extremely simple. Three inventions above all contributed to making these two schools of music so different. The first was that of counterpoint, which was unknown to the ancients, as is by now acknowledged by all scholars after the evidence produced by the illustrious Padre Martini.[2] The second is that of present-day musical notation, which is easier and much more practical than that of the ancients, who were unable distinctly and clearly to express the com-

---

1. Hebrew music must have been most perfect, indeed superior to that of any other nation, whether ancient or modern. This would not be difficult to prove if the scope of our work so permitted. However, the results achieved in this art by a people such as the Jews during their republic, who because of their religion and inclination were cut off from all other nations, died with the republic itself. Thus their achievements in no way furthered the perfection of the music that spread through all the civilized nations of antiquity.
2. Giovanni Battista Martini, *Storia della musica* (Bologna, 1757–81); see the excerpt in Ch. 4. [BJB]

poser's concepts. The last is the invention of instruments having more octaves than those used by the Greeks, none of whose instruments went beyond three octaves, if we are to believe what has come down to us concerning their instrumental music. Clearly, music that puts such inventions to good use will enrich its aesthetic qualities more easily than another that has not been able to profit from them. Let us now discuss the element of pathos in this art.

§3. WHEREIN LIES THE QUALITY OF PATHOS IN MUSIC. Each passion carries with it a particular tone of voice, which is quite different from that of a man who is tranquil. In fact, without seeing a person and without knowing his real mood, we can determine simply from the tone of his voice not only whether he is in the grip of some emotion, but even its very nature, whether it is disdain, happiness, or fear. The ancient orators clearly differentiated these tones in terms of their corresponding emotion. In order to suit the tone of his harangues better, Gracchus would hide a slave behind him who would suggest with a flute either this or that pitch, as it best fit the various parts of his allocution.[3]

Pathos in music consists in imitating these tones; we are thus powerfully induced to feel the same emotions evoked by the imitated tones, reproducing in our imagination the very emotions we had formerly experienced while listening to such tones. For example, a compassionate tone recalls to my imagination the notion of similar tones that I had previously heard uttered by unhappy people, and together with such ideas the confused ideas of the feelings of compassion that I had then felt are rekindled through an association of ideas. Such an association is necessarily contained in the ideas that were already present in my mind. In like manner, the portrait of a person either feared, loved, or hated awakens in us the same emotions formerly aroused by the person himself, who is the archetype of that imitation or portrait. This is precisely the effect that the element of pathos in music has on the human spirit. Nor does this action remain in the spirit; it also passes to our entire body. This happens as those confused ideas related to previously experienced emotions are paralleled and, I would say, echoed, within our very being, by an emotion similar to that which had formerly accompanied the aforementioned agitations of our soul.

This shows that the element of pathos, not only in music but in all the pleasurable arts, acts on the mechanical part of our emotions, but only indirectly, and not directly as it does on our sense organs. Nevertheless, I am of the opinion (no matter what the learned natural philosophers, which I am not, may think) that music also has a direct action on the mechanism of the passions, that is, on the nerves, on which this mechanism rests. First of all, it seems beyond

3. Cicero, *De oratore*, bk. 3 [§225].

doubt that, among the nerves of the human body, some are particularly apt to serve the passions (hereafter they will be referred to as *diathetic nerves*), which are those that wind through the chest and stomach regions and belong mainly to the vagus and intercostal nerves, and even to some branching off the fifth pair.[4] Everyday experience enables anyone to notice that an emotional reaction inevitably produces a corresponding motion in the aforementioned regions of the body. Such agitations, which we experience every time we are overcome by some passion, induced the ancients to set the seat of our affections in these regions. For instance, they set the emotion of love in the liver, that of anger in the bile, that of laughter in the spleen, and so on. From the close connection between the reaction of these nerves and the emotions, it happens that when some illness alters one of these particular systems, it causes a person to be moved by sadness, disdain, or happiness, without any motive and without his soul's being concerned with any object corresponding to those emotions. This is the reason that when those in delicate health suffer from such blind emotions, they usually complain of a contraction of the chest nerves and those of neighboring regions. Because of the function of these nerves in relation to the emotions, each emotion has its own special physiognomy, since these nerves, especially those of the fifth pair, send out branches to the different parts of the face. These branches are stimulated by the movement that the emotions create in those nerves that descend toward the chest, and which we include among the diathetic nerves. This is also the origin of weeping, which accompanies sadness, happiness, compassion, and other emotions; laughter, which goes with yet other emotions; and a quavering and almost halting voice, which accompanies them all, as they are all effects of the stimulation of the same diathetic nerves, and especially of the branches that they transmit to the tear ducts, to the muscles of the cheeks, the mouth, the diaphragm or transverse septum, and to the larynx. Lastly, according to Willis,[5] this is what constitutes one of the major differences between our bodily structure and that of animals. Humans have a multitude of nerves, especially in the chest and bowel regions, whereas animals have very few. Since they are incapable of feeling emotions, they do not need the nerves that in our bodies preside over the emotions, but only those pertaining to the vital functions.[6] All

4. By saying, however, that these nerves preside over the emotions, we do not wish to imply that they are not also important as far as the vital functions are concerned.

5. Thomas Willis (1621–75), a physician and pioneer investigator of the anatomy of the brain. He was Sedleian professor of Natural History at Oxford University and one of the founder Fellows of the Royal Society. Planelli may have read his *Cerebri Anatome* (1664) or his *Pathologiae cerebri et nervosi generis specimen* (1667). [BJB]

6. I do not know, however, whether the natural philosophers are content with Willis's justification, it seeming to me that, without resorting to the passions, the reason for such a difference is to be found in the difference that exists between the position of the human body and that of

this further confirms that we have a category of nerves that are in charge of the emotions, and these are precisely those we have called diathetic. It also seems clear that our nerves, like the strings of an instrument, have a specific sound. There is an unquestioned principle in acoustics whereby any sound necessarily sets in motion all those bodies in the vibrational field that it produces in the air; if these bodies possess a definite pitch, it is precisely the unison or another consonant with that sound; on the other hand, the sound gives no movement whatever to those other bodies that lack a definite pitch. It is for this reason that we can frequently observe an instrumental or vocal sound not only moving the strings of musical instruments comprised within that vibrational field, but even crystals, vases of silver or of some other metal, windowpanes, and any other body that by chance possesses a sound that is consonant with one sounding at the same time. We also experience such a vibrating effect on our nerves, to the extent that, while listening to a sound, we often feel a trembling sensation in some part of our body. Therefore, our nerves also have a definite sound, or, what amounts to the same thing, are disposed to a definite sound. It follows that (1) they will be directly and necessarily moved by music containing sounds that are consonant with those to which they are naturally inclined, and (2) that a musical mode based on sounds that are consonant with those of the diathetic nerves will necessarily and directly move such nerves. Because of the agreement that exists between the latter and the emotions, their oscillations will awaken the passion that corresponds to the particular motion produced in them.

Such are the considerations that have come to my mind, and they lead me to think it extremely likely that music has a direct effect on the workings of our emotions. This direct effect seems to be borne out by the sway that music holds over the human soul, which is greater than that exercised by any other faculty, and especially by the purely mechanical effects that music often produces. It is also borne out by music's effectiveness in curing diseases, a property observed from the most ancient times and frequently witnessed even today, particularly in the healing of those who in Apulia are said to be affected by tarantism. Such effects are never said to have been produced by painting, sculpture, or by any of the other fine arts.

I have deemed it necessary to expound briefly my viewpoint as regards the direct effect that music exerts on the workings of our passions, for it may possibly be relevant in the following chapter in determining the style of theater music.

---

animals. This is because the vital functions in a horizontally positioned body, as that of animals, do not require as much strength as a perpendicularly positioned body, as is the human, part of whose fluids must ascend vertically.

§4. ANOTHER DIFFERENCE BETWEEN ANCIENT AND MODERN MU-
SIC. In terms of pathos, it must be admitted, modern music is vastly inferior to
that of the ancients. The Greeks succeeded in analyzing this part of their music
so perfectly that they soon discovered all the modes apt to excite and control a
given passion.[7] Each of these modes normally corresponded to a passion in the
listener, as is unanimously affirmed by the ancients, who bore ample testimony
to what they experienced in themselves and in others, as history itself confirms.[8] Without that, if the Lydian mode, for example, had not normally
sparked cheerfulness in listeners, because of the rare examples observed of such
an effect it could not have been claimed absolutely that such a mode aroused
cheerfulness, and much less could everyone have agreed (as indeed they do)
to make use of that mode only when wishing to dispose the listeners to that
emotion.

Therefore, the ancients drew greater benefit from a poor music than we do
from one that is particularly rich. If we asked a Greek which mode was needed
to instill a given mood, he would know well which one to choose. Today, however, this same question would throw the worthiest composer in Italy into confusion; we often see an aria composed, say, in F minor that had previously been
sung to us in E major, and one that was formerly *parlante* become a heavily
ornamented aria, and another that previously proceeded slowly, guided by a
phlegmatic duple meter, suddenly reappear, almost like a galop, in rapid a cappella tempo.

It is not that modern composers do not at times succeed in producing pathos, but it costs them a continuous and often useless mental effort, whereas the
Greeks achieved such results simply by observing the rules that applied to that
aspect of music. The difference between our composers and the Greeks is the
same as that between one who does not know the rules of practical arithmetic,
and someone who is clearly able to use them. It is quite possible that the former,
just as exactly as the latter, can find the right answer, but the former will have
found it belatedly and with great effort, while the latter will have done so
quickly and easily. The former will always fear he has made a mistake, and he
will repeat his calculations a thousand times yet never be certain; the latter, being sure that his rules are infallible, will find in those very rules proof of the
correctness of his calculation.

7. The Phrygian mode, for example, inspired a sense of scorn among its people, and a warlike
spirit, whereas the Lydian mode begot cheerfulness and the desire to dance, and so on.
8. In this respect, it is well known that Timotheus caused Alexander to fly into a rage and rush
for his arms by means of the Phrygian mode. Then, by suddenly shifting to the Dorian mode, he
calmed the irate monarch. As Aristotle reports, the famous musician Olympius instilled a
wondrous ardor in people's hearts. Plutarch (in *De musica*) reports that Terpander, another excellent musician, suppressed a riot in Sparta by means of his art. It is said that the Spartans themselves

If I am not mistaken, that the element of pathos was so regular and certain in ancient music, and is so uncertain and irregular in modern music, is due principally to three reasons. The first is the difference in aesthetics between the two. Music that flaunts an aesthetics that is too rich, too varied, and refined inevitably makes it impossible for its own sounds to leave their mark on the mind and body of the listener. In a melody made up of rapid notes, trills, arpeggios, runs, mordents, divisions, and sudden leaps, no sooner does a sound reach the auditory nerves than its effect is totally nullified by that of another sound immediately following, which in turn is followed closely by a myriad of other equally brief sounds. The mind of the listener has neither the time nor the ability to discern, in the midst of all these sounds, those he formerly perceived as producing pathos, nor time for his imagination and memory to reproduce and perceive the affecting ideas bound up with those sounds. Contemporary, complex harmony makes sounds all the more uncertain and difficult to distinguish, especially when, as usually happens, consonance and dissonance go hand in hand.

If such music can have no effect on the imagination or on memory, it will have even less on the diathetic nerves, as the oscillation produced in them by a sound is no sooner begun than interrupted by another sound that is completely different. Experience shows that when such music is performed next to instruments that are at rest, none of these will be shaken or moved to sound, as they surely would be by music that made use of clearer and steadier sounds. Therefore, ancient music, the aesthetics of which was not so refined, had a greater effect upon the diathetic nerves, the imagination, and on memory, upon which pathos in music depends.

The second reason is the concept modern composers have of music, which is different from that of the ancients. Today, music is treated as an art whose main purpose is to please the sense of hearing. All those who compose it have virtually no other aim in mind but to make music commendable to the ear. Therefore, although they have found the true and invariable laws governing melody and harmony, they have not discovered those that regulate the element of pathos in art.

The Greeks, on the contrary, perceived music as destined not so much to appease the ear as to move and regulate the emotions, which, through the pleas-

---

sang sweet songs in battle to control their fear. However, once while fighting against the Messenians, the musician Tyrtaeus, realizing that the Spartans were falling back, by changing from the Lydian to the Phrygian mode obtained victory for them, for the Phrygian mode sparked the courage in the Spartans that the Lydian mode had dulled. It is also narrated that a precipitous and rapid music stirred some youths to such a rage that they rushed to set fire to the house of a courtesan. The musician, however, being instructed by Pythagoras to change his mode, calmed the hearts of those young men. Similarly, it is said of Pythagoras that, with music, he pacified the spirits of a youth set raving by amorous passion. Theophrastus, as is written, employed the same means to calm the enraged.

ant medium of music, they directed toward objects more perfect and more worthy of the human soul. Music, thus used, is the most effective minister of virtues. Therefore Athenaeus assures us that, by means of music, the Greeks taught the duties of religion and morality, and the deeds and examples of illustrious men.[9] This helps us to understand what Polybius[10] wrote about the two peoples of Arcadia, one of which, having adopted the use of music, became virtuous and cultivated, while the other, having contempt for music, remained barbarous and corrupt.

Not even during festivities, merrymaking, weddings, or banquets did Greek music lose sight of its purpose. The singer whom Agamemnon left with Clytemnestra did not apply himself to entertaining that princess with purely aesthetic music. Instead, he sought to instill in her soul the love of her absent husband and of the virtues necessary in a regent, with the result that Aegisthus could not bend her to his desires until he had done away with her singer.[11]

How were the Greeks able to form such an exact idea of music? It was because they were led by their own experience. They had been instructed by means of music and owed their culture to it. Linus, Orpheus, Cadmus, and Amphion[12] called on the Greeks to abandon the brutal life that they had led up to then in the company of wild beasts, and to enjoy the delights of civilized society under the protection of the laws. Music was the means they used to humanize, as it were, those bestial souls. This is why it was allegorically fabled that, with the sound of the lyre, they were able to tame the savage beasts and to induce the stones themselves to build cities. Through music, those men, who until then had been undeserving of bearing that name, and who perhaps did not even consider themselves such, began to taste the delights of social life, worthy of rational beings. With song accompanied by the harmony of a musical instrument they were taught their duties toward the Supreme Being; the laws of a nascent homeland were promulgated; the norms of justice, friendship, and conjugal love were instilled, as were those of courtesy, charity, compassion for others, and military courage.[13]

9. Athenaeus, *The Deipnosophists*, bk. 14, 627F–628A. [LAH-S]

10. [*Histories*], bk. 4 [ch. 20. The excerpt is cited in Athenaeus, bk. 6; this passage appears in translation in Strunk, *Source Readings,* 50–51. BJB]

11. Homer, *Odyssey* 3.267–72. [LAH-S]

12. On Orpheus and Amphion see n. 13. The perhaps mythical Linus is mentioned as a musician in ancient literature; he was known as a composer of laments. Cadmus was the husband of Harmonia. [BJB]

13. "Silvestres homines sacer interpresque deorum / caedibus, et victu foedo deterruit Orpheus; / dictus ob hoc lenire tigres rabidosque leones, / dictus et Amphion Thebanae conditor arcis / saxa movere sono testudinis et prece blanda / ducere quo vellet. Fuit haec sapientia quondam / publica privatis secernere, sacra profanis, / concubitu prohibere vago, dare iura maritis, / oppida moliri, leges incidere ligno"; Horace, *Ars poetica* 391–99. ["Orpheus, in the care of

The Greeks, then, who had directly experienced music's effectiveness in awakening and governing the emotions, were instructed by this very experience to form the right idea about this discipline. This is why music enjoyed such a high place among them. Pythagoras, for example, considered it the source of all morality, and he demanded that his disciples begin and end the day with music.[14] Plato[15] speaks of music as heaven's greatest gift, and "as having been given by the gods not only to delight the ear, but also to restore order and harmony in the human soul, and to banish errors and voluptuousness." Other philosophers of that nation spoke similarly, and especially Plutarch, for whom all intellectual and moral virtues derived from music. Indeed, what could they not expect from an art destined to such noble use? Is it not true that the fastest way to acquire intellectual and moral virtues is through intense emotions governed by reason?

From this we can see where those moderns went astray. Paying no mind to the nature of Greek music, and judging it as they do ours, they considered the ancients extravagant and ridiculous for holding their music in such esteem.

The favorable concept that the Greeks had of their music led them to cultivate it with great diligence, not so much the part that gratifies the ear as the part that moves the soul. They made music such a basic tenet of their education that Themistocles was considered uneducated and uncivilized when, having been asked to play the lyre at a banquet, he answered that "he did not know how to play it and that he had devoted all his endeavors to making his homeland prosperous and formidable."[16] The Greeks' most eminent wise men and their most expert philosophers were practitioners of this elegant and useful art.[17] In my

the gods and interpreter of their will, deterred wild men from slaughter and foul living; for this he was said to have tamed raging tigers and lions; Amphion too, who founded Thebes' citadel, was said to move stones with the sound of the lyre and lead them where he would with enticing song. Once upon a time wisdom consisted in distinguishing public from private, sacred from profane, forbidding unregulated intercourse of the sexes, giving law to the married, building towns, carving laws on wood." LAH-S]

14. Iamblichus, *Vita Pythagorea*, ch. 25.

15. [Freely cited] from Plutarch, *De superstitione* 5 [*Moralia* 167B, himself paraphrasing Plato, *Timaeus* 47D. LAH-S]

16. Plutarch, *Life of Themistocles* 2.4.

17. Laertius [2.19] provides us with the names of Socrates' two music teachers, Damon and Lampon [not in Diogenes, and a soothsayer, not a musician; confused with Sophocles' reputed music teacher Lamprus (Athenaeus 1.20F)?], who were famous in their time. Plutarch [Pseudo-Plutarch, *De musica* 17 (*Moralia* 1136F)] informs us that Plato's teachers were Dracon, the Athenian, and Metellus [*recte* Megillus], from Agrigento, who were likewise famous in their day. Arcesilaus was taught music by Xanthus, a celebrated Athenian musician [Diogenes Laertius 4.29], to say nothing in particular of the Pythagoreans, who, as we said, began and ended each day with music. The greatest men Greece could boast all wrote about the art of music: men such as Simmias, Aristotle, Theophrastus, Aristoxenus, Democritus, and Epicurus, all illustrious Greek philosophers, and Antisthenes himself, who founded the sect of the Cynics. [Additions by LAH-S.]

opinion, this is the third reason why the element of pathos in ancient music was far more ordered and precise than ours. Music was performed by the flower of literate men of a nation where the fine arts attained a degree of perfection they had never before known, nor would know after. This nation's taste was systematic, but it degenerated into a sort of mania that aimed at systematizing any discipline, no matter how reluctant. Lastly, this nation abounded in sublime minds, who enhanced the study of music thanks to their training both in the sciences and the fine arts. It is no wonder that musical pathos, which had been cultivated so diligently by such a nation, became ordered and systematic, and reached such perfection.

However, opera in our day fares quite differently. It is true, thanks be to God, that our century is not culturally inferior to any of Greece's more flourishing ages. But those among us who profess music are not those who constantly broaden the boundaries of human knowledge, as it was with the Greeks. Indeed, our philosophers consider it extremely shameful to know how to play an instrument with refinement. Today, things have reached such a pass that those who would flaunt indifference, and affect a stoic attitude, display insensibility and boredom toward any kind of harmony. Such literary hypocrisy would even induce the genial Mencke[18] to bare his teeth. Therefore, since music today is not practiced by our philosophers, their sense of pathos could not benefit much, like those who cannot advance without the aid of philosophy. Of the advancements of that art, only its aesthetic quality progressed, as it needs to be judged only by the ear.

We have touched upon these matters concerning ancient and modern music because what we have observed will help us to understand better the subject matter of the next chapter. We have noted how far still the element of pathos in our music is from reaching perfection, and what course it should follow in order to reach it, for if it lacks this quality, not only can it not hope to provide us with a refined and lasting pleasure, but it strangely eclipses the beauty of our theatrical presentations.

II. *The style of theater music*

§1. THE FIRST LAW OF THIS STYLE. Music was admitted to the world of theater in order to enhance the power of words in drama, to which it is united and with which it has a common aim: to stimulate a given emotion.[19] This is the origin of the particular style that this kind of music needs in order to fulfill the task of both sustaining the words and moving the emotions.

---

18. "Menchenio," i.e. Johann Burchard Mencke, *De charlataneria eruditorum declamationes duae* (Leipzig, 1715); the identification was made by Francesco Degrada. [BJB]

19. See Sec. 1, Ch. 2 ["In what the perfection of opera consists"].

First of all, *theater music requires few notes*. The reason is that music padded with notes, whether simultaneous or successive, is incapable of producing pathos, as we have shown in the preceding chapter. It should be added that the fragmented effect produced by a succession of very short notes in a singer's voice reveals the composer's artifice, and as everyone knows, overt artifice is proscribed in dramatic action, as it destroys verisimilitude.

Not only reason but also experience aptly bear out what we have set forth with regard to this law governing theatrical style. If any theater music rich in pathos is examined, it will be found to contain fewer notes than even one of those deadly trills that are so fashionable today. Furthermore, it can never happen that a song made up of many notes will produce pathos in the theater, or strengthen the emotional charge of the words. Such a song may well be pleasing to the ear; yet aside from the insipidness of that pleasure, compared with one springing from deeper emotions, it constitutes an abuse of the fine arts to use their aesthetic elements separated from those of pathos, and especially with respect to operas, which, as we have said, use those arts only to add vigor and support to dramatic emotion, which their aesthetic elements are incapable of doing. Children provide us with a particularly clear example of the effects of these two types of music. When listening to music made up of few notes, whether instrumental or vocal, children show signs of enjoyment and start bouncing about in their fashion. None of these signs, however, is observable when they listen to other kinds of music, overladen with notes. Further evidence of this is provided by the type of music commonly called *Tarantella,* as it is employed to treat those affected by tarantism. This marvelous music, which produces such extraordinary effects on the mind and body of these sufferers, is composed of only twenty tones that are neither too low nor too high. It would lose all value and fail to produce any of the aforementioned effects, if a player were to diminish it, as they say, by turning it into a banal mixture of many fast notes.

§2. THE SECOND LAW. *This style abhors tones that are too high and too low.* Pathos consists of a just medium.

Not long ago, there appeared in one of Europe's most illustrious theaters a talented female singer, endowed with a voice so high-pitched that it possibly had no equal. With her finch-like voice she inspired a sense of wonder in all who listened to her—but nothing more than wonder. Not only was her voice incapable of serving dramatic passion, it did not even appease the ear, as passages executed high on the fingerboard of a violin are similarly incapable of doing. Voices that are too low are likewise incapable of conveying a sense of pathos. This can easily be proved by selecting a song that moves you; transposing it to a higher or lower pitch will suffice to make it lose all its moving qualities. We can thus understand how the Greeks attained such heights with this type of music, even though, as we pointed out, they had no instrument capable of spanning more than three octaves. This kind of music is most compatible with moderate tones, for if it is to move the emotions, it must imitate the human voice, which rarely possesses tones that are too high or too low. Those rare voices indulging in excesses of this sort sound ridiculous and are ill adapted to the gravity of tragic performances.

§3. The third law. *Theatrical style prefers songs that are performed in a parlante rather than an ornamented style.* Do you want a powerful recipe to deprive an energetic song of force? Sprinkle it with a good dose of the world's most beautiful ornaments. This manner of singing is totally alien to vocal music. The latter's function is so to enhance the power of words that the ideas they contain can be vividly conveyed to the listener. An "a," an "e," or an "o," trilled for the duration of many notes, and sometimes many beats, conveys nothing to the listener's spirit, and just when the listener anxiously attempts to penetrate the mood of those characters who attract his interest, he begins to hear those drawn-out yawning sounds, which, with the promise of an exotic pleasure, extinguish instead of enhance the pleasure of pathos. Furthermore, is it not an intolerable breach of verisimilitude to interrupt the flow of an idea in the very midst of its meaning, indeed in the middle of a word, in order to give way to a spate of inarticulate sounds? Is it not comical to see a serious character deliberately stop, with open mouth, to gurgle a long ornamental passage?

This strange manner of singing was introduced in theaters by those ambitious singers who, so as not to leave anything untried, took up the style of instrumental music. They thus acquired a broader range in which to display their vocal flexibility by imitating those mordents, tremolos, runs, trills, and arpeggios that are so effective when performed on some instruments. However, they ignored the fact that music, no less than any of the other fine arts, has different styles, which can only be confused through lack of experience, and that the style of vocal music has to be much more sober and austere than the instrumental.

Never has this manner of singing been more fashionable in our theaters than it is today. The marvelous voice of a famous contemporary female singer[20] has made our composers delirious. Since she began to appear in European theaters and let her inimitable, distinctive, and totally novel trilling be heard, everything in theaters has become trill. Entranced by this novel musical spell, audiences

20. L. S. G. [La Signora Gabrielli. Caterina Gabrielli (1730–96) was one of the outstanding sopranos of the eighteenth century. She sang throughout Italy and in Vienna (where Metastasio was her protector), and also in St. Petersburg (while Traetta was there) and London. Her technical expertise was matched by her charms. BJB]

were convinced they were hearing for the first time the only style truly worthy of operatic music. The *maestri di cappella,* similarly touched by such magic, imagined they were entering a new musical world. Setting foot in that enchanted land, and looking with proudly compassionate eyes at the Scarlattis, Pergolesis, and Vincis, who from the other world could not share in such a discovery, they blessed the heavens (as did the first Spaniards who reached America) for having destined them to be born in this age. Woe to anyone who would have dared challenge this musical novelty! He would have been set upon immediately by a pack of fanatics. This is why the few people of good taste who had not been swayed by the allurements of this new siren, and who knew that the days of Timotheus and Terpander had long passed,[21] thought it best not to protest against this novelty. They refrained from complaining, though they clearly realized that, while the style of that female singer could perhaps do honor to a psaltery or lute player, singing needed a completely different kind of music.

It is high time that composers like Cafaro, Jommelli, Piccinni, Traetta, and Sacchini took true vocal music in hand and brought it again to the stage, leaving that usurped style to instrumental music, where it belongs. In fact, even instrumental music should make a careful and moderate use of such an intricate style. For then (and the expert masters know it full well) music can be called perfect, when it possesses that apparent facility, in which

sibi quivis
Speret idem, sudet multum frustraque laboret
Ausus idem.[22]

This most difficult faculty constitutes the perfection not only of music, but of all its sister arts. For example, it is this which makes Cicero's eloquence superior to Seneca's, Petrarch's muse to Marino's, ancient architecture to Gothic, the tranquillity of Greek statues to the vehemence and liveliness of some modern sculptors.

From *Dell'opera in musica. Trattato del cavaliere Antonio Planelli dell'Ordine Gerosolimitano* (Naples, 1772), 98, 103–31; modern edition by Francesco Degrada (Fiesole: Discanto, 1981), 55, 57–71.

21. Two ancient Greek musicians famed for their innovations: Timotheus of Miletus (fourth century B.C.) for adding an eleventh string to the kithara and replacing the enharmonic genus with the chromatic, Terpander (seventh century B.C.) for introducing the seven-stringed lyre, the lyric *nomos,* and instrumental preludes to recitals of epics. See also above, n. 8, where Timotheus the flute player is confused with Timotheus of Miletus. [BJB]

22. "If anyone should hope to do the same for himself, having made the same venture he would sweat a great deal and labor in vain" (Horace, *Ars poetica* 240–42). [LAH-S]

FRANCESCO MILIZIA
from *Complete Formal and Material Treatise*
on the Theater (1794)

On the Essence of Music

The essence of music lies in imitation. The essence of imitation lies in the true expression of an emotion that one wishes to display. Every expression must be consonant with what has to be expressed. It is like a tailor-made suit. Thus, each expression requires unity, truth, clarity, simplicity, brio, originality, and elegance. Painting, with its contours and colors, expresses the appearances of an infinite number of animate and inanimate bodies. Poetry, with its verses, expresses whatever is in nature. Music, with its songs and sounds, expresses the verses, that is, the expressions of poetry. Consequently, music can be divided into two parts. If it imitates and expresses non-passionate sounds, then it corresponds to landscape painting; if it expresses animate sounds that produce emotion, then it is a narrative painting.

The musician is no freer than the painter; he is forever subjected to the comparisons that people draw between his works and those of nature. If, for example, he has to depict a storm, a brook, or a breeze, the sounds he must use are all in nature, and it is to nature that he must turn in order to find them. If he has to depict something that does not exist in nature, as the cries of the earth, or the shuddering of a ghost emerging from a tomb, his ideas must always correspond to and resemble natural things. Art can neither create nor destroy expressions; it cannot depart from nature. Art can only regulate, enhance, and refine these expressions, but their foundation must always remain utterly natural.

If music is a painting, what kind of painting would it be if the painter had drawn bold lines on his canvas, together with patches of the most vibrant colors, with no resemblance whatever to any familiar object? Similarly, what kind of song or sound would it be that expressed nothing? Monstrous indeed would be that music which expressed the complete opposite of what it ought to signify. Music is a universal language, which speaks by means of sounds. Therefore, if it is not understood, it is a clear indication that art has warped nature instead of perfecting it. Rich as nature may be for musicians, if the meaning enclosed in the latter's expressions cannot be understood, then it is no longer richness, but rather an unfathomable and therefore useless idiom.

Music must of necessity follow poetry, because music lacks its own means of explaining the reasons for its various impressions. Thus, without poetry, music's imitations of nature and of passions would be very vague and indefinite. Tender and sweet arias that can express love can also express similar sensations such as benevolence, friendship, and compassion. How can music distinguish sensations of scorn from those of terror or other violent agitations of the heart? Music therefore must always faithfully adhere to poetry, as did ancient music, which followed poetry closely, expressing exactly its rhythm and measure, and applying itself to poetry only to make the latter more splendid and majestic. If the declamation, or even the simple reading, of an excellent lyrical drama makes us weep, what power then would it not receive from the enchantment of music, when embellishing without overwhelming it? What impression would it not produce upon a sensitive audience?

Our music, however, which was once subordinate to poetry, as it should be, has become poetry's tyrant and despot. Present-day musicians no longer understand the art of imitating the harmony of verse and of displaying poetic grace. Indeed, they demand that poets write short, truncated, prosaic, and irregular verses, without rhythm and harmony. At times, they go so far as to compose their arias first and then have some poetaster tack on whatever words come into his imagination, so that one can hardly recognize that our *opera* is sung in verse, and it could rightly be entitled *music without poetry.*

Since our music has thrown off the yoke of poetry, it is no longer imitative, it no longer expresses anything, and it produces no effect. It has become a collection of thoughts, often excellent, but unconnected and meaningless, as useless as Raphael's Vatican arabesques, so prized and so irrational. No matter how well planned music is in all its tones, how geometric in terms of harmony, if it lacks meaning it will be like a prism that displays the most beautiful colors but does not make a picture. It will delight the ears, but prove tedious to the spirit.

Thus, if music is to be restored to its twofold objective of delighting the senses and predisposing the heart to virtue, it must be guided by poetry and express its emotions. Only then will there be an end to the common criticism that accuses operatic characters of singing and trilling while tormenting themselves and going off to their deaths. Such censure is based on the disconnection that usually exists between song and words. When the passions speak, the trills must stop. If music were adapted to poetry well, then all the irksome improprieties that now afflict opera would disappear. However, for this to be achieved, either the poet needs to be a composer, or the composer a poet. When these two rare talents cannot be found together, let the composer at least have the discretion to come to an understanding with the poet, and be convinced once and for all that music is a more powerful, livelier, and warmer expression of the concepts and emotions of the soul expressed by the poetry. Lully, in fact, depended on Quinault, Vinci on Metastasio. If the composer behaves in this way, he will secretly be pleased with his music, which will prove more narrative, more clearly meaningful, and devoid of vagueness and obscurity. The worst music is that which is totally lacking in character.

Lastly, our Italian music must be wary of another evil, that of constant change. Music that was pleasing twenty years ago cannot be tolerated today. Even were Apollo the composer of an opera, once it has been produced, Heaven forbid that it be mounted a second time, not even after thirty years. The same drama can be staged as many times as one wishes, but the music must always be different. This is one of the foremost reasons why music has become something of a fad, full of passing fancies and whimsicalities, and is now charged with decline after Vinci and Pergolesi, just as architecture in the manner of Borromini.[1] That is, because of the desire to surprise by means of novelty, composers have lost sight of the need to imitate the beauty of nature, and thus to please and instruct.

After these preliminary notions on music in general, let us now consider how they apply to the various parts of the drama.

ON THE OVERTURE[2]

The overture is both the opening of our operas and their first drawback. The ingredients of every overture are a pair of allegros, a slow section, and a deafening noise. Once you have heard one, you have heard them all. It is always a meaningless part that every drama is allowed to contain.

Nevertheless, it is evident that an overture should be like the exordium of an opera, and it is universally known that the exordium must be drawn from the very viscera of the subject that is to be represented. From this, two necessary consequences may be derived:

1. Each opera must have its own overture, one that in some way announces the action and prepares the audience to receive those emotional impressions that result from the entire drama.

2. Each overture must be meaningful.

Our overtures, on the contrary, are so lacking in meaning that the same one could be applied to any drama whatever. Any music that depicts nothing is simply noise. Were it not for habit, which alters everything, such music would procure no more pleasure than a string of harmonious and sweet-sounding words wanting both order and logical connection. The celebrated Tartini never

---

1. The architect Francesco Castelli, called Borromini (1599–1667); the façades of his Roman churches are outstanding examples of Baroque architecture, in which he sought to soften the colossal and symmetrical constructions of his predecessors with undulating façades and nervous decorative elements, creating elements of surprise. [BJB]

2. In this and much of the remainder of the passage Milizia paraphrases Algarotti (see above, pp. 236–39), to the point of unabashed plagiarism in some phrases. [KKH]

composed a sonata that did not express some composition by Petrarch; nor did he ever lose sight of his intended subject.[3] These sonatas, however, although rich in meaning, are only half alive, as they lack the expression of song, which is the very soul of music.

On the Recitative

The din of the overture is followed by the recitative, which is both dull-sounding and neglected by composers and singers alike, and which no one thinks of listening to any longer. In truth, its insipidity and monotony are insufferable. Yet it is the very foundation of opera.

All things in this world, and especially human emotions, have their rests and intervals, and the art of the theater demands that in this respect the course of nature be observed. At performances one cannot always be bursting with laughter or bathed in tears. The leading characters are not always moved by the same intensity of feeling; they alternate between moments of emotional passion and of calm. Those in subordinate roles, no matter how involved in the action, cannot have the same passionate excesses as their heroes. Lastly, even the most pathos-inspiring situation becomes so only by degree; it needs to be prepared, and its effect depends in large measure on what has preceded and led up to it.

There are thus two distinct tempos in opera: the calm and the passionate. The composer must concentrate all his efforts on finding two musical genres that are essentially different and capable of conveying respectively the language of tranquillity and that of the emotions, in all their forcefulness, variety, and disorder. This last genre makes up what is known as the *aria,* the former what is called *recitative.*

When characters on stage discuss, deliberate, linger, and converse together, it would be most inappropriate for them to sing and trill: they must recite. But what will this recitative of theirs be? Performing it in the usual way is soporific; nor can it simply be spoken: an opera that is alternately spoken and sung would be as incongruous as ice and fire. How then to proceed?[4]

3. Tartini's habit of choosing poetic subjects for his instrumental works was also remarked upon by d'Alembert; see Ch. 2, p. 90. [BJB]

4. In the outstanding M. Rousseau's lyrical scene *Pygmalion,* which was performed at Lyons with great success [1770], the words were never sung, and music merely served to fill in the intervals necessary in recitation. With this spectacle Rousseau wanted to convey an idea of Greek *melopoeia* and of ancient Greek theatrical recitation. This is why he wanted the music to be expressive and to depict both the situation and, as it were, the particular emotion the author himself felt. Some sections of the music were composed by Rousseau himself, and the rest by M. Coignet. Why is such an example, which was so successful in France, not imitated in Italy? Would it be so shameful to correct our ways? [Horace Coignet (1735–1821), an amateur violinist, singer, and composer in Lyons, wrote 24 of the 26 instrumental interludes for *Pygmalion;* the music was very popular in France. BJB]

The masters of this art have proved that the foundation of the recitative must be a harmony closely patterned on nature, in other words, something halfway between ordinary speech and melody. Therefore, it must be varied and draw its form and soul from the quality of the words. At times, it must be as rapid as the flow of words themselves, and at times it must proceed slowly. Above all, it must stress those inflections and those accentuations that the power of the emotions has the strength to convey to the expressions.

To be persuaded of the truth of this assertion, one has only to observe recitative that is accompanied by instruments and is called *obbligato*. Why is it that we listen to it with both attention and pleasure, if not because it is natural? Therefore, let all recitative be similar to the *obbligato;* then, instead of being boring, it will become delightful, and the more delightful it is, the more natural and expressive it will be.

Such harmonious recitative would result in a further advantage, that of avoiding the ugly break that occurs between an ordinary recitative and an aria, which shoots off in the middle of things like a rocket gone wild. Certainly there has to be an appreciable difference between the recitative and the aria, but not a leap as from the earth to the sky. Who bursts out in a fit of passion without having first experienced it in various degrees?

On Arias

An *aria* is the development of an interesting situation; it is the peroration and recapitulation of the scene. With four short lines provided by the poet, the composer attempts to express not only the main idea of his character, but also all the associated ones and the gradations. The more ably the composer divines the most secret stirrings of the human soul in each situation, the more beautiful will his aria be. It is here that he must unfold all the riches of his artistry by joining the magic of harmony with that of melody, and the authority of the voices with that of the instruments. The performance of the aria will then be divided between song and gesture, as it requires not only an able singer but also a competent actor. This is what an aria should be. Let us see what it is at present.

The aria begins not with singing, but rather with those introductory ritornellos, which are always useless and often annoying, and which enfeeble the action. This happens because the actor is obliged to stand there with his hands in his belt, waiting for the ritornello to end—which it does not readily do—before giving vent to the passion seething within his breast.

At last he sings, but a host of instruments will so drown his voice that only from time to time will some remote cry or shout be heard. Why such a rabble of violins? Why do away with the violas, which are midway between violins and basses? Why not reintroduce lutes and harps, whose pizzicato gives the ripienos a certain sparkle?

Those arias in which the voices compete with a trumpet or an oboe, exchanging question and answer until they are breathless, elicit the most enthusiastic applause. What then is imitated? What poetic emotion is expressed? Each aria should be discreetly accompanied by different types of instruments, so that each instrument suits the nature of the words, thus effecting a proper expression of a particular emotion.

He who sings the highest notes in arias is the best, that is, the least melodious. Who does not see that the high notes are for music what the brightest colors are for painting?

Those frequent passages from one musical pole to another, when not required by emotion or a particular feeling, are true interruptions of the musical sense.

What are those endless repetitions of words, verses, of complicated, disordered, and mixed parts if not a maze? Words are not to be repeated unless in the order dictated by the emotions.

The first part of an aria is usually a display of pyrotechnics, the second a boring lamentation, from which one returns to the first part, which (come what may) has to be repeated four times in its entirety and separately in countless fragments so that each member of the audience can leave the theater utterly satiated. The foremost musical minds cannot suffer so much music.

Maestri di cappella are normally very careful to express the words of an aria. They sweeten the notes at the words *calma, sposo, padre* (calm, husband, father); they express the word *cielo* (heaven) with high notes and the words *terra* (earth) and *inferno* (hell) with low ones; they impetuously glide over words like *fulmini* (lightning) and *tuoni* (thunder), and with a dozen vocal outbursts forcefully express the words *mostro furioso* (furious monster). But these and other similar childish devices are not those that express the condition of the soul or the sense of an aria; they only explain a few words, and destroy the overall feeling. The same problems are to be found in the duets.

The choruses are even more poorly produced; they are so insipid that no one deigns to listen to them anymore. Yet if they were properly laid out by a poet, and expressed with simplicity the sentiments of a people voicing their hatred of a tyrant's cruelty by means of brief imprecations, or applauding a beneficent hero with joyful acclamations, they would become pleasing and interesting, at least if they were set to expressive music.

Choruses can even be sung in recited tragedies, as was once done in Ferrara in the case of Giraldi's *Egle,* Lollio's *Aretusa,* and Tasso's *Aminta.*[5] These tragic choruses should always praise virtue, condemn vice, and console the unfortunate. These choruses should be set either to plaintive or cheerful music, or a mixture of the two, according to their subject matter. This gives pleasure and relief to the listeners who are at times tired and filled with the powerful effects produced by the tragedy itself. In this way, they can catch their breaths and rest at the end of each act, since the choruses serve as appropriate intermezzos, unlike those most unsuitable ones that are at present used both in tragedies and comedies.

From what has been said so far, it clearly seems that the great illness of modern Italian music lies in excess. This excess has given rise to ornamentation of all types, flourishes, trifles, embroideries, and all sorts of oddities. These, in turn, have caused us to lose sight of the main aim of music, which consists in expressing poetic sentiment in the most natural and simple manner, so as to touch the heart in the most vivid way possible. Do you really want touching ariettas, capable of etching themselves in everyone's memory? Then have them depict and express the poet's feelings; have them be as natural as possible, or, as they say, speaking (*parlanti*). Only beautiful simplicity can imitate nature. It was this simplicity that made Vinci and Pergolesi famous. Intricate artistic embellishments may cause surprise, but they fail to go to the heart.

If you want music to be simple and touching, use more melody and less counterpoint. Counterpoint is made up of various parts: one is high and quick-paced, the other low and slow, and both must exist together and strike the ears at the same time. How then can counterpoint produce in the soul a given passion, which requires a specific rhythm? Happiness requires a very fast tempo, with an intense and high-pitched tone; sadness requires a slow tempo, with a restrained and low-pitched tone. Melody, on the other hand, always proceeds at the same tempo and with the same tone up to the end, and is thus particularly suited to arousing a given emotion. Melody does not require such profound learning as does counterpoint, but it does require exquisite taste and the greatest discretion in judgment.

Proof of this are those musical intermezzos[6] and short comic operas, which

5. Milizia evidently did not know the works firsthand, for Giovanni Battista Giraldi Cintio's *Egle* (1545; the music by Antonio dal Cornetto is lost), Alberto Lollio's *Aretusa* (1563; music by Alfonso della Viola, lost), and Torquato Tasso's *Aminta* (1573) are all pastorals. [BJB]

6. From the days of ancient chivalry up to the beginning of the last century, it was customary at the feasts of distinguished princes and lords to perform a sort of dumb show between one course and another with the aid of machines, that is, a theatrical representation in which there were human figures, strange animals, trees, mountains, rivers, seascapes, and boats. All this was interspersed with characters and birds that moved about the hall or on the tables, representing actions evoking warlike and chivalric deeds, especially those of the Crusades. Such amusements, which served to entertain the dinner guests between one course and the other, were called *entremets,* that

are more pleasing than heroic operas because their music is simpler and expresses the subject matter better, both in its entirety and its separate parts. These operas are composed with greater simplicity, as they usually concern very ordinary characters who cannot be expected to perform all the secrets of the art or the treasures of learning. This is why composers are compelled to keep to what is simple, and with simplicity imitate nature. It is the burlesque opera *La serva padrona* that caused Italian music to triumph in France.

Thus, properly composing an opera requires much more than just a few hours stolen from libertine pursuits, as some composers boast. Long and serious meditation is required to understand thoroughly and to express a drama, both in its entirety and in its parts.

From *Trattato completo, formale e materiale del teatro* (Venice, 1794; repr. Bologna: Forni, 1969), 50–59.

VITTORIO ALFIERI
Preface to *Abele: Tramelogedia* (1796)

Having conferred an unusual name on this theatrical production of mine (whatever it may be), I feel compelled to provide a brief explanation of the title I have given it.

Tramelogedy, a term which time will judge either barbarous or Italian, seemed to me the most appropriate to characterize this work, about which it will perhaps be easier for me to say what it is not than what it is.

It is not tragedy, since it violates various basic rules of the tragic genre, and it avails itself of means that a sound tragedy cannot and absolutely must not allow.

It is not comedy, since its action depicts characters who, on account of their antiquity, are most venerable, its reversals (*peripezie*) are doleful, and its outcome is supremely tragic. Although because of the simplicity of its subject matter it seems to bear some analogy with a pastoral, it is nevertheless quite different because of the extremely complex manner in which it develops and progresses, the marvelous elements it contains, and the denouement of the plot.

---

is, "between courses." From these were derived the *intermezzos* in theaters. Perhaps the *desserts,* which today are in fashion at meals, have their origin in those *entremets.* Today, however, the term *entremets* means a more general and voluptuous kind of luxury that is repeated daily and presents us with all the sensual laxity or the boredom of the Sybarites. He who thinks too much of his table thinks too little of virtue.

It is not drama (in the current meaning of the term): if we speak of musical drama, this work of mine in no way resembles the genre, both because it strictly observes unity of action and approximately two-thirds of its scenes are written and recited in tragic style. If then we speak of drama (in the sense of domestic tragedy), my composition resembles it even less because, as I have already pointed out, it deals with lofty characters and constantly draws on the marvelous and the supernatural.

It is not tragicomedy, because those parts that are not tragic are in no way comic.

Nor, finally, could anyone familiar with this art say that my poem resembles Greek tragedy, in which the melody of the choruses is intertwined in such a way that it can justly be called melotragedy. Being sound and logical, this title would be ill suited to my work, which is perhaps illogical and certainly is extravagant. In Greek tragedy the marvelous also occurs at times, but always in strict observance of the three unities of place, time, and action. There the choruses are sung by real characters, who also recite iambic verse and engage in dialogue with heroic figures, and they are continually inserted into every act of the tragedy. In my composition, on the other hand, both the singing and the fictitious characters remain almost completely separated from the tragic ones. Although these two different categories of performers both tend toward the same end, each usually operates on his own, in precisely the way that in epic poems the "celestial mechanics" separately arrange among themselves those supernatural interventions that, through extraordinary means, will then influence the heroes' actions.

Opera-tragedy, then, would be the term that most appropriately defines a tragedy mixing melody and marvelous elements, such as mine is. However, wanting to use a title that would do it justice, I have, so to speak, inlaid the word *melos* in the word *tragedy*, in such a way as not to spoil the ending of the latter, and not worrying about the root of the word itself. For had I paid attention to it, I would certainly not have split up τράγος, fearing that the pedants would not have left me alone. However, I wanted this rather extravagant term immediately to convey the author's extravagant intention of grafting elements of sung epic onto tragedy, yet without diminishing in the least the full tragic effect of the fifth act. I myself would be the first to acknowledge that this genre (if indeed it is a genre) is monstrous, and ought never to be admissible in any sound poetics. People will say to me: why then invent such a genre and use it? I shall therefore attempt to justify this too.

Certainly I was not encouraged by the silly and childish vanity of wanting to be regarded as the inventor of a new dramatic genre. I knew only too well that true literary laurels are earned only by writing perfect examples of genres that have already been established, never by inventing new and worse ones. However, since I was writing in Italian for Italians, I could not totally divorce myself from that country's uses and abuses, and think or not think about Italy. This region of Europe lies in an almost complete political void, a fact that cannot help but influence its non-entity or its false and abject moral, literary, and especially theatrical position. This being the case, very few if any tragedies worthy of the name are written there, and certainly none is ever passably performed, because there are no actors, no spectators, no connoisseurs, and no one willing to pay. Thus, being accustomed to wasting away in their theaters, without even having real theater, Italians have found a cloying auditory pastime in opera; in these would-be theaters of theirs, they have become progressively incapable of exercising any of those intellectual faculties required to feel, enjoy, judge, or even understand a real tragedy. In short, Italian audiences are all ears and no mind, and such long-eared judges can only beget more and more long-eared writers and actors. For this as well as for many other reasons, we have rightly become the laughingstock of the rest of Europe.

This motive alone prompted me, from the very first years of my literary career, to see whether it might not be possible to offer such an audience a mixed spectacle and, by means of their ears, use a fruitful deception of their intellects in order to instill in them a taste for tragedy. At the time when I was writing (or thought I was writing) some real tragedies, I preferred not to mix in this spurious genre among them, in order not to diminish their worth. Hence for my *Abele* I composed only the supporting structure, and I devised five other tramelogedies, but put off writing them out until I had finished the tragedies. Various circumstances then upset this plan of mine, so that only the one tramelogedy that I had already sketched out did I undertake to complete. I totally gave up the idea of bringing the other five to completion: if this genre is such that it will prove successful, another writer will be able to compose many others on the model of this one, and improve upon it. If, conversely, this genre proves unperformable, it will have been to my advantage to have written only one, rather than six.

After this preamble, it remains to give some explanation of the purpose, means, and execution of this monstrous spectacle, and to explain how it can function. Much like scaffolding used to prop up a building, which, being slowly removed, enables the edifice itself to stand straight and tall, this work of mine could serve as a go-between, so to speak, catering to the future taste and understanding of true and simple tragedy. In due course the latter would take the place of tramelogedy, should this genre succeed in reopening the necessary channels of communication between intellect and hearing, which today, to the misfortune of Italians, are totally disconnected in their theaters.

He who would write tramelogedies (in case anyone, prompted by this attempt of mine, should undertake a similar task) should first choose subjects far removed from us in time, customs, and place, but ones that can be realistically adapted to the marvels of religion, without seeming too unlikely or laughable. He should then use extreme care in distributing the miraculous episodes, which is the musical part, so that they enhance the tragic effect without spoiling it, indeed increasing it whenever possible. And at the same time in the tragic part he should incorporate episodic and marvelous parts, though tragedy should dominate in such a way that no one can doubt the primacy of the tragic over the musical part. The two, however, must be so cohesive and interlaced that the operatic part cannot be removed without maiming the tragedy, nor the tragedy removed without destroying the entire work. It is not easy for me to explain my ideas to everyone with the utmost clarity, this being a new subject and partly dependent on the imagination. I hope, however, that for those who understand the art, these few words of mine, which are then commented on in the *Abele* that follows them, will succeed in explaining or indicating the author's intention through the piece itself.

In whatever way the poem is subsequently divided, care must be taken to have the fifth act consist solely of tragedy, without interrupting or in any way spoiling the catastrophe by including some melodious element. The catastrophe could indeed be increased, once acted out, by adding to it some melodious passage, but this must always be done with discretion because, as the purpose of this spectacle is to move the listeners intellectually and emotionally, and not to leave them with a simple buzzing of music in their ears, its ending must be absolutely tragic. What is more, it will be through the author's dexterity in handling these two parts properly that the listeners, thinking they have come to see an opera, will have, as it were, ingested a tragedy. The latter will have been presented to them in much the same way as sick children are restored to health, by taking medicine from sugar-rimmed glasses.

As regards distribution, I have preferred to have the first act of my tramelogedy consist entirely of opera, the second of tragedy, the third and the forth of mixed tragedy, and the fifth again entirely of tragedy, except for the very end, where the few verses uttered by God's voice are like a *deus ex machina*. Others will do as they wish. I too, had I completed the other tragedies, would have varied the distribution in each one, according to the requirements of the various subjects.

The religious cults of the ancient Egyptians, Persians, Jews, Chaldeans, Arabs, Indians, Celts, and Scots, indeed of the Greeks themselves, and among contemporary peoples such as the Mexicans and Peruvians, since they are very remote in location, can offer ample material for this kind of drama, for they are all abundantly provided with the marvelous, which is necessary to this type of work; they can furthermore prove to be ever new, diverse, and effective sources of it. In terms of poetry, the field is extremely broad. The competent poet can cut a splendid figure, as can the able tragedian. Together, these two sublime branches of poetry can vie with one another without one damaging the other. An author can mix events drawn from tradition, fables, and history with the aforementioned religious cults and customs of those remote nations. He can also totally invent situations, as long as he presents them under the guise of familiar names and of realistic events, in conformity with the customs and the political situation of those places where the actions he narrates are supposed to have occurred.

He who wishes to have either this or some other tramelogedy based on such foundations performed must first procure the services of two different theatrical companies: one of tragic actors and one of singers. Each, with their different skills and, moreover, mostly appearing in separate scenes, must cooperate toward the same end. The tragic actors will expect to recite a tragedy in which some singers will be introduced, without disturbing them in the least. On the other hand, the singers (who are at present more presumptuous, more ignorant, and by far more spoiled than actors) will expect that the tragic actors, for their convenience and rest, will allow them an intermezzo between one act and another. Their pride being thus flattered—or deluded—and they themselves being seduced by generous wages, they will perhaps unwittingly serve the general purpose of the performance.

If this genre could produce the miracle of instilling in Italians a love of tragedy, I would then perhaps hold myself worthy of esteem for having been instrumental in promoting it. I would hope, although I do not regard it as positive, that this genre might develop and spread to a certain extent, especially as I am quite certain that it would soon be replaced by a sounder and truer type of tragedy, which would banish tramelogedy, as all things that are monstrously hybrid should be banished. This particular monster, however, will at least have proved useful in paving the way for real tragedy, which has hitherto been so difficult to achieve.

If, on the other hand, my reckless attempt to create something false, when there was already so much falsity, should produce only errors and monsters still worse than this *Abele*, I will be happy to have been the only person to have made such an attempt, and equally happy that such a genre be born and die without begetting any other.

However, this type of performance, being very spectacular, will easily please the general public. As a novelty, and also partly false, it will also please those many admirers of the novel and the false. At the same time, tramelogedy will require the protection of princes and those who govern, and of those who are rich and powerful. For it can never be properly staged in theaters, or be fully successful, without enormous expenditure on costumes, scenery, and performers. This intrinsic dependence, which is typical of this genre and makes it all the less pleasing to me, would appear to be a significant obstacle in the way of its success. Yet this very same reason could also work to its advantage. Princely nuptials, a coronation, a glorious peace, or some other similar celebration could perhaps provide the opportunity of attempting, for novelty's sake, the representation of a tramelogedy with all its necessary pomp. At such an occasion, the prince's purse can at least partially, if not entirely, make up for the lack of ability and judgment on the part of the authors, if indeed they were authors, for even a mediocre composition, with the magic help of a *maestro di cappella,* singers, dancers, actors, scenery, and costumes, will nevertheless greatly delight the general public. This is also one of the main reasons why I myself, more as a stepfather than as a father, judge tramelogedy to be far inferior to true tragedy. The latter, with only five or six characters who truly know their art, will enthrall the hearts and minds of the listeners without in the least involving the other senses, and without superfluous, grandiose apparatus.

In conclusion, I hope that Italy (if not through me, then through some other author) will some day have real theater, in which each art will have its proper place, and that opera, confined within its natural boundaries of fictional, playful, and amorous themes, will no longer usurp divine tragedy's primacy. These two theatrical genres are too diverse in their effects for a healthy nation to allow them even to compete on equal terms. Opera debases and enfeebles the mind, while tragedy uplifts, ennobles, and fortifies it. May tramelogedy thus partly pave the way for this necessary and important change, whereby Italians, rising from their effeminate opera to the virility of tragedy, will similarly arise from the nullity of their political condition to the dignity of a true nation.

From *Abele* (1796), in *Tutte le opere di Vittorio Alfieri,* ed. P. Cazzani (Milan: Mondadori, 1957), 1213–19.

PIETRO METASTASIO
Letter to Saverio Mattei, at Naples (1770)

Vienna, 5 April 1770

A few tasks are enough, my most revered Signor don Saverio,[1] to take up all the activity of a tired, worn out, and aged individual such as myself. Having had

---

1. Saverio Mattei (1744–95), a man of many talents, was a scholar of near eastern languages, a musician, and a lawyer. His Italian translations in the style of Metastasio of the "poetic books" of the Bible from the original Hebrew were first published in 1766–74 as *I libri poetici della Bibbia tradotti dall'ebraico originale, ed adattati al gusto della poesia italiana con note e dissertazioni.* So popular were they that thirteen editions were printed during the eighteenth and early-nineteenth

more than I could cope with in the past weeks, I pray your most illustrious Lordship, if not to forgive, at least to excuse the involuntary delay in my response to your recent letter, which is as learned as it is obliging. From the very beginning, I have not hidden from you my physical inability to undertake such a laborious task. Hence, despite my inability, you are now obliged to back me up.

Prudens emisti vitiosum, dicta tibi est lex.[2]

Our young and indefatigable composer[3] is very surprised by the excessive favor your most illustrious Lordship has accorded her music. Her ambition was set much lower, and therefore she is convinced she is indebted to such a kind supporter for most of the enthusiastic words expressed in her praise. In order to experience the effect of her work, she arranged a private rehearsal of the noted Psalm in her chambers.[4] There were only the most necessary instruments, the four inevitable voices, which were a little less than mediocre. The singers' parts had not been doubled for the ripienos, and so this sort of painting lacked all the enchantment of chiaroscuro. Nevertheless, I am compelled to confess that the varied, delightful, and unusual harmony of her composition greatly exceeded the expectation of both myself and the few initiates who had been admitted to such a private event. I took care to distribute copies of the poetry to the audience, and exulted at the general applause for the translator's excellent work. I hope your most illustrious Lordship will not have overlooked this indispensable act of diligence.

I shall now discuss the just merit that accrues to your learned book, which has so rapidly required a new octavo edition.[5] I would not, however, want the

---

centuries. Among the best known and loved were Mattei's translations from the Book of Psalms, which were set to music by various composers. [KKH]

2. "Well knowing what you were doing, you have bought defective goods; the terms have been stated"; Horace, *Epistles* 2.2.18. [EF]

3. Marianne [von] Martínez (1744–1812), daughter of Nicolò, in whose house Metastasio lived in Vienna. She took harpsichord lessons from Haydn and was a talented composer. Among other things, she set to music Metastasio's oratorio *Isacco, figura del Redentore.* The poet saw to her education and left her a legacy. [EF] In a previous letter to Mattei, of 18 Dec. 1769, Metastasio had mentioned sending him a packet containing "your most beautiful Psalms set to music by mademoiselle Marianne Martinetz." [KKH]

4. The Psalm to which Metastasio refers here is probably *Salmo L: Miserere, trasportato in versi italiani dal Signor D. Saverio Mattei,* Marianne Martínez' setting for four voices and orchestra of Psalm 50 (Vulgate; Psalm 51 in the King James version), known in Italy as the "Miserere" from its first line: "Have mercy upon me, o Lord." It was probably the best known of all Mattei's Psalm translations and was also set to music by Jommelli. See Bruno Brunelli, ed., *Tutte le opere di Pietro Metastasio,* 5 vols. (Milan: Mondadori, 1943–54), 4:893, note to Letter 1821. [KKH]

5. Metastasio is referring to *The Poetic Books of the Bible* [see note 1] "admirably translated into Italian meter by the most learned Don Saverio Mattei" (see his *Estratto dell'arte poetica* in Brunelli, ed., 2:1068.) [EF]

original quarto edition to remain incomplete. The three volumes you courteously sent me, which are temporarily bound only to the extent convenient for the reader, impatiently await their fellow volumes in order to be uniformly adorned in the elegant binding they deserve. Up to now, they have so sweetly and profitably occupied my time that I certainly would not be able to deprive them of this small token of my gratitude.

I should share with you my feelings on the merits of ancient and modern music? Ah, my cruel don Saverio! This means thrusting me into a maze from which you know full well I would never be able to escape, even were I equipped with all the necessary tools, or were I still in the flower of my strength. What reasonable comparison can ever be made between things that are not known? I am convinced of the true and splendid magnificence of Jewish music, and do not think it permissible to doubt the efficacy of the Greek; however, I would not be able to form a just opinion of their different systems. I too know very well that there is only one music in all nature, that is, "a delightful harmony produced by the proportions of the highest and lowest sounds, and of the fastest and slowest tempos." But who will supply me with Ariadne's thread so that I will not lose my way amidst these proportions? They depend mainly on the proper division of a series of sounds, and such a division has, I believe, always been and is manifestly imperfect. How can I think otherwise, when I hear great composers arguing whether the interval from one tone to another should consist of five, seven, or nine steps? Or when I notice that some consider the interval of a fourth to be a dissonance, while others think it a perfect consonance? Or again, if I see that when a harpsichord is tuned exactly in accordance with the divisions of our system, it is clearly out of tune? And if, in order to remedy this difficulty, tuners have to start forming a widened fifth in the middle of the keyboard by ear, which they call *allegra* (that is, out of tune), so that, by adjusting the rest of the tuning on the basis of it, the defect itself is divided and therefore becomes imperceptible? Who can tell me if the ancients were more successful than we with the exactness of this division, which is no less subject to error than is the calendar? Or, who can tell me what devices they used, as we do, to cover up these flaws? After having read Plutarch's boring list of the inventors of every musical innovation;[6] after having learned from him and from the Greek masters, edited by the illustrious Meibom,[7] about "the hypate, the nete, the diapason, the diatessaron, the diapente, the tetrachords, the diatonic, chromatic, and enharmonic genera, the Dorian, Phrygian, and Lydian modes," and all the ancient musical terms, will I be more enlightened? Will I be able to formulate a

---

6. Pseudo-Plutarch, *De musica* (Περὶ μουσικῆς). [EF]

7. *Antiquae musicae auctores septem. Graece et latine*, ed. Marcus Meibom (Amsterdam, 1652). Metastasio also referred to it in *Estratto dell'arte poetica*, in *Opere*, ed. Brunelli, 2:964. [EF]

clear definition of all these terms fit to frighten children? How is it possible to draw comparisons in the midst of such obscurity? It may well be, indeed it is quite likely, that what appears to me a pitch-dark night will seem as clear as day to others who are more perceptive, and less foreign to this vast and terrifying province than I. But I do not believe that, because of this, they will possess the knowledge necessary to make a sound comparison between ancient and modern music. Music is the object of one of the senses, and the senses, either through their own physical alterations or through those caused by various external trappings, change their taste from one season to the next, and from one century to another. A banquet prepared according to Apicius' recipes[8] would today prove nauseous to the hardiest of stomachs; the much touted *Bacchi cura Falernus ager,*[9] in the judgment of modern palates, produces a wine fit for galley slaves; bitter and dreadful coffee, which, according to Redi,[10] is worse than poison itself, has become for almost everyone alive the most delicious drink—and who knows if this did not happen in the end with Redi himself? The ariettas that once enchanted our forebears are for us today tedious and unbearable dirges. Thus, wherein lies music's perfection, since it is subject to the dictates of taste, which changes so much from one moment to the next? How can I ever come up with a sure norm that will enable me to know when taste judges correctly or when it is incoherent? "But," you will object, "this skepticism of yours is beside the point. I also can doubt, and am I not particularly curious to learn how you go about doubting. What I desire to know is your idea of ancient and modern music, for it seems to me absolutely impossible that, despite so many doubts, you have not yet formulated an idea on this matter." This is very true, my dear don Saverio. Our imagination, which is ever active and reckless, is satisfied with the most frivolous grounds upon which to construct immediately the most whimsical images. It is enough for me to hear mention of Cairo or Peking for those vast cities, which I have never seen, to appear before my eyes. Thus, if your Lordship is happy to have me convey ideas of this type, I am ready to satisfy you.

It seems to me, my most revered friend, that the music of the ancients was much simpler, but much more effective than the modern, and that, on the other hand, the modern is more artful and marvelous than the ancient. When I

8. Marcus Gavius Apicius, a pleasure-lover in the age of Tiberius, putative author of a collection of culinary recipes entitled *De re coquinaria.* [EF]

9. Metastasio is referring to the territory of Falernum, in the region of Campania, which was famous in antiquity for its excellent wine, and was consequently dear to Bacchus. [EF]

10. Francesco Redi (1626–98), poet, physician, and polymath, who made the god Bacchus, praising Tuscan wines to Ariadne, declare: "Beverei prima il veleno, / Che un bicchier, che fosse pieno / Dell'amaro e reo caffè" (I would sooner drink poison than a beaker full of bitter, wicked coffee); *Bacco in Toscana: Ditirambo di Francesco Redi* (Florence, 1685), ll. 188–90. [LAH-S]

hear that Plato wanted everyone in his republic to study music, as the necessary foundation of every science and virtue;[11] when I read that in Greece not only all the poets, but also all the philosophers, army commanders, and even the governors of the republics were excellent musicians, I conclude that music must then have demanded much less study than does ours, for our music requires that one devote half a lifetime to become a mediocre artist. Consequently, their music was simpler than ours. To prove that our music is more artful than that of the ancients, it seems sufficient to cite (besides numerous other reasons) modern counterpoint, thanks to which as many as twenty-four completely different melodies can be sung together at the same time, producing an extremely sweet harmony, unknown to the ancients. That it was indeed unknown to the ancients is amply demonstrated by the writings, especially on the science of harmonics, by the most learned maestro, Padre Martini.[12] He will give you the scientific and historical reasons why the ancients did not possess, nor could possess, this kind of music, and he will explain how that concord of diverse voices, which is mentioned in a few passages by ancient authors, and which constitutes the rather weak evidence on which supporters of the opposite theory base their opinion, must have consisted of singing at the fourth, fifth, and octave, but always the very same melody. In fact, had such a significant invention been known to the Greeks, who can think that they would have made so little noise about it? It should be added that all the imperfect ancient ways of notating music (which we know of today) made it impossible for them to master the complexities involved in modern counterpoint. The ability to express as we now do all the differences of pitch and rhythm on a single five-line staff; the ability to superimpose one melody on another and to perceive at a glance all their connections, was, in my opinion, absolutely necessary for the invention of counterpoint. And as you of course know well, this manner of writing music dates back to no further than the eleventh century.

The fact that ancient music was more effective than modern music seems to me to depend on the diametrically opposed role of modern and ancient singers. Theater is the throne of music. It is in the theater that music unfolds all the pomp of its enchanting powers, and it is thence that the prevailing taste spreads to the people. The theaters of the ancients were vast squares; ours are very restricted halls. In order to make themselves heard by the innumerable spectators, ancient theater actors had to possess that *vox tragoedorum* that Cicero prescribed for his orator.[13] To develop such a voice, those who were

11. See *Republic*, bk. 3, 401Dff. [EF]

12. Giovanni Battista Martini, *Storia della musica* (Bologna, 1757–81); excerpts are given above, Ch. 4. [BJB]

13. Cicero, *De oratore* I.28. [EF]

chosen to perform in such theaters had to begin strengthening their voices when they were very young to make them loud, firm, clear, and forceful. This they achieved through vocal exercises quite different from those practiced in our day. Our singers, on the other hand, needing to strive much less in order to make themselves heard, have forsaken that laborious type of training. Instead of laboring to make their voices firm, robust, and sonorous, they endeavor to make them light and pliant. With this new method they have achieved that amazing vocal flexibility that elicits the audience's resounding applause; but a voice that is minced into particles, and thus weakened, in singing arpeggios, runs, and trills can indeed produce the kind of pleasure that is aroused by sheer amazement, and must be preceded by a syllogism. But it can never arouse the kind of pleasure immediately produced by the vigorous physical impression of a clear, firm, and robust voice, which strikes our auditory organs with a forceful- ness equal to that of delight, and causes its effects to penetrate to the innermost recesses of our soul. A simple example will enable anyone who so wishes to as- certain how great this difference is. The singers of the Papal Chapel, although instructed from their earliest childhood in the techniques of the modern school, when admitted to that chorus are compelled, under the threat of severe punish- ment, to abandon completely all the applauded ornaments of common singing. They are further constrained to get used (to the extent that they are still able) to holding and sustaining their voices. Even the famous *Miserere* by the renowned Palestrina,[14] which so enraptured and utterly moved me when I heard it sung in Rome by the papal singers, bored me when I heard it performed in Vienna according to that most excellent style currently in fashion.

I have often hoped that our church music could give us some idea of what ancient music was like, for when St. Gregory regulated the music of our liturgy at the end of the sixth or the beginning of the seventh century, the public the- aters were still open, and it seemed natural to me that any music composed in that time had to bear the influence of whatever style was then popular in the theaters. However, as the style in vogue in those theaters must already have been barbarized, as was everything else in that era, what performers could reproduce it for us now, if at present it is just as impossible to sing a maxima as it was in ancient times to crowd thirty-two notes into one beat? . . .

From Pietro Metastasio, *Opere,* ed. Mario Fubini and Ettore Bonora (Milan and Naples: Ricciardi, 1968), 790–95. Most of the notes are taken from this edition. Charles Burney in- cluded a translation of this letter (misdated 25 April) in his *Memoirs of the Life and Writings of the Abate Metastasio,* 3 vols. (London: G. G. and J. Robinson, 1796), 2:396–407.

14. Although Palestrina wrote several settings of the *Miserere,* it is more likely that Metastasio is referring to Allegri's famous *Miserere;* its particular style of performance (not the composition itself) was jealously guarded in the Papal Chapel. [BJB]

Chapter Six

German Musical Culture and the Controversy regarding Bach

THE WEEKLY JOURNAL *Der critische Musikus,* directed by the composer and theoretician Johann Adolf Scheibe and published in Hamburg from 1737 to 1740, is of particular interest for its polemical articles regarding Johann Sebastian Bach. This chapter contains a brief passage by Scheibe, in which he sums up the reasons why the great musician was criticized, and a lengthy answer in Bach's defense by Johann Abraham Birnbaum. Scheibe criticizes Bach in the name of simplicity and melodiousness, accusing him of useless and cerebral complications in counterpoint and harmony; Birnbaum tries to defend him simply by denying the accusations, without perhaps grasping the originality of his music, which sounded so antiquated to modern ears! Scheibe's journal carried numerous other articles on the controversy regarding Bach, which show that German music was by then moving in a different direction. Even Bach's few supporters tried to rehabilitate the great master by stressing his modernity. Perhaps only his son Carl Philipp Emanuel praises his father's achievement as a composer of five- or six-voice fugues.

The writings excerpted here from the treatises of Johann Mattheson, Johann Joachim Quantz, Leopold Mozart, and Friedrich Wilhelm Marpurg all belong to the same genre. They are essentially didactic writings in which the authors offer practical instruction on how to be a competent performer, or, in Mattheson's case, an orchestral leader. However, these treatises, which are undoubtedly interesting if we are to understand the instrumental practice of the age, the habits of the composers and performers, and many other aspects of the music and its written form, also contain precious information of an aesthetic and philosophical nature. They all presuppose the "doctrine of affections" and, by means of their didactic instructions addressed to students, more or less explicitly purport to show the best way to imitate and convey the various affects (or, as we would say today, the various feelings) to the listener, to respect the composer's intentions faithfully and effectively. What they all set out to find is the bridge between sounds, harmonic progressions, embellishments, melodic patterns and the world of the affections. The intermediary role of the words is no longer taken into account: these are instrumentalists, and they have faith in the power of sounds and instruments.

With his *Der vollkommene Capellmeister* (The Complete Music Director, 1739), Johann Mattheson has left us a veritable encyclopedia of musical practice in his day in Germany.

Johann Joachim Quantz, the famous flute player (Frederick the Great was one of his students), drew up an authentic musical vocabulary of the passions in his treatise *Versuch einer Anweisung die Flöte traversiere zu spielen* (A Treatise on How to Play the Flute, 1752). The author suggests that the performer must make himself one with the passions he is to reproduce.

Leopold Mozart, Wolfgang's father, in his *Versuch einer gründlichen Violinschule* (A Treatise on the Fundamentals of the Violin, 1756), in the excerpt given here, dwells on the particular skill that is required of an orchestral player, who, to a certain extent, must be more knowledgeable than a soloist. The stress is always laid on the performer's need to "find the affect and perform it correctly, just as the composer intended it."

In his *Anleitung zum Klavierspielen* (Guide to Playing Keyboard Instruments, 1755–61), Friedrich Wilhelm Marpurg, musician and author of numerous musical treatises, gives us valuable information on harpsichord technique. The pages quoted here concern a problem of fundamental importance in Marpurg's time, that of embellishments. Marpurg stresses that they ought to be written by the composer so that they will not be left up to the will of the performer. They are an integral part of a composition and, if their complete and accurate notation is ignored, a performer risks betraying the author's intentions.

The famous treatise by one of J. S. Bach's sons, Carl Philipp Emanuel Bach, *Versuch über die wahre Art das Clavier zu spielen* (Essay on the True Art of Playing Keyboard Instruments, 1753–62), again addresses the general themes of interpretation that had already appeared in the works of other authors: to move, to convey emotions to the heart, to speak to the imagination: these are skills that a performer acquires if he does not limit himself to "playing the right notes" but knows how to grasp the "true emotional content of a piece." The general assumption is that "a musician can move others only if he himself is moved."

Finally, in his numerous theoretical works Mattheson laid the foundations of a new style based on sensibility rather than on rules and the authority of the ancients. It is from this perspective that his affirmations regarding the autonomy of taste as a specific organ for the appreciation of music and art are to be understood. His ideas "On Musical Taste" are set forth in the second part of *Die neueste Untersuchung der Singspiele* (1744).

JOHANN ADOLF SCHEIBE
Passage on J. S. Bach from a Letter of 1737

Mr. — is the most eminent among the music-makers (*Musikanten*) of —. He is an extraordinary artist on the clavier and organ; so far he has met only one with whom he could vie for superiority. I have heard this great man play on various occasions. His dexterity is amazing, and it is almost incomprehensible how he can cross and stretch his fingers and feet so peculiarly and quickly, how he can perform the widest leaps without introducing a single wrong note, or how he can make such vehement movements without shifting his body.

This great man would be the admiration of entire nations if he had more pleasantness, and if he did not allow a bombastic and confused style to suffocate naturalness in his pieces, or obscure their beauty through excessive artifice. Since he judges according to his own fingers, his pieces are exceedingly difficult to play, for he demands that singers and instrumentalists perform with their throats and instruments exactly what he is able to play on the keyboard. This, however, is impossible. All styles of playing, every little embellishment, and everything that involves playing "by the method," as it is called, he writes out in actual notes; this deprives his pieces not only of the beauty of harmony, but it also renders the melody imperceptible. In short, he is to music what Herr von Lohenstein once was to poetry.[1] Pompousness has led both from naturalness to artificiality, from sublimity to obscurity. One admires the onerous toil and the exceptional effort of both, but they have been applied in vain because they contend with reason.

From a purportedly anonymous letter (actually by Scheibe) published in the sixth issue of *Der critische Musikus,* dated 14 May 1737; taken from the second, revised and enlarged edition (Leipzig, 1745; repr. Hildesheim: Olms, 1970), 62.

1. Daniel Kaspar von Lohenstein (1635–83), poet, novelist, and author of tragedies of a distinctly moral emphasis and baroque style. [BJB]

JOHANN ABRAHAM BIRNBAUM
from *Impartial Remarks on a Dubious Passage in the Sixth Issue of* Der critische Musikus (1738)

In one part the author of this passage praises the court composer, in another he criticizes him all the more sharply. After close examination, I have found the praise conferred on him to be incomplete but the mistakes attributed to him to be unreasonable. I shall demonstrate both clearly.

The court composer is called the most eminent among the music-makers (*Musikanten*) of Leipzig. This expression is much too base and is not compatible with the epithets "extraordinary artist," "great man," and "admiration of entire nations," which the author later bestows on the court composer. Customarily, we call music-makers those whose main occupation is some sort of musical practice. They are called upon, indeed often doing it voluntarily, to make audible by means of musical instruments the pieces composed by others. Indeed, not even most of this lot bear the name, but only the lowest and worst; thus there is almost no distinction between music-makers and beer-hall fiddlers. But if one of these musical practitioners is an extraordinary artist on his instrument, he is not called a music-maker but a virtuoso. Least of all does this contemptuous name befit great composers or those who conduct musical ensembles. The reasonable reader now may judge for himself if proper credit is given to the court composer by calling him the most eminent among music-makers. In my opinion it is just as if I were to give honorable commendation to a thoroughly educated man by calling him the ranking member of the bottom class of schoolboys. The court composer is a great composer, a master of music, a virtuoso on the organ and clavier who has no equal; but by no means is he a music-maker. . . .

In the words immediately following, the author praises the court composer as "an extraordinary artist on the clavier and organ." I could point out here that the word "artist" sounds too much like artisan, and talking in these terms would be just as contrary to the common usage of language as referring to great philosophers, orators, and poets as artists in thinking, speaking, and writing verse. . . .

Next, the author discloses in somewhat more detail what he considered laudable and admirable in this great man, whom he himself heard play on various occasions. He admires the enormous dexterity of his hands and feet. He deems it incomprehensible how it is possible to make such fast and vehement movements of the hands and feet "without shifting his body," or to play such wide leaps "without introducing a single wrong note." That is all quite true; yet, such a judgment, too, would have been made by someone, after all, who does not thoroughly understand music. But since the author wishes to be considered as someone whose judgment is elevated above common taste, I am quite surprised that he has not mentioned much more significant circumstances, which easily would have come to mind to any learned connoisseur of true musical perfection. Why does he not praise the astonishing amount of unusual and well-executed ideas; the modulations of a single subject through the keys, with the most charming variations; the truly remarkable skill of playing all the notes clearly and with complete uniformity, even at the fastest tempo; the extraordinary skill in rendering the most difficult keys with the same speed and accuracy as the easiest one; and, on the whole, a general pleasantness combined with artistry? . . .

He begins with criticizing Bach's pieces for a lack of "pleasantness," that is, melodies without dissonance, or as others would say, who do not understand the matter any better, that do not please the ear. To dismiss this accusation, a memorable passage from the English *Spectator* may suffice. It says: "Music is not destined only to please gentle ears, but also those that know how to differentiate a rough tone from a pleasant one";[1] that is, those who know how to employ and to resolve dissonances properly and skillfully. True pleasantness in music consists in a connection and alternation of consonances and dissonances, without violating harmony. The nature of music demands the same. Without such alternation, the various passions, especially mournful ones, cannot be expressed according to their nature. One would violate commonly known rules of composition if they were set aside. The careful judgment of a musical ear, which does not follow vulgar tastes, accepts this alternation and rejects those ditties consisting only of consonances as something of which one soon wearies. It is most obvious in his compositions how carefully the court composer observes this alternation and how thoroughly pleasant his harmony is. The enthusiastic approval of those whose musical ear has not been corrupted by some sort of newfangled taste corroborates this. Consequently, the reproach by the author is unfounded. And this conclusion will remain valid until he rightfully dismisses the presumed notion of "pleasantness" and replaces it with a better one.

The court composer, in addition, is accused of depriving his pieces of naturalness through a "bombastic and confused style." These are harsh and obscure words. What does "bombastic" mean in music? Is it to be understood as in

---

1. *The Spectator*, Tuesday, 3 April 1711, from an essay by Addison. Birnbaum mistranslated the passage, perhaps inadvertently; Addison wrote: "Musick is not design'd to please only Chromatick Ears, but all that are capable of distinguishing harsh from disagreeable Notes." In a footnote, Scheibe pointed out that Addison had said nothing at all about pleasantness in music. [BJB]

oratory, where bombast refers to wasting splendid adornments on trivial things, thereby underscoring even more their contemptuousness? If one draws on external and superfluous splendor without realizing the essential beauty? If one lapses into base, forced, and foolish trifles and confuses reasonable thoughts with childish ideas? I concede that such mistakes regarding music may be committed by those who do not understand or are unable to apply the rules of composition; yet to accuse the court composer of them would constitute the coarsest abuse. This composer does not, after all, squander his splendid ornaments on drinking songs or lullabies, or silly and galant pieces. His church compositions, overtures, concertos, and other musical works contain embellishments that are always appropriate to the theme he wishes to develop. Thus the author's contention is worthless, since it is obscure and cannot be proven. Consequently, the subsequent comparison of the court composer with Herr von Lohenstein is a notion belonging to the category of objectionable ornaments, and thus it is itself a pompousness of style.

What does "confused" mean in music? Inevitably one has to consult the definition of the word if one is to guess the author's opinion. As far as I know, "confused" refers to something having no order, and whose individual parts are intermixed and entangled so oddly that one cannot discern where each belongs. If this is what the author means, he must be reproaching the court composer for having no order in his compositions, and that everything is so bewildering that one cannot make sense of it. If the author is serious in passing such judgment, I am almost forced to believe that some confusion has affected his own thoughts that does not allow him to discern the truth. Wherever the rules of composition are followed to the letter, inevitably there must be order. I surely hope that the author does not consider the court composer to be a violator of these rules. Moreover, it is certain that the voices in pieces by this great master of music interact marvelously together, all without the least confusion. They proceed together and against each other, each in its proper place. They separate and reunite at the proper time. Each voice is distinguished by some specific variation, even though they often imitate each other. They flee and follow each other, without ever creating the impression of the slightest irregularity in their anticipation and pursuit of one another. If all this is executed as it should be, there is nothing more beautiful than this harmony. . . .

Now it has been demonstrated sufficiently that there is nothing bombastic or confused to be found in the court composer's pieces; consequently, they cannot be devoid of naturalness, that is, of pleasant melody and harmony, which is at issue here. Rather, the praiseworthy endeavors of the court composer are aimed at presenting this very naturalness with the help of artistry in its most splendid appearance to the world.

That is exactly what the author does not want to admit. He says explicitly that the court composer "obscures the beauty of his pieces through excessive artifice." This sentence is contrary to the nature of true art, the question here. The essential aims of true art are to imitate nature and, if necessary, to assist it. Without doubt, if art imitates nature, naturalness must radiate everywhere from works of art. Consequently, in those matters where art—including music—imitates nature, it is impossible for it to be deprived of naturalness. For art to assist nature it must seek to preserve it or to improve its condition, but not to destroy it. Many things that appear quite misshapen in nature will acquire the most beautiful appearance once art has developed them. Thus art lends nature the beauty it is lacking and enhances that which is already present. The greater the art, that is, the more diligently and carefully it applies itself to improving nature, the more the resulting beauty shines forth. Thus, again, it is impossible that the greatest art could obscure the beauty of a thing. Should it be possible, then, for the court composer to deprive his musical pieces of naturalness and to obscure their beauty by applying the greatest art in their composition? . . .

The last matter for which the author criticizes the compositions of the court composer is this: All voices proceed simultaneously and with the same degree of complexity, so that no main voice—presumably a treble voice is meant—can be discerned. Yet I could not find sufficient reason to establish that melody necessarily must be placed in the treble voice, or that the simultaneous progression of all voices is a mistake. On the contrary, the nature of music suggests the opposite. The harmony becomes much more perfect if all voices interact. Consequently, this is not a mistake, but a musical perfection. And I am fairly surprised that the author considers it a mistake, since this conforms with the Italian style so highly appreciated everywhere today, especially in church compositions. The author may simply consult the works of Palestrina among the old composers, Lotti and others among the newer, and he will find there not only that all voices interact continuously, but also that each consists of an individual melody that harmonizes well with all the others.

I shall not go further into the matter whether the author of the passage that I have just examined would not decide that he has unjustly blemished the reputation and merit of such a great man, if he would take to heart the reasons presented above, and that he ought to regret his unreasonable judgment. Undoubtedly he has rushed to conclusions and, perhaps, he was not even sufficiently familiar with the court composer. If he had been, I am sure he would have granted him the same kind of praise that he has given to the famous Herr Graun. Just by changing one word, he could have said: "A great Augustus honors him with favors and rewards his accomplishments; this is sufficient praise. He who is loved by such a great and prudent prince surely must truly be skilled."[2] Considering this, he would not have dared to criticize a man whose least perfection he is not able to imitate. Indeed, he would have considered that criticism is not difficult, but that those who find fault with everything are always the furthest removed from doing it better. I, and all reasonable admirers of the great Bach, wish the author more salutary thoughts in the future, and, after having accomplished his musical journey, the successful start of a new life free of unnecessary censoriousness.

From *Unparteyische Anmerkungen über eine bedenkliche Stelle in dem sechsten Stücke des critischen Musikus,* originally published with a dedication to Bach in Lorenz Mizler, *Neu eröffnete Musikalische Bibliothek* (Leipzig, April 1738); it was republished by Scheibe, with his own footnotes, in the second edition of *Der critische Musikus* (Leipzig, 1745; repr. Hildesheim: Olms, 1970), 833–58, from which the excerpt is taken. Further rejoinders followed.

JOHANN MATTHESON
from *The Complete Music Director* (1739)

3. On Sound in Itself, and on the Natural Philosophy of Music

1. Most books on music make a great fuss about numbers, measures, and weights. Hardly a word is said, however, about sound and about the very substantial physiological aspect of this science; instead it is passed over quickly, as if it meant little or nothing.

2. But such a procedure is all wrong: sound is the only subject of music, just as hearing is its object; numbers and what is associated with them, on the other hand, are merely assistants and necessary helpers in the art of harmonic measurement, with whose assistance the external appearance and size of intervals may be examined and comprehended. It will therefore be most necessary to inquire more closely into the nature of sound.

3. In reading the best and oldest writers on music, we find that they describe

2. The quotation, concerning Carl Heinrich Graun (1703/4–1759), Frederick the Great's Kapellmeister, changes the word "Friederich" to "August" (the Elector of Saxony, Frederick Augustus II); Scheibe's remarks on Graun had appeared immediately following those on Bach (p. 63 of the 1745 edition of *Der critische Musikus*). [BJB]

sound as "an incident where the singing voice only expands once" or as "the smallest part of a voice proceeding to sing," etc.[1] No edification may be gained from this, however, since such a description does not in the least touch upon the actual nature of sound. And one must be fairly astonished to find such a description in Aristoxenus bearing the title "Definitio soni" [the definition of sound].[2]

4. We could include numerous inadequate descriptions of this kind from Aristotle, Boethius, and Ptolemy at this point, if that would serve any purpose. We shall cite in a note only Kircher's uncommonly complicated definition,[3] which may be simplified here thus: "sound is a certain quick movement and collision of the smallest particles of air that perceptibly enter the ear."

5. Hereafter, it is necessary to discuss the matter more in respect to its nature if the reader is to have a clear understanding of the essence of sound and its actual formation. This is much more useful than to waste time with numerous mathematical formulas and arithmetical whims.

6. If everything were motionless, it would also be completely still; one would not be able to perceive any sound, indeed not even the slightest noise, to say nothing of a euphonious concord. Hence one must conclude that all sound, singing, and resonance can result from nothing but motion, by means of which the surrounding air has indirectly been agitated, divided, propelled, struck, and pushed. In this process, three aspects must be distinguished: what moves must be considered an *agens* (active), what is moved a *patiens* (passive), and the

---

1. "Vocis casus, cantui aptus, in unam ⟨in⟩tensionem"; Euclid, *Introductio harmonica*, p. 1. "Vocis cantui aptae pars minima"; Aristides Quintilianus, *De musica*, bk. 1, p. 9. "Vocis concinnae casus in unam tensionem"; Bacchius Senior, *Introductio artis musicae*, p. 2 etc. [Mattheson took all these references from the translations by Marcus Meibom, *Antiquae musicae auctores septem* (Amsterdam, 1652), where the treatises are paginated separately. The *Introductio harmonica* is now ascribed to Cleonides. Mattheson's translations do not give an adequate understanding of the theorists' definitions of sound, which in any case refer not to the physical phenomenon but to the unit of melody. Translated from the Greek, they are: "The musical incidence of a voice on a single pitch" (Cleonides); "It is the smallest part of the musical voice" (Aristides); "It is the incidence of the musical voice on a single pitch" (Bacchius). LAH-S]

2. *Elementa harmonica*, bk. 1, p. 15 [also taken from Meibom].

3. "Sonus est qualitas passibilis successiva ex aëris vel aquae interceptione, elisioneque, sonantium corporum collisionem insequente, producta, sensum auditus movere apta" [Sound is a passible quality successive upon the trapping and squeezing of air or water produced following the collision of sounding bodies, apt to move the sense of hearing]; Athanasius Kircher, *Musurgia universalis* (Rome, 1650), vol. 1, p. 3. More on this subject may be found in Jean Pierre de Crousaz, *Traité du Beau* (Amsterdam, 1715), ch. 11; in the third part of the *Orchestre* [Mattheson, *Das forschende Orchestre, oder desselben dritte Eröffnung;* Hamburg, 1721], in a number of places, as shown in the index, and in the second edition of the *Organisten-Probe* [*Johann Matthesons Grosse General-Bass-Schule. Oder: der exemplarischen Organisten-Probe zweite, verbesserte und vermehrte Auflage;* Hamburg, 1731], p. 158f.

means by which the effect of this movement is communicated to the ear must be considered the *vehiculum*.

. . .

12. When these principles are applied more closely to the actual theory of acoustics, it will easily be apparent that the first kind of motion mentioned above [the impact of two hard bodies] pertains to all string instruments, which are set in motion by tangents [of clavichords], quills [of harpsichords], bows, fingers, etc., including all those instruments where mallets and tightened hides come into contact, and thus the collision of two dense bodies, used most commonly in music. For even if the solidity of the bodies varies—some quills, for example, are made of metal, others of raven feathers—they are more or less dense bodies, as are the hair on a bow or the ball of a finger.

13. We count among the second kind of motion, to mention it briefly, all wind instruments, since a thin and fluid substance, that is, breath, strikes a firm and dense one, be it wood, silver, brass, or something else.

14. To the third kind, however, belong all those sounding instruments whose tightened strings divide the air, whereby a firm body operates upon a soft one.

15. Nothing sounds more delightful or pleasant, however, than one soft air [column] dividing another most gently and artistically, such as the human voice alone can accomplish in highest perfection. Its superiority derives from the fourth kind of motion, by which two soft bodies of the same kind delightfully meet without any violent movement in the process of singing.

. . .

49. The fifth part of the natural philosophy of sound, which is closely related to the preceding one (inasmuch as weaknesses of the body are closely tied to the state of mind), is the most noble and the most important of all. It investigates the effects of well-ordered sounds on the emotions and passions of the soul.

50. This is, for obvious reasons, a great and extensive matter of no little utility, which appears to be more indispensable to a practical musician than a theorist, even though it is concerned primarily with pure contemplation.

51. The theory of temperaments and dispositions (about which Descartes[4] is especially worth reading since he has contributed a great deal to music) is here of special use, because it teaches how to differentiate the feelings of the listeners and the effect of the sounding phenomena upon them.

52. What are the passions? How many are there? How do they arise, and how are they stimulated? Should they be eradicated, tolerated, or cultivated? To

---

4. *De passionibus animae* [*Les Passions de l'âme* (Amsterdam, 1650 and later editions)].

consider these questions seems more incumbent on an accomplished philosopher than an actual music director. Yet it is indispensable for him to know at least that the dispositions of the human mind are the true matter of virtue, and that the latter is nothing other than a well-organized and judiciously moderated disposition of the mind.

53. Without passion, without affect, there is no virtue. If our passions are ailing, they must be cured, and not slain.

54. It is a fact that those affects which by nature are most inherent in us are not the best, and thus they must be reduced and kept under control. This is a part of ethics with which an accomplished composer must be absolutely familiar, if he wishes clearly to distinguish virtue and vice in his music, and if he wishes to kindle love for the former and abhorrence for the latter in the mind of the listener. It is the true purpose of music to be an example of propriety for others.

55. Natural philosophers are able to describe how our emotions actually—that is, physically, as it were—occur; and it is of great advantage to a composer if he is not ignorant in these matters.

56. For instance, since joy is perceived as an expansion of our vital spirits, it follows rationally and naturally that I can express this affect best by large and expanded intervals.

57. If it is known, on the other hand, that sadness is a contraction of such subtle parts of our body, one can easily imagine that small and the smallest intervals are the most appropriate to this passion.

58. Furthermore, if we consider that love is based on a diffusion of the spirits, we will adjust the art of composition accordingly and proceed with corresponding relations of sounds (with expansive and extravagant intervals).

59. Hope is an elevation of the mind or the spirits; despair is the complete collapse of the same. These are matters that can be represented quite naturally by sounds, especially if other elements contribute (in particular, the tempo). And in such manner one will be able to form a mental conception of all emotions, and organize one's inventions accordingly.

60. To list here each and every emotion would surely be too tedious; only the most distinguished ones must not be left untouched. Love, to be sure, ought to be ranked above all others, since it holds a place more eminent than any other passion in musical matters.

61. In this respect, what matters is that the composer distinguish exactly the degree, type, or kind of love he is confronted with, or which he selected as his subject. The diffusion of spirits mentioned above, from which this emotional tendency generally and specifically originates, can be expressed in many ways, and it is impossible to treat all kinds of love in the same manner.

62. The author of amorous compositions must draw on his own experi-

ence, be it current or past; and he will find in himself or in his own affect the best model to organize his expressions in sound. However, if he has no personal experience of this noble passion nor any vivid feeling for it, he should not occupy himself with it: he would be more successful with anything else but this most gentle emotional disposition.

. . .

65. Although desire cannot be separated from love, it is to be distinguished from it in that the latter refers to the present, the former, however, to the future, and at times it harbors within itself more vehemence and impatience. All yearning, longing, wishing, striving, and desire, be they moderate or impetuous, belong here; and the invention and composition of sounds must be arranged according to desire's manifold qualities, taking into account also the natural qualities of what is desired or wished.

66. Sadness occupies a not insignificant area in the land of affects. In sacred matters, where this passion is the most salutary and moving, it includes everything that represents repentance and sorrow, penitence, contrition, lamentation, and recognition of our misery. In such circumstances, "sorrow is better than laughter" (Eccles. 7:3). Besides, an author already mentioned suggests a good reason why most people would rather listen to sad than to joyous music, namely: "Almost everybody is unhappy."[5]

67. In secular matters, where sadness serves no particular purpose, there is still an infinite number of opportunities for this mortal emotion and its various gradations and mixtures, each of which—as with any other emotion—may occasion a particular invention or expression according to its measure through diverse concentrations of sounds and intervals.

68. Next to love, he who wishes to express sadness well in sound must feel and perceive it himself much more than any of the other passions; otherwise, all so-called *loci topici* (rhetorical commonplaces) will go up in smoke. The reason is that being sad and being in love are closely related to each other.[6]

69. Certainly, all other emotions too must be felt deeply by the composer, if they are to be represented naturally. Yet, since this worldly sadness is most contrary to human self-preservation, for "the sorrow of the world worketh death"; "heaviness in the heart of man maketh it stoop"; "by the sorrow of the heart the spirit is broken"; "a broken spirit drieth the bones"; "sadness slayeth many"; and "it saps the strength";[7] and since men are often inclined to take joyless joy

5. La Mothe le Vayer, vol. 1, p. 550. [From his "Discours sceptique sur la musique," in *Œuvres de François de La Mothe Le Vayer,* 3d ed. (Paris, 1662), 1:550. BJB]

6. "Qui dit amoureux, dit triste"; Roger, comte de Bussy-Rabutin, *Les Mémoires.* [First edition Paris, 1696; in the Amsterdam, 1731 edition it is found on p. 244 of vol. 2 and is a line from one of his "Maximes d'amour." BJB].

7. 2 Cor. 7:10; Prov. 12:25, 15:13, 17:22; Ecclus. 30:23, 38:18.

in sadness, it takes more coercion if one wishes to participate in this emotional tendency and yet does not actually feel it within oneself.

70. Joy, on the contrary, is far more natural than sadness; and perhaps because it is such a friend of life and health, the mind approves of it more easily in imagination and acceptance. Still, it can wreak irreparable harm when abused by malicious people.

71. The best use of a properly joyous music surely should be sought (yet without excluding legitimate delights) in the praise of God and in joyous thanksgiving for his ineffable and numberless blessings. Daily, indeed hourly, we have every cause and opportunity to bring about this expansion of our spirits and tension of our nerves: let us prefer the sound of joyful music in churches or at home in honor and praise of God (provided it is presented with due modesty) to all other joyous music-making; and, in the words of the Apostle, "rejoice evermore" and "rejoice in the Lord alway, and again I say, Rejoice."[8] God does not wish sorrowful sacrifices,[9] and he cannot commend cheerfulness too highly to his people.[10]

72. Pride, arrogance, haughtiness, and the like are customarily depicted or expressed musically in their own colors and sounds, whereby the author mostly refers to a daring and conceited character. This creates an opportunity to employ all kinds of splendid-sounding figures demanding a special seriousness and bombastic movement; never, however, do they include many fleeting or descending passages, but continuously strive to ascend.

73. The counterparts to these emotions are humility, patience, etc., which are treated in a lowering manner in music, without inserting anything uplifting. These latter passions correspond to those mentioned before in that they do not tolerate jesting or trifling any more than arrogance itself.

74. Obstinacy deserves its own place among the affects suitable to musical speech and useful to composition. It can be represented well by various so-called *capricci* or bizarre ideas, if, that is, such obstinate musical figures are employed in one or the other voice, and one is determined not to change them under any circumstance. There is a kind of counterpoint known to the Italians by the term *perfidia*,[11] and which to some extent belongs in this category. . . .

75. As far as wrath, zeal, revenge, rage, fury, and all related violent emotions are concerned, they are indeed more easily suited to all kinds of inventions in

---

8. 1 Tim. 5 [actually 1 Thess. 5:16]; Phil. 4:4.

9. Deut. 26:14, with Luther's annotation. [Deut. 26:14 says "I have not eaten thereof in my mourning," to which Luther has added the annotation: "God's sacrifice should be joyful, pure, and holy, and therefore nothing of it should be eaten in sorrow." BJB]

10. Deut. 16:11, 14, 15, etc. Ps. 100[:2], "Serve the Lord with gladness: come before his presence with singing," etc.

11. Literally "treachery," a name for ostinato figures of all sorts. [BJB]

music than the genial and pleasant passions, which need to be treated more subtly. Still, it will certainly not suffice to rumble about continuously, or to make a crude racket, racing madly to and fro; nor will these affects be evoked simply by multi-tailed notes, as many people think. Instead, each of these harsh characteristics demands a particular manner and, notwithstanding the forceful expression, each must nonetheless be fashioned with an appropriately melodious character, as expressly required by our general principle, of which we ought never lose sight.

76. Beloved jealousy is frequently turned to use in the arts of music and poetry; and since this state of mind is composed of seven other passions—among which burning love ranks in first place, followed by mistrust, desire, revenge, sadness, fear, and shame—it is easy to imagine that numerous inventions in the combinations of sound can be derived from it, all of which must direct their ultimate intentions toward a certain restlessness, vexation, ferocity, and misery, according to their nature.

77. Hope is a pleasant and flattering matter: it consists of a joyful desire, which fills the mind with a certain courage. Hence this affect requires the most attractive composition for the voice and the sweetest mixture of sounds in the world. These are incited, as it were, by courageous desire, yet in such a manner that—even though joy is only moderate—that courage will animate and stimulate all. This results in composition of the best blend and union of sounds.

78. Those affects that are, so to speak, to be set against hope and that consequently inspire a contrary arrangement of sounds are fear, pusillanimity, despondency, etc. Here also belong fright and terror, which invite—if they are properly understood and if one has distinct images of their natural characteristics—appropriate progressions of sound corresponding to the condition of the emotion.

79. For although the musical profession should concern itself primarily with grace and pleasure, it also works at times with dissonant sounds or harsh-sounding themes and appropriately strident instruments to represent not only matters adverse and unpleasant, but even horrible and dreadful, in which the mind occasionally finds a particular kind of delight.

80. Just as despair is the most extreme degree or the brink to which cruel fear can drive us, so is it easily realized that this passion, if it is to be expressed naturally, may lead us to peculiar extremities of all kinds in our sounds, even to the furthermost; and thus it may result in exceptional cases and peculiar, absurd, and excessive tonal constructions.

81. It remains to mention compassion, which plays a by no means insignificant part in the science of music, since it consists of two main tendencies—namely, love and sadness—of which one alone would suffice to animate our sounds to the utmost.

82. That I would be allowed to turn composure into an emotion I doubt, since a calm and composed heart is free of all external movement, quiet and happy within itself. Yet since this condition has its distinguishing characteristic, and since it can be well presented naturally through a gentle unanimity, the composer of course ought to notice and observe various points: regardless of what it may be called, he may not assign it the first place, nor the last, in his natural philosophy of sound, even though it readily occupies the latter (because of its calmness).

. . .

86. My humble advice at the end of this chapter, which connects the natural philosophy of sound with the doctrine of the affects in certain necessary ways, is as follows: One ought to choose one or the other good, or very good, poetic work in which nature is vividly depicted, and strive to distinguish exactly the passions contained therein. For without doubt, the things of many a composer or judge of music would turn out better, if only he himself now and then realized what he actually wished to achieve.

87. Yet, so much is lacking in this, that people do not know their own will, or never examine their intentions; and most vocal and instrumental compositions, even by those claiming to be great masters (I almost said, powerful orators), are written down without planning, without moral or laudable intentions, just as the Tartars shoot an arrow aimlessly into the air. One is satisfied if the sound pleases the ears, no matter how it agrees with the precepts of nature and morality.

88. According to an expression of a great Church Father, who is highly esteemed by everyone, regardless of belief, there is much superfluous matter in singing and playing, that is, in sound itself, even though it pleases the ears.[12] For when the precepts of nature and morality, which I present here as a pair, are passed over, neither reason nor wisdom can take delight. Silly chatter holds the floor.

89. Even if it were more beautiful in its external appearance than Venus, it is nothing but a graceful and pretty body without an intelligent soul: pleasant notes and lovely sounds—but the singing does not touch the heart. Is it any wonder, then, with matters in such a state—that is, with the true theory of the nature of sound, including the corresponding science of human emotions, completely being ignored—that only the poor, naive, and conceited listener's ears are tickled, but his heart and thought are not thereby inspired? These are,

---

12. "Multa in canendo & psallendo, quamvis delectent, vilissima sunt" [many things in singing and playing, though they delight, are worthless]; Augustine, *De musica*, bk. 1. But why should I mention this book? Our theological scholars do not know it and everybody else even less, the music-makers least of all.

in Horace's words, *nugae canorae;* or, according to St. Paul's words, tinkling cymbals; or, in good French, *des niaiseries harmonieuses,* which I shall not attempt to translate, though I understand it well.

From Ch. 3, "Von der Natur-Lehre des Klanges," in *Der vollkommene Capellmeister* (Hamburg, 1739; repr. Kassel: Bärenreiter, 1954), 9–11, 15–20. There is an English translation by Ernest C. Harriss, *Johann Mattheson's Der vollkommene Capellmeister: A Revised Translation with Critical Commentary* (Ann Arbor: UMI Research Press, 1981).

JOHANN JOACHIM QUANTZ
from *A Treatise on How to Play the Flute* (1752)

XII
HOW TO PLAY AN ALLEGRO

24. The passions frequently change in an allegro as well as in an adagio. The performer must try to understand each one and endeavor to express it appropriately. It is therefore necessary to examine whether the piece to be performed contains only cheerful thoughts, or whether other thoughts, of a different nature, may be linked as well. In case of the former, a continuous liveliness must be maintained throughout the piece. But in case of the latter, the rule mentioned above applies. Cheerfulness is represented in short notes—according to the measure, they may be eighth notes, sixteenths, or, in alla breve time, quarter notes in leaping or stepwise motion—and expressed by brisk tonguing. Stateliness is represented by long notes, supported by fast movement of the voices below, as well as by dotted notes. The dotted notes must be attacked sharply and in lively manner by the performer. The dots are held long, and the notes directly following are made very short. Occasionally a trill may be added to the dotted notes. Boldness is represented by notes of which the second or third is dotted, thus precipitating the first notes. Here one must take care not to rush too much, in order to avoid making it sound like ordinary dance music. In a concerto one may temper this somewhat irregularly and make it more pleasing through modest performance. Flattery is expressed by slurred notes moving stepwise up or down, or likewise by syncopated notes of which the first half may be played gently, and the other may be intensified by movement of the chest and lips.

25. The main ideas, which are the principal guideline to the expression, must be carefully distinguished from intermingled ideas. Thus if there are more

cheerful than majestic or flattering ideas present in an allegro, then it must be played chiefly fast and bright. However, if stateliness is the character of the main idea, then the piece in general must be performed more seriously. If flattery is the principal affect, calmness must rule. . . .

XVIII
How to Judge a Musician and Music[1]

87. If, after due consideration, one knows to select the best in musical style of various peoples, the result will be a mixed style, which now one may very well call the German style without overstepping the bounds of modesty. This is not only because the Germans were the first to chance upon it, but also because it has been introduced in various parts of Germany many years ago and is still flourishing; and it has been well received in Italy, France, and other countries.

88. Provided that the German nation will not abandon this style; if it continues to develop it, as her most famous composers have done; if the new generation of composers, like their predecessors, will apply themselves to studying their mixed style, as well as the rules of composition, more thoroughly than unfortunately happens today; if they will not simply be contented with composing pure melody and arias for the theater, but will also practice the church style and instrumental music; if, for a reasonable union and mixture of thoughts in their own pieces, they will take as models those composers who are generally well received and emulate their manner of composition and fine style (without becoming accustomed to adorning themselves with borrowed plumes, as is done by many, and copying or rehashing a principal idea or the entire context from this or that one); if, rather, they will invest their own power of imagination to display and develop their talent without being detrimental to others, and become composers instead of just remaining copyists; if German instrumentalists will not allow themselves to be led astray by bizarre and comical procedures, as has been said above about the Italians, but will take as a model the style of those who sing and perform with reasonable style; if, moreover, the Italians and the French will emulate the Germans in mixing styles, just as the Germans have imitated them in matters of style; if, I say, all this were observed unanimously, then in time a good universal style in music could be introduced. Indeed, this is not at all improbable, because neither the Italians nor the French—but more the enthusiasts of music among them than the professional musicians—are quite satisfied any longer with their own purely national style,

---

1. Beginning with paragraph 52 of Ch. 18 Quantz takes up the question of national styles (he prefers the word "tastes"), arguing that they should be international, universal, and rational. In the last paragraphs of the book he sums up his recommendations. [BJB]

and for some time they have taken greater pleasure in certain foreign compositions than in those of their own country.

89. In a style consisting of a mixture of the styles of various nations, like the present German style, each nation recognizes something similar to its own, and this is bound to be pleasing. In view of all ideas and experiences mentioned so far in respect to the distinction of styles, one cannot avoid preferring the pure Italian over the pure French style. But anybody will admit that a mixed style compounded of the best of both the former (which by itself is not as solid as it once was but has become very daring and bizarre) and the latter (which has remained too simplistic) without doubt must be more universal and pleasing. For a music that is accepted not only by a particular country, a particular province, or only by this or that nation, but instead is accepted and favored by many nations—indeed, if it cannot help but being accepted for the reasons mentioned above—this music, if it is founded on reason and sound perception, must indisputably be the best.

From *Versuch einer Anweisung die Flöte traversiere zu spielen* (Berlin, 1752; repr. Kassel: Bärenreiter, 1983); in the 3d ed. of 1789 (repr. Kassel: Bärenreiter, 1953), 116, 332–34. There is an English translation by Edward R. Reilly, *On Playing the Flute*, 2d ed. (New York: Schirmer, 1985). Extensive excerpts from Ch. 18 are given in Strunk, *Source Readings*, 577–98.

LEOPOLD MOZART
from *A Treatise on the Fundamentals of the Violin* (1756)

XII
On the Correct Way of Reading Music and Good Performance in General

3. It is by far more artistic to read musical pieces by great masters correctly according to the written instruction, and to play according to the affects governing the piece, than to study the most difficult solos and concertos. After all, the latter does not require much understanding. And if enough skill has been acquired to work out fingerings, one can learn the most difficult passages by oneself, if only by dint of plenty of practice. The former, however, is not as easy. One must observe not only exactly what is marked and prescribed, and not play differently from what has been written down, but also play with a certain sensitivity; one must immerse oneself in the affect that is to be expressed; and one must apply and perform in a good and certain manner all bow strokes, slurs,

attacks of notes, forte and piano, and, in short, everything that belongs to the tasteful performance of a piece. And this manner of performance can only be achieved through sound judgment and long experience.

4. Now one may conclude for oneself whether a good orchestral violinist ought not to be valued much higher than a pure soloist. The latter can play everything as he likes and arrange the performance according to his own intent, even his own ability. The former must be proficient in understanding immediately the style, ideas, and expressions of various composers and perform them correctly. The soloist may simply practice at home to produce everything clearly, and others have to follow him; the orchestral player, however, must play everything at sight, and often even passages that are contrary to the natural order of the measure;[1] and usually he must adjust his playing to others. A soloist can play his concertos reasonably well, even laudably, without having great insight into the music in general, if only he can perform clearly. A good orchestral violinist, however, must have many insights into music as a whole, into composition, and into the variety of characters; indeed, he must have an especially ready ability to carry out his duties with honor, particularly if he intends in time to be the leader of an orchestra. Some perhaps believe that there are more good orchestral violinists than soloists. They are mistaken. Certainly, there are plenty of bad accompanists; good ones, however, are rare: everybody wants to play solo these days. I shall leave it to those composers who have had their music played in orchestras consisting only of soloists to describe what they are like. Few soloists read well, since they always add something according to their own imagination, and since they are accustomed to taking notice only of themselves, rarely of others.[2]

5. Thus, one ought not to play solo before knowing how to accompany well. First one must know how to apply all variations of the bow stroke; understand how to use forte and piano at the right place and in the right proportion; learn how to distinguish the character of pieces; and how to perform all passages according to their own requisite taste; in a word, one must first be able to read correctly and gracefully the work of many skilled people before setting about playing concertos and solos. In a painting it is immediately apparent whether its creator is a master of drawing. By the same token, many a performer would play his solo more reasonably if he had ever performed a symphony or trio ac-

---

1. *Contra metrum musicum.* I have already discussed this in Ch. 1, part 2, para. 4, note *d.* And I do not know what I ought to think when I see an aria by one of those Italian composers who are all the rage now that runs so counter to the measure that one would think that a student had written it.

2. I am by no means referring to those great virtuosos who, in addition to their extraordinary talent in playing concertos, are also good orchestral players. These are men who are truly worthy of the greatest admiration.

cording to the style required, or if he had learned to accompany an aria with the right affect and according to its particular character. I shall endeavor to provide some short rules that may be used for the performance of music.

6. It is well known that one should tune one's instrument well and exactly with others, and my reminder in this case may appear superfluous. Yet, since there are often many people even among those who aspire to play first violin who do not tune their instruments together, I find it very necessary to point it out here, and even more so since all others ought to tune their instruments according to the first violinist. If one performs with an organ or clavier, however, the tuning should be adjusted to these instruments; if neither one is present, the pitch will be taken from a wind instrument. Some players first tune the A-string, others the D-string. Both are correct as long as they tune carefully and exactly. One reminder: the pitch of string instruments always falls in warm rooms, and rises in cold ones.

7. Before beginning to play one must carefully examine and consider the piece. One must decide on the character, tempo, and kind of movement required by the piece, and carefully look for any passages that on first sight may appear unimportant, but which may not be played easily because they demand a special kind of performance or expression. Finally, during the execution itself one should take pains to find the affect and perform it correctly, just as the composer intended it. Since sadness often alternates with cheerfulness, one must attempt to render both according to their nature. In a word, one must play in such a manner that one will be moved by it oneself.[3]

8. From this it follows that the prescribed pianos and fortes must be observed precisely, without grinding on continuously on one level. Indeed, one often has to alternate soft and low by oneself without directions and know how to apply each at the proper place; this means, as painters would call it, light and shadow. Pitches raised by a sharp or a natural should always be played somewhat stronger, but the subsequent notes should return to the previous level. For example,

Likewise, pitches suddenly lowered by a flat or a natural must be stressed. For example,

3. Bad enough that many give no thought to what they are doing, but play the notes as if in a dream, or as if they were playing only for themselves. They do not even notice if they are two beats ahead, and I would wager that they would end the piece several measures early, if their neighbor or the leader himself did not warn them.

Half notes, if they appear among short notes, are customarily played with a strong attack and then diminished in tone. For example,

Even many quarter notes are played in the same manner. For example,

This is the expression that a composer in fact demands when he places an *f* and *p*, namely forte and piano, under one note. Once the note is played with a strong attack, however, the bow should not be taken off the string—as some do rather awkwardly—but the bow must continue on so that the tone will still be heard and diminish only gently.

From *Versuch einer gründlichen Violinschule* (Augsburg, 1756), 258–61. The third edition (Augsburg, 1787) is available in reprint (Leipzig: Breitkopf & Härtel, 1956; Leipzig: VEB Deutscher Verlag für Musik, 1969). There is an English translation by Edith Knocker, *A Treatise on the Fundamental Principles of Violin Playing*, 2d ed. (Oxford: Oxford University Press, 1985). The complete Ch. 12 is translated in Strunk, *Source Readings*, 599–608.

FRIEDRICH WILHELM MARPURG
from *Guide to Playing Keyboard Instruments* (1755–61)

2. On Embellishments

1. In contrast to intentional, arbitrary embellishments [of composition], embellishments of performance (*Spielmanieren*) are called *essential* because they are used throughout every piece. A piece may well be performed without those arbitrary ornaments, but never without these little essential adornments; and no instrument calls for them more than the keyboard.

2. But as unpleasant and harsh as a performance is when stripped of any embellishments, it is just as loathsome when all notes are garnished with orna-

ments. The former makes the most excellent compositions blunt and raw, the latter renders the melody itself unrecognizable. A musician who applies a trill to every note appears to me like a conceited beauty who curtseys at every word.

3. But where can one learn which note to ornament, or in which part of a melody this or that embellishment ought to be used? One should seek out published music in which all kinds of embellishments are written out. One should listen to performers with a reputation for playing gracefully; and one should seek to listen to their performances of pieces with which one is already familiar. In this way one can cultivate one's taste and acquire practice in it at the same time. For it is impossible to derive rules suitable to all possible occasions as long as music remains an inexhaustible sea of change, and one person's feelings differ from another's. As an experiment, give a piece of music that has no written-out embellishments to ten different performers, each of whom plays according to the good taste of the time, and ask them to apply embellishments. In certain cases many will perhaps agree; in others, however, all will differ. Each one will ornament according to his own particular taste: one performer will have more ornaments, one will have fewer; one will use a trill where another will only play a turn; this player will use an appoggiatura where another will employ a mordent, and vice versa.

4. From this it is apparent how important it is, if a composer wishes it to be clearly understood that a piece is to be played in such a way and not otherwise, that he must write out all embellishments—regardless of how slight they may be—just as precisely as he indicates the tempo above the first clef. Without these indications he runs the risk of having his compositions misinterpreted, if not completely botched. He ought to imagine that other performers playing his compositions are in the same position as he is when asked to perform unfamiliar pieces. Just as he can scarcely guess the intention of the composer if it is not properly indicated, so others will not be able to guess his intention.

5. All embellishments are to be indicated either by certain signs or by small auxiliary notes, or they are to be written out regularly like other notes and incorporated into the measure. The first manner is necessary with certain embellishments that cannot be expressed conveniently by notes, as for instance a trill. If it were written out in notes and a performer were to obey the indicated speed of the alternating notes, it would be as difficult for him as it would be for the accompanist or continuo player to accompany a solo at the keyboard by playing the thorough-bass from a four-part score. These signs, however, ought not to be multiplied without necessity; no special signs are needed if something can be expressed easily and conveniently with the notes themselves. Therefore one makes use, secondly, of certain small auxiliary notes that are played within the time value of a given main note; notwithstanding the time value, they are not reckoned as part of the measure, but the execution of the division is left to the

performer. Since this frequently may cause confusion, it may be necessary, thirdly, to write out certain embellishments properly like the other notes and to fit them appropriately into the measure, so that the proper effect is not lacking.

6. Finally, the embellishments used in good performance today are as follows:

the vibrato (*Bebung*)
accented and unaccented appoggiaturas
the compound appoggiatura
the slide
the turn
the trill
the mordent
the arpeggio

From *Anleitung zum Klavierspielen* (Berlin, 1755–61; repr. New York: Broude Bros., 1969; Hildesheim: Olms, 1970), I. Hauptstück, welches die theoretischen Grundsätze des Clavier-spielens enthält, IX. Abschnitt. Von den Manieren, pp. 43–45.

CARL PHILIPP EMANUEL BACH
from *Essay on the True Art of Playing Keyboard Instruments*
(1753–62)

III
On Performance

1. It is undeniably prejudiced to believe that the strength of a keyboard player consists purely in dexterity. One may have the most dexterous fingers, be able to play simple and double trills, understand the art of fingering, be proficient in sight-reading, however many clefs may occur in the course of a piece; one may be able to transpose everything extempore without difficulty, reach tenths and even twelfths, play runs and leaps of all kinds with crossed hands, and more besides; and yet despite this, not be a clear, pleasing, or moving keyboard player. We know all too well from experience that technically adept and nimble professional players possess just these qualities, and that they indeed amaze both ear and eye by means of their fingers; but they do not touch the emotions of the listener. They surprise the ear without delighting it; they daze the mind without satisfying it. I do not wish to deny the proper praise of impro-

visation. It is praiseworthy to be proficient in it, and I advise everyone to develop it as much as possible. A mere technician, however, may by no means lay claim to the true accomplishments of a performer: to affect the ear more than the eye, and the heart more than the ear, with gentle emotions, and to transport it wherever he wishes. Only rarely is it possible to perform a piece at first sight according to its true content and affect. The most experienced orchestras often rehearse more than once works that, in terms of their notes, appear easy enough. Most technicians will do no more than hit the notes; how much will not, indeed must not, the coherence and continuity of melody suffer, even if there is not the slightest stumbling in respect to harmony? It is an advantage of the keyboard that one may reach a higher level of dexterity than on other instruments. But one should not abuse this advantage. It should be saved until dexterity is really needed, without immediately exceeding the tempo. To show that I do not question the merit of dexterity, nor its usefulness and necessity, I myself demand that the exercises in G and F minor and the runs of very small note values in the C minor one be played as rapidly but as clearly as possible. In some foreign places there is a very great tendency to play the adagios too fast and the allegros too slow. It is not necessary to spell out what a contradiction this is. Still, I do not mean to condone those sluggish and stiff-handed players who lull one to sleep by their complacency, who under the pretext of melodiousness do not know how to enliven the instrument, and who deserve all the more reproach for the tiresome execution of their boring conceptions than those mere heroes of dexterity. The latter, at least, are capable of improvement; their fire can be damped, if they are urged explicitly to moderate their tempo. The opposite, however, has only little or no effect on the annoying hypochondriac nature that filters through limp fingers. Both, of course, play their instrument only mechanically; a moving performance demands good heads capable of submitting to certain reasonable rules and performing their pieces accordingly.

2. Yet in what does good performance consist? In nothing other than the ability to make musical thoughts perceptible by singing or playing according to their true content and affect. It is possible to present one and the same thought to the ear so differently that it will hardly sense that it was the same thought.

3. The means of performance are the loudness and softness of tones, their stress, their speeding up, legato, staccato, vibrato (*Beben*), arpeggiating, tenuto, ritardando, and accelerando. Whoever uses these means at the wrong time or not at all performs poorly.

4. Thus, good performance may immediately be recognized when all notes and their proper embellishments are played with facility at the right time, at the appropriate volume, and with a touch suited to the true nature of the piece. This leads to a rounded, pure, and flowing manner, and the performance be-

comes clear and expressive. To the same end, one should test beforehand the condition of the instrument one is playing in order to avoid too heavy or too light a touch. Some keyboards do not produce a perfect and clear tone unless they are struck hard; others, however, have to be played very gently or the response of the tone will be exaggerated. I have mentioned this before, and I repeat it here: one ought to try to depict rage, anger, and other violent affects in a more reasonable manner than is generally done, that is, not by exaggerated force of touch, but by harmonic and melodic figures. Even in the most rapid passages each note must have its proper force; otherwise the touch is uneven and inarticulate. These passages are commonly speeded up by the use of trills.

5. The liveliness of an allegro is usually represented by detached notes, the tenderness of an adagio by held and slurred notes. In performance one has to see to it that these characteristics of the allegro and adagio are observed, even if they are not indicated in the pieces, and even if the player does not yet have sufficient insight into the affect of the piece. I emphasize "usually," however, since I know very well that all kinds of notes may appear in all kinds of tempi.

6. Some people play stickily, as if they had glue between their fingers. Their attack is too slow since they hold the notes too long. Others, to improve this, play them too short, as if the keys were red-hot. Both make a poor effect. The middle road is best. But I am speaking here generally; at the right time, all sorts of touch may be appropriate. . . .

13. A musician cannot move others unless he himself is moved. Thus he must of necessity be able to immerse himself in all the affects he wishes to arouse in his listeners; he must communicate his feelings to them in such a way as best to move them to empathy. In languid and sorrowful passages he must appear languid and sorrowful. One must see and hear it in him. The reverse is true with passionate, cheerful, and other kinds of ideas, when he immerses himself in these affects. No sooner is a passion stilled than another is excited, and thus he passes constantly from one to another. This is especially the case in pieces that are highly expressive, be they conceived by the performer himself or by somebody else; in the latter, the performer must feel the same passion within himself that the author of the piece intended at its composition. An excellent means for the keyboard player to capture the heart of the listeners is to become proficient in improvising fantasias. That this cannot be brought off without the least gestures will be denied only by those unfeeling players who sit like a carved figure in front of the instrument. Certainly, just as unattractive gestures are improper and harmful, good ones are conducive to helping the listeners with our intentions. Those opposed to them, even the most skillful players, often do injustice to the most beautiful pieces. They do not know what the music contains because they cannot express it; but when they hear such pieces performed by another player, who is capable of gentle feelings and who has mastered the art of

performing, they learn to their amazement that their works contain more than they had known and believed. Clearly, a good performance can even elevate an ordinary piece and win it applause.

14. In view of the multitude of affects that music is capable of evoking, it is obvious how many special gifts a musician must possess, and how much prudence he must bring to bear on them: not only must he consider his listeners and, according to their level of education, the content of the works he intends to perform, but he must also take into consideration the location of the performance and other additional circumstances. Since nature has so wisely endowed music with such diversity that it can be enjoyed by everyone, the musician, too, has the duty, insofar as he is able, to satisfy all kinds of listeners.

From *Versuch über die wahre Art das Clavier zu spielen* (Berlin, 1753–62; repr. Leipzig: Breitkopf & Härtel, 1957), Drittes Hauptstück, pp. 115–18, 122–23. There is an English translation by William J. Mitchell, *Essay on the True Art of Playing Keyboard Instruments* (New York: W. W. Norton, 1948).

JOHANN MATTHESON
from *The Latest Study of the Opera* (1744)

I
ON MUSICAL TASTE

1. Taste, in its figurative sense, is that internal sensibility, selection, and judgment by which our intellect reveals itself in matters of feeling. If the tongue has its own intellect—as Pliny[1] would have it—than so, too, the intellect has its own tongue with which it tastes and examines its objects.

2. Nature, reason, and the experience of art are our guides. Wherever these lead us hand in hand, we shall always encounter pleasure by means of true taste; there is infallibly to be found the sound basis of all knowledge. Whatever is good and healthy to eat will taste good as well;[2] but whatever tastes good is not necessarily good and healthy to eat.[3] We ought not to mistake the causes for means and effects.

[1]. This seems to be a faulty recollection of Pliny, *Natural History*, 11.174: "intellectus saporum caeteris in prima lingua, homini et in palato" (Other creatures recognize tastes with the tip of their tongue, man also on his palate). [LAH-S]
[2]. For example, young chicken, mature pikes.
[3]. For example, spices, confectionery, etc.

3. Though the taste examines and judges, it can never draw final conclusions. It represents a convenient vehicle, as it were, to reach the proper purpose. Yet, no matter how convenient a coach may be, it still can turn over.

4. It used to be said: there is no disputing taste; to each his own. When the French wish to indicate that a matter admits no rules or deliberation, they say: "C'est une affaire de gout!" If the ultimate object is considered, however, it is quite otherwise.

5. I remember the years when gentlemen did not drink Pontac. Anybody wishing to avoid being suspected of bad taste would abstain from dry red wine. Champagne and sweet Spanish wine, on the other hand, were much in vogue. Everyone fell in with this.

6. Then the tide turned. Sweet wines were completely forgotten, and the tart juices pressed from blue and brown grapes were much preferred. Here, too, nobody wished to swim against the current. The reigning taste prevailed everywhere.

7. Things seem much the same with respect to musical taste,[4] of which we shall give here a small example. To begin with, it may simply be asserted that the soul of musical art is not subject to such fluctuations of taste that it often turns completely around within the space of a hundred years or, indeed, even in less time; rather, it consists of correspondences between measures of sound and time and human emotions.

8. Taste, then, ought not to be called the cause of pleasure; we may perhaps better consider it a result. Contrariwise, one imagines that something tastes good only if it pleases; but it should please only if it tastes good. Still, the pleasant movement and the refined and judicious order of sounds are always the main cause of pleasure; taste is only a means to that purpose.

II

9. Accordingly, a modern composer should not trouble himself to acquire the least formal education or knowledge of rules. Instead, he should simply follow one or two general practical principles. This is the fashion. This is a sample of the magnificent taste of our times. It does play quite a different tune.

10. Is it not necessary for him to learn what harmonic relationships are? Whether a unison can be an interval? Whether a fundamental bass can be read in many different ways? Still less, what effect contrary motion has, or even what false relations are? Does he really need to discover how many and what kinds of keys there are, how to distinguish them, what their properties are, etc.? None of

4. From Nicolas Ragot de Grandval, *Essai sur le bon goust en musique* (Paris, 1732); an excerpt in German translation appears in *Niedersächsische Nachrichten von Gelehrten Sachen* (1733), 83.

this follows the latest taste. Let it be said in a word: there are only two keys: a hard or major key, and a soft or minor key; that is, the former contains a major third, the other, however, a minor third. That will suffice, and it is not necessary to refer to the beloved ancients, who were still prattling about a major and minor semitone, which nowadays has been completely forgotten.

11. By no means should one distinguish between the species of diatonic, chromatic, and enharmonic steps, but instead proceed unfailing to mix all the strings of the genera in one aria in the most curious manner—the more outrageous, the better!—so as to distance oneself all the more from antiquated cranks through such novel concoctions, indeed, distinguish oneself altogether.

12. Anyone may use ♭♭♭ and ♯♯♯ according to his own discretion, and hilariously jumble accidentals, so that no one has the slightest idea what they mean. That is just what French chefs do, whose greatest pleasure and honor consists in preparing a meal whose ingredients are unrecognizable to the human tongue and unidentifiable by a watchful eye. One may conveniently use the enharmonic sign (as they call it) instead of the chromatic and boldly claim them to be *sinonima* (not *synonyma;* that would be too pedantic). By the same token, one may claim that ♭ lowers a pitch as much as ♯ raises it. Chromatic signs may only divide whole steps; enharmonic signs, however, divide semitones, etc. Opponents will soon be silenced. Should someone be so bold as to maintain that *synonyma* are not *homonyma,* he would just be laughed at—and deservedly, too, for his mouthful of Greek! Who among us, after all, understands it?

13. Yet, all pleasantry aside, a modern music director must still be able to read somewhat, no matter how little: not as a matter of taste, but rather as an unavoidable necessity. To scribble misshapen letters, to spell incorrectly—this means nothing. As the saying goes: scholars paint poorly. This manner of writing endears a gentleman all the more to some ladies, particularly sopranos: birds of a feather flock together. By today's standards of taste, a word correctly spelled is likely to be a misprint, originating in scholarly ignorance. Even a little borrowed Latin, etc., may be inserted unexpectedly; the reader may be assured, however, that we would delete it immediately, if we knew what it meant or who wrote it.

14. Nowadays one would point a finger at a composer who knew a thing or two about the Latin language. We prefer to leave this to learned explorers of comets, whose star is approaching its *nodum descendentem* (descending node). Should anyone be asked by chance to respond in Latin to a Latin letter dealing with the craft, he can simply answer haughtily that he has been through all that textbook stuff long ago, and has not concerned himself with it for ages. If he is still obliged to set a Latin church piece, he can accomplish it perfectly well with Polish quantities of syllables: everybody nowadays likes it in good Polish. In particular, sarabands, gigues, courantes, etc., are just right for performances of a

Te Deum laudamus, or of a *Laudate Domino,* as long as they are indicated by "fugue," "canon," "double counterpoint," etc.—in Italian, of course. So much for learning.

From Part 2, "Die musikalische Geschmacksprobe, worin die heutigen allergalantesten Mittel und Wege zur Niedlichkeit des Gesanges und Klanges nachdrücklich anpreiset," of *Die neueste Untersuchung der Singspiele, nebst beygefügter musikalischen Geschmacksprobe* (Hamburg, 1744; repr. Kassel: Bärenreiter, 1975), 123–28.

Chapter Seven

Toward the Revaluation
of Instrumental Music

THE EIGHTEENTH CENTURY, which witnessed the full development and triumph of instrumental music, was at the same time rather meager in straightforward statements by critics, theorists, and philosophers on the value and function of pure music, either on its expressive or imitative power or on its right of admission to Parnassus, together with its elder sister, vocal music. Instead, more or less radical condemnations of instrumental music, as a meaningless arabesque geared only to the satisfaction of mere auditory pleasure, are more frequent. Nevertheless, there are several authors, and even some musicians, who enable us to discern, between the lines, that pure music was by then acquiring full rights of citizenship among the arts, and hence far from being regarded as a mere sonorous arabesque. However, they never come out with explicit and, perhaps for those days, rash statements of principle on the value of instrumental music, much less on its superiority to vocal music, as was to happen a few decades later in the years of the Sturm und Drang. The numerous treatises on instrumental performance practice written in the second half of the eighteenth century leave not the slightest doubt that instrumental music was by then implicitly considered a powerfully expressive art.

The sections gathered here, taken from treatises by Mattheson (*Der vollkommene Capellmeister*, 1739) and Quantz (*Versuch einer Anweisung die Flöte traversiere zu spielen*, 1752), as well as one by Diderot and Bemetzrieder (*Leçons de clavecin et principes d'harmonie*, 1771) in which the expressive power inherent in each slightest change in the harmonic framework of a composition is stressed, show that a new evaluation of instrumental music in the context of eighteenth-century culture was coming into its own.

Further indications confirming this evolution of Enlightenment thought are to be found among English philosophers. Several thinkers and writers, from Shaftesbury to John Dennis, up to James Harris, Edmund Burke, and Charles Avison, who was the most directly interested in music, bear out this tendency. It is significant that the last of these, although living in England, where instrumental music was already very widespread (at least in terms of popularity), should take as a reference point of musical excellence, even more than Handel with his by then celebrated oratorios, the two Italian musicians Benedetto Marcello and Francesco Geminiani, who were better known for their instrumental than their vocal music (see the sections in this chapter taken from Avison's treatise, *An Essay on Musical Expression,* 1753).

In the thinking of these writers, even those whose musical interests were only marginal, the concept of *expression* constitutes the key to a new approach to instrumental music, valued in terms of its formal and expressive importance. The classical aesthetics of imitation, in fact, ranked music last among the arts precisely because of its scarce (or non-existent) imitative capacity. Only a revaluation of the emotions and the discovery of the autonomy of the world of feelings with respect to that of reason made it possible to grasp the importance of those arts lacking a model in nature, but possessing a powerful symbolic significance, such as music, whose power lay precisely in its capacity to "affect the Heart and raise the Passions of the Soul" (Avison). Empirical philosophy, which quickly spread from England to the rest of Europe, and especially to France, represents the cultural soil in which this gradual change in ways of relating to music in general began to mature. The classicizing concept of harmony and beauty, seen as a limpid balance of parts ordered according to traditional rules, was replaced by the idea of the sublime and of the positiveness of what is infinite and indeterminate. The power of expression is linked more to the sublime than to what is beautiful, to what is indefinite and obscure rather than to what is clear and well-defined. Music, therefore, precisely because of its indeterminacy (which does not mean *meaninglessness*) is perhaps closer to the sphere of expression. Its power is based precisely on a certain lack of clarity and, more exactly, on its strong evocative power. The way was then open for a revaluation of music not only as a complement to poetic language, or as its support, but as an autonomous and perfectly self-sufficient language, capable of expressing and arousing feelings, at times even to a greater extent than the other arts.

JOHANN MATTHESON
from *The Complete Music Director* (1739)

25
ON THE ART OF PLAYING INSTRUMENTS

1. The science and art of playing instruments well, of presenting certain principles and rules thereof (all of which originate from one source, including the entire theory of acoustics), and especially the art of composing skillfully for instruments, is called *organica*, or, commonly, instrumental music, since it deals with external tools, and it attempts with these to imitate the human voice so that everything may sound and sing properly.

2. It follows as the first and irrefutable truth of this essay that he who wishes to compose for instruments or play them properly must thoroughly understand the art of singing, and thus he must know more than a mere singer. Because of his actual pursuits, he may in fact not be a vocalist, since the gift of a beautiful voice is not bestowed on everybody.

3. This is the reason why far more people apply themselves to the art of playing than the art of singing. Here in Hamburg, for instance, one may encounter a hundred instrumentalists for every ten singers. In all places it will probably be the same.

4. Thereafter, the *organicus* should devote himself with diligence and earnestness to one instrument above all others, and he should not imagine himself being or becoming a master to the same degree on every instrument. Such flights of fancy result in mastering a little of everything, but nothing completely.

5. On the other hand, no one, especially not those who wish to compose, should apply himself so intensely and exclusively to one instrument that he forgets all the others. At the least he must have sufficient knowledge of all common instruments to be able to distinguish

their volume
their range or compass
their style or manner of performance
their application.

6. If someone, for example, would have a viola da gamba compete with trumpets and timpani, or would lead an oboe down to g, or would treat a chalumeau like a Waldhorn, or would use the flute far more often than the

violins, he would be the butt of ridicule even if otherwise he played the clavier very beautifully. No one should think that there are not enough people who would act even more foolishly, if such customs were not conventionally avoided. Stax gives us examples of this.[1] But convention is not an art form, and it is not based on principles that can be taught, or from which conclusions may be drawn that could lead to satisfactory understanding.

7. Here a question comes to mind: why cornetts and trombones, which once were closely related and came to mind first among professional players as well as composers, apparently have completely disappeared from our churches —at least hereabouts—as if they had been declared unfit? The former instrument, because of its harshness, is very penetrating, whereas the other sounds rather magnificent and fills a large church excellently. Anyone is free to answer this question.

8. Although it will be left to every virtuoso to examine and describe his particular instrument, we still want to give a small model or sample, just as we did in the preceding chapter on external appearance, of an attempt to describe the use of the noblest instrument. First, we shall describe briefly the volume of the organ; secondly, its range; thirdly, its performance practice; fourthly, its application; and fifthly, as an addition, the best-known and most skilled masters or organists of our time. Hereafter it will be easy to elaborate on this and on other statements.

9. As far as the volume of a great organ is concerned, perhaps no other instrument in the world compares with it. It can imitate to good effect almost all other kinds of instruments, including even the human voice.

10. The more opportunity an organist has to utilize the volume of his instrument, however, the more he must apply it with moderation. At musical performances he will consider the number of singers participating and their accompaniment, so that his playing will not overpower them but that the singers especially will always prevail.

11. If, on the other hand, he is accompanying two or three choirs, and his part indicates *organo maggiore,* then he may pull out all the stops. If he cannot otherwise see, the time must be beaten to him by a special conductor. He should not contradict it.

12. A good musical ear and sound judgment are required to prevent the organ from dragging or rushing ahead. The former is a mistake common among

1. *Der critische Musicus,* p. 62 [pp. 84–85 in the 1745 edition]. [Mattheson refers to Scheibe's ridicule of the composer Stax, who introduced trumpets and timpani in an aria in a sacred composition, completely covering the words of the dying protagonist, and began a lively theatrical composition with a lugubrious overture. BJB]

most older organists; the latter, however, occurs among keyboard players who are still young and fiery. With age everything becomes more sluggish—in these as well as in other matters.

13. If the organ is to be played with the congregation, it must be determined whether they are strong or weak, whether all are fully assembled, or merely half, or even if no more than a quarter is present. As more arrive, the organ must swell as well; and as the congregation gradually disperses, the stops of the organ should diminish, too.

14. Yet everything must be so adjusted that the organ predominates in this case and keeps the roaring layman[2] on pitch (I dare not say, in check). This is exactly the opposite in the performance of formal music: here the organ is subordinate to the chorus; there the congregation must orient itself to the organ and must be governed and mastered by it. There is nothing more disgraceful or aggravating than when the voices of the congregation go flat, especially in winter and gloomy weather, and a weak organ cannot keep the balance.

15. Finally, it must be noted in regard to the volume of the organ—which often deafens even the organist—that it almost appears necessary to have a precentor or someone similar standing near the organ, who follows the singing of the congregation as it slows down or rushes ahead, and thus helps the organist keep pace with them. How often mistakes of this sort occur is only too well known.

16. The range of an organ keyboard in the upper manual commonly corresponds to that of the harpsichord, or at least it should. Hence, it is no trifling mistake that some organs contain the so-called short octaves; in others (even in some newly built and unveiled with much fanfare) C$\sharp$ and D$\sharp$ are nowhere to be found in pedal and manual.

17. The saving of costs here is no excuse at all, since far more was spent on useless child's play and dull figurines than possibly could have been saved in this case. This is organ construction for the eyes, not the ears. It is like cutting out a human's spleen and liver and giving him two noses instead. I mention this here since it had been forgotten in the previous chapter, where it actually belongs.

18. Just as the organ is the strongest instrument, it also has the widest range or compass. It not only reaches up to three whole octaves above the ordinary harpsichord but, by means of 32-foot basses, it also extends down in a marvelous manner to two octaves below, and thus it contains nine whole octaves with all their divisions, that is, 108 different pitches.

19. Anybody who knows what an artist is capable of playing on only three octaves (for instance, on a violin) can easily imagine what remarkable things

---

2. The ancients spoke of "laicus clamans," in contrast to the "clerus sonans."

can be produced on an organ. Here he has the fullest concord: both hands are equally active; both feet are occupied in addition; by coupling (*copula*) the various keyboards, the manual stops sound together with the pedals, or two manual keyboards are connected in such a manner that when one is played the other one sounds together with it and plays the stops drawn.

20. Now, thirdly, we shall discuss style, or the manner in which or by means of which the organ must be played or used, which is the most important and significant point. Style cannot be described as a manner of writing, but it must necessarily be called a manner of performance, unless all things performed or to be performed were to be written down.

21. There are—excluding here thorough-bass, a science essential to every harpsichord player and organist—four main genres: the prelude, the fugue, the chorale, and, finally, the actual improvisation of a fantasia or postlude.

22. As far as the first is concerned, preludes have a threefold use, which hardly three organists of those I know appreciate properly or understand systematically and clearly. Undoubtedly, the main use of the prelude, which should always be energetic and short rather than too long, is to prepare the listener for the principal matter that follows or the singing of the selected chorale.

23. The second use is to structure and divide precisely the time devoted to the divine service, so that, for example, a short hymn is accompanied by a longer prelude, a long hymn, however, by a shorter prelude. In this manner, the half or full hour reserved for congregational singing will suffer no curtailment or prolongation, but "Let all things be done decently and in order," as St. Paul tells us (1 Cor. 14:40).

24. The third use of a prelude is to make a skillful and imperceptible transition from the sometimes quite contrary key of the preceding hymn or piece to the next. And even though it is no novelty for today's lascivious ears if, for instance, a recitative ends in G major and is immediately followed by an aria in A minor (often with good reason, to arouse our attention), such a procedure is not acceptable for an unmusical congregation: there a smooth connection is needed, that is, an appropriate prelude.

From Part 3 of *Der vollkommene Capellmeister* (Hamburg, 1739; repr. Kassel: Bärenreiter, 1954), 470–72. There is an English translation by Ernest C. Harriss, *Johann Mattheson's Der vollkommene Capellmeister: A Revised Translation with Critical Commentary* (Ann Arbor: UMI Research Press, 1981).

JOHANN JOACHIM QUANTZ
from *A Treatise on How to Play the Flute* (1752)

XVII
ON THE DUTIES OF ACCOMPANISTS IN GENERAL

10. If an orchestra is to be good, it must strive for a good execution that is appropriate to the nature and characteristics of each piece. The piece may be gay or melancholy, grandiose or jesting, daring or flattering, or whatever it may be; thus it must be performed in the passion that it is supposed to express. If one is accompanying a concertante part, the accompanist must always follow the performance of the soloist, whatever happens. There must be no partiality, so that the work of one is performed well and that of another is performed poorly: everyone must strive to execute what has been submitted to him—regardless of who composed it—with the same enthusiasm as if it were his own work, lest he disserve the creditable reputation of a musician as an honest man.

. . .

12. Not only does every piece and, in particular, every passion impose certain rules and restrictions on performance, but the location and purpose of the music do so as well. For example, church music demands more splendor and seriousness than music for the theater, which permits more liberties. If certain daring and odd thoughts that are not very appropriate in church should have been inserted into a piece of church music by the composer, the accompanists, particularly the violinists, should endeavor as much as possible to conceal, restrain, and make them gentler through a modest performance.

13. Good performance, which is appropriate to its subject matter, must also extend to comic music. An interlude (intermezzo), which represents a caricature or the opposite of a serious vocal composition and which is set by the composer with common and lowly ideas rather than serious ones, and which has no other object than criticism and laughter, must be accompanied, if it is to fulfill its purpose, in a lowly, common manner, and not like a serious opera, especially in the burlesque arias. The same is to be observed in a ballet of common character, since, as has already been mentioned, the accompaniment must participate in both serious and comic matters.

14. The performance, however, must not only be good and appropriate to each piece, but it must also be even and consistent among all members of a good orchestra. One will admit that a speech by one makes a greater impression than by another. If one were to perform a German tragedy in which the dramatis

personae all were supposed to be born in the same country, using actors speaking a variety of dialects—for instance, High German, Low German, Austrian, Swabian, Tyrolean, Swiss, etc.—the differences in pronunciation would render even the most serious tragedy ridiculous. In music, the situation is almost the same, if every participant were to play in his own particular manner. For example, if one were to form an orchestra of such individuals, some of which played only according to the Italian taste, some only according to the French, and others played still differently from these two manners, then, even if each were sufficiently skilled in his manner, the performance nevertheless would have the same effect as the tragedy mentioned above, because of the dissimilarity in the style of performance. Indeed, the flaw would be even greater, since in a tragedy one speaks only after another; in music, however, all play mostly simultaneously. It is a common belief that if only the principal part is performed by skilled people, the others do not matter much. But just as a little vinegar will spoil even the best wine, so it happens in music, too, if only some voices are played well and the others, even only one, are played badly.

15. When he performs a ripieno part, every soloist must to a certain extent renounce the skill he displays when giving a concert or playing a solo; and, in contrast to the freedom he is allowed when standing out alone, he must submit to slavery, so to speak, when he accompanies. Thus he may not add anything that could obscure the melody in any way, especially if the part is scored for more than one player. Otherwise he would cause great confusion in the melody, because it is impossible for one to guess the thoughts of the other all the time. For example, if one were to apply only one unspecified appoggiatura, and the other to play the note without embellishment, the result would be a bad dissonance, with no preparation or resolution, and it would greatly offend the ear, especially in slow pieces. If one were to perform the prescribed appoggiaturas not in their proper tempo, but shorten the long ones and lengthen the short ones, it would make an equally poor effect because of the others playing along differently. Ritornellos above all must be performed without any arbitrary additions. These additions are reserved for the soloist. Some have the bad habit of occasionally applying all kinds of tomfoolery already in the ritornello, and on that account they forget to read the notes properly. Some end arias strangely with a full-voiced multiple stop, where none is called for. They seem to have learned this from beer-hall fiddlers. Even worse is when they play a few open strings on the violin immediately after the conclusion of an aria. If the aria, for example, is written in E-flat major, and thereupon they immediately try an E and A, one can easily imagine what a beautiful effect it makes.

16. Since the beauty of an orchestra depends mainly on the ability of all its members to play uniformly, and since it is indispensable that their leader per-

form in an accomplished manner appropriate to each piece, it is also incumbent on every individual member of the orchestra to conform to the leader in such matters, not to resist his instructions, and not to consider it a shame to submit to reasonable and necessary authority, without which no good music can ensue. Only rarely one will encounter a long-established orchestra that is not made up of both good and bad performers; this will be noticed most easily if for a small concert one selects alternately only parts of the orchestra. Both the young and the old will be found among them. Neither the age nor the youth of its members make an orchestra good, but only the good discipline and order they keep. An old ripieno player, if he is still in command of his powers, and if he has been trained under good leadership, can render better service than many a young performer, who perhaps has a greater facility in mastering difficult passages, but who has less experience; and, in addition, he is perhaps not willing to submit to the necessary authority. Very often the old, if they have been trained under poor leadership, as well as the young, who may have too high an opinion of their performing skills, turn rebellious: the latter because of their supposed dexterity, the former, however, because of prejudice, or because of their seniority. Frequently the old maintain that too much is expected of them, if they are to submit to a leader who is not as rich in years as they are. The young, however, imagine themselves to have all the skills necessary to a leader, notwithstanding that the duties of a good leader are plentiful. How can an orchestra exist or improve if rebelliousness, envy, hatred, and disobedience reign among its members, instead of cooperative and pliant minds? What becomes of even and harmonious performance, if each one follows his own head?

17. To further harmonious performance, one additional rule should be taken to heart by anyone who aspires to be a good musician or accompanist: during the performance of a musical composition, he must avail himself of the art of simulation. Simulation is not only permitted, it is even of the utmost necessity, and it does not violate ethical behavior. If one attempts, as much as possible, to be the master of one's passions in daily life, it will not be difficult at any time during a performance to place oneself into the affect the piece demands. Then one will perform really well and always from the soul. Without a mastery of the laudable art of simulation one remains a mere craftsman and not a true musician, even if one knows every species of counterpoint by heart and can play all kinds of difficult passages on one's instrument. Although, unfortunately, many dissimulate very often in their daily lives, in music they rarely practice the desirable art of simulation.

18. An honest musician ought not to be obstinate or overly insistent on his rank. For example, a skilled violinist need not be ashamed if he has to play second violin or even viola, in case of need. In their own way, and in many

pieces, these demand a skilled player just as much as the first violin. The highest and most solid rank is given to an honest musician by his skill, and this he may show on one instrument as well as on another.

From *Versuch einer Anweisung die Flöte traversiere zu spielen* (Berlin, 1752; repr. Kassel: Bärenreiter, 1983); in the 3d ed. of 1789 (repr. Kassel: Bärenreiter, 1953), 245–49. There is an English translation by Edward R. Reilly, *On Playing the Flute*, 2d ed. (New York: Schirmer, 1985).

DENIS DIDEROT
AND ANTON BEMETZRIEDER
from *Keyboard Lessons and Principles of Harmony* (1771)

The Teacher: Now that the four consonances in all the modulations present no difficulties for you, the word *dissonance* may be uttered in your presence.

The Pupil: What are you saying? Is discord also combined with harmony?

The Teacher: Assuredly, and it plays the same role here as in the universe: it is pain that sharpens pleasure; darkness that brings out light; weariness to which pleasure owes its sweetness; a cloudy day that makes a clear one beautiful; vice that serves as cosmetic to virtue; ugliness that heightens the radiance of beauty. It is through opposition that qualities are distinguished; the magic of painting consists in the play of light and shadow. Poets of exquisite taste have often mixed a melancholy notion into the happiest and most sensual images; the latter become more interesting for it; a little noise in the distance lends an inconceivable charm to silence; a pensive being relegated to the corner of a lonely landscape adds to the impression of solitude. Unrelieved happiness becomes insipid.

The Pupil: Despite your poetic tirade, I do not think I have ever wished to season goodness with evil.

The Teacher: We learn the value of the two greatest possessions in life—health and freedom—only when we have lost them.

The Pupil: That is certainly putting it nicely: habit removes the sweetness from possession and makes privation more bitter; and on that note, let me compliment you.

The Teacher: On what?

The Pupil: Guess.

The Teacher: I don't know.

The Pupil: You don't know? Why, on your reconciliation with my dearest friend.

The Teacher: And this friend is?

The Pupil: Moral philosophy. Everything you've just told me is pure moral philosophy.

The Teacher (*irritated*): Mademoiselle, begin in C. After C, E, G play G, B, D, F, and finish with C, E, G. What do you think of that?

The Pupil: I think it shows two examples of your principles at the same time. This little fit of temper has brought out your natural sweetness, and never have C, E, G pleased me so much; G, B, D, F will reconcile me to passing difficulties, and I will hate only the long dissonances of life. So G, B, D, F is a dissonance.

The Teacher: Yes, mademoiselle. Dissonant harmony is composed of three thirds, G, B, D, F, according to the first four odd numbers, 1, 3, 5, 7.

The Pupil: In that case, nothing is easier than dissonant harmony. I know it all. It has just one note more than the consonance that has two thirds in the order of the first three odd numbers. So there are twenty-four dissonances; let me play—I see, I see. All I have to do is add a third above the consonance. There's nothing to it!

The Teacher: The way you are going about it? Dissonant harmonies cannot exist alone. They lead to consonances, the only points of rest in music.

The Pupil: I suspected as much.

The Teacher: The consonant harmony of the tonic is the main point of rest in modulation. Let us look for a dissonance that leads to it. The consonance of the dominant follows that of the tonic very well, which succeeds it well in turn. You have tested this in a harmonic phrase in all the keys.

You must have felt that C, E, G satisfies the ear before and after G, B, D, F. So what is G, B, D, F?

The Pupil: The dissonant harmony of the dominant in C.

The Teacher: G is the root of the consonance of the dominant, and it's also the root of the dissonance.

G, B, D form the consonance of the dominant, thus the note F, alone, when added, forms the dissonance, and that is because it is linked to the root G.

Notice that the B, the D, and the F in G, B, D, F are dissonant with the principal consonance C, E, G: B with C; D with C and E; F with E and G.

These dissonances are the true pointers, the true paths that lead the dissonant harmony of the dominant to the consonant harmony of the tonic.

Conclude from this that in the harmonic phrase of four consonances, I have not been arbitrary in following the order found there, for though G, B, D is consonant harmony, it is nevertheless dissonant harmony with C, E, G, the principal consonance that must end the phrase.

The Pupil: Those conclusions are not otherwise obvious.

The Teacher: Ask your father. He will tell you that in all the fine arts, phenomena are subtle, that the cause of phenomena is subtle as well, and that the sensible man—who knows that the slightest hint of preference ultimately causes men to get carried away, and who is aware that this hint is often very secret, even for the one whose preference is determined by it—is delighted to have uncovered it and carefully avoids quibbling.

From *Leçons de clavecin et principes d'harmonie* (Paris, 1771; repr. New York: Broude Bros., 1966), Septième dialogue et troisième leçon d'harmonie, pp. 154–57. The preface is signed by Diderot, whose daughter was Bemetzrieder's pupil. Diderot evidently was the moving force behind the writing and publication of this treatise. Although he claims that he did no more than to revise Bemetzrieder's teutonic French (protesting just a bit too much), his ideas are inseparably interwoven throughout the treatise, and not just in the portions of the dialogue attributed to "the Philosopher." Within the decade it was translated into English and published in London: *Music made easy to every capacity, in a series of dialogues; being practical lessons for the harpichord, laid down in a new method, so as to render that instrument so little difficult, that any person, with common application, may play well; become a thorough proficient in the principles of harmony; and will compose music if they have the genius for it in less than a twelvemonth. Written in French by Monsieur Bemetzrieder . . . and published at Paris, (with a preface) by the celebrated Monsieur Diderot, the whole translated, and adapted to the use of the English student, by Giffard Bernard* (London, 1778–79). The complete treatise was republished in Diderot's *Œuvres complètes*, ed. J. Assézat, vol. 12 (Paris, 1876), and has recently been edited by Jean Mayer and Pierre Citron, with an introduction by Jean Varloot, in the *Œuvres complètes, édition critique et annotée*, ed. H. Dieckmann and J. Varloot, vol. 19 (Paris: Hermann, [1983]), 56–391; the excerpt is found on pp. 196–98.

CHARLES AVISON
From *An Essay on Musical Expression* (1753)

3. ON MUSICAL EXPRESSION, SO FAR AS IT RELATES TO THE COMPOSER

So much concerning the two Branches of Music, *Air* and *Harmony:* Let us now consider the third Circumstance, which is *Expression.* This, as hath been already observed, "arises from a Combination of the other two; and is no other than a strong and proper Application of them to the intended Subject."

From this Definition it will plainly appear, that Air and Harmony, are never to be deserted for the Sake of Expression: Because Expression is founded on them. And if we should attempt any Thing in Defiance of these, it would cease to be *Musical Expression.* Still less can the horrid Dissonance of Cat-Calls deserve this Appellation, though the Expression or Imitation be ever so strong and natural.

And, as Dissonance and shocking Sounds cannot be called Musical Expression; so neither do I think, can mere Imitation of several other Things be entitled to this Name, which, however, among the Generality of Mankind hath often obtained it. Thus the gradual rising or falling of the Notes in a long Succession, is often used to denote Ascent or Descent, broken Intervals, to denote an interrupted Motion, a Number of quick Divisions, to describe Swiftness or Flying, Sounds resembling Laughter, to describe Laughter; with a Number of other Contrivances of a parallel Kind, which it is needless here to mention. Now all these I should chuse to stile Imitation, rather than Expression; because, it seems to me, that their Tendency is rather to fix the Hearers Attention on the Similitude between the Sounds and the Things which they describe, and thereby to excite a reflex Act of the Understanding, than to affect the Heart and raise the Passions of the Soul.

Here then we see a Defect or Impropriety, similar to those which have been above observed to arise from a too particular Attachment either to the *Modulation* or *Harmony*. For as in the first Case, the Master often attaches himself so strongly to the Beauty of *Air* or Modulation, as to neglect the *Harmony;* and in the second Case, pursues his Harmony or Fugues so as to destroy the Beauty of Modulation; so in this third Case, for the Sake of a forced, and (if I may so speak) an unmeaning Imitation, he neglects both Air and Harmony, on which alone true Musical Expression can be founded.

This Distinction seems more worthy our Notice at present, because some very eminent Composers have attached themselves chiefly to the Method here mentioned; and seem to think they have exhausted all the Depths of Expression, by a dextrous Imitation of the Meaning of a few particular Words, that occur in the Hymns or Songs which they set to Music. Thus, were one of these Gentlemen to express the following Words of *Milton,*

Their Songs
Divide the Night, and *lift* our Thoughts to Heav'n.[1]

It is highly probable, that upon the Word *divide,* he would run a *Division* of half a Dozen Bars; and on the subsequent Part of the Sentence, he would not think he had done the Poet Justice, or *risen* to that *Height* of Sublimity which he ought to express, till he had climbed up to the very Top of his Instrument, or at least as far as a human Voice could follow him. And this would pass with a great Part of Mankind for Musical Expression, instead of that noble Mixture of sol-

---

1. Milton, *Paradise Lost* 4, l. 688. [BJB]

emn Airs and various Harmony, which *indeed* elevates our Thoughts, and gives that exquisite Pleasure, which none but true lovers of Harmony can feel.

Were it necessary, I might easily prove, upon general Principles, that what I now advance concerning Musical Imitation is strictly just; both, because Music as an imitative Art has *very confined Powers,* and because, when it is an Ally to Poetry (which it ought always to be when it exerts its mimetic Faculty) it obtains its End *by raising correspondent Affections* in the Soul with those which ought to result from the Genius of the Poem. But this has been already shewn, by a judicious Writer,[2] with that Precision and Accuracy which distinguishes his Writings. To his excellent Treatise I shall, therefore, refer my Reader, and content myself, in this Place, with adding two or three practical Observations by way of corollary to his Theory.

1st, as *Music* passing to the Mind through the Organ of the Ear, can imitate only *by Sounds and Motions,*[3] it seems reasonable, that when *Sounds* only are the Objects of Imitation, the Composer ought to throw the mimetic Part entirely amongst the accompanying *Instruments;* because, it is probable, that the Imitation will be too powerful in the *Voice* which ought to be engaged in *Expression* alone; or, in other Words, in raising correspondent Affections with the Part.[4] Indeed, in some Cases, Expression will coincide with Imitation, and may then be admitted universally: As in such *Chromatic Strains* as are mimetic of the Grief and Anguish of the human Voice.[5] But to the Imitation of Sounds in the *natural* or *inanimate* World,[6] this, I believe, may be applied as a general Rule.

2dly, when Music imitates *Motions,* the Rythm, and Cast of the Air, will generally require, that both the vocal and instrumental Parts coincide in their Imi-

---

2. Vide three Treatises of *J. H.* the second concerning Poetry, Painting, and Music. [James Harris, *Three Treatises. The First Concerning Art. The Second Concerning Music, Painting and Poetry. The Third Concerning Happiness* (London, 1744). BJB]

3. Vide Page 57 in the above Treatise [the third paragraph of this excerpt].

4. I cannot bring a finer Illustration of my Meaning, than from the old Song in *Acis* and *Galatea.*

> Hush ye pretty warbling Quire,
> Your thrilling Strains
> Awake my Pains,
> And kindle soft Desire, &c.

Here the great Composer has very judiciously employed the vocal Part in the nobler Office of expressing, the Pathos, the plaintive Turn of the Words, while the symphony and Accompaniment very chearfully imitates the singing of *the warbling Quire.* But had Mr HANDEL admitted this *Imitation of Sound* into the vocal Part, and made it imitate the *thrilling Strains of the Birds* by *warbling Divisions,* it is manifest the Expression would have been much injured; whereas, according to his Management of it, the *Imitation* greatly assists the Expression.

5. As to take Mr *H*[andel]'s own Example, the Chorus of Baal's Priests in *Deborah. Doleful Tidings how ye wound.*

6. Such as the Noise of Animals, the Roar of Thunder, Ocean, &c. The Murmur of Streams.

tation. But then, be it observed, that the Composer ought always to be more cautious and reserved when he applies this Faculty of Music to *Motion,* than when he applies it to Sound, and the Reason is obvious; the Intervals in Music are not so strictly similar to animate or inanimate Motions, as its Tones are to animate or inanimate Sounds. Notes ascending or descending by large Intervals, are not so like the Stalking of a Giant,[7] as a Flow of even Notes are to the murmuring of a Stream;[8] and little jiggish Slurrs are less like the Nod

7. Mr *H*[andel] has himself quoted a Passage in *Acis* and *Galatea, "See what ample Strides he takes,"* as imitative of the *Walk* of *Polypheme:* but, I apprehend, the Majesty of that Air rather affected him by an *Association of Ideas,* than any great Similarity in the Imitation.

An Association of this Kind, seems to have struck the Author [François Raguenet] of the *Paralèle des Italiens et des François en ce qui regarde la Musique* "Pour la Conformité (says he) de l'Air, avec le sens des paroles, je n'ay jamais rien entendu, en matière de Symphonies, de comparable à celle qui fut exécutée à Rome, à l'Oratoire de S. Jerôme de la Charité, le jour de la Saint Martin de l'année 1697, sur ces deux mots, *mille saette, mille flèches:* c'étoit un Air dont les Notes étoient pointées à la manière des Gigues; le caractère de cet Air imprimoit si vivement dans l'âme l'idée de flèche; et la force de cette idée seduisoit tellement l'Imagination, que chaque violon paroissoit être un arc; & tous les Archets, autant de flèches décochées, dont les pointes sembloient darder la Symphonie de toutes Parts; on ne sauroit entendre rien de plus ingenieux & de plus heureusement exprimé."

We may learn from this, how far *musical Imitation,* simply considered, may amuse the Fancy of many who are less susceptible of the more delicate and refined Beauties of *Expression.* The particular Felicity of the *Frenchman,* in the musical Performance here described, seems to have depended on this Similitude, *viz.* that every *Violin* appeared as a *Bow,* and all the *Bows,* like so many *Arrows shot off,* the *Points* of which, seemed to *dart* the Symphony through all its Parts. Perhaps, so far as *Imitation* was necessary, his Observation might be just. But were this an Argument, that the Business of *Imitation* was superior to every other in musical Composition, it would reduce the noblest Species of it, still lower than the *Extravaganzi* of the instrumental Performances which we have noted in the Chapter on Modulation. [Part of the quotation from Raguenet is given above in Ch. 1. BJB]

8. Here let me quote with Pleasure, the Air which Mr HANDEL has adapted to those charming Words of MILTON [*Il Penseroso,* ll. 141–54].

> Hide me from Day's garish Eye,
> While thee Bee, with honied Thigh,
> At her flow'ry Work does sing,
> And the Waters murmuring;
> With such Concert as they keep,
> Entice the dewy-feather'd Sleep.
> And let some strange mysterious Dream,
> Wave at his Wings in airy Stream
> Of lively Portraiture display'd,
> Softly on my Eyelids laid.
> Then, as I wake, sweet Music breath,
> Above, about, and underneath;
> Sent by some Spirit, to Mortals good,
> Or th' unseen Genius of the Wood.

Here the Air and the Symphony delightfully imitate the humming of the Bees, the murmuring of the Waters, and express the Ideas of Quiet and Slumber; but what, above all, demands this Eulogium, is the Master-Stroke of accompanying the Voice with Trebles and Tenors, only till he comes to these Words, "Then, as I wake, sweet Music breath," where *the Bass begins* with an Effect that

of *Alexander*,[9] than certain Shakes and Trills are to the Voice of the Nightingale.[10]

3dly, as Music can only imitate Motions and Sounds, and the *Motions* only imperfectly; it will follow, that musical Imitation ought never to be employed in representing Objects, of which Motion or Sound are not the principal Constituents. Thus, to Light, or Lightning, we annex the Property of Celerity of Motion; yet it will not follow from thence, that an extremely swift Progression of Notes will raise the Idea of either one or the other; because, as we said, the Imitation must be, in these Cases, very partial.[11] Again, it is one Property of Frost to make Persons shake and tremble; yet, a tremulous Movement of Semitones, will never give the true Idea of Frost: though, perhaps, they may of a trembling Person.

4thly, as the Aim of Music is to affect the Passions in a pleasing Manner, and as it uses Melody and Harmony to obtain that End, its Imitation must never be employed on *ungraceful Motions,* or *disagreeable Sounds;* because, in the one Case, it must injure the *Melody* of the Air, and in the other, the *Harmony* of the Accompanyment; and, in both Cases, must lose its Intent of affecting the Passions *pleasingly.*

5thly, as Imitation is only so far of Use in Music, as when it aids the Expression; as it is only analogous to poetic Imitation, *when Poetry imitates* through mere natural Media,[12] so it should only be employed in the same Manner. To make the Sound eccho to the Sense in descriptive Lyric, and, perhaps, in the cooler Parts of Epic Poetry is often a great Beauty; but, should the tragic Poet labour at shewing this Art in his most distressful Speeches; I suppose he would

---

can be felt only, and not expressed. [From Handel's *L'Allegro, il Penseroso, ed il Moderato,* Part 2, no. 26. BJB]

I have chosen to give all my Illustrations on this Matter from the Works of Mr HANDEL, because no one has exercised this Talent more universally, and because these Instances must also be most universally understood.

9.   With ravish'd Ears,
        The Monarch hears,
        Assumes the God,
        Affects to nod,
        And seems to shake the Spheres.

In which Air I am sorry to observe, that the *Affectation* of imitating this Nod, has reduced the Music as much below the Dignity of the Words, as *Alexander's* Nod was beneath that of *Homer's Jupiter.* [Handel, *Alexander's Feast,* Part 1, no. 7 BJB]

    10.   Vide [Milton], *Il Penseroso* [ll. 61–62].

        Sweet Bird that shuns the Noise of Folly,
        Most musical, most melancholly.

    11. What shall we say to excuse this same great Composer, who, in his Oratorio of *Joshua,* condescended to amuse the vulgar Part of his Audience, by letting them *hear the Sun stand still.*

    12. *H*'s Treatises, p. 70 [see above, n. 2].

rather flatten than inspirit his Drama: In like Manner, the musical Composer, who catches at every particular Epithet or Metaphor that the Part affords him,[13] to shew his imitative Power, will never fail to hurt the true Aim of his Composition, and will always prove the more difficient in Proportion as his Author is more pathetic or sublime.

What then is the Composer, who would aim at true musical Expression, to perform? I answer, he is to blend such an happy Mixture of Air and Harmony, as will affect us most strongly with the Passions or Affections which the Poet intends to raise: and that, on this Account, he is not principally to dwell on particular Words in the Way of Imitation, but to comprehend the Poet's general Drift or Intention, and on this to form his Airs and Harmony, either by Imitation (so far as Imitation may be proper to this End) or by any other Means. But this I must still add, that if he attempts to raise the Passions by Imitation, it must be such a temperate and chastised Imitation, as rather brings the Object before the Hearer, than such a one as induces him to form a Comparison between the Object and the Sound. For, in this last Case, his Attention will be turned entirely on the Composer's Art, which must effectually check the Passion. The Power of Music is, in this Respect, parallel to the Power of Eloquence: if it works at all, it must work in a secret and unsuspected Manner. In either Case, a pompous Display of Art will destroy its own Intentions: on which Account, one of the best general Rules, perhaps, that can be given for musical Expression, is that which gives Rise to the Pathetic in every other Art, *an unaffected Strain of Nature and Simplicity.*[14] . . .

---

13. To give but one Instance, how many Composers hath the single Epithet, WARBLING, misled from the true Road of Expression, like an *ignis fatuus,* and bemired them in a *Pun?*

14. Whatever the State of Music may have been among the ancient *Greeks,* &c. or whether it was actually capable of producing those wonderful Effects related of it, we cannot absolutely determine; seeing all the Uses of their *Enharmonic Scale* are totally lost; and of their musical Characters, which should have conveyed to us their Art, slender Traces any where to be found. From the Structure of their Instruments, we cannot form any vast Ideas of their Powers:[a] They seem to have been far inferior to those in Use at present: but which, indeed, being capable of as much Execution as Expression, are only rendered more liable to be abused. Thus, the too great Compass of our modern Instruments, tempting as well the Composer as Performer, to exceed the natural Bounds of Harmony, may be one Reason why some Authors have so warmly espoused the Cause of the ancient Music, and run down that of the modern.[b]

I believe that we may justly conclude, that the Force and Beauties of the ancient Music, did not consist so much in artful Compositions, or in any Superiority of Execution in the Performance: as in the pure Simplicity of its Melody; which being performed in Unisons, by their vast Chorusses of Voices and Instruments, no Wonder the most prodigious Effects were produced.[c] Since the Time of GUIDO ARETINO,[d] the Laws and Principles of Harmony have been considerably enlarged, and by rendering this Art more intricate and complex, have deprived it of those plain, though striking Beauties, which, probably, almost every Hearer could distinguish and admire. And, I don't know whether this will not go some Way, towards determining the Dispute concerning the superior Excellency of ancient and modern Music. It is to be observed, that the Ancients, when they speak

We might soon arrive at a very different Style and Manner, as well in our Compositions as Performance; did we but study the Works of the best Chapel-Masters abroad, as CALDARA, LOTTI, GASPARINI, and many others, whose excellent Compositions ought surely to be better known, and rescued from the Possession of those churlish Virtuosi, whose unsociable Delight is to engross to themselves those Performances, which, in Justice to their Authors, as well as the World, they ought freely to communicate.[15]

We may clearly discern the Effects of such a Commerce as is here proposed, with the Works of the greatest Masters. The immortal Works of CORELLI, are in the Hands of every one; and accordingly we find, that from him many of our best modern Composers have generally deduced their Elements of Harmony. Yet there remains something more to be done by our present Professors: they ought to be as intimately conversant with those other great Masters, who, since CORELLI's Time, have added both Taste and Invention; and, by uniting these, have still come nearer to the Perfection of the *General-Harmonic Composition*.

---

of its marvellous Effects, generally consider it as an Adjunct to Poetry. Now, an Art in its Progress to its own absolute Perfection, may arrive at some intermediate Point, which is its Point of Perfection, considered as an Art joined to another Art; but not to its own, when taken separately. If the Ancients, therefore, carried Melody to its highest Perfection, it is probable they pushed the musical Art as far as it would go, considered as an Adjunct to Poetry: but Harmony is the Perfection of Music, as a single Science. Hence then we may determine the specific Difference between the ancient and modern Compositions, and consequently their Excellency.

[a]Calmet's *Dissertation sur la Musique des Anciens.* [Augustin Calmet, *Dissertations sur la poésie et la musique des Anciens en général et des Hébreux en particulier* (Amsterdam, 1723). BJB]

[b]Sir William Temple's *Works,* vol. 1, p. 162. [For the full reference, see above, p. 195, n. 4. BJB]

[c]Bonnet, *Histoire de la Musique* [see above, Ch. 4].

[d]Aretino lived in the eleventh Century.

15. The *Motetts* of CALDARA, are noble, pathetic, and finely adapted to the Purposes here mentioned. LOTTI and GASPARINI, have also composed various Pieces for the Service of the Church. But, as only the Fame of them hath, as yet, reached me, I can only suppose them of a Character, equal at least to their other Compositions, the Perusal of which, have often afforded me a very singular Pleasure.

There is a Composition for the Church, which the Connoisseurs, acquainted with its Beauties, esteem as inimitable in its Way; namely, the *Stabat Mater,* &c. of the Baron D'ASTORGA. This Nobleman had many Excellencies, as a Composer, and chiefly a simplicity of Harmony, and an affecting Style in *many* of his Airs and Duetts, which, undoubtedly, he has thrown, in some peculiar Manner, into the Performance here mentioned.

If ever I have the Felicity of seeing this Work, I shall expect to find it more equally conducted than the *Stabat Mater* of PERGOLESE. For, though it is the distinguished Character of this latter Composer, to have succeeded in the *complaining, or sorrowful Style;* yet I have often thought there was wanting, in several Movements of his *Stabat Mater,* the just Distinction, which ought always to be observed, between the Tenderness or Passion of a Theatrical Scene, and the Solemnity of Devotion. [Emanuele d'Astorga (1680–?1757) is a colorful and mysterious character. The *Stabat mater* is his only sacred work known; it enjoyed immense success in England for nearly a century after Avison's report. BJB]

The numerous Seminaries in *Italy* seldom fail of producing a Succession of good Masters: from these we might select such Pieces as would greatly contribute to the real Solemnity of the Cathedral Service. While others again of a different Kind, might be compiled and fitted for Concertos, or other musical Purposes; so that there would never be wanting a Variety of Examples and Subjects, for the Practice of all Students in Harmony whatever: and, by an assiduous Application to a greater and more comprehensive Style than we have hitherto attempted; we should soon be able to acquire so true a Taste, as would lay a sure Foundation for the forming our own Masters.[16]

If it should be asked, who are the proper Persons to begin a Reform in our Church Music? It may be answered, the Organists of Cathedrals, who are, or ought to be, our *Maestri di Capella,* and by whom, under the Influence and Protection of their Deans, much might be done to the Advancement of their Choirs: nor would they find any Difficulty in accomplishing this useful Design, as there are many Precedents to direct them, both from Dr ALDRIDGE and others,[17] who have introduced into their Service the celebrated PALESTINA and CARISSIMI with great Success. And if this Method, when so little good Music was to be had, hath been found to advance the Dignity and Reputation of our Cathedral Service; how much more may be expected at this Time, from the Number and Variety of those excellent Compositions that have since appeared; and which may be easily procured, and adapted to the Purposes here mentioned.

An Improvement of this Kind might be still more easily set on Foot, were there any History of the Lives and Works of the best Composers; together with an Account for their several *Schools,* and the *characteristic Taste,* and *Manner* of each: A Subject, though yet untouched, of such extensive Use, that we may reasonably hope it will be the Employment of some future Writer.

Painting has long had an Advantage of this Kind, but whether it has profited by such Advantage, may at present, perhaps, be disputed. However, I think, if both these Arts are not now in the State of Perfection which one might wish, it ought not to be attributed to the Want of Genii, but to the Want of proper

16. The *Italians* are allowed to excel all other Nations in the Arts of Painting and Music, but the Reason is more obvious in the former than latter; for the Recourse to the *antique* which *Italy* afforded to Painting, must be the chief Cause of its Excellence in that Art. Music could have no such external Assistance. The Goths had rooted out all Tracks of the ancient Melody. How then must we account for the superior Genius, which the *Italians* have, since that Time, discovered in regard to Music? Not from the chimerical Hypothesis of Air, Climate, Food, &c. but from the public and national Care, which has ever attended it in that Country, so different from the Treatment it meets with in *England.*

17. Henry Aldrich (1648–1710) bequeathed his music library, rich in Elizabethan and Italian music, to Christ Church, Oxford, with which he was long associated; he himself adapted music by Palestrina and Carissimi to English words. [BJB]

Encouragement, from able and generous Patrons, which would excite them to more laudable Pursuits; many Professors in both the Sciences having alike employed their Talents in the lowest Branches of their Art, and turned their Views rather to *instant Profit*, than to *future Fame*.[18]

Thus, and thus alone, can we hope to reach any tolerable Degree of Excellence in the nobler Kinds of musical Composition. The Works of the greatest Masters are the only Schools where we may *see*, and from whence we may *draw*, Perfection. And here, that I may do Justice to what I think the most distinguished Merit, I shall mention, as Examples of true *Musical Expression*, two great Authors, the one admirable in *vocal*, the other in *instrumental* Music.

The first of these is BENEDETTO MARCELLO, whose inimitable Freedom, Depth, and comprehensive Style, will ever remain the highest Example to all Composers for the Church: For the Service of which, he published at *Venice*, near thirty Years ago, the first fifty Psalms set to Music.[19] Here he has far excelled all the Moderns, and given us the truest Idea of that noble Simplicity which probably was the grand Characteristic of the ancient Music. In this extensive and laborious Undertaking, like the divine Subject he works upon, he is generally either grand, beautiful, or pathetic; and so perfectly free from every Thing that is low and common, that the judicious Hearer is charmed with an endless

18. In reflecting on the State of Music in *England*, I have often thought, that it might not be altogether foreign to the Design of some periodical Memoir of Literature, to have an Article sometimes, giving an Account and Character of the best musical Compositions.

As a Precedent, I shall here take the Liberty to consider a late Performance in such a cursory Manner, as may, perhaps, be proper enough on the Publication of other musical Works hereafter. *La Musique raisonée &c. par Mr le Compt. St Germain*, published by *Walsh* [ca. 1750], pr. 1*l*.1*s*. This Collection of Airs, in the Opera Style, are most of them set for a *Soprano*, some few for the *Conter-Alto*, and accompanied with Violins, &c. in four Parts.

In these Pieces the Author has shewn a peculiar Genius in the tender and complaining Style, but which require a Performer, like himself, to do them Justice: this single Species of musical Expression seems to run through the whole Collection, for, though he often aims to express different Passions, yet there is still wanting a sufficient Variety to keep up the Attention, when more than one of these Airs are performed at a Time. Nevertheless, when they are intermixed with other Performances in the Concert, they have then, in a particular Manner, a very pleasing Effect.

Some general Idea like this, of our musical Essays, on their first Appearance, would not only incite a Spirit of Emulation among the Composers, and render their Works more worthy the public Notice; but might also prove a more effectual Restraint to the Publishers, not to be so careless and dilatory on their Part: for however inadvertent our Composers may be, in putting their Works incorrect out of their Hands, their Printers are seldom behind them in that point.

19. This Work is contained in eight Volumes in Folio. The first four were published in the Year 1724. And the whole came out complete two Years after, under the following Title, *Estro Poetico Armonico, Parafrasi sopra Salmi, Poesia di* GIROLAMO ASCANIO GIUSTINIANI, *Musica di* BENEDETTO MARCELLO *Patrizi Veniti, Venezia,* 1726. There are some Pieces of instrumental Music published in *London*, and said to be composed by BENEDETTO MARCELLO, a *Venetian* Nobleman; but as these are very mean Performances, they cannot be supposed to come from the same great Author. [Twelve sonatas for flute or violin were published in London in 1732 as op. 1; op. 2, six cello sonatas, was published in the same year. BJB]

Variety of new and pleasing Modulation; together with a Design and Expression so finely adapted, that the Sense and Harmony do every where coincide. In the last Psalm, which is the fifty-first in our Version, he seems to have collected all the Powers of his vast Genius, that he might surpass the Wonders he had done before.

I do not mean to affirm, that in this extensive Work, every Recitative, Air, or Chorus, is of equal Excellence. A continued Elevation of this Kind, no Author ever came up to. Nay, if we consider that Variety which in all Arts is necessary to keep alive Attention, we may, perhaps, affirm with Truth, that *Inequality* makes a Part of the Character of Excellence: That something ought to be thrown into Shades, in order to make the Lights more striking. And, in this Respect, MARCELLO is truly excellent: If ever he seems to *fall*, it is only to *rise* with more astonishing Majesty and Greatness.[20]

To this illustrious Example in *vocal*, I shall add another, the greatest in *instrumental Music;* I mean the admirable GEMINIANI; whose Elegance and Spirit of Composition ought to have been much more our Pattern; and from whom the public Taste might have received the highest Improvement, had we thought proper to lay hold of those Opportunities which his long Residence in this Kingdom has given us.

From *An Essay on Musical Expression,* 2d ed. (London, 1753), Part II, On Musical Composition, pp. 56–70, 93–103. The first edition was published in 1752. The first excerpt and a later one are given in Lippman, *Musical Aesthetics* 1:190–99.

20.   Far the greatest Part
Of what some call Neglect, is study'd Art.
When *Virgil* seems to trifle in a Line,
'Tis like a Warning-Piece which gives the Sign,
To wake your Fancy and prepare your Sight,
To reach the noble Height of some unusual Flight.
                    Roscom. *Ess. on translated Verse.*

[Wentworth Dillon, Earl of Roscommon, *An Essay on Translated Verse* (London, 1684). BJB]

Chapter Eight

Sensism and Empirical Currents

S O FAR AS MUSIC is concerned, sensism and empiricism undoubtedly represent a minority trend in Europe, compared with classical rationalism. Even though many Encyclopedists had come into contact with English empiricism, such influences were nevertheless marginal. In the lively pages devoted to opera in *The Spectator*, the London journal to which Joseph Addison contributed, the usual criticisms of opera's inverisimilitude are not accompanied by any remarks of an intellectualistic or moralistic nature. For Addison, opera's only end is "to gratify the senses, and keep up an indolent attention in the audience." His criticisms therefore are directed toward this end. Of far greater philosophical and aesthetic weight are the remarks by Jean-Baptiste Dubos, taken from his treatise *Réflexions critiques sur la poésie, la peinture et la musique* (first published in 1719), in which a good many sections are devoted to music. Influenced by Locke and English empiricism, as well as French classicism, Dubos's work was widely read throughout Europe during the eighteenth century, and his thoughts on music served as a model for Rousseau. The first original formulation of an aesthetics of taste is found in Dubos's *Réflexions*. Sensism is also the starting point of Pietro Verri's thinking. In his observations on music he refers back to cultural relativism, already present in some Encyclopedists, for whom every country and every people is sensitive only to its own music. Music is essentially an "exciter of the passions," but "the means to excite the passions change in accordance with changes in the various degrees of longitude and latitude." Its function is to alleviate man's "unnamed sorrows," that is, sadness. If men were always happy, Verri notes in alluding to Dubos's *Réflexions,* perhaps the fine arts, and music in particular, would not exist.

JOSEPH ADDISON
from *The Spectator* (1711)

Spectatum admissi risum teneatis?
(Admitted to the sight, would you not laugh?)
Horace, *Ars poetica* 5

An Opera may be allowed to be extravagantly lavish in its Decorations, as its only Design is to gratify the Senses, and keep up an indolent Attention in the Audience. Common Sense however requires, that there should be nothing in the Scenes and Machines which may appear Childish and Absurd. How would the wits of King *Charles's* time have laughed, to have seen *Nicolini* exposed to a Tempest in Robes of Ermin, and sailing in an open Boat upon a Sea of Paste-Board? What a Field of Raillery would they have been let into, had they been entertain'd with painted Dragons spitting Wild-fire, enchanted Chariots drawn by *Flanders* Mares, and real Cascades in artificial Land-skips? A little Skill in Criticism would inform us that Shadows and Realities ought not to be mix'd together in the same Piece; and that Scenes, which are designed as the Representations of Nature, should be filled with Resemblances, and not with the Things themselves. If one would represent a wide Champian Country filled with Herds and Flocks, it would be ridiculous to draw the Country only upon the Scenes, and to crowd several Parts of the Stage with Sheep and Oxen. This is joining together Inconsistencies, and making the Decoration partly Real and partly Imaginary. I would recommend what I have here said, to the Directors, as well as to the Admirers, of our Modern Opera.

As I was walking the Streets about a Fortnight ago, I saw an ordinary Fellow carrying a Cage full of little Birds upon his Shoulder; and, as I was wondering with my self what Use he would put them to, he was met very luckily by an Acquaintance, who had the same Curiosity. Upon his asking him what he had upon his Shoulder, he told him, that he had been buying Sparrows for the Opera. "Sparrows for the Opera," says his Friend, licking his Lips, "what are they to be roasted?" "No, no," says the other, "they are to enter towards the end of the first Act, and to fly about the Stage."[1]

---

1. The absurdities listed by Addison come from Handel's *Rinaldo e Armida,* his first opera performed on the English stage, at King's Theatre, Haymarket in February 1711. The libretto, based on the well-known episode in Tasso's *Gerusalemme,* was by Giacomo Rossi, translated by Aaron Hill; hence "two poets of different nations." The sparrows were let loose during the aria "Augelletti che cantate." [EF]

SENSISM AND EMPIRICAL CURRENTS

This strange Dialogue awakened my Curiosity so far that I immediately bought the Opera, by which means I perceived that the Sparrows were to act the part of Singing Birds in a delightful Grove: though upon a nearer Enquiry I found the Sparrows put the same Trick upon the Audience, that Sir *Martin Mar-all* practised upon his Mistress;[2] for, though they flew in Sight, the Music proceeded from a Concert of Flagellets and Bird-calls which was planted behind the Scenes. At the same time I made this Discovery, I found by the Discourse of the Actors, that there were great Designs on foot for the Improvement of the Opera; that it had been proposed to break down a part of the Wall, and to surprize the Audience with a Party of an hundred Horse, and that there was actually a Project of bringing the *New-River* into the House, to be employed in Jetteaus and Water-works. This Project, as I have since heard, is post-poned till the Summer-Season; when it is thought the Coolness that proceeds from Fountains and Cascades will be more acceptable and refreshing to People of Quality. In the mean time, to find out a more agreeable Entertainment for the Winter-Season, the opera of *Rinaldo* is filled with Thunder and Lightning, Illuminations, and Fire-works; which the Audience may look upon without catching Cold, and indeed without much Danger of being burnt; for there are several Engines filled with Water, and ready to play at a Minute's Warning, in case any Accident should happen. However, as I have a very great Friendship for the Owner of this Theater, I hope that he has been wise enough to *insure* his House before he would let this Opera be acted in it.

It is no wonder, that those Scenes should be very surprizing, which were contrived by two Poets of different Nations, and raised by two Magicians of different Sexes. *Armida* (as we are told in the Argument) was an *Amazonian* Enchantress, and poor Seignior *Cassani*[3] (as we learn from the persons represented) a Christian Conjuror (*Mago Christiano*). I must confess I am very much puzzled to find how an *Amazon* should be versed in the Black Art, or how a Christian should deal with the Devil.

To consider the Poets after the Conjurors, I shall give you a Taste of the *Italian*, from the first Lines of his Preface: *Eccoti, benigno Lettore, un Parto di poche Sere, che se ben nato di Notte, non è però aborto di Tenebre, mà si farà conoscere Figlio d'Apollo con qualche Raggio di Parnasso.* "Behold, gentle Reader, the

2. In *Sir Martin Mar-all, or the Feigned Innocence,* a comedy by Dryden translated from Molière's *L'Étourdi,* the ridiculous Sir Martin pretends to serenade his mistress, holding a lute and making grimaces, while it is really his servant Warner who is playing and singing. There is a similar episode in Rostand's *Cyrano.* [EF]

3. Giuseppe Cassani (fl. 1700–28), an Italian alto castrato. He arrived in London in 1710 and was a member of the Queen's Theatre company for two years; the part of the Mago was composed expressly for him. [BJB]

Birth of a few Evenings, which, tho' it be the Offspring of the Night, is not the Abortive of Darkness, but will make it self known to be the son of *Apollo,* with a certain Ray of Parnassus." He afterwards proceeds to call Seigneur *Hendel* the *Orpheus* of our Age, and to acquaint us, in the same Sublimity of Stile, that he Composed this Opera in a Fortnight. Such are the Wits to whose Tastes we so ambitiously conform our selves. The Truth of it is, the finest Writers among the Modern *Italians,* express themselves in such a florid form of Words, and such tedious Circumlocutions, as are used by none but Pedants in our own Country; and at the same time, fill their Writings with such poor Imaginations and Conceits, as our Youths are ashamed of, before they have been Two Years at the University. Some may be apt to think, that it is the difference of Genius which produces this difference in the Works of the two Nations; but to show there is nothing in this, if we look into the Writings of the old *Italians,* such as *Cicero* and *Virgil,* we shall find that the *English* Writers, in their way of thinking and expressing themselves, resemble those Authors much more than the Modern *Italians* pretend to do. And as for the Poet himself, from whom the Dreams of this Opera are taken, I must entirely agree with Monsieur *Boileau,* that one Verse in *Virgil,* is worth all the *Clincant* or Tinsel of *Tasso.*[4]

But to return to the Sparrows; there have been so many Flights of them let loose in this Opera, that it is feared the House will never get rid of them; and that in other Plays they may make their Entrance in very wrong and improper Scenes, so as to be seen flying in a Lady's Bed-Chamber, or perching upon a King's Throne; besides the Inconveniences which the Heads of the Audience may sometimes suffer from them. I am credibly informed, that there was once a Design of casting into an Opera, the Story of Wittington and his Cat,[5] and

---

4. Addison had little understanding and appreciation of the Italians of his time, as can be seen from his *Remarks on Several Parts of Italy* (1705); on the other hand, he had unbounded admiration for the ancient Romans, to whom he compared his English contemporaries. The passage he alludes to in Boileau comes from Satire IX:

> Tous les jours à la cour un sot de qualité
> Peut juger de travers avec impunité;
> À Malherbe, à Racan, préférer Théophile,
> Et le clinquant du Tasse à tout l'or de Virgile. [EF]

5. The puppeteer Powell, perhaps taking up Addison's suggestion, put on a *Whittington* against *Rinaldo e Armida;* the story of Whittington and his prodigious cat has many parallels in European folk literature. Whittington, while in the service of a London merchant, Mr. Fitzwarren, sent his cat, his only possession, on an overseas expedition as his share in the commercial speculation of his master; the king of Barbary, who was plagued with mice and rats, acquired the cat for an enormous sum. In the meantime, Whittington, mistreated by the cook he served as scullery boy, fled London. But at Holloway he heard the sound of the bells of St. Mary le Bow in London, which seemed to say: "Turn again Whittington, Lord Mayor of London." Thus he returned to the Fitzwarren house, and subsequently became mayor of London. The true Richard Whittington was mayor of London at various times between 1397 and 1419. [EF]

that in order to it, there had been got together a great Quantity of Mice; but Mr. *Rich,* the Proprietor of the Play-House,[6] very prudently considered that it would be impossible for the Cat to kill them all, and that consequently the Princes of his Stage might be as much infested with Mice, as the Prince of the Island was before the Cat's arrival upon it; for which Reason, he would not permit it to be Acted in his House. And indeed I cannot blame him; for, as he said very well upon that Occasion, I do not hear that any of the Performers in our Opera, pretend to equal the famous Pied Piper, who made all the Mice of a great Town in *Germany* follow his Musick, and by that means cleared the Place of those little Noxious Animals.

Before I dismiss this Paper, I must inform my Reader, that I hear there is a Treaty on Foot between *London* and *Wise,*[7] who will be appointed Gardiners of the Play-House, to furnish the opera of *Rinaldo* and *Armida* with an Orange-Grove; and that the next time it is Acted, the Singing Birds will be Personated by Tom-Tits: The Undertakers being resolved to spare neither Pains nor Money for the Gratification of the Audience.

From *The Spectator,* no. 5 (6 March 1711).

JEAN-BAPTISTE DUBOS
from *Critical Reflections on Poetry, Painting, and Music* (1740)

XLV
On Music Itself

It remains for us to speak of music as the third of those means that men have invented to give new force to poetry and enable it to make a greater impression on us. As the painter imitates the lines and colors of nature, so the musician imitates the tones, accents, sighs, inflections of the voice—in short, all those sounds with which nature itself expresses its sentiments and passions. All of

6. Christopher Rich, director of the Theatre Royal, Drury Lane. [EF]
    7. A famous firm of gardeners; they explained their methods in *The Retir'd Gard'ner* (a translation of two French books by F. Gentil and the Sieur Louis Liger) of 1711, and gave a detailed description of the Dutch gardens of Count Tallard at Nottingham. [EF]

these sounds, as we have already shown, have a marvelous power to move us, because they are the signs of the passions, instituted by nature, from whom they have received their energy, whereas articulated words are only arbitrary signs of the passions. Articulated words draw their meaning and value solely from the men who established them and who were able to give them currency only in a given country.

To make its imitation of natural sounds more capable of moving and pleasing, music has reduced this imitation to a continuous melody, called the "subject." This art has discovered two further ways of rendering song more pleasing and moving. One is harmony, and the other is rhythm.

The chords of which harmony is composed hold great appeal for the ear, and the convergence of the different parts of a musical composition that form these chords contributes further to the expression of the sound that the musician attempts to imitate. The basso continuo and the other parts greatly contribute to the melody's ability to express more perfectly the subject of the imitation.

What we call *measure* and *movement* in music, the ancients called rhythm. Now measure and movement give a musical composition its soul, so to speak. The science of rhythm, by showing how to vary the measure appropriately, relieves music of a uniformity of movement that would soon make it boring. In the second place, rhythm is able to add a new verisimilitude to the imitation of which a musical composition is capable, because the rhythm reinforces the imitation of the progression and movement of noises and natural sounds that was already being imitated through melody and harmony. Thus rhythm adds another dimension of verisimilitude to imitation.

Music imitates, then, with the aid of melody, harmony, and rhythm. "In cantu tria præcipue notanda sunt, harmonia, sermo, et rithmus. Harmonia versatur circa sonum. Sermo circa intellectum verborum et enunciationem distinctam. Rithmus circa concinnum cantici motum" ["Three things above all are to be observed in song: harmony, speech, and rhythm. Harmony is concerned with sound, speech with the understanding of words and their distinct enunciation, rhythm with the elegant movement of songs"]. In this same way painting makes its imitations with the help of line, contrast, and local colors.

The natural signs of the passions that music brings together, and that it uses skillfully to increase the energy of the words it sets in song, must therefore make them more capable of moving us, because these natural signs have a marvelous power to stir our emotions. They receive this power from nature itself. "Nihil est enim tam cognatum mentibus nostris, quam numeri atque voces, quibus et excitamur, et incendimur, et lenimur, et languescimus" ["Nothing is so akin to our minds as rhythm and melody, by which we are aroused and inflamed and soothed and made languid"], says one of the most judicious observers of human affections.[1] In this way the pleasure of the ear becomes the pleasure of the heart. Thus songs were born; and the observation that would have been made—that words had quite a different force when they were sung than when they were recited—gave rise to setting stories to music on the stage, and we came round gradually to singing an entire dramatic piece. These are our operas.

There is thus a certain truth in operatic recitatives, and this truth consists in the imitation of the tones, accents, sighs, and sounds that are naturally appropriate to the sentiments that the words contain. The same truth can be found in the harmony and rhythm of the whole composition.

Music did not content itself with imitating in its melodies the inarticulate language of man, and all the natural sounds that he instinctively uses. This art attempted further to imitate all the sounds most capable of making an impression on us when we hear them in nature. Music uses only instruments to imitate these sounds, in which no words are articulated, and we commonly call these imitations *symphonies*. Yet *symphonies* actually play, so to speak, different roles in our operas, and they do so very successfully.

In the first place, although this music is purely instrumental, it contains nonetheless a true imitation of nature. In the second place, there are several sounds in nature capable of producing a great effect on us, when we are made to hear them at the right moment in the scenes of a drama.

The truthfulness of the imitation of a *symphonie* consists in the resemblance of this *symphonie* to the sound it is meant to imitate. There is truth in a *symphonie* composed to imitate a storm when its melody, harmony, and rhythm cause us to hear a noise similar to howling winds and moaning waves crashing together or breaking over the rocks. An example is the *symphonie* that imitates a storm in Marais's opera *Alcione*.[2]

So although these *symphonies* do not imitate verbal expression, they are able nonetheless to play roles in dramatic pieces, because they help to interest us in the action by creating an impression approximating that of the noise itself, were we to hear it in the same circumstances as we hear the *symphonie* that imitates it. For example, the imitation of the noise of a storm that is about to drown a character in whom, at that moment, the poet has had us take great interest, affects us just as would the noise of a storm about to drown a person for whom we felt great interest and warmth, if we were within hearing distance of this actual storm. It would be useless to repeat here that the *symphonie*'s impression could not be as genuine as the impression that the true storm would make on

1. Cicero, *De oratore* 3.197.
2. Marin Marais, *Alcione* (Paris, 1706). [BJB]

us; for I have already said several times that the impression made on us by the imitation is much less forceful than the impression made by the thing imitated. "Sine dubio in omni re vincit imitationem veritas" ["Without a doubt in all things truth exceeds imitation"].[3]

It is thus not surprising that *symphonies* move us greatly, although their sounds, as Longinus says, "are but simple imitations of an inarticulate noise, and if it may be so expressed, of sounds that possess only half of their being, and half a life."[4]

This is why the inarticulate song of instruments has been used in all countries and in all ages to move the hearts of men and to instill certain feelings in them, principally on the occasions when these feelings could not have been inspired through the power of speech. . . .

There is then verisimilitude in instrumental music, as in poetry. As the poet must conform his fictions to a conventional truth, so the musician must conform to this truth in the composition of his *symphonies*. Let me explain. Musicians often compose *symphonies* to express noises that we have never heard and that perhaps never existed in nature. Such are, for example, the earth howling when Pluto leaves the underworld, the winds whistling when Apollo inspirits the Pythia, the noise made by a ghost coming out of its tomb, and the trembling foliage of the oaks of Dodona.[5] There is a conventional truth for these *symphonies*. The "convenientia finge" of Horace[6] has its place here as in poetry. We know when the required degree of verisimilitude has been met. It is certainly present when the *symphonies* have an effect approximating the effect that the noises they imitate could have had, and when they seem to us to be in keeping with these noises that we have not heard and of which we have nonetheless a vague idea in relation to other noises that we have heard. Thus it is said of *symphonies* of this sort, as well as of those that imitate actual noises, that they are truly expressive, or they are not expressive. The *symphonie* of the tomb from

---

3. Cicero, *De oratore* 3.215.

4. Longinus, *On the Sublime*, ch. 32 [Dubos quotes it in French, but not from the translation by Boileau, *Traité du sublime ou du merveilleux dans le discours* (Paris, 1674). In modern editions of Longinus it occurs in 39.3: "The notes of the lyre, though they have no meaning, also, as you know, often cast a wonderful spell of harmony with their varied sounds and blended and mingled notes. Yet all these are but spurious images and imitations of persuasion, not the genuine activities proper to human nature of which I spoke" (as translated in D. A. Russell and M. Winterbottom, *Ancient Literary Criticism: The Principal Texts in New Translations* [Oxford: Clarendon Press, 1973], 497). The notion of the sublime became widely influential in eighteenth-century thought. The treatise is no longer thought to be by Longinus but to date from the first century A.D. BJB].

5. The ghost scene, discussed below, comes from Lully's *Amadis*, first performed at Paris, 18 January 1684. The music depicting the trembling foliage comes from Destouches's *Issé*, Paris, 1697. [BJB]

6. Horace, *Ars poetica* 119. [BJB]

Amadis[7] is praised, as is that of the opera *Issé*,[8] for imitating nature well, although nature has never been observed in the circumstances in which these *symphonies* intend to copy it. Thus although they are, in a certain sense, the product of pure invention, they nevertheless contribute greatly to making the performance touching and the action moving. For example, the funereal accents of the *symphonie* that Lully placed in the scene from the opera *Amadis*,[9] in which the ghost of Ardan comes out of his tomb, make as much of an impression on our ear as the spectacle and declamation make on our eyes. Our imagination, set upon in the same moment by the organ of sight and that of hearing, is much more moved by the appearance of the ghost than if our eyes alone had been captivated. . . .

The basic principles of music are thus the same as those of poetry and painting. Like poetry and painting, music is an imitation. Music cannot be good if it is not in keeping with the general rules governing the choice of subjects, verisimilitude, and several other points in these two arts. As Cicero says: "Omnes artes quae ad humanitatem pertinent, habent quoddam commune vinculum et quasi cognatione quadam inter se continuantur" ["For all arts that pertain to human culture have a common link and are, so to speak, joined together by a common kinship"].[10]

Just as there are people who are more moved by color than by the expression of passion in painting, there are also people who are sensitive only to the charm of the melody or to the richness of the harmony in music, and who do not pay enough attention to whether this melody is a good imitation of the sound it is supposed to imitate, or whether it is suited to the meaning of the words it sets. They do not require that the musician match the melody to the sentiments contained in the words that he sets to music. They are satisfied if the melodies are varied, graceful, or even unusual, and it is enough for them that they express in passing a few words of the text. The number of musicians who conform to this taste is all too great, as if music were incapable of producing anything better. If they set to music, for example, the verse of the psalm *Dixit dominus* that begins with the words "De torrente in via bibet," they concentrate only on expressing the speed of the torrent in its flow, instead of adhering to the meaning of the verse, which contains a prophecy of Christ's Passion.[11] However, the expression of a word cannot be as moving as the expression of a feeling, unless the word itself contains a feeling. If the musician contributes something to the ex-

---

7. Lully's opera; see above, n. 5. [BJB]
8. See above, n. 5. [BJB]
9. Act III.
10. Cicero, *Pro Archia* 1.2.
11. Ps. 110:7 [109 Vulg.]: He shall drink of the brook in the way: therefore shall he lift up the head. [BJB]

pression of a word that is only part of a sentence, he must do so without losing sight of the general meaning of the sentence he is setting to music.

I would gladly rank music in which the composer has not known how to use his art to move us on the same level as paintings that are merely well colored and poems that are merely well versified. Just as the beauties of execution must serve in poetry, as in painting, to set into motion the beauties of invention and the strokes of genius that portray the nature they imitate, so the richness and variety of chords, the charms and the novelty of melodies, must serve in music only to imitate and embellish the imitation of the language of nature and of the passions. What we call the science of composition is a servant, so to speak, that the musician's genius must keep in its employ, as the poet's genius must do with his gift for rhyming. All is lost, if I may be forgiven this image, if the slave becomes the mistress of the house, and if she is allowed to arrange it according to her liking, like a building made only for her. I even think all poets and musicians would feel as I do, if it were no easier to adhere strictly to rhyme than to sustain a poetic style, or to find—without abandoning truth—melodies that are at once natural and graceful. But one cannot be moving without genius, and it suffices to have practiced the art, even if one has applied oneself to it without such genius, to compose knowledgeably in music, or to rhyme richly in poetry.

XLVI
Some Reflections on Italian Music. The Italians Cultivated This Art only after the French and the Flemish

This discourse seems to lead me naturally to speak of the difference between Italian and French taste in music. I am speaking of contemporary Italian taste, today much farther removed from that of the French than it was during the pontificate of Pope Urban VIII. Although nature does not change, and it seems consequently that taste in music should not change, it has nonetheless been changing in Italy for some time. Music is fashionable in that country, as are clothes and carriages in France.

Foreigners find that we understand movement and meter better than the Italians, and that we are thus more successful than the Italians in that part of music that the ancients called rhythm. Indeed, the most skillful violinists in Italy would give a bad performance—I will not say of Lully's character pieces —but even of a gavotte: "Itali longioribus utuntur flexibus, unde ridentur à Gallis, veluti qui in uno formando plasmate utrunque exhauriunt pulmonem. Galli praeterea in suo cantu rhythmum magis observant quam Itali, unde fit ut apud illos complura occurrant cantica quae concinnos et elegantes admodum habent motus" ["The Italians use longer ornamentations, which makes the

French laugh, like those who exhaust both lungs with one trill. Moreover, the French observe the meter much better in their music than do the Italians, so that one finds among them many songs with a well-formed, indeed elegant, movement"].[12] Although Italians study meter a great deal, it seems nonetheless that they do not understand rhythm, and they are not able to make use of it for expression, or adapt it for imitation, as well as we do. . . .

XLVII
Which Poetry Is Most Suited to Be Set to Music

Now I shall be so bold as to assert that, generally speaking, music is much more effective than simple declamation; that music gives greater force to poetry than declamation, when this poetry is suited to be set to music. But it is imperative that all the poetry be equally suited, and that the music can give it the same energy.

We have said that poetry should express feelings in simple terms, but that it should present to us all the other subjects about which it speaks in images and pictures. We have shown that music must imitate in its melodies the tones, sighs, accents, and all of those sounds not articulated by the voice that are the natural signs of our feelings and passions. It is very easy to infer from these two truths that poetry containing feelings is most suited to be set to music, and that poetry containing pictures is not well suited to it.

Nature herself furnishes, so to speak, the melodies appropriate to the expression of feelings. We could not even begin to recite poetry containing tender or touching sentiments convincingly without sighing, without using the accents and *ports de voix* that a man gifted with a talent for music easily brings into a continuous song. I am certain that Lully did not search very long for the melody of the verses Medea speaks in the opera *Thésée:* "Mon coeur aurait encore sa première innocence / S'il n'avait jamais eu d'amour" (My heart would have retained its innocence, if it had never known love).[13]

There is more. The man of genius, who composes to words like these, finds that he has composed a variety of melodies without even having thought to do so. Each feeling has its own tones, its accents, and its sighs. So the musician, in setting poetry of the kind we have been discussing, creates melodies as varied as Nature herself.

Poetry containing pictures and images, what is often called poetry *par excel-*

---

12. Isaac Vossius, *De poematum cantu et viribus rythmi* (Oxford, 1673), 123. [The quotation has been corrected after the original. BJB]

13. From Act II, sc. 1 of Lully's *tragédie lyrique,* first performed at Saint-Germain on 12 January 1675. [BJB]

lence, does not allow the composer as many opportunities for success. Nature furnishes almost nothing toward its expression. Art alone helps the composer who might wish to set to music lines such as those in which Corneille paints such a magnificent portrait of the Triumvirate:[14]

> Le méchant par le prix au crime encouragé,
> Le mari dans son lit par sa femme égorgé:
> Le fils tout dégouttant du meurtre de son père
> Et sa tête à la main demandant son salaire, etc.

> [The evil man whom profit urges to crime,
> The husband slain by his wife while in bed,
> The son still dripping from his father's murder
> Who comes, head in hand, asking for his pay, etc.]

Indeed, the composer, obliged to set such lines of poetry to music, would not find many possibilities for melody in the natural declamation of the words. He must therefore have recourse to melodies that are more noble and imposing than expressive, and since Nature offers him no help in varying these melodies, they end up all sounding the same. Music adds almost no force to verses whose source of beauty is in images, while it dulls their impression by slowing down their articulation. A good poet of verse for music, however rich he may be in inspiration, will hardly ever use in his works verses such as those by Corneille that I have cited. So the reproach made to Quinault when he composed his first operas—that his verses were devoid of those images and pictures that make poetry sublime—is ill-founded. What was considered a defect in his poetry was in fact a merit. But we in France had not yet understood what constituted the merit of verses written to be set to music. Until then we had composed only songs; and as these little poems were destined only for the expression of a few sentiments, they had not occasioned the observations on poetry written to be set to music that we have subsequently been able to make. As soon as we had become acquainted with operas, the philosophical mind, which excels at bringing truth to light, provided that it follows the path of experience, brought us to the discovery that poetry full of images and, generally speaking, the most beautiful poetry, is not the most likely to succeed in music. There is no comparison to be made between the two stanzas that I am about to cite when they are declaimed. The first is from the opera *Thésée* written by Quinault:[15]

> Doux repos, innocente paix,
> Heureux, heureux un cœur qui ne vous perd jamais.
> L'impitoyable amour m'a toujours poursuivie,

---

14. *Cinna,* Act I, sc. 3, lines 199–202. [BJB]
15. In Lully's setting, Act II, sc. 1.

N'était-ce point assez des maux qu'il m'avait faits?
Pourquoi ce Dieu cruel avec de nouveaux traits
Vient-il encor troubler le reste de ma vie?

[Sweet repose, innocent peace,
Happy, happy is the heart that never loses you.
Unpitying love has always pursued me,
Were those injuries he had done me not enough?
Why does this cruel god come with new arrows
To trouble what remains of my life?]

The second is from the *Idylle* at Sceaux, by Racine:[16]

Déjà grondaient les horribles tonnerres
Par qui sont brisés les ramparts,
Déjà marchait devant les étendards
Bellone les cheveux épars,
Et se flattait d'éterniser les guerres
Que ses fureurs soufflaient de toutes parts.

[Already the horrible thunder was rumbling,
The thunder with which ramparts are broken,
Already before the banners Bellona
Was marching, her hair flying,
And she prided herself on the perpetual wars
That her fury blew in from every direction.]

These two stanzas were very far from achieving equal success in music.
Thirty people can recall the first for every one who recalls the second. Yet both
were set to music by Lully, who even had ten more years of experience when he
composed the *Idylle* at Sceaux. But the first contains the natural sentiments of a
heart excited by a new passion. Only one image, one of the simplest, appears,
that of Cupid unleashing his arrows on Medea. The lines from Racine contain
the most magnificent images with which poetry may be adorned. All those who
can forget for a moment the effect created by these verses when sung will rightly
prefer Racine to Quinault.

It is generally agreed today that the poetry of Quinault is very well suited to
be set to music, due to the very point upon which his verses were criticized
when opera began; I mean to say by the nature of their poetic style. What has
always had to be acknowledged is that these verses are well suited to music due

16. Lully's one-act divertissement *Idylle sur la paix*, on a libretto by Racine (*Œuvres complètes*,
ed. Raymond Picard [Paris, 1951], 1:992–95), was first performed at Sceaux on 16 July 1685. [BJB]

to the structure of their composition and the arrangement of the words considered as simple sounds.

From *Réflexions critiques sur la poésie, la peinture et la musique*, 4th ed. (Paris, 1740), 1:435–41, 448–50, 451–56, 468–74. The first edition was published in 1719. The seventh edition of 1770 has been reprinted by Slatkine Reprints (Geneva, 1967). There is an English translation by Thomas Nugent, *Critical Reflections on Poetry, Painting and Music* (London, 1746; 2d ed., 1748; repr. New York: AMS Press, [1978]).

PIETRO VERRI
from "Music" (1765)

Almost all nations in the world have some type of music, but very few nations take delight in music that is foreign to them. This gives rise to the reasonable suspicion that man has a natural disposition to develop an artificial delight through sounds. This delight, however, is purely artificial, and never intrinsically inherent in the nature of the thing itself. All nations consider as music that kind to which their education has accustomed them; they consider what is called music by others to be barbarous noise, to which they have not trained their ear through repeated listening. The music of the Chinese, of the Hottentots, of the Peruvians, of the Iroquois, even that of Europeans, ceases to be music when it is exported; once it is foreign, it becomes a barbarous roaring of an ill-tuned babble. I dare not lift the veil beneath which scholars of geometry hide from the layman their ingenious investigations based on the comparison of quantity. I dare not violate the sacred recesses where, with keen eyes intent on exploring the mysteries of nature, one considers whether a sound is a small bundle of several consonant pitches corresponding to some given string lengths, among which a certain proportion is unfailingly preserved. Such investigations, mainly undertaken in recent times by the most praiseworthy and distinguished minds of our century, are not the object of my essay, in which I wish to deal with *music* and not *harmony*.

First of all, then, I ought to state what I mean by the word *harmony:* it is that compound sensation deriving from the combination of several tones that strike the ear simultaneously. It seems that harmony has certain physical and universal laws, and that every ear must judge it on this basis; thus it seems that all mankind must agree in calling some sweeter and more natural combinations *consonant,* and others that are harsher and more foreign *dissonant.* Nor do I propose to settle anything at all in this matter. I merely wish to write what I think about music; and by music I mean what others call melody, that is, a particular style in which one sound follows another, which varies either in terms of tempo, or discontinuity, or the distance from one voice to another, or, lastly, of the varying techniques of holding back or projecting the voice itself with greater energy. In short, by music I mean a succession of sounds that awakens in music lovers various emotions, such as tenderness, daring, compassion, pride, and all the other emotions that, as if by magic, are aroused by sounds. Therefore, I shall divide all that is included under the universal name of music into three categories; simple sound, harmony, and music.

I consider simple sound to be a mere weaving in language of words that contain no idea at all; I would compare harmony to a series of words judiciously representing a reasoned statement; music to me is similar to a series of words which, being properly declaimed, are apt to awaken our emotions. Thus, music is eloquence in the realm of harmony. I do not know whether what we call eloquence—the art of arousing emotions—is, in terms of the various means it uses, universal to all mankind. Rather, I am inclined to believe that, although the people of each nation can be moved by an eloquent orator, nevertheless since the sensibilities of various peoples (owing to different forms of legislation and the physical differences of climates in which they live) are widely divergent, the art of eloquence also must vary with the sensibilities of the listeners. Although the principle of this art, which consists of reaching man's heart and thus determining his emotions, is both universal and immutable, nevertheless the means to achieve this end have to adapt to and follow the various routes available in each nation. Such doubts as come to my mind would require the help of travelers. If, for the benefit of human knowledge, the likes of Chardin, La Caille, Maupertuis, and La Condamine could be multiplied,[1] and travelers to remote places would always prefer, as did these worthy men, the pleasure of being precise and truthful and the lasting fame of posterity to the ill-directed desire to impose on their fellow countrymen for a few years, eventually to be discredited and heaped together with the novelists, then we could not only expound our doubts (to which a little philosophy often gives rise), but also the

---

1. Jean Chardin (1643–1713), French traveler to the Indies and Persia, author of *Le Récit du roi de Perse Soliman III* (1670); Nicolas Louis de La Caille (1713–62), French astronomer; during his four-year expedition to the Cape of Good Hope (1750–54) he catalogued 10,000 stars; Pierre Louis Moreau de Maupertuis (1698–1759), French mathematician and one of the leading French scientists of the century; his expedition to Lapland in 1736–37 verified the flattening of the earth in the polar regions; Charles Marie de La Condamine (1701–74), French geographer; his expedition to Peru in 1735–44 resulted in astronomical observations confirming Newton, as well as the discovery of curare and india rubber. [BJB]

true and proven theories of many important things that are all the more certain for being based on many indisputable facts.

Music then, as an exciter of the passions, is an art that is perhaps universal. However, as it depends on the different modes of thinking of different peoples, it must modify its means in order to excite the passions in accordance with changes in the various degrees of longitude and latitude. Perhaps what I call music is nothing more than the specific occasion for which we ourselves generate the passions we attribute to music. Perhaps music is nothing more than random spots on a wall, or clouds just as randomly meeting in the sky, in which men of particularly lively and vivid imagination easily perceive all sorts of objects, clearly drawn and ready to be painted. In fact, how else could we explain that frequently observed phenomenon that upon hearing the same singer and the same instrumentalist some are totally and visibly moved, and express their rapture in their facial muscles, by their physical restlessness and involuntary exclamations of applause, or, as if oblivious to every other object, appear to be absorbed and mesmerized by the magic of art; while at the same time others, endowed with a most exquisite and delicate sensibility for distinguishing both the beauty and the defects of the other arts, listen motionless and emotionless —indeed almost out of courtesy—to the same music? They attentively notice every minimal defect and those tiny oversights that are sometimes purposely left in musical compositions so that, just as harsh and deliberate brushwork enhances the delicate brushwork of a stone surface, the same effect occurs on the sweetness and the dignity of music.

If we divide mankind into two categories, one of music lovers and the other of those indifferent to music, we shall find that the latter are in the majority. If among the music lovers we exclude all those who are hypocrites so far as music is concerned, who feign to enjoy it only because they believe that by so doing they display refined taste; and, if from this category we further exclude those who, only because they are encouraged by others, claim to be music supporters (when in reality they are all pseudo-lovers of music, who with their undiscriminating applause at times exalt to the stars the most mediocre things, thereby mortifying those composers who put their hearts and souls in their music); I say, if we exclude all those who do not deserve inclusion, we would perhaps discover that the number of those who really love music is much smaller than is commonly thought. This further convinces me that the exquisite pleasure music produces by delightfully moving our emotions is utterly artificial and developed through the artful flexibility that experience and training have conferred upon our senses. However, as the origin of the pleasure that music arouses in us is not in the intrinsic nature of things, this does not mean that, being produced in us, it is not an authentic pleasure that sweetly moves sensitive souls. Nor for this reason should we cherish it less. A philosopher, who knows the wisdom of parsimony in the exercise of life's innocent pleasures, would put his reason to bad use if he were to resort to it in order to diminish musical sensibility by uncovering the intrinsic inconsistency of the means that music employs to arouse that very sensibility.

The truths of this genre are always obtained at a very high price, and I prefer those blessed moments of sweet delirium that from time to time I experience when listening to real music to all the discoveries that might be made about the most difficult problems concerning its nature. I could go on at great length if I wished to present my readers with a pompous display of erudition, but such is not my intention. Plato's opinions on music and the wonders of Greek theater, and the fables about its therapeutic virtues, and other such antiquated notions or errors do not suit my purpose.

Wherein lies the magic that music uses to excite our passions? With what art can one hope to excite them? These problems are so complex that it is easier to feel them than to define them with words. I find that even one solo voice can excite my emotions; I find that even when someone talks to me, there are tones of voice that grate on my ear, and others I find most agreeable, and this aside from the particular relationship I may have with the person talking to me. When I hear someone singing, this difference is much greater. I notice that there are some voices that, being naturally impassioned, need only sing a few notes to arouse my emotions from listlessness and spark them with the sweet impress of music. There are also some instruments that are naturally appealing to my ear, particularly the oboe. I certainly do not expect every ear that is musically inclined to react in the same way, as I speak only of what I personally experience. I believe, however, that every sensitive ear distinguishes between impassioned and non-impassioned voices. I also notice that the simplest and most natural things are those that make a greater impression. Music, like architecture, requires the purity, the nudity, so to speak, of the Tuscan style. Gothic ornamentation, arabesques, and artistic whimsicalities heaped one upon the other occasionally arouse admiration, very often tedium, but never delight. A plaintive aria, sung by an impassioned voice, can hardly fail to produce its effect. A *parlante* aria in which the composer has managed to produce a melodic line that represents the meaning of the words in a natural manner will assuredly prove successful. But as soon as human voices start vying with nightingales, flitting up and down endless musical scales, leaping recklessly from the highest to the lowest notes, and incessantly quavering with such inconstancy that it is barely possible to keep up with them, then the performances may well elicit the applause of the professionals, but hardly that of those who are genuinely sensitive to music.

I make a significant distinction between the judgment of performers and that of those who are especially fond of music. The former, in the main, love their work only for the profit they derive from it. They have become so used to what they do that they have grown insensitive to the force of music, and consider it a laborious task that they are constrained to perform in order to make a living. I also notice that the various performers each have, depending on their particular training or their natural bent, strong and weak points. While some are exceedingly precise even with the most difficult notes, others distinguish themselves for the incredible range of their vocal agility, while yet others succeed particularly well in brilliant vocal passages, and so on. Thus, instead of giving themselves up wholeheartedly, and without bias, to the power of music, and of judging it by the effects it produces on the mind (which, for those who are sensitive to music, is the only real touchstone), performers generally demand from other professionals the sort of mastery that their own conceit has led them to prefer above all others.

There is nothing more distressing than to see composers who thoroughly understand the laws of harmony and, like the constructors of anagrams, are most skillful in their practical application, inverting and re-inverting consonances and dissonances feet first or head first, without even attempting to excite human emotions and without ever feeling them. This distress then turns into a contempt of sorts when, while listening to their compositions, my imagination takes over and, by bolstering the effects of the music, lets me experience all those sensations that the composer himself ignored. My self-respect is offended, and I feel that someone, without losing his composure, is mocking my sensibility, and I would expect that person, if he is to stir my excitement, at least to go to the trouble of first exciting himself. In short, I transfer to music the feelings that are common to lovers, the desire to share emotions.

There are many things in music that I find utterly useless, and that could be termed musical pedantry. One of these is the trill. The penultimate note of each melodic phrase must contain a trill; every aria must end with a prolonged vocal outburst, that is, a cadenza, and the penultimate note must contain a trill. And what pleasure can that vocal quavering and that inconstant oscillation from one note to the other, which is called a trill, ever awaken in the senses? And even if in some situations the artifice known as the trill could be used to express either a nightingale's song, the rustling of leaves, or something similar, how can it ever arouse any emotion in us if we constantly misuse it by systematically turning it into a final embellishment of all musical thoughts? I do not know if cadenzas are always necessary at the end of arias, but I believe not. However, even if they are to be included, I believe they can be made to end very gracefully even without trills, with a well-placed appoggiatura. I know that the voices that go straight to my heart are those that are neither too low nor too high; those which, because of a hidden association with my mind, seem to me impassioned; those voices which, as they develop, describe a curve, so that they never form angles, as it were, nor ever grate on my ears. I know that my heart is moved when one of these firm and steady voices sweetly flows over various half-steps, and touches unexpected minor harmonies. In such passages from one pitch to another there is no break whatever, but rather a very short but most ingenious route that, by imperceptible degrees, blends one tone with another without my becoming aware exactly when this occurs.

Oh how many times do we find we must say of some arias what the illustrious author of *Mondi*, M. Fontenelle, was wont to say: "Music, what do you want?"[2] One listens to wondrously intoned arias, sung with prodigious agility, with perfectly even voice, with the strictest observance of tempo, with trills, with an admirably long cadenza sung all in one breath, and we ask: "Music, what do you want?" I still do not know, if you do not awaken any emotion in me. I have listened to voices that could not be reproached for being in any way defective, and yet my heart hurled against them the greatest of all reproaches, because it felt nothing. Tightrope walkers are paid to spark our amazement; musicians are paid to move our emotions; and yet most musicians want to be tightrope walkers.

"La musica," in *Il Caffè* 2 (10 August 1765); repr. in *Il Caffè: ossia Brevi e vari discorsi distribuiti in fogli periodici,* ed. Sergio Romagnoli (Milan: Feltrinelli, 1960), 343–47.

PIETRO VERRI
from *Discourse on the Nature of Pleasure and Sorrow* (1774)

VIII
THE PLEASURES OF THE FINE ARTS SPRING
FROM UNNAMED SORROWS

Music, painting, poetry, and all the fine arts have at their foundation unnamed sorrows; such that, if I am not mistaken, were men perfectly healthy and happy, the fine arts would never have been born. These ills are the source of all of life's most delicate pleasures. In fact, if we examine man when he is truly happy, content, and lively, we will find him insensitive to music, painting, po-

2. Misquoted by Verri (who turns it to his own purposes), Fontenelle's famous remark was actually "Sonate, que me veux-tu?" The book Verri mentions is *Entretiens sur la pluralité des mondes* (1686), a guide to the universe written for laymen. [BJB]

etry, and every fine art, unless his previous artistic propensities continue out of habit, mechanically, to spark his interest, or unless his vanity leads him to flaunt his sensitivity and he then becomes a hypocrite. A healthy individual whose heart is brimming with joy is the furthest removed from artistic feeling. The latter increases with the awareness of our frailty, our needs, and our fears. A man who is sad and whose ear is sensitive to harmony will delight in the melody of a fine concerto. He will grow tender, he will experience a sweet agitation of emotions, and he will enjoy real physical pleasure: the unnamed sorrow whence his sadness sprang will rapidly subside as his heart is absorbed by music and freed from the sad, confused, and unknown sensations of sorrows that he vaguely felt. In fact, to escape the sadness that torments him, man helps himself and attempts to embellish and to animate through his imagination the effect of the fine arts. No matter how ill-disposed his heart may be to enthusiasm, just as he will perceive facial expressions in various attitudes in the random position of clouds, similarly, he will imagine many emotions in musical variations, along with many objects and situations to which the composer himself will never have given a thought. Music is a unique art in which the composer enables the listener to share his efforts in obtaining an illusory effect. A fine painting or a sublime poem will have some effect even on those who have neither taste nor feeling for such art forms. Fine music, however, will always remain a meaningless noise to those whose ears are not attuned to such positive enthusiasm. The reason, as we have already pointed out, is that music leaves more to the imagination of the listener. Therefore, the same music will please different people at the same time, while the sensations it produces in them will be very different. Some will find it extremely simple and naive; for others it will prove tender and impassioned; yet others will find it harmonious and full-sounding, and so on. Such diversity will occur less frequently when judging either painting or poetry because, as I said, in these art forms the artist is active, while the listener, even if he possesses an exquisite sensibility, is almost completely passive. With music, however, the listener has to go above himself. Depending on the dispositions of his heart, he will react differently in different situations, and the sensations produced by the same object will also vary according to the different occasions.

From *Discorso sull'indole del piacere e del dolore* (Milan, 1774), §VIII; modern edition in *Del piacere e del dolore e altri scritti*, ed. R. De Felice (Milan: Feltrinelli, 1964), 38–39.

Chapter Nine

The Ancients and the Moderns

ARALLEL TO THE *querelle des Bouffons,* which, as we have said, was a musical manifestation of the *querelle des anciens et des modernes,* in Italy we encounter a polemic between the defenders of ancient music, which can mean either the Greeks or Palestrina and Renaissance polyphony, and those of modern music, which means the most recent composers.

Padre Martini, who is often mentioned polemically by Vincenzo Manfredini, was the champion defender of the ancients. Antiquity became identified with counterpoint, and counterpoint was placed in opposition to melody. Counterpoint represented the world of rules, whose correct observance always guaranteed the composer's success. Melody represented "good taste" and was thus subject to the whims of fashion. Antonio Eximeno, a Spanish Jesuit, mathematician, and theorist, was a generation younger than Padre Martini, from whom he hoped to obtain a letter of approval for his weighty *Dell'origine e delle regole della musica colla storia del suo progresso, decadenza e rinnovazione* (1774), which he wrote in Rome after the expulsion of the Jesuits from Spain. Martini, however, did not grant his approval. There was no common ground between the two: Eximeno was steeped in Encyclopedist culture, an admirer of Dubos, Condillac, and Rousseau, and all his efforts were directed toward showing that music has nothing to do with mathematics. In the preface to his treatise, which we have included in this chapter, he anticipates his conclusions, affirming that "music evolves from those modifications of language that enable it to delight the ear and touch the heart." Rousseau's teachings were by then accepted by all European culture, and his theses were used as theoretical support by the defenders of modern music.

Approximately a decade later, the theorist and man of letters Esteban de Arteaga, another Spanish Jesuit who had been expelled from Spain in 1767 and moved to Italy, wrote a major work in three volumes. *Le rivoluzioni del teatro musicale italiano dalla sua origine fino al presente* (1783–88) is a sort of history of Italian opera aimed at demonstrating the superiority of the music of past centuries in contrast to that of his day, which was by then on the way to decadence. The cause of such decadence was the domination of music over poetry. The purpose of music, when it was no longer an instrument of poetry, was "only to tickle the ear," and it forgot "to move the heart" and "to render the meaning of words, which ought to be the principal and sole task of dramatic music." For Arteaga, the progress of instrumental music was to blame, as it had even crept into opera, leading it to sure downfall.

A few years later, the polemic between the defenders of the ancients and those of the moderns was revived by the brilliant polemicist Vincenzo Manfredini, with his essay *Difesa della musica moderna e de' suoi celebri esecutori* (1788). Manfredini responded principally to the arguments put forth by Arteaga and Padre Martini, and set out to defend not only the music of his day, but in particular its instrumental music. The concept of progress informs all his reasoning: everything makes progress and music cannot contradict this universal law. Furthermore, the concept of progress also serves to defend the autonomy of instrumental music; indeed, the separation of music and poetry is also a result of progress. Both arts are perfected and "such a separation had to ensue naturally as the two art forms developed and improved." The polemic pitting the ancients against the moderns, the advocates of counterpoint against those of song, of melody against harmony, reached its final stage with Manfredini. The crisis that beset Italian opera and the birth of the sonata style were by then shifting the focus of interest toward other themes and other problems.

ANTONIO EXIMENO (Y PUJADES)
from *On the Origin and the Rules of Music, with the History of Their Development, Decline, and Renewal* (1774)

PREFACE

A combination of circumstances, with which I cannot acquaint the reader without writing a lengthy novel, induced me four years ago to direct my attention to music. I was persuaded that the study of this subject would prove rather easy, since I was well versed in the principles of mathematics, which is commonly supposed to be the basis of music. I was soon convinced, through my own experience, that mathematical theory has nothing to do with the practice of music. Had I kept my first lessons in counterpoint, which I studied following the rules that Padre Kirkero purports to derive from numbers,[1] I would have the most decisive document on this matter, and the most apt to stop up men's ears, or to move stones to laughter. Although the suspicion that mathematics in no way applies to music had already dawned on me, I nevertheless rejected such a thought as vain, on consideration that at least music theory could be a part of mathematics, as are several other things that this science includes, and which are all useless to the practical application of the arts, like the subtleties of the Aristotelian school. Therefore, on the one hand, I continued to practice counterpoint under the tutelage of a teacher, and on the other I formulated for myself a mathematical theory of music. After having toiled greatly to perceive some light amidst the obscurities of Signor Tartini's treatise on harmony,[2] with his sextuple harmonic, and with the three harmonies called First, Fourth, and Fifth, which make up the scale, I came up with a little theory of my own, which, as happens with writers, seemed to me rather good. But in the midst of this theory and the daily exercise of composing, I was completely in the dark so far as practice was concerned. My teacher praised many of my exercises; in fact, he often said to me that he could not understand how, having so little practice, I was able to write the parts so well, especially the basses. However, I did this all gropingly, and I found it most annoying that one day he would praise my exercise, and the next he would criticize it, and I could never tell why. My despair grew as I continued to read works on theory in which I found only a jumble of rules concerning fundamentals (*regole de Canto fermo*), which I soon perceived to be false and misleading, especially as I saw those very rules constantly being violated in the most beautiful compositions. What is the point, I asked myself, of a rule that forbids the leap of a diminished fifth, when this interval often proves so pleasant to the ear? Why am I obliged to follow the rule of preparing every dissonance, when the seventh and the diminished fifth are constantly being used without preparation? Why is it an unforgiveable sin for a pupil to write parallel fifths, since I come across them in the works of the most celebrated composers? What rule am I given to transpose from one key to another? Everyone told me that, in order to understand these things, long practice in singing or playing was necessary. "Good God!" I would say to myself, what manner of art is this? I realize that in no art can one acquire facility or good taste without practice. But the principles of art can be understood perfectly well without it. I have never been an architect, and yet I know why a building is solid and beautiful. I am not able to write another *Aeneid,* but nevertheless I can at least partly

---

1. Athanasius Kircher, *Musurgia universalis* (Rome, 1650). [BJB]

2. Giuseppe Tartini, *Trattato di musica secondo la vera scienza dell'armonia* (Padua, 1754), or *De' principi dell'armonia musicale contenuta nel diatonico genere* (Padua, 1767); the Preface to the latter is given above in Ch. 3. [BJB]

explain the reason why it is a masterpiece. Is it possible that the art of music lacks true principles, or general and infallible rules, and that everything concerning it must be learned with great effort, as a dog learns to become a watchdog, or to carry a lantern in its mouth before its master? Utterly dispirited by such considerations, I sent music to God (not to say in some other direction), and spent a year without giving any thought to the subject, and without even wanting to hear anything about it. Yet from time to time I felt compelled by nature to delve into this divine art, which, due to the subtleties of the speculative theorists and the inconsistencies of the practical ones, had become a mystery, or rather a veritable chaos. It is indeed very true that chance, rather than study, gives rise to the soundest observations. On the morning of Pentecost, I was in Saint Peter's Basilica while Signor Niccolò Jommelli's divine *Veni Sancte Spiritus* was being sung. I found myself inwardly reciting the words together with the singer, just as forcefully as if I were reciting them to a congregation to move them to devotion, and I suddenly realized that my voice was moving along in a manner that, although obscure, was very similar to that of the singer. No one can imagine how enlightened I then felt about music; it was like emerging from a dark cave into the open sunlight. Thus, I said to myself, music is only a prosody, the purpose of which is to imbue language with gracefulness and expression. What correlation is there between prosody and mathematics? As any clearly perceived truth is wont to do, this simple observation so emboldened me that I went back to the study of music.

Up to this point, I had read only Signor Tartini's confusing treatise, along with a few authors on practical music. However, I also knew that some competent people, whose works I had not had the opportunity of reading, had applied to music fundamental ideas taken from mathematics and physics. Among these, the most renowned were Signor Euler and Signor Rameau, together with his interpreter Signor d'Alembert. The fame these authors justly enjoyed in the literary world made me tremble and fear that any attempt I might make to reduce music to pure prosody was both useless and naive. Yet this very thought had made such an impression on me that I took heart and set out to examine the writings of the abovementioned authors. Fortunately, my long study of mathematics had already persuaded me of the false evidence of this science, or rather of the abuses to which some hypothetical truths of geometry had been subjected during our times in order to give certain suppositions, which were in part uncertain and in part utterly false, the appearance of proven truths. This is why the algebraic formulas that Signor Euler uses to put together a new algebraic treatise on music did not frighten me.[3] Indeed, for me his treatise was the

---

3. *Tentamen novae theoriae musicae ex certissimis harmoniae principiis dilucide expositae* (St. Petersburg, 1739). [BJB]

most authentic evidence supporting my reservations on mathematics, seeing so famous a geometrician use mathematics to found a new, purely illusory theory of music. I was more worried by Signor Rameau, who, having been an excellent practical musician, and having written in a country where even the women have a smattering of physics and mathematics, would seem not to be so easily mistaken in deriving the principles of music from these sciences. In fact, Signor Rameau provides some very helpful rules in practical matters. And although as far as mathematics is concerned his theory is as useless as Signor Euler's, at first glance his considerations on physics are surprising, and almost convince us that nature actually does produce in sounding strings phenomena capable of instructing men how to combine certain sounds in order to produce harmony.[4] This part of Signor Rameau's theory has a greater appearance of truth in Signor d'Alembert's short treatise entitled *Elémens de la musique*.[5] In this work, the great philosopher and mathematician, purging Signor Rameau's theory of its false suppositions and palpable contradictions, reduces it to a series of clear and concise propositions that have rendered Signor Rameau's musical theory worthy of being compared with Newton's theory of physics. However, in the end I realized that the last propositions of that theory destroyed the first, and that between the physical phenomenon, which serves as its basis, and the rules of harmony there is only a chance relationship, similar to so many other situations that often deceive philosophers who mistake coincidence for cause and effect. Thus, I am compelled to state that all the books on musical theory written after Pythagoras up to our day are ill-founded and full of illusions and falsehoods. What impression could I imagine such a statement would have on the public, for which the prejudice of authority holds such sway? Especially as I had to do away with all the difficult combinations of calculations, numbers, and proportions with which music has been muddled, for people generally suppose to be true what they do not understand rather than what is simple and clear. This thought would certainly have kept me from publicly expressing my ideas on other subjects; but as I considered music theory something of little consequence and of no importance to the general public, I decided to combat, in Book One of the Part One, the very ancient and widespread prejudice that music is a part of mathematics.

Having taken this first step, it was my duty to show in Book Two that music evolves from those modifications of language that enable it to delight the ear

---

4. Among the many writings on music by Rameau that he could have read, Eximeno is probably referring to the *Traité de l'harmonie réduite à ses principes naturels* (Paris, 1722); an excerpt is given above in Ch. 3. [BJB]

5. *Elémens de musique, théorique et pratique, suivant les principes de M. Rameau* (Paris, 1752 and several later editions). [BJB]

and touch the heart. These modifications concern both the stress and the quantity of the syllables, which no philosopher ever thought should be regulated by means of mathematical rules. The more observations I made on the common speech of men, and especially on that of women, the more I became convinced of this truth. I have often set myself to speaking while playing the harpsichord, and, noting the variations of my voice, I subsequently found them in the strings of that instrument. Above all, I had no hesitations at all as regards music's identity with prosody when, upon examining the prosodies of the most cultivated languages, which were once Greek and Latin, I saw that the rules on accents generally tend to produce, in ordinary speech, a series of musical cadences, and that the entire variety of tempos and notes that music uses are the same as the feet in Greek and Latin poetry. Since these things have a common origin in language, it follows that language, prosody, and music must all proceed from a common source. I could have stopped short of investigating this common origin, leaving everyone free to embrace whatever he considered the most plausible opinion explaining the origin of language. However, not only would the first source of music have remained confused and doubtful, I would also not have been able to explain what taste and genius consist of, nor why music has progressed without either a real theory or real rules governing practice. For this reason I resolved to show how and why man speaks. Thus, here I am again, committed to demonstrating the fallacy of another common bias.

The true principle underlying man's actions is often confused with the observations that govern or accompany them. It is said that man learns to speak through reason, because when he speaks he reasons. Furthermore, despite the fact that man has many activities in common with brute animals, it is supposed that in the latter these activities proceed from instinct, while in man they do so from reason. I consider this a great error. Man and beast both eat because of the same principle; but man often accompanies this activity with thought, while animals do not. Herein lies the difference between man and beast. Man cannot learn through reason to give his bodily organs those movements that suit every activity. It is equally impossible for man to understand how he must use his mouth and tongue to articulate words as it is for the beast to know which nerves it must activate in order to bring food to its mouth, chew, and swallow. These activities must, in all living beings, proceed from a common instinct or from an inborn impress that renders the movements of their organs virtually autonomous and conducive to the maintenance of life and to those activities that are proper to each living species. Without this innate impress it is impossible to understand certain natural inclinations in man that begin to develop when he is very young, and which, moreover, cannot possibly be acquired through teaching or thought processes. In my opinion, this innate impress or instinct is the basis of language, with all the modifications that make it delightful. Man is thus superior to beasts not only because he is endowed with thought but also because he instinctively bears a feeling of humanness impressed upon him by nature, which is the source of virtue, and which is beyond the scope of animal instinct.

From *Dell'origine e delle regole della musica, colla storia del suo progresso, decadenza e rinnovazione* (Rome, 1774; repr. Hildesheim: Olms, 1983), 1–10.

ESTEBAN DE ARTEAGA
from *Revolutions of the Italian Musical Theater from Its Origin to the Present* (1785)

II
PARTICULAR CAUSES OF THE PRESENT DECADENCE OF OPERA

The difficulties associated with our musical system did not prevent composers from creating partial wonders, and from bringing each of the various musical branches to the degree of perfection of which it was capable. If modern music no longer has that moral purpose to which the Greeks destined it, and if all the parts that go to make up opera now lack that relationship and total combination of elements that the Greeks had developed through long practice over many centuries, and the mutual relation assisted by legislation, it can nevertheless adapt itself marvelously to the objective that it sets itself, which is to flatter the senses with graceful and brilliant modulations, and these can be marshaled to a certain unity, which, if it does not fully satisfy the severe demands of reason, is nonetheless sufficient to seduce the imagination with pleasant illusions. Some Italian composers and quite a few modern poets have put into practice what philosophy had long declared to be a certainty, namely, that variations in the Beautiful are legion, that the wellsprings of delight in the fine arts and *belles lettres* were not fully tapped by the ancients, that the barbarity of our methods was capable, to a certain extent, of being refined and polished, and that, even with a system different from that of the Greeks, the power of genius could give rise to new fountainheads of true, intimate, and unprecedented pleasure. Thus, out of the unfortunate condition of music in certain centuries, and the inability to apply it to poetry, was born recitable tragedy, which in many ways is preferable to its sung version. Thus, the loss of ancient prosody gave birth to rhyme, which so delights us in the poems of Ariosto, Camoens, and Tasso, as in the verses of Boileau, Pope, Garcilaso, and Racine. And thus from the strange confusion of many voices in church music came the sublime compositions of Palestrina, Carissimi, Marcello, and Handel. Finally, from the crude plays performed in Prà della Valle,[1] or in Florence during May Day, there subsequently developed spectacles that let us experience the wonders of masters such as Vinci, Pergolesi, Jommelli, and Metastasio.

Thus we must look beyond the aforementioned reasons to discover the causes of the present decadence of Italian opera. If it cannot legitimately be expected of composers, singers, poets, and dancers to put their respective skills to exactly the same use as was customary twenty centuries ago, it is nevertheless reasonable to demand that they not deform the talents with which they have been endowed. They are to blame for the confusion and disconnectedness that prevails, and especially for the endless abuses that have taken root in each of these branches. They are to blame for the lack of illusion and verisimilitude that now characterizes humanity's most beautiful invention, and that renders it incoherent, grotesque, and ridiculous. Nor would it be just to blame the arts for the defects of the artists. Therefore, having decided to make known, in the following chapters, to what extent the latter have contributed to the total decline of opera, I shall start with composition, and I affirm that the first and capital fault of contemporary theater music is that it has too little philosophy and too much refinement; its sole objective is to tickle the ear, not touch the heart, which ought to be its one and only task. This sad state of affairs will continue as long as the imitation of nature, and of what is true, grand, simple, and capable of engendering pathos, continues to be neglected in favor of childish pursuits, caricatures, and false ornaments. Praise is offered to second-rate maestros, but the works of the greatest composers of the past are neither studied nor imitated. Everyone wants to be original in his own right and open up new paths; however, as these can be found only in the examination of nature, which present-day composers ignore, and in profound meditation, of which they are incapable, their inventions amount to no more than a whimsical style, a false refinement that flatters their vanity, but utterly destroys music.

In order to see whether or not my assertion is exaggerated, let us briefly consider, from a practical standpoint, the method that is commonly used in singing an aria. No sooner has the male or female singer ended the recitative than the instruments start playing a sonata or prelude called "ritornello." The purpose of

---

1. Arteaga alludes to a reference found by Apostolo Zeno to a sacred *rappresentazione* performed at Prà della Valle (near Padua) during Easter of 1243, as possibly the oldest mention of Italian theater. We would recognize this as liturgical drama, but it was not clear to eighteenth-century writers whether it included speaking parts, let alone music. [BJB]

this short sinfonia is to inform the spectators, in the manner of a proem or preamble, of the general emotion that is to reign in the aria. When the instruments stop playing, the singer's voice starts to sing the first part of the aria, alone and without accompaniment, dividing and dismembering its periods. Let us take as example the following aria:

> Vedrai col tuo periglio
> Di questo acciaro il lampo,
> Come baleni in campo
> Sul ciglio al donator.[2]

The aria begins with the word *vedrai* (you will see) repeated three times, and *acciaro* (sword) twice. Two minutes are then spent in rapid passagework on the word *lampo* (lightning); *come come* (how), *sul ciglio sul ciglio* (on the brow) are repeated twice. The first two lines

> Vedrai col tuo periglio
> Di questo acciaro il lampo

are repeated with the usual confusion of notes, and then we go on to the next two lines, where a few minutes are spent on that most beautiful *baleni* (flashes of lightning). Can we now believe that the aria is ended? Certainly not. The singer pauses, and the instruments fill the interval, repeating with their sound the same emotions that were conveyed through song. And, as if the audience had not sufficiently understood or as if the aria had been sung using the language of the Hottentots, for which the music was to act as a dictionary, the singer has to drive it home to his listeners all over again, repeating the words in the same order. Therefore, again and again those *vedrai, baleni,* and *lampo* are repeated, with the singer running up and down the notes with headlong ornamentations and a thousand sixteenth notes. Finally he gets to the cadenza, that interminable cadenza where the audience has to wait half an hour before the

2. I have chosen as a case in point the same aria that Saverio Mattei cites in his essay on the philosophy of music, since, needing an example of contemporary abuse, it was indifferent to me and to others whether this or another one was chosen. The attentive reader will notice that my manner of analyzing this aria is quite different from Signor Mattei's; contenting himself with the first ideas that come to his mind, he forgoes analysis and design, touching here and there the "defects" and the "disjointed" things. [The reference is to *La filosofia della musica o sia la riforma del teatro. Dissertazione,* published in the third volume of Metastasio's *Opere* (Naples, 1781). Despite Arteaga's remark, his analysis is largely a condensed paraphrase of Mattei's. BJB] [The aria is from Act I, scene 2 of Metastasio's *Alessandro nell'Indie,* one of his most frequently set librettos. It is not clear which setting Arteaga had in mind, but the wording here varies slightly from that of the original libretto of 1729, the version found in all the editions of Metastasio's works. In that version the first two lines read: "Vedrai co*n* tuo periglio / Di questa *spada* il lampo." See Bruno Brunelli, ed., *Tutte le opere di Pietro Metastasio* (Milan: Mondadori, 1943–54), 1. KKH]

singer gets beyond the *a* of *donator,* which is his favorite vowel. The singing stops, but are we then out of the thicket? Oh dear! The instrumental music starts up again on its own, in order to give the emotion all possible variety of expression, until the first part is over. And the second? Oh, this experiences the same misfortune that befalls the younger sons of illustrious families, who have to languish in straitened circumstances while the elder son lives in luxury and affluence. Its lot is to be dispatched rapidly with a few notes, without the subdivision, division, or repetition of periods that is characteristic of the first part. The only exception is when, between the vocal pauses, the orchestra from time to time offers some help to the singer. Should the reader ask me the reason for such diversity, I would have to claim ignorance. Be this as it may, have we now at least reached the halfway point of our voyage? He who so believed would be mistaken. This is only the first way station, where our horses can rest and gather their strength for the long ride ahead. The ritornello, the singer, and the first part of the aria start anew, and the same to and fro is repeated twice with the same array of notes and ornaments.

I know very well that this method is not without its advantages. I know that in music some repetition is necessary to etch the emotions of the song in the listener's heart with greater incisiveness; were they neither well understood nor forcefully stressed, they would fail to make an impression. I know that the ritornello is included in order to reawaken the listeners' excessively languid attention, and to enable the singer, weary after the long voyage of the recitative, to catch his breath. I know that the desire to develop all the exquisite nuances of harmony, by varying an emotion in a thousand ways, forms the musical base of that broad array of notes that one notices in compositions. Yet I also know that, owing to the composers' scant training and lack of experience, this method has become a source of infinite blunders. Let us attempt to examine them separately with the impartiality that befits a philosopher, who writes only out of love for the truth, and not out of hatred for, or connivance with, anyone. Let us avoid setting forth any opinion not corroborated by the eternal and general concepts governing ideal beauty, before which all prejudices disappear like fog pierced by the rays of the sun.

Beginning with the use to which instrumental music is usually put, it seems to me that the perfection that modern composers have attempted to achieve over half a century has greatly contributed to the ruin of opera. In the happy days of Leo, Pergolesi, and Vinci, those outstanding masters concentrated only on asserting the authority of singing and poetry, and not that of the instruments. Most judiciously, they realized that, instrumental music being nothing more than a commentary upon words, it would be utter stupidity to allow it to prevail over the voices and the emotions, just as a grammarian who praised

Servius' or de la Cerda's explanations of Virgil's *Aeneid* rather than the divine poet's own text would have to be taxed with ignorance.[3] All music's energy then lay in giving expression to the text, and the orchestra's only task was to provide the words with a sober and *sotto voce* accompaniment. Such simplicity soon ceased to please fickle audiences and capricious composers. Therefore, both the number and types of instruments were increased; accompaniments gradually became richer; orchestras acquired greater force and vigor, mainly in the hands of Galuppi ("il Buranello"), Hasse, and Jommelli. Even these composers, however, knew how to keep orchestral music in check, avoiding excesses. They reckoned that instrumental music should be to poetry what brilliance of color is to a well-conceived drawing, or the sharp contrasts of light and shadow are to figures.[4] From Jommelli's time onward, this part of opera has developed beyond belief. The number of violins has multiplied excessively; place has been made in orchestras for the noisiest instruments; and what is worse, this has happened without observing the proper relationship between these instruments and the nature of what they are to represent. Side drums, kettledrums, bassoons, hunting horns—everything is amassed in order to create a din. One could say that some arias accompanied in this manner represent the engagement of two armies on the field of battle.

What singer can raise his voice above the roar of the harmony, the many sounds heaped up one upon the other, the millions of notes required by the number and variety of the parts? What poetry can avoid becoming jumbled and encumbered? All the more so because another, no less minor, fault is progressively taking root, namely, the density of notes. In ancient scores, notes were large and given ample space, which resulted in open, energetic, and distinct sounds. Notes are now so minute that they are incapable of producing a lasting impression; their only function is to enfeeble, as it were, the forcefulness of a sound, breaking it up into parts that are too weak because they are too labored. In the same way, the excessive use of diminutives in the style makes poetry much too soft and diluted.[5] Furthermore, by following one another so rapidly and confusedly, the notes choke the singer's voice so that little or nothing is heard. And so, instead of instrumental and vocal music going together, instead of instruments supporting the voice, as order and nature would require, the former overwhelms the latter, so that it can reasonably be said that it is the instruments that sing, not the singer. Everyone can see for himself how damag-

3. Servius (fifth century B.C.) wrote the chief ancient commentary on Virgil; J. L. de la Cerda (seventeenth century) was the first great modern commentator on Virgil. [LAH-S]

4. Gluck. In the Preface to the music of *Alceste*. [See below, Ch. 10. BJB]

5. Today one might say of the style that reigns in music what Seneca said of the style of Maecenas: "laudem suam corrupit orationis portentosissimae deliciis" ["he ruined this praise by the affectations of his utterly unnatural prose style"]. [*Epistulae morales* 114.7. LAH-S]

ing such a defect is to the illusion of the spectator: hearing no more than the noise of the instruments, and not knowing to what words or sentiments the harmony refers, the various emotions awakened in him are useless, since they lack a precise object. And so he perceives no more verisimilitude or interest in the opera than he would find in a simple concert. Fontenelle's "sonata, what do you wish?" is most appropriate here.

From Stefano Arteaga, *Le rivoluzioni del teatro musicale italiano dalla sua origine fino al presente*, 3 vols. (Bologna, 1783–88; repr. Bologna: Forni, 1969), vol. 2 (1785): 42–51. A second edition was published in Venice in 1785.

VINCENZO MANFREDINI
from *Defense of Modern Music and Its Celebrated Performers* (1788)

My Replies are now concluded, and, consequently, the reason to enlarge my defense of modern music and its excellent performers, be they professionals or dilettantes. Yet so just and sound is the cause, that it did not even require the support of lengthy argumentation. Be this as it may, anyone who thought that Signor Arteaga was the only one to believe that modern music does not rival the ancient would be greatly mistaken. In fact, Arteaga simply followed in the footsteps of various erudite men and learned composers who went so far as to consider a defect what in reality is a virtue,[1] which only goes to prove that preconceived ideas, the great enemies of truth, are sometimes adopted even by great men. In my opinion, this happens because of a principle that is common to all the arts, but which should not apply to music and to the other arts of genius. Innovation, without which, as I said earlier, all the arts would still be in their infancy, has always prompted artists, especially those fully formed and accepted, to raise their voices against it and cry anathema, perhaps because they

1. In the music of our day (says the abovementioned Padre Martini) one seeks only variety of ideas, intervals most apt to excite the senses and arouse the most tender and delicate emotions, and the blending of those movements, figures, and instruments that are more surprising and exciting, and create more noise. In singers and players, one seeks what is on the lips of all maestros and is called *good taste* (see *Storia della musica*, vol. 2, p. 281). All this, which Padre Martini has said in a derogatory tone, in my opinion is the highest praise that can be bestowed on modern music. If only, God willing, Padre Martini's assertions would come true: that composers would always seek delicate and tender expressions when warranted, and that singers and players would always seek *good taste*, without which no music can ever be perfect.

nurture too much veneration for tradition, or because they themselves are incapable of being innovative. It is certain, however, that if in any art innovation
was to be sought, and the way of rendering it more pleasing and expressive, it
ought to be in music, which, as was said, was among the last of the arts to have
been revived; and only recently has it been brought, if not to the peak, at least
near to perfection, thanks especially to those sublime geniuses and inventors
who have been able to overcome the barriers of prejudice by means of innovation. Such men have rendered and continue to render music more pleasant,
more expressive, and truer than almost all that of the ancients, which abounded
in *parts, fugues, imitations, ligatures,* and *counter-subjects;* in short, it was more
harmonic than melodic. This is why very many concur that instrumental music
has now reached a degree of perfection that ancient instrumental music never
achieved.

For what else does this musical genre contain if not *cantilene,* or melodies
that are livelier, more pleasant, and expressive than those of the ancients, whose
melodies almost all derive from vocal music, of which instrumental music has
been and always will be a follower and companion? It is indeed true that instrumental music is mostly a copy and imitation of vocal music. When it does not
sing, it does not express; in other words, when it says nothing, it is worth nothing. If instrumental music has greatly improved, this has occurred only after the
improvement of vocal music. He who denies this can deny anything. However,
to convince oneself that modern music, whether instrumental or vocal, is absolutely better than ancient music, it suffices to compare good modern compositions with ancient ones, and to notice the difference between the music written
in various periods and that of fine modern composers. The latter, by dint of
repeated efforts, have been able to remedy inverisimilitude, incongruity, and
prejudices. This was so as, being new, the art of music required sufficient time
in order to reach the degree of excellence that it had not yet achieved. This
happy task has been reserved to our century, which was destined, if not to render them completely perfect, at least to brighten and greatly improve some arts
and sciences, among which music certainly ought to be included. In fact, there
is an extraordinary difference between music written sixty, forty, or twenty years
ago, and that of today. To believe either that such a diversity depended, and still
depends, on the fact that music lacks a fixed style or that it is at present in a
declining state seems fallacious, and put forth too easily by those who, not
knowing this art or not having properly exercised it, are unable to form a sound
judgment. It is natural that all those arts and sciences that have not yet reached
perfection must undergo some change. As music (as I have often said, and
which is incontrovertible) was among the last arts to be revived, in order to
become cultivated, and to improve, it has had to suffer no mean number of

alterations, which some authors take to be imperfections, when indeed just the opposite is true.

Furthermore, one should also remember that music, being a very rich art, like poetry, painting, etc., has many different styles and tastes, and likewise many manners. Therefore, it is necessary to know them all, and to know in depth about music, in order to decide whether or not a given style, or taste, is good or bad; or if a particular manner is better or worse than another, or if both are valid. I also think that among each of the fine works in a given genre, and the various good authors, it is not so easy to make comparisons as to which is better; each can be excellent for some praiseworthy aspect or another. He who would claim, for example, that Raphael's *Santa Cecilia* is a better and more beautiful work than Guido [Reni]'s *San Pietro*, or [Ariosto's] *Orlando furioso* than [Tasso's] *Gerusalemme liberata*, or Pergolesi's *Stabat* than Jommelli's *Miserere*, etc., or the opposite, would certainly be reasoning poorly, as each of these beautiful works has its own particular merit, as do their respective authors, who themselves are to be admired and not compared. The same can be said for many other things, provided they are good: each has its own merit and can be the most perfect in its own genre. But let us examine separately the main reasons why some, who prefer ancient music, believe the music of our *opere serie* to be in decline (it would be too ignorant to claim that, starting from the time Buranello flourished up to now, *opera buffa* has not made incredible strides). Such detractors go about saying: "one can no longer hear a truly cantabile aria"; "today, only rondòs, clatter, and bravura arias are performed . . . and this is so because the singers no longer know how to sing . . . it is the orchestra that sings, etc." These critics should know that the word *rondò*, which comes from the French, is often incorrectly used, as not all the arias partly resembling rondòs are true rondòs: they are grand and sublime arias that contain two motives, or subjects, one slow and the other spirited, which are repeated only twice. These arias are certainly superior to the so-called ancient "cantabile arias," in that they are more natural, genuine, and expressive.

First of all, many cantabile arias of thirty and forty years ago contained a great deal of passagework, that is, ornamentations, deliberately included so that the singer might show his ability by altering them. As this passagework was almost always alien to the sentiment of the words and to the character of the aria, it was greatly detrimental to expression, truth, the power of the action, etc.

Secondly, such things as repeating the words of the first part of an aria four times, and those of the second only once; having two and sometimes four cadenzas; being condemned to die and going off to meet death with calm and serenity; saying one has to leave and never leaving; vocalizing on words before having ended them, etc., were all badly conceived, and, consequently, very harmful to the demands of verisimilitude and reason, even though at times they were found even in the arias of renowned authors, who wrote them either out of excessive subservience to the singers, or out of habit. How much more pleasant and natural are our arias, especially those with two clearly distinct subjects and tempos? Even if they do contain some passagework, it is almost nothing compared to the amount that was customary in the past. Furthermore, these arias are free from such drawbacks as the da capo, the cadenza, etc. They end forcefully and with an expression that suits the situation and the tempo in which they are performed. However, not all the arias written some years back, and have a cadenza, a da capo, etc., are imperfect. Some are most perfect, and written by excellent composers. This was possible because, as I have said, music is rich in styles and manners. Thus, the composer must exert the utmost care in finding these styles, which are and always will be beautiful, especially when adapted to precise occasions and situations. Moreover, it is true that the aforementioned two-tempo arias, although they do bear some resemblance to them, are not real rondòs, but grandiose and heroic arias: their composers rarely and perhaps never called them rondòs. In fact, they did not even use this term to describe genuine rondòs, calling them cavatinas instead, that is, short arias, as in fact they are, such as Gluck's "Che farò senza Euridice," Galuppi's "Idol mio, che fiero istante," and Sacchini's "Idol mio se più non vivi,"[2] and many others of this genre.

As for those arias called *arie di bravura*, which were written in past years, not overlooking merits where they exist, many contain much passagework, or ornaments, which greatly undermine their effect. Our arias also contain them, but are much closer to the emotion of the words, and more tasteful because they are more varied. In short, they are more uniform and in keeping with the motives and characters of the arias. Thus they are not annoying, or boring, or out of place, but highly interesting and pleasing. Hence I conclude by saying that if modern arias are more perfect than the ancient for the aforementioned reasons, it is also true that our singers, in contrast to the ancients, have the possibility of singing with greater expression and ease. And if the orchestra also sings, so much the better, because music is nothing but song. It suffices that it sing well; that is, that the instruments not play too much in unison with the singing part, in order not to cover it and that the words may be understood clearly. When the singer performs, the instruments, so to speak, should be the servant; they should play only a few notes, and do so softly. However, when both poetry and circumstances require a more significant instrumental accompaniment, a sort

2. Gluck's aria is the noted rondò from his opera *Orfeo ed Euridice* (Vienna, 1762). Those by Galuppi and Sacchini have not been identified. [KKH]

of melody that is more *parlante* and richer, this must be composed so as to enable the main melody, which must always be that of the singer, to stand out and not be overwhelmed. Such a task, however, is well within the skills of our fine composers, orchestras, and players, as well as our excellent singers.[3] If, then, Signor Arteaga continues to object that most composers do not write music as they should, that most singers do not touch the heart, and that most players do not play with clarity and expression, such objections (as I hope I have already demonstrated) are frivolous, and form an insufficient basis on which to infer that music has suffered a decline. In all the arts and sciences there will always be those who are less able, and those who are less than perfect.

I cannot conclude this defense of modern music more appropriately than by making public Maestro Sacchini's sincere and just praise of modern music, of which, before his death in Paris last year, he was one of the finest inventors. As he wrote this eulogy while in the French capital, and in a language different from ours, perhaps not all Italians are familiar with it. I discuss it here most willingly because, as it contains much musical doctrine, it can prove instructive to young composers; it also serves as eulogy, as it were, of the celebrated Maestro Piccinni. Besides being Sacchini's mentor, Piccinni has been and continues to be one of the finest pillars and creators of modern music (which means the best music), yes, the best without a doubt, for it is so obvious that good modern music is superior not only to the most ancient, but in general also to music written fifty to sixty years ago, and for many reasons, but chiefly melody, which is the most essential part of all music. In his previously cited letter on French music,[4] Rousseau wrote that Corelli, Bononcini, Vinci, and Pergolesi were the first to have composed music, meaning by this that music written by earlier composers could not be defined as such, being insufficiently melodious, too artificial, and full of counterpoint. To these four composers must be added the two Scarlattis (Alessandro and Domenico), Porpora, Marcello, Handel, Clari, etc. Nevertheless, our good music surely excels that of these great maestros

---

3. I should like to make it clear that, throughout this *Defense,* I am speaking and have always spoken only of fine musicians. I willingly agree with Signor Arteaga, and with those who asserted it before him, that there are many mediocre and ineffectual performers who perhaps were born to do anything but take up music. I also agree that many composers often ruin melody by covering and entangling the singing part with a jumble of inappropriate and ill-conceived accompaniments. They also make use of certain extravagant novelties, which violate the soundest laws of modulation, naturalness, and verisimilitude, perhaps to cater to the tastes of those who lack musical understanding, while they should do just the opposite; what comes from the unqualified is not true praise. I also fully admit that a most brazen theatrical style has made its way into churches, something highly unsuitable and contrary to the spirit of devotion. But I shall never concede that all composers have been guilty of such shortcomings, and consequently of having brought about the decline of music. Instead, music is greatly beholden to those fine modern composers who have raised and continue to raise it to a level of perfection it had not reached in the past.

4. *Lettre sur la musique françoise* (Paris, 1753 and later editions). [BJB]

(with the exception of Pergolesi, of whom there are some compositions that, so to speak, in a single point of time were both invented and perfected by that sublime genius). As I have already said, modern music is superior to ancient music in its most essential part, which is without the slightest doubt good melody, which consists in delightful and varied singing. If we examine the music by the aforementioned authors, with the exception of Pergolesi, we will find much counterpoint and much learning, but little melody, and consequently little naturalness and variety. Generally, their style is that of the *stretto fugato*, that is, excessively continuous imitation. What I mean is that, because they were lacking in invention, a few ideas or a few *cantilene* were enough for them to write a complete and lengthy composition. I leave it to those who have even a simple idea of what good taste is to imagine how monotonous and boring this type of music can be. How much more preferable is the music of fine modern composers (among whom, however, are also to be included Pergolesi, Leo, Durante, Hasse, Galuppi, Jommelli, Traetta, and various others, who greatly helped to improve the art, and have left monumental works that will always be good and beautiful, although they were written many years ago). By adapting and uniting harmony to melody, an imitative style to an ideal and varied style, art to nature, etc., their music does not prove so uniform and tedious but pleases both the connoisseurs and the amateurs.

The same applies to modern fugues. Because they are interspersed and interwoven with new thoughts not deriving from those of the fugues themselves, are they not so much more pleasing and perfect than the ancient ones? Let us then agree and candidly admit that ancient music was never so animated, well worked out, and expressive as is modern music. I realize full well that Algarotti, Sulzer, Brown, Padre Martini, and many others with whom Signor Arteaga agrees in many respects were of a different mind. Yet not all the music they considered imperfect was truly so, nor indeed is ours. I do not know how, if those illustrious men had listened and paid careful attention to so much good and expressive music, written by so many fine modern composers, still alive, they would have dared criticize it. Furthermore, having heard so much music by Hasse, Buranello, Jommelli, Perez, Gluck, etc., how could they ignore its superiority to ancient music and the progress it was still making? Did they perhaps expect it to be totally good and beyond criticism, and, like the goddess Minerva, born fully shaped and perfect? And why attribute to music the many abuses to which operas are often subject, and which stem from far more serious abuses, such as the poor way operas are produced at the hands of almost all the impresarios, or the refusal to give way to the poet, to the composer, etc.? Nevertheless, despite such maladies, fine composers have always done their utmost to enhance and improve music. Their incentive is not the enticement of considerable reward, nor the justice that is rendered them (which happens rarely), but the very nature of their art, which is the same for all arts that depend on genius and inspiration. Excellence is not achieved in the arts simply by means of gold, honors, and great application, but through a totally natural inclination, and after the repeated efforts of our predecessors have made it easier for us to attain artistic excellence. But it is now time to discuss the eulogy mentioned above.

From *Difesa della musica moderna e de' suoi celebri esecutori,* conclusion (Bologna, 1788; repr. Bologna: Forni, 1972), 189–202.

Chapter Ten

The "Querelle" between the Gluckists and the Piccinnists

THE LAST *querelle* to enliven French culture in the second half of the century is that between the supporters of Gluck and Piccinni. Less violent than the former *querelles*, it was less impassioned and perhaps slightly more contrived. It is generally accepted that Gluck and his Italian librettist Ranieri de' Calzabigi emerged victorious, in part because their rival, the meek Italian musician Niccolò Piccinni, reluctantly involved in the controversy, was not all that far from Gluck's ideas. The true mastermind of the reform was undoubtedly the poet Ranieri de' Calzabigi, a native of Livorno. During his stay in Paris, when he published an edition of Metastasio's works in his *Dissertazione su le poesie drammatiche del signor Abate P. Metastasio* (1755), he expressed ideas that already foreshadowed the reform his first libretto for Gluck, *Orfeo ed Euridice* (1762), was to bring about. The preface to *Alceste* (1769), signed by Gluck but in reality inspired in every detail by Calzabigi, contains in synthesis all the aesthetic principles of the reform. It is easy to see how this work represented a harmonious condensation and fusion of the Encyclopedists' demands (of a forceful art, which touches the heart, and is simple and expressive) and those of the classicists (dramatic coherence, poetic and literary dignity, elimination of the "abuses" and of useless virtuosity).

The positions assumed by Gluck's supporters (La Harpe) and Piccinni's (Marmontel) revived and exaggerated aesthetic themes of the previous disputes. Marmontel's reasons for taking sides against Gluck were those that go back to the French classical tradition, which Batteux had so aptly expressed in his essay *Les Beaux-arts réduits à un même principe* (1746). According to Batteux, art imitates nature, but must go beyond it by selecting its best features, discarding what reality presents as ugly and unpleasant. Thus, Gluck's expressivity was indeed deemed forceful, but also unpleasant and jarring, in that it was too raw: "His accents, if not embellished by imitation, will only produce, as in nature, the impression of suffering." It is curious that, in this case, the model of "beautiful nature" was identified with Italian opera and not with the French classical tradition. Melodious singing had the function of softening expressions that were too forceful, of attenuating them, and of conferring upon them a "noble elegance."

La Harpe rightly distanced himself from the Gluck–Piccinni polemic, as he recognized in the two musicians the same expressive force and the same dramatic intensity. Hence Gluck's *Orfeo ed Euridice* represented for La Harpe "the first example of an opera in which the music was never separate from the action, and in which the words and the melody formed a truly dramatic whole from beginning to end."

In his essay *Observations sur la musique, et principalement sur la métaphysique de l'art* (1779), Michel-Paul Guy de Chabanon also kept to an intermediate position in this dispute, admitting that both sides were right. Music and melody must never reach the level of harshness; they must not sacrifice pleasingness to expression. At times, Gluck risked putting too much truth in "the wrenching cry that intermittently breaks through the song of the weeping Thracians."

These writings marked the end of the eighteenth-century *querelles*. The conflicting sides tended to exchange roles; the arguments put forward by those of one side were adopted by those of the other. In reality, the scope of musical issues was also changing. The final excerpts reproduced here, three letters that Mozart wrote to his father in 1781, show how profound transformations were by then also taking place in opera. Mozart was neither a theoretician nor a philosopher, but through his words one easily becomes aware that the problems connected with opera had already changed, that the distance between comic and serious opera was no longer so clear, nor that between Italian and French opera, between harmony and melody, or between the prevalence of music or poetry. For Mozart, all opera came down to music, and it was the musician who should guide the librettist. Emotions could indeed be violent; it was not a question of reducing expression, but rather of resolving it immediately in the language of music, which must reign supreme and "make everything else forgotten."

RANIERI DE' CALZABIGI

from *Essay on the Dramatic Poetry of the Abbé P. Metastasio*

(1755)

I must force myself to abandon this part of my observations on Metastasio's poetry, as the enrapturing pleasure it gives me would persuade me to continue;

but it is time to end, and to conclude with a truly Pindaric hymn in praise of Lycidas, the presumed victor, in his tragedy *L'Olimpiade:*[1]

> Del forte Licida
> Nome maggiore
> D'Alfeo sul margine
> Mai non suonò.
> Sudor più nobile
> Del suo sudore
> L'arena Olimpica
> Mai non bagnò.
> L'arti ha di Pallade,
> L'ali ha d'Amore:
> D'Apollo, e d'Ercole
> L'ardir mostrò.
> No, tanto merito,
> Tanto valore
> L'ombra de' secoli
> Coprir non può.

> (Than Lycidas a nobler name
> For fortitude renown'd,
> Did ne'er along his winding stream
> Alpheus' shores resound.
> No hero e'er more bravely stood,
> In combat hand to hand;
> No mightier labours e'er bedew'd
> The fam'd Olympic sand.
> Minerva's arts are his in fight,
> The wings of Love in speed;
> Nor Phoebus' or Alcides' might
> Can Lycidas exceed.
> Such worth, such valorous deeds display'd,
> For ages shall endure:
> No time with dark oblivion's shade
> Such honors shall obscure.)[2]

Those who through long study of Greek and Latin models have acquired a knowing eye for the beauties of divine poetry do not need me to alert them to the poetic gems that shine throughout this quotation. They can see for them-

1. The text is a chorus at the beginning of Act II, scene 6 of Metastasio's opera libretto *L'Olimpiade* (1733). [KKH]
2. The English translation is from Pietro Metastasio, *Dramas and Other Poems,* translated from the Italian by John Hoole, 3 vols. (London: Otridge, 1800), 1:114–15. [KKH]

selves that Metastasio's poetic wonders can compare with what is most pictur-esque and beautiful in the works of both the ancients and the moderns, which I could easily show by examples, had I undertaken to write a book. For me it is sufficient to have demonstrated, in the limited scope I have set myself, what I stated at the beginning, namely, that Metastasio's dramatic compositions are perfect tragedies wrought in compliance with the authentic laws prescribed to us by the ancients, and that, just like the most celebrated ones, they are replete with all the wonders that one might wish for in this genre. This will also serve as an answer to those who too rashly go about spreading the word that our tragic theater is utterly debased, and that in it one no longer sees verisimilitude, proper disposition, or interest. These presumptuous opinions, written with such a careless air, need to be rebutted, lest those who do not understand our language get the impression that they are incontrovertible truths.

In my opinion, the power, variety, and beauty of our music depend on the majesty, forcefulness, and brilliant images of Metastasio's poetry. The harmony that even a cursory reading enables us to discover in his verses immediately strikes our composers, supplying them with the musical splendor that elicits admiration and respect even from the most biased. I believe that it cannot be denied that the poetry most suited to music is the most beautiful poetry, and that the music most suited to words is the most beautiful music; consequently, the nation that has a more expressive poetry for its music will also have a more effective music, which in turn will be able to produce a sweeter and livelier sen-sibility in the hearts of the listeners. A composer who attempts to awaken ten-derness, compassion, and terror by adapting sounds to words that are inept, harsh, affected, bombastic, and meaningless will labor in vain. For the musician to be able to depict fear or love harmonically it is not enough that the poet has made Pluto or Cupid speak, or that he has set the action of his drama in Hell or in the realm of Venus; if the musician himself does not first feel the different impressions of these two different affects in his heart, if he is not at first fright-ened or moved to tenderness, if he has not filtered the emotions his heart has experienced into his words, if his styles are not different in consequence, as Virgil's are when describing Dido's amorous transports and when illustrating the pains of Hell, then he will not find harmonies that correspond to his sub-ject. Feeling no emotion while he composes, as the poet felt nothing while writ-ing his verses, he will produce only a jumble of muddled and ineffective sounds, similar to an excellent engraver forced to ply his burin on a poor design; no matter how artfully he goes about his task, his copper will always reflect the faults of the designer.

There are some who suppose that music is independent of poetry, and that a composer can make up for the defects of the words with the excellence of the harmony. However, they can easily see for themselves how far they are from the truth by examining whether, for example, the nascent dawn could be better rendered with sounds as described in the following verses:

> Ici se lève l'aurore
> Qui brille et dure toujours.
> Les Jours sereins, les beaux jours
> S'empressent ici d'éclore.
> Heureux qui finit son cours,
> Et voit naître ici l'aurore
> Qui brille et dure toujours.[3]

or in Tasso's verses:

> Non si destò fin che garrir gli augelli
> Non sentì lieti, e salutar gli albori;
> E mormorare il fiume, e gli arboscelli,
> E coll'onda scherzar l'aura, e co' fiori.[4]

> (The birds awak'd her with their morning song,
> Their warbling music pierc'd her tender ear;
> The murmuring brooks and whistling winds among
> The rattling boughs and leaves their parts did bear.)[5]

Or if Hell could be more harmonically represented with these verses by Dante:

> Diverse lingue, orribili favelle,
> Gemiti di dolore, accenti d'ira,
> Voci alte, e fioche, e suon di man con elle.[6]

> (Uncouth tongues, horrible utterances were blent
> with words of woe, accents of anger, sound
> of hands that joined with voices loud and faint.)[7]

or else with that lengthy allocution entitled "The Chorus of Furies and Demons":

> Qu'au gré de nos fureurs
> La haine, le parjure,
> L'audace, l'imposture

3. Calzabigi drew his example from Jean-Philippe Rameau's opera *Castor et Pollux* (1737), Act IV, scene 2: "Air d'une ombre heureuse." [KKH]

4. *Gerusalemme liberata*, VII, 5. [BJB]

5. The English version is taken from *Jerusalem Delivered*, the Edward Fairfax translation newly introduced by Roberto Weiss (Carbondale, IL: Southern Illinois University Press, 1962). [KKH]

6. *Inferno*, Canto III, 25–27. [BJB]

7. The English version as found in *The Divine Comedy*, text with translation in the metre of the original by Geoffrey L. Bickersteth (Cambridge, MA: Harvard University Press, 1965). [KKH]

Remplissent la nature
De nouvelles horreurs.
Qu'on invente des crimes
Pour outrager les Cieux.
Tombez dans nos abîmes,
Misérables victimes
Des vengeances des Dieux.

It is clear that a composer cannot make anything harmonious out of these verses, and by just seeing them entitled "Chorus of Demons," he can put nothing more into them than a great din. His music, therefore, will be noisy, but inexpressive. If one might suggest that the composer, finding the first lines quoted above to be void of images suited to his music, adapt some beautiful music to them by having in mind those other lines by Tasso, on which he will construct a sinfonia, since Tasso's verses will not be presented to the audience during the performance, the composer's sinfonia, although following the charms of those verses exactly, will only come out as a jumble and a useless heap of sounds, in which no one will find the nascent dawn except those who had already discovered it.

That precept by Horace mentioned earlier:[8]

Si vis me flere, dolendum est
Primum ipsi tibi

(If you wish me to weep, you must first grieve yourself)

How well this could be placed in the mouth of the composer to remind the poet! Seen in this light, we realize the indispensable connection that there must be between poetry and music, so that, by helping each other in turn, they can win over the listeners' hearts, and move their emotions as they please, according to what they wish to express.

It was decided by the ancient masters, and the modern have seen fit to conform to their judgment, that without verisimilitude there can be no sustained interest, which, like the vibrations produced by striking a taut string, lasts in varying degree for the entire duration of the dramatic action. Aristotle observes that events that the spectator does not suppose can happen to himself produce no interest whatever; nor is he shaken by situations in which he could never imagine finding himself.[9] Following these principles, besides having already pointed out that in general the poetry of French opera is not suited to music, we shall acknowledge that French operatic tragedies can never be interesting, and we shall have two highly convincing reasons whereby we can be persuaded of

---

8. *Ars poetica* 102–3. [BJB]
9. *Poetics* 1453ᵃ 4–6. [BJB]

the greater elegance and livelier expression of Italian music. In our dramatic poetry, both in that of the poet we are discussing and in Zeno's,[10] and even in that of his predecessors, not only verisimilitude, but truth itself, as it were, shines everywhere. Their poetry presents famous names, historic events, and deeds that are well known, or that have been only slightly altered to suit the audience's taste. In it the passions dominate, emotions are portrayed, both true and imagined denouements are introduced; but in each case verisimilitude is always respected. In this way the spectator can readily imagine being in those same situations himself, wherefore he is easily induced to deplore, abhor, pity, and fear in the fictitious characters that which he can well deplore, abhor, pity, and fear in the people he knows, and perhaps even in himself.

From the preface to his edition of the librettos of Metastasio in *Dissertazione su le poesie dram-matiche del signor Abate P. Metastasio*, vol. 1 (Paris, 1755), pp. clxxxvi–cxciii.

RANIERI DE' CALZABIGI and CHRISTOPH WILLIBALD GLUCK
Preface to *Alceste* (1769)

YOUR ROYAL HIGHNESS

When I undertook to write the music for *Alceste*, I determined to strip it completely of all those abuses, whether introduced by the mistaken vanity of the singers, or by the excessive obligingness of the composers, that have long been disfiguring Italian opera and have turned the most magnificent and beautiful of all the spectacles into the most ridiculous and boring. I determined to restrict music to its true function, namely, to enhance poetry in terms of expression and the situations it relates, without interrupting the action or numbing it with useless and superfluous ornaments. And I thought music ought to do for the poetry what lively colors and the contrast of light and shadow do for a correct and well-ordered drawing, animating the figures without modifying their contours. Therefore, I have taken care not to halt a singer in the heat of his dialogue to make him wait through a boring ritornello, nor stop him in mid-word on a

---

10. Apostolo Zeno (1688–1750), Metastasio's great predecessor as a librettist of Italian opera. [BJB]

favorable vowel, either to display the agility of his beautiful voice in a long melisma, or to wait for the orchestra to give him time to catch his breath for a cadenza. I did not think it necessary to rush through the second part of an aria, when this second part was the most impassioned and important, just to allow time regularly to repeat the words of the first part four times, and to end the aria where perhaps the meaning does not end in order to give the singer more leeway to show how he can vary a passage in so many different ways, according to his whim. In short, I have attempted to do away with all those abuses against which common sense and reason have been crying out in vain.

I have felt that the overture should inform the listeners beforehand of the nature of the action that is about to be represented, to sum up, as it were, its subject; that the instrumental passages should be used in proportion to interest and emotion, above all to avoid that sharp break in the dialogue between aria and recitative; and that they should not cut off the sentence illogically or interrupt the heat and power of the action inopportunely.

Finally, I have deemed it my greatest task to seek the beauty of simplicity, and I have avoided making a display of complexities at the expense of clarity. I have not judged any novelty estimable unless it immediately and naturally flows from the situation and the expression; and there is no convention that I have not felt free to sacrifice for the sake of effect.

These are my principles. It was my good fortune that the libretto lent itself so well to my design, for the celebrated author, envisaging a new plan for dramatic opera, has substituted for flowery descriptions, superfluous comparisons, and sententious and cold moralism the language of the heart, strong passions, interesting situations, and an ever-varied spectacle. Success has justified my maxims, and the unanimous approval that I have received in such an enlightened city has shown me that simplicity, truth, and naturalness are the great principles of what is beautiful in all artistic productions. All this notwithstanding, and despite repeated entreaties by the most respected people encouraging me to publish my opera, I have been sensible of the great risk one runs in countering such widespread and deep-rooted prejudices, and I have deemed it necessary to protect myself with the most powerful patronage of YOUR ROYAL HIGHNESS, and implore you to grant me the favor of prefacing my work with your august name, which rightly enjoys the favor of enlightened Europe. Only the great patron of the fine arts, who rules a nation that has the glory of having revived them from a state of universal oppression and of having produced in each its highest example, in a city that has always been the first to shake off the yoke of common prejudices and pave the way to perfection, only he can undertake to reform this noble spectacle, in which all the fine arts have so large a part. Should this come to pass, mine will be the credit of having laid the foundation stone, and in this public testimonial of your lofty patronage, for the favor of which I am privileged, I have the honor to declare myself, in all humility, Your Royal Highness's

Most humble, devoted, and obliged servant,
Christoforo Gluck

Preface to *Alceste* (Vienna, 1769). A facsimile appears in *The New Grove Dictionary of Music and Musicians* (London, 1980), 7:466. The letter is also translated in Strunk, *Source Readings,* 673–75.

JEAN-FRANÇOIS MARMONTEL
from *Essay on the Progress of Music in France* (1777)

The question that has been considered for some time now, concerning the type of theatrical music that should be adopted in France, will only be decided when the nation's taste, enlightened and formed by custom, will have achieved in this art, still almost new to France, what it has done in poetry, that is, when it has exhausted comparisons, and, through experimentation, has determined the precise nature of the beautiful. Until then, we shall have only a vague and confused sense of what is lacking in our music, of the character that is suitable to it, and of the beauties of which it is susceptible. The current state of our taste must therefore be doubt, concern, questioning, and a prudent distrust of the illusions of the systematic spirit and the seductions of novelty. Let us remember how slowly, and after how many errors, a sound and just idea of beauty, in all the arts, was established among us; and may this lesson serve to show us how to remain ignorant of what we have not learned. . . .

And so, when the French had no music other than the elegant but monotonous declamation of Lully, and the simple and easy airs that he mixed in with his scenes, they loved their music, and they were right to do so: art and taste had reached the same point.

Rameau came along to teach them that much greater effect could be gained from harmony. His music seemed uncivilized to them, because it was more learned than Lully's, less easy, and less analogous to the character of their language; they became accustomed to it, however, and as it had more force, greater richness, and less monotony, they developed a passion for it. Rameau had adopted Lully's style of declamation, but altered and slowed it down to an excessive and unbearable degree by the empty ornaments with which it was burdened. He made the mistake of not restoring its original simplicity. But he supported it with a more energetic harmony; in the monologues of *Dardanus* and *Castor*,[1] he suggested a moving recitative; he came closer than Lully to the accents of tragedy; he composed sublime choruses; he displayed all the richness of a creative genius in his dance pieces; and through the inexhaustible variety of the characters that distinguish them, the happy choice of the passages of which they are composed, the movement that animates them, and the mixture and dialogue of the instruments he uses, he made himself a reputation in this genre that would be difficult to extinguish.

When he was in his decline and the lyric stage was beginning to feel the effects of the weakening of his genius, a few *bouffons*, escaped from Italy, came along to let the French hear an animated and piquant music, full of wit and gaiety, in which all the subtleties of expression could be felt, in which art, making light of its difficulties, reconciled strength with grace, the precision of movement with the elegance of form, and the charm of melody with the magic of harmony.

From that moment, the French realized that something was missing in their vocal music. Pergolesi's had made them feel the effects of rhythm and meter (*du nombre et de la mesure*), the gradations of light and dark, the intelligence of design, the cohesion and unity of accompaniment with melody, the great secret of the musical period in the construction of arias. From that moment French vocal music began to seem to us inanimate, without character or color.

But we held fast to habit, or rather opinion: for we were convinced that our language was receptive neither to rhythm nor to the inflections of Italian music. A deep hatred for innovators took hold, and not without some reason. The art of enjoyment, in all things, consists in making our desires coincide with the means: a curse on the age in which knowledge surpasses talent and ability too much! Only a sense of malaise and an uneasy feeling of want and need may result from it.

Persuaded as we were that the beauties of Italian music were inaccessible to the French language, we had then to be afflicted with the distaste it inspired in us for the only music we had been given; thus we saw the Lully and Rameau factions, enemies up to that point, cease their domestic war and unite their forces to defend their homeland. Nothing could be more amusing than this confederation of the two French musics, incompatible for twenty years and all at once reconciled in order to oppose the invasion of a foreign music; but it is quite true that since that time there has been no distinction made between the two, and they have fought together to the very end for their common survival. . . .

---

1. *Dardanus* (libretto by C.-A. Le Clerc de la Bruyère) was first performed on 19 November 1739; *Castor et Pollux* (libretto by P.-J. Bernard) was first performed on 24 October 1737. [BJB]

They hasten to warn us against this seduction in journals, in gazettes, in the evening paper; they rail incessantly against Italian music, analyze Gluck's as profoundly as they analyzed the Apocalypse, and announce that his music, revived from Greeks, is the only one that is expressive, the only one that is dramatic. They would like, if it were possible, to persuade us never to listen to any other music, and to commit ourselves to following Ulysses' example, in order to protect us from the song of the sirens. That would undoubtedly be a sure means of preserving for Gluck the authority they want him to exercise; but what best serves his fame may not best serve our pleasure: it may not be true that he is the only musician in Europe capable of expressing passions; it may not be true, as they would have us believe, that harshness and asperity are essential to good music; it may not be true that a broken, mutilated melody is the most beautiful, the most touching, and that unity, fullness, and continuity weaken it. We are assured that this is so; but the reasons given are not clear and may not be sound.

For example, we are told that in the theater one must have a type of music that is not melodic, that is, which abstains from any kind of design and periodic form; that such music is far more natural and passionate when it is composed of broken movements, aborted motives, and rhythms that are disordered and disconnected.

That may be so; but if we were to hear an author of prose dramas treat the harmonious verses of Virgil, Racine, or Voltaire with scorn, saying to us: "Were Dido, Hermione, and Orosmane meant to speak in beautiful verse? If I wished to do so, I too could have this continuous elegance, this rhythmic and easy style, this melodious language; but all of this art only distorts and weakens nature. Listen to my prose: it is uncultivated, neglected, full of harshness, and crude; but it is only the more genuine for it, closer to nature." Would not this man be just as right as his counterparts in music? And would it be necessary, on his word, to consider Virgil, Racine, and Voltaire to be corrupters of taste?

The object of the arts that move the soul is not only emotion but the pleasure that accompanies it. It is therefore not enough for emotion to be strong, it must also be pleasing. This principle is acknowledged in poetry, painting, and sculpture: we know that the firm rule of the ancients was never to allow grief to distort the features of beauty. The Dying Gladiator, Niobe, and Laocoön are examples of this. Not that a convulsive facial expression would not have been far more frightening; rather, the pain it would have inflicted would not have been mixed with pleasure. The Greeks took the same care in tragedy to grant the most violent passions, either in action or in language, all the charm of expression: force itself had its own elegance. Virgil, Racine, and Voltaire have followed the example of the Greeks.

Why then should we not practice in music what has been done in poetry? Passions are expressed with cries, howls, wrenching and terrible sounds; but these accents, if they are not embellished when imitated, will, as in nature, create only an impression of suffering. If we simply wished to be moved, we could go among the common people to hear a mother who has lost her son, or children who have lost their mother: here no doubt the expression of grief is artless, and here too it is most forceful. But what pleasure would these wrenching emotions give us? The sharp point of grief that moves us in the theater must leave some balm in the wound. This balm is the pleasure of the mind, or of the senses; and the cause of this pleasure, in poetry, is the sublimity of thoughts, of sentiments and images, the noble elegance of expression, the charm of beautiful verse. In music, the same pleasure must combine with impressions of grief; and the reason for this is in the musician's art, as in that of the poet—in the art of giving to musical expression a charm that the airs, the laments, and the dire or grievous accents of passion do not possess in nature. It is therefore as strange an idea to wish to banish melodious song from opera as to wish to prohibit beautiful verse in tragedy. But it is an even stranger idea to mix declamation with fragments of mutilated song. Why not finish a song that you begin? Or why begin a song you do not wish to finish? What good is an intermittent declamation that seems to soar rapidly, but then suddenly falls back down and drags itself along heavily? There is only one excuse for the imitator who distances himself from nature: it is to procure for us the pleasures of art.

In a word, melody without expression is worth little; expression without melody is something, but not enough. Expression and melody, each to the highest degree to which they may rise together: that is the problem of art. It remains to be seen who will provide us with a solution to this problem. . . .

On the one hand they tell us that Gluck has created a type of dramatic music undreamed of by Italian composers. On the other hand, they ask precisely what this creation is. Except for accent, they say, Gluck's recitative is the same as in Italy. He has almost always written an accompaniment for it, and the sound of the orchestra has covered the defects of his Teutonic modulations: force has often substituted for accuracy of expression; but in having his recitative accompanied, he has only imitated to excess the obbligato recitative of Italian opera; his choruses are assuredly not more dramatic than those of Rameau; he has set characters into action, moved them about on the stage, and we must be grateful to him; but to say of him that "Prometheus has shaken his torch," and that "the statues have come to life"[2] is to express in a truly magnificent fashion what is anything but a wonder! His duets aspire to resemble the duets in dialogue, bet-

---

2. This quotation comes from an anonymous letter originally published in the *Journal de Politique et de Littérature* and included in Leblond's collection of *Mémoires* (1781) under the title "Défense de M. Gluck," reprinted in *Querelle des Gluckistes et des Piccinnistes*, ed. Lesure, 1:108. (For the full titles see the source note at the end of the excerpt.) [BJB]

ter constructed than his, that he heard in Italy. Here is what those who do not wish to believe in his creative genius reply.

They have tried to make us admire "how," in an overture, "the composer after having linked the beginning to the subject, not through some vague relationship but through the forms themselves, hurls all the instruments onto the same note at once; how, after having risen together and in unison up to the octave of this note, these instruments divide and compete, each on its own, toward preparing the soul for a great event; how, in order to maintain the feeling of the rhythm, weakened by the quickness with which the upper parts move, the composer has the instruments strike an anapestic rhythm."[3] All of this is no doubt excellent; but it is the language of experts, which the common crowd does not understand.

The distinctive character of Gluck's music would then be in what the Italians call "rocky and rugged" (*escarpée et raboteuse*) harmony; in the broken and incoherent modulations of his arias, in the disparate and mutilated passages of which they are composed, in the negligence, intentional or not, with which he chooses his motives and follows his designs, with which he gives analogy and fullness to his song. But one may question whether this is a model of art, an invention of genius.

Let us draw the firm conclusion that Gluck's true merit lies in having seen "in French opera," as his apologist says, "the outline of a magnificent spectacle, in which only the music was lacking; to have found in Italian music colors suited to painting all the affections of the soul," and to have tried to "compose great paintings with them."[4] But did he paint these scenes in the colors of beautiful music? This is what admirers of easy, regular, and melodious song have disputed.

Much is said of the force, the energy, and the vigor of the sounds Gluck obtains from his orchestra or from the lungs of his singers; and one must admit that no one has ever made the trumpets rumble, the strings whirr, or the voices bellow as has he. But who knows if Italian melody and harmony do not also have some force in their simplicity, with less effort? In all the theaters of Europe, we have felt the effects of countless touching passages in which singing was not noise; and if the impressions of the singing were not to be as violent as those of noise and cries, is the ear or the soul of the French then so insensitive that it needs these profound disturbances in order to be moved? For those who wish only to be stirred, Shakespeare would be preferable to Racine: and so, by the

---

3. This quotation comes from the *Lettre de M. L'A. A** à Madame d'**** [i.e. the Abbé François Arnaud and Mme d'Augny], first published in the *Gazette de Littérature* (?1774); it is also included in Leblond's collection, reprinted in *Querelle*, ed. Lesure, 1:29–30. [BJB]

4. From the same letter cited in n. 2, p. 107. [BJB]

same reasoning that grants Gluck's music exclusive preference over Italian music, English tragedy is considered superior to our own; but this new school of taste has not been fashionable in Paris. By doing excessive honor to the German musician—I mean by considering him the Shakespeare of music, which from the perspective of genius must flatter him infinitely—we do not say that on his account the Racines of Italy must be excluded from the theater.

We know full well that Italian opera, such as it is, would not succeed in France: it would seem barren, cold, sad, and languishing: tragedy, in its austerity, is not made for opera; all of Metastasio's talent was unable to give it a character it did not have. Singing is a fantastic or magical language: its verisimilitude stems from the marvelous elements in the plot. We are prepared to hear Armide, Roland, or Proserpine sing; but we would feel repugnance at hearing Alexander, Regulus, Caesar, or Cato sing. We have a theater devoted to history; this is the theater of pathos *par excellence;* and it would be impossible for opera to rival tragedy, without the variety and magnificence of the scenery and the festive elements (*fêtes*) that the marvelous provides.

It is thus not Italian opera but Italian music that must be introduced on the French stage. But Italian music, we are told, is merely a warbling of birds; nothing could be more contrary to the expression of feeling, and especially strong passions, than those arias in which a brilliant voice seems to flit about on a sound.

This is assuredly not what we must envy in Italian opera. But do they wish to persuade us that its airs, which the Italians call bravura arias, destined to display the voice in all its brilliance, are Italian music at its best and in its essence? The Italians themselves admit that this is a vain luxury, an abuse of their riches: this is not what they propose that we imitate in their opera. The sublime element of their music, the one they genuinely admire, is obbligato recitative; those with the greatest character are very natural songs and very expressive, but also very melodious, and there are an infinite number of this sort in their operas. We have heard nothing else in our concerts for several years; while, through an inconceivable coincidence, Gluck's music is almost never performed in our concerts. His partisans are thus truly right in saying that "Italian music is concert music"; but they are not equally right in asserting that "it is not music for the theater."

Italian music has known different ages, like Latin and French literature. Its taste has been purified, then corrupted, and then corrected. The Italians sought a pure and beautiful simplicity, found it, and appreciated it; they tried to surpass it, and burdened musical expression, like poetic expression, with false brilliance and *concetti;* they realized their error and returned to beautiful simplicity. Such is the circle through which taste has run in Italy. It is still, one must admit, too indulgent of the ear; it still seeks to delight even at the expense of expression; but this is an occasional evil, and the example is without consequence.

In forming their opera from tragedy, the Italians have distorted both one and the other. Tragedy has lost its progression, its gradations, its eloquence, its knowing portraits of character and customs; in this state of mutilation, it no longer has anything that redeems its constant sadness: it was therefore necessary to grant it the freedom of a type of singing that relieves the ear from its dreariness and soothes the spectator overcome by five hours of boredom. Whereas French opera, naturally embellished by the charm of festive elements and the magnificence of the marvelous, needs no other adornment; and the music, varied by the events of the spectacle, can conform to the objects it depicts without being dull and sad.

In Italy, the voices produced by the climate or contrived by a cruel art are so light, so flexible, so dazzling to the ear, if I dare say so, that it is hardly likely that a people, accustomed to hear them rival the most brilliant and sweetest instruments, would renounce this pleasure and allow composers to deprive them of it by practicing a more austere style; let us add that composers, slaves to the caprices and vanity of the singers, are obligated, in spite of themselves, to produce for these singers an abundance of passages that display their brilliance. But in France, where the voices of theatrical heroes have a more masculine character, where the voices of the women themselves are more sensitive than brilliant, where the composer dominates and establishes the law, art is not exposed to the same seductions of habit and bad taste. Nothing then prevents excellent Italian music—that which refines and even strengthens expression without distorting it—from being transplanted in all of its force and purity to our stage.

From *Essai sur les révolutions de la musique en France* (Paris, 1777), 1–6, 12–16, 24–31. Reprinted in Abbé Leblond (= Gaspard Michel), *Mémoires pour servir à l'histoire de la révolution opérée dans la musique par M. le Chevalier Gluck* (1781), in turn reprinted in *Querelle des Gluckistes et des Piccinnistes: Texte des pamphlets avec introduction, commentaires et index,* ed. François Lesure, 2 vols. (Geneva: Minkoff Reprint, 1984), 1:153–90.

JEAN-FRANÇOIS DE LA HARPE
From *Lyceum, or Course in Ancient and Modern
Literature* (1803)

IV
ON ITALIAN OPERA COMPARED WITH OURS, AND ON CHANGES
THAT THE NEW MUSIC CAN INTRODUCE IN FRENCH OPERA

It may be said that progress in opera has been divided equally between the Italians and ourselves, according to the nature of each of the two peoples: they have perfected the music, and we the drama. Not having, strictly speaking, any tragic theater, they must have little idea of the pleasure one may derive during two to three hours from purely dramatic emotions prolonged by a sustained illusion, emotions that have been so dear and familiar to us, going back even before Corneille, that is, more than a hundred and fifty years. Truly good tragedy, among the moderns, originated in France, and we had a taste for it even before this taste was elucidated, as may be seen by the success of Tristan and Mairet.[1] It was only an instinct at the time when we were transported by the latter's *Sophonisbe* and the former's *Mariamne*. From *Le Cid* onwards,[2] this taste became an ever more lively, and at the same time more refined, passion. Among the Italians, it is music that is native. It is a fruit of the soil, and they have made every effort to encourage its cultivation. When you see the enthusiasm with which they listen to music, they appear to be natural musicians; and as they have learned to know and appreciate music very early, two natural effects result: trained taste becomes severe in its judgment, and they will not tolerate mediocre music; intense feeling exhausts itself quickly, and each year they demand new music. It is perhaps also for this same reason that they do not much care for listening to music for an entire evening: there is no emotion that lasts three hours, unless it completely occupies the soul, and the ear is at least halfway attuned to the pleasure that music gives to those who love it passionately. The Italian ear is very sensitive, and it is for this very reason that it scarcely pays attention, except to a few superior pieces, in the course of a performance much

1. François L'Hermite, known as Tristan L'Hermite (ca. 1601–65), French poet, dramatist, and novelist; his *Mariamne* (1636) rivaled Corneille's *Le Cid* in popularity. Jean Mairet (1604–86), French dramatist, was the first to apply classical precepts to French drama; *Sophonisbe* (1634) was considered the first real French tragedy. [BJB]
2. Corneille's *Le Cid* was in fact written in the same year as Tristan's *Mariamne*, 1636. [BJB]

longer than ours: these pieces throw Italians into a kind of intoxication, and their senses then need to rest.

You will recognize the influence of the climate, and the customs that accompany it, in the way the Italians attend an opera. They visit each other, they make conversation, they gamble in their boxes, they eat there, they come and go, as if they were at home. Sedentary almost the entire day, for Italians the evening is the time for action and movement, and distractions are necessary in a performance five to six hours long. Their attention returns only with the expectation of pleasure, when it is a question of hearing the aria, the virtuoso, and the soprano. Is it surprising—given these universal inclinations—that they have had only bad opera with beautiful music? This is bound to happen when one is passionate about one and not much interested in the other. Voltaire has said that music killed tragedy for the Italians, and he was right. It is not, however, for lack of poetic talent that Italian opera has remained so imperfect; a nation that can take great pride in a poet such as Metastasio cannot say that it is devoted exclusively to music because the words are bad. It has only itself to blame for the uneven quality of the librettos (*poëmes*), which has become almost the rule, given the necessity of expanding the plot in order to find a place for the singers. But in spite of all the vices of the whole, a clever and knowledgeable people could not fail to recognize the genius of the poet in the interest these plots hold, and in the beauty of the dialogue and the style that have assured the reputation of Metastasio. Yet it is at the court of Vienna, and not in his own country that this famous writer has enjoyed rewards and honors; and in Italy a good composer earns more by himself alone than twenty authors, and a talented singer more than all the composers and all the poets. We know, moreover (and it is proven daily), that there is neither a scene nor a situation that may not be sacrificed, without the least scruple, to make room for an aria that is much in demand or a virtuoso who is much in fashion. So it is that neither good composers nor good singers are ever lacking; but if by chance one has a poet, it is nature who summons him and foreigners who give him his rightful place.

"Honos alit artes."[3] Just as the strictly intellectual arts are little valued in Italy, so have they been honored in France; and what was an object of indifference in one country has been one of society's chief interests in the other. The Frenchman—who is more active due to a cooler climate, more devoted to the pleasures and especially to the pretensions of the mind, due to a disproportionate vanity that has always been one of his traits—the Frenchman is capable of abandoning everything, tolerating anything, for the sole pleasure of having seen any novelty, in order to exercise his right to judge. This was evident daily in the age of literature, for we can so designate the time when literature was a social

3. "Glory is the nourishment of the arts" (Cicero, *Tusculan Disputations*, 1.2).

force, just as we may call the past ten years the age of ignorance, in which the latter has been a universal power. This excessive desire for things intellectual was to grant a singular importance to authors as a class, provided that they were not absolutely devoid of any ability. . . .

As a man of genius, Gluck had felt that if music was too often lacking in expression in French opera, in Italian opera what expression it had was entirely contained in a few arias and independent of the drama as a whole. He must have felt this defect all the more in that, at the very moment when good music was gaining credit among us, it was beginning to be corrupted, in some re-spects, in Italy. Wealth breeds overindulgence; and too great an indulgence for singers, whose vocal chords lent themselves with astonishing facility to all the efforts and all the tricks of which the human voice is capable, had more than once led composers, even the most renowned, away from the principles estab-lished by those who first created the art of fine singing. These frivolous tri-umphs of the throat, whose natural domain is in ballets and *fêtes*, whose sole aim is to amuse the ear and eyes, had usurped a place even on the stage, where music must always conform to the situation and the character; and in this way they degenerated from the rich and noble simplicity of the models. Even those who provided them, the finest composers since Pergolesi, sometimes yielded to the passion that Italians showed for these tours de force that appeared to be the wonders of singing; but tours de force are never truly wonders of art, which is doubtless not nature, although they have been so thoroughly confused in con-temporary poetics. Art must always retrace nature to its favor; and note that the beauties of nature always appear effortless, because Nature always hides her work; and art must do the same. Good judges, still numerous in the land of music, were not taken in by this sort of charlatanism, which they looked upon as the degradation of an imitative art; and one of them, Martini, went so far as to say that Italian music had become brazen (*sfacciata*). But a beautiful woman, though she wears make-up, does not cease to be beautiful; to find her true com-plexion again, one need only remove the make-up. Gluck, who like all German artists was familiar with Italian music, had put on Calzabigi's *Orfeo* in Rome, a weak drama in which verisimilitude is sometimes strained,[4] but which had the

---

4. If anything can demonstrate how permissive we have become on the question of verisimili-tude in opera when we are moved by the music, it is the scene between Orpheus and Eurydice and the strange quarrel they have with one another. Just as the movement of curiosity and amorous impatience that Virgil attributes to Orpheus is natural and interesting, so is it absurd that Eurydice takes it into her head to quarrel with Orpheus because he does not look at her. There is assuredly nothing more pressing for her than to leave the underworld; she has this moment within her grasp, and she pauses, in the most obstinate folly, refusing to move until her lover looks at her and de-spairing at no longer being loved. What woman then will believe that she is loved, if not she whose lover has come even to Hades to find her? Of all the lovers' quarrels, this is certainly the most

novel merit of unity of action and a subject engaging in its simplicity. It was all the more successful in that, of all of Gluck's operas, *Orfeo* is the one in which he used the most singing, and in which, without equaling the melodies of Piccinni, Sacchini, Paisiello, etc., he came much closer to doing so than he has since. But he produced the first example of an opera in which the music was never separate from the action, and in which the words and the melody formed from beginning to end a truly dramatic whole, something he alone could do. However, he had to yield to what is called bravura; an aria had to be sung (at the end of the first act, "L'espoir renaît dans mon âme"), in a style which is a bit too glittery, but more excusable coming from Orpheus in a moment of joy than it would have been elsewhere; moreover, this aria was not by Gluck.[5]

He soon realized that his plan for opera (although it was the right one) could not bring about a revolution in Italy. This revolution was awaited in France, where boredom made the opera ripe for innovation: *Orphée* was received quite differently there than in Italy. The *air de situation* "J'ai perdu mon Eurydice," the romance "Objet de mon amour," and the duet "Quels tourments insupportables!" were certainly the most beautiful things that had been heard in this theater. The air that Orpheus sings to the demons, "Laissez-vous toucher par mes pleurs," did not produce as great an effect, perhaps because too much was expected of it, and because it is easier to measure feeling—which is common to everyone—than imagination heightened by the fantastic elements of the story. But the infernal "No," contrasting with the lament of Orpheus; the chorus in mourning around Eurydice's tomb in the first act, and the name of "Eurydice," that cry of love and grief so effectively interjected in the intervals where it expressed everything by itself alone; the chorus of the underworld, and even the dance pieces—everything had a quality of theatrical illusion that up until then had been lacking in this type of spectacle. . . .

The most recent work of Piccinni, *Didon*,[6] seems to me to combine almost everything one could desire in an opera: it was the greatest success of this illustrious artist, and it is perhaps his masterpiece, at least among his French operas. *Didon* could be better written, I admit, but it is very well designed, well composed in the spirit of the genre, and full of the feeling called for, that of touching

---

extravagant; but the duet makes up for everything. [Early performances include Florence, 1771 and Naples, 1774, but none is recorded in Rome. BJB]

  5. The attribution to Ferdinando Bertoni (1725–1813) is now disbelieved: the original music is by Gluck and was reused by Bertoni in his *Tancredi* (1767), then used again by Gluck for the Paris version of *Orphée*, whereupon he was accused of having plagiarized Bertoni. See Tom Hammond, "A Note on the Aria di bravura 'L'espoir renaît dans mon âme'," in Patricia Howard, *C. W. von Gluck: Orfeo* (Cambridge Opera Handbooks; Cambridge, 1981), 109–12. [BJB]

  6. *Didon*, libretto by Marmontel, first performed at Fontainebleau, 6 December 1783. Piccinni had set Metastasio's *Didone abbandonata* in 1770. [BJB]

pity which, in my view, is worth a great deal more than the horror that has been produced all too unsparingly since Gluck and which even tragedy admits only with all of the care and attention of art. I know of nothing better conceived, nothing more beautiful than the scene in which Dido prepares for death, than the calm and concentrated despair with which she keeps her secret, even from her sister, and waits only for the repose of death, while priests offer a sacrifice to the spirit of her husband Sychaeus, asking that he return to his widow the peace of mind she has lost. All of this is in Virgil, I know; but all of it combined has the greatest dramatic and musical effect. Recall the song of the religious chorus:

> Dieu de l'oubli, dieu du repos,
> Rends à Didon des jours paisibles;
>
> (God of forgetfulness, good of repose,
> Return to Dido more peaceful days)

and recall the frightening silence she maintains in the midst of this scene and this song, at the sight of the pyre to which Aeneas's spoils are brought and which she is about to mount. It is here, it seems to me, that the action and the music reinforce one another most effectively and produce the most penetrating emotion, with neither one missing the mark; this is the true perfection of opera. It was felt deeply, and through thirty consecutive performances, which troubled at least one faction that could not be pacified. It is sad and even shameful that a foreign artist, who brought us new pleasures, was so long the target of scorn heaped upon him by a cabal as clever as it was untiring in its efforts to do harm, and was reduced finally to leaving France, the homeland of the arts, which had called him to her, and whose ingratitude he could now recount. His enemies, who could only be the enemies of genius, triumphed at his retreat, and there could not have been a better demonstration that it was not music, but their own opinion, that they loved.

We have yet to consider this opinion in itself; and as I am now more indifferent to it than ever, I would not take the trouble, if it did not touch on dramatic art and consequently enter into the topics I must discuss. Certainly I care very little whether Gluck is preferred to Piccinni, or Piccinni to Gluck; and having little stake in the matter, I care even less about my own opinion. But we have already seen that the system proposed by the Gluckists leads directly to a confusion of opera with tragedy; and as this error is an immediate consequence of their doctrine, and serves no less than to pervert the genres, it is my duty to combat it, as I have undertaken to do.[7] And what justifies the detail into which I have entered here on music is the fact that our opera has united music with

---

7. In the article "Opera," in the preceding century [the earlier part of his book, dealing with seventeenth-century literature. BJB]

drama; and false principles based on this alliance compromise the two arts equally and cannot touch one without having an influence on the other. The proof of this may be seen in most of the operas produced since Gluck. The tyranny of fashion appears to have subjugated composers of recognized talent, and neither art nor spectacle may be seen to have gained by it.

From Ch. 6, "De l'Opéra," in *Lycée, ou Cours de littérature ancienne et moderne*, 17 vols. (Paris, 1799–1805), vol. 12 (1803): 153–59, 172–75, 195–98.

MICHEL-PAUL GUY DE CHABANON
From *Observations on Music and Principally on the Metaphysics of Art* (1779)

VIII
EXPRESSION IN SONG DOES NOT CONSIST IN THE IMITATION
OF THE INARTICULATE CRY OF THE PASSIONS

What extraordinary assertions have been made about music, ever since one has lost sight of the fact that its primary component is melody? All the power of the art, it has been said, consists in imitating the inarticulate cry of the passions. But how can a song be made from a cry? This is what troubles me. Can the principle be reduced to inserting a passionate cry into an air? This is then no more than a chance effect of art and of the air; it is no longer its depth, its foundation, and its essence.

It cannot be denied, I believe, that music is susceptible of gaiety; this is among the sentiments that are closest to it. And what is the inarticulate cry of gaiety? Laughter. Yet you would search in vain for the imitation of laughter among these tambourins, provençales, and allemandes,[1] which spread a feeling of lightheartedness through a crowd and move the listeners to fits of joy. Have you not observed that the gaiety that music inspires does not carry over into laughter? It soothes the limbs and makes the whole body feel light and refreshed. I know of nothing less joyful in music than the airs to which actors are made to laugh in the theater; the actor laughs, but the music does not accompany him. The musical gestures meant to mimic laughter destroy its gaiety and make it seem rather sad in nature.

1. Various types of dance music, indispensable in French opera. [BJB]

The *Stabat* is commonly considered to express grief; there is no imitative cry to be found in it.[2]

Gluck, whose genius—more than any other, unless I am mistaken—has sought and achieved musical expression, has often inserted plaintive notes in a melodious song to suggest the accents of grief, and on these notes he invites the singer to approximate natural expression. At the first performance of *Orphée*,[3] the leading actor came a bit too close. He gave too lifelike a rendition of the wrenching cry that intermittently breaks through the song of the weeping Thracians:[4] he became aware of it, and softened the tone. He had, in some way, gone beyond the bounds of his art and come too close to nature; an instinctive sense of what was fitting brought him back within the natural limits of taste. Imitation lost its lifelike quality, but it became more musical and was therefore more appreciated.

Many of our passions have no particular cry associated with them, and yet music may express them. Instruments, incapable of imitating the cries of the human voice, are nonetheless eloquent interpreters of musical energy and expression. "Naturâ ducimur ad modos: neque aliter enim evenerit ut illi quoque organorum soni, quanquam verba non exprimunt, in alios, atque alios ducerent motus auditorem."[5] Quintilian does not say in this passage that the instruments affect us because they imitate words and cries. He says: "Nature has made us sensitive to melody. Otherwise, would it be possible, for instruments, which articulate no words, to inspire so many different responses in us?" Here is the whole truth of the matter: "Nature has made us sensitive to melody; Naturâ ducimur ad modos." Any music pleasing to those well-versed in melody is certainly melodious. But how can music express passions without imitating speech or cries? Insofar as it is able, music combines the diverse sensations it produces with our various sentiments. This is the point we shall develop further. . . .

XXII
On Harmony Joined with Melody

Up to now we have limited ourselves to the simplest idea one may have of music, that is, melody alone. Let us complete this idea and reconstitute the art

---

2. Chabanon probably refers to Pergolesi's *Stabat mater,* which enjoyed great renown in the eighteenth century. [BJB]

3. The first performance of the French version of Gluck's opera took place in Paris on 2 August 1774. [BJB]

4. La Harpe also referred to this passage; see above. [BJB]

5. "We are naturally drawn to music, for it could not otherwise have come about that even the sounds of instruments, although they do not express words, should lead the listener into one emotion after another"; Quintilian, *Institutio oratoria* 9.4.10. [LAH-S]

in its entirety, by restoring to it one of its most essential accessories, harmony.

The reader should not expect here a scientific treatise on chords and how to use them. In this chapter, as in the rest of the work, we consider the metaphysical aspect of music more than its material or technical aspects. Instead of repeating what the most scholarly theorists have said about the formation and use of chords, we shall limit ourselves to a few observations, made more for those unschooled than those well-versed in music.

It is certainly a phenomenon worth noting that several sounds may coexist, each of which the ear may distinguish, whose combined impression produces only one clear and distinct sensation. Among all of our senses, hearing alone is susceptible of such a sensation, composite and simple at the same time, and music alone is capable of making us feel it. When different noises are perceived simultaneously, they cancel each other out. When several people speak at the same time, no one succeeds in making himself heard. But let several voices simultaneously sing parts that have been set out harmonically, and the ear, distinguishing each of them, receives the impression of these combined voices as it would the impression of a single voice. In this mixture of sounds brought together by harmony, the melody is clearly and distinctly revealed: it is the result of everything the ear hears. If the secondary sounds added to the melody are not those prescribed by the harmony, from that very moment unity is destroyed, the melody vanishes, and there remains nothing but disorder and incomprehensible confusion.

It is impossible to imagine a melody that does not include a bass and harmonic parts, just as it is impossible to imagine a series of chords, pleasing to the ear, from which a melodious song could not be drawn. Thus harmony exists implicitly in melody, and melody in harmony. One cannot say which gives rise to which; each engenders the other, and implicitly therefore they cannot exist one without the other.

It would be an interesting experiment for a European, finding himself transported among savages, to let them hear, with the embellishment of harmony, the songs they are accustomed to sing in unison. What would be the effect of this first impression on them? Would it be unwelcome or pleasing? Would the musical instinct of these primitive men lead them to distinguish first the melody from among the other parts, by subordinating all the accompanying parts to it? These questions can only be clarified by experiment. The result one might obtain would demonstrate to what extent the appreciation of harmony is natural to man and to what extent the sensation received is artificial, deliberate, and contrived.

Harmony seems to derive immediately from the nature of sound, since every reverberating sound produces its harmonics. A bell that has been struck sounds its third and fifth, as well as its fundamental tone. By its very nature, then, sound never exists alone; it comes into being accompanied by its partials.

Play an instrument in a room where there are twenty others, and the strings of all these instruments will shake and quiver each time the one being played produces a sound analogous to their own. But these strings remain silent and insensitive to all other sounds; they experience no vibration.

One cannot play two strings together on the same instrument without a resulting indistinct resonance of a third sound, lower than the other two, but which blends them together, as if to say that it belongs to them and cannot be separated from them.[6]

Such are the principal experiments that reveal to us the sympathetic relation of sounds and their essential coexistence. These experiments serve as a foundation for the scholarly speculations of theorists. We shall content ourselves here with the observation that the third sound resulting from the resonance of the other two, far from being a true bass, may not—in any number of cases—be associated with the two sounds that produce it. The reason for this is that these two sounds, depending on the movement of the melody, belong to one key or another, and the established key often rejects the sound produced by the reverberation. See the example below:

The resonances of a sounding body may be considered the cradle of harmony, the first elements of a theory of chords. This is not to say that we owe to this experience the art of writing music in several parts. This practice began long before the phenomenon of resonance had been observed. Instinctive discoveries, in this case as in all others, anticipated the discoveries of science.

Much as one may be legitimately surprised that the ancients did not know harmony, so one may be astonished that the moderns have extended the theory of harmony so far. How is it that the former, made aware through the ear's sensations of the affinity of certain sounds, did not attempt to combine them in their songs? And how could the latter have dared to associate sounds that dissonance seems to make incompatible?

The effect of some dissonances is so harsh and crude that it inflicts a type of

6. This is the phenomenon first described by Tartini as the "third sound," or combination tone; see above, p. 149, n. 2. [BJB]

suffering on the instrument that produces them. Play two notes a tone apart on the violin and you will feel the surface of the instrument tremble violently, as if they would break it apart. Let a consonance follow, and the rough shaking subsides. The instrument then enjoys the same calm and tranquillity as the ear.

Yet our whole system of harmony is composed equally of consonance and dissonance. The arbiters of harmony, it is true, have compromised with the ear to make it admit certain discords. The rule for preparing and resolving them consists first in producing one of the notes of which the chord is composed, then bringing to it that hostile sound whose proximity frightens it, and finally making it disappear altogether so that a friendlier sound may follow. Only under these conditions will the ear adapt itself to dissonance and tolerate momentary discomfort in order to rest more pleasantly afterwards amid better-suited sounds. Thus in life do short trials contrast with happiness and make the appreciation of it sweeter.

Those little schooled in music may imagine that since each sound has its own harmonics, the art of composition consists merely in joining them to the fundamental sound, and keeping them always in concert with it. But this method would produce confusion; art prescribed a different one. When melody sets twenty or thirty notes to playing lightheartedly together, harmony often establishes a single bass note in response. This is not to say that the twenty notes above it belong to the bass and are among its harmonics. But melody deceives the ear, throws it off track, and makes it hear the notes as if they derived from this low sound.

Melody thus reigns supreme in music, even when considered from the perspective of harmony. Melody arranges the materials that harmony furnishes and makes the secondary parts sound, each according to its rank within the whole. It is melody again that carries the principal tune from the voice to the instruments at its will, and from one instrument to another. How could one follow the melody through these transmigrations without the ready instinct of a trained ear?

There is no reason (even in the theater) for the human voice always to sing the main part, that is, the most interesting one. If you maintain that the singer who is present onstage and guiding the action attracts the greatest attention from the audience, I will answer that the orchestra is no less present than the singer, and no less intimately tied to the action. I would add that the orchestra has at its disposal a hundred voices, as powerful in their diversity as in their coming together, and that the singer has but one, infinitely limited in its modes of performance.

Just so has Renaud's monologue in the second act of *Armide*[7] been defended,

7. Opera by Gluck.

or rather praised. The principal melody is played by the instruments, and it is fitting that the orchestra express these words: "Ce fleuve coule lentement, etc." (this river flows slowly).

This brings us to a natural observation. If music were essentially an imitative art, melody, accompaniments, everything should converge unanimously toward imitation. We see, however, that in the most moving arias and the most touching adagios the accompaniment departs from imitation and plays melodiously about the subject.[8] In pieces where the accompaniment strives to depict certain effects, the upper part frees itself from this imitative constraint and ends up simply singing.

A universal principle of harmony, according to which one could admit or reject certain sequences of chords, has long been sought. I doubt this principle will ever be found. The simplest and most general rule one can give to students is to link chords that follow one another with one or several notes common to them. This principle admits exceptions, and some very fortunate ones, for there is no sweeter and smoother harmony than a series of descending sixths. Yet these successive chords are not linked by any note preserved from one to the other. For want of the principle sought, here is the one I propose. All harmony from which a simple and natural melody flows is good and in accordance with the rules. Harmony that produces only irritating and difficult melodies does not deserve to be admitted. Keep this sort of harmony at the very most for those preludes in which the performer wishes to dazzle with his skill rather than his taste. For in these skillful combinations, harmony can be, if you will, harsh and bristling; fleeing the common path, let it make its way through the brush and briar. But this roundabout route will never be counted among harmony's natural processes: it is rather a licentious digression, a learned ecstasy. Harmony is tributary and subject to melody. It should not dare anything without the consent of its sovereign. Let this truth be the first and the last of those we must establish.

From *Observations sur la musique, et principalement sur la métaphysique de l'art* (Paris, 1779; repr. Geneva: Minkoff, 1969; Slatkine Reprints, 1971), Ch. 8, pp. 64–67, and Ch. 22, pp. 203–15. Chapters 2–10 are translated in Lippman, *Musical Aesthetics* 1:295–318.

8. See "Che farò senza Euridice" [from Gluck's *Orfeo*]. The accompaniment plays lightly underneath the melody. This is even more noticeable in the aria "Alceste au nom des Dieux" [from Gluck's *Alceste*]. The same observation could be made about most Italian arias.

WOLFGANG AMADEUS MOZART
Three Letters to His Father (1781)

Vienne ce 12 de May
1781

Mon très cher Père!

From my last letter you know that I have asked the Prince[1] for my discharge, since he himself told me to do so; for already in the first two audiences he said to me, "If you will not serve me properly, clear off!" He will deny it, of course, but it is as true as God is in heaven. Is it any wonder, then, that I have agreed to "clear off," after getting all worked up because of "knave, scoundrel, rascal, negligent fellow," and other similar expressions so dignified in the mouth of a prince? On the following day I gave Count Arco[2] a petition to present to his Grace, and I also returned my travel money, which consisted of 15 florins and 40 kreutzer for the coach, and 2 ducats for living expenses. He accepted neither; instead he assured me that I could not resign without having your consent, Father. "That is your duty," he said to me. I assured him that I knew my duty to my father as well and perhaps better than he, and that I should be sorry if I had to learn it only from him. "Very well, if he is satisfied, you may request your discharge; and if he is not, you may request it anyway," he answered. A fine distinction! All the pleasantries the Archbishop expressed toward me during the three audiences, especially during the last one, and the news that this grand man of God had given me now had such a splendid effect on my body that at night I had to leave the opera in the middle of the first act to go home and lie down. For I was very feverish, trembling all over, and staggering like a drunkard in the alley. I also stayed at home the following day, yesterday, and spent the whole morning in bed, having taken tamarind water.

The Count was also so kind as to write many flattering things about me to his father, which you have probably had to swallow already. There will probably be some fantastic passages in it, but if one writes a comedy and seeks applause, one must exaggerate a little and not stick too closely to the truth of the matter; and you must give these gentlemen credit for their assiduity.

---

1. Archbishop Hieronymus Colloredo, Mozart's patron. [BJB]
   2. Count Karl Joseph Felix Arco (1743–1830). At the time he was high chamberlain at the Salzburg court. [BJB]

Without getting into a rage—for I value my health and life, and am only sorry that I am forced to do this—I will present the main accusation with respect to my service: I did not realize that I was a valet, and that was my undoing. I was supposed to waste a couple of hours every morning in the antechamber. Of course I was told occasionally that I should show myself, but I don't recall that it was my duty to do so; and I only came when the Archbishop specifically sent for me.

Now I will confide in you briefly my firm resolve, so that the whole world may hear it: if I can receive a salary of 2,000 florins from the Archbishop of Salzburg, and only 1,000 at another place, I shall go to that other place. Instead of the other 1,000 florins, I shall enjoy my health and peace of mind. Thus I hope that with all the fatherly love that you have bestowed on me to such a high degree from childhood on—and for which I can never be grateful enough in all my life, least of all in Salzburg—I hope that you will write nothing about this whole matter and consign it to deepest oblivion, if you wish to keep your son healthy and happy. For only a word about it would suffice to set my blood boiling again, and yours too, if you will only admit it.

Now farewell, and be glad that you don't have a coward for a son. I kiss your hands a thousand times, embrace my sister with all my heart, and am forever your most obedient son,

Wolfgang Amadè Mozart

Vienne ce 26 de Septembre
1781

Mon très cher Père!

Forgive me for making you pay more postage the other day! But I had nothing necessary to write, and I thought you would enjoy it if I gave you some idea about the opera.[3] The opera [text] began with a monologue, and I asked Herr Stephani[4] to turn it into a short arietta, and to make a duet after Osmin's song, instead of both characters chattering. We thought of giving the role of Osmin to Herr Fischer,[5] who certainly has a superb bass voice (nevertheless the Archbishop said to me that he sang too low for a bass, and I assured him that he would sing higher in the future). One must take advantage of such a man, especially since he has

---

3. *Die Entführung aus dem Serail*, first performed at the Burgtheater on 16 July 1782. [BJB]
   4. Gottlieb Stefanie, Jr. (1741–1800), Mozart's librettist. At the time he was director of the National Singspiel. His personal qualities were universally deplored, but Mozart appreciated his willingness to accommodate the libretto to the composer's wishes. [BJB]
   5. The basso profundo Johann Ignaz Ludwig Fischer. [BJB]

the local public on his side. In the original libretto Osmin has only a little
song to sing and nothing else, except the trio and the finale. Now he has
another aria in the first act, and he will get another one in the second. I
have given the whole aria to Herr Stephani; the main part of the music
was already finished before Stephani even knew a word. You only have
the beginning and the ending, which must make a good effect: to turn
Osmin's rage comical, it is set to Turkish music. In the composition of
the aria, I let his beautiful low tones gleam (in spite of the Salzburg
Midas). The section "drum beim Barte des Propheten," etc., is set in the
same tempo, but with fast notes. Since his rage keeps growing, and one
thinks the aria is already at an end, the allegro assai—in a completely
different tempo and another key—is bound to make the best effect: a
man in such a vehement state of rage exceeds all order, measure, and intention; he doesn't know himself, and so the music must not know itself
anymore. Since the passions, however, whether vehement or not, must
never be expressed to a point that disgusts; and since the music must
never offend the ear, even in the most horrible situations, but must still
please it—in short, always remain music—I have not chosen a remote
key to accompany F, the key of the aria, but a related one—not the key
most closely related, D minor, but one further removed, A minor. Now
comes Belmonte's aria in A major, "O wie ängstlich, o wie feurig"; you
see how it is expressed—the affectionately beating heart is already indicated, with the two violins in octaves. This is the favorite aria of everybody who has heard it—mine, too. And it was entirely written to suit
Adamberger's voice.[6] You see trembling and shaking, you see the swelling
of his throbbing breast, portrayed by a crescendo. You hear the whisper-
ing and sighing, expressed by the first violins with mutes and a flute in
unison.

The Janissary chorus has everything that can be desired of a Janissary chorus: short and cheerful, and written entirely for the Viennese.
Constanze's aria I sacrificed somewhat to the fluent throat of Mlle
Cavalieri.[7] In "Trennung war mein banges Los. Und nun schwimmt
mein Aug in Thränen" I have tried to express as much as Italian bravura
permits. Thus I changed the "hui" into "schnell": "doch wie schnell
schwand meine Freude," etc. I don't know where our German poets have
their brains: if they don't understand the theater as far as opera is con-

---

6. Josef Valentin Adamberger, the leading tenor. [BJB]
    7. Caterina Cavalieri (Franziska Kavalier), who had studied with Salieri, had a brilliant so-
prano voice. [BJB]

cerned, at least they shouldn't let the characters talk as if confronted with a herd of pigs.[8] Hui, swine!

Now the trio, the finale of the first act. Pedrillo has introduced his master as an architect, so that he may have an opportunity to meet Constanze in the garden. Bassa Selim has taken him into his service. Osmin, the steward, who knows nothing of all that, is an uncouth brute and the impertinent arch-enemy of all foreigners, and won't let them into the garden. The introduction is very short, and since the text demands it, I have written it fairly well for three voices. But then the pianissimo section in major, which must go very quickly, begins immediately. The ending will be rather noisy, which is just what the end of an act requires: the more noise, the better; the shorter, the better, so the people will not cool down from applauding.

Of the overture you have no more than fourteen measures. It is very short and alternates continuously between forte and piano; the Turkish music comes in at the forte. It modulates on and on through the keys and, I believe, one will not be able to fall asleep to it, even if he has not slept for a whole night. Now here's the rub: the first act has been ready for more than three weeks; in the second act, the carousal duet, "per li signori vieneri,"[9] which consists of nothing but *my* Turkish tattoo, is already completed. But I cannot do any more since the whole story is being changed, and that on my request. At the beginning of the third act, there is a charming quintet or, better, a finale: I'd rather put it at the end of the second act. To accomplish this, a great change must be made; indeed, an entirely new plot has to be devised. And Stephani is up to his ears in work, so I must have a little patience. Everybody carps about Stephani, and it may be that he is friendly only when face to face with me. But, to be sure, he is arranging the libretto for me, and exactly as I want it. By God, I don't expect more of him! This, now, is gossip about the opera, but I cannot help it. Please send me the march I mentioned last time. Gylofsky[10] says that Daubrawaik[11] will come soon. Fräulein von Auerhammer[12] and I are anxiously awaiting the two dou-

8. "Hui" is an interjection meaning "whoosh," which Mozart considered more suited to scattering pigs. [BJB]

9. The duet "Vivat, Bacchus," when Pedrillo gets Osmin drunk; Mozart thought it would appeal to the Viennese. [BJB]

10. Franz Xaver Gilowsky (1757–1816), a friend of Mozart's, later a witness at his wedding. [BJB]

11. The court councillor Johann Baptist Anton Daubrawa (1731–1810). [BJB]

12. Josepha Barbara Auernhammer (1758–1820); Mozart taught her piano and dedicated to her his op. 2, six violin sonatas. [BJB]

ble concerti[13]—I hope we shall not wait as vainly as the Jews for the Messiah. Now, adieu, and farewell. I kiss your hands a thousand times, and my dear sister, whose health, I hope, has improved, I embrace with all my heart. I am forever your most obedient son,

W. A. Mozart

Vienne ce 13 d'Octobre
Mon très cher Père!   *1781*

Fräulein von Auerhammer and I thank you for the concerti. Yesterday, M. Marchal brought the young Herr von Mayern[14] up to my room, and in the afternoon I drove out and fetched my things. M. Marchal hopes to become steward to Count Jean Esterhatzy,[15] and Count Kobenzel[16] has given him a letter of recommendation. He said to me, "J'ai donné une lettre à Monsieur votre protégé," and when he spoke again to Marchal, he said to him, "D'abord que j'aurai de réponse, je le dirai à M. Mozart, votre protecteur."

Now about the text of the opera. As far as Stephani's work is concerned, you are surely right. Still, the poetry is quite suitable to the character of the stupid, crude, and malicious Osmin. And I am well aware that the verse is not of the best, but it corresponds so well to my musical thoughts, which have gone round and round in my head beforehand, that it could not fail to please me. And I would like to wager that no deficiency will be noticed at its performance. As for the remaining poetry of the piece, I wouldn't sell it short. Belmonte's aria, "O wie ängstlich," etc., could hardly have been written better for music. Except for the "hui" and "Kummer ruht in meinem Schoß" (for sorrow can't rest), the aria really isn't bad, especially the first part. Besides, in an opera the poetry simply has to be the obedient daughter of the music. Why are the Italian comic operas, in spite of their miserable librettos, so successful everywhere, even in Paris, where I witnessed it myself? Because music reigns supreme, and everything else is forgotten. An opera must please all the more if the plot has been worked out well and the words have been written for the music, and not stuck in to obtain some miserable rhyme here and there—or even entire strophes that ruin the composer's idea—

13. K. 365 (316a) and Mozart's arrangement of K. 242. [BJB]

14. Probably Johann Baptist Mayr (1764–1819); his companion has not been identified. [BJB]

15. Count Johann Nepomuk Esterházy (1754–1840), a very active member of the Wiener Gesellschaft für Musikfreunde. [BJB]

16. Count Johann Philipp Cobenzl (1741–1810); from 1779 he was *Vize-Hof- und Staatskanzler.* Mozart frequently visited his country house in the summer of 1781. [BJB]

which, by God, do not contribute anything to improve the quality of a theater performance but rather harm it, no matter what it may be. Music cannot do without verse, but rhyme for the sake of rhyme is the worst of all. Those gentlemen who proceed so pedantically will always fail together with the music.

It is best if a good composer, who understands the theater and is able to make suggestions, and a clever poet, as a true phoenix, come together. Then one doesn't need to fear the applause of the ignorant. Poets always remind me of trumpeters with their professional antics! If we composers were to follow the rules so closely—which once were acceptable, when one didn't know any better—we would produce music just as useless as the librettos they produce. Now I think I have rattled on about enough foolish stuff; now I must inquire about the matter I am most interested in, dear Father, namely, your health. In my last letter I recommended two remedies for dizziness, which may appear useless to you if you don't know them. I have been assured, however, that they surely would bring about relief, and the prospect of knowing you healthy made the assurance believable and certain to me. Thus I couldn't possibly refrain from heartily suggesting them to you, with the utmost hope that you won't need them or, in the worst case, that they may contribute to your full recovery. My sister, I hope, will continue to recover. I kiss her with all my heart, and your hands, dearest and best Father, a thousand times, always your most obedient son

W. A. Mozart

As soon as I have received the watch, I shall give yours back. Adieu.

From *Mozart, Briefe und Aufzeichnungen: Gesamtausgabe,* ed. Wilhelm A. Bauer and Otto Erich Deutsch, vol. 3 (Kassel: Bärenreiter, 1963), 112–14, 161–64, 166–68. Most of the notes are drawn from this edition.

Biographical Dictionary

This dictionary provides brief identifications of seventeenth- and eighteenth-century authors, composers, and musicians who have not been annotated in the text. For the most part it includes persons mentioned more than once, as well as authors of the excerpts.

ADDISON, JOSEPH (1672–1719). English essayist, poet, and dramatist, best known for his contributions to the journals *Tatler* and *Spectator*. Having spent four years on the Continent, he became greatly interested in opera and, desirous of seeing England develop an opera of her own, he wrote a libretto, *Rosamond,* set to music by Thomas Clayton (1707); the project failed on musical grounds (according to Burney, Addison "never manifested a greater want of taste and intelligence in Music than when he employed Clayton to set his opera of Rosamond"). In addition to his literary pursuits, he held various political offices, becoming Secretary of State in 1717. His essay on the absurdities of the staging of Handel's *Rinaldo* (1711) is excerpted in Ch. 8.

AGOSTINI, PIETRO SIMONE (ca. 1635–80). Italian composer. Active in Genoa and Rome, in between intrigues and military adventures he composed operas, cantatas, and some sacred works. Tosi admired his cantatas, linking him with Stradella (*Opinioni de' cantori,* 1723).

ALBINONI, TOMASO GIOVANNI (1671–1751). Italian composer. Independent financially, he held no fixed position but devoted himself to composing, producing over forty-eight operas besides sacred music, cantatas, and instrumental music. His operas were performed throughout Italy, and in 1722 he was commissioned to write one for a wedding in Munich. Adaptations and pasticcios of his operas had great success in London and Hamburg.

ALEMBERT, JEAN LE ROND D' (1717–83). French philosopher and mathematician. He wrote the *Discours préliminaire* to Diderot's *Encyclopédie,* summarizing and classifying the arts and sciences and showing the progress of knowledge; he also contributed numerous articles on mathematics. His interests were wide-ranging and included both literary criticism and music theory. In the latter field, in addition to some thirty articles for the *Encyclopédie* (some in collaboration), his simplification and explanation of the theories of Rameau, *Elémens de musique, théorique et pratique, suivant les principes de M. Rameau* (1752) became a standard work; in 1757 it came out in a German translation by Friedrich Wilhelm Marpurg. The present anthology contains excerpts from his *De la liberté de la musique* (1781) (Ch. 2).

ALFIERI, VITTORIO (1749–1803). Italian poet and dramatist. The weight of his literary output lies in his tragedies, which he sought to imbue with a strong moral tone. His attempt at fusing opera with tragedy in a new genre he labeled "tramelogedy," exemplified in his *Abele* (excerpts from the preface are given in Ch. 5), was unsuccessful, and he abandoned the five other tramelogedies he had planned.

ALGAROTTI, FRANCESCO (1712–64). Italian man of letters and writer. He traveled widely and corresponded with the major literary figures of the day, notably Voltaire and Metastasio. Talented as a popularizer of knowledge, he published works on architecture, painting, and music, and even wrote a book on "Newtonism for ladies." During his residence in Berlin (in the service of Frederick the Great) and Dresden (as adviser to Augustus III, Elector of Saxony and King of Poland) he became involved in opera productions, rewriting Italian librettos. His *Saggio sopra l'opera in musica* (1755), a widely read work that was translated into English, German, French, and Spanish, is excerpted in Ch. 5.

ARTEAGA, ESTEBAN DE (STEFANO ARTEAGA) (1747–99). Spanish writer on aesthetics and music. Forced to leave Spain in 1767 upon the expulsion of the Jesuits, he came to Italy, left the Order, and studied at the University of Bologna (1773–78). His musical interests were furthered by Padre Martini's library and led to his three-volume history of Italian opera, *Le rivoluzioni del teatro musicale italiano dalla sua origine fino al presente* (1783–88; 2d enlarged ed., 1785), excerpts from which are given in Ch. 9.

AUGUSTINI. *See* Agostini

AVISON, CHARLES (1709–70). English composer, organist, and writer on music. His *Essay on Musical Expression* (1752), the first example of English music criticism (and therefore controversial, provoking numerous responses), treats the relation of music to emotions, contemporary composers and their styles (in which he championed Geminiani, with whom he had studied, and Marcello, whose *Estro poetico-armonico* he edited), and instrumental performance. Two excerpts are included in Ch. 7.

BACH, CARL PHILIPP EMANUEL (1714–88). The most famous of Bach's sons, he was a composer, keyboard player, and theorist. University-educated, he was at home in the literary as well as the musical world; he spent the major part of his career first in the service of Frederick the Great, then succeeded Telemann as Kantor and music director in Hamburg. His widely influential book, *Versuch über die wahre Art das Clavier zu* *spielen* (1753–62), grew out of his experiences as accompanist to Frederick. In it he discusses ornamentation, continuo playing, accompaniment, and improvisation, with special attention to fingering. Excerpts are given in Ch. 6.

BACH, JOHANN SEBASTIAN (1685–1750). German composer and keyboard player. He was famed in his lifetime as a virtuoso keyboard player (see the remarks by Scheibe and Birnbaum in Ch. 6), but his posthumous fame rests on the strength and originality of his compositions, which influenced generations of composers.

BALDASSINI, ANTONIO LUIGI (b. ca. 1650). Italian violinist. He published sonatas for two violins and violone in Rome in the 1690s.

BARETTI, GIUSEPPE MARC'ANTONIO (1719–89). Italian critic. After his literary career in Italy ended in controversy, he came to England in 1751, where he assisted in Italian opera and taught Italian. He was a friend of Dr. Johnson, who acquainted him with English literature, and was well known in the literary circle of the Thrale family, whose eldest daughter he taught Italian—she was later to become Burney's pupil on the harpsichord. A prolific writer in English and Italian, he published two facetious pamphlets on opera in London (1753), but his best-known work is an Italian–English dictionary (1760). Upon returning to Italy for a period, he founded and edited in Venice the *Frusta letteraria* (1763–65), a satiric journal modeled on Addison's and Steele's *Spectator*. He was well placed to answer Samuel Sharp's criticism of Italian customs; an excerpt on opera appears in Ch. 4.

BASSANI, GIOVANNI BATTISTA (ca. 1657–1716). Italian composer, violinist, and organist. For much of his career he was associated with Ferrara, both at the Accademia della Morte and at the cathedral. In 1712 he became *maestro di cappella* at S. Maria Maggiore in Bergamo. Although he composed operas, oratorios, Masses, cantatas, and other liturgical and secular works, he was best known for his trio sonatas for strings; Burney admired him greatly as a violinist.

BEMETZRIEDER, ANTON (1743 or 1748–ca. 1817). French theorist and music teacher of Alsatian origin. He moved to Paris in 1770, where it was his good fortune to have Diderot's daughter as a pupil. Diderot attended her lessons and became so interested in the philosophical problems they raised that he encouraged Bemetzrieder to write a treatise, *Leçons de clavecin, et principes d'harmonie* (1771), in which philosophical conversations are included. Although Diderot disclaimed authorship (apart from the Preface), there can be no doubt that the work is a collaborative effort. (An excerpt is given in Ch. 7.) In 1781 Bemetzrieder moved to London, where he continued to teach and write pedagogical treatises. None show either the literary or the philosophical merits of his first, collaborative effort with Diderot.

BENEVOLI, ORAZIO (1605–72). Italian composer. He held posts in various Roman churches before becoming Kapellmeister to Archduke Leopold Wilhelm in Vienna in 1644, returning to Rome after two years. He specialized in sacred music for four choirs.

BIRNBAUM, JOHANN ABRAHAM (1702–48). German writer. He taught philosophy, rhetoric, and law at the University of Leipzig and was personally acquainted with Bach. His rejoinder to Scheibe's attack on Bach's keyboard style is excerpted in Ch. 6.

BONNET, JACQUES. *See* Bourdelot

BONONCINI, GIOVANNI (1670–1747). Italian composer and cellist. He studied in Bologna with Colonna, achieving the distinction at age fifteen of acceptance into the Accademia Filarmonica and publication of three books of instrumental music. A highly prolific composer, especially of vocal music, he was much admired throughout Europe; he lived and worked in Vienna, Berlin, Rome, London, Paris, and Lisbon. His opera *Il trionfo di Camilla* (1696) became a huge success (there were sixty-three performances in London from 1706 to 1709); its arias were much admired for their sensitive text setting and were praised for their expressive character.

BONTEMPI, GIOVANNI ANDREA ANGELINI (ca. 1625–1705). Italian composer, castrato singer, theorist, and historian. His reputation in the seventeenth century was as a singer and composer of opera (*Il Paride* of 1662 was the first Italian opera performed in Dresden; he had been in the service of the Elector of Saxony since 1650). In the eighteenth century he was remembered mainly as a theorist; he wrote a treatise on counterpoint and the first history of music in Italian, *Historia musica* (1695), more interesting for its remarks about contemporary practice than about the music of the ancients.

BOURDELOT. Three members of this family collaborated in preparing the earliest French history of music, *Histoire de la musique et de ses effets depuis son origine jusqu'à présent* (1715). It was begun by Pierre Bourdelot (1610–85), physician to Louis XIII and amateur music lover. Upon his death his nephew Pierre Bonnet-Bourdelot (1638–1708), also a royal physician, having inherited his uncle's library and papers, continued with the history. When he in turn died, his brother, Jacques Bonnet (1644–1724) took over the task of preparing the book for publication, making his own contribution. The historical part relies heavily on anecdotes gathered from secondary sources, but his remarks on the contemporary musical scene are valuable. Excerpts are given in Ch. 4. Jacques Bonnet also wrote an early history of dance and ballet, *Histoire générale de la danse* (1724).

BOUSSET, RENÉ DROUARD DE (1703–60). French composer and organist. He wrote *airs* and sacred cantatas and some instrumental music.

BROSSES, CHARLES DE (1709–77). French magistrate and writer. Intensely interested in Roman history, art, and archeology, he undertook a trip to Italy in 1739–40. His highly informative observations were recorded in a series of letters, published posthumously. Excerpts from one of these, on the habits of Italian theatergoers, are given in Ch. 4.

BROWN, JOHN (1715–66). English clergyman, writer, and amateur musician. In his *Dissertation on the Rise, Union, and Power, the Progressions, Separations, and Corruptions, of Poetry and Music* (1763) he systematically surveyed the development of music, dividing it into thirty-six hypothetical stages. He was particularly interested in the relation of music and poetry in primitive societies and deplored their separation (in the course of "a supposed civilization"), which extinguished music's moral force. Excerpts are given in Ch. 4.

BURANELLO. *See* Galuppi

BURNEY, CHARLES (1726–1814). English composer, organist, teacher, man of letters, and writer on music (it would not be unjust to call him a musicologist). His great *General History of Music from the Earliest Ages to the Present Period* (1776–89) was preceded by extended research trips to the Continent, where he met many musicians and heard much music; from his travel diaries he drew two books that have proved as interesting today as they were in his own time: *The Present State of Music in France and Italy: or the Journal of a Tour through those Countries, undertaken to collect Materials for a General History of Music* (1771) and *The Present State of Music in Germany, the Netherlands, and the United Provinces* (1773). The preface to his *History* is given in Ch. 4.

CAFARO, PASQUALE (1716–87). Italian composer. He spent his entire life in Naples, where he held various appointments in the royal chapel; many of his cantatas celebrate events in the royal family. Apart from a few operas, he concentrated on sacred music.

CALDARA, ANTONIO (ca. 1670–1736). Italian composer. A native of Venice, he was first choirboy, then cellist at St. Mark's; in 1699 he became *maestro di cappella* to the Duke of Mantua, and then moved to Rome in the service of Prince Ruspoli; in 1716 he became Fux's successor as Vice-Kapellmeister at the imperial court in Vienna, which required the composition of numerous occasional works. He was a prolific composer of oratorios and operas.

CALZABIGI, RANIERI DE' (1714–95). Italian writer and librettist. At first an admirer and later a severe critic of Metastasio, whose works he published in 1755 in Paris (where he lived from 1750 to ca. 1759), Calzabigi's major contribution was his collaboration with Gluck, challenging the Metastasian form of Italian serious opera; he wrote the librettos for *Orfeo ed Euridice*, *Alceste* (the preface to which is given in Ch. 10), and *Paride ed Elena*.

CAMPRA, ANDRÉ (1660–1744). French composer. He was regarded in his time (by Lecerf de la Viéville) as the foremost among the composers after Lully. He came to Paris in 1694, when he was appointed *maître de musique* at Notre-Dame; in view of this position, his first theatrical works were published anonymously. He invented the *opéra-ballet*, in which he combined (in his words) French "délicatesse" with Italian "vivacité"; its first example, *L'Europe galante* (1697), was an immediate success, and in 1700 he left Notre-Dame to be a conductor at the Opéra.

CARISSIMI, GIACOMO (1605–74). Italian composer. From 1629 to his death he was *maestro di cappella* at the Collegio Germanico in Rome. Now remembered chiefly for his oratorios and cantatas, Carissimi enjoyed a posthumous reputation in the eighteenth century, deriving from his influence on his German and French pupils (notably Charpentier); he was viewed favorably by the earlier writers (Bonnet called him "the greatest musician that Italy has produced") but distantly by others (de Brosses warned in 1739–40 that he was by then terribly old-fashioned). In England, too, his music was greatly admired, to the extent of being copied and reworked, by Handel and others.

CELANO. *See* Corsi

CESTI, ANTONIO (1623–69). Italian composer and singer. He was the outstanding composer of his generation, excelling in cantatas and operas, written for Venice, Innsbruck, and Vienna.

CHABANON, MICHEL-PAUL GUY DE (1729 or 1730–1792). French man of letters, librettist, and writer on music. Although he started out, and continued, as a violinist and composer, Chabanon's main interests were literary, both as a librettist and as an observer of the musical controversies besetting French opera. Excerpts from his *Observations sur la musique, et principalement sur la métaphysique de l'art* (1779) are given in Ch. 10.

CHARPENTIER, MARC-ANTOINE (1643–1704). French composer. He studied with Carissimi in Rome, bringing back an Italianate style that is especially evident in his numerous sacred works. He began collaborating with Molière after the quarrel with Lully and produced a fair number of works for the stage, but only a few operas. At the time of his death he held the prestigious post of *maître de musique* of the Sainte-Chapelle in Paris.

CLARI, GIOVANNI CARLO MARIA (1677–1754). Italian composer. After studying with Colonna in Bologna, where he became a member of the Accademia Filarmonica, he eventually was made *maestro di cappella* at Pistoia, returning to his native Pisa in 1724. Although he composed relatively little and seems never to have left Italy, his music (especially the chamber duets and trios for voice) was well known in England, and Handel thought well enough of it to use five of his duets in *Theodora* (1750).

COLLASSE, PASCAL (1649–1709). French composer. As Lully's secretary he was called upon to compose the inner voices of vocal works; he enjoyed the master's support in life but was denied the pension and house willed to him and then had to defend himself against charges of plagiarism. Only one of his operas was successful, *Thétis et Pélée* (1689).

COLONNA, GIOVANNI PAOLO (1637–95). Italian composer, organist, and teacher. After study in Rome, he spent most of his career in his native Bologna, first as organist, then as *maestro di cappella* in S. Petronio and other churches. Most of his music is sacred.

CORELLI, ARCANGELO (1653–1713). Italian composer, violinist, teacher, and director. He spent his entire career in Rome. His surprisingly small output, consisting mostly of solo sonatas, trio sonatas, and concertos, stands in marked contrast to the reputation he enjoyed throughout Europe as a virtuoso violinist ("the new Orpheus of our days," according to Angelo Berardi) and director. Most of his works were published during his lifetime, facilitating a flood of imitations.

CORNEILLE, PIERRE (1606–84). French dramatist; one of the greatest French writers for the theater, equally at home in comedy and tragedy. The alarming success of his *Cid* (1636) earned him the censure of the Académie for having disregarded the three unities. They were respected, though not unreasonably so, in his later tragedies, which are characterized by a grandeur of style matching the representation of heroic figures as they confront moral dilemmas. In his own works he was reluctant to accord music more than an incidental role, but his plays served as the basis of many later opera librettos.

CORSI, GIUSEPPE (also known as Celano, after his birthplace; d. after 1690). Italian composer. He was a pupil of Carissimi; like his master, he was a composer of motets and cantatas.

COUPERIN, FRANÇOIS (1668–1733). French composer, harpsichordist, and organist. The most illustrious member of a large family of musicians, and the major French figure between Lully and Rameau, he was named *organiste du roi* in 1693, becoming the king's harpsichordist in 1717. Although remembered chiefly for his many *pièces de clavecin*, he also composed organ music, sacred and secular vocal music, and chamber music.

CRÉBILLON, PROSPER JOLYOT DE (1674–1762). French dramatist. His tragedies, incorporating violent episodes and emphasizing the complications of love, were well regarded.

DAGINCOUR (DAGINCOURT, D'AGINCOURT), FRANÇOIS (1684–1758). French composer, organist, and harpsichordist. Most of his life was spent in Rouen. Little of his music is known apart from the *Pièces de clavecin* (1733), dedicated to the queen.

DESTOUCHES, ANDRÉ CARDINAL (1672–1749). French composer. He abandoned a career as a soldier to begin the study of music when he was in his early twenties, and achieved a notable success with *Issé*, a *pastorale-héroïque* (1697). After he was appointed inspector general of the Académie Royale de Musique in 1713 he largely relinquished composition in favor of administration; he was also *surintendant*, then *maître de musique de la chambre*, and organized concerts for Queen Maria Leszczyńska.

DIDEROT, DENIS (1713–84). French philosopher and writer. He devoted nearly twenty years of his life to the *Encyclopédie* (1747–66), the ideal undertaking for a man endowed with such great curiosity. His writings ranged from philosophy, religion, and natural science to aesthetics, art criticism, drama, and novels. An interest in music (both acoustics and aesthetics) runs throughout his works, and it was he who contributed the articles on musical instruments to the *Encyclopédie*. Excerpts from his *Additions à la Lettre sur les sourds et les muets* (1751) and his satiric novel *Le Neveu de Rameau* are included in Ch. 2, two passages from his *Principes généraux de la science du son* in Ch. 3, and an excerpt from a harmony lesson taught by Anton Bemetzrieder, from the *Leçons de clavecin et principes d'harmonie*, in Ch. 7.

DUBOS, JEAN-BAPTISTE (1670–1742). French diplomat, historian, and critic. Postings to Italy, Germany, England, and elsewhere widened his acquaintances (which included Locke) and his firsthand knowledge of the arts. He became a member of the Académie Française in 1720 and its secretary in 1723. His best-known work, which went through many editions and was translated into several languages, is the *Réflexions critiques sur la poésie, la peinture et la musique* (1719), one of the earliest considerations of musical aesthetics; an excerpt is given in Ch. 8.

DURANTE, FRANCESCO (1684–1755). Italian composer and teacher. In 1728 he became *primo maestro* at the Conservatorio dei Poveri di Gesù Cristo in Naples; his early years, as other periods of his life, are obscure, but he taught in other Neapolitan conservatories, and among his students were Pergolesi, Terradellas, Traetta, Sacchini, Piccinni, and Paisiello (to name only the composers mentioned in the present anthology). Exceptionally, he composed no operas; it was his church music that won him long-lasting international attention.

EULER, LEONHARD (1707–83). Swiss mathematician, scientist, and philosopher. He was one of the greatest mathematicians in all history. His early work on acoustics, *Dissertatio physica de sono*, set the foundation for his treatise on music, in which he laid down mathematical laws for the theory of consonance, *Tentamen novae theoriae musicae, ex certissimis harmoniae principii dilucidae expositae* (St. Petersburg, 1739), which also includes a theory of modulation. His musical theories were disseminated to a wider public in a series of letters written to a German princess, published in French in 1768 and translated into German and Italian.

EXIMENO Y PUJADES, ANTONIO (1729–1808). Spanish theorist. Expelled from Spain in 1767 for being a member of the Jesuit order, he went to Italy, where he began the study of music, for which he thought his mathematical background would ideally prepare him. His disillusion on that account and subsequent illumination on the true nature of music are set out in the preface to his *Dell'origine e delle regole della musica* (1774) (see Ch. 9). His argumentative nature embroiled him in controversies with the major writers of his day, notably Padre Martini, but he also criticized Tartini, Rameau, and Euler.

FOGGIA, FRANCESCO (1604–88). Italian composer. He spent the earlier part of his career in Germany and Austria, but from 1646 he was *maestro di cappella* successively in three Roman churches. He was considered the last successor of Palestrina, combining a contrapuntal style with continuo bass.

FONTENELLE, BERNARD LE BOVIER DE (1657–1757). French philosopher and poet. Having failed at drama (he was the nephew of Corneille), he found success as an essayist and popularizer of science. His perplexed remark on instrumental music— "Sonate, que me veux-tu?"—was taken almost as a rallying cry by those who could find no meaning in music without words.

FORKEL, JOHANN NIKOLAUS (1749–1818). German theorist, music historian, and bibliographer. In a lifelong association with the University of Göttingen, he was organist, concert master, and then music director. He also taught music theory. Accorded the status of *Magister* in 1787, he turned his attention to completing his *Allgemeine Geschichte der Musik*, the first volume of which was published in the following year (an excerpt is given in Ch. 4). His other major contributions were his *Allgemeine Litteratur der Musik* (1792), an annotated bibliography that was a model of its kind, and his biography of J. S. Bach, based on information from Bach's sons (1802).

FUX, JOHANN JOSEPH (ca. 1660–1741). Austrian composer and music theorist. He was court composer to three Habsburg emperors, from 1698 until his death. His main work was sacred music in contrapuntal style (both with and without instruments), for which he took Palestrina as his model. In 1725 he published a book that was to serve generations of students of counterpoint, *Gradus ad Parnassum*, a dialogue between "Aloysius" and "Josephus," thinly veiled references to the master Palestrina and the pupil Fux. (Excerpts are given in Ch. 3.)

GALUPPI, BALDASSARE (1706–85). Italian composer, conductor, and instrumentalist. Frequently referred to as Buranello, after his birthplace, the Venetian island Burano, he received his early training in Venice. Two years spent in London assured his success with English audiences, but it was after his return to Venice in 1743, when he took up *opera buffa* in conjunction with Goldoni, that he made his greatest contribution to the history of opera (Burney considered him second only to Jommelli).

GASPARINI, FRANCESCO (1661–1727). Italian composer and teacher. As *maestro di musica* at the Ospedale della Pietà in Venice (1701–13) he hired Vivaldi as violin master, bringing the conservatory a reputation as one of the finest. Gasparini composed numerous operas during this period. After 1713 he returned to Rome; for a period he was *maestro di cappella* to Prince Ruspoli. As a teacher he counted among his pupils Domenico Scarlatti, Quantz, and Benedetto Marcello, and gained international renown for his treatise on playing the harpsichord.

GEMINIANI, FRANCESCO (1687–1762). Italian violinist, composer, teacher, and theorist. A virtuoso violinist, he spent much of his career in England and Ireland. Much appreciated as a teacher, late in life he began publishing treatises, including *The Art of Playing on the Violin* (1751), written not for beginners but for advanced players, and especially valuable for its transmission of the Italian tradition of performance.

GLUCK, CHRISTOPH WILLIBALD (1714–87). Bohemian-Austrian composer. Little is known of the early part of his career; he seems to have been mostly self-taught. Only in 1741 in Milan did he start composing opera; with a libretto by Metastasio, *Artaserse* proved a highly successful debut. From then on Gluck devoted himself almost entirely to opera. His travels took him to London (where two operas were not particularly well received, his performance on musical glasses quite the contrary), Hamburg, Dresden, and finally to Vienna, though it was not until 1752 that he settled permanently there, having finally found a position as Konzertmeister, then Kapellmeister to the Prince of Saxe-Hildburghausen. In Vienna Gluck became involved with the French theater; his experiences with it paved the way for his so-called reform of opera. The revival of Italian opera in Vienna in 1760 led to Gluck's collaboration with the librettist Ranieri de' Calzabigi in *Orfeo ed Euridice* (1762), *Alceste* (1767), and *Paride ed Elena* (1770); the principles of their reform are stated in Calzabigi's Preface (signed by Gluck) to the printed score of *Alceste* (included in Ch. 10). In the last phase of his career Gluck moved to Paris (1773) with the idea of renewing French *tragédie lyrique;* his setting of *Iphigénie en Aulide,* based on Racine, was a great success and was followed by three more French operas, and a revision in French of *Orphée et Euridice* (1774) and *Alceste* (1776). The last two years of his French sojourn were marred by the disputes between his supporters and those of Piccinni. He returned to Vienna in 1779, where he hoped to compose a German opera, but ill health brought his career to an end.

GRASSI, FRANCESCO (fl. ca. 1700). Italian composer. He was *maestro di cappella* at S. Giacomo degli Spagnuoli in Rome and later at the Gesù and composed sacred music.

GRAVINA, GIAN VINCENZO (1664–1718). Italian jurist, dramatist, and critic. Although he held the chair of civil, and then canon, law at the Roman university La Sapienza and published numerous works on the law, both in Latin and Italian, he was most famous for his *Ragion poetica* (1708). In 1710 he adopted and educated the twelve-year-old Antonio Trapassi, who later took the name Pietro Metastasio. Excerpts from Gravina's *Della tragedia* (1715) are given in Ch. 1.

GRIMM, FRIEDRICH MELCHIOR, FREIHERR VON (1723–1807). German writer, critic, and diplomat, resident in Paris. With no training in music, he leapt into music criticism with an attack on Destouches' *Omphale,* revived in 1752. At first favorable to

Rameau, he turned against him under Rousseau's influence, satirizing French opera in his mock-biblical *Le Petit Prophète de Boehmischbroda* (excerpts are given in Ch. 2). He was initially hostile to Gluck's *Orfeo ed Euridice*, but liked the French version; nevertheless, he remained a firm italophile, siding with the Piccinnists in the 1770s. During Mozart's boyhood visit to Paris in 1763–64 Grimm's influence at court assured a favorable reception; but when the composer returned in 1778 Grimm proved instead to be a hindrance. Grimm contributed the article on "Poème lyrique" (libretto) to the *Encyclopédie*; excerpts are given in Ch. 2.

HASSE, JOHANN ADOLF (1699–1783). German composer; for fifty years at midcentury one of the most performed in Europe. His popularity in Italy led to his being called "il caro Sassone" (the dear Saxon—though he was from north Germany); he spent nearly a decade there, from 1722 to 1730. For much of the rest of his career he worked in Dresden, where he was Kapellmeister to the Elector of Saxony, but with frequent periods in Italy. In both places he composed and performed operas, many on librettos by Metastasio, but he also wrote church music and instrumental music. He passed his final active years in Vienna, writing his last opera, *Il Ruggiero*, when he was seventy-two. It was on a libretto by Metastasio (his last), whom Hasse supported against the proponents of Calzabigi's and Gluck's "reform" opera. Hasse retired to Venice, where he spent his last years composing church music and revising earlier works. His wife Faustina Bordoni, one of the most fêted sopranos of the 1720s and 1730s, sang in many of his works. Burney characterized Hasse as "the most natural, elegant, and judicious composer of vocal music, as well as the most voluminous now alive, equally a friend to poetry and the voice."

HAWKINS, JOHN (1719–89). English attorney, antiquarian, and historian of music. He became interested in music in his twenties, and was apparently an amateur violinist and cellist; membership in both the Academy of Ancient Music and the Madrigal Society indicate his interest in older music. Sixteen years of research preceded his *General History of the Science and Practice of Music* (1776) (the Conclusion is given in Ch. 4). The five volumes of this work appeared some seven months after Burney's first volume of his own *General History*; inevitably comparisons were made (largely instigated by Burney), Hawkins getting the worst of it on organization, style, and his antagonism to modern music. Yet the thoroughness of his research, especially in original sources, invites admiration, and his book can still be read with profit—and surprise (according to Tassoni's *Dieci libri di pensieri* of 1620, the sweetness of Gesualdo's compositions is due to his imitation and improvement of "that melancholy and plaintive kind of air which distinguishes the Scots melodies").

JOMMELLI, NICCOLÒ (1714–74). Italian composer. He was one of the most influential Italian opera composers of the eighteenth century. After studying in Naples, he worked in Bologna, Venice, and Rome before accepting a position at Stuttgart in 1753, becoming Ober-Kapellmeister to the Duke of Württemberg. Here he built up the orchestra, which played an increasing role in his operas. He heightened dramatic effectiveness by using obbligato instruments in his recitatives and freeing the aria from its da capo restraints; he also gave greater prominence to ensembles and choruses. With his last operas, written after his return to Naples in 1769, his attempts to introduce this style into Italy largely failed.

LA HARPE, JEAN-FRANÇOIS DE (1739–1803). French dramatist and critic. He was literary critic of the *Mercure de France*. He joined Marmontel in supporting Italian composers against Gluck. In 1786 he opened a Lycée on the rue Saint-Honoré, at which he offered a course in literature to the public; the success of this enterprise led to the publication of the first work to survey the history of literature, *Lycée, ou Cours de littérature ancienne et moderne*, published in seventeen volumes between 1799 and 1805. Three excerpts are included in Ch. 10.

LALANDE, MICHEL-RICHARD DE (DELALANDE) (1657–1726). French composer, organist, and harpsichordist. By 1729 he had reached the rank of *surintendant* of the king's music, and composer of the royal chapel and chamber. Though he wrote instrumental music and works for the stage (ballets, divertissements, and pastorales), he is most remembered for his imposing *grands motets*.

LAMOTTE (LA MOTTE), ANTOINE HOUDAR DE (1672–1731). French dramatist, librettist, and poet. He found immediate success with his first libretto, for Campra's *L'Europe galante* (1697), and became much in demand. After election in 1710 to the Académie Française he turned to weightier matters. He entered the quarrel between the ancients and the moderns on the latter side, producing a version of the *Iliad* arranged for contemporary taste.

LECERF (LE CERF) DE LA VIÉVILLE, JEAN-LAURENT, SEIGNEUR DE FRE-NEUSE (1674–1707). French author and poet. He is best known as a defender of the French style of Lully, set forth in his reply to François Raguenet's claims for the superiority of Italian music. Excerpts from his *Comparaison de la musique italienne et de la musique française* (1704–6) are given in Ch. 2.

LECLAIR, JEAN-MARIE (L'AÎNÉ) (1697–1764). French composer, violinist, and dancer. He made his career in France and the Netherlands, serving royal patrons. Having studied in Italy, he could play equally well in both French and Italian styles, and sought to combine the two in his compositions. Most of his music for the theater is lost.

LEGRENZI, GIOVANNI (1626–90). Italian composer and organist. Beginning as an organist in Bergamo, he culminated his career in the position of *maestro di cappella* at St. Mark's in Venice. He is one of the major figures in the development of the late Baroque style, explored in opera, sacred music, and instrumental music.

LEO, LEONARDO (1694–1744). Italian composer and teacher. He wrote his first opera at the age of nineteen in Naples, where he spent his whole career. After Hasse's departure and the death of Vinci Leo became the foremost composer in Naples, with a particular gift for comic opera, often in Neapolitan dialect. He taught Piccinni and Jommelli. He also composed much sacred music, which influenced his secular music in its use of contrapuntal writing.

LOCATELLI, PIETRO ANTONIO (1695–1764). Italian composer and violinist. His reputation as a virtuoso violinist had spread northward by the time he settled in Amsterdam in 1729, where he spent the rest of his life, teaching and conducting an orchestra. The reaction to both his music and his playing was quite mixed.

LOTTI, ANTONIO (ca. 1667–1740). Italian composer and teacher. A pupil of Legrenzi at St. Mark's in Venice, he too ended his career as *maestro di cappella* there, having taught Bassani and Galuppi. He also taught music at the Venetian Ospedale degli Incurabili, writing sacred works for its female choir. Composing at a time of stylistic change, he adapted his contrapuntal style without difficulty to neoclassical taste.

LULLY, JEAN-BAPTISTE (1632–87). French composer of Italian origin; also a dancer, violinist, and instrumentalist. He was the central figure in France in his own century and the reference point for many of the debates on opera in the following century. His *ballets de cour*, written in the earlier part of his career, and the *comédies-ballets* of the middle period culminated in the *tragédies lyriques*, the first true French operas, which he developed in a fruitful collaboration with his main librettist, Quinault.

MANFREDINI, VINCENZO (1737–99). Italian theorist and composer. He spent the years 1758–69 in Russia, where in 1762 he became *maestro di cappella* of the emperor's Italian opera company, later serving under Catherine II. Eclipsed by Galuppi, he returned to Italy and concentrated on composing instrumental music and writing treatises. He became embroiled with Arteaga over the latter's *Le rivoluzioni del teatro musicale italiano* (1783), publishing his *Difesa della musica moderna* in response in 1788. An excerpt is given in Ch. 9.

MARCELLO, BENEDETTO (1686–1739). Italian composer, writer, and teacher. A member of a Venetian patrician family, he studied law and held a number of administrative positions. At the same time he continued his musical and literary interests; he was a member of the Accademia Filarmonica in Bologna and the Roman Arcadia. He started publishing his own music in 1708, winning international acclaim with his *Estro poetico-armonico* (1724–26), settings of Italian psalm paraphrases. His biting satire *Il teatro alla moda* (1720) had not lost its relevance by the time of its last edition in 1761. An excerpt is given in Ch. 1.

MARMONTEL, JEAN-FRANÇOIS (1723–99). French librettist, writer, and man of letters. He directed the *Mercure de France* from 1758 to 1760. A member of the Académie Française from 1763, he became permanent secretary in 1783, succeeding d'Alembert. He contributed several articles to the *Encyclopédie*, including those on criticism and on declamation. His attack on Gluck and championship of Piccinni and Italian melody, *Essai sur les révolutions de la musique en France* (1777), became a focal point of the *querelle;* excerpts are given in Ch. 10.

MARPURG, FRIEDRICH WILHELM (1718–95). German writer, composer, and theorist. Although he composed keyboard and vocal music, his main work was as editor and author of didactic works on keyboard, thoroughbass, and composition, as well as an important study of fugal technique illustrated in many works of his contemporaries, including Bach. He also edited three different journals, to which he was the main contributor. An excerpt from his *Anleitung zum Klavierspielen* (1753–62) is given in Ch. 6.

MARTELLO, PIER JACOPO (1665–1727). Italian poet, librettist, and writer. He was one of the founders of the Bologna branch of the Arcadia. A visit to Paris in 1713, where he met the leading French men of letters, led to his *Della tragedia antica e moderna* (1715); an excerpt is given in Ch. 1.

MARTINI, GIOVANNI BATTISTA (1706–84). Italian historian of music, teacher, and composer, known as "Padre Martini." A man of wide-ranging interests and an inquiring mind, he made equally important contributions to the history of music (*Storia della musica,* 3 vols., 1761–81; it remained incomplete, never reaching beyond Greek music) and the theory and practice of counterpoint (*Esemplare ossia saggio fondamentale pratico di contrappunto sopra il canto fermo,* 1774–75). He had many famous pupils, whom he prepared for admission to the Accademia Filarmonica in Bologna (including Mozart, J. C. Bach, Jommelli, and Grétry). With the aid of his many correspondents in Italy and abroad he collected a splendid library of some 17,000 volumes (now the basis of the Civico Museo Bibliografico Musicale in Bologna). He was also a prolific composer, with a particular fascination for canonic writing.

MATTEI, SAVERIO (1742–95). Italian man of letters and librettist, author of biographies of Jommelli and Metastasio. His most famous work was a translation of the Psalms into Italian verse, some of which were set to music. His proposals for the reform of opera appear in *La filosofia della musica o sia la riforma del teatro. Dissertazione* (1781, in the third volume of Metastasio's *Opere*). A letter written to him by Metastasio is given in Ch. 5.

MATTHESON, JOHANN (1681–1764). German composer, writer on music, and theorist. In his youth a musical prodigy, both as singer and keyboard player, he turned to scholarly pursuits in connection with his duties as secretary to the English ambassador to Hamburg, while at the same time composing and conducting at the cathedral and court. After he became totally deaf in 1735 he produced his most famous books, which cover the breadth of eighteenth-century German music in a highly informative and original way. In particular, he codified the doctrine of affections, set forth the principles and art of thoroughbass and improvisation, and made a lexicon of 149 famous musicians. Excerpts from *Der vollkommene Capellmeister* (1739) are given in Chs. 6 and 7, and from *Die neueste Untersuchung der Singspiele* (1744) in Ch. 6.

MELANI, ALESSANDRO (1639–1703). Italian composer. He spent the earlier part of his career mainly in Pistoia. In 1667 he became *maestro di cappella* at S. Maria Maggiore in Rome, then at S. Luigi dei Francesi. In addition to sacred music, he contributed to the second Roman school of opera, writing the first opera to take Don Juan as subject, *L'empio punito* (1669).

METASTASIO, PIETRO (1698–1782). Italian poet and librettist; probably the single most influential figure in the history of eighteenth-century Italian opera. His real name was Antonio Trapassi; he was adopted as a child by Gian Vincenzo Gravina, who hellenized his name, educated him, and made him his heir. Metastasio wrote his first original opera libretto, *Didone abbandonata*, in 1724, and soon afterwards his works were in great demand throughout Italy and all of Europe. In 1730 he succeeded Apostolo Zeno as poet laureate at the Austrian court; much of his work thereafter was commissioned for special events at court in Vienna. His thorough knowledge of the conventions of Italian *opera seria*, which his librettos were largely responsible for shaping, and the melodious quality of his verse assured his success. For more than a century nearly all of his twenty-seven opera librettos were set many times by over 300 composers.

MILIZIA, FRANCESCO (1725–98). Italian architect and writer. Author of numerous works on architecture and the fine arts, he also translated works on natural history and mathematics. An excerpt from his *Trattato completo, formale e materiale del teatro* (1794) is given in Ch. 5.

MOURET, JEAN-JOSEPH (1682–1738). French composer. Beginning as a singer, he rose to music director of various courts and institutions, including the Paris Opéra from 1714 to 1718. He spent his last twenty years as composer-director of the Comédie-Italienne. In addition, he composed for and directed the Concert Spirituel from 1728 to 1734. Writing in the generation between Lully and Rameau, Mouret was particularly successful with comic elements and lifelike characters.

MOZART, LEOPOLD (1719–87). German composer, violinist, and theorist. At the age of thirty-seven (the year of Wolfgang's birth) he published the work that was to establish his international reputation, *Versuch einer gründlichen Violinschule* (1756), an excerpt from which is given in Ch. 6. Within four years he had given up composing and teaching, carrying out the minimum of his duties as composer to the court and chamber at Salzburg, to devote himself to the artistic education of the "miracle."

MOZART, WOLFGANG AMADEUS (1756–91). Austrian composer. A child prodigy, carefully nurtured by his father Leopold, he grew into one of the most celebrated and beloved composers of all time, excelling in every genre he touched. Three of his letters to his father, discussing the composition of the opera *Die Entführung aus dem Serail*, are given in Ch. 10.

MURATORI, LUDOVICO ANTONIO (1672–1750). Italian historian and writer. A man of immense industry and wide-ranging interests, pursued as librarian of the Duke of Modena, he is chiefly remembered for the great series *Rerum italicarum scriptores* (1723–51), a collection of sources on the history of Italy, *Antiquitates italicae medii aevi* on sources of the Middle Ages, and *Annali d'Italia*, the first complete history of Italy. He also wrote on medicine, law, liturgy, inscriptions, poetics, and many other subjects. An excerpt from his *Della perfetta poesia italiana* (1715) is given in Ch. 1.

NEWTON, ISAAC (1642–1727). English scientist and mathematician, author of the law of gravitation. Although he was interested in practical and theoretical music in his youth, especially Greek music, his studies remained in manuscript; his contemporaries knew only his analogy between the colors of the spectrum and just intonation.

NICOLINI (NICOLO [NICOLA] GRIMALDI) (1673–1732). Italian alto castrato. One of the most famous castrato singers, he made his early career in Naples, but was soon in demand in Rome, Bologna, and Venice. In 1708 he went to England, where he was lionized, ensuring the popularity of Italian opera in London. He was equally praised for his acting ability.

PAISIELLO, GIOVANNI (1740–1816). Italian composer; one of the most influential opera composers of the late eighteenth century. Trained at the Conservatorio di S. Onofrio in Naples, he began his career with operas for Bologna, Modena, Venice, and Parma in 1764–65. His reputation soon reached Russia, and in 1776 he accepted the invitation to become *maestro di cappella* to Catherine II, remaining in St. Petersburg until 1784, when he returned to Naples to serve the king. Personally invited to France by Napoleon, Paisiello spent two years in Paris (1802–4), but returned to Naples as director of music to Joseph Napoleon Bonaparte. He wrote over eighty operas, of which the comic ones such as *Il barbiere di Siviglia* were the most popular, as well as in his last years a considerable amount of sacred music.

PEREZ, DAVID (1711–78). Italian composer. Trained in Naples, he served in Palermo and Naples at the beginning of his career. With the success of his operas in Genoa, Florence, and Naples, he was called to Lisbon in 1752, and spent the remainder of his life as *maestro di cappella* to the king of Portugal. Perez was considered one of the great mid-eighteenth-century composers of *opera seria*, ranked with Hasse and Jommelli.

PERGOLESI, GIOVANNI BATTISTA (1710–36). Italian composer. Between the time he left the conservatory in Naples in 1731 and his death five years later he composed an astonishing amount of music, sacred and secular (if genuine; problems of attribution abound), but his posthumous fame rests on the impact his *Serva padrona* made on Parisian audiences in 1752, where it sparked the *querelle des Bouffons* and became the rallying cry of the progressives, led by Jean-Jacques Rousseau. His last work, the *Stabat mater*, was equally famous.

PERRAULT. The two brothers Charles (1628–1703) and Claude (1613–88) were instrumental in securing the establishment of French opera. Charles, a noted author remembered today for his tales such as *La Belle au bois dormant* (The Sleeping Beauty), promoted Lully and Quinault. He published his defense of modern French music in *Parallèle . . . des anciens et des modernes* (1688–97). Claude, a polymath, wrote some of the first scientific studies of acoustics. He supported his brother in defending the richness of modern music over the simplicity of ancient Greek music, as well as the emerging form of opera.

PERTI, GIACOMO ANTONIO (1661–1756). Italian composer. At the age of thirty-five he became *maestro di cappella* at San Petronio in Bologna, a position he held for sixty years. His many sacred works are balanced by a fair number of operas, most no longer extant.

PICCINNI, NICCOLÒ (1728–1800). Italian composer; a central figure in Italian and French opera in the second half of the eighteenth century. He had early success with comic opera in Naples, and became the darling of Roman opera in the years 1758–73. Burney, who easily believed Sacchini's assertion that Piccinni had written 300 operas (a more sober estimate is 130), called him "full of fire and genius." His most famous work, *La buona figliuola*, is from this fertile period. After the Roman public turned against him, he accepted an invitation to France, where he found himself embroiled in the controversy over Gluck's renewal of French opera; supported by Marmontel, who adapted librettos for him, he succeeded with the public, fusing French forms with Italian style.

PISTOCCHI (PISTOCCO), FRANCESCO (1659–1726). Italian composer, castrato singer, and teacher. He was much in demand for his contralto voice, both in Italy and Germany. In later years, living in Bologna, he was sought out as a teacher; one of his pupils was Giovanni Battista Martini.

PITONI, GIUSEPPE OTTAVIO (1657–1743). Italian composer and writer on music. Active at many churches in Rome, he was particularly known for his polychoral music, in which he carried on the Palestrina style, infusing it with modern stylistic elements. He also collected biographical notices on earlier musicians that are still useful.

PLANELLI, ANTONIO (1747–1803). Italian writer. An early interest in chemistry gave way to literary studies. Two excerpts from his *Dell'opera in musica* (1772) are given in Ch. 5.

PLUCHE, NOËL-ANTOINE (1668–1761). French writer. A professor of humanities, then of rhetoric at Reims, he was forced to leave his post because of Jansenist sympathies. In Rouen he taught physics to the son of Lord Stafford, which led to his best-known work, *Le Spectacle de la nature,* published in nine volumes between 1732 and 1750. Two excerpts are given in Ch. 2.

POLLAROLO (POLLAROLI), CARLO FRANCESCO (ca. 1653–1723). Italian composer and organist. He had already made a career as an opera composer in Brescia before becoming second organist at St. Mark's in Venice in 1690; by 1692 he was *vicemaestro di cappella.* A steady stream of operas ensued; he wrote some 85 altogether. He was also musical director of the Ospedale degl'Incurabili, the Venetian conservatory.

PORPORA, NICOLA (1686–1768). Italian composer and teacher. He studied at the Conservatorio dei Poveri di Gesù Cristo in Naples until about 1706, when he embarked on a career that was to make him notable connections and bring international fame: he set texts by the young Metastasio and was the teacher of the castratos Farinelli and Caffarelli, and briefly of Johann Adolf Hasse; later in life, in Vienna, Haydn was his valet and pupil. From 1733 to 1736 Porpora composed for the Opera of the Nobility in London, set up to rival Handel. In a long and restless career he produced both secular and sacred operas, cantatas, oratorios, and a small number of instrumental works.

QUANTZ, JOHANN JOACHIM (1697–1773). German flutist, composer, and writer on music. He began as an oboist, but switched to transverse flute, absorbing much of his style from a violinist friend. A European tour from 1724 to 1727 took him to Italy, France, and England, which ensured his reputation and a market for his compositions. Having tutored the Prussian Crown Prince on the flute, he joined Frederick's service when he became king in 1740. Quantz's comprehensive *Versuch einer Anweisung die Flöte traversiere zu spielen* (1752) is addressed not only to flutists; it considers performance practice and includes a survey of current styles. Excerpts are given in Chs. 6 and 7.

QUINAULT, PHILIPPE (1635–88). French dramatist, librettist, and poet. In his early years he studied literature and law. He found success as a poet in 1668, and became a member of the Académie Française in 1670. In 1668 he began collaborating with Lully, an association that would last eighteen years. Their first pastorale was *Les Fêtes de l'Amour et de Bacchus* (1672); it was followed by two ballets and eleven *tragédies lyriques.* Quinault drew on mythological and chivalric themes, with episodes of the marvelous as well as dance interspersed, and set the course of French opera for well over a hundred years.

RACINE, JEAN (1639–99). French poet and dramatist. His early works were occasional ones for court, where he found Louis XIV's favor. He achieved greatest renown with the ten tragedies, distinguished by their supple verse and psychological depth, that he wrote in the space of ten years, eclipsing Corneille's fame. After *Phèdre* (1677) Racine retired to become the king's historiographer. Though an attempt to produce a libretto for Lully in 1674 failed (Louis commanded Lully to work with Quinault instead), in 1685 they collaborated in *L'Idylle sur la paix.* Later Racine wrote two more tragedies, *Esther* (1689) and

Athalie (1691), set to music by Moreau, who showed respect for Racine's intention with music of reserved simplicity and clarity of text setting.

RAGUENET, FRANÇOIS (ca. 1660–1722). French man of letters. His wide interests comprised theology and history. His interest in music, deriving from his experiences with Roman opera during a visit in 1697, led him to write his *Paralèle des italiens et des français* (1702); intended to be objective on the virtues of the two styles, it aroused a storm of protest on the part of Lecerf de la Viéville and a pamphlet war ensued. An excerpt is given in Ch. 2.

RAMEAU, JEAN-PHILIPPE (1683–1764). French composer and theorist. He spent his early years as an organist, mostly in Clermont Cathedral. His theoretical bent was soon evident with the publication in 1722 of his *Traité de l'harmonie*, in which he developed a new theory of harmony, based on the fundamental sound, from which he derived the notion of harmonic generation, the fundamental bass, and harmonic inversion. An excerpt is given in Ch. 3. After his move to Paris Rameau began writing vocal music; he produced his first opera, *Hippolyte et Aricie*, at the age of fifty. Many dramatic works followed, including comic opera and *opéras-ballets*, but Rameau thought his theoretical work more important, engaging in polemics when it was criticized. An excerpt from his late work, *Observations sur notre instinct pour la musique et sur son principe* (1754) also appears in Ch. 3.

ROSSI, LUIGI (ca. 1597–1653). Italian composer. He was the leading Italian composer in Rome by 1640, especially appreciated for his chamber cantatas and operas. His fame in France dates from the performance of his *Orfeo* at the French court in 1647.

ROUSSEAU, JEAN-JACQUES (1712–78). Swiss philosopher, writer, and composer. Rousseau's ideas on music, exalting the natural over the artificial, prizing melody over harmony as closer to human emotions, derive from his philosophical notions in general, in which civilization is seen as a corrupting influence, stifling freedom and equality and removing man from his natural state. He had already attempted composition, including opera, before he discovered Italian opera (and other music) while he was secretary to the French ambassador in Venice in 1743–44; it was a turning point in his musical experiences and laid the foundation for what was to become a crusade to revolutionize French music. With *Le Devin du village* (1752), modeled on Pergolesi's *La serva padrona*, Rousseau succeeded in showing that the French language could be reconciled with Italian melody. He followed this with his *Lettre sur la musique française* (1753), a wounding attack on French opera and a manifesto of the pro-Italian side of the *querelle des Bouffons*. He wrote a number of other occasional pieces on music, often expressed in letters, and is the author of an idiosyncratic *Dictionnaire de musique* (1768). Excerpts from his *Essai sur l'origine des langues* are given in Ch. 2.

SACCHINI, ANTONIO (1730–86). Italian composer and teacher. Early success in Naples led him to abandon the conservatory where he was teaching to make a career as an opera composer in Rome and northern Italy. He settled in Venice in 1768 as musical director of the Conservatorio dell'Ospedaletto, where he gained a reputation as a vocal teacher. From 1772 to 1781 he worked in London, where his operas impressed Burney—not so his dissolute lifestyle, which forced him to flee to France to escape his creditors. In Paris he was enlisted by the Piccinnists and caught in the cross fire. His French operas had mixed success, with the exception of *Œdipe*, performed in the year after his death, which remained in the repertory until 1830.

SCARLATTI, ALESSANDRO (1660–1725). Italian composer. He spent his formative years in Rome, where his first opera, *Gli equivoci nel sembiante* (1679) was a huge success. Throughout his career, which was divided between Rome and Naples, he enjoyed princely patronage, and he amply rewarded his protectors with a steady stream of operas, serenatas, oratorios, and several hundred cantatas.

SCARLATTI, DOMENICO (1685–1757). Italian composer, keyboard player, and teacher, son of Alessandro. Little is known of his early career, spent mostly in Rome, where he concentrated on vocal music, including opera. By 1719 he had left for Portugal; in Lisbon he taught the king's daughter Maria Barbara harpsichord, and moved to Spain when she married the Spanish crown prince Fernando in 1728. For the remainder of his career Scarlatti lived in Madrid, where he composed his best-known works, over 500 keyboard sonatas.

SCHEIBE, JOHANN ADOLF (1708–76). German composer, writer on music, and theorist. Although his father was an organ builder, Scheibe decided to take up music at a rather late stage, after university study in law. Failing to obtain a position as an organist, he turned to composition and to criticism, founding the journal *Der critische Musikus* in 1737. A slighting notice on Bach's keyboard style (see Ch. 6) elicited lively rejoinders that clarify Scheibe's aesthetic position, influenced by Enlightenment philosophers, in which he emphasized natural simplicity and good taste. He spent the years from 1740 to his death in Denmark.

SHARP, SAMUEL (?1700–78). English surgeon. He spent part of his apprenticeship in France, where he met Voltaire. Apart from his *Letters from Italy,* deriving from his tour in 1765–66, all his other books are medical, including *A Treatise on the Operations of Surgery* (1739), which went through many editions. Excerpts from his letters on opera in Naples in November and December 1765 appear in Ch. 4.

STRADELLA, ALESSANDRO (1639–82). Italian composer. Of an aristocratic family, he wrote many of his works on commission, principally for noble patrons (leaving time for intrigues of various sorts—his life was, literally, the stuff of opera plots). He composed many cantatas and considerable stage music; his instrumental music is notable for the early use of concerto grosso instrumentation.

SULZER, JOHANN GEORG (1720–79). Swiss mathematician and aesthetician. He was editor of the *Allgemeine Theorie der schönen Künsten* (Leipzig, 1771–72 and subsequent editions), an encyclopedia of the arts; the articles on music were written by Johann Philipp Kirnberger and J. A. P. Schulz.

TARTINI, GIUSEPPE (1692–1770). Italian composer, violinist, theorist, and teacher. An early marriage (1710) relieved him of studies for the priesthood, allowing him to take up music seriously; after hearing Veracini play, he polished his own technique to the point that he was hired as first violinist at Il Santo in Padua in 1721. Except for the years 1723–26, spent in Prague, he worked in Padua, where he had many pupils. Various versions of his treatise on the violin exist, one of which was published in French in 1771. Tartini set great store on his speculative works; having discovered the phenomenon of the difference tone ("terzo suono"), he built a whole musical system around it, set forth in his *Trattato di musica secondo la vera scienza dell'armonia* (1754). His ideas proved controversial, and he was moved to defend himself in several publications. The preface to his *De' principi dell'armonia musicale contenuta nel diatonico genere* (1767) appears in Ch. 3.

TERRADELLAS, DOMÈNECH (DOMINGO) (1713–51). Spanish composer. After studying in Naples he achieved great success with his *Merope* in Rome in 1743. He wrote two operas in London in 1746–47 and visited Paris thereafter; Rousseau reports on a conversation with him.

TORELLI, GIUSEPPE (1658–1709). Italian composer. He was hired as a violinist at San Petronio in Bologna in 1686, where he remained with the exception of four years in Germany and Vienna. He wrote many sonatas, sinfonie, and concertos, and enlarged the repertory of trumpet music.

TRAETTA, TOMMASO (1727–79). Italian composer. Like many Italian opera composers, he began his career in Naples, where he studied with Porpora and Durante. In 1758 he moved to Parma, where he undertook a setting, translated and adapted, of the libretto of Rameau's *Hippolyte et Aricie*, with a view to integrating French and Italian styles; he used some of Rameau's music as well. His setting of *Armida* (1761, for Vienna) was likewise adapted, from Quinault's libretto for Lully. Personal and musical relations between Traetta and Gluck were fruitful for the two. A period in Venice beginning in 1765 led to the composition of his best-known comic operas; he then succeeded Galuppi at the court of Catherine II in 1768, where he stayed until 1775. He found London still enthralled to Sacchini, and finally returned to Venice, again producing comic operas.

VERRI, PIETRO (1728–97). Italian economist and man of letters. As an economist, he held various offices in Milan. His literary interests led him to write a history of Milan (1783–99), and together with his brother Alessandro and other Milanese intellectuals he founded the journal *Il Caffè*, of which he was editor during its short life (1764–66); one of the articles he wrote for it is given in Ch. 8. An excerpt from his *Discorso sull'indole del piacere e del dolore* (1774) appears in the same chapter.

VINCI, LEONARDO (ca. 1696–1730). Italian composer. Trained in Naples, he became *pro-vicemaestro* of the royal chapel in 1725. From 1728 he also taught at the Conservatorio dei Poveri di Gesù Cristo, where Pergolesi was among his pupils. He began with comic operas in Neapolitan dialect, then moved to *opere serie*, which were commissioned throughout Italy; several of the later ones were on librettos by the young Metastasio. His music was long remembered after his death, and his last opera, *Artaserse* (1730), was performed frequently. Burney praised him for the clarity of his melodies, disentangled from fugues and other complications.

VOLTAIRE (FRANÇOIS MARIE AROUET, CALLED) (1694–1778). French writer. A lasting enemy of oppression and superstition, he wrote on many subjects and in many genres: philosophy, history, anti-religious tracts, satires, drama, and poetry. He spent time in England, Berlin, Geneva, and Ferney before returning to Paris in triumph at the age of eighty-four. Many of his dramas were set to music, but few in his lifetime.

Bibliography

This short bibliography is not intended to offer the reader an exhaustive survey of eighteenth-century music. The field is vast, and pertinent bibliographical material is often hard to come by. Rather, it includes a few brief but indispensable suggestions on a limited number of basic general works on aesthetic thought in the age of the Enlightenment. These works are very helpful as general reference texts, and also include a few anthologies, or general histories, treating eighteenth-century writers at length.

Allen, Warren Dwight. *Philosophies of Music History: A Study of General Histories of Music 1600–1960.* New York: American Books, 1939. Repr.: New York: Dover Publications, 1962.

Brown, Howard Mayer, and Stanley Sadie, eds. *Performance Practice: Music after 1600.* London: Macmillan, 1989; New York: W. W. Norton, 1990.

Coward, Georgia, ed. *French Musical Thought 1600–1800.* Ann Arbor: UMI Research Press, 1989.

Dahlhaus, Carl. *Esthetics of Music.* Translated by William Austin. Cambridge: Cambridge University Press, 1982.

Dahrenberg, Karl H. *Studien zur englischen Musikästhetik des 18. Jahrhunderts.* Hamburg: W. de Gruyter, 1960.

Della Corte, Andrea. *La critica musicale e i critici.* Turin: Unione Tipografico-Editrice Torinese, 1961.

Écorcheville, Jules-Armand. *De Lully à Rameau (1690–1730): L'esthétique musicale.* Paris: Fortin, 1906.

Flaherty, Gloria. *Opera in the Development of German Critical Thought.* Princeton: Princeton University Press, 1978.

Fubini, Enrico. *Gli enciclopedisti e la musica.* Turin: Einaudi, 1975.

———. *History of Music Aesthetics.* Translated by Michael Hatwell. London: Macmillan, 1990.

———. *Gli illuministi e la musica.* Milan: Principato, 1969.

Giazotto, Remo. *Poesia melodrammatica e pensiero critico nel '700.* Milan: Bocca, 1952.

Goldschmidt, Hugo. *Die Musikästhetik des 18. Jahrhunderts und ihre Beziehungen zu seinem Kunstschaffen.* Zürich and Leipzig: Rascher, 1915.

Graf, Max. *Composer and Critic: Two Hundred Years of Musical Criticism.* New York: W. W. Norton, 1946.

Heartz, Daniel. "From Garrick to Gluck: The Reform of Theatre and Opera in the Mid-Eighteenth Century," *Papers of the Royal Musical Association,* 94 (1967–68), 111–27.

Hirschberg, Eugen. *Die Encyclopädisten und die französische Oper im 18. Jahrhundert.* Leipzig: 1903.

Jullien, Adolphe. *La Musique et les philosophes au XVIIIe siècle.* Paris: Baur, 1873.

Launay, Denise, ed. *La Querelle des Bouffons: Texte des Pamphlets avec introduction, commentaires et index.* 3 vols. Geneva: Minkoff Reprint, 1973.

le Huray, Peter, and James Day, eds. *Music and Aesthetics in the Eighteenth and Early-Nineteenth Centuries.* Cambridge: Cambridge University Press, 1981.

Lippman, Edward A. *A History of Western Musical Aesthetics.* Lincoln, Nebr.: University of Nebraska Press, 1992.

————, ed. *Musical Aesthetics: A Historical Reader.* 3 vols. New York: Pendragon, 1986–91.

MacClintock, Carol, ed. *Readings in the History of Music in Performance.* Bloomington: Indiana University Press, 1979.

Morgenstern, Sam, ed. *Composers on Music.* London: Faber and Faber; New York: [Bonanza], 1956.

The New Grove Dictionary of Music and Musicians. Edited by Stanley Sadie. 20 vols. London: Macmillan, 1980.

The New Grove Dictionary of Opera. Edited by Stanley Sadie. 4 vols. London: Macmillan; New York: Grove's Dictionaries of Music, 1992.

Oliver, Alfred Richard. *The Encyclopedists as Critics of Music.* New York: Columbia University Press, 1947.

Portnoy, Julius. *The Philosopher and Music.* New York: The Humanities Press, 1954.

Serauky, Walter. *Die musikalische Nachahmungsästhetik im Zeitraum von 1700 bis 1850.* Münster: Helios, 1929.

Snyders, Georges. *Le Goût musical en France aux XVIIe et XVIIIe siècles.* Paris: Vrin, 1968.

Stefani, Gino. *Musica barocca, poetica e ideologia.* Milan: Bompiani, 1978.

Strunk, Oliver. *Source Readings in Music History.* New York: W. W. Norton, 1950.

Venturi, Franco. *Italy and the Enlightenment: Studies in a Cosmopolitan Century.* Translated from the Italian by Stuart Woolf. Edited with an Introduction by Stuart Woolf. London: Longmans, 1972.

Verba, Cynthia. *Music and the French Enlightenment: Reconstruction of a Dialogue 1750–1764.* Oxford: Oxford University Press, 1993.

Weiss, Piero, and Richard Taruskin, eds. *Music in the Western World: A History in Documents.* New York: Schirmer Books; London: Collier Macmillan, 1984.

Index

415

Burney on, 185–88; Hawkins on, 194–95; Martini on, 173–77; Metastasio on, 266–69; Muratori on, 39–40, 44–45; Planelli on, 244–48; Rousseau on, 93, 99–100
as a "cri animal," 17, 110–11, 378–79
and emotions (*see also* pathos in music), 7–8, 10, 16–17, 34, 45–46, 56, 70, 94–95, 98, 103–4, 122, 134, 138, 141, 258, 271, 274, 300, 312, 315, 325, 330, 348, 368, 386; C. P. E. Bach on, 292–95; Mattheson on, 279–85; Milizia on, 252–55; Verri on, 334–39
and freedom, 14–16, 85, 102–3
mathematical foundations, 21, 341
compared with painting, 252, 324–25, 328–29
and poetry, common origin of, 8, 12, 15, 30, 36–37, 92–93, 99, 161–69, 235, 345
theories of development of, 12, 99–101, 164–69, 216
theory of physiological effect (*see also* tarantism), 98, 103, 241–43, 245, 280

Naples, 72, 202–3, 205, 208–12, 214
nature vs. art, 83, 134, 239, 331, 358, 369, 375, 379
Birnbaum on, 276
Lecerf on, 6, 76
Martini on, 179
Milizia on, 252, 258–59
Newton, Isaac, 344, 406
Nicolini (Nicolo Grimaldi), 70n, 321, 406
Nigitti, Francesco, 40n

Olympius, 244n
opera
behavior of audience at, 47, 113, 127, 203–5, 209, 214, 373–74
as corruption of tragedy, 7–8, 20, 25, 35, 38–39, 43–46
criticism of, 6–8, 11, 19–20, 22–24, 35, 172, 206–7, 264; by Algarotti, 233–39; by Arteaga, 346–51; by Marcello, 60–65; by Milizia, 253–58; by Muratori, 41–47; by Planelli, 249–51
economics of, 50, 58, 62, 204–6, 211–15, 263–64, 374
immorality of, 19–20, 35, 39–41, 46n
overture, 236, 254, 365, 370
plots, 44, 51–52, 124–26, 171, 207, 261–62, 364, 374, 388
reform of, 22–25, 231–32, 234, 358, 364, 369, 376
relative value of music and words (*see* words vs. music)

requirements of libretto (*see also* words vs. music), 23, 61, 110–11, 171, 207, 215, 253, 331–32, 361, 374; Grimm on, 120–28; Martello on, 50–53, 58–69; Mozart on, 385–89; Muratori on, 42–46
role of impresario, 62, 64, 205, 213, 235, 356
set design, 42, 49–51, 91, 206, 321–24
theories on origin of, 8, 120–21, 169–71, 347
opera houses
description of, 203–4, 209–12
Académie Royale de Musique (Opéra), 85, 86, 106, 113–19
Argentina, 202–3
Capranica, 70n, 202
King's Theatre (London), 215n, 321
Teatro alle Dame (Aliberti), 202–3
Teatro dei Fiorentini, 209
Teatro della Valle, 202, 204, 208
Teatro Nuovo, 209
Teatro Reale (San Carlo), 203, 209–11, 213
Théâtre Italien, 89
Theatre Royal, Drury Lane, 324n
Tordinona, 202–3
organ, 195, 302–4
Orpheus, 246
Ottoboni, Pietro, Cardinal, 199

Padua, 201
Paisiello, Giovanni, 376, 406
Palestrina, Giovanni Pierluigi da, 72n, 276, 317, 347; *Miserere*, 269
Papal Chapel, 72n, 200n, 269
Paris, 87, 159, 200, 202, 355, 371, 388
Pascal, Blaise, 85, 110
Pasquini, Bernardo, 58
pathos in music (*see also* music: emotions in), 142, 241, 244–45, 249–50
Pausanias, 64, 188
Perez, David, 356, 406
perfidia, 282
Pergolesi, Giovanni Battista, 110, 117, 126, 251, 254, 258, 347, 349, 355–56, 367, 375, 406; *Livietta e Tracollo* (*La contadina astuta*), 106, 208; *Il maestro di musica*, 208; *La serva padrona*, 15, 85, 106, 108n, 208, 259, 406; *Stabat mater*, 106, 109n, 316n, 353, 379, 407
Peri, Jacopo, 236
Perrault, Charles, 8, 407
Perrault, Claude, 407
Perti, Giacomo Antonio, 58, 72n, 407
Pherecrates, 99
Philidor, François-André Danican: *Le Jardinier et son seigneur*, 105n; *Le Maréchal ferrant*, 108

Teach Yourself VISUALLY™

Samsung® Galaxy S®5

by Guy Hart-Davis

Visual
®
A Wiley Brand

Teach Yourself VISUALLY™ Samsung® Galaxy S®5

Published by
John Wiley & Sons, Inc.
10475 Crosspoint Boulevard
Indianapolis, IN 46256

www.wiley.com

Published simultaneously in Canada

Wiley publishes in a variety of print and electronic formats and by print-on-demand. Some material included with standard print versions of this book may not be included in e-books or in print-on-demand. If this book refers to media such as a CD or DVD that is not included in the version you purchased, you may download this material at http://booksupport.wiley.com. For more information about Wiley products, visit www.wiley.com.

Library of Congress Control Number is available from the Publisher.

ISBN: 978-1-118-91931-6 (pbk); ISBN: 978-1-118-91965-1 (ebk); ISBN: 978-1-118-91932-3 (ebk)

Manufactured in the United States of America

10 9 8 7 6 5 4 3 2

Trademark Acknowledgments

Contact Us

For general information on our other products and services, please contact our Customer Care Department within the United States at (877)762-2974, outside the United States at (317)572-3993, or fax (317)572-4002.

For technical support, please visit www.wiley.com/techsupport.

Credits

Sr. Acquisitions Editor
Katie Mohr

Project Editor
Dana Lesh

Technical Editor
Andrew Moore

Copy Editor
Dana Lesh

Editorial Assistant
Paige Newman

Sr. Editorial Assistant
Cherie Case

Project Coordinator
Emily Benford

About the Author

Guy Hart-Davis is the author of *Teach Yourself VISUALLY Android Phones and Tablets; Teach Yourself VISUALLY iPhone 5s and iPhone 5c; Teach Yourself VISUALLY iMac,* Third Edition; *iMac Portable Genius,* Fourth Edition; and *iWork Portable Genius,* Second Edition.

Author's Acknowledgments

My thanks go to the many people who turned my manuscript into the highly graphical book you are holding. In particular, I thank Katie Mohr for asking me to write the book; Dana Lesh for keeping me on track, guiding the editorial process, and editing the text skillfully and with a light touch; and Andrew Moore for reviewing the book for technical accuracy and contributing helpful sugggestions.

How to Use This Book

Whom This Book Is For

This book is for the reader who has never used this particular technology or software application. It is also for readers who want to expand their knowledge.

The Conventions in This Book

① Steps

This book uses a step-by-step format to guide you easily through each task. Numbered steps are actions that you must perform; bulleted steps clarify a point, step, or optional feature; and indented steps give you the result.

② Notes

Notes give additional information — special conditions that may occur during an operation, a situation that you want to avoid, or a cross-reference to a related area of the book.

③ Icons and Buttons

Icons and buttons show you exactly what you need to click to perform a step.

④ Tips

Tips offer additional information, including warnings and shortcuts.

⑤ Bold

Bold type shows command names, options, and text or numbers you must type.

⑥ Italics

Italic type introduces and defines a new term.

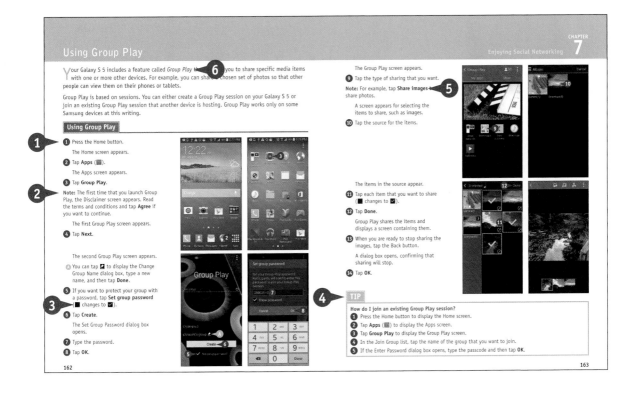

Table of Contents

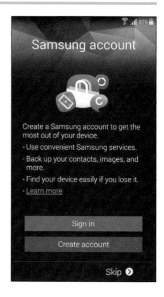

Chapter 3	Working with Text and Voice

Table of Contents

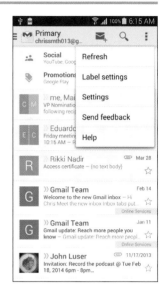

Chapter 6   Making Calls and Texting

Chapter 7   Enjoying Social Networking

Table of Contents

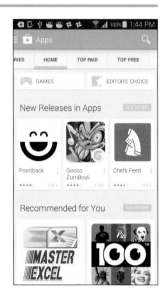

Chapter 10   Taking Photos and Videos

Chapter 11   Using Maps and Other Built-in Apps

Table of Contents

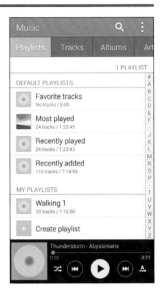

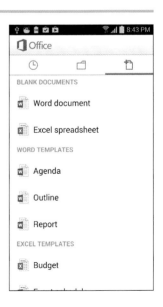

CHAPTER 1

Getting Started with Your Galaxy S 5

In this chapter, you will set up your Galaxy S 5, meet its hardware controls, and learn to navigate the TouchWiz interface. You will also learn to transfer files to your Galaxy S 5 from your PC or Mac.

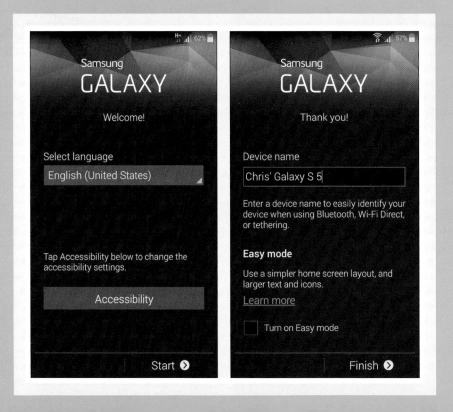

Get Your Galaxy S 5 Ready for Use

Your first move is to get your Galaxy S 5 ready for use by unboxing it, installing the battery, and setting the phone to charge. Samsung recommends charging the battery fully before using your phone for the first time, even if the battery is already partly charged when you install it.

You may also need to install a SIM card if your carrier has not already installed one. You can also install a memory card to supplement the Galaxy S 5's built-in memory.

Get Your Galaxy S 5 Ready for Use

1 Open the box and remove its contents.

2 Verify that the Galaxy S 5 itself and the components are all present and undamaged.

Note: The box normally includes the phone, a battery, a USB cable, a charger, and a quick start guide.

3 If the Galaxy S 5 has protective stickers on its front or back, peel them off.

4 Put your thumbnail in the cover-removal indentation and pull off the back cover.

5 Slide the SIM card into the SIM slot.

Note: The contacts face downward.

6 Push the SIM card fully into the SIM slot.

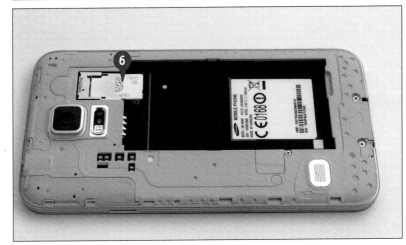

7 Optionally, insert a memory card in the memory slot above the SIM card.

8 Unwrap the battery and insert it in the battery compartment. Align the contacts at the top of the battery with the contacts at the top of the battery compartment.

9 Put the back cover back on, pressing to secure each of the catches.

10 Connect the USB end of the USB cable to the power adapter.

11 Plug the power adapter into a power socket.

12 Connect the other end of the USB cable to your Galaxy S 5.

A charging readout appears on-screen.

13 Leave the Galaxy S 5 to charge until the battery readout shows that the battery is fully charged.

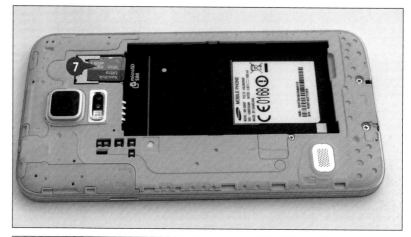

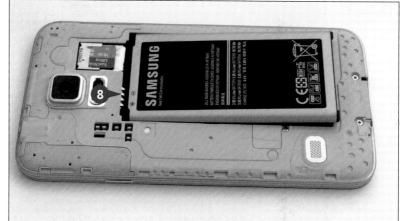

TIP

Must I charge the battery fully before using my Galaxy S 5?

Like many hardware manufacturers, Samsung recommends charging the battery fully before using it. Experts disagree on whether this is essential, but unless you are in an extreme hurry, it is a good idea. Some experts recommend conditioning the battery by charging it fully and discharging it fully three times before starting a more normal regime of partial charging whenever it suits you. Few people manage this.

If you must use the Galaxy S 5 before charging the battery fully, do not worry. You can replace the battery easily at only moderate expense if necessary.

Meet the Galaxy S 5's Hardware and Controls

Your Galaxy S 5 has an impressive amount of hardware, including the main camera and the screen-side camera, the speaker and earpiece, and the headset jack.

The Galaxy S 5 has three physical buttons: the Power button on the right side, the volume rocker on the left side, and the Home button below the screen. The phone also has two soft buttons, the Recent Apps button to the left of the Home button and the Back button to the right.

Meet the Galaxy S 5's Hardware and Controls

1 Press and hold the Power button for a couple of seconds.

The Galaxy S 5 vibrates to indicate that it is starting.

At the top of the screen are the following:

Ⓐ The earpiece for making phone calls.

Ⓑ The front camera.

Ⓒ The proximity/gesture sensor.

Ⓓ The light sensor.

Ⓔ The notification light.

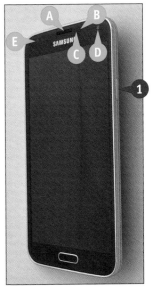

Ⓕ As the Galaxy S 5 starts, its name and model number appear on-screen.

Ⓖ The Home button, which incorporates the fingerprint sensor, is at the bottom of the screen.

On the left side of the Galaxy S 5 is the volume rocker.

H You press the upper part of the volume rocker to increase the volume.

I You press the lower part to decrease the volume.

On the back of the Galaxy S 5 are the following:

J The main camera lens.

K The flash for the main camera.

L The speaker.

At the top of the Galaxy S 5 are the following:

M The headset jack.

N The microphone for the speakerphone.

O The infrared LED.

When the Galaxy S 5 finishes startup, you can perform the initial setup routine, as explained in the next section, "Perform the Initial Setup Routine."

TIP

What is on the bottom of my Galaxy S 5?
On the bottom of your Galaxy S 5 are the multipurpose jack and another microphone. You use the multipurpose jack to connect your Galaxy S 5 to your computer or other devices, such as an HDTV you are using to display photos. The microphone at the bottom of the Galaxy S 5 is the one that picks up your voice when you are making a phone call and holding the phone to your face.

Perform the Initial Setup Routine

To get your Galaxy S 5 working, you must perform the initial setup routine. This is a one-time procedure in which you select essential settings and connect the phone to a wireless network.

The first time that you turn on your Galaxy S 5, it displays the Welcome screen. You can then choose which language to use, connect to a Wi-Fi network, and set up your Google account on the phone. You can also choose other settings, such as backup and restore settings and Google and location settings.

Perform the Initial Setup Routine

1 Turn on your Galaxy S 5 by pressing and holding the Power button on the right side for a couple of seconds.

Your Galaxy S 5 vibrates to indicate that it is starting, and the Welcome screen appears.

2 Tap **Select Language**.

3 Tap the language that you want to use.

4 Tap **Start**.

The Wi-Fi screen appears.

5 Tap the Wi-Fi network to which you want to connect.

The dialog box for connecting to the network opens.

6 Type the password for the network.

A You can tap **Show password** (■ changes to ✓) to display the password.

7 Tap **Connect**.

Your Galaxy S 5 connects to the network.

B The "Connected to Wi-Fi network" readout appears briefly.

8 Tap **Next**.

9 Read the end user license agreement.

10 Tap this option (■ changes to ✓).

11 Tap **Yes** or **No thanks** (◉ changes to ⦿) to control whether your Galaxy S 5 sends error log data to Samsung.

12 Tap **Next**.

The Got Google? screen appears.

13 Tap **Yes** to set up your Google account.

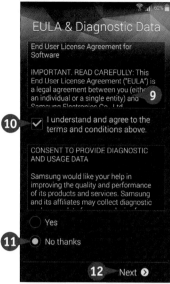

The Sign In screen appears.

14 Type your Gmail account name.

15 Type your password.

16 Tap the Next button (▶).

A confirmation dialog box opens.

C You can tap a link, such as **Terms of Service** or **Privacy Policy**, to display the linked information.

17 Tap **OK**.

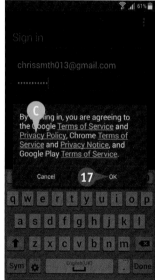

TIPS

What is Smart Network Switch?

Smart Network Switch is a feature that enables your Galaxy S 5 to switch automatically from a Wi-Fi network to the cellular network to maintain its Internet connection. Turning Smart Network Switch on may cause your Galaxy S 5 to use the cellular connection when you want to use Wi-Fi, so it is best to leave Smart Network Switch off during initial setup.

Should I create a Google account if I do not have one?

If you do not already have a Google account, you should create one at this point. Having a Google account enables you to get the most out of your Galaxy S 5.

continued ▶

During the initial setup routine, you can choose whether to back up the data from your Galaxy S 5 to your Google account. You can also decide whether to allow apps to determine your location and send anonymous location data to Google's servers, and whether to allow Google's location service to scan for Wi-Fi networks even when Wi-Fi is turned off. Google uses the data provided to improve location accuracy.

Perform the Initial Setup Routine (continued)

18 Tap this option (■ changes to ✓) if you want to back up data to your Google account and restore from it.

19 Tap this option (■ changes to ✓) to allow apps to use your location.

20 Tap this option (■ changes to ✓) to allow your Galaxy S 5 to scan for Wi-Fi networks even when Wi-Fi is off.

21 Tap this option (■ changes to ✓) to receive messages from Google Play.

22 Tap ▶.

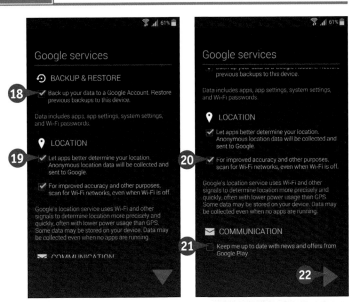

The Entertainment screen appears.

23 Tap **Not now**.

The This Phone Belongs To . . . screen appears.

24 Type your first name.

25 Type your last name.

26 Tap ▶.

The Samsung Account screen appears.

Ⓐ You can tap **Sign In** to sign in with your existing account or **Create account** to start a new account.

㉗ Tap **Skip**.

The Dropbox screen appears.

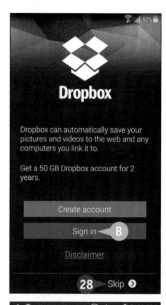

Ⓑ You can tap **Sign in** to sign in to your existing Dropbox account.

㉘ Tap **Skip**.

The Samsung Galaxy screen appears.

㉙ Edit the contents of the **Device name** box so that it shows the name you want for your Galaxy S 5.

㉚ Tap **Finish**.

The Home screen appears, and you can start using your Galaxy S 5.

TIP

Should I back up my Galaxy S 5 to my Google account?

Backing up your Galaxy S 5 to your Google account is a good idea unless you prefer not to store sensitive data online, no matter how securely. Backing up to your Google account enables you to restore your data if your Galaxy S 5 suffers a failure.

If you have backed up a previous Android device to your Google account, you can restore your data to your Galaxy S 5. This feature enables you to set up your Galaxy S 5 with your settings, contacts, and other data quickly and easily.

Set Up Fingerprint Recognition

Your Galaxy S 5 includes a fingerprint-recognition feature that helps you to keep your valuable data and personal items secure against intruders. After setting up fingerprint recognition, you can unlock your Galaxy S 5 by swiping a finger across the Home button. This is easier and quicker than using a passcode, and it is unique to you.

You set up fingerprint recognition by scanning your finger in various positions. Set up fingerprint recognition for multiple fingers in case you abrade the skin on your fingertip or injure your finger.

Set Up Fingerprint Recognition

1 Pull down from the top of the screen with one finger.

The Notifications panel opens.

2 Tap the Settings button (⚙).

The Settings app opens.

3 In the Quick Settings section, tap **Finger Scanner** (◉).

The Finger Scanner screen appears.

4 Tap **Fingerprint manager**.

Note: When you display the Fingerprint Manager screen, your Galaxy S 5 displays a Disclaimer screen. Tap **Do not show again** (■ changes to ✓) and then tap **OK**.

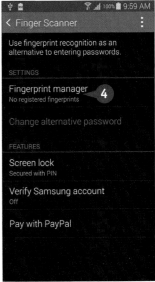

The Register Fingerprint screen appears.

5 Swipe your finger down over the Home button repeatedly.

A The indicator shows your progress.

The Enable Fingerprint Lock dialog box opens.

6 Tap **OK**.

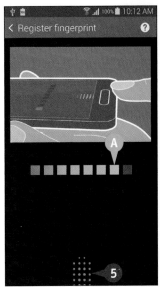

The Screen Unlock Settings screen appears.

7 Tap **Fingerprint**.

The Finger Scanner screen appears.

B The "Fingerprint lock turned on" message appears briefly.

C You can tap **Fingerprint manager** to register another fingerprint as a backup.

D You can tap **Verify Samsung account** to set up your fingerprint to verify your Samsung account.

E You can tap **Pay with PayPal** to set up your fingerprint for paying via PayPal.

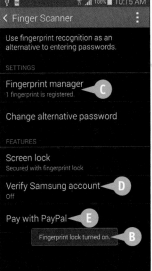

TIP

How can I make the fingerprint sensor recognize my finger?

Make sure that you swipe your finger across the middle of the Home button, not across either side of the button. You can swipe in any direction, but because the Home button is close to the bottom of the phone, you may find swiping your finger accurately to be easier if you hold your Galaxy S 5 in one hand and swipe the finger on the other hand. If your finger is too narrow to cover most of the Home button, try using your thumb instead.

Connect to a Wireless Network

To get the most use out of your Galaxy S 5, you likely need to connect it to several wireless networks in different locations. Many wireless networks broadcast the network name, and often you need to provide only the password to make a connection. To connect to a wireless network that does not broadcast its name, you need to type the name to identify the network and then provide the password. For some networks, you may need to specify an IP address or proxy server details.

Connect to a Wireless Network

Display the Wi-Fi Screen

1 Pull down from the top of the screen.

The Notifications panel opens.

2 Tap and hold **Wi-Fi** (🛜).

The Wi-Fi screen appears.

Connect to a Wireless Network That Broadcasts Its Name

Ⓐ If the **Wi-Fi** switch is set to Off, set it to **On**.

1 Tap the network to which you want to connect.

A dialog box opens for connecting to the network.

2 Type the password.

Ⓑ You can tap **Show password** (⬛ changes to ☑) to display the characters.

3 Tap **Connect**.

Your Galaxy S 5 connects to the wireless network.

Connect to a Wireless Network That Does Not Broadcast Its Name

1 On the Wi-Fi screen, tap **Add Wi-Fi network**.

The Add Wi-Fi Network dialog box opens.

2 Type the network name.

3 Tap **Security** and then tap the security type, such as **WPA/WPA2/FT PSK**.

4 Tap **Password** and type the password.

5 Tap **Connect**.

Your Galaxy S 5 connects to the network.

Connect to a Network and Specify Settings

1 Tap the network.

2 Type the password.

3 Tap **Show advanced options** (■ changes to ✓).

4 To set proxy server information, tap **Proxy**, tap **Manual**, and then choose the settings.

5 To set IP address information, tap **IP settings**, tap **Static**, and then choose the settings.

6 Tap **Connect**.

Your Galaxy S 5 connects to the network.

How do I stop using a particular wireless network?

On the Wi-Fi screen, tap the network's name. In the dialog box that opens, tap **Forget**.

Is there an easier way to set up a wireless network?

Yes, if the wireless network has Wi-Fi Protected Setup (WPS) and you have physical access to the wireless router. If so, display the Wi-Fi screen, tap the Menu button, and then tap **WPS push button**. On your router, press the WPS button to set up the network connection automatically.

Explore the User Interface and Launch Apps

When you press the Power button or the Home button to wake your Galaxy S 5 from sleep, Android displays the lock screen. You then unlock your phone to reach the Home screen, which contains a Favorites tray of icons for running frequently used apps, shortcuts to apps, and the Apps icon for accessing the full list of apps installed.

You can add other icons to the Home screen as needed. When you launch an app, its screen appears. From the app, you can return to the Home screen by pressing the Home button. You can then launch another app.

Explore the User Interface and Launch Apps

1 Press the Home button.

The phone's screen lights up and displays the lock screen.

Note: You can use various means of unlocking the lock screen. The default is the swipe explained here.

2 Swipe across the screen.

The Home screen appears.

Note: If your Galaxy S 5 displays an app instead of the Home screen, press the Home button.

3 Tap **Apps** (▦).

The Apps screen appears.

4 Tap the app that you want to use, such as **Calculator** (▨).

The app opens.

5 Use the app as needed.

Note: For example, tap the buttons to perform a calculation.

A In the Calculator app, the result appears here.

6 Press the Home button.

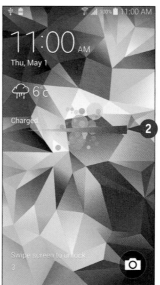

The Home screen appears.

7 Tap **Apps** (▦).

The Apps screen appears.

8 If the screen is full of apps, swipe your finger from right to left across the screen.

Note: If the Apps screen is not full, most likely there is no second screen of apps to display. In this case, swiping left displays the Widgets screen.

The next screen of apps appears.

9 Tap the app that you want to launch.

The app opens, and you can start working in it.

Using Multi Window

Your Galaxy S 5 includes a feature called *Multi Window* that enables you to view two apps at the same time. Multi Window can be useful for both work and play and even lets you play music or video from two apps at the same time.

Multi Window works with only some of the apps on your Galaxy S 5, the apps that appear on the Multi Window panel. You may need to enable Multi Window in the Settings app before you can use it.

Using Multi Window

Enable Multi Window

1 Pull down with two fingers from the top of the screen.

The Quick Settings panel opens.

2 Tap **Multi window**.

Multi Window turns on.

Display Multiple Apps with Multi Window

1 Press and hold the Back button.

A You can also tap the handle to display the Multi Window panel.

The Multi Window panel appears on the left of the screen.

2 Tap and hold the first app that you want to display and then drag it to the upper pane.

Note: This example uses **Gallery** (◨).

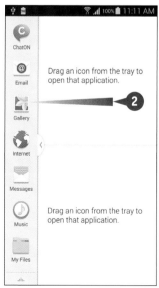

The app opens in the upper pane.

3 Tap and hold the second app that you want to display.

4 Drag it to the lower pane.

Note: This example uses **Music** (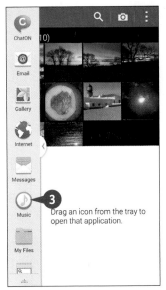).

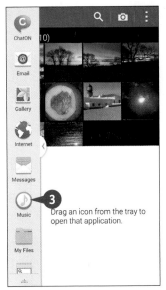

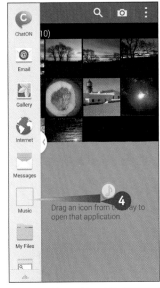

The second app opens, and you can start using it. For example, in Music, you can tap a song to start playing it.

5 Tap the window that you want to make active.

6 Tap and drag the split bar handle to resize the windows.

B You can tap the handle to display the Multi Window panel so that you can open another app in Multi Window.

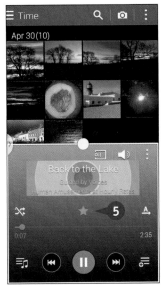

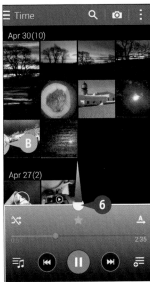

TIP

How do I stop using Multi Window?

You can turn Multi Window off temporarily by pressing and holding the Back button until the Multi Window handle disappears from the left side of the screen.

If you no longer want to use Multi Window at all, disable it. Pull down with two fingers from the top of the screen to open the Quick Settings panel and then tap **Multi window**.

continued ▶

M ulti Window enables you to rearrange the apps in the upper window or the apps in the lower window independently of each other, so you can display the apps that you need at the same time. For quick access, you can create pairs of apps that you typically use together.

You can also switch the apps in the upper window and the lower window easily, copy text from the app in one window to the app in the other window, or insert a screenshot of one window's contents in the other window.

Using Multi Window (continued)

Close an App in Multi Window

1 Tap the window that you want to close.

2 Tap the split bar handle.

The Multi Window controls appear.

3 Tap Close (⊠).

The selected app closes.

If two or more apps are open in Multi Window, the next app appears. If only one app is open, that app switches to full screen.

Switch the Positions of Apps in Multi Window

1 Tap the split bar handle.

The Multi Window controls appear.

2 Tap the Switch Windows button (⤢).

The windows switch positions.

Copy Text from One App to Another

1 In Multi Window, display the source app and the destination app for the text.

2 Tap the split bar handle.

The Multi Window controls appear.

3 Tap the Copy button (⌷).

4 Drag a paragraph to the destination app.

The text appears in the destination app.

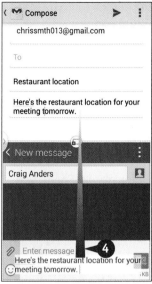

Insert a Screenshot of One App in Another App

1 Display the source app and the destination app for the screenshot.

2 In the source app, display the content that you want to include in the screenshot.

3 Tap the split bar handle.

The Multi Window controls appear.

4 Tap ⌷.

5 Drag the content to the destination app.

The screenshot appears in the destination app.

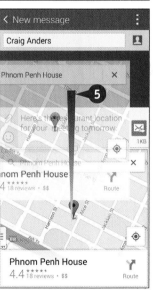

TIP

How do I create a pair of apps?

1 In Multi Window, display the two apps in the arrangement that you want.

2 Press and hold the Back button to display the Multi Window panel.

3 Tap the Commands button (⌨) to display a pop-up panel containing commands.

4 Tap **Create** (⊞) to display the Create a Paired Window dialog box.

5 Edit the suggested name as needed.

6 Tap **OK**. The app pair then appears on the Multi Window panel.

Navigate with Gestures

To navigate the TouchWiz user interface smoothly and swiftly, you can use seven main gestures. To trigger the default action for an item, you tap it and then raise your finger off the screen. To access extra functionality, you tap and hold until you get a response. To select text or zoom in on content, you double-tap. To scroll from one screen to another, you swipe right, left, up, or down. To move a shorter distance, you drag a finger across the screen. To zoom in or out, you place two fingers on the screen and pinch outward or inward.

Navigate with Gestures

1 Press the Home button.

The Home screen appears.

2 Tap **Apps**.

The Apps screen appears.

3 Tap **Maps** (⊞).

Note: This section uses the Maps app as an example, but you can use these gestures in most apps.

The Maps app opens and displays the area around your current location.

4 Swipe right by moving your finger rapidly from the left side of the screen to the right side.

The map scrolls freely, following the direction that you swiped.

5 With one finger, double-tap an item of interest on the screen.

Note: The double-tap gesture is also called *double-touch*.

The map zooms in on the area.

Note: In Maps, double-tapping zooms in by increments. You can zoom out by the same increments by double-tapping with two fingers.

6 Place your thumb and finger together on the screen and pinch outward.

The map zooms in on that point.

7 Tap and hold a road on the screen for a moment.

Note: The tap-and-hold gesture is also called a *long press*.

A pin appears on the map and a banner appears at the bottom of the screen.

8 Tap the banner.

The information panel opens.

9 Tap **Street View** on the information panel.

The Street view of the location appears, showing photos of the road.

10 Tap the screen and drag to the right.

The view moves to the left.

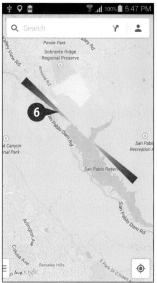

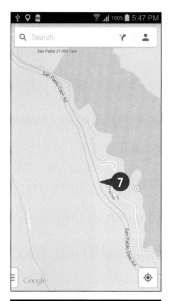

TIPS

What is the difference between swiping and dragging?
Swiping is a more expansive gesture than dragging and does not involve a specific object on the screen. You swipe to move from one screen to another, whereas you drag to move an object within a screen.

What other gestures can I use with my Galaxy S 5?
Your Galaxy S 5 supports several gestures other than those explained in this section. You learn about these other gestures in Chapter 2, "Customizing Your Galaxy S5."

Using the Notifications Panel

Your Galaxy S 5 integrates a wide range of different types of alerts into the Notifications panel, a panel that you can pull down from the top of the screen over whichever app or screen is currently displayed. You can quickly open the Notifications panel from the Home screen or almost any other screen. With the Notifications panel open, you can go to the app that raised a particular alert, dismiss an alert, dismiss all alerts, or simply close the panel.

Using the Notifications Panel

Open the Notifications Panel

1 Press the Home button.

The Home screen appears.

Note: You can open the Notifications panel from the Home screen or from almost any Android app. A few apps, such as the Camera app, are exceptions.

2 Tap the status bar at the top of the screen and drag downward.

The Notifications panel opens.

Open the App That Raised an Alert

1 In the Notifications panel, tap the alert.

The app opens and displays the source of the alert.

You can now work in that app.

2 Drag or swipe open the Notifications panel when you want to work with other alerts.

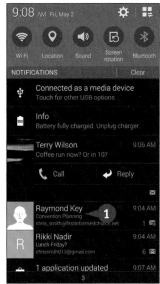

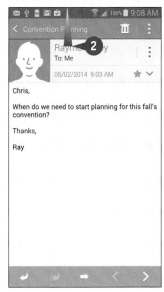

Dismiss One or More Alerts

1 To dismiss an alert, swipe the alert to the left or right.

The alert disappears from the list.

2 To dismiss all alerts, tap **Clear**.

Android dismisses all the alerts that do not require your attention.

The Notifications panel closes.

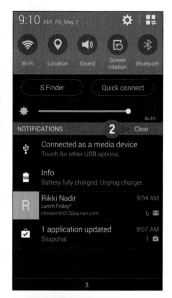

Close the Notifications Panel Manually

1 If you do not dismiss all alerts, as explained in the preceding subsection, tap the bar at the bottom of the Notifications panel and drag it upward to close the panel.

Note: You can also swipe up from the bottom of the screen to close the Notifications panel.

The Notifications panel closes, and Android displays the Home screen or the app that was last open.

TIPS

To open the Notifications panel, do I drag down or do I swipe down?

You can either drag or swipe. Dragging the status bar down enables you to peek at the contents of the Notifications panel without opening it fully. Swiping opens the Notifications panel fully so that you can see its contents.

What other actions can I take in the Notifications panel?

When you miss a phone call, you can tap **Call back** in the notification to return the call or tap **Message** to send a text message instead. When you receive a notification for new e-mail messages, drag your finger down the notification to expand the list of messages so that you can decide how to handle them.

Using the Toolbox

Your Galaxy S 5 includes a feature called the *Toolbox* that enables you to keep apps that you use frequently right at hand. You can display the Toolbox from the Quick Settings bar or the Quick Settings panel, position it wherever suits you on the screen, and run an app from it with a couple of taps of your finger.

The Toolbox comes with a default selection of apps, but you can quickly customize it to contain up to five of the apps that you find the most useful.

Using the Toolbox

Display the Toolbox and Open an App

1 Pull down from the top of the screen with two fingers.

The Quick Settings panel opens.

2 Tap **Toolbox** (◉ changes to ◉).

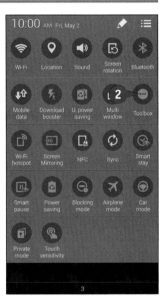

The Toolbox appears.

Note: You can reposition the Toolbox by tapping it and dragging it to where you want it to appear.

3 Tap the Toolbox.

The Toolbox opens.

4 Tap the app that you want to open.

The app opens, and you can work with it.

Customize the Toolbox

1 Tap and hold the Toolbox.

The Edit and the Remove buttons appear.

2 Drag the Toolbox to the Edit button.

The screen for customizing the Toolbox appears.

3 Tap each app that you want to add to the Toolbox (■ changes to ✔).

Note: The Toolbox can contain up to five apps.

4 Tap **Save**.

5 Tap the Toolbox.

The Toolbox opens, showing the apps that you selected.

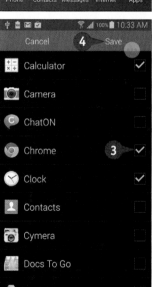

How do I display the Toolbox from the Quick Settings bar?

Pull down from the top of the screen to display the Quick Settings bar, scroll the Quick Settings bar left, and then tap the **Toolbox** button (⬤).

Is there another way to edit the Toolbox?

Yes — you can also edit the Toolbox from within the Settings app. Pull down from the top of the screen with two fingers to open the Quick Settings panel and then tap and hold **Toolbox** (⬤) to display the Toolbox screen in Settings. You can then set the **Toolbox** switch to **On** and tap **Edit** to edit the apps in the Toolbox.

Download and Install Samsung Kies

Samsung provides an app called *Kies* for managing its phones and tablets. You can use Kies to copy files — such as songs, videos, and other media files — between your Galaxy S 5 and your PC or Mac. Kies also enables you to back up your Galaxy S 5 to your PC or Mac and restore files from backup if necessary.

To use Kies, you must download it and install it on your computer. If you do not intend to use Kies to manage your Galaxy S 5, skip this section and the following one.

Download Kies

To get Kies, open your web browser, such as Internet Explorer in Windows or Safari on the Mac. Enter www.samsung.com in the address box and press **Enter** or **Return** to go to the Samsung website, which automatically redirects you to the website for your country or region. Type **kies** in the Search box and press **Enter** or **Return** to search for Kies, and then click the appropriate search result to go to the Kies page. Click **Download for Windows** or **Download for Mac OS** to download the version of Kies for your operating system. If your browser prompts you to choose between saving the downloaded file and running it, select the option for saving it.

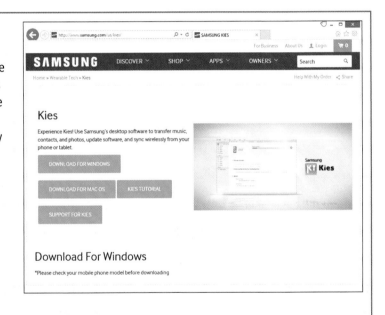

Install Kies in Windows

After downloading the Kies setup file for Windows, run the file, either by clicking the **Run** button when your browser prompts you or by double-clicking the file in a File Explorer window. If the User Account Control dialog box opens, confirm that the verified publisher is Samsung Electronics and click **Yes**. The installation routine then runs, displaying information screens as it does so.

When the Installation Complete dialog box appears, click **Create Shortcut on Desktop** only if you want to create a Kies shortcut on the desktop. Click **Run Samsung Kies 3** if you want to run Kies immediately, as you probably do. Then click **Finish**.

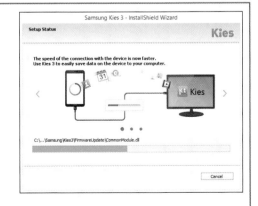

Install Kies on the Mac

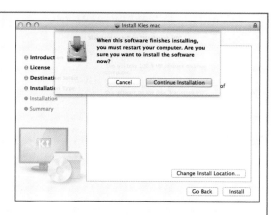

When your Kies download finishes on the Mac, OS X may automatically open a Finder window showing the contents of the disk image file. If not, click **Downloads** on the Dock to open a Finder window showing your Downloads folder, and then double-click the Kies disk image file to open it.

Save any unsaved work in your open apps before running the installer because the installation requires restarting OS X. Then, in the Finder window called *KiesMac,* double-click the **KiesMac.pkg** file to start the installer. Follow through the screens of the installer, accepting the Kies end user license agreement and choosing either to accept the default install location — usually the best choice — or to specify a different location. When the installer warns you that you must restart your computer after the software finishes installing, click **Continue Installation**. On the screen that announces, "The installation was successful," click **Restart**.

Launch Kies

After installing Kies, you can launch it using the normal technique for your computer's operating system.

In Windows 8, move the mouse pointer to the lower-left corner of the desktop to display the Start button, click **Start** to display the Start screen, navigate to the Apps section, and click **Samsung Kies 3**.

On OS X, click the Launchpad button () on the Dock to display the Launchpad screen and then click **Kies** (   ).

Kies opens and prompts you to connect your device. You can then sync files as explained in the following section, "Sync Files from Your Computer."

Sync Files from Your Computer

You can load files on your Galaxy S 5 by connecting it to your PC or Mac via a USB cable and transferring files using the Samsung Kies app. Kies provides an easy way to copy media files between your computer and your Galaxy S 5, so you can use Kies to load your Galaxy S 5 with music, copy photos you take on your Galaxy S 5 to your computer, and so on.

This section shows Kies running in Windows, but Kies on OS X works in almost exactly the same way.

Sync Files from Your Computer

1 On your PC, click **Samsung Kies 3**.

Note: In Windows 8, the Samsung Kies 3 icon appears on the Start screen. In Windows 7 and earlier versions, you find the icon on the Start menu.

Kies opens.

2 Connect your Galaxy S 5 to your PC via the USB cable.

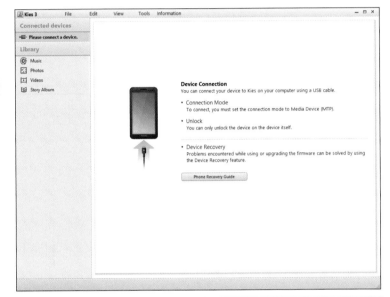

Kies detects your Galaxy S 5 and establishes a connection.

A Your Galaxy S 5 appears in the Connected Devices list.

B The Internal Memory readout shows how much of the phone's internal memory has been used and how much is free.

C The External Memory readout shows how much of the SD card has been used and how much is free.

3 In the Library section of the sidebar, click the item you want to sync.

In this example, the contents of your PC's music library appear.

4 Click each item that you want to sync (☐ changes to ☑).

D You can click the check box on the heading bar (☐ changes to ☑) to select all the files.

5 Click the Send Selected Music to Device button (☐).

6 Click **Internal memory** or **External memory**, as appropriate.

Note: It is a good idea to keep plenty of internal memory free so that you can shoot photos and videos without risking running out of space.

Kies copies the files to the memory you chose.

E The Finished readout appears in the status bar.

7 Click the Disconnect button (☒).

Kies disconnects your Galaxy S 5.

8 Disconnect the USB cable from your Galaxy S 5.

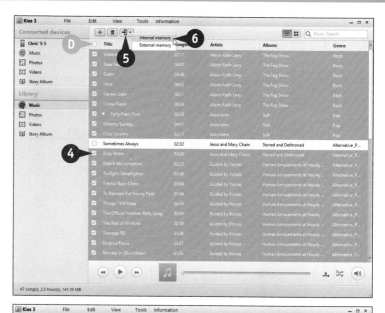

TIP

Can I connect my Galaxy S 5 to my PC or Mac via Wi-Fi?

You may be able to connect your Galaxy S 5 wirelessly by using the Kies Air app from Samsung. Kies Air is available only in some markets and has received mixed reviews, so it is a good idea to search for and read the latest reviews before you install it.

After installing Kies Air on your Galaxy S 5, you run the app to create a wireless connection to which you can connect a web browser. You can then use the web browser to manage the files on your Galaxy S 5.

CHAPTER 2

Customizing Your Galaxy S 5

To make your Galaxy S 5 work the way that you prefer, you can configure its many settings. In this chapter, you will learn how to access the most important settings and use them to personalize your Galaxy S 5. You will discover how to control notifications, audio preferences, screen brightness, and other key aspects of your phone's behavior.

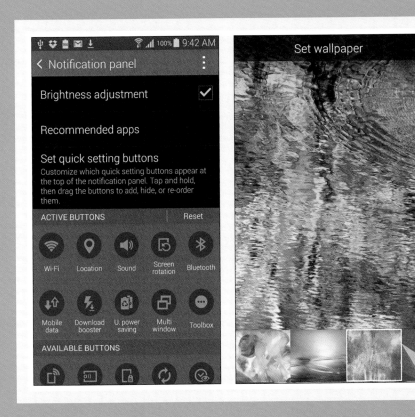

Find the Settings That You Need

Your Galaxy S 5 contains hundreds of settings that enable you to make the phone work the way you prefer. You can access some of these settings through the Notifications panel, but to reach the full range of settings, you open the Settings app and then select the category that you need.

Some apps provide access to settings through the apps themselves instead of through the Settings app. If you cannot find the settings for an app in the Settings app, look within the app itself.

Find the Settings That You Need

Using the Quick Settings Bar and Quick Settings Panel

1 Pull down from the top of the screen.

The Notifications panel opens.

A You can tap a button on the Quick Settings bar to turn that feature on or off.

B You can tap and hold a button on the Quick Settings bar to display the screen of associated settings.

2 Tap the Quick Settings bar and scroll left.

C Other icons appear on the Quick Settings bar.

3 Tap the Quick Settings button (⊞).

The Quick Settings panel appears.

D You can tap a button on the Quick Settings panel to turn that feature on or off.

E You can tap and hold a button on the Quick Settings panel to display the screen of associated settings.

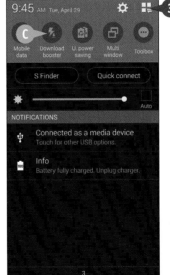

Navigate the Settings App

1 Pull down from the top of the screen.

The Notifications panel opens.

2 Tap the Settings button (⚙).

The Settings app opens.

3 Tap a section heading bar to collapse (⌃ changes to ⌄) or expand (⌄ changes to ⌃) the section.

4 Tap the button for the settings screen that you want to display.

You can now choose settings on the screen.

5 Tap the screen's name or the Back button to return to the previous screen.

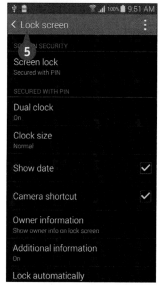

TIP

How do I choose settings within an app?
Open the app by tapping its button on the Home screen or the Apps screen. Tap the Menu button (such as ⋮, ⋮, or ⋮) to display the menu and then tap **Settings**. The Settings screen opens, and you can tap its buttons and options to choose settings. Tap the Back button or tap the button in the upper-left corner of the screen when you are ready to return to the app.

Customize the Quick Settings Bar and Quick Settings Panel

The Quick Settings bar gives you instant access to useful settings directly from the Notifications panel. With another tap, you can display the Quick Settings panel, which provides access to further settings.

Both the Quick Settings bar and the Quick Settings panel are time-savers in their default state, but you can customize both to contain the buttons that you find most useful. You can rearrange the buttons so that they appear in your preferred order, enabling you to access key settings more quickly.

Customize the Quick Settings Bar and Quick Settings Panel

1 Pull down from the top of the screen.

The Notifications panel opens.

2 Tap ⊞.

Note: You can also open the Quick Settings panel by pulling down from the top of the screen with two fingers.

The Quick Settings panel opens.

3 Tap the Edit button (✎).

The Notification Panel screen appears.

Ⓐ The Active Buttons list shows the buttons currently on the Quick Settings bar.

Ⓑ The Available Buttons list shows the buttons that you can add to the Quick Settings bar.

4 Tap **Brightness adjustment** (■ changes to ☑) if you want the Brightness controls to appear on the Notifications panel.

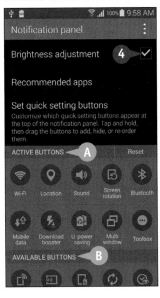

5 To add a button to the Quick Settings bar, tap the button in the Available Buttons list and then drag it to the Notification Panel list.

Note: You can drop the dragged button on another button to swap the two buttons.

6 To remove a button from the Quick Settings bar, tap and hold the button in the Notification Panel list and then drag it to the Available Buttons list.

7 To change the order of buttons on the Quick Settings bar, tap and hold a button in the Notification Panel list and then drag it to where you want it to appear.

8 When you finish customizing the Quick Settings bar, tap the Back button.

The Quick Settings panel appears, showing the buttons in their new order.

TIP

How can I restore the Quick Settings bar to its original set of buttons?

1 Pull down from the top of the screen to open the Notifications panel.

2 Tap ⊞ to open the Quick Settings panel.

3 Tap ▨ to display the Notification Panel screen.

4 Tap **Reset** to open the Reset dialog box.

5 Tap **OK**.

The Quick Settings bar is reset.

Choose Which Notifications to Receive

Some apps on your Galaxy S 5 can display notifications to alert you to events such as calendar items, incoming e-mail messages, and software updates becoming available. Notifications enable you to keep track of important information, but you likely want to choose which notifications you receive rather than receive notifications for everything. You can choose which apps can give you notifications. You can also choose whether to have the blue LED blink to alert you to notifications you have missed while the screen was turned off.

Choose Which Notifications to Receive

Choose Notifications

1 Pull down from the top of the screen.

The Notifications panel opens.

2 Tap ⚙.

The Settings screen appears.

3 In the Applications section, tap **Application manager** (⊞).

The Application Manager screen appears.

4 Swipe left one or more times until the All list appears.

5 Tap the app for which you want to configure notifications.

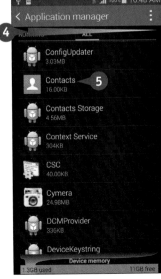

The App Info screen appears.

6 Tap **Show notifications** (■ changes to ✔) if you want to receive notifications for this app.

7 Tap **App info**.

The Application Manager screen appears.

8 Repeat steps **5** to **7** to choose settings for other apps as needed.

Set the Blue LED to Blink for Missed Notifications

9 Tap **Application manager** on the Application Manager screen.

The Settings screen appears.

10 In the Quick Settings section, tap **Display** (▣).

The Display screen appears.

11 Tap **LED indicator**.

The LED Indicator screen appears.

12 Tap **Notifications** (■ changes to ✔).

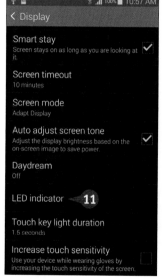

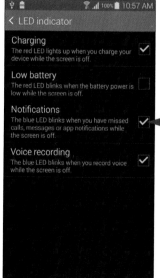

TIP

What does the red LED indicator mean?

When the screen is off, the red LED indicator conveys two messages:

- **Constant red LED:** This indicates that the battery is charging. You can turn on this notification by tapping **Charging** (■ changes to ✔) on the LED Indicator screen.
- **Blinking red LED:** The red LED blinks to warn you that the battery power is low. You can turn on this notification by tapping **Low battery** (■ changes to ✔) on the LED Indicator screen.

Choose Volume and Sound Settings

Your Galaxy S 5 enables you to control the playback volume of sounds and music in two ways: by pressing the physical volume buttons on the left side of the phone and by using on-screen controls.

You can control which audio feedback your Galaxy S 5 gives by choosing settings on the Sound screen. You can set the ringtone and vibration, specify the default notification sound, and choose whether to play sounds to give feedback when you take actions such as tapping the screen or locking the screen.

Choose Volume and Sound Settings

1 Pull down from the top of the screen.

The Notifications panel opens.

2 Tap and hold **Sound** (🔊).

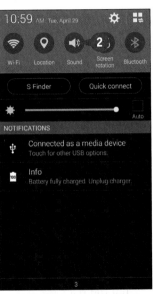

The Sound screen appears.

3 Tap **Volume**.

The Volume dialog box opens.

4 Drag the **Ringtone** slider to set the ringtone volume.

5 Drag the **Music, video, games and other media** slider to set the volume for these items.

6 Drag the **Notifications** slider to set the notifications volume.

7 Drag the **System** slider to set the volume for system sounds, such as for screen taps.

8 Tap **OK**.

You are returned to the Sound screen.

9 Tap **Vibration intensity**.

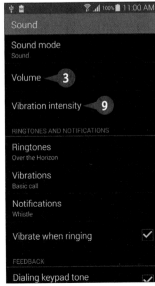

The Vibration Intensity dialog box opens.

⑩ Drag the sliders as needed.

⑪ Tap **OK**.

You are returned to the Sound screen.

⑫ Tap **Ringtones** and select the ringtone.

⑬ Tap **Vibrations** and select the vibration pattern.

⑭ Tap **Notifications** and select the default notification sound.

⑮ Tap **Vibrate when ringing** if you want vibrations and ringing together.

⑯ Tap the options in the Feedback section to choose which sounds to play.

⑰ Tap **Sound when tapped** if you want to hear sounds when you tap keys on the keyboard.

⑱ Tap **Vibrate when tapped** if you want vibrations when you tap keys.

⑲ Tap the Back button.

The Home screen appears.

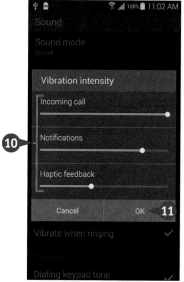

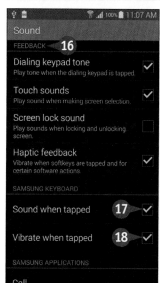

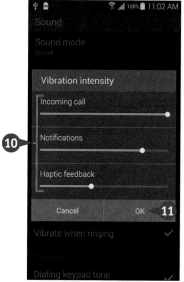

TIP

What does the Sound Mode button do?

The Sound Mode button enables you to switch among having your Galaxy S 5 play sounds, having it vibrate, and having it be mute and still. Tap **Sound mode** on the Sound screen in the Settings app to display the Sound Mode dialog box and then tap **Sound**, **Vibrate**, or **Mute** (■ changes to ◉), as needed.

Set the Display Options and Wallpaper

You can change the brightness of your Galaxy S 5's display as needed. You can use the Automatic Brightness feature to automatically adjust the display brightness to a level that suits the ambient brightness that the light sensor detects.

You can customize the Home screen or the lock screen by changing the wallpaper that appears in the background. You can choose a picture of your own from the Gallery app, select a built-in static wallpaper, or pick a live wallpaper that shows changing patterns.

Set Display Options and Wallpaper

Adjust the Screen Brightness

1 Pull down from the top of the screen.

The Notifications panel opens.

2 Drag the **Brightness** slider to set the brightness.

3 Tap **Auto** (■ changes to ✓) if you want to turn on Automatic Brightness.

Note: You can also change the brightness by tapping **Brightness** on the Display screen in Settings.

Set the Wallpaper

1 Pull down from the top of the screen.

The Notifications panel opens.

2 Tap ⚙.

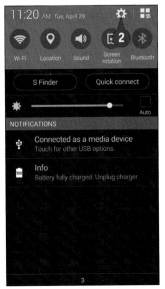

The Settings screen appears.

3 In the Quick Settings section, tap **Wallpaper** (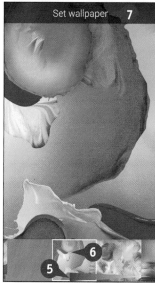).

The Wallpaper screen appears.

4 Tap **Home screen**, **Lock screen**, or **Home and lock screens**, depending on which screen you want to affect.

Note: This example uses the Home screen.

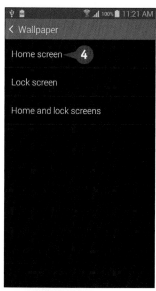

The Set Wallpaper screen appears.

5 Scroll the thumbnails left or right.

6 Tap the thumbnail for the wallpaper that you want.

7 Tap **Set wallpaper**.

Settings applies the wallpaper.

8 Press the Home button.

The wallpaper appears, and you can judge how well it works with your desktop items.

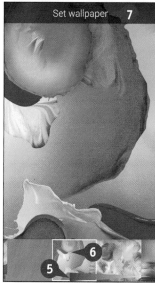

TIP

How do I use one of my photos as wallpaper?

On the Wallpaper screen, tap **Home screen**, **Lock screen**, or **Home and lock screens**. Tap the **More Images** button to display the Complete Action Using dialog box, tap **Gallery**, and then tap **Just once**. The Gallery app appears, which contains photos that you have taken with the Camera app as well as photos from other sources. Tap the album or collection that contains the photo and then tap the photo. When the photo opens, drag the selection handles to select the appropriate part of the photo and then tap **Done**.

Choose Location Access Settings

Your Galaxy S 5 can determine your location using three sources: satellites in the Global Positioning System (GPS), known wireless networks, and cellular phone towers. Android and your apps can use your location data to tag your photos, customize your searches, and provide local information where appropriate. Android enables you to choose whether to allow location access and — if you permit it — which means of determining your location to allow. You control location access separately for Google apps and for other apps.

Choose Location Access Settings

1 Pull down from the top of the screen.

The Notifications panel opens.

2 Tap and hold **Location** (🔵).

The Location screen appears.

3 Set the **Location** switch to **On**.

The Location Consent dialog box opens, requesting your permission for Google's location service to collect anonymous data.

4 Tap **Agree** or **Disagree**.

5 Tap **Mode**.

The Locating Method screen appears.

6 Tap **High accuracy**, **Power saving**, or **GPS only** (🔘 changes to 🔵).

7 Tap **Locating method**.

8 Tap **My places**.

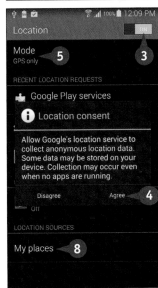

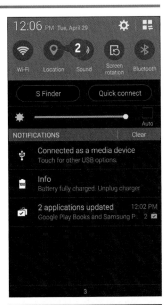

The My Places screen appears.

9 Tap **Home**.

The Home screen for Location settings appears.

10 Tap **Select method**.

Note: Your Galaxy S 5 can identify a location by map, by a wireless network, or by a nearby Bluetooth device. For example, you can use your home wireless network to identify your home and your car's Bluetooth device to identify your car.

The Select Method dialog box opens.

11 Tap **Maps**, **Wi-Fi**, or **Bluetooth** (⬤ changes to ⭘).

Note: This example uses **Wi-Fi**.

12 Tap **OK**.

The Wi-Fi screen appears.

13 Tap the wireless network that identifies the location.

The wireless network's name appears on the Home screen.

14 Tap **Done**.

Note: You can now tap **Office**, **Car**, or the Add button (➕) on the My Places screen to add another location.

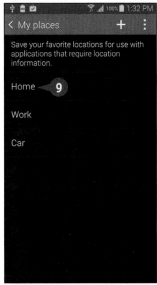

 TIP

Should I grant location access when apps request it?

That is entirely up to you. Each time an app requests location access, verify that it has a good reason for using location data and is not just snooping on your movements. Granting location access to apps can help you to get more out of your Galaxy S 5, but it also raises privacy concerns. For example, allowing social-media apps to access your location enables your friends to keep up with your movements but can also enable people to stalk you. Similarly, adding location information to your photos enables you to sort them by location, which is helpful. But if you post photos containing location information online, other people can tell exactly where you took the photos.

Secure Your Galaxy S 5

For security, you should apply a screen lock with a Personal Identification Number (PIN) to your Galaxy S 5. To unlock the phone, you must enter the PIN. For tighter security, you can use a password, which offers greater entropy than a PIN and so is harder to crack. You can also encrypt your Galaxy S 5, as explained in the following section, "Encrypt Your Galaxy S 5"; to encrypt, you must use a PIN or password of six characters or longer.

Secure Your Galaxy S 5

1 Pull down from the top of the screen.

The Notifications panel opens.

2 Tap ⚙.

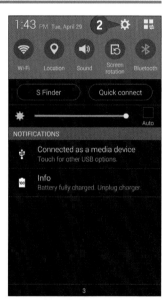

The Settings app opens.

3 In the Quick Settings section, tap **Lock screen** (🔒).

The Lock Screen screen appears.

4 Tap **Screen lock**.

Note: If your Galaxy S 5 currently has a screen lock applied, you must unlock it before you can proceed. For example, if a pattern is applied, you must draw the pattern on the Confirm Pattern screen.

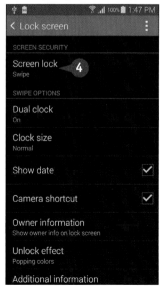

The Select Screen Lock screen appears.

5 Tap **PIN**.

The Select PIN screen appears.

6 Type a PIN of four digits or more.

7 Tap **Continue**.

A second Select PIN screen appears, prompting you to confirm your PIN.

8 Type the same PIN.

9 Tap **OK**.

The Lock Screen screen appears.

10 Tap **Lock instantly with power key** to enable locking by pressing the Power button.

A You can tap **Dual clock** or **Clock size** to configure the lock screen clock.

11 Tap **Lock automatically**.

The Lock Automatically dialog box opens.

12 Tap the appropriate option, such as **Immediately**.

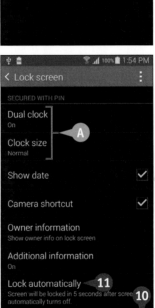
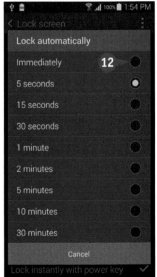

Instead of a PIN, how else can I secure my Galaxy S 5?
On the Select Screen Lock screen, you can choose four other methods of unlocking the screen. **Swipe**, the default method in which you swipe your finger across the screen, provides no security. **Pattern** requires you to draw a pattern on a grid of nine dots and provides medium security. **Fingerprint** requires you to swipe one of your fingers across the scanner built into the Home button; this method provides good security but requires a PIN as a backup. **Password** requires you to type a password and provides high security. Alternatively, choose **None** to disable locking altogether.

Encrypt Your Galaxy S 5

After securing your Galaxy S 5 with a password, you can protect your data further by encrypting it. Encryption encodes the data using a digital key, helping ensure that the data can be read only by someone who unlocks the Galaxy S 5 with the password.

Before encrypting your Galaxy S 5, you must charge its battery fully. During encryption, the phone must be connected to a power source. Android requires two sources of power to ensure that encryption can finish successfully because encryption failing may cause data loss.

Encrypt Your Galaxy S 5

1 Connect your Galaxy S 5 to a power source and charge the battery fully.

2 With the Galaxy S 5 still connected to the power source, pull down from the top of the screen.

The Notifications panel opens.

3 Tap ⚙.

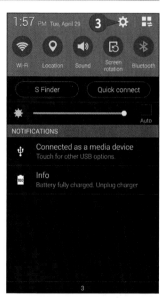

The Settings app opens.

4 In the System section, tap **Security** (🔒).

The Security screen appears.

5 Tap **Encrypt device**.

Note: If your Galaxy S 5 has no password applied or if the password is shorter than six characters, you are prompted to set an unlock password. Tap **Set screen lock type** and follow the prompts.

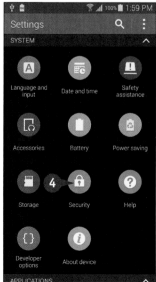

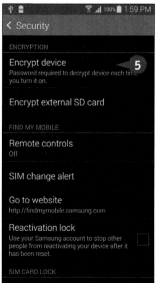

The Encrypt Device screen appears.

Note: If your Galaxy S 5 is not plugged into a power source, the Encrypt Device button is dimmed to indicate that it is unavailable.

6 Tap **Encrypt device**.

The Confirm Password screen appears.

7 Type your password.

8 Tap **Continue**.

The Confirm Encryption screen appears.

9 Tap **Fast encryption** (■ changes to ✔) to encrypt only used memory space.

10 Tap **Encrypt device**.

Your Galaxy S 5 is encrypted.

The Enter Your PIN or Password to Use the Encrypted Device Memory screen appears.

11 Type your password.

12 Tap **Done**.

The lock screen appears, and you can unlock your Galaxy S 5 by typing your password.

TIPS

Do I need to encrypt my Galaxy S 5?
You need to encrypt it only if you store highly sensitive or valuable personal or business data on it. If you use your phone mostly for enjoying media and browsing the web, a PIN or password probably offers adequate protection.

How do I remove encryption from my Galaxy S 5?
The only way to remove encryption is to perform a factory data reset, which wipes all data from your Galaxy S 5 and restores it to the factory settings. You can then set up the phone again from scratch. See Chapter 14, "Troubleshooting Your Galaxy S 5," for instructions on performing a factory data reset.

Choose Language and Input Settings

Android enables you to choose which language to use for its user interface. Android supports many languages, and you can switch quickly among them as needed. Android also provides various ways of entering text, ranging from assorted keyboard layouts to using speech to input text with the Google Voice feature. You use the Language and Input screen in Settings to configure your UI language and input methods.

Choose Language and Input Settings

1 Pull down from the top of the screen.

The Notifications panel opens.

2 Tap 🔧.

The Settings app opens.

3 In the System section, tap **Language and input** (🅰).

The Language and Input screen appears.

4 To change the language, tap **Language**, tap the desired language on the Language screen, and then tap the Back button.

5 Tap the **Samsung Keyboard** 🔧.

The Samsung Keyboard Settings screen appears.

6 Tap **Select input languages**.

Note: If the Input Languages dialog box opens, tap **OK** to update the language list.

The Input Languages screen appears.

7 Tap the option for each input language to use.

A You can tap **Update** to update a language's data.

B You can tap a language to download it.

8 Tap **Input languages**.

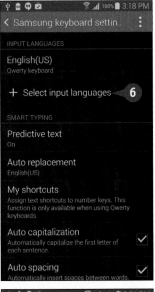
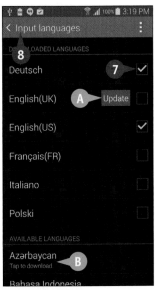

You are returned to the Samsung Keyboard Settings screen.

9 Choose options in the Smart Typing section. See the Tip for details.

10 Scroll down.

11 Choose options in the Key-Tap Feedback section to control which feedback occurs when you tap a key.

C You can tap **Reset settings** to reset the keyboard settings to their defaults.

TIP

What do the options in the Smart Typing section do?
Set **Predictive text** to **On** to display suggestions for completing the current word. Tap **Predictive text** and use the options that appear to customize the sources for predictive text. With predictive text on, set **Auto replacement** to **On** to have the predicted word automatically inserted when you tap the space bar or a punctuation key. Tap **Auto capitalization** (■ changes to ✓) to automatically capitalize the first word of each sentence or paragraph. Tap **Auto spacing** (■ changes to ✓) to insert spaces between words automatically. Tap the **Auto punctuate** option (■ changes to ✓) to insert a period by typing two spaces.

Customize the Home Screens

ndroid enables you to customize the Home screens on your Galaxy S 5. You can add the apps and widgets that you find the most useful and remove any apps or widgets that you do not need. You can reposition the apps and widgets on each Home screen to suit your preferences, and you can customize the Favorites tray at the bottom of the Home screen with apps that you use frequently. You can also resize the widgets to their optimum sizes.

Customize the Home Screens

Place an App on a Home Screen

1 Press the Home button.

The Home screen appears.

2 Swipe left or right to display the Home screen on which you want to place the app.

A You can also tap the dot that represents the Home screen.

3 Tap **Apps** (⊞).

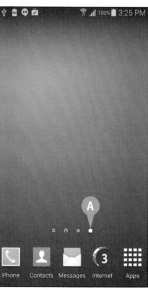

The Apps screen appears.

Note: You can change the view by tapping ⋮, tapping **View as**, and then tapping **Custom** or **Alphabetical order** (⬤ changes to ◉).

4 Tap and hold the app that you want to add to the Home screen.

The Home screen appears with the app on it.

5 Drag the app to where you want it to appear and then release the app.

The app's button appears on the screen.

Customize the Favorites Tray

1 Press the Home button.

The Home screen appears.

2 Swipe left or right to display the Home screen that contains the button that you want to put in the Favorites tray.

3 Tap and hold the button until it becomes movable.

4 Drag the button to the existing button that you want to replace and then release it.

The buttons switch places.

Place a Widget on the Home Screen

1 Press the Home button.

The Home screen appears.

2 Tap a dot or swipe left or right to display the Home screen on which you want to place the widget.

3 Tap and hold an empty space on the Home screen.

The customization options appear.

4 Tap **Widgets** (▦).

TIP

What are widgets?

Widgets are miniature apps that display useful information or give you quick access to frequently used apps. For example, the Dual Clock widget enables you to see the time in two locations at once. The Gmail widget displays the contents of an e-mail folder, and you can tap a message to open it in the Gmail app. Your Galaxy S 5 comes with a wide range of built-in widgets, but you can also download other widgets from the Play Store and other online sources.

continued ▶

If you put many apps on your Home screens, you may want to create folders to separate the apps into convenient categories. After creating and naming a folder, you drag icons to the folder to add apps to it.

You can create folders both on the main part of the Home screen and in the Favorites tray. After creating a folder, you can populate it with as many apps as needed. You can quickly open an app from within the folder, and you can remove an app from the folder if necessary.

Customize the Home Screens (continued)

The Widgets screen appears.

5 Tap and hold the widget that you want to add.

The Home screen appears with the widget on it.

6 Drag the widget to where you want it and then release it.

Note: After you add the widget, you may need to choose options for it. For example, the Gmail widget displays the Choose Folder dialog box so that you can select the folder to display.

Resize a Widget

1 Press the Home button.

The Home screen appears.

2 Tap a dot or swipe left or right to display the Home screen that contains the widget.

3 Tap and hold the widget.

A An outline and adjustment handles appear around the widget.

4 Drag a handle to resize the widget.

5 Tap outside the widget to deselect it.

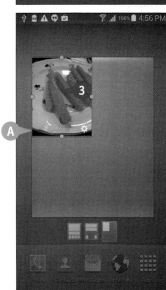

Create a Folder

1 Press the Home button.

The Home screen appears.

2 Tap a dot or swipe left or right to display the Home screen that contains the app that you want to put into a new folder.

3 Tap and hold the app.

The folder controls appear.

4 Drag the app to the **Create folder** button () and drop it there.

The Create Folder dialog box opens.

5 Type the name for the folder.

6 Tap the Add button (➕).

7 Tap each app that you want to add to the folder (⬛ changes to ☑).

8 Tap **Done**.

Android adds the apps to the folder.

Note: To launch an app from the folder, tap the folder so that the folder's contents appear and then tap the app.

TIPS

How do I remove an app or a widget from the Home screen?

Tap and hold the app or widget until the Remove button appears at the top of the screen. Drag the app or widget to the Remove button and then drop it.

How do I remove an app from a folder?

Tap the folder to open it, tap and hold the app's button, and then drag the app's button out of the folder and drop it in open space on the Home screen.

Customize the Lock Screen

Android enables you to customize the lock screen, the screen that appears when you turn on your Galaxy S 5 or wake it from sleep. You can add the dual clock feature to the lock screen, showing the time in your home city and — when you are roaming — in your current location. You can also display the date, your owner information, and weather and pedometer information.

In order to be able to take photos quickly, you can add the Camera shortcut to the lock screen.

Customize the Lock Screen

1 Pull down from the top of the screen.

The Notifications panel opens.

2 Tap ⚙.

Note: If you set the screen lock method to None, the lock screen does not appear, and you cannot set options for it.

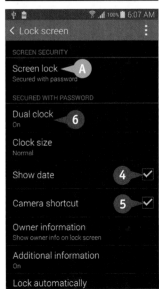

The Settings app opens.

3 In the Sound and Display section, tap **Lock screen** (⬛).

The Lock Screen screen appears.

Ⓐ You can tap **Screen lock** to choose a different means of screen locking if necessary.

4 Tap **Show date** (⬛ changes to ✅) to show the date.

5 Tap **Camera shortcut** (⬛ changes to ✅) to show the Camera shortcut.

6 Tap **Dual clock**.

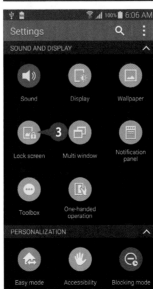

The Dual Clock screen appears.

7 Set the **Dual clock** switch to **On**.

8 Tap **Set home city**, tap the appropriate time zone on the Set Home City screen, and then tap the Back button.

9 Tap **Dual clock**.

10 Tap **Clock size** and tap **Small**, **Normal**, or **Large** (changes to).

11 Tap **Owner information**.

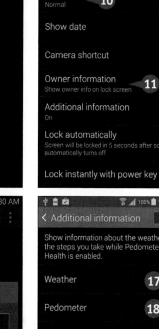

12 Type your information.

13 Tap **Show owner info on lock screen** (changes to).

14 Tap **OK**.

15 Tap **Additional information**.

The Additional Information screen appears.

16 Set the **Additional information** switch to **On**.

17 Tap **Weather** (changes to).

18 Tap **Pedometer** (changes to).

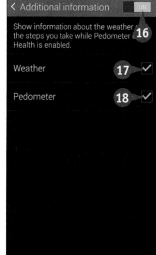

TIP

What screen lock method should I choose for security?
Use the Fingerprint screen lock if you are content with medium security; use the Password screen lock if you need top security. To secure your Galaxy S 5 effectively, tap **Lock automatically** on the Lock Screen screen and then tap **Immediately** (changes to). You should also tap **Lock instantly with power key** (changes to) so that you can lock your Galaxy S 5 at a moment's notice by pressing the Power button.

Set Up Sleep and Daydream

To conserve battery power, your Galaxy S 5 automatically goes to sleep after a period of inactivity. You can control how long this period is.

Android includes Daydream, a feature similar to screen savers on computers. By turning on Daydream and choosing settings, you can make your Galaxy S 5 display animations, photos, or information in the Flipboard app on-screen while it sleeps or charges.

Set Up Sleep and Daydream

1 Pull down from the top of the screen.

The Notifications panel opens.

2 Tap ⚙.

The Settings app opens.

3 In the Quick Settings section, tap **Display** (▣).

The Display screen appears.

4 Tap **Screen timeout**.

The Screen Timeout dialog box opens.

5 Tap the period of inactivity to allow before your Galaxy S 5 goes to sleep, such as **15 seconds**.

6 Tap **Daydream**.

The Daydream screen appears.

7 Set the **Daydream** switch to **On**.

8 Tap the theme that you want to use (⬛ changes to ⚫).

9 Tap ⚙ to the right of the theme, if it appears.

The settings screen for the theme appears.

10 Tap the option that you want to use (⬛ changes to ☑).

A You can tap **Select all** to select all the options.

11 Tap the Back button.

The Daydream screen appears.

12 Tap **Preview**.

The Daydream theme appears, and you can preview it.

13 Press the Home button.

The lock screen appears, and you can unlock it using your usual method.

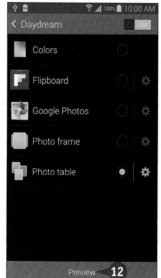

TIP

What is the difference between the Photo Frame theme and the Photo Table theme?
The Photo Frame theme shows one photo at a time and is good for enjoying your photos. Generally speaking, Photo Frame works better on Android tablets than on Android phones, simply because tablets' larger screens make the photos easier to view than phones' smaller screens do. The Photo Table theme gradually arranges miniature versions of your photos onto a table-like surface and is more of a decorative effect.

Set Up Accessibility Features

Android provides a range of accessibility features that enable you to make your Galaxy S 5 easier and more convenient to use. These features range from general accessibility features, such as enabling or disabling automatic rotation of the screen, to features for helping with vision, hearing, or mobility problems. You can configure these features by opening the Settings app and working on the Accessibility screen.

Set Up Accessibility Features

Display the Accessibility Screen and Choose Vision Accessibility Features

1 Pull down from the top of the screen.

The Notifications panel opens.

2 Tap ⚙.

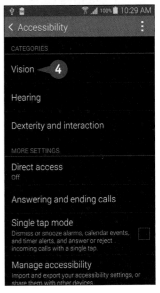

The Settings app opens.

3 In the Personalization section, tap **Accessibility** (⬛).

The Accessibility screen appears.

4 Tap **Vision**.

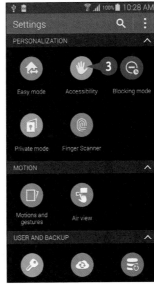

The Vision screen appears.

5 Tap **Font size**.

The Font Size dialog box opens.

6 Tap the font size, such as **Small** ( changes to ○).

7 Tap **Magnification gestures**.

The Magnification Gestures screen appears.

8 Set the **Magnification gestures** switch to **On**.

9 Tap **Magnification gestures**.

The Vision screen appears.

10 Tap **Negative colors** (■ changes to ✔) if you want to invert the screen colors.

11 Tap **Text-to-speech options** if you want to configure the Text-to-Speech feature.

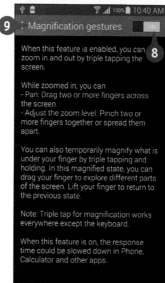
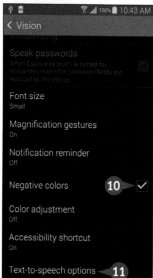

TIP

How do I use the Magnification Gestures feature?

After setting the **Magnification gestures** switch to On, triple-tap the screen to zoom in or out. After zooming in, drag two or more fingers across the screen to pan around. Pinch inward or outward with two fingers to adjust the zoom level. You can also triple-tap and hold to magnify an item temporarily; while holding, move your finger around the screen to pan to different areas.

continued ▶

On the Accessibility screen, you can configure several vision-related features. You can increase the font size to make text easier to read, turn on magnification gestures to enable easy zooming, or invert the screen colors to improve visibility. You can also configure how the Text-to-Speech feature reads on-screen content.

Android also provides several hearing-related accessibility features. You can adjust the sound balance, use mono audio for a single earphone, or turn off all sounds. You can also make the camera light flash to alert you to notifications.

Set Up Accessibility Features (continued)

Choose Hearing Accessibility Features

1 On the Accessibility screen, tap **Hearing**.

The Hearing screen appears.

2 Tap **Flash notification** (■ changes to ✔) to make the Camera light flash when notifications arrive.

3 Tap **Turn off all sounds** (■ changes to ✔) to turn off all sounds temporarily.

A You can tap **Samsung subtitles (CC)** to configure subtitles on Samsung services.

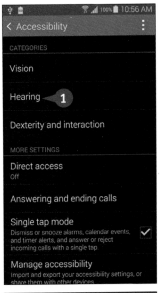

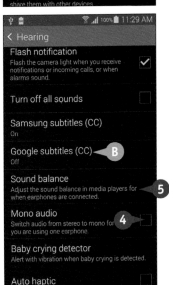

B You can tap **Google subtitles (CC)** to configure subtitles on Google services.

4 Tap **Mono audio** (■ changes to ✔) to play mono audio.

Note: This is useful when you use an earphone.

5 Tap **Sound balance**.

6 Drag the slider toward the Left end or the Right end, as needed.

7 Tap **Set**.

8 Tap **Hearing**.

The Accessibility screen appears.

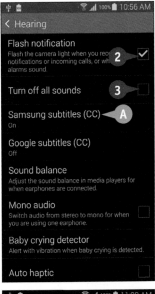

Choose Direct Access Settings

1 On the Accessibility screen, tap **Direct access**.

The Direct Access screen appears.

2 Set the **Direct access** switch to **On**.

3 In the Accessibility Settings area, tap each item — **Accessibility**, **TalkBack**, **Negative colors**, and **Interaction control** — that you want to appear in the Direct Access dialog box (■ changes to ✓).

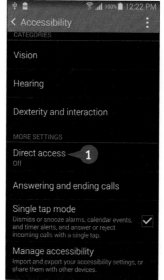

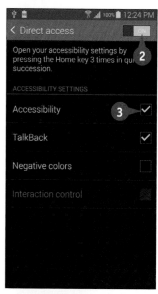

Choose Settings for Answering/Ending Calls

1 Tap **Answering and ending calls**.

2 In the Answer Calls By area, tap each answering method — **Pressing the Home key**, **Voice control**, and **Waving hand over device** — that you want to use (■ changes to ✓).

3 Tap **Pressing the power key** (■ changes to ✓) to end calls by pressing the Power button.

TIP

How can I transfer my accessibility settings to another device?

On the Accessibility screen, tap **Manage accessibility** to display the Manage Accessibility screen. There, you can transfer your accessibility settings in two ways:

- Tap **Import/Export** to display the Import/Export dialog box, which enables you to import a file to or export a file from either My Files or the SD card.

- Tap **Share via** to copy the accessibility settings to an SD card and then insert the card in the other device and import the settings.

Using TalkBack and Explore by Touch

Android includes a feature called *TalkBack* that can read the items on the screen for you. TalkBack can be a big help when you find it hard to see what your screen is displaying. TalkBack says the name of the current screen or dialog box and announces the items that you tap on the screen, enabling you to navigate by listening. After you turn on TalkBack, you can also use the Explore by Touch feature, which announces the name of the item under your finger on the screen.

Using TalkBack and Explore by Touch

1 Pull down from the top of the screen.

The Notifications panel opens.

2 Tap ⚙.

Note: Android cannot use TalkBack at the same time as some other features, such as Air Gesture, Smart Screen, and Multi Window. If these features are enabled when you turn on TalkBack, Android disables them.

The Settings app opens.

3 In the Personalization section, tap **Accessibility** (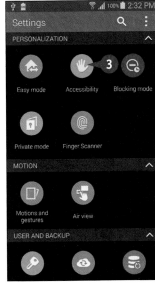).

The Accessibility screen appears.

4 Tap **Vision**.

The Vision screen appears.

5 Tap **TalkBack**.

The TalkBack screen appears.

Note: The first time you turn on TalkBack, a tutorial runs. Follow through it, tapping once to select a button and tapping again to press it.

6 Set the **TalkBack** switch to **On**.

7 Tap **OK**.

8 Tap **Settings**.

The TalkBack Settings screen appears.

9 Tap **Use pitch changes** (■ changes to ✔) to use a lower-pitched voice for keyboard feedback.

10 Tap **Use proximity sensor** (■ changes to ✔) to stop TalkBack when you bring your Galaxy S 5 to your face.

11 Tap **Speak caller ID** (■ changes to ✔) to have TalkBack announce incoming callers.

12 Tap **Explore by touch** (■ changes to ✔) to use Explore by Touch.

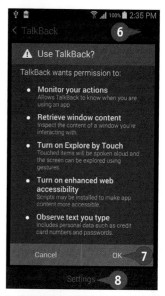

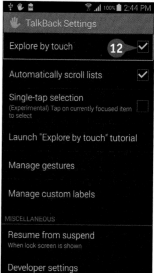

TIP

What other settings can I choose for TalkBack?

Tap **Keyboard echo** and then tap **Always speak typed keys**, **Only for on-screen keyboard**, or **Never speak typed keys** (◉ changes to ◉) in the Keyboard Echo dialog box. Tap **Vibration feedback** (■ changes to ✔) to receive TalkBack feedback via vibration. Tap **Focus speech audio** (■ changes to ✔) to make your Galaxy S 5 decrease the volume of any other audio it is playing while TalkBack is speaking. Tap **Manage gestures** to display the Manage Gestures screen, on which you can configure gestures for controlling your Galaxy S 5.

Set Up and Use Kids Mode

Your Galaxy S 5 includes a Kids mode that enables you to restrict the apps and content that a user can access. As its name suggests, Kids mode is primarily intended for children, and its design reflects this.

To use Kids mode, you normally need to install the app from a widget on a Home screen panel. You can then run Kids mode, set a PIN to lock it, and create a profile for the child who will use it.

Set Up and Use Kids Mode

1 Press the Home button.

2 Swipe left one or more times to locate the Kids Mode widget (📷).

Note: If the Kids Mode widget (📷) does not appear on a Home screen panel, add it as explained in the section "Customize the Home Screens," earlier in this chapter.

3 Tap **Kids Mode** (📷).

The Install Application dialog box opens.

4 Tap **OK**.

The Kids Mode screen appears.

5 Tap **Install**.

Your Galaxy S 5 installs the app.

6 Tap **Kids Mode** (📷) on the Home screen panel.

The Kids Mode introductory screen appears.

7 Tap **Set PIN**.

The Enter Your New PIN screen appears.

8 Type the PIN.

The Confirm Your New PIN screen appears.

9 Type the PIN again.

The Kid's Profile screen appears.

10 Use the controls to create the profile for your child.

11 On the Allow Applications screen, tap each app that you want to allow your child to use (☐ changes to ☑).

12 When Kids mode opens, hand your Galaxy S 5 to your child.

13 To exit Kids mode, tap the Exit button (▧) and then type your PIN.

TIP

What are the apps in Kids mode?

▨ is a media viewer for pictures, voice recordings, and media files. ▨ is a camera app for taking photos and videos. ▨ is a drawing app, ▨ is an audio player, and ▨ is a video player. The wrapped packages (▨) represent the apps that you have allowed in the child's profile.

CHAPTER 3

Working with Text and Voice

You can input text into your Galaxy S 5 using the on-screen keyboard, the continuous input features, and voice input. You can also control your Galaxy S 5 with your voice by using features such as voice search and Car mode.

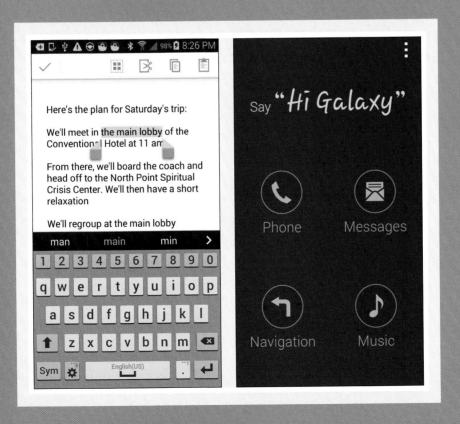

Using the On-screen Keyboard and Continuous Input

The most straightforward way to enter text in an app is by tapping the keys on the on-screen keyboard. Android automatically displays this keyboard when you tap an input field. The keyboard appears at the bottom of the screen by default, but you can move it elsewhere if you prefer.

The keyboard has a feature called *continuous input* that enables you to enter a word by tapping its first letter, keeping your finger on the screen, and then sliding your finger to each of the other letters in turn.

Using the On-screen Keyboard and Continuous Input

Open an App That Accepts Text Input

1 Press the Home button.

The Home screen appears.

2 Tap **Apps** (▦).

The Apps screen appears.

3 Tap the app, such as **Gmail** (✉).

4 Open a document in which to input text, such as by tapping the New Message button (✉).

In this example, a new message opens.

Type on the On-Screen Keyboard

1 Tap here.

A The keyboard switches to uppercase at the beginning of a sentence.

2 Start typing.

Note: After the first letter of the sentence, the keyboard types lowercase letters unless you tap ⬆. You can turn on Caps Lock by double-tapping ⬆.

B The Suggestions bar shows suggestions.

3 Tap **>** to see more suggestions.

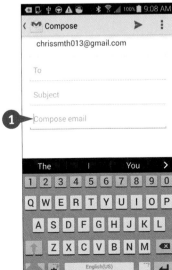
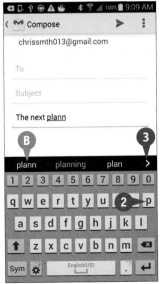

The Suggestions panel opens.

4 If a suggestion is correct, tap it to enter it. Otherwise, keep typing.

C The word appears in the document.

5 Tap the first letter of the next word and, keeping your finger on the screen, move to each of the remaining letters in turn.

D The blue line shows the last part of the path your finger has followed.

6 Lift your finger off the screen.

The word appears in the document.

7 Tap **Sym**.

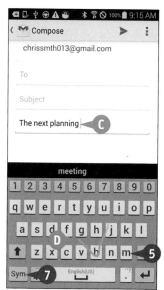

The first screen of the Symbols keyboard appears, showing widely used symbols.

8 Tap **1/2**.

The second screen of the Symbols keyboard appears, showing other symbols.

9 Tap the symbol that you want to insert.

10 Tap **ABC**.

The letters keyboard appears again.

How do I turn on continuous input?

1 Pull down from the top of the screen.

2 Tap ⚙ to open the Settings app.

3 Tap **Language and input** to display the Language and Input screen.

4 Tap ⚙ to the right of Samsung Keyboard to display the Samsung Keyboard Settings screen.

5 In the Keyboard Swipe area, tap **Keyboard swipe** to display the Keyboard Swipe screen.

6 Tap **Continuous input** (⬤ changes to ◉).

Work with Different Keyboards

Your Galaxy S 5 provides several different keyboards to enable you to enter text and other items quickly in your documents. For example, you can type on a standard keyboard or a floating keyboard, insert *emoticons* — smiley characters and similar graphics — in your documents, or enter text by handwriting with your finger on the screen. To access these features, you tap and hold the button to the left of the spacebar and then tap the appropriate icon on the pop-up panel that appears.

Work with Different Keyboards

Open an App That Accepts Text Input

1 Press the Home button.

The Home screen appears.

2 Tap **Apps** (▦).

The Apps screen appears.

3 Tap the app, such as **Gmail** (✉).

4 Open a document in which to input text, such as by tapping ✉.

In this example, a new message opens.

Explore the Available Keyboards

1 Tap here.

Ⓐ The keyboard appears.

2 Tap and hold this button, which shows the last-used keyboard, such as regular (▦), emoticon (☺), or voice input (🎙).

Note: You can tap that button to switch straight to the last keyboard that you used.

The keyboard panel appears.

3 Tap the Voice Input button (🎙).

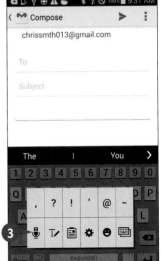

The voice input keyboard appears.

4 Speak the text that you want to enter.

B You can tap **Tap to pause** to turn off the microphone.

Note: The microphone automatically turns off after several seconds of inactivity.

C You can tap **Tap to speak** to turn on the microphone again.

5 Tap the Keyboard button (⌨).

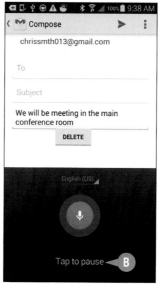

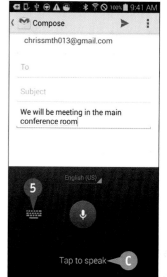

The keyboard appears.

6 Tap and hold 🎤.

The keyboard panel appears.

7 Tap the Emoticon button (☺).

The Emoticon keyboard appears.

D You can tap a tab to display another set of emoticons.

8 Tap the emoticon that you want to insert.

The emoticon appears in the document.

9 Tap **ABC**.

The regular keyboard appears.

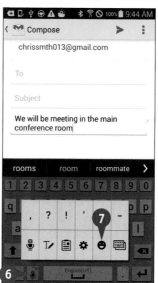

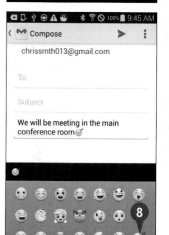

TIPS

How do I display the floating keyboard?
Tap ⌨ on the keyboard pop-up panel to switch to the floating keyboard, which you can reposition by dragging the dotted handle at the top. To return to the normal keyboard, tap ⌨.

What does the T icon on the keyboard pop-up panel do?
T⁄ is the Text button; tap it to turn on handwriting recognition. You can then write with your finger on the panel that appears. Your Galaxy S 5 recognizes the text and inserts it in the document.

Edit Text and Use Cut, Copy, and Paste

Your Galaxy S 5 makes it easy to edit existing text in documents and to select part or all of the text. You can cut selected text from the document or copy it to the clipboard and then paste it elsewhere in the same app or another app. Cutting text removes the selection from the document, whereas copying text leaves the selection in the document. The clipboard can contain multiple items, and you can paste each item as many times as you need.

Edit Text and Use Cut, Copy, and Paste

Edit Text

1 Open the document that you want to edit.

2 Tap where you want to position the insertion point.

The arrow for moving the insertion point (▉) appears.

3 If necessary, drag ▉ to move the insertion point.

4 Edit the text as needed.

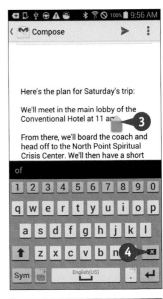

Select Text and Use Cut, Copy, and Paste

1 Tap and hold a word.

2 Drag ▉ or ▉ to extend the selection as needed.

Ⓐ You can tap ▦ to select all the text.

3 Tap ▤ to copy the text.

Ⓑ You can tap ▨ to cut the text.

Ⓒ You can tap ▨ to delete the text.

Ⓓ You can tap ☑ to turn off selection mode.

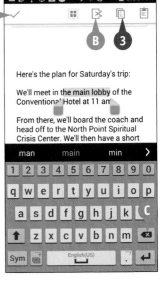

4 Tap where you want to paste the copied text.

Note: If you want the text you paste to replace existing text, select that text before pasting.

5 Tap 📋.

The Paste button appears.

6 Tap **Paste**.

The copied text appears in the document.

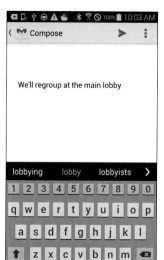

Paste Multiple Items

1 Tap and hold this button.

The keyboard panel appears.

2 Tap 📋.

The Clipboard pane appears.

3 Tap the item that you want to paste.

E The item appears in your document.

4 Tap another item that you want to paste.

F You can tap **Clear** to clear the contents of the clipboard.

5 Tap the Close button (✉).

TIP

Can I transfer the contents of the clipboard to my computer?
You cannot access the Android clipboard directly from your computer, but you can easily transfer the contents of the clipboard using workarounds. For example, begin a new e-mail message in the Gmail app or the Email app and address it to an e-mail account that your computer can access. You can then paste items from the clipboard and send the message.

Using Voice Input and Voice Search

Android enables you to enter text and search terms by speaking. The ability to input text by talking is called *voice input,* and this can be a great way of creating documents quickly. You access voice input directly from the on-screen keyboard in any app that accepts it.

The ability to search via voice is called *voice search*. Android implements voice search as a separate app that you launch from the Apps screen. You can search for web pages or identify music that is playing.

Using Voice Input and Voice Search

Use Voice Input

1 Open a new document by following steps **1** to **4** in the section "Work with Different Keyboards."

2 Tap where you want to input text.

3 Tap and hold this button.

The keyboard pop-up panel opens.

4 Tap 🎤.

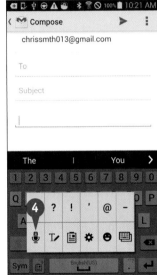

The Voice Input pane appears.

5 Speak the text.

The text is entered in your document.

Ⓐ You can tap **Tap to pause** to turn off the microphone.

Ⓑ You can tap **Delete** to delete your latest entry.

Ⓒ You can tap an underlined word or phrase to display a menu of possible corrections.

The keyboard appears.

6 Tap 🎤.

The Voice Input screen appears, and you can dictate more text.

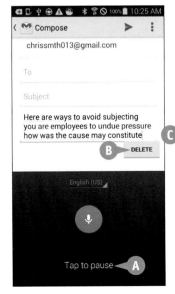

Use Voice Search

1 Press the Home button.

The Home screen appears.

2 Tap **Apps** (▦).

The Apps screen appears.

3 Tap **Voice Search** (🎤).

The Voice Search screen appears.

4 Speak your search terms.

D The gray circle indicates that your input is being processed.

E The interpreted words are displayed.

After you finish speaking, the search results are displayed.

5 Tap the result that you want to see.

Your default browser, such as Chrome, displays the web page.

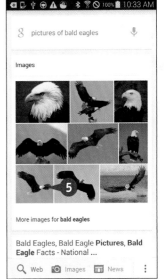

TIP

How do I look up the current song using voice search?

1 Press the Home button to display the Home screen.

2 Tap **Apps** (▦) to display the Apps screen.

3 Tap **Voice Search** (🎤) to open the Voice Search screen.

4 Tap the Music button (♫) to start Voice Search listening to the music. After analyzing a snippet of the music, Voice Search displays matches. You can tap **Google Play** to open the Play Store app and display the song.

Using S Voice

Voice enables you to take actions by using your voice to tell your Galaxy S 5 what you want. S Voice requires an Internet connection because the speech recognition runs on Samsung's servers.

You can use S Voice either with your Galaxy S 5's built-in microphone or with the microphone on a compatible headset. Unless you are in a quiet environment or you hold your Galaxy S 5 close to your face, a headset microphone normally gives better results than the built-in microphone.

Using S Voice

Open S Voice

1 Press the Home button twice.

S Voice opens.

Note: If this does not open S Voice, press the Home button, tap **Apps** (▦), and then tap **S Voice** (◉). Tap the Menu button, tap **Settings**, and then tap **Open via the home key** (■ changes to ✅).

A S Voice activates the microphone (🎤) but turns it off (🎤) if you do not speak.

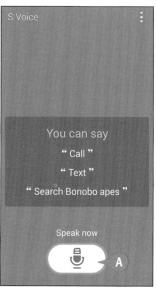

Wake S Voice and Give a Command

1 If the "Tap Mic" prompt appears, say, "Hi, Galaxy" or tap the microphone (🎤 changes to 🎤).

B S Voice displays a prompt.

2 Speak your command.

Note: For example, you can say, "Set alarm for 5:30 a.m."

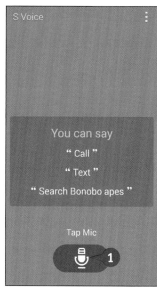

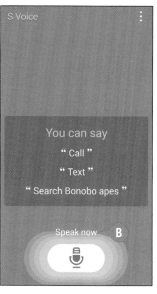

C S Voice displays its interpretation of what you said.

D Depending on the command, S Voice prompts you for further instructions.

Note: In this example, S Voice asks whether it should save the alarm.

3 Give the appropriate command, such as "Yes."

E S Voice acts on your command, such as saving an alarm.

F You can say, "Hi, Galaxy" or tap the microphone to make the microphone active again.

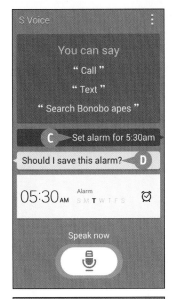

Open an App from S Voice

1 If the "Tap Mic" prompt appears, say, "Hi, Galaxy" or tap the microphone (🎙 changes to 🎙).

G S Voice displays a prompt.

2 Say, "Open" and the app's name.

Note: For example, say, "Open Gmail," to open Gmail.

S Voice displays its interpretation of what you said and opens the app.

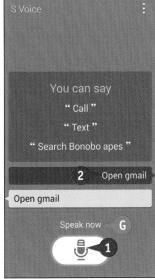

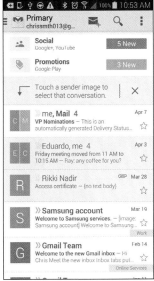

TIP

What other actions can I take with S Voice?

You can take many other actions, including these:

- **Dial a call.** Say, "Call Alice Smith mobile."
- **Send a text.** Say, "Text Sam message where are the car keys."
- **Start a memo in Memo.** Say, "Memo keynote for convention."
- **Schedule an event.** Say, "New event breakfast with Tiffany 8 a.m. October 1st at El Torito."
- **Create a task.** Say, "New task mend the broken window."

Using Car Mode

Your Galaxy S 5 includes a Car mode, also known as *hands-free mode* or *driving mode,* that automatically reads out the details of incoming calls and the text of new notifications when it is activated. You can turn Car mode on at any time, but it is primarily useful in situations when you cannot use your hands to manipulate the phone, such as when you are driving a vehicle.

Before using Car mode, it is a good idea to configure its settings to make sure that you receive only those calls and notifications you want.

Using Car Mode

1 Pull down with two fingers from the top of the screen.

The Quick Settings panel opens.

2 Tap **Car mode** (changes to).

A Warning screen appears while Car mode loads.

Note: The first time that you access Car mode, you must accept its terms and conditions.

The Car Mode screen appears.

A The "Say 'Hi Galaxy!'" prompt indicates that your Galaxy S 5 is listening for a wake-up call but not for instructions.

3 Say, "Hi Galaxy!"

Note: You can also tap the screen to wake up Car mode.

The Speak Now prompt appears.

4 Speak the command that you want your Galaxy S 5 to execute.

Note: For example, say, "Play 'Over the Horizon'" to play the song "Over the Horizon."

Your Galaxy S 5 executes the command and displays the appropriate screen, such as the Music screen.

B You can say, "Hi Galaxy!" and give another command, such as "Next song."

Car mode automatically displays its main screen after a few seconds of inactivity.

You can say, "Hi Galaxy!" and give other commands as needed.

5 When you are ready to stop using Car mode, pull down from the top of the screen with two fingers.

The Quick Settings panel opens.

6 Tap **Car mode** (changes to).

Your Galaxy S 5 turns Car mode off.

TIP

How can I change the language used in Car mode?

1 In Car mode, tap the Menu button ( ) to open the menu.

2 Tap **Settings** to display the Settings screen.

3 Tap **Language** to display the Language screen.

4 Tap the language that you want to use (changes to).

Setting Up Communications

To unleash the communications power of your Galaxy S 5, you can set up your e-mail accounts in the Gmail app and the Email app, import your contacts, and configure the S Planner calendaring app.

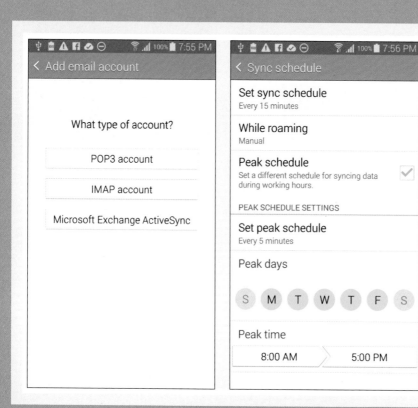

Set Up Your Gmail Accounts

Android's Gmail app enables you to send and receive e-mail using your account on Google's Gmail service. Android walks you through the process of setting up your primary Gmail account as you set up your device for the first time or as you add an account to it. If you have other Gmail accounts, you can add them manually at any time.

To start adding a Gmail account, you open the Settings app and use the Add Account command on the Accounts screen.

Set Up Your Gmail Accounts

1 Pull down from the top of the screen.

The Notifications panel opens.

2 Tap the Settings button (⚙).

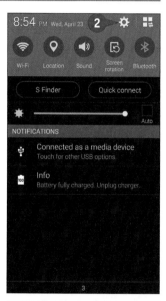

The Settings app opens.

3 In the User and Backup section, tap **Accounts** (◉).

The Accounts screen appears.

4 Tap **Add Account**.

The Add Account screen appears.

5 Tap **Google**.

The Add a Google Account screen appears.

6 Tap **Existing**.

A You can tap **New** to create a new account.

7 Type your e-mail address and password.

8 Tap Next (▶).

The Terms of Service dialog box opens.

9 Tap **OK**.

The Google Services screen appears.

10 Tap **Keep me up to date with news and offers from Google Play** (☑ changes to ▪) if you do not want to receive Google Play news and offers.

11 Tap **OK**.

The Set Up Payment Info screen appears.

12 Tap **Add credit or debit card** or **Redeem** if you want to set up a means of payment. Otherwise, tap **Not now**.

The Account Sign-in Successful screen appears.

13 Tap the options to select the services you want (▪ changes to ☑).

14 Tap ▶.

Your Gmail account is now set up.

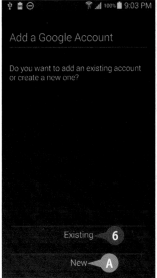

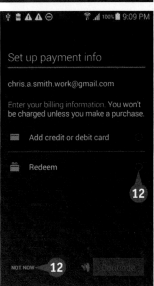

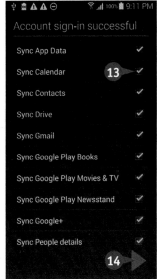

TIP

Which items should I sync with my Gmail account?
To get the most out of your Galaxy S 5, it is usually helpful to sync most, if not all, of the items that appear on the Account Sign-in Successful screen. If you want to sync only essential items and not entertainment items, sync App Data, Calendar, Contacts, and Gmail with your account.

Choose Essential Settings for Gmail

The Gmail app provides a wide variety of settings that enable you to control your e-mail account closely. To get the most out of Gmail on your Galaxy S 5, spend a few minutes exploring the settings that you can change and choosing options that suit your needs.

When customizing Gmail, start with the General settings category, which contains settings that apply to all your Gmail accounts. After that, move on to choose account-specific settings for each Gmail account.

Choose Essential Settings for Gmail

1 Press the Home button.

The Home screen appears.

2 Tap Apps (▦).

The Apps screen appears.

3 Tap **Gmail** (✉).

Note: If Gmail is not on the Apps screen that appears first, swipe right or left until you find it.

Your Inbox appears.

4 Tap the Menu button (⋮).

5 Tap **Settings**.

The Settings screen appears.

6 Tap **General Settings**.

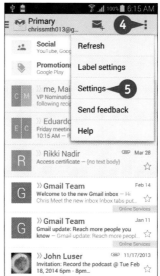

The General Settings screen appears.

7 Tap **Archive & delete actions**.

The Archive & Delete Actions dialog box opens.

8 Tap **Show archive only**, **Show delete only**, or **Show archive & delete** (◻ changes to ◉), as needed.

You are returned to the General Settings screen.

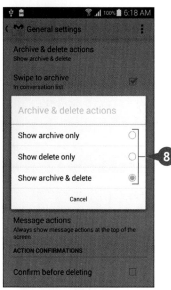

9 Tap **Swipe to archive** (◻ changes to ☑) to enable archiving a conversation by swiping.

Note: If you selected **Show delete only** in the Archive & Delete Actions dialog box, **Swipe to Delete** appears instead.

10 Tap **Auto-advance**.

The Advance To dialog box opens.

11 Tap **Newer**, **Older**, or **Conversation list** (◻ changes to ◉), as needed.

12 Tap **Message actions**.

TIP

What does the Advance To setting control?
The Advance To setting controls which conversation Gmail displays after you deal with the current conversation by archiving it or deleting it. Select **Newer** to display the next conversation, select **Older** to display the previous conversation, or select **Conversation list** to display the list so that you can tap the conversation you want to view next.

continued ▶

Gmail enables you to turn on or off action confirmations for deleting messages, archiving messages, and sending messages. The confirmations can be especially useful if you use your Galaxy S 5 while in motion or on public transit. But if you find the action confirmations unnecessary, turn them off.

You can designate the Inbox of one or more of your accounts as the Priority Inbox. Priority Inbox analyzes your incoming messages and grades them into three categories: "Important and unread," "Starred," and "Everything else."

Choose Essential Settings for Gmail (continued)

The Message Actions dialog box opens.

13 Tap **Always show**, **Only show in portrait**, or **Don't show**, as needed.

14 In the Action Confirmations area, choose which action confirmations to use by tapping **Confirm before deleting**, **Confirm before archiving**, or **Confirm before sending** (☐ changes to ☑).

15 Tap the Gmail button (✉).

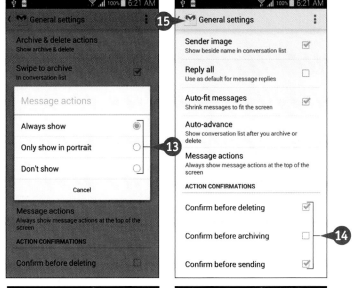

The Settings screen appears.

16 Tap the account that you want to configure.

The Settings screen for the account appears.

17 Tap **Inbox type**.

The Inbox Type dialog box opens.

18 Tap **Default Inbox** or **Priority Inbox** (◻ changes to ◉), as needed.

Note: The settings available change depending on which you choose.

19 Tap **Notifications** (◻ changes to ☑) to receive notifications.

20 Tap **Priority inbox sound & vibrate.**

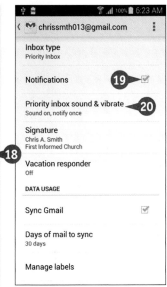

The Priority Inbox screen appears.

21 Tap **Sound** and choose the sound.

22 Tap **Vibrate** (◻ changes to ☑) if you want vibration notifications.

23 Tap ☑.

The Settings screen appears.

24 Tap **Sync Gmail** (◻ changes to ☑).

25 Tap ☑.

The Settings screen appears.

26 Tap ☑.

Your Inbox appears.

Why might I want to hide pictures in messages?

This can help preserve your privacy. A sender can add to a message not the picture itself but a link to the image file on a server on the Internet. When you open the message, Gmail downloads the image from the server. The server's logs can store the details of the download, enabling the sender to tell that you have read the message, when you read it, and the IP address from which your computer connected. If you hide pictures in messages, Gmail displays placeholder boxes for the picture areas. After establishing that a message is harmless, you can tap a placeholder to download its picture.

Set Up Your Other E-mail Accounts

As well as the Gmail app for accessing Google's Gmail service, your Galaxy S 5 includes an app called *Email*. You can use this app to access other types of e-mail accounts than Gmail. Before you can use the Email app, you must set up each account that you want to use in it and choose the account settings. You can set up many types of accounts by using only the account's e-mail address and password. For other accounts, you may need more information, such as the names of the incoming and outgoing mail servers.

Set Up Your Other E-mail Accounts

1 Press the Home button.

The Home screen appears.

2 Tap **Email** (icon).

The Email Accounts screen appears.

Note: If you have already set up an account, your Inbox appears. Tap the Menu button, tap **Settings**, and then tap **Add account**.

3 Type your e-mail address.

4 Type your password.

5 Tap **Next**.

Note: If Email sets up your account without further details, the Account Options screen appears. Go to step **17**.

The Add Email Account screen appears.

6 Tap **POP3 account**, **IMAP account**, or **Microsoft Exchange ActiveSync** to specify the account type.

The Incoming Server Settings screen appears.

7 Edit the username if necessary.

8 Edit the server address and security type if necessary.

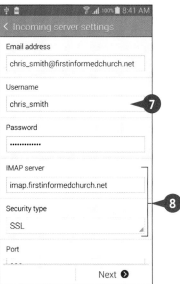

9 Change the port number if necessary.

10 For an IMAP account, enter the path prefix if necessary.

11 Tap **Next**.

12 Type the server name.

13 Tap the pop-up menu and select the security type.

14 Tap **Require sign-in** (☐ changes to ☑) if your e-mail provider requires you to sign in.

15 Edit the username if necessary.

16 Tap **Next**.

17 Choose options for syncing your e-mail messages.

18 Tap **Sync Email** (☐ changes to ☑).

19 Tap **Next**.

20 Type the name to display for the account.

21 Type your name as you want it to appear.

22 Tap **Done**.

Your Inbox appears.

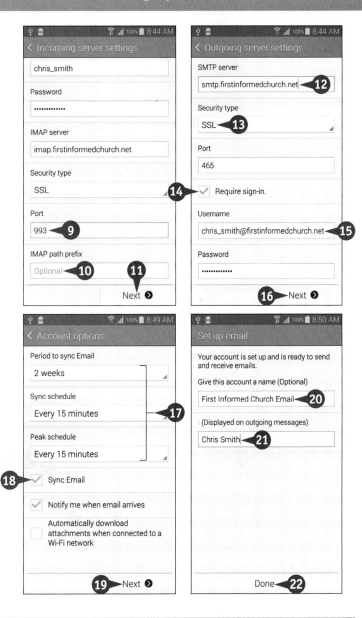

TIPS

What is the username for my e-mail account?
Your username is typically either the same as your e-mail address, such as csmith@example.com, or just the part before the @ sign, such as csmith. Your username may be different for the incoming and outgoing mail servers. If neither works, ask your e-mail provider.

What security type and port should I use?
This depends on your e-mail provider, so ask if possible. Many providers use SSL and port 993; for some, you may need to select **SSL (Accept all certificates)**. Some use TLS and port 143; you may need to select **TLS (Accept all certificates)**. Do not use the **None** setting for the **Security type** pop-up menu.

Set Your Default Account and Signatures

If you set up multiple e-mail accounts in the Email app, set the appropriate e-mail account to be the default account. This is the account from which the Email app sends messages unless you choose another account.

To help complete your e-mail messages without having to type the same information repeatedly, you can create e-mail signatures. A *signature* is text, such as your name and contact information, that the app automatically adds to the end of each message you create.

Set Your Default Account and Signatures

1 Press the Home button.

The Home screen appears.

2 Tap **Email** (⊚).

Ⓐ If ⊚ does not appear on the Home screen, tap **Apps** (▦) and then tap **Email** (⊚).

Your Inbox appears.

3 Tap the Menu button (▤).

4 Tap **Settings**.

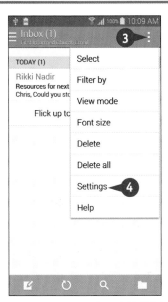

The Settings screen appears.

5 Tap **Manage accounts**.

The Manage Accounts screen appears.

Ⓑ "(Default)" appears on the current default account.

6 Tap the account that you want to make the default account.

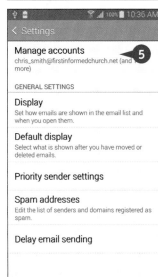

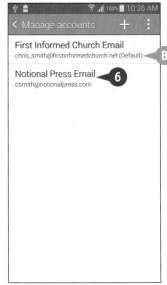

92

The settings screen for that account appears.

7 Tap **Default account** (☐ changes to ☑).

8 Tap **Signature**.

The Signature screen appears.

9 Set the **Signature** switch to **On**.

10 Tap **Edit signature**.

Note: E-mail convention is to keep signatures fairly short. A signature typically gives the sender's contact information and sometimes adds a quote.

The Edit Signature screen appears.

11 Type the text that you want to use for the signature.

12 Tap **Done**.

The Signature screen appears.

13 Tap the Back button four times to return to your Inbox.

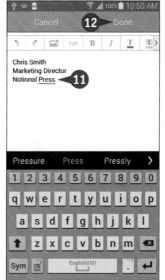

TIPS

How do I create a signature in the Gmail app?

In the Gmail app, tap ⋮ and then tap **Settings**. Tap the account that you want to affect and then tap **Signature**. Type the signature in the Signature dialog box and then tap **OK**.

How do I change the name that Email displays for an e-mail account?

In the Email app, tap the Menu button and then tap **Settings**. Tap **Manage accounts** to display the Manage Accounts screen and then tap the account that you want to rename. Tap **More settings** to display the More Settings screen and then tap **Account name**. Type the name in the Account Name dialog box and then tap **OK**.

Choose How and When to Get Your E-mail

The Email app can get your e-mail messages by using two different technologies, Push and Fetch. With Push, the e-mail server pushes your new messages to the app as soon as the server receives them. With Fetch, the app periodically checks the server for new messages and downloads any it finds. Push is normally more convenient than Fetch, but some e-mail providers do not support Push. In this case, you must use Fetch instead. You can configure the interval at which Fetch retrieves your e-mail. You can also check manually for e-mail at any point.

Choose How and When to Get Your E-mail

1 Press the Home button.

The Home screen appears.

2 Tap **Email** (⊚).

A If ⊚ does not appear on the Home screen, tap **Apps** (▦) and then tap **Email** (⊚).

Your Inbox appears.

3 Tap ⋮.

4 Tap **Settings**.

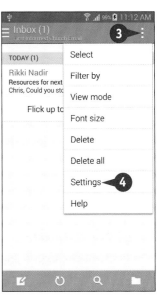

The Settings screen appears.

5 Tap **Manage accounts**.

The Manage Accounts screen appears.

6 Tap the account for which you want to choose sync settings.

The settings screen for the account appears.

7 Tap **Sync settings**.

The Sync Settings screen appears.

8 Tap **Sync Email** (☐ changes to ☑) if you want to sync e-mail.

B You can tap **Limit retrieval size** to display the Limit Retrieval Size screen, which enables you to set the maximum message size to retrieve.

9 Tap **Sync schedule**.

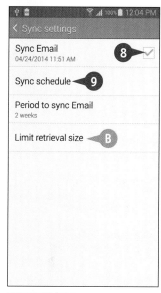

10 Tap **Set sync schedule**.

The Set Sync Schedule dialog box opens.

11 Tap the appropriate option (☐ changes to ⦿).

12 Tap **While roaming**.

The While Roaming dialog box opens.

13 Tap **Manual** or **Use above settings** (☐ changes to ⦿), as needed.

14 Tap the Back button several times to return through the settings screens to your Inbox.

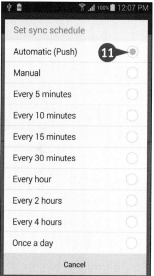

TIPS

How do I set up a peak schedule?

1 Tap **Peak schedule** (☐ changes to ☑).

2 Tap **Set peak schedule** to display the Set Peak Schedule dialog box.

3 Tap the appropriate option, such as **5 minutes** (☐ changes to ⦿).

4 Tap the **Peak days** letters to toggle them on or off. A green circle indicates a peak day.

5 Tap the two **Peak time** buttons to set the start time and end time.

Can I choose between Push and Fetch for Gmail?

No. At this writing, Gmail does not enable you to choose between Push and Fetch.

Set Up and Use the Priority Inbox

The Gmail app includes a feature called *Priority Inbox* that helps you to identify the messages that need your attention urgently. Priority Inbox is especially useful if you receive many e-mail messages.

Priority Inbox attempts to identify your important messages so that it can present them to you separately from your less-important messages. To use Priority Inbox, you turn on the feature in Gmail's settings. You can then display your Priority Inbox in Gmail and work through its contents.

Set Up and Use the Priority Inbox

1 Press the Home button.

The Home screen appears.

2 Tap **Apps** (▦).

The Apps screen appears.

3 Tap **Gmail** (✉).

Note: If Gmail is not on the Apps screen that appears first, swipe right or left until you find it.

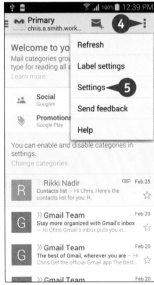

Your Inbox appears.

4 Tap ⋮.

5 Tap **Settings**.

The Settings screen appears.

6 Tap the account for which you want to set up Priority Inbox.

The settings screen for the account appears.

7 Tap **Inbox type**.

The Inbox Type dialog box opens.

8 Tap **Priority Inbox** (⊙ changes to ⦿).

Options for configuring Priority Inbox appear.

9 Tap **Priority inbox sound & vibrate**.

The Priority Inbox screen appears.

10 Tap **Sound**, tap the sound in the Ringtones dialog box (⦿ changes to ○), and then tap **OK**.

11 Tap **Vibrate** (☐ changes to ☑) to receive vibrations.

12 Tap **Notify for every message** (☐ changes to ☑) if you want notifications for each message.

13 Tap ᴹ three times to return to your Inbox.

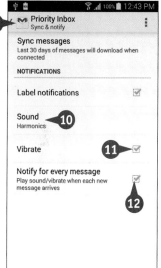

How do I use Priority Inbox?

In Gmail, tap the pop-up menu in the upper-left corner of the screen and then tap the name of the Priority Inbox that you want to display.

How does Priority Inbox work?

Priority Inbox collects any messages in conversations you and Gmail have labeled as important. You can mark a message as important by tapping ⋮ and then tapping **Mark important**. Gmail automatically labels messages as important for various reasons, such as messages from people you contact frequently. Even if Priority Inbox seems to be catching all your important messages, check your other messages in case any vital ones have ended up with your less-important messages.

Your Galaxy S 5's Contacts app enables you to manage your contacts. The Contacts app syncs contact data from your Google account, so your Google Contacts automatically appear in the Contacts app. You can also sync contacts from other e-mail accounts or import contacts manually. If you have many contacts, you may want to display only one group of them — for example, only your Facebook contacts or only your Corporate contacts. You can do this easily, but you can also create a custom display group that contains exactly the contacts you want to see.

Choose Which Contacts to Display

1 Press the Home button.

The Home screen appears.

2 Tap **Contacts** (📇).

Ⓐ If 📇 does not appear on the Home screen, tap **Apps** (▦) and then tap **Contacts** (📇).

The Contacts app opens.

3 Tap ⋮.

4 Tap **Settings**.

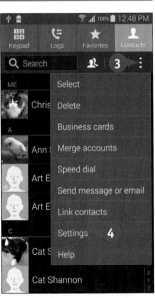

The Settings screen appears.

5 Tap **Contacts**.

The Settings screen for contacts appears.

6 Tap **Contacts to display**.

B To display an existing group, tap its option (⬤ changes to ◉) and skip the remaining steps in this section.

7 To create a custom group of contacts, tap the Settings button (⚙).

8 Tap the heading of an account whose listing is collapsed (⌄ changes to ⌃).

9 Tap each group that you want to include (⬛ changes to ✓).

10 Tap **Done**.

You are returned to the Contacts Settings screen.

11 Tap the Back button.

The Settings screen appears.

12 Tap the Back button again.

The Contacts screen appears, showing the contacts in the group that you chose.

C The Contacts in Custom View heading or Contacts in *account* heading indicates which contacts are displayed.

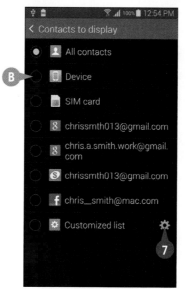

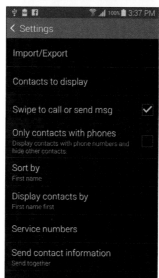

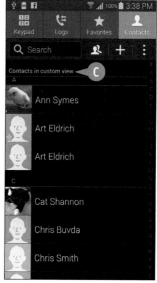

TIP

How do I display all my contacts again?

1 In the Contacts app, tap the **Contacts in Custom View** heading or the **Contacts in *account*** heading to jump straight to the Contacts to Display screen.

2 Tap **All contacts** (⬛ changes to ◉). Contacts displays the Contacts screen again, now showing all your contacts.

Import Your Contacts

Your Galaxy S 5 can sync contacts with your Google account or with other e-mail accounts that you set up, such as Exchange Server. But if you have contact data stored elsewhere, you will need to import it into the Contacts app. You can import contact information from vCard files, a widely used format, by sending the files to your Galaxy S 5 or by placing the files on it. If you have the contacts stored on a SIM card that fits into your Galaxy S 5, you can insert the SIM card and import the contacts from it.

Import Your Contacts

Import Contacts Attached to an E-mail Message

1 In the Email app, tap the message to open it.

2 Tap the attachment button.

The attachment or attachments appear.

Ⓐ You can tap **Download** to save the attachments to your Download folder. Normally, it is more helpful to import them.

Note: In Gmail, the attachment appears below the message body. Tap ▭ to display the Create Contact under Account dialog box.

3 Tap **Preview**.

A preview of the file appears.

4 Tap **Save**.

The Create Contact under Account dialog box opens.

5 Tap the account to which you want to add the contacts.

Ⓑ Android imports the contacts to the account that you chose.

6 Tap the Back button twice.

Your Inbox appears.

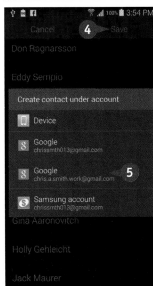

Import Contacts from a File

1 Copy the file to the Download folder on your Galaxy S 5 using Samsung Kies or a similar app.

2 In the Contacts app, tap ▤.

3 Tap **Settings**.

4 Tap **Contacts**.

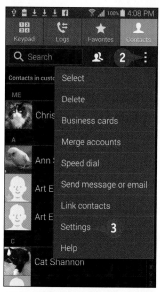

5 Tap **Import/Export**.

The Import/Export Contacts dialog box opens.

6 Tap **Import from USB storage**.

The Save Contact To dialog box opens.

7 Tap the account to which you want to add the contacts.

The Select vCard File dialog box opens.

8 Tap **Import all vCard files** (■ changes to ◉).

9 Tap **OK**.

The Contacts app imports the contacts.

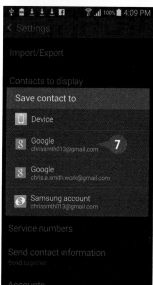

TIP

How do I create vCard files containing my contacts?

In Windows, first open the Contacts folder in an Explorer window. Select the contacts to export and then click **Export** on the toolbar. In the Export Windows Contacts dialog box, click **vCards (folder of .vcf files)** and then click **Export**. On the Mac, click **Contacts** (▩) if it appears on the Dock; otherwise, click **Launchpad** on the Dock and then click **Contacts** (▩) on the Launchpad screen. In the Contacts app, select the contacts to export and then drag them to the desktop or to a Finder window.

Choose S Planner Notifications and Reminders

The S Planner app on your Galaxy S 5 is a useful tool for tracking your time commitments. You can easily add your events to S Planner, send invitations to other people for meetings and shared appointments, and accept invitations to events that other people create.

To help you remember your plans, S Planner can notify you of upcoming events by playing sounds, vibrating, and displaying pop-up messages. You can choose your notifications and control when they appear by working on the Settings screen for S Planner.

Choose S Planner Notifications and Reminders

1 Press the Home button.

The Home screen appears.

2 Tap **Apps** (▦).

The Apps screen appears.

Note: If S Planner is not on the Apps screen that appears first, swipe right or left until you find it.

3 Tap **S Planner** (📅).

The S Planner app opens.

4 Tap the Menu button (⋮).

5 Tap **Settings**.

The Settings screen appears.

6 In the Event Notification section, tap **Select alert type**.

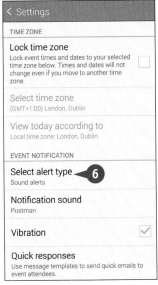

The Select Alert Type dialog box opens.

7 Tap **Sound alerts** (⚪ changes to ⦿) if you want to receive alerts.

OR

7 Tap **Status bar notifications** (⚪ changes to ⦿) if you want to receive notifications in the status bar.

You are returned to the Settings screen.

8 Tap **Notification sound**.

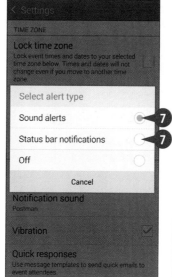

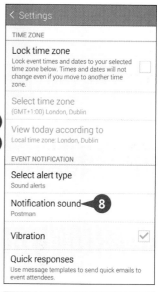

The Notification Sound dialog box opens.

9 Tap the ringtone that you want to hear (⚪ changes to ⦿).

10 Tap **OK**.

You are returned to the Settings screen.

11 Tap **Vibration** (☐ changes to ☑) if you want your Galaxy S 5 to vibrate when S Planner raises a notification.

12 Tap the Back button.

The S Planner screen appears, showing your calendars.

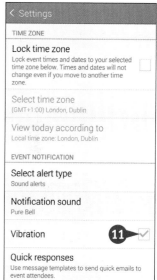

TIP

What are quick responses in S Planner?

Quick responses are pieces of boilerplate text you can insert quickly in your replies to calendar invitations. To set up your quick responses, open S Planner, tap ▤, and then tap **Settings**. Scroll down to the bottom of the screen and then tap **Quick responses** to display the Quick Responses screen. There, you can tap an existing quick response to edit it, tap the Add button (➕) to create a new quick response, or tap the Delete button (🗑) to delete existing quick responses.

Choose Week and Time Zone Settings

S Planner enables you to choose whether to display the week number in the year — from Week 1 to Week 52 — for reference. You can also choose which day to use as the start of the week: Saturday, Sunday, Monday, or the default for the locale you are using.

If you travel to different time zones, you may need to specify in which time zone S Planner should show event dates and times. Otherwise, S Planner uses your current location's time zone for your events.

Choose Week and Time Zone Settings

1 Press the Home button.

The Home screen appears.

2 Tap **Apps** (▦).

The Apps screen appears.

Note: If S Planner is not on the Apps screen that appears first, swipe right or left until you find it.

3 Tap **S Planner** (🗓).

The S Planner app opens.

4 Tap ⋮.

5 Tap **Settings**.

The Settings screen appears.

6 Tap **Show week numbers** (☐ changes to ☑) if you want to display the week numbers.

7 Tap **First day of week**.

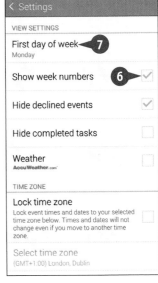

The First Day of Week dialog box opens.

8 Tap the appropriate option, such as **Sunday** (◯ changes to ◉).

You are returned to the Settings screen.

9 Tap **Lock time zone** (☐ changes to ☑) if you want to lock your event times and dates to a particular time zone.

10 Tap **Select time zone**.

The Select Time Zone dialog box opens.

11 Scroll up or down as needed and then tap the option for the time zone (◯ changes to ◉).

You are returned to the Settings screen.

12 Tap the Back button.

The S Planner screen appears, showing your calendars.

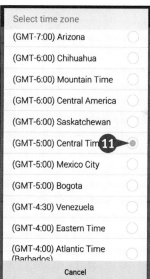

TIP

What does the Hide Declined Events option do?

Tap **Hide declined events** (☐ changes to ☑) if you want to prevent events to which you were invited but you declined from appearing in your calendar. Depending on your business life and social life, you may find it helpful to see those events you have declined as well as those you have accepted; if so, deselect **Hide declined events** (☑ changes to ☐).

CHAPTER 5

Networking and Communicating

Your Galaxy S 5 can connect to cellular networks, wireless networks, and wireless hotspots. It can also connect via Bluetooth and transfer data wirelessly using the Android Beam and S Beam features.

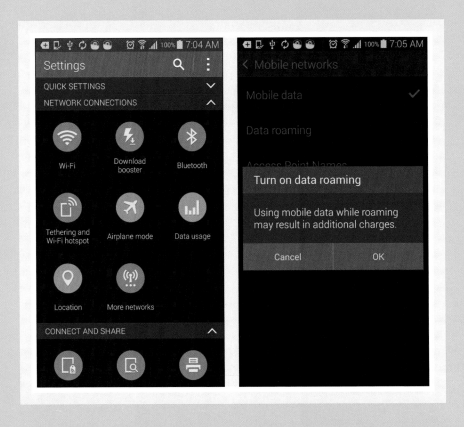

Control Wi-Fi, Bluetooth, and Cellular Access

Your Galaxy S 5 can connect to cellular networks, to Wi-Fi networks, and to other devices via Bluetooth. Normally, you want to keep your Galaxy S 5 connected to the cellular network so that you can make or receive calls and access the Internet when no Wi-Fi connection is available. But when you do not need or may not use the cellular network, you can turn on Airplane mode to cut off all connections. Turning on Airplane mode turns off Wi-Fi and Bluetooth connections as well, but you can also turn Wi-Fi and Bluetooth on and off independently when necessary.

Control Wi-Fi, Bluetooth, and Cellular Access

Turn On Airplane Mode

1 Pull down from the top of the screen with two fingers.

The Quick Settings panel opens.

2 Tap **Airplane mode** (☒).

The Turn on Airplane Mode dialog box opens.

3 Tap **OK**.

Ⓐ The Airplane Mode icon (☒) appears on the status bar.

Note: To turn off Airplane mode, pull down from the top of the screen with two fingers, tap **Airplane mode** (☒), and then tap **OK** in the Airplane Mode dialog box.

Turn Wi-Fi On

1. Pull down from the top of the screen with one finger.

   The Notifications panel appears.

2. Tap **Wi-Fi** (📶).

   Your Galaxy S 5 turns Wi-Fi on (📶 changes to 📶) and connects to a known Wi-Fi network if one is available.

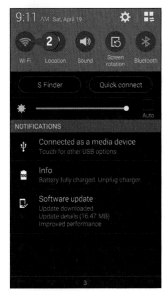

Turn Bluetooth On

Ⓑ When Wi-Fi is on, 📶 appears in the status bar.

1. Pull down from the top of the screen with one finger.

   The Notifications panel appears.

2. Tap **Bluetooth** (❋).

   Your Galaxy S 5 turns on Bluetooth.

Note: When Bluetooth is on, ❋ appears in the status bar.

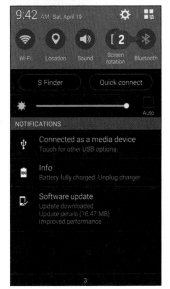

When should I use Airplane mode?

Airplane mode is designed for use on airplanes, but you can also use it any other time you want to take your Galaxy S 5 offline, such as in the movie theater or during important meetings.

Should I turn Bluetooth on or leave it off?

Turn Bluetooth on when you want to use Bluetooth devices with your Galaxy S 5. If you use Bluetooth devices frequently, leave Bluetooth on. Otherwise, turn Bluetooth off to save battery power and avoid unintentional Bluetooth connections.

Connect Bluetooth Devices

Your Galaxy S 5 enables you to extend its functionality by connecting devices that communicate using the wireless Bluetooth technology. Bluetooth is a networking protocol that is limited to short distances — typically up to about 30 feet — and modest transfer speeds. For example, you can connect a Bluetooth headset and microphone so that you can listen to audio and make and take phone calls. Alternatively, you can connect a Bluetooth keyboard so that you can quickly type e-mail messages, notes, or documents.

Connect Bluetooth Devices

1 Pull down from the top of the screen.

The Notifications panel opens.

2 Tap and hold **Bluetooth** (❄ or ❄).

The Bluetooth screen appears.

3 If the **Bluetooth** switch is set to Off, set it to **On**.

A By default, your Galaxy S 5 is not visible to other Bluetooth devices. You can make it visible for two minutes by tapping its check box (■ changes to ✔).

4 Turn on the Bluetooth device and make it visible.

5 Tap **Scan**.

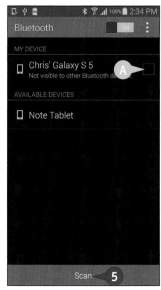

The Available Devices list shows available Bluetooth devices.

6 Tap the device to which you want to connect.

Note: When connecting a keyboard, type the code shown in the Bluetooth Pairing Request dialog box.

Your Galaxy S 5 pairs with the device, and the device moves to the Paired Devices list.

7 Tap the Settings button (⚙) for the device.

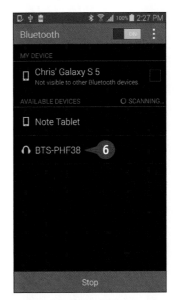 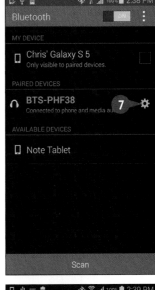

The Paired Bluetooth Device screen appears.

8 In the Profiles list, tap each option that you want to use (■ changes to ✓).

Ⓑ You can tap **Unpair** if you want to remove the device's pairing.

9 Tap **Rename**.

The Rename dialog box opens.

10 Type the name that you want to use.

11 Tap **OK**.

The new name is assigned to the device.

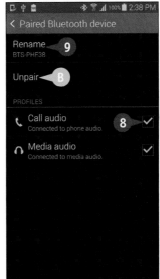 

TIPS

What else can I do with Bluetooth?
You can connect your Galaxy S 5 to a Bluetooth-enabled computer or another Bluetooth-enabled device so that you can transfer files from one to the other. File transfer via Bluetooth is slow compared to Wi-Fi, but it can be handy if the files are not too large.

Where do I find the files I receive via Bluetooth?
On the Bluetooth screen in the Settings app, tap the Menu button (⋮) to open the menu and then tap **Received files**. Your Galaxy S 5 displays the Received Files screen, showing the files. Tap the file that you want to open.

Control Data Roaming and Cellular Usage

Your Galaxy S 5 has a data-roaming feature that enables you to access the Internet using carriers other than your regular cellular carrier. With data roaming, you can use your Galaxy S 5 in a location where your carrier does not provide Internet service.

Using data roaming may incur extra charges, especially when you use it in a different country. For this reason, you may prefer to keep data roaming off most of the time and turn it on only when you need it. Normally, you will want to use data roaming only when no wireless network connection is available.

Control Data Roaming and Cellular Usage

1 Pull down from the top of the screen.

The Notifications panel opens.

2 Tap 🔧.

The Settings screen appears.

Note: If the Quick Settings section is expanded, tap the Collapse button (▲) to collapse it. If the Network Connections section is collapsed, tap the Expand button (▼) to expand it.

3 Tap **More networks**.

The More Networks screen appears.

4 Tap **Mobile Networks**.

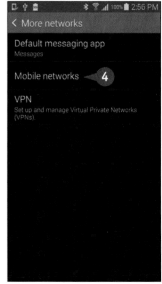

The Mobile Networks screen appears.

5 Tap **Data roaming** (■ changes to ☑) if you want to use data roaming.

The Turn On Data Roaming dialog box opens, warning you that roaming may incur extra charges.

6 Tap **OK**.

You are returned to the Mobile Networks screen.

7 Tap ◁.

The More Networks screen appears.

8 Tap ◁.

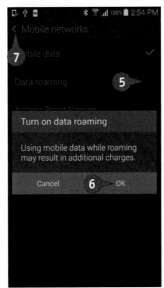
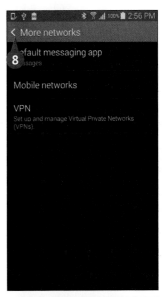

The Settings screen appears.

9 Tap **Data usage**.

The Data Usage screen appears.

10 Tap **Set mobile data limit** (■ changes to ☑).

11 Tap **Data usage cycle** and set the cycle's dates.

12 Drag the red **limit** bar (■) up or down to set the data limit.

13 Drag the orange **warning** bar (■) up or down to set the warning level.

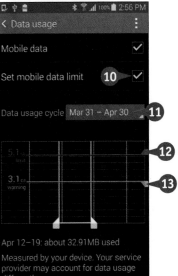

TIPS

How can I see how much data I have used during a particular period?
On the Settings screen, tap **Data usage** to display the Data Usage screen. Drag the two vertical bars to set the start and end of the period and then look at the usage figure that appears below the histogram.

How can I turn off cellular data altogether?
On the Mobile Networks screen, tap **Mobile data** (☑ changes to ■) and then tap **OK** in the Mobile Data dialog box. If you exhaust your cellular data allowance, you might want to turn off cellular data until the start of the next billing period.

Your Galaxy S 5 supports the Wi-Fi Direct standard for establishing wireless connections directly between devices instead of connecting through a wireless access point. By using Wi-Fi Direct, you can quickly connect your Galaxy S 5 to another Wi-Fi Direct–enabled device, such as a smartphone or a tablet, and share data or transfer files.

Wi-Fi Direct in effect turns one of the devices into a miniature access point for the wireless network. Your Galaxy S 5 enables you to connect to multiple devices simultaneously via Wi-Fi Direct.

Connect to a Wi-Fi Direct Device

Connect to Another Wi-Fi Direct Device

1 Pull down from the top of the screen.

The Notifications panel opens.

2 Tap and hold **Wi-Fi** (📶).

The Wi-Fi screen appears.

3 Tap 🔡.

4 Tap **Wi-Fi Direct**.

The Wi-Fi Direct screen appears.

Settings automatically scans for other Wi-Fi Direct devices.

5 Start Wi-Fi Direct on the device to which you want to connect.

Note: If your Galaxy S 5 stops scanning before Wi-Fi Direct is ready on the other device, tap **Scan** to scan again.

6 Tap the device to which you want to connect.

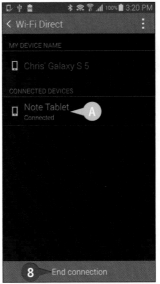

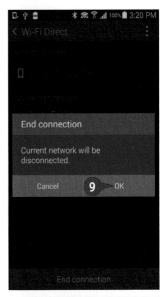

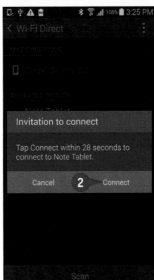

Ⓐ The device appears in the Connected Devices list.

7 Share files with the other device.

Note: For example, open a photo, tap ◄, and then tap **Wi-Fi Direct** (📧) in the Share Via dialog box.

8 When you finish using Wi-Fi Direct, tap **End Connection**.

The End Connection dialog box opens.

9 Tap **OK**.

The connection is closed.

Accept a Wi-Fi Direct Connection from Another Device

1 Go to the Wi-Fi Direct screen.

When you receive a request for a connection, the Invitation to Connect dialog box opens.

2 Tap **Connect**.

Settings establishes the connection.

3 When you finish using Wi-Fi Direct, tap **End Connection**.

The End Connection dialog box opens.

4 Tap **OK**.

TIPS

How do I connect to multiple devices using Wi-Fi Direct?
Display the Wi-Fi Direct screen and then tap **Multi connect**. Settings displays the Multi Connect screen, showing a list of available devices. Tap **Select all** (■ changes to ✓) if you want to connect to all the devices; otherwise, tap the option for each device (■ changes to ✓) to which you want to connect and then tap **Done**.

Why do some Wi-Fi Direct devices not appear on the Multi Connect screen?
Only some Wi-Fi Direct devices support the multi connect feature. The Multi Connect screen displays only devices that support multi connect.

Using USB Tethering

Your Galaxy S 5 can share its cellular connection with your computer or other devices. You can connect your computer to your Galaxy S 5 via USB tethering to share the phone's connection. Alternatively, you can turn your Galaxy S 5 into a portable Wi-Fi hotspot, as discussed in the section "Using a Portable Wi-Fi Hotspot," or use Bluetooth tethering, as discussed in the section "Using Bluetooth Tethering," both in this chapter. USB tethering is for one computer only, whereas portable Wi-Fi hotspots and Bluetooth tethering enable you to connect multiple devices.

Using USB Tethering

Turn Tethering On or Off

1 Pull down from the top of the screen with two fingers.

The Quick Settings panel opens.

2 Tap and hold **Wi-Fi hotspot** (■).

The Tethering and Wi-Fi Hotspot screen appears.

3 Tap **USB tethering** (■ changes to ✅).

Ⓐ The "Tethering or hotspot active" message appears in the status bar.

Your computer starts using your Galaxy S 5's Internet connection across the USB cable.

Note: Windows usually picks up the Internet connection seamlessly, but you may need to set a Mac to use the connection, as explained on the facing page.

4 Press the Home button.

The Home screen appears.

Ⓑ The Tethering icon appears in the status bar.

⑤ When you are ready to turn off USB tethering, pull down from the top of the screen.

The Notifications panel appears.

⑥ Tap **Tethering or hotpot active**.

The Tethering and Wi-Fi Hotspot screen appears.

⑦ Tap **USB tethering** (☑ changes to ■).

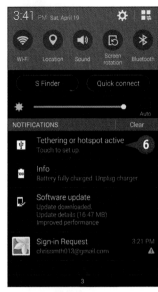

Set Your Mac to Use a Tethered Connection

① On your Mac, click the System Preferences button (▦) on the Dock.

The System Preferences window opens.

② Click **Network**.

The Network preferences pane appears.

③ In the left pane, click your Galaxy S 5.

④ Click **Apply**.

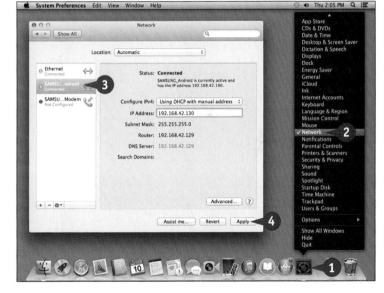

TIP

Why does my Galaxy S 5 not appear in Network preferences on my Mac?
You may need to install a driver, a piece of software that enables your Mac to use the USB connection on your Galaxy S 5. The HoRNDIS driver available at http://joshuawise.com/horndis enables OS X to use your Galaxy S 5 this way.

To install HoRNDIS, you must allow apps downloaded from anywhere. Click ▦ on the Dock, click **Security & Privacy**, click **General**, and then click **Anywhere** in the Allow Applications Downloaded From area. You may need to click the lock icon and type your password to make these changes.

Using a Portable Wi-Fi Hotspot

Your Galaxy S 5 can access the Internet from anyplace that has a suitable connection to the cellular network. It can also act as a Wi-Fi hotspot to share that Internet access with your computer and other devices. This feature is called a *portable Wi-Fi hotspot*. In order for your phone to be able to act as a portable Wi-Fi hotspot, your cellular carrier must permit it. Many carriers charge an extra monthly fee for using a portable Wi-Fi hotspot, so before you try it, read your carrier's policy and be careful not to exceed your cellular data allowance.

Using a Portable Wi-Fi Hotspot

1 Pull down from the top of the screen with two fingers.

The Quick Settings panel appears.

2 Tap and hold **Wi-Fi hotspot** (▨).

The Tethering and Wi-Fi Hotspot screen appears.

3 Tap **Portable Wi-Fi hotspot**.

The Portable Wi-Fi Hotspot screen appears.

4 Tap ▤.

5 Tap **Configure**.

A You can tap **Allowed devices** to set up a list of devices allowed to connect to the hotspot.

B You can tap **Timeout settings** to choose the interval after which the hotspot automatically turns off.

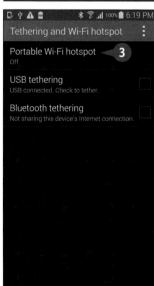

You can use your device as an Internet AP (access point) using Portable Wi-Fi hotspot, and connect a maximum of 10 other devices to it via Wi-Fi. The connected devices will have access to the Internet via your mobile network.

You can create an allowed device profile and set the connection mode for it.

Using Portable Wi-Fi hotspot consumes more battery power and increases your data usage.

The Configure Wi-Fi Hotspot dialog box opens.

6 Type a name for the Wi-Fi hotspot.

7 Tap **Security** and then tap **WPA2 PSK**.

8 Tap **Password** and type a password of eight characters or more.

C You can tap **Show password** to verify the password.

9 Tap **Save**.

10 Set the **Portable Wi-Fi hotspot** switch to **On**.

The Attention dialog box opens, warning you that turning on the portable Wi-Fi hotspot will turn off Wi-Fi.

11 Tap **OK**.

D Instructions appear for connecting your computers or devices to the portable hotspot's wireless network.

12 Connect your computers or devices.

E The devices appear in the Connected Devices list.

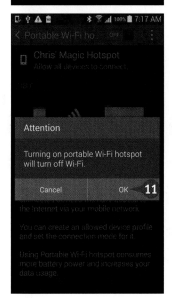

How can I control which devices can connect to my portable Wi-Fi hotspot?

First, set a password as described in this section and share it only with those people you want to be able to connect. Second, on the Portable Wi-Fi Hotspot screen, tap ▦, tap **Allowed devices**, and then use the Allowed Devices screen to create a list of allowed devices identified by names and by their MAC addresses. The MAC address is an identifier burned into the physical network adapter. To learn your Galaxy S 5's MAC address, open Settings, tap **About device**, tap **Status**, and then look at the Wi-Fi MAC Address readout.

Using Bluetooth Tethering

Your Galaxy S 5 includes a Bluetooth tethering feature that enables you to share the phone's Internet connection with other devices via Bluetooth. By turning on Bluetooth tethering, you can connect other devices to the Internet through your Galaxy S 5.

Bluetooth tethering can be convenient, but it is best to use it only for devices that cannot share your Galaxy S 5's connection via the portable Wi-Fi hotspot feature. This is because Wi-Fi gives both faster transfer speeds and greater range than Bluetooth.

Using Bluetooth Tethering

1 Pull down from the top of the screen with two fingers.

The Quick Settings panel appears.

2 Tap and hold **Wi-Fi hotspot** (▧).

The Tethering and Wi-Fi Hotspot screen appears.

3 Tap **Bluetooth tethering** (■ changes to ✓).

Ⓐ A message appears telling you that Bluetooth visibility has been turned off.

Note: If you have already paired the other Bluetooth devices with your Galaxy S 5, skip to step **7**.

4 Pull down from the top of the screen.

120

The Notifications panel appears.

5 Tap and hold **Bluetooth** ().

The Bluetooth screen appears.

6 Tap the button for your Galaxy S 5 (■ changes to ✔) to make your Galaxy S 5 visible via Bluetooth for two minutes.

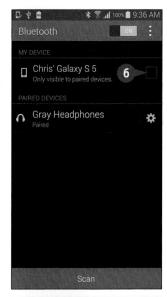

7 Connect your other devices to your Galaxy S 5's hotspot via Bluetooth.

Ⓑ If the Bluetooth Pairing Request dialog box opens, tap **OK**.

8 If the Bluetooth screen is displayed, tap the Back button.

You are returned to the Tethering and Wi-Fi Hotspot screen.

9 When you finish using the shared connection, tap **Bluetooth tethering** (✔ changes to ■).

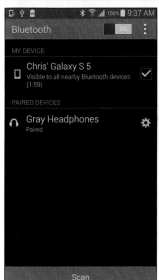

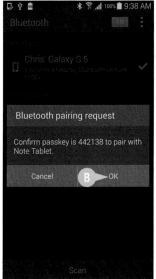

TIP

How fast is Bluetooth?
Both the latest versions of Bluetooth, Bluetooth version 3 and Bluetooth version 4, have a maximum theoretical data transfer speed of 24 megabits per second, or Mbit/s. Apps can use only some of Bluetooth capacity. But because the Internet connection your Galaxy S 5 is sharing is likely to be substantially slower than Bluetooth's maximum transfer rate, sharing your Internet connection via Bluetooth is adequate for light usage. For heavier usage, use Wi-Fi for mobile devices or USB tethering for a computer.

Manage Your Wireless Networks

To conserve your cellular data allowance, you should use wireless networks whenever possible. Your Galaxy S 5 can connect both to wireless networks that broadcast their network names and to *closed* networks, ones that do not broadcast their names. The network name is formally known as the *service set identifier* (SSID). Your Galaxy S 5 can switch automatically between Wi-Fi networks and cellular networks.

The first time that you connect to a Wi-Fi network, you provide the network's password. Your Galaxy S 5 then stores the password for future connections.

Manage Your Wireless Networks

Connect to an Open Wireless Network

1 Pull down from the top of the screen.

The Notifications panel opens.

2 If Wi-Fi is off (📶), tap **Wi-Fi** (📶 changes to 📶).

3 Tap and hold **Wi-Fi** (📶).

The Wi-Fi screen appears.

4 Tap the network to which you want to connect.

Note: If the network has no password, your Galaxy S 5 connects to it without prompting you for one.

A dialog box for connecting to the network opens.

5 Type the password.

A You can tap **Show password** (⬛ changes to ✅) to view the password.

6 Tap **Connect**.

Your Galaxy S 5 connects to the network.

Connect to a Closed Wireless Network

1 On the Wi-Fi screen, tap **Add Wi-Fi network**.

The Add Wi-Fi Network dialog box opens.

2 Tap **Network SSID** and type the network name.

3 Tap **Security** and select the security type, such as **WPA/WPA2/FT PSK**.

4 Tap **Password** and type the password.

5 Tap **Connect**.

Your Galaxy S 5 connects to the network.

Make Your Galaxy S 5 Forget a Wireless Network

1 On the Wi-Fi screen, tap and hold the network's name.

A dialog box opens. The dialog box's title bar shows the network's name.

2 Tap **Forget network**.

Your Galaxy S 5 forgets the network.

Note: After telling your Galaxy S 5 to forget a network, you can join the network again, but you will need to enter its password.

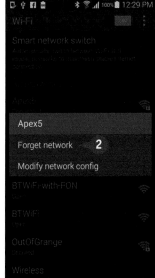

TIP

What is Smart Network Switch, and should I use it?

Smart Network Switch is a feature that enables your Galaxy S 5 to switch automatically to a cellular connection if the Wi-Fi connection becomes unstable or disappears. When your Galaxy S 5 is using a patchy or intermittent Wi-Fi connection and you can afford to use your cellular connection instead, turn on Smart Network Switch by tapping **Smart network switch** (■ changes to ☑) on the Wi-Fi screen. When you are using a reliable Wi-Fi network, it is best to keep Smart Network Switch turned off.

Log in to Wi-Fi Hotspots

hen you are in town or on the road, you can log in to Wi-Fi hotspots to enjoy fast Internet access without using your Galaxy S 5's data allowance. You can find Wi-Fi hotspots at many locations, including coffee shops and restaurants, hotels, airports, municipal areas, and even parks and highway rest stops.

Some Wi-Fi hotspots charge for access, whereas others are free. If you travel extensively, it is worth signing up for a plan that provides long-term access to Wi-Fi hotspots.

Log in to Wi-Fi Hotspots

1 Pull down from the top of the screen.

The Notifications panel opens.

2 If Wi-Fi is off (⬛), tap **Wi-Fi** (⬛ changes to 📶).

3 Tap and hold **Wi-Fi** (📶).

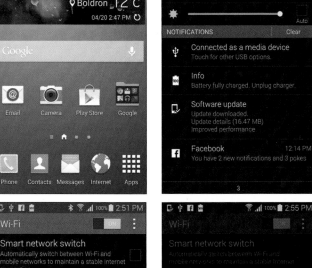

The Wi-Fi screen appears.

4 Tap the network to which you want to connect.

5 Tap **Connect**.

Your Galaxy S 5 connects to the network.

6 Press the Home button.

The Home screen appears.

⑦ Tap **Internet** ().

The Internet app opens and displays a login page for the hotspot.

⑧ Type the login information.

⑨ Tap the button for logging in.

Your Galaxy S 5 logs in to the hotspot, and you can begin using the Internet connection.

⑩ When you finish using the hotspot, pull down from the top of the screen.

The Notifications panel opens.

⑪ Tap and hold **Wi-Fi** ().

The Wi-Fi screen appears.

⑫ Tap the wireless network's name.

The network's dialog box opens.

⑬ Tap **Forget**.

Your Galaxy S 5 forgets the network.

TIP

What precautions should I take when using Wi-Fi hotspots?
The main danger is that you may connect to a malevolent network. To stay safe, connect only to hotspots provided by reputable establishments — for example, national hotel chains or restaurant chains — and avoid hotspots run by unknown operators. Even then, it is best not to transmit any private information that may interest eavesdroppers. When you finish using a Wi-Fi hotspot that you do not plan to use again, tell your Galaxy S 5 to forget the network: Display the Wi-Fi screen, tap the Wi-Fi network's name, and then tap **Forget** in the dialog box that opens.

Transfer Data Using Android Beam

Android includes a feature called *Android Beam* that enables you to transfer data wirelessly between your Galaxy S 5 and other Android devices. Android Beam uses a technology called *Near Field Communications* (NFC), which allows NFC-enabled smartphones and tablets to automatically establish a radio connection when you bring them to within a few inches of each other.

You can establish an NFC connection by bringing the back of your Galaxy S 5 to the back of another NFC-enabled device briefly. NFC is great for transferring contacts, photos, and other data that you want to share quickly and effortlessly.

Transfer Data Using Android Beam

Turn On Android Beam

1 Pull down from the top of the screen with two fingers.

The Quick Settings panel opens.

2 Tap and hold **NFC** (▨).

The NFC screen appears.

3 Set the **NFC** switch to **On**.

4 If Android Beam is Off, tap **Android Beam**.

The Android Beam screen appears.

5 Set the **Android Beam** switch to **On**.

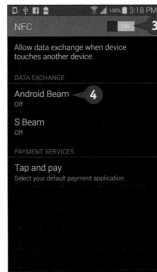

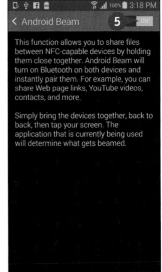

Send a File via Android Beam

1 Open the app that contains the file you want to transfer.

Note: This example uses a contact in the Contacts app.

2 Bring your Galaxy S 5 back-to-back with the other NFC-enabled Android phone or tablet.

The Touch to Beam prompt appears.

3 Tap **Touch to beam**.

Your Galaxy S 5 sends the file.

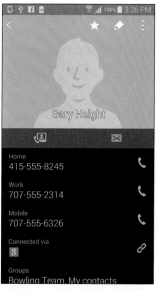
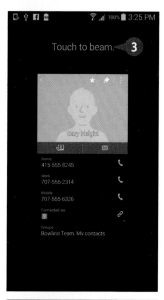

Receive a File via Android Beam

A When someone starts to send you a file via Android Beam, your Galaxy S 5 displays an Incoming Beam message.

1 Pull down from the top of the screen.

The Notifications panel opens.

The Beam Complete notification appears.

2 Tap **Beam complete**.

The file opens in an app that can handle the file.

Why can my Galaxy S 5 not connect to another Android device via Android Beam?

If you have turned on NFC and enabled Android Beam on both your Galaxy S 5 and the other device, the problem is most likely that you have not brought the NFC chips close enough to each other. Hold your Galaxy S 5 back-to-back with the other device and move it around the other device until both devices vibrate. You have then found the right location to use for Android Beam connections.

What happens when my Galaxy S 5 receives data via Android Beam?

Your Galaxy S 5 accepts the data, but it may prompt you to decide where to store it. For example, if the Contacts app receives a contact, it may prompt you to choose the account in which to place that contact.

Transfer Data Using S Beam

I n addition to Android Beam, your Galaxy S 5 includes a feature called *S Beam*. S Beam is a Samsung-proprietary technology for transferring data wirelessly between two devices. At this writing, only some Samsung devices support S Beam.

You establish an S Beam connection in a similar way to an Android Beam connection: You bring the back of your Galaxy S 5 to the back of another S Beam–enabled device. For S Beam to work, you must first enable both NFC and S Beam in the Settings app on both devices.

Transfer Data Using S Beam

Turn On S Beam

1 Pull down from the top of the screen with two fingers.

The Quick Settings panel opens.

2 Tap and hold **NFC** (▨).

The NFC screen appears.

3 Set the **NFC** switch to **On**.

4 If S Beam is Off, tap **S Beam**.

The S Beam screen appears.

5 Set the **S Beam** switch to **On**.

Note: When you set the S Beam switch to On, Settings automatically sets the NFC switch to On if it is off.

A The "Both S Beam and Android Beam turned on" message appears briefly.

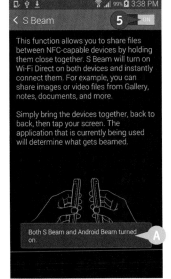

Send a File via S Beam

1 Open the relevant app and display the file that you want to transfer.

2 Bring your Galaxy S 5 back-to-back with a Samsung phone or tablet that supports S Beam, has the feature enabled, and is unlocked.

3 Tap **Touch to beam**.

B Your Galaxy S 5 prompts you to separate the devices.

4 Move the devices apart.

The file is transferred.

Receive a File via S Beam

C When someone starts to send you a file via S Beam, your Galaxy S 5 establishes the connection.

D Your Galaxy S 5 receives the file.

E You can tap **Cancel** to cancel the transfer.

TIP

When should I use S Beam instead of Android Beam?

Generally, it is best to use S Beam instead of Android Beam any time both the devices support S Beam. S Beam uses NFC to create a Wi-Fi Direct connection between the two devices, giving faster transfer speeds than Bluetooth. The only disadvantage to S Beam is that connections may take longer to establish than Android Beam connections.

CHAPTER 6

Making Calls and Texting

Your Galaxy S 5 not only enables you to make phone calls anywhere, including easy conference calls, but also to send and receive text messages and multimedia messages and to enjoy video chat via Google's Hangouts service.

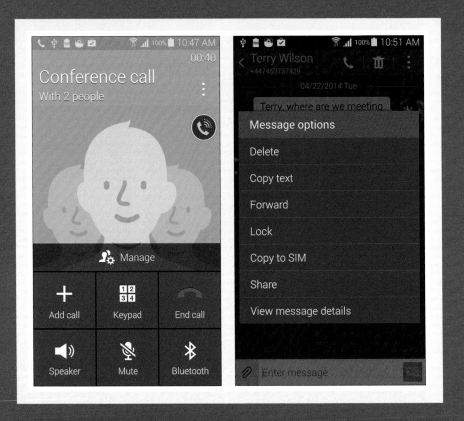

Make Phone Calls

Your Galaxy S 5 enables you to make phone calls anywhere you have a connection to the cellular network. You can make a phone call by dialing the phone number using the keypad, but you can place calls more easily by tapping the appropriate phone number for a contact or by using your call logs. When you need other people near you to be able to hear both ends of the phone call you are making, you can turn on the speaker.

Make Phone Calls

Open the Phone App

1 Press the Home button.

The Home screen appears.

2 Tap **Phone** (📞).

The Phone app opens and displays the screen that you used last, such as Contacts.

Note: You can also place a call quickly to a phone number Android has identified. For example, you can tap an underlined phone number that represents a link on a web page.

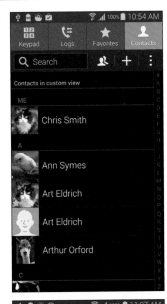

Dial a Call Using the Keypad

1 Tap **Keypad** (📱).

The Keypad screen appears.

2 Tap the number keys to dial the number.

A You can tap **Add to Contacts** to add this phone number to your contacts.

B You can tap the Menu button (⋮) and then tap **Add 2-sec pause** or **Add wait**.

3 Tap the Dial button (📞).

Your Galaxy S 5 places the call.

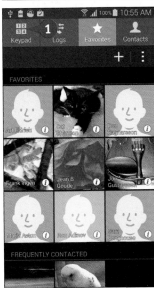

Take a Call Using a Headset

1 Connect your headset to your Galaxy S 5.

When you receive an incoming call, the phone ringtone plays in the headset, and the screen turns on if it is off.

B The lock screen shows the caller's name and phone details — for example, "Mobile" or the phone number.

Note: If you are listening to music or watching a video when you receive a call, Android automatically fades and pauses the audio.

2 Press the clicker button on the headset to take the call.

The lock screen shows the caller's name and the call duration.

3 Press the clicker button on the headset when you are ready to end the call.

After the call ends, your Galaxy S 5 locks again.

4 Press the Home button or the Power button.

The lock screen appears.

TIPS

Can I take other actions using my headset?
This depends on the model of headset and how it is designed to work with your Galaxy S 5. Some headsets include a button that you can press to mute a call or press and hold to place the call on hold. Explore your headset's controls or read its documentation to find out all that you can do with it.

What does the Bluetooth button on the call screen do?
You tap this button to switch the call to a Bluetooth headset that you have previously paired with your Galaxy S 5.

Make a Conference Call

When you need to talk to more than one person at a time, you can make a conference call using your Galaxy S 5. This capability is great for both business calls and social calls. To make a conference call, you simply call the first participant and then add each other participant in turn.

During a conference call, you can talk in private to individual participants as needed. You can also drop a participant from the call without affecting the other participants.

Make a Conference Call

1 Press the Home button.

2 Tap **Phone** ().

3 Tap **Contacts** ().

The Contacts screen appears.

4 Tap the picture for the contact that you want to call first.

The Quick Info panel opens.

5 Tap .

The phone numbers appear.

6 Tap the appropriate phone number.

Your Galaxy S 5 places the call.

7 After the contact answers the call, tap **Add call** ().

The Keypad screen appears.

8 Tap **Contacts** ().

The Contacts screen appears.

9 Locate the contact and tap the second phone number to call.

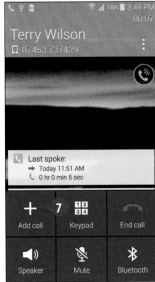

The Phone app places the first call on hold and places the second call.

Ⓐ The first call is on hold.

10 Tap **Merge** (⊳⊲).

The Phone app merges the calls and displays the Conference Call readout.

Ⓑ You can add another participant by repeating steps **7** to **10**.

11 Tap **Manage**.

The list of participants appears.

Ⓒ You can tap the Split button (⧉) to speak privately to a participant.

Ⓓ You can tap the Hang Up button (☎) to hang up on a participant.

12 When you are ready to end the call, tap **End call** (☎).

The Phone app ends the call.

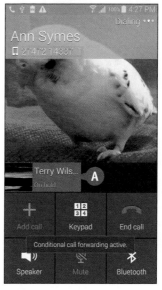

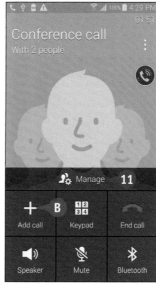

TIPS

How many participants can I include in a conference call?
This depends on your cellular carrier. Contact your carrier's support department to find out the limit.

How do I use other apps during the conference call?
Press the Home button to display the Home screen and then launch an app from there or from the Apps screen. Alternatively, press and hold the Home button to display the Recent Apps list and then tap the app to which you want to switch. The status bar shows a green shade to indicate the call is continuing. To return to the call, pull open the Notifications panel and then tap the Phone button (📞) below the Quick Settings bar.

Call Using Call Logs and Frequent Contacts

To help you make phone calls quickly and easily, the Phone app provides call logs, a Favorites list, and a Frequently Contacted list.

Your call logs track the phone numbers that you have called and those that have called you. You can filter the call logs to show only calls you have missed, only outgoing calls, or only incoming calls. The Frequently Contacted list automatically gathers the contacts whom you call and who call you most often. Favorites is a list to which you can manually add people whom you want to be able to contact easily.

Call Using Call Logs and Frequent Contacts

Call Using the Call Logs

1 Press the Home button.

2 Tap **Phone** (📱).

3 Tap **Logs** (📋).

The Logs screen appears.

4 Tap the Logs pop-up menu.

5 Tap the call log that you want to view.

Note: For example, tap **Received calls** to see only the calls that you received.

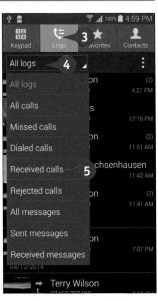

The call log appears.

6 Tap the contact's picture.

The Quick Info panel opens.

7 Tap 📱.

The phone numbers appear.

8 Tap the phone number.

The Phone app places the call.

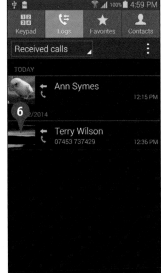

Call Using Your Favorites and Frequently Contacted List

1 Press the Home button.

The Home screen appears.

2 Tap **Phone** ().

The Phone app opens.

3 Tap **Favorites** (⭐).

Ⓐ The upper section of the Favorites screen shows the Favorites list.

4 Drag up to scroll down to the end of the Favorites list.

Ⓑ The Frequently Contacted list appears.

5 Tap the contact that you want to call.

The contact's record appears.

Note: If you are offered a choice of phone numbers, tap the phone number that you want to call.

The Phone app places the call.

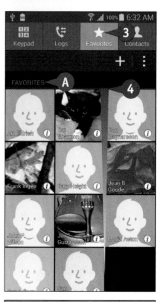

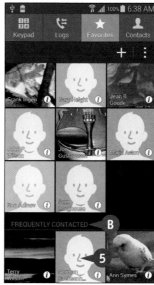

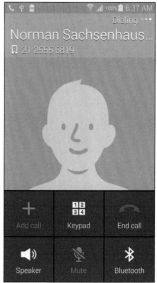

TIP

How do I turn a contact into a favorite?

Tap the contact's name on the Contacts screen to display the contact record and then tap the Favorites star (⭐ changes to ⭐).

To remove a contact from the Favorites list, you can display the contact record and tap the Favorites star (⭐ changes to ⭐). Alternatively, display the Favorites screen, tap 🔡, and tap **Remove from Favorites**. Phone displays a check box for each favorite. Tap each favorite that you want to remove and then tap **Done**.

Send and Receive Text Messages

Your Galaxy S 5 enables you to send text messages to other smartphone users. The messages can use either SMS or MMS. SMS stands for *Short Message Service* and transmits text-only messages. MMS stands for *Multimedia Messaging Service* and transmits messages that can contain text, photos, videos, sounds, or other data.

The Messages app automatically switches between SMS and MMS as needed. For example, when you start a new message, Messages uses SMS. If you add a photo to the message, Messages changes the message seamlessly to MMS.

Send and Receive Text Messages

1 Press the Home button.

The Home screen appears.

2 Tap **Messages** (▢).

A If Messages (▢) does not appear on the Home screen, tap **Apps** (▦) and then tap **Messages** (▢).

The Messages app opens.

3 Tap the New Message button (▨).

The New Message screen appears.

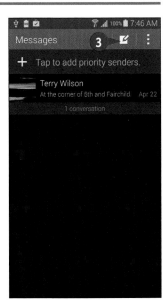

4 Tap the To field, which has the prompt "Enter recipients," and start typing the contact's name or phone number.

A list of matching contacts appears.

5 Tap the contact that you want.

B The contact's name appears in the To field.

6 Tap the text field, which has the prompt "Enter message," and type the message.

7 To add pictures, video, or audio to the message, tap the Attach button (▨).

The Attach dialog box opens.

8 Tap the type of item you want to attach.

Note: If the Complete Action Using dialog box opens, tap the appropriate app. For example, tap **Gallery** for attaching an image. Then tap **Always** if you want to use this app each time or tap **Just once** to use the app only this time.

The appropriate app opens, such as Gallery.

9 Tap the album that contains the photo you want to send.

The album opens.

10 Tap the photo that you want to attach. A green check mark (✓) appears on the photo.

11 Tap **Done**.

C The photo appears in the message.

D The "Converting to multimedia message" pop-up appears briefly while Messages converts the SMS message to an MMS message.

12 Tap the Send button (✉).

Messages sends the text.

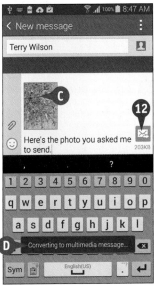

TIP

Why do videos I send via MMS look so jerky and grainy?

MMS messages are limited in size, so you can send only a small amount of video that uses a low resolution and high compression. If you record a video, the Camera app limits it to 295 kilobytes, which typically records between 10 and 20 seconds, depending on the subject. Similarly, the Voice Recorder app limits an audio recording to 295 kilobytes, which records around three minutes of audio at moderate quality. To transfer longer or higher-quality audio or video, use a different means, such as Dropbox.

Manage Your Text Messages

If you send and receive many text messages, you may find the Messages app's interface soon becomes full of messages, making it difficult to navigate among them. To keep your messages under control, you can forward messages to others and delete messages that you do not need to keep. You can either delete individual messages from a conversation, leaving the other messages, or delete an entire conversation that you no longer need.

Manage Your Text Messages

Forward or Delete a Message

1 Press the Home button.

The Home screen appears.

2 Tap **Messages** (☐).

Ⓐ If Messages (☐) does not appear on the Home screen, tap **Apps** (▦) and then tap **Messages** (☐).

The Messages app opens.

3 Tap the conversation that contains the message.

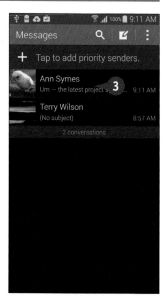

The conversation appears.

4 Tap and hold the message that you want to forward or delete.

The Message Options dialog box opens.

5 Tap **Forward**.

OR

5 Tap **Delete**.

If you tap **Forward**, Messages starts a new message containing the forwarded message. You can then address the message and tap ☒.

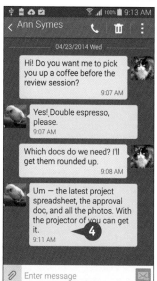

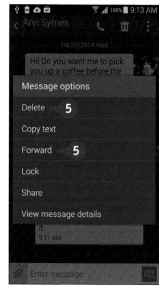

Delete Conversations

1 Press the Home button.

The Home screen appears.

2 Tap **Messages** (▨).

B If Messages (▨) does not appear on the Home screen, tap **Apps** (▦) and then tap **Messages** (▨).

The Messages app opens.

3 Tap ▮.

4 Tap **Delete**.

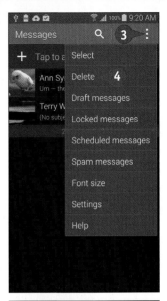

The Delete screen appears.

5 Tap each conversation that you want to delete (▮ changes to ☑).

C You can tap **Select all** to select all the conversations (▮ changes to ☑).

6 Tap **Done**.

The Delete Conversation dialog box opens.

7 Tap **OK**.

The Messages app deletes the selected conversations.

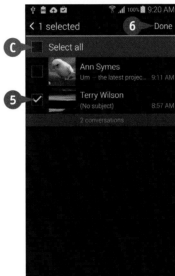

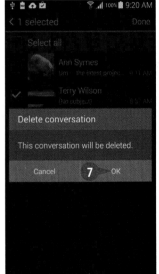

TIP

How do I save a photo I receive in a message?

1 On the message screen, tap and hold the photo to display the Message Options dialog box.

2 Tap **Save attachment** to display the Save Attachment dialog box.

3 Tap the name of the file (▮ changes to ☑).

4 Tap **Save**.

Android saves the photo in the Download folder, which you can access through the Gallery app.

Chat with Hangouts

Google's Hangouts feature enables you to enjoy audio and video chats with your contacts who have Google+ accounts. Google Hangouts runs on Windows PCs, Macs, and Linux computers as well as Android and iOS phones and tablets, so you can chat with a wide range of people.

To use Google Hangouts, your Galaxy S 5 must be connected to either a wireless network or the cellular network. Using a wireless network is preferable because you typically get better performance and do not use up your cellular data allowance.

Chat with Hangouts

1 Press the Home button.

The Home screen appears.

2 Tap **Apps** (▦).

The Apps screen appears.

3 Tap **Hangouts** (▣).

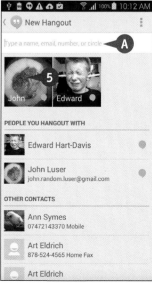

The Hangouts screen appears.

4 Swipe left.

The New Hangout screen appears.

5 Tap the name in the Suggested People list or the Other Contacts list.

A You can also tap this prompt, start typing identifying information, and then tap the appropriate match.

B You can tap **Anyone else?** to invite other participants.

6 Tap .

If the call is accepted, your contact's video feed appears on-screen.

C Your own video appears in an inset window.

7 To control the call, tap the screen.

The on-screen controls appear.

D You can tap 🎤 to mute your microphone (🎤 changes to 🎤).

8 Tap 🔊 to display the Audio panel, which enables you to select the audio output.

E You can tap 📷 to turn off the video camera (📷 changes to 📷).

9 To switch to another hangout, tap the Hangouts button (▤).

The Hangouts screen appears.

10 Tap the hangout that you want to view.

11 Tap 📷 when you are ready to end the call.

TIPS

What is the Switch Cameras button for?
Tap the Switch Cameras button (📷) to switch between your Galaxy S 5's front and rear cameras. Hangouts uses the front camera at first, making it easy to show your face. But you may want to show something else to the person with whom you are chatting; in this case, use the rear camera.

Why might I turn off my video camera?
Turning off your video camera enables you to prevent the other people in the hangout from seeing things you do not want to show, but you might also turn off video if your connection is too slow to transmit the video feed at a satisfactory refresh rate. If the video stutters or freezes, you may prefer to try an audio-only call instead.

Using Blocking Mode

Your Galaxy S 5 includes a feature called *Blocking mode,* which enables you to block notifications when you do not want to receive them.

You can choose which features to block, such as incoming calls and notifications. You can specify a set time for blocking, such as when you sleep, or turn Blocking mode on manually at any time that suits you. You can allow specified contacts to interrupt you while blocking is turned on.

Using Blocking Mode

1 Pull down from the top of the screen with two fingers.

The Quick Settings panel appears.

2 Tap and hold **Blocking mode** (🔲).

The Blocking Mode screen appears.

3 Set the **Blocking mode** switch to **On**.

4 Tap **Block incoming calls** (■ changes to ✓).

5 Tap **Turn off notifications** (■ changes to ✓).

6 Tap **Turn off alarm and timer** (■ changes to ✓).

7 Tap **Always** (✓ changes to ■).

8 Tap **From**.

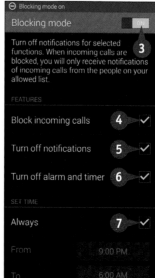

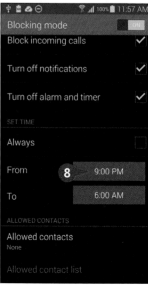

A dialog box for setting the time opens.

9 Tap the spin dials and the AM/PM control to set the time.

10 Tap **Set**.

11 Tap **Allowed contacts**.

The Allowed Contacts dialog box opens.

12 Tap **None**, **All contacts**, **Favorites**, or **Custom** (■ changes to ●), as appropriate.

Note: This example uses **Custom**.

The Allowed Contact List screen appears.

13 Tap **Add**.

A screen for selecting the contacts appears.

14 Tap each contact (■ changes to ✓) you want to add to the list of contacts whom you allow to disturb you when Blocking mode is on.

15 Tap **Done**.

The contacts appear in the list.

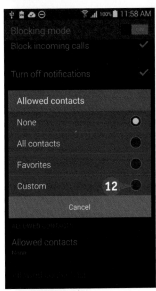

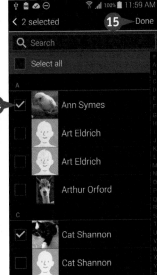

TIP

How do I turn Blocking mode on or off manually?

The easiest way to turn Blocking mode on or off manually is to pull down from the top of the screen with two fingers, displaying the Quick Settings panel, and then tap **Blocking mode** (◙ changes to ◙ or ◙ changes to ◙). You can also turn Blocking mode on or off by opening the Settings app, going to the Personalization section, tapping **Blocking mode** (◙) to display the Blocking Mode screen, and then setting the **Blocking Mode** switch to **On** or **Off**, as needed.

CHAPTER 7

Enjoying Social Networking

Your Galaxy S 5 enables you to enjoy social networking all day long anyplace you can access the Internet. You can network with Google+ or Facebook, tweet with Twitter, and use Group Play and Samsung's ChatON service.

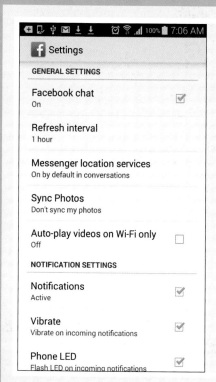

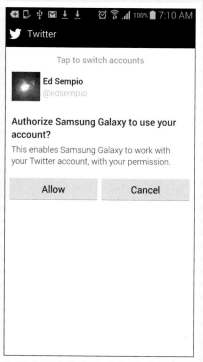

Set Up Google+

By setting up Google+ on your Galaxy S 5, you can log in to Google's social network and stay connected to your contacts wherever you go.

Google+ includes a range of social-networking features. You can use the Google Circles feature to organize your contacts into different groups for easy communication; share your photos in moments using the Instant Upload feature; and chat with your family, friends, and colleagues using Google Hangouts. If you are not already a Google+ member, you can sign up on your Galaxy S 5.

Set Up Google+

1 Press the Home button.

The Home screen appears.

2 Tap the **Google** folder (▦).

The Google folder opens.

3 Tap **Google+** (▨).

The Google+ Profile screen appears.

Note: If you are already a Google+ member, the Google+ screen appears. Go to step **8**.

4 Type your name or accept the suggested name.

5 Tap the **Gender** pop-up menu and select your gender.

6 Tap **Get Started**.

The Link Picasa Web Albums with Google+ screen appears.

7 Tap **Link and Continue**.

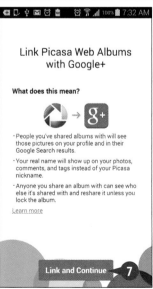

The Google+ screen appears.

8 Tap the Menu button (⚏).

9 Tap **Settings**.

The Settings screen appears.

Ⓐ You can tap **Auto Backup** to set up automatic backups for your photos and videos. See the Tip for details.

10 Tap your account name.

The settings screen for the account appears.

11 Tap **Notifications**.

12 Set the **Notifications** switch to **On** to receive notifications.

13 Tap **Ringtone** and select the ringtone.

14 Tap **Vibrate** (☐ changes to ☑) if you want vibrations for notifications.

15 Tap **Who can notify me** and select who can notify you.

16 Tap the Posts and Mentions options (☐ changes to ☑) to control which notifications you receive.

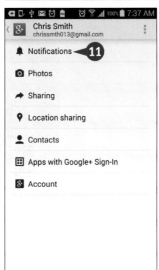

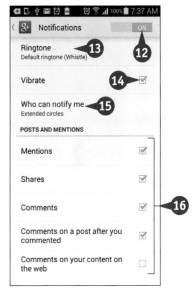

TIP

What is the Auto Backup feature?

The Auto Backup feature enables you to automatically back up your new photos and videos to the Google Photos service. To enable this feature, tap **Auto Backup** on the Settings screen and set the **Auto Backup** switch to **On**. You can then tap **Photo size** to choose whether to store photos at their full size, for which Google Photos gives you 15GB of space, or at the standard size of 2048 pixels, for which Google Photos gives you unlimited free storage. You can also choose options to control when to back up photos and videos or tap **Back up all** to back them all up immediately.

Navigate Google+

After you have set up Google+ on your Galaxy S 5, you can run the Google+ app to enjoy social networking. From the Circles screen that Google+ displays at launch, you can easily view the posts for one or more circles, comment on posts, or post your own photos. You can write posts, share moods, and even shoot new videos and post them immediately.

Navigate Google+

1 Press the Home button.

The Home screen appears.

2 Tap the **Google** folder (▦).

The Google folder opens.

3 Tap **Google+** (g+).

The Google+ Home screen appears.

4 Tap the Circles pop-up menu.

5 Tap the circle that you want to display.

Note: For example, tap **Friends**.

The posts for that circle appear.

6 Tap **Photo** (◉) to share a photo.

Ⓐ From a posts screen, you can also tap **Location** (◉) to share your location, **Mood** (◉) to share a mood, or **Write** (✎) to write a post. Tap an existing post to comment on it.

The Select Photos screen appears.

Ⓑ You can tap 📹 to record a video.

Ⓒ You can tap 📷 to take a photo.

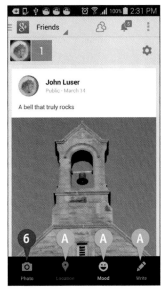

7 Tap the photo or photos to share.

8 Tap **Select**.

9 Tap the pop-up button and choose the circle with which you want to share the picture.

10 Type any needed text.

11 Tap **Location** (◉) if you want to add your location.

12 Tap **Share**.

Google+ shares the photo and text.

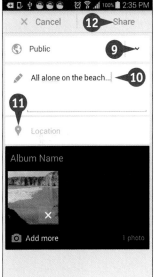

What are Google circles?

On Google+, *circles* are separate groups within your social network. Google+ provides circles called Friends, Family, Acquaintances, and Following to get you started, enabling you to associate your contacts with different groups. You can also access the What's Hot circle and the Nearby circle, create your own custom circles, and share data only with particular circles. For example, you may want to share some items with your friends but not with your family or acquaintances.

Set Up Your Facebook Account

Your Galaxy S 5 comes with the Facebook app already installed. If you have a Facebook account, you likely want to set up your account on your Galaxy S 5 so that you can access Facebook anytime. You can use Facebook's tool for finding friends among your contacts, and you can choose settings to make the Facebook app work the way you prefer.

After you log in to your Facebook account, the app automatically keeps you logged in so that you can easily post your own updates and see updates from others.

Set Up Your Facebook Account

1 Press the Home button.

The Home screen appears.

2 Tap **Apps** (▦).

The Apps screen appears.

3 Tap **Facebook** (f).

The Facebook login screen appears.

4 Type your Facebook login name.

Note: You can also log in by using your Galaxy S 5's phone number.

5 Type your password.

6 Tap **Log In**.

Note: You can tap **Find Friends** and follow the prompts to add suggested friends and invite your contacts to join you on Facebook.

7 Tap the Menu button (☰).

8 Tap **App Settings**.

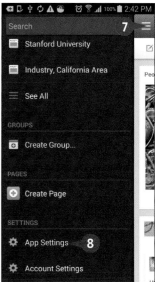

The Settings screen appears.

9 Tap **Facebook chat** (☐ changes to ☑) to turn on Facebook chat.

10 Tap **Refresh interval**.

The Refresh Interval dialog box opens.

11 Tap the refresh interval that you want (◯ changes to ◉).

You are returned to the Settings screen.

12 Tap **Messenger location services**.

13 Tap **Location is on** (☐ changes to ☑) if you want your messages to include your location by default.

14 Tap **OK**.

15 Tap **Auto-play videos on Wi-Fi only** (☐ changes to ☑) to turn off auto-play on cellular connections.

16 In the Notification Settings area, tap the options you want to enable (☐ changes to ☑).

17 Tap the Back button.

The Facebook screen appears.

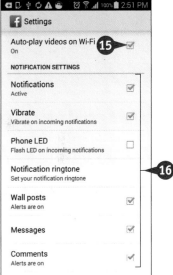

TIPS

Should I use the Find Friends feature?

Find Friends can be helpful for building your Facebook network, but evaluate each friend suggestion carefully before adding a friend. Similarly, send Facebook invitations only to selected contacts, not to your entire contacts list.

How do I sync photos?

On the Settings screen, tap **Sync Photos** to display the Photo Syncing screen, on which you can specify which photos to sync. Facebook enables you to sync all the photos from the Gallery app, but unless you take photos with especial care, it is better to upload photos only after reviewing them for quality and content.

Navigate Facebook

After setting up your account, you can use the Facebook app for social networking. On your Facebook home page, you can see what is new in your social network and quickly access other pages. On these pages, you can take other actions, such as accepting or rejecting friend requests, reading your messages, and reviewing your notifications. You can also easily post updates to let your friends know your news and submit friend requests.

Navigate Facebook

1 Press the Home button.

The Home screen appears.

2 Tap **Apps** (▦).

The Apps screen appears.

3 Tap **Facebook** (◼).

Your Facebook home page appears.

Ⓐ You can tap **Like** to like an item.

Ⓑ You can tap **Comment** to comment on an item.

4 Tap a person's name to display that person's profile.

Ⓒ You can tap **Message** to send a message to the person.

Ⓓ You can tap **About** to see more about the person.

5 Tap the Friend Request button (◪).

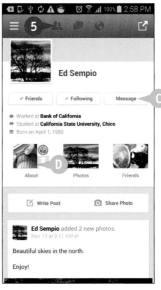

Your friend requests appear.

E You can tap **Confirm** to confirm a friend.

F You can tap **Not Now** to postpone the decision about a friend request.

6 Tap the Messages button (□).

Your messages appear.

G You can tap **New Message** (□) to start writing a new message.

7 Tap the Notifications button (□).

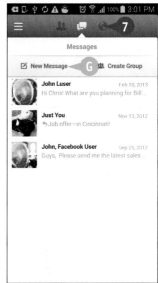

Your notifications appear.

H You can tap a notification to open it. You can then take actions, such as responding to a poke.

8 Tap ☰.

9 Tap the area of Facebook that you want to display.

Note: For example, tap **Nearby Places** to display the Nearby Places screen.

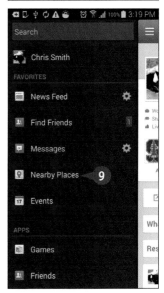

TIP

How do I log out of Facebook on my Galaxy S 5?

You do not need to log out of Facebook. You can simply stay logged in so that you can quickly access your social network at any time. But if you decide to log out, tap the Menu button to display the menu panel and then tap **Log Out**. In the Log Out dialog box that opens, tap **Confirm**. The Facebook app then logs you out of the service.

Set Up Your Twitter Account

Your Galaxy S 5 comes with the Twitter app installed. If you like tweeting on the Twitter microblogging service, reading other people's tweets, or both, you will probably want to set up your Twitter account on your Galaxy S 5 so that you can enjoy Twitter anywhere.

After entering your username and password, you can choose whom to follow on Twitter. You can also configure settings for Twitter by working on the Settings screen.

Set Up Your Twitter Account

1 Press the Home button.

The Home screen appears.

2 Tap **Apps** (▦).

The Apps screen appears.

3 Tap **Twitter** (🐦).

The Welcome to Twitter screen appears.

4 Tap **Sign In**.

Ⓐ You can tap **Create my account** to create an account for the e-mail address shown.

The Sign In screen appears.

5 Type your username or e-mail address.

6 Tap **Sign in using password** if you want to sign in using your password.

Ⓑ Alternatively, tap **Sign in via Text Message** to sign in via text.

7 Type your password.

8 Tap **Upload my address book** (☐ changes to ☑) if you want to upload your address book to Twitter.

9 Tap **Sign In**.

The Authorize Samsung Galaxy to Use Your Account? screen appears.

10 Tap **Allow**.

The Find Your Friends screen appears.

C You can tap **Skip** to skip finding your friends.

11 Tap **Follow** and proceed through the remaining screens of Find Your Friends.

The Who to Follow screen appears.

12 Tap 🖼 to follow an account.

13 Tap **Finish**.

Note: If the message "Twitter would like to use your current location to customize your experience" appears, tap **OK** or **Don't Allow**, as appropriate.

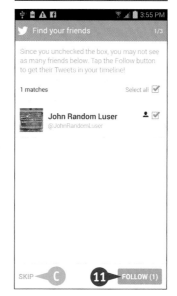

What settings can I select for Twitter?

Tap the Menu button and tap **Settings**. You can choose settings including these:

- Tap **Add account** to add another Twitter account.
- Tap **Sound effects** (☐ changes to ☑) to turn on sound effects.
- Tap **Font size** to set the font size.
- Tap **Notifications timeline** to set timeline filters.

Send Tweets

After you set up your Twitter account on your Galaxy S 5, you can use the Twitter app to send tweets. A tweet can consist of nothing but text, but you can also add a new photo you take or an existing photo on your phone. You can also add one or more hashtags, such as #politics or #kittens, to help readers locate your tweets. You can add your location to your tweets when you want to share that information with others.

Send Tweets

1 Press the Home button.

The Home screen appears.

2 Tap **Apps** (▦).

The Apps screen appears.

3 Tap **Twitter** (🐦).

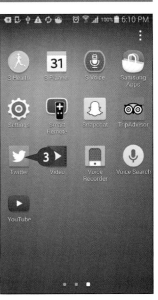

Your Twitter Home screen appears.

4 Tap **What's happening?**.

The screen for creating a tweet appears.

5 Type the text of your tweet.

A The counter shows the number of characters remaining.

B You can tap the Camera button (📷) to take a photo to add to your tweet.

6 To add a photo that is already on your Galaxy S 5, tap the Photo button (🖼).

The Photos panel opens.

7 Scroll as needed and then tap the photo that you want to use.

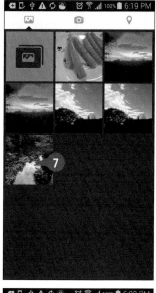

The Edit Photo screen appears.

C You can swipe left one or more times to apply a filter to the photo.

D You can use the three buttons at the bottom of the screen to edit the photo. See the Tip for details.

8 Tap **Done**.

The photo appears in your tweet.

9 Tap 📍 if you want to add your location to the tweet.

10 Tap **Tweet**.

Twitter posts the tweet.

TIP

How do I edit a picture for inclusion in a tweet?

Tap the Effects button (🔘) to view thumbnails of the available effects so that you can compare them. You can then tap the effect you want to apply. Tap the Enhance button (🪄) to enhance the photo's colors; if the result is unsatisfactory, tap 🪄 again to restore the photo to its previous state. Tap the Crop button (⬜) to display the Move and Scale controls. Drag the corners of the cropping frame to adjust the cropping or tap the photo in the frame and move it to show the appropriate part. When the crop is correct, tap **Apply**.

Using Group Play

Your Galaxy S 5 includes a feature called *Group Play* that enables you to share specific media items with one or more other devices. For example, you can share a chosen set of photos so that other people can view them on their phones or tablets.

Group Play is based on sessions. You can either create a Group Play session on your Galaxy S 5 or join an existing Group Play session that another device is hosting. Group Play works only on some Samsung devices at this writing.

Using Group Play

1 Press the Home button.

The Home screen appears.

2 Tap **Apps** (▦).

The Apps screen appears.

3 Tap **Group Play**.

Note: The first time that you launch Group Play, the Disclaimer screen appears. Read the terms and conditions and tap **Agree** if you want to continue.

The first Group Play screen appears.

4 Tap **Next**.

The second Group Play screen appears.

Ⓐ You can tap ✎ to display the Change Group Name dialog box, type a new name, and then tap **Done**.

5 If you want to protect your group with a password, tap **Set group password** (■ changes to ✔).

6 Tap **Create**.

The Set Group Password dialog box opens.

7 Type the password.

8 Tap **OK**.

The Group Play screen appears.

9 Tap the type of sharing that you want.

Note: For example, tap **Share images** to share photos.

A screen appears for selecting the items to share, such as images.

10 Tap the source for the items.

The items in the source appear.

11 Tap each item that you want to share (■ changes to ✓).

12 Tap **Done**.

Group Play shares the items and displays a screen containing them.

13 When you are ready to stop sharing the images, tap the Back button.

A dialog box opens, confirming that sharing will stop.

14 Tap **OK**.

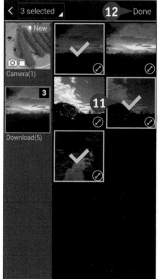

TIP

How do I join an existing Group Play session?

1 Press the Home button to display the Home screen.

2 Tap **Apps** (▦) to display the Apps screen.

3 Tap **Group Play** to display the Group Play screen.

4 In the Join Group list, tap the name of the group that you want to join.

5 If the Enter Password dialog box opens, type the passcode and then tap **OK**.

Explore Samsung ChatON

Samsung's ChatON is a mobile communications service run by Samsung. ChatON is available in more than 120 countries worldwide and runs on several operating systems, including Android, iOS, and Windows Phone. By running the ChatON app on your Galaxy S 5, you can connect to the ChatON network and communicate via text chat, audio chat, or video chat.

To use ChatON, you must set up a Samsung account and register your phone number.

Launch ChatON

To get started with ChatON, launch it as normal: Press the Home button to display the Home screen, tap the **Apps** button to display the Apps screen, and then tap **ChatON** ().

If ChatON does not appear on the Apps screen on your Galaxy S 5, tap the Play Store button ( ) on the Apps screen to open the Play Store app. You can then search for *ChatON*, download the app, and install it.

Register with ChatON and Sync Your Contacts

The first time you run ChatON, you must accept the terms and conditions and the privacy policy. You can read these by tapping **Terms and conditions** and **Privacy policy** on the Terms and Privacy screen that appears. Tap **Accept** on the Terms and Privacy screen if you want to proceed.

Next, you use the Registration screen to register your Galaxy S 5's phone number on the ChatON network. ChatON then automatically prompts you to sync your contacts. Tap **Include SIM contacts** (changes to) to include any contacts on your phone's SIM card. Then tap **OK**.

Navigate the ChatON App's Screens

After your Galaxy S 5 connects to the ChatON service, the ChatON app displays its main screens. You navigate the ChatON app's screens by tapping the four tabs near the top of the screen. Tap **Contacts** to display the Contacts screen, which shows your chat contacts. Tap **Chats** to display your ongoing chats. Tap **My page** to display the My Page screen, which enables you to post notes about your status for others to view. Tap **More** to display the More screen, which gives you access to features such as the LIVE services and the ChatON Shop.

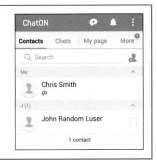

Add Contacts

From the Contacts screen, you can add other contacts to your Contacts list by searching for them. Tap the Add Contact button (▣) to display the Add Contact screen and then tap the means of searching: Tap **Suggestions** (▣) to display the list of contact suggestions, tap **Tell friends** (▣) to send a download link to a friend you want to encourage to join ChatON, tap **Phone number** (▣) to search by phone number, or tap **Email** (@) to search by e-mail address.

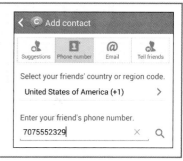

Chat with a Contact via Text

From the Contacts screen, tap a contact to display the Quick Info window and then tap **Text Chat** (▣). On the chat screen that appears, tap the "Enter Message" prompt, type a message, and then tap the Send button (▣). You can tap ▣ to send a file via chat or ▣ to enter an emoticon, or smiley, character.

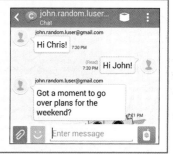

Chat with a Contact via Audio or Video

From the Contacts screen, tap a contact to display the Quick Info window and then tap the Audio Chat button (▣) to place an audio call. ChatON places the audio call across the Internet, but it rings on the recipient's phone using a similar interface to that of a regular phone call.

From the Quick Info window, you can also tap the Video Chat button (▣) to place a video call.

CHAPTER 8

Working with Apps

An *app* is software that provides specific functionality on a computer. Your Galaxy S 5 comes with many apps built in, and you can install further apps to make your phone perform the tasks that you need. You can download apps from Google's Play Store or other sources, run them as needed, and switch quickly from app to app. You also can update your apps to keep them running well.

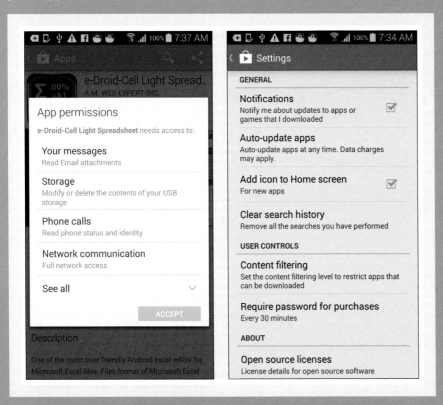

When you need to use an app on your Galaxy S 5, you run the app. You can run any app from the Apps screen, but you can also put apps on the Home screen for quick access.

Your Galaxy S 5 can run many apps simultaneously. Each app appears full screen by default, so you work in a single app at a time, but you can switch from app to app as needed. You can also run apps in Multi Window as explained in Chapter 1, "Getting Started with Your Galaxy S5."

Switch Quickly from One App to Another

Launch Multiple Apps

1 Press the Home button.

The Home screen appears.

2 Tap **Apps** (▦).

The Apps screen appears.

3 Tap the first app that you want to open.

Note: This example uses **Clock** (▽).

The app opens.

4 Press the Home button.

The Home screen appears.

5 Tap **Apps** (▦).

The Apps screen appears.

Note: If necessary, swipe left or right to display the icons for other apps.

6 Tap the second app that you want to open.

Note: This example uses **Calculator** (▦).

The app opens.

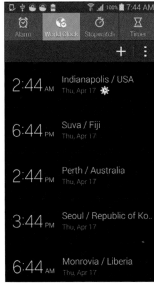

Switch Quickly among Running Apps

1 With a running app displayed, tap the Recent Apps button.

The Recent Apps list appears.

The apps at the bottom of the list are the ones that you have used most recently.

2 If necessary, pull down to scroll the list to display other apps.

3 Tap the app that you want to use.

The app's screen appears, and you can start using the app.

TIP

Can I do anything else from the Recent Apps list?
You can also display an app's information or remove the app from the Recent Apps list. To display the app's information, tap and hold its icon in the Recent Apps list and then tap **App info** on the pop-up menu that appears. To remove an app, either swipe it left or right off the list or tap and hold and then tap **Remove from list** on the pop-up menu.

Explore the Play Store

Your Galaxy S 5 comes with a wealth of apps that enable you to perform everyday tasks. For example, you can surf the web using the Chrome app or the Internet app, send and receive e-mail messages on Google's Gmail service using the Gmail app, and keep track of events using the S Planner app. When you need to perform tasks beyond the capabilities of your existing apps, you can add other apps. To get apps, you can run the Play Store app, which gives you access to Google Play, a service that contains apps Google has approved for use on Android devices.

Explore the Play Store

1 Press the Home button.

The Home screen appears.

2 Tap **Play Store** (▶).

A If Play Store (▶) does not appear on the Home screen, tap **Apps** (▦) to display the Apps screen and tap **Play Store** (▶).

The Play Store app opens and displays the Google Play screen.

3 Tap **Apps**.

The Apps area appears.

B Tap **Games** to display the Games section.

C Tap **Editors' Choice** to see apps selected by the Google Play editors.

D Tap **See More** in the Recommended for You section to see recommended apps.

4 To browse Google Play by categories, tap **Categories** or swipe right.

The Categories screen appears.

5 Tap the category that you want to view.

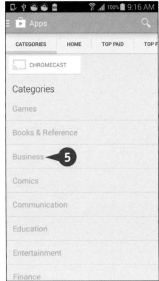

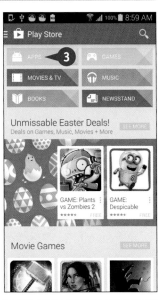

The category's screen appears, and you can browse the apps that it contains.

⑥ Tap the Play Store button (📼) or tap the Back button.

The Categories screen appears.

⑦ Swipe left twice.

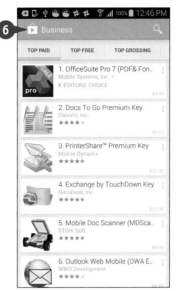

The Top Paid screen appears, showing the top apps for which people pay.

⑧ Swipe left once.

Ⓔ You can also tap **Top Free** to display the Top Free screen.

The Top Free screen appears, showing the top free apps.

Note: Swipe left again to reach other screens: Top Grossing, Top New Paid, Top New Free, and Trending. Swipe right to go back to the other screens.

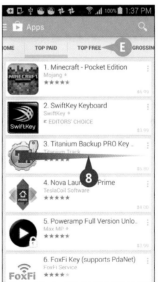

TIP

How can I see which apps I have previously bought on Google Play?

From the Google Play screen or from one of the main screens, such as the Top New screen, tap 📼 to display the menu panel and then tap **My apps**. The My Apps screen appears, showing your Installed list first. From the list, you can see the apps that you have installed on your Galaxy S 5. Tap the **All** tab to display the All list, which shows all the apps you have bought, including apps you have not installed on your Galaxy S 5.

Find and Download Apps from the Play Store

Browsing the Play Store gives you an idea of the many types of apps available. But when you need to find a particular app, search instead and then explore the list of matches. When you find an app you want, you can download and install it.

As part of the installation process, you must review the permissions the app requires on your Galaxy S 5. If you are prepared to grant these permissions, you can complete the installation; if not, you can cancel it.

Find and Download Apps from the Play Store

1 Press the Home button.

The Home screen appears.

2 Tap **Play Store** (▶).

A If Play Store (▶) does not appear on the Home screen, tap **Apps** (▦) to display the Apps screen and tap **Play Store** (▶).

The Play Store app opens and displays the Google Play screen.

3 Tap **Apps**.

The Apps screen appears, showing the Home list.

4 Tap the Search button (🔍).

The Search box and keyboard appear.

B The pop-up menu shows any recent searches you have performed. You can repeat a search by tapping it in the pop-up menu.

C You can search using your voice. Tap 🎤 and then speak the terms when the "Speak now" prompt appears.

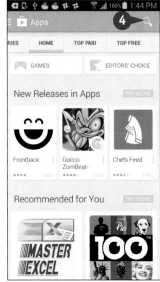

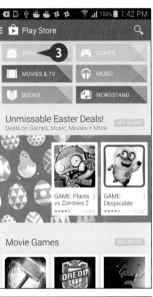

5 Type your search terms.

D The pop-up menu displays suggestions. If one of them is suitable, tap it. Otherwise, finish typing your search terms.

6 Tap the Search button (🔍) on the keyboard.

A screen of search results appears.

7 Tap the result that you want to view.

The app's screen appears.

8 Tap ▶ to view a video of the app.

9 Read the description and, below it, the user reviews.

10 Tap **Install** if you want to install the app.

The App Permissions dialog box opens.

11 Read the list of permissions.

E You can tap **See all** to display the full list of permissions.

12 Tap **Accept** if you want to complete the installation. Otherwise, tap the Back button to cancel the installation.

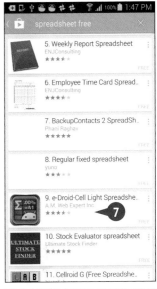

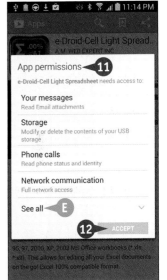

TIP

What permissions should I grant to an app?

This depends on the app, so you must decide depending on what the app does. For example, an app that creates files needs the Modify or Delete the Contents of Your USB Storage permission; similarly, an app that can open e-mail attachments needs the Read Email Attachments permission. But you must be suspicious of any app that wants to access sensitive data such as your contacts but does not have a good reason to do so.

Update Your Apps

Software developers often update their apps to remove bugs and to add new features. To keep your Galaxy S 5's apps running well, you should install app updates when they become available. Most updates for paid apps are free, but you must usually pay to upgrade to a new version of an app.

You can update all your apps at once or update a single app at a time. Normally, updating all your apps is most convenient, but you may sometimes need to update a single app without downloading all the available updates.

Update Your Apps

Display the My Apps Screen

1 Press the Home button.

The Home screen appears.

2 Tap **Play Store** (▷).

A If Play Store does not appear on the Home screen, tap **Apps** (⊞) to display the Apps screen and tap **Play Store**.

The Play Store app opens.

3 Tap **Play Store** (▷).

4 Tap **My apps**.

The My Apps screen appears.

Update a Single App

1 Tap the button for the app, such as **Google+**.

The app's screen appears.

B You can view the What's New section to see what is new in this version of the app, read user reviews, and decide whether to install the update.

2 Tap **Update**.

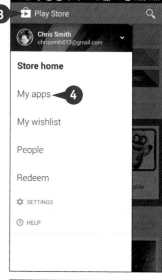

174

The App Permissions dialog box opens.

③ Read the permissions.

⊙ The New readout marks a change in permissions from the previous version.

④ Tap **Accept**.

The app's screen appears again.

The Play Store app downloads and installs the update.

Ⓓ You can tap **Open** to open the updated app.

⑤ Tap 🔲.

The My Apps screen appears.

Update All Installed Apps

① Tap **Update All**.

The Play Store app downloads and installs all the updates.

Ⓔ The updated apps appear in the Recently Updated list.

You can now press the Home button to return to the Home screen.

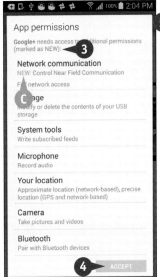

Remove an App

Each app that you install takes up some of your Galaxy S 5's storage space. When you no longer need an app that you have installed, you can remove it. The app remains available to you on Google Play, so you can reinstall it later if necessary. You can remove an app either by using the Apps screen or by using the App Info screen for the app. You cannot remove the apps that come built into Android, only the apps you have installed.

Remove an App

Using the Apps Screen

1 Press the Home button.

The Home screen appears.

2 Tap **Apps** (▦).

The Apps screen appears.

3 Tap the Menu button (▤).

4 Tap **Uninstall/disable apps**.

Ⓐ ⊘ indicates an app that you can uninstall or disable.

Note: You can swipe left or right to display a different screen of apps.

5 Tap the app that you want to remove or disable.

A confirmation dialog box opens.

6 Tap **Uninstall**.

Android removes the app.

7 Press the Home button to go to the Home screen.

176

Using the App Info Screen

1 Press the Home button.

The Home screen appears.

2 Tap **Play Store** (▶).

B If Play Store does not appear on the Home screen, tap **Apps** (▦) to display the Apps screen and tap **Play Store**.

The Play Store app opens.

3 Tap **Play Store** (▶).

4 Tap **My apps**.

The My Apps screen appears.

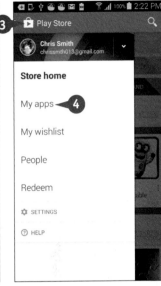

5 Tap **Installed**.

The list of apps installed on your Galaxy S 5 appears.

6 Tap the app that you want to remove.

The app's screen appears.

7 Tap **Uninstall**.

A confirmation dialog box opens.

8 Tap **OK**.

The Play Store app uninstalls the app.

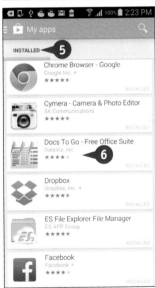

TIP

How do I reinstall an app I have removed?

1 Press the Home button to display the Home screen.

2 Tap **Apps** (▦) to display the Apps screen.

3 Tap **Play Store** (▶) to open the Play Store app.

4 Tap **Play Store** (▶) and then tap **My Apps**.

5 Tap **All** to display the All list.

6 Tap the app to display its screen.

7 Tap **Install**.

Choose Which Apps to Update Automatically

Your Galaxy S 5 enables you to update apps either manually or automatically. Updating apps automatically makes it easy to take advantage of the bug fixes and new features that developers add to their apps. You can choose to update all apps automatically or just some apps.

Automatic updates may involve downloading large amounts of data, so unless you have an unlimited cellular plan, it is better to set your Galaxy S 5 to download updates only when it is connected to a Wi-Fi network.

Choose Which Apps to Update Automatically

Display the My Apps Screen

1 Press the Home button.

The Home screen appears.

2 Tap **Play Store** (▶).

A If needed, tap **Apps** (▦) to display the Apps screen and tap **Play Store**.

The Play Store app opens.

3 Tap **Play Store** (▶).

4 Tap **My apps**.

The My Apps screen appears.

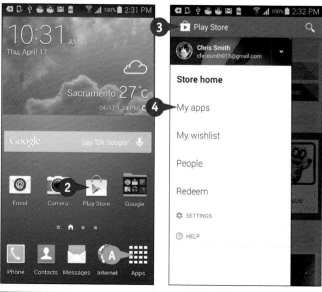

Set All Your Apps to Update Automatically

1 Tap the Menu button (▤) or **Play Store** (▶).

2 Tap **Settings**.

The Settings screen appears.

3 Tap **Auto-update apps**.

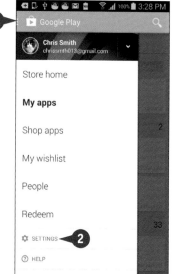

The Auto-Update Apps dialog box opens.

4 Tap **Auto-update apps over Wi-Fi only** (⃝ changes to ◉).

B Tap **Auto-update apps at any time. Data charges may apply** (⃝ changes to ◉) only if you have an unlimited data plan.

C The Settings screen shows the setting that you chose.

5 Tap 🔄.

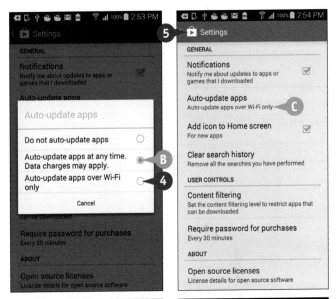

The My Apps screen appears.

Control Automatic Updates for an Individual App

1 Tap **Installed**.

The Installed list appears.

2 Tap the app.

The app's App Info screen opens.

3 Tap ⋮.

4 Tap **Auto-update** (☐ changes to ☑).

5 Tap 🔄.

The My Apps screen appears again.

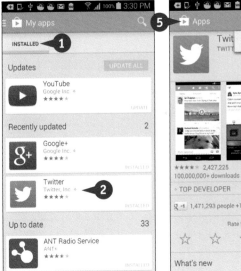
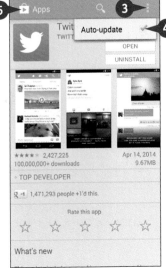

TIP

How can I reach the App Info screen quickly?

If the app is running, you can display its App Info screen quickly by using the Recent Apps list. Follow these steps:

1 Tap the Recent Apps button to display the Recent Apps list.

2 Tap and hold the thumbnail for the app whose App Info screen you want to display.

3 On the pop-up menu that opens, tap **App info**.

Install an App Manually

You can install an app manually by using a technique called *sideloading*. To sideload, you first acquire a package file containing the app. You then transfer the package file to your Galaxy S 5, enable the installation of apps from unknown sources, and finally install the app.

Understanding When to Use Manual Installation

Sideloading is primarily useful for installing apps that are not available on the Google Play service. For example, you may need to sideload an app that your company or organization provides.

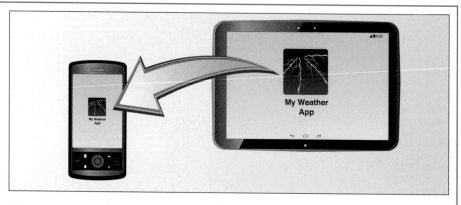

Sideloading can also be useful for installing an app that is available for other Android devices but not for your Galaxy S 5. Be aware that apps that you download from sources other than Google Play may contain malevolent code. It is wise to search the web for reviews of an app before installing it.

Install an App That Enables Sideloading

To sideload apps, you need a suitable file-management app on your Galaxy S 5. You use this app to install the app that you are sideloading. To get your Galaxy S 5 ready to sideload, open the Play Store app and install a file-management app such as ES File Explorer, shown here, or Astro File Manager. Both these apps are free and are easy to use.

Get the Package File for the App That You Will Sideload

Each app comes in a distribution file called a *package file* from which you install the app. If you already have the app on another Android device, use a file-management app to copy the file to a backup, creating a package file. For an app provided by your company or organization, download the package file from the company's or organization's site. For other apps, download the package file from an online repository, but be wary of malevolent content.

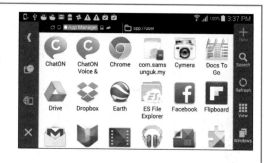

Transfer the Package File to Your Galaxy S 5

After acquiring the package file for the app that you want to sideload, you need to transfer the file to your Galaxy S 5. You can transfer the file in several ways. If the package file is on your computer, use Windows Explorer or the Finder to copy or move the file to an SD card and then insert the card in your Galaxy S 5. Otherwise, use an online storage service such as Dropbox. If the package file is small, you can also transfer it via e-mail or Bluetooth.

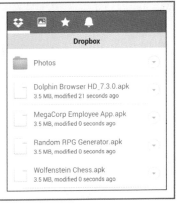

Enable Installation of Apps from Unknown Sources

By default, Android prevents you from installing apps from sources other than Google Play. So before you can sideload an app on your Galaxy S 5, you must set Android to allow the installation of apps from unknown sources. Pull down at the top of the screen to display the Notifications panel and then tap ⚙. On the Settings screen, tap **More** to display the More screen. Tap **Security** to display the Security screen and then tap **Unknown sources** (■ changes to ✔). In the Unknown Sources dialog box that opens, tap **OK**.

Sideload the App

After copying the package file to your Galaxy S 5 and setting Android to allow the installation of apps from unknown sources, you can sideload the app. Open the file-management app that you installed, such as ES File Explorer or Astro File Manager, and then tap the package file. When the screen listing the app's required permissions appears, read the permissions carefully and decide whether to proceed with the installation. After you install the app, you can run it from the Apps screen like any other app.

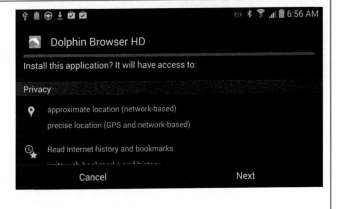

CHAPTER 9

Browsing the Web and E-mailing

For browsing the Web, your Galaxy S 5 includes the Internet app and the Chrome app. For sending and receiving e-mail, your Galaxy S 5 offers both the Email app and the Gmail app.

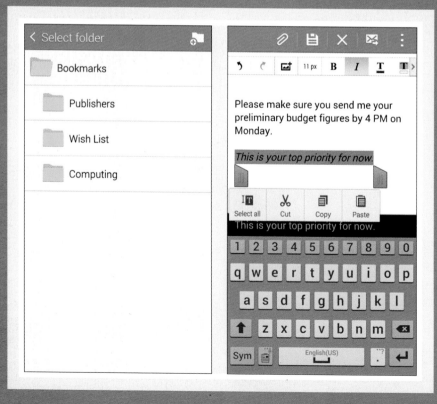

Browse the Web

Your Galaxy S 5 includes two apps for browsing the web, Samsung's Internet app and Google's Chrome app. Both browsers are full featured, and you may choose to use either or both. This chapter shows Internet, but you likely want to explore Chrome as well.

Using Internet, you can quickly go to a web page by entering its address in the address box or by following a link from another page. You can browse by opening a single web page at a time or by opening multiple pages in separate windows and switching back and forth among them as needed.

Browse the Web

Open Internet and Navigate to Web Pages

1 Press the Home button.

The Home screen appears.

2 Tap **Internet** (⬛).

Ⓐ If Internet does not appear on the Home screen, tap **Apps** (⬛) and tap **Internet** (⬛).

Internet opens.

Your home page appears.

3 Tap the address box.

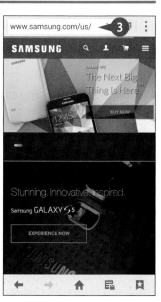

4 Type the address of the page that you want to open.

5 Tap **Go**.

Internet displays the page.

6 Tap a link on the page.

Internet displays the linked page.

Ⓑ After going to another page, you can tap ⬅ to go back to the previous page. You can then tap ➡ to go forward to the page from which you just went back.

Open Multiple Web Pages and Navigate among Them

1 In Internet, tap the Window Manager button ().

The Window Manager screen appears.

2 Tap the New Window button ().

Internet opens a new window and displays the Quick Access screen.

3 Tap the address box and go to the page that you want.

4 To switch to another web page, tap .

The Window Manager screen appears.

C You can tap to close a window.

5 Tap the window that you want to display.

The window appears full screen.

TIPS

How do I get the full version of a web page instead of the mobile version?

You can display the regular version of the current web page by tapping the Menu button () and then tapping **Desktop view** (■ changes to ✓). Some pages are programmed to prevent mobiles from requesting the desktop version of the page, so this does not always work.

What else can I do from the Window Manager screen?

You can close a window by swiping its thumbnail off the screen to the right. You might find this move easier than tapping .

Create Bookmarks for Web Pages

The Internet app enables you to create a bookmark for any web page that you want to be able to access again easily. When you return to the bookmarked page, Internet displays the current version of the page, which may have changed since you bookmarked it.

You can give each bookmark a descriptive name to help yourself identify the web pages, and you can organize your bookmarks into folders to keep them in a logical order.

Create Bookmarks for Web Pages

1 Press the Home button.

The Home screen appears.

2 Tap **Internet** (◙).

A If Internet does not appear on the Home screen, tap **Apps** (▦) and tap **Internet** (◙).

Internet displays the last page that you visited.

3 Navigate to the web page that you want to bookmark.

4 Tap the Bookmark button (★).

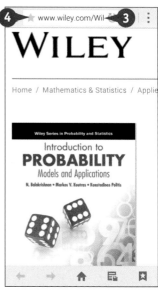

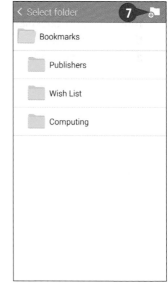

5 Type the name for the bookmark.

Note: You can accept the default name, but it is helpful to type a more descriptive name.

6 If the folder bar shows the folder in which you want to store the bookmark, go to step **12**. Otherwise, tap the folder bar.

The Select Folder screen appears.

7 If the folder that you want to use already exists, tap it and go to step **12**. If not, tap here.

The New Folder screen appears.

8 Type the name for the new folder.

9 Tap the existing folder in which to store the new folder (⭕ changes to ⦿).

10 Tap **Done**.

The Select Folder screen appears.

The new folder appears in the list.

11 Tap the new folder.

The Add Bookmark screen appears, now showing the folder that you selected.

12 Tap **Save**.

Internet saves the bookmark.

The web page appears again.

B The Bookmark star is now gold (⭐), indicating that Internet has a bookmark for the page. You can tap ⭐ to delete the bookmark.

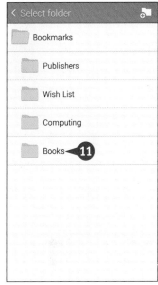

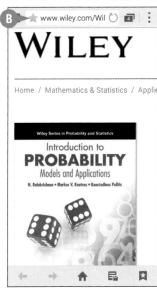

TIP

How do I delete a bookmark?

1 In the Internet app, tap the Bookmarks button (⭐) to display the Bookmarks screen.

2 Navigate to the bookmark by tapping the folder or folders that contain it.

3 Tap ⋮ and then tap **Delete**. A check box appears on each bookmark.

4 Tap each bookmark that you want to delete (☐ changes to ☑).

5 Tap **Done**.

Internet deletes the bookmark.

Using Bookmarks, Saved Pages, and History

To save your having to type web addresses, the Internet app provides bookmarks, saved pages, and the history. As explained in the preceding section, "Create Bookmarks for Web Pages," you can create a bookmark for any web page. You also can save a web page for future reading in its current state. The history records the web pages that you visit, creating a log that enables you to return to any of the pages, unless you turn on Incognito mode.

Using Bookmarks, Saved Pages, and History

Display the Bookmarks Screen

1 Press the Home button.

The Home screen appears.

2 Tap **Internet** (◉).

A If Internet does not appear on the Home screen, tap **Apps** (▦) and tap **Internet** (◉).

Internet displays the last page that you visited.

3 Tap 🔖.

The Bookmarks screen appears.

Open a Bookmarked Web Page

1 Navigate to the appropriate bookmarks folder by tapping the folder.

2 Tap the bookmark.

Internet displays the web page.

Save a Web Page for Future Reading

1 In the Internet app, navigate to the page that you want to save.

2 Tap ⋮.

3 Tap **Save page**.

Internet saves the page.

Ⓑ The message "Page saved in Saved pages" appears briefly.

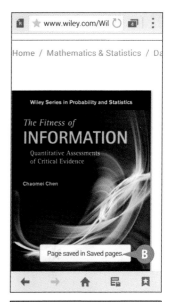

Open a Saved Page

1 In the Internet app, tap the Saved Pages button (▤).

The Saved Pages screen appears.

2 Tap the saved page that you want to view.

The saved page appears.

Note: To delete saved pages, tap ⋮ and tap **Delete**. Tap each saved page to delete (☐ changes to ☑), and then tap **Done**.

How can I browse the web without the history recording the pages that I visit?

You can turn on Incognito mode, which prevents the history from recording the list of pages. In the Internet app, tap ⋮ to display the menu and then tap **Incognito mode**. The Incognito Mode dialog box opens, explaining that pages you view in this window will not appear in your browser history or your search history. Tap **OK**.

When you finish using Incognito mode, tap ▧ to display the Window Manager screen and then close the Incognito Mode window by tapping ⊖ or by swiping it to the right off the list of windows.

Search for Information

To find information with the Internet app, you often need to search using a search engine. The Internet app offers a choice of search engines and enables you to switch from one to another as you want. Your choice of search engines may vary depending on your country or region, but many Galaxy S 5 models offer Google Search, Yahoo!, and Bing. Experiment with these search engines to find out which gives you the most suitable results.

Search for Information

1 Press the Home button.

The Home screen appears.

2 Tap **Internet** (icon).

A If Internet does not appear on the Home screen, tap **Apps** (icon) and tap **Internet** (icon).

Internet displays the last page that you visited.

3 Tap the address box.

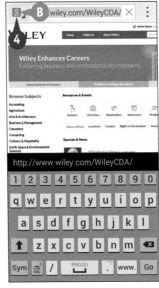

The address box expands.

B This button shows your current search engine, such as Google Search (icon), Yahoo! (icon), or Bing (icon).

Note: At this writing, Yahoo and Bing use the same icon, (icon).

4 Tap the button.

5 Tap the search engine that you want to use.

C The icon for the search engine appears.

6 Type your search terms.

Internet displays suggested searches based on the search terms.

7 If a search is suitable, tap it. Otherwise, finish typing, and then tap **Go** on the keyboard.

The search results appear.

8 To restrict the search to a particular type of result, tap a link at the top, such as **Images**.

The matching search results appear.

Note: You can tap a search result to view the web page in the same window. But often it is better to open results in separate windows so that you can return to the search results if needed.

9 Tap and hold a search result.

The Actions dialog box opens.

10 Tap **Open in new window**.

Internet opens the web page in a new window.

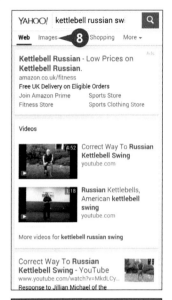

TIP

How can I search using a search engine that does not appear on the pop-up menu?
You can search using any search engine that you can find on the web. Open a web page to the search engine and then perform the search using the tools on the page. If you plan to use this search engine frequently, create a bookmark for it or tap the Menu button and then tap **Add shortcut to Home** to add the page to your Home screen.

Fill in Forms Using Auto Fill Forms

If you fill in web forms on your Galaxy S 5, you can save time by turning on the Auto Fill Forms feature and setting it up to suit your needs. Auto Fill Forms can automatically fill in standard form fields, such as name and address fields, using the information from one or more profiles that you enter. If you create only a single profile, Auto Fill Forms uses that profile; if you set up multiple profiles, you can choose among them as needed.

Fill in Forms Using Auto Fill Forms

① Press the Home button.

The Home screen appears.

② Tap **Internet** (🌐).

Ⓐ If Internet does not appear on the Home screen, tap **Apps** (▦) and tap **Internet** (🌐).

Internet displays the last page that you visited.

③ Tap ⋮.

④ Tap **Settings**.

Note: You may need to scroll down to reveal the Settings item on the menu.

The Settings screen appears.

⑤ Tap **Auto fill forms**.

The Auto Fill Forms screen appears.

⑥ Tap **Auto fill forms** (☐ changes to ☑).

⑦ Tap **Add profile**.

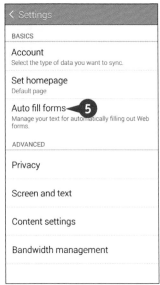

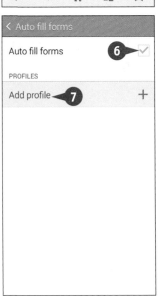

The Add Profile screen appears.

8 Type your name in the Full Name box.

Note: To move from one field to the next, either tap another field or tap **Next** on the keyboard.

9 Type your company name if applicable.

10 Type your address information.

11 Type your phone number.

12 Type your e-mail address.

13 Tap **Save**.

The Auto Fill Forms screen appears.

B The profile appears in the Profiles list.

C You can tap **Add profile** to add another profile.

14 Tap **Auto fill forms**.

The Settings screen appears.

15 Tap **Settings**.

The web page appears again.

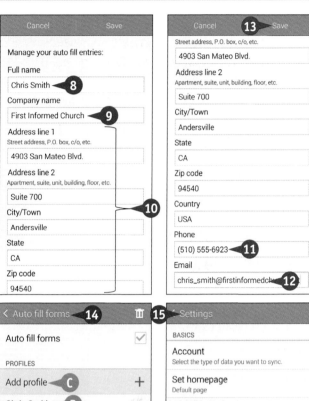

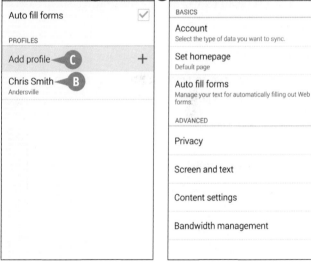

TIP

How do I use Auto Fill Forms to fill out a form?

After turning on the Auto Fill Forms feature and setting up your profiles as shown here, you can navigate to a web page that contains a form with name and address fields. The first time that you tap a form field for which your profile contains the appropriate information, Internet displays a pop-up button showing that information. Tap the pop-up to insert the information in the field. Internet automatically inserts the other available information in the matching fields on the form.

Tighten Up Your Browsing Privacy Settings

The web contains many sites that provide useful information or services, but it also contains sites that try to infect computers with malevolent software — *malware* for short — or lure visitors into providing sensitive personal or financial information. Although Google has built Android to be as secure as possible, it is wise to apply high-security settings. You can choose privacy settings, disable JavaScript, and block pop-ups and cookies.

Tighten Up Your Browsing Privacy Settings

1 Press the Home button.

The Home screen appears.

2 Tap **Internet** (⬤).

A If Internet does not appear on the Home screen, tap **Apps** (⌗) and tap **Internet** (⬤).

Internet displays the last page that you visited.

3 Tap ⋮.

4 Tap **Settings**.

Note: You may need to scroll down to reveal the Settings item on the menu.

5 Tap **Privacy**.

The Privacy screen appears.

6 Tap **Suggest search terms and Web addresses** (☐ changes to ☑) to use suggestions.

7 Tap **Preload available links** to preload links.

8 Tap **Remember form data** to store your form data.

9 Tap **Remember passwords** to store usernames and passwords.

10 Tap **Delete personal data**.

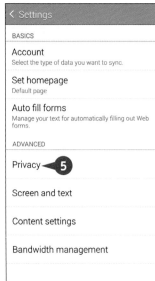

The Delete Personal Data dialog box opens.

11 Tap each option that you want to delete (☐ changes to ☑).

12 Tap **Done**.

13 Tap **Privacy**.

The Settings screen appears.

14 Tap **Content settings**.

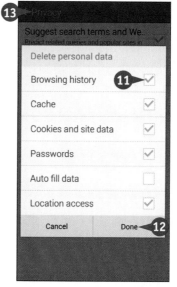

The Content Settings screen appears.

15 Tap **Accept cookies** (☐ changes to ☑) to accept cookies.

16 Tap **Turn on location** only if you want to allow location access.

17 Tap **Turn on JavaScript** only if you want to enable JavaScript.

18 Tap **Block pop-ups** to block pop-up windows.

19 Tap the Back button twice.

The web page appears again.

TIP

What are cookies, and what threat do they pose?

A *cookie* is a small text file that a website places on a computer or device to identify it in the future. Cookies are helpful for many sites, such as shopping sites in which you add items to a shopping cart, but when used by malevolent sites, cookies can pose a threat to your privacy. You can deselect **Accept cookies** to make Internet refuse cookies, but this prevents many legitimate websites from working properly. So normally it is best to set Internet to accept cookies.

Read Your E-mail Messages with Email

After setting up your non-Gmail e-mail accounts, as explained in Chapter 4, "Setting Up Communications," you can use the Email app to send and receive e-mail messages. You can easily read your incoming e-mail messages, reply to messages that you have received, and write new messages as needed.

If you have set up multiple e-mail accounts in the Email app, you can display either a single account's Inbox or use the Combined Inbox view to display the messages from all your accounts in the same list.

Read Your E-mail Messages with Email

1 Press the Home button.

A The badge shows the number of unread messages.

2 Tap **Email** (📧).

B If Email (📧) does not appear on the Home screen, tap **Apps** (▦) and tap **Email** (📧).

Your Inbox appears.

3 If you have set up multiple accounts in Email, tap ☰ to choose the Inbox to view.

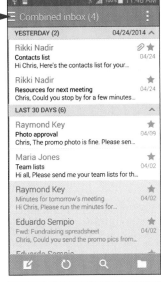

4 Tap the Inbox or other folder that you want.

C Each message preview shows the sender's name, the subject line and time or date, and the first part of the message.

D The sender of an unread message appears in boldface on a white background.

E A read message appears on a gray background.

F This number shows how many unread messages you have.

5 Tap the message that you want to read.

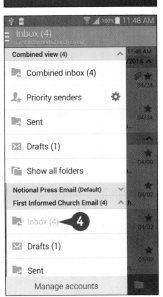

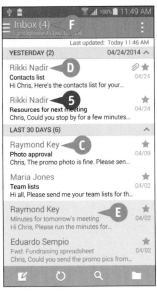

The message opens.

G You can tap 🗑 to delete the message.

6 When you want to display the next message, tap ▶.

H You can tap ◀ to display the previous message.

7 To see the message at a larger size, rotate your Galaxy S 5 to Landscape orientation.

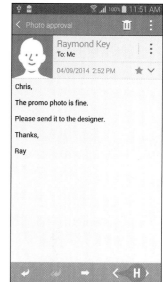

The message appears in Landscape orientation.

8 When you finish reading messages, tap the message's subject or tap the Back button.

The folder or your Inbox appears.

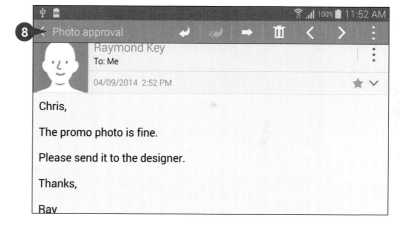

TIP

How do I move a message to a different folder?

In the Inbox or other folder, tap 📃 and then tap **Select**. Tap each message that you want to move (☐ changes to ☑). Tap 🗂 to open the Move dialog box and then tap the folder to which you want to move the message.

If you have opened the message for reading, tap 📃 to open the menu and then tap **Move** to open the Move dialog box. Tap the folder to which you want to move the message.

Reply to or Forward a Message with Email

When replying to an e-mail message, you can reply only to the message's sender or to the sender and all the other recipients in the To field and the Cc field. Email automatically adds **Re:** to the beginning of the subject line to indicate that the message is a reply.

Other times, you may need to forward a message that you have received to one or more people. Email adds **Fwd:** to the beginning of the subject line to indicate that the message has been forwarded.

Reply to or Forward a Message with Email

Open the Email App and the Message

1 Press the Home button.

The Home screen appears.

2 Tap **Email** (⊚).

Ⓐ If Email (⊚) does not appear on the Home screen, tap **Apps** (▦) and tap **Email** (⊚).

Your Inbox appears.

3 Tap the message that you want to open.

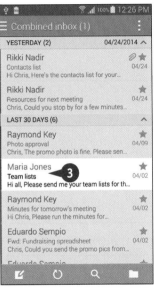

The message opens.

4 To see the recipients list for the message, tap the Expand arrow (▽).

The recipients pane opens.

Ⓑ You can tap the Add to Contacts button (▨) to add an address to the Contacts app.

Ⓒ You can tap the Collapse arrow (△) to collapse the recipients pane again.

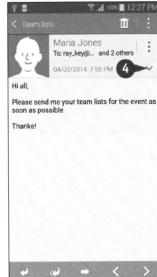
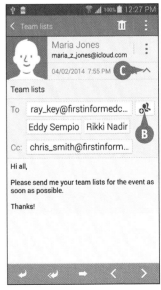

198

Reply to the Message

1. In the open message, tap ◀.

   Email creates a reply.

2. Type the text of the reply.

   Ⓓ You can tap ◀ to display the pop-up toolbar, which contains controls for formatting the message.

3. Tap **Original message** (☑ changes to ☐) if you want to remove the original message.

4. Tap ✉.

   Email sends the reply.

Forward the Message

1. With the message open, tap the Forward button (▭).

   Email creates a forwarded message.

2. Enter the recipient in the **To** field.

Note: You may need to tap the Back button to display the To field.

3. Type any text needed for the forwarded message.

4. Tap ✉.

   Email sends the message.

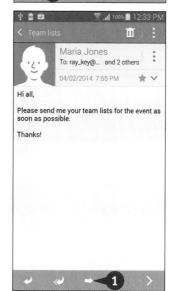

TIP

How do I reply to all the recipients of a message?

When you need to reply to all the recipients of the open message, tap the Reply All button (▣) instead of ◀. The Email app starts a reply to all the recipients, both those in the To field and those in the Cc field; if the message had any Bcc recipients, you do not see their names, and the reply does not go to them. You can remove any To or Cc recipients to whom you do not want to reply. When the recipient list is to your satisfaction, compose the reply and tap ✉ to send it.

Write and Send E-mail Messages with Email

The Email app enables you to write and send new messages easily on your Galaxy S 5. You can use the data in the Contacts app to address your outgoing messages quickly and accurately. If the recipient's address is not one of your contacts, you can type the address manually.

Write and Send E-mail Messages with Email

1 Press the Home button.

The Home screen appears.

2 Tap **Email** (⊚).

Ⓐ If needed, tap **Apps** (▦) and tap **Email** (⊚).

Your Inbox appears.

3 Tap the New Message button (✉).

Note: If you have set up multiple accounts and are using Combined view, Email creates the new message in the default account.

Email creates a new e-mail message.

Ⓑ You can tap ✉ to expand the address area, tap **From**, and then tap a different account in the Select Email Address dialog box.

4 Tap the **To** field and start typing the recipient's address.

A pop-up menu displays possible matches from the Contacts app.

5 Tap the appropriate entry. If it does not appear, finish typing the address.

The recipient's name appears.

C If necessary, add other recipients by tapping the **To** field or tapping ✉ and then tapping the **Cc/Bcc** field.

6 Tap the **Subject** field and type the subject for the message.

7 Tap the body field.

Email scrolls the message up, hiding the message headers.

8 Type the body of the message.

9 If you need to apply formatting, tap ◁.

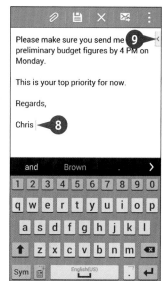

The toolbar appears.

10 Select the text that you want to format.

11 Tap the formatting that you want to apply.

Note: Tap *I* to apply italics, ⧉ to change the font size, **B** to toggle boldface, **T** to select the font color, or **T** to select the background color.

12 Tap ✉.

Email sends the message.

How can I add multiple recipients to a message easily?

Tap the **To** box or the **Cc/Bcc** box. If you tap **Cc/Bcc**, the Cc box and Bcc box appear; tap the appropriate one. Tap ⚊ to the right of the selected box to display the Contacts list. Tap each contact that you want to include (■ changes to ☑) and then tap **Done**.

What are the buttons on the toolbar?

The toolbar buttons are Undo (↰), Redo (↱), Insert Multimedia (⊡), Font Size (⧉), Bold (**B**), Italic (*I*), Font Color (**T**), Background Color (**T**), Numbered List (▤), Bulleted List (▤), Indent (▤), and Decrease Indent (▤).

Send and Receive Files with Email

The Email app enables you to send files via e-mail by attaching them to outgoing messages and to receive files attached to incoming messages. E-mail can be a fast and convenient way to exchange files with others or to move them among your computers and devices. But because most e-mail servers reject messages with attachments larger than several megabytes, it is best to use e-mail only for relatively small files.

Send and Receive Files with Email

1 Press the Home button.

The Home screen appears.

2 Tap **Email** (⊙).

A If Email (⊙) does not appear on the Home screen, tap **Apps** (▦) and tap **Email** (⊙).

Your Inbox appears.

3 Tap ✎.

Email creates a new e-mail message.

4 Tap the **To** field and start typing the recipient's address.

The list of matches appears.

5 Tap the recipient.

Email enters the recipient's name.

6 Tap the **Subject** field and type the subject.

7 Tap the Attach button (∅).

The Attach dialog box opens.

8 Tap the source of the file that you want to attach, such as **My Files**.

The source opens — the My Files app in this example.

9 Navigate to the folder that contains the file.

10 Tap the check box for each file (■ changes to ☑) that you want to attach.

Note: Do not tap the filename because doing so opens the file.

11 Tap **Done**.

The file appears in the document.

Ⓑ You can tap ▬ to remove an attachment.

12 Tap the body field.

Email scrolls the message up, hiding the message headers.

13 Type the body of the message.

14 Tap ✉.

Email sends the message and the attached file.

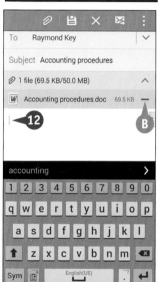

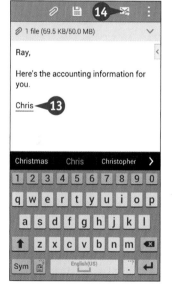

How do I receive a file attached to an e-mail message?
In your Inbox, an e-mail message with an attachment displays 📎. Tap the message to open it and then tap **Attachments** to display the Attachments pane. Tap the **Preview** button to preview the file — assuming that your Galaxy S 5 has an app that can display the file — or tap **Save** to save the file to your Download folder. If you save the file, you can use My Files or another file-management app to open the file from the Download folder.

Reply to or Forward a Message with Gmail

Your Galaxy S 5 is fully integrated with Google's Gmail service, enabling you to read, write, and manage your messages no matter where you go. Android walks you through the process of setting up your Google account during the initial setup, so you normally set up your main Gmail account at that point; if you have multiple Gmail accounts, you can add the other accounts later, as explained in Chapter 4. You are then ready to read, reply to, and forward e-mail messages in Gmail.

Reply to or Forward a Message with Gmail

Open the Gmail App and a Message

1 Press the Home button.

The Home screen appears.

2 Tap **Apps** (▦).

The Apps screen appears.

3 Tap **Gmail** (✉).

Your Gmail Inbox appears.

A You can tap ✉ to display the navigation panel.

B Each message appears with the sender's name, the subject, and a message preview.

C The sender and subject of unread messages appear in boldface on a white background.

D Read messages appear on a light-gray background.

4 Tap the message that you want.

E You can tap 🗑 to delete the message.

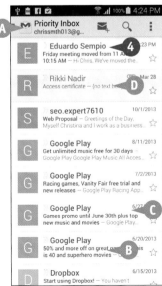

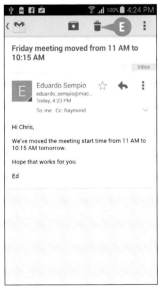

Reply to the Message

1 Tap ⬅.

Gmail creates a reply.

2 Type the text of the reply.

3 Tap **Quote Text** (☐ changes to ☑)
if you want to include the original
message in your reply.

4 Tap **Respond Inline** if you want to
respond to the original message
paragraph by paragraph.

5 Tap ➤.

Gmail sends the message.

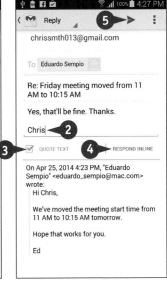

Forward the Message

1 Tap ⋮.

2 Tap **Forward**.

⑤ You can tap **Reply all** if you need
to reply to all To and Cc recipients.

Gmail creates a forwarded message.

3 Tap the **To** field and address the
message.

4 Tap the **Compose email** field and
type any message needed.

5 Tap ➤.

Gmail sends the message.

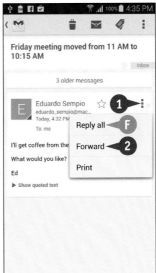

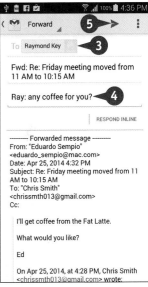

TIP

What is the point of the Respond Inline feature?

Responding inline is useful when you need to answer an e-mail message one point at a time and make clear
to which part of the original message your paragraphs refer. When you tap **Respond Inline**, Gmail sets up
the reply so that you can edit the original message and add the paragraphs of your reply between the
paragraphs of the original message for clarity.

Write and Send E-mail Messages with Gmail

Using your Galaxy S 5, you can send e-mail messages any place and any time. You can send a message using any Gmail account that you have set up, and you can either choose recipients from your Contacts list or simply type in their e-mail addresses. You can send a message to either a single recipient or multiple recipients, include carbon-copy recipients, and even add blind carbon-copy recipients if necessary.

Write and Send E-mail Messages with Gmail

1 Press the Home button.

The Home screen appears.

2 Tap **Apps** (▦).

The Apps screen appears.

3 Tap **Gmail** (✉).

Your Gmail Inbox appears.

4 Tap the New Message button (✉).

The Compose screen appears, with the insertion point in the To field.

5 Start typing the recipient's name or e-mail address.

A pop-up menu displays possible matches from your Contacts list.

6 Tap the recipient.

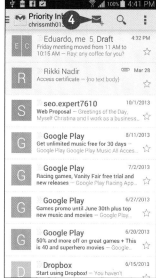

The recipient's name appears as a button in the To field.

Note: You can add another recipient by starting to type his or her name or e-mail address.

7 To add Cc or Bcc recipients, tap ⋮.

8 Tap **Add Cc/Bcc**.

The Cc and Bcc fields appear.

9 Tap the **Cc** or **Bcc** field.

10 Start typing the recipient's name or address.

11 Tap the appropriate match.

12 Tap the **Subject** field and type the subject.

13 Tap the **Compose email** field and type the body of the message.

14 Tap ➤.

Gmail sends the message.

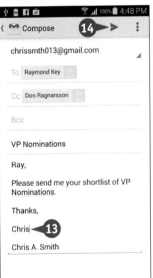

TIP

How can I enter my contact details quickly in an e-mail message?

You can enter your contact details by using a signature. In Gmail, tap ⋮ and then tap **Settings** to display the Settings screen. Tap the Gmail account in which you want to create the signature and then tap **Signature** to open the Signature dialog box. Type the text for the signature, pressing Return (⏎) to create new lines or paragraphs as needed. Tap **OK** to close the Signature dialog box.

Now, when you create a new message, a reply, or a forwarded message, Gmail inserts your signature automatically at the end of the body text.

Send and Receive Files with Gmail

Gmail enables you to send and receive files with e-mail messages. You can send files by attaching them to outgoing messages; similarly, you can receive files that others attach to messages they send to you. Sending and receiving files via e-mail is fast and convenient, provided that the total size of files attached to a message is below the size limit for any of the mail servers involved. These limits vary, so it is prudent to err on the side of caution.

Send and Receive Files with Gmail

1 Press the Home button.

The Home screen appears.

2 Tap **Apps** (▦).

The Apps screen appears.

3 Tap **Gmail** (✉).

Your Gmail Inbox appears.

4 Tap ✉.

The Compose screen appears, with the insertion point in the To field.

5 Start typing the recipient's name or e-mail address.

A pop-up menu displays possible matches from your Contacts list.

6 Tap the recipient.

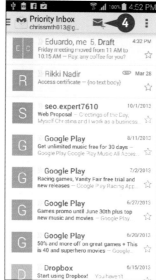

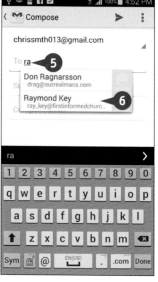

Gmail enters the recipient's name.

7 Tap the **Subject** field and type the subject.

8 Tap the body area and type any body text needed.

9 Tap ⋮.

10 Tap **Attach file**.

The Open From panel appears.

11 Tap the source for the file, such as **Dropbox**.

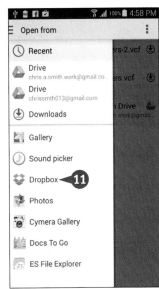

The source opens.

12 Tap the file that you want to attach.

B A button for the file appears in the message.

13 Tap ▷.

Gmail sends the message and the attached file.

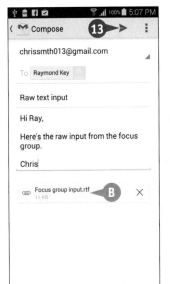

TIP

How big of a file can I send via Gmail?

If you are sending the file from your Gmail account to another Gmail account, the maximum file size is 25MB per message — but because encoding an attachment for sending via e-mail adds some overhead, the actual file size must be smaller.

If you are sending the file from your Gmail account to a non-Gmail account, you can determine the maximum file size only by trial and error. Generally speaking, it is unwise to send a file larger than 5MB — including the encoding overhead — via e-mail.

Label and Archive Your Messages with Gmail

To keep your Inbox under control, you should archive each message that you no longer need in the Inbox and delete any message that you do not need to keep. Before archiving a message, you can apply one or more labels to it.

Labels enable you to categorize messages so that you can find them later. You can label, archive, or delete a single message at a time, or you can select multiple messages in your Inbox and label, archive, or delete them all at once.

Label and Archive Your Messages with Gmail

Open Gmail

1 Press the Home button.

The Home screen appears.

2 Tap **Apps** (▦).

The Apps screen appears.

3 Tap **Gmail** (✉).

Gmail opens, and your Inbox appears.

Select Messages, Label Them, and Archive Them

1 Tap the icon to the left of a message.

☑ appears on the message's icon.

The selection bar appears.

2 Tap the icon for each message that you want to label or archive.

Ⓐ The readout shows how many messages you have selected.

3 Tap ⋮.

4 Tap **Change labels**.

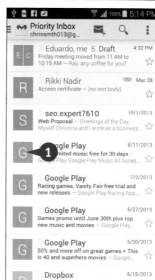

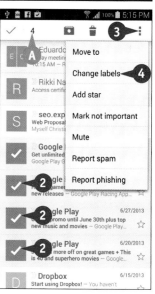

The Change Labels dialog box opens.

⑤ Tap each label that you want to apply (☐ changes to ☑).

⑥ Tap **OK**.

Ⓑ The label or labels that you selected appear on the messages.

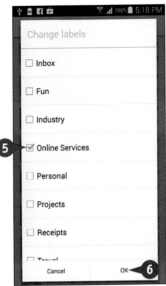

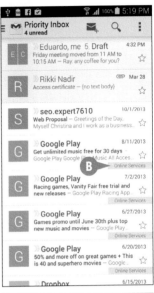

⑦ Tap the icon to the left of each message you want to archive.

☑ appears on the icon of each message that you tap.

⑧ Tap the Archive button (▣).

Gmail archives the messages and removes them from the Inbox.

Ⓒ You can tap **Undo** to undo the archiving.

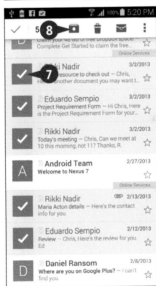

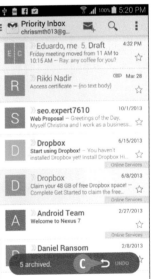

TIPS

How do I file my messages in folders?

Gmail uses labels instead of folders. So instead of moving a message to a folder, you apply one or more labels to it and then archive it. To retrieve the message, you use the label or labels rather than opening the folder as you would in most other e-mail apps.

How can I create new labels for marking my messages?

At this writing, you cannot create new labels directly in the Gmail app. Instead, open Internet or another browser, log in to your Gmail account, and create the new labels in the browser.

Browse by Label and Search with Gmail

After you apply labels to your e-mail messages, as explained in the preceding section, "Label and Archive Your Messages with Gmail," you can use the labels to browse through your messages and find the ones that you need. Browsing is useful when you need to look at a selection of messages to find the right one.

Another way to find a particular message is to search for it. Searching is the fastest approach when you can identify one or more keywords contained in the message.

Browse by Label and Search with Gmail

1 Press the Home button.

The Home screen appears.

2 Tap **Apps** (▦).

The Apps screen appears.

3 Tap **Gmail** (✉).

Gmail opens, and your Inbox appears.

4 Tap ✉.

The navigation panel opens.

Note: You may need to scroll down to reach the Recent Labels section or the All Labels section.

5 Tap the label by which you want to browse.

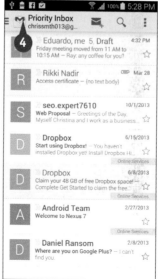

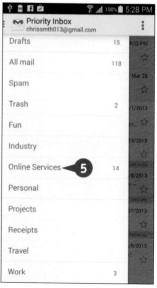

The messages marked with that label appear.

Ⓐ You can tap a message to open it.

⑥ To search, tap 🔍.

Ⓑ The Search Mail box appears.

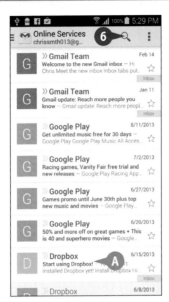

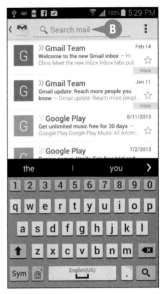

⑦ Type your search terms.

Note: If you have searched before, Gmail displays a pop-up menu containing your recent searches below the Search Mail box. You can tap a recent search to perform it again.

⑧ Tap 🔍.

Gmail searches and displays a list of matching messages, if any.

Ⓒ You can tap a message to open it.

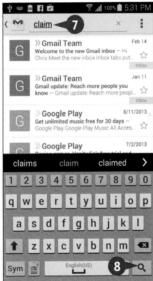

How can I delete messages instead of archiving them?

① In Gmail, tap ⋮ to display the menu.

② Tap **Settings** to display the Settings screen.

③ Tap **General settings** to display the General Settings screen.

④ Tap **Archive & delete actions** to display the Archive & Delete Actions dialog box.

⑤ Tap **Show delete only** (◯ changes to ◉).

⑥ Tap **Swipe to delete** (☐ changes to ☑).

Now you can tap a message in a conversation list and swipe left or right to delete it.

CHAPTER 10

Taking Photos and Videos

Your Galaxy S 5 includes two cameras, a high-resolution rear one and a lower-resolution front one, that you can use to take photos or videos with the Camera app.

Take Photos with the Camera App

Your Galaxy S 5 includes a high-resolution rear camera that you can use to take photos and a lower-resolution front camera — on the screen side of the phone — that enables you to take photos and videos of yourself or to enjoy video calls.

To take photos with the cameras, you use the Camera app. This app includes capabilities for zooming in and out and for using the flash to light your photos and a video clips, plus a rich tone or HDR — High Dynamic Range — feature for improving the exposure, lighting, and color balance in your photos.

Take Photos with the Camera App

1 Tap the Home button.

The Home screen appears.

2 Tap **Camera** (◉).

Ⓐ If Camera (◉) does not appear on the Home screen, tap **Apps** (▦) and then tap **Camera** (◉).

The Camera app opens, and the screen shows where the camera lens is pointing.

3 Aim your Galaxy S 5 so that your subject appears in the middle of the photo area.

Note: If you need to take tightly composed photos, get a tripod and a mount that fits your Galaxy S 5. You can find various models on Amazon, eBay, and photography sites.

4 Tap the Shutter button (◉).

The Camera app takes the photo.

5 Tap the thumbnail.

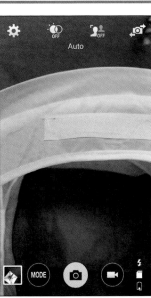

The photo that you just took appears.

B The controls at the top and the filmstrip at the bottom appear at first. They disappear if you do not use them for a few seconds.

6 Swipe left to display other photos on the camera roll.

7 Tap the screen.

The controls reappear, and you can use them to navigate, manipulate, edit, and share the photos. See the other sections in this chapter for details.

C You can tap a thumbnail in the filmstrip to display that photo or video.

8 Tap the Back button.

The Camera app appears again.

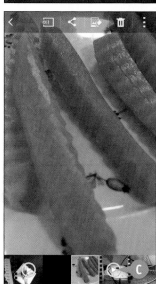

TIP

How do I switch to the camera on the screen side?

Tap the Switch Cameras button (▨) to switch from the main camera on the back of the Galaxy S 5 to the camera on the screen side. The screen-side camera has more limited capabilities than the main camera and is designed for video chat and for taking self-portraits. Tap ▨ again when you want to switch back to the main camera.

Using Zoom and Manual Focus

Your Galaxy S 5's Camera app enables you to zoom in so that your subject appears larger. Zoom is useful when you cannot get the lens close enough to make the subject the size that you want. After zooming in, you can zoom back out as needed.

The Camera app focuses automatically on whatever is in the middle of the picture. This works well for many photos, but when your subject is not in the middle of the picture, you can improve the focus by focusing manually on it.

Using Zoom and Manual Focus

Using Zoom

1 Tap the Home button.

The Home screen appears.

2 Tap **Camera** ( ).

A If Camera ( ) does not appear on the Home screen, tap **Apps** ( ) and then tap **Camera** ( ).

The Camera app opens, and the screen shows where the camera lens is pointing.

3 Aim the camera at your subject.

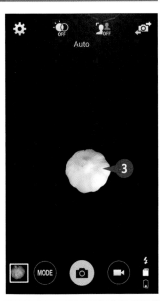

4 To zoom in, place two fingers together on the screen and pinch outward.

The zoom indicator appears.

B The number at the top of the zoom indicator shows the zoom level — for example, ×3.1.

5 Tap .

The Camera app takes the photo.

Note: You can also zoom in and out by pressing the Volume buttons on the side of the Galaxy S 5.

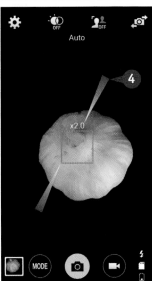

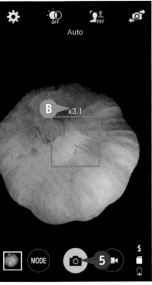

Using Manual Focus

1 Aim the lens at your subject.

Note: Zoom in as described earlier in this section if the subject is too far away.

C The Camera app focuses on the center of the screen. The green circle indicates that focusing is complete.

2 Tap where you want to place the focus.

D A white circle containing a split focus circle appears as you tap.

The focus changes.

Objects that are closer or farther away than the focal point may go out of focus.

3 Tap again to move the focus.

The focus changes.

The light metering may change too.

4 When you are satisfied with the focus, tap ◙.

The Camera app takes the photo.

TIPS

Why do my pictures become grainy when I zoom in?
Your Galaxy S 5's camera uses digital zoom, not optical zoom. Digital zoom zooms in by enlarging the pixels that make up the picture, so when you zoom in a long way, the pictures can become grainy as the pixels become larger. By contrast, optical zoom uses moving lenses to zoom in, thus retaining full quality even at extreme zoom.

How can I add optical zoom to my Galaxy S 5?
You can add optical zoom by using an external lens. Some lenses come built into a case, whereas other stick or clip onto the Galaxy S 5. You might also consider a Galaxy K Zoom, a version of the Galaxy S 5 that has a built-in full-size lens with 10× optical zoom.

Using the Flash and High Dynamic Range

Your Galaxy S 5 includes a flash for lighting your photos. You can switch among three flash settings: On uses the flash for every photo, Auto lets the Camera app decide whether to use the flash, and Off disables the flash.

The Camera app includes a High Dynamic Range (HDR) mode, which is also sometimes called *Rich Tone mode*. High Dynamic Range mode takes several photos in immediate succession with varying exposure settings. It then combines the photos into a single photo that — in theory — has a better color balance and intensity than a single photo.

Using the Flash and High Dynamic Range

Using the Flash

1 Tap the Home button.

The Home screen appears.

2 Tap **Camera** (⊙).

Ⓐ If Camera (⊙) does not appear on the Home screen, tap **Apps** (▦) and then tap **Camera** (⊙).

The Camera app shows where the camera lens is pointing.

3 Aim the camera at your subject.

4 Tap ⚙.

The Settings panel appears.

Ⓑ The flash icon indicates the flash status: Auto (⚡A), On (⚡), or Off (⚡⊘).

5 Tap the current flash icon as needed to cycle through the settings.

Note: The cycle is On, Auto, Off. This example has it set to On (⚡).

6 Tap ⚙.

The Settings panel closes.

7 Tap ⊙.

The Camera app takes the photo.

Using High Dynamic Range

1 In the Camera app, tap the HDR button (📷 changes to 📷).

The HDR preview appears. You may notice that the color balance of the photo changes.

2 Compose your photo by aiming the lens and zooming as needed.

3 Optionally, tap to specify the point on which to focus.

4 Tap 📷.

The Camera app takes the photo.

C You can tap the thumbnail to view the photo.

TIP

Is there any disadvantage to using High Dynamic Range, or should I use it all the time?
It is best to use High Dynamic Range only when you need it. Taking HDR photos takes longer than taking a regular photo, so you cannot shoot photos in rapid succession or capture motion successfully. When possible, use a tripod for your HDR photos to ensure that each photo has exactly the same alignment. If you move your Galaxy S 5 while shooting HDR photos, the Camera app prompts you to hold the phone steady.

Using Other Camera Modes

Your Galaxy S 5's Camera app offers a wide variety of camera modes that enable you to take different types of photos. You can switch quickly among the modes by tapping the Mode button and then tapping the mode that you want on the Mode panel that appears.

The default mode is Auto, which gives good results for general shooting. But it is worth spending time exploring the other modes and learning which modes are best for producing the types of photos that you typically want to take.

Using Beauty Face Mode

Use Beauty Face mode when you are capturing a portrait of a person and want to make the photo look as good as possible. Beauty Face mode detects the area of the frame occupied by the face and applies an airbrush effect to minimize or hide blemishes.

Beauty face

Using Shot & More Mode

The Galaxy S 5's intriguingly-named Shot & More mode enables you to take a burst of photos and then pick and choose among them. When you tap **Shot & more**, the Camera app switches to a mode where tapping 🔘 takes a burst of photos over several seconds. The Camera app then presents you with a choice of five modes, some of which may be available only depending on the subject and nature of the burst of photos.

Shot & more

Best Photo mode lets you choose which photo or photos to keep from the burst. Best Face is for group shots, enabling you to combine faces from different photos into a single group photo. Drama Shot is for encapsulating movement and action; it lets you combine different frames into a single photo to convey a sequence of motion. Eraser enables you to erase unwanted parts of the photo, such as someone walking past in the background. Panning Shot enables you to blur the background to hide unwanted moving objects.

Using Virtual Tour Mode

Use Virtual Tour mode when you want to create a virtual tour of a room, building, or location. When you turn on Virtual Tour mode and tap 🔘, the Camera app provides on-screen directions for aiming the camera lens and either moving forward or turning from side to side to take the photos needed. When you finish taking the photos, the Camera app automatically assembles a short video containing the virtual tour. If you have a steady hand or — better — you use a monopod or Steadicam rig, the results can be impressive.

Virtual tour

Using Dual Camera Mode

Use Dual Camera mode when you want to superimpose a photo of yourself, taken with the screen-side camera, on a photo that you take with the main camera. When you switch to Dual Camera mode, the picture from the screen-side camera appears in a stamp-like frame on the picture from the rear camera. You can tap the frame and resize it; you can also drag it to a different part of the picture. When you are ready to take the photo, tap 🔘 as usual. Dual Camera mode works for video as well as for still photos.

Dual camera

Adding Further Modes

To supplement the modes that come with the Camera app, Samsung provides extra modes that you can download. Tap **Mode** and then tap **Download** to access these modes, which at this writing include Surround Shot, Animated Photo, Sports Shot, and Sound & Shot. Surround Shot mode enables you to take a surround photo by combining multiple photos. Animated Photo mode creates an animated photo consisting of a short segment of video that you manipulate. Sports Shot mode helps you capture fast movement. Sound & Shot mode lets you capture the audio background to provide context for a photo.

Download

Take Panoramic Photos

One of the Camera app's most impressive modes is Panorama mode, which enables you to take panoramic photos easily. You can take panoramic photos either horizontally or vertically. Taking a horizontal panorama produces a long, low photo looking around a single point; taking a vertical panorama produces a tall, narrow photo looking up and down.

To take a panoramic photo, you turn on Panorama mode by using the Mode panel and then follow the prompts that appear.

Take Panoramic Photos

1 Tap the Home button.

The Home screen appears.

2 Tap **Camera** (⚫).

Ⓐ If Camera (⚫) does not appear on the Home screen, tap **Apps** (▦) and then tap **Camera** (⚫).

The Camera app opens.

The screen shows where the camera lens is pointing.

3 Tap **Mode**.

The Mode list appears.

4 Tap **Panorama**.

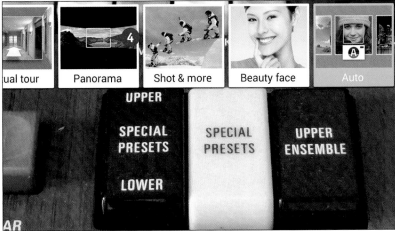

The Panorama controls appear.

5 Aim the camera at your subject.

6 Tap 📷.

The Camera app starts capturing the panorama.

B The arrow shows you which way to turn the camera.

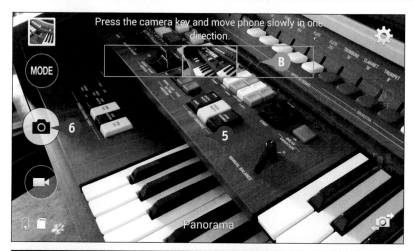

7 Turn the camera to follow the guide.

C The Panorama controls show what you have captured so far.

8 Either tap ⏹ to stop capturing the panorama or complete the circuit, causing the Camera app to stop the capture automatically.

TIP

How can I take better panoramic photos?

The Panorama feature is designed for handheld use, so it takes a robust approach to minor imperfections in the interest of producing a workable photo. But you can take better panoramas by using a device to steady your Galaxy S 5 as you shoot. Most standard tripods tend to be better for taking vertical panoramas than horizontal panoramas, but a monopod can be good for taking horizontal panoramas. A Steadicam rig can also help. If you prefer to be unencumbered, try a camera foot strap against which you apply tension to keep the camera steady.

Using Selective Focus

The Galaxy S 5 includes a feature called *Selective Focus* that enables you to manipulate the focus after taking a photo. First turn on Selective Focus and then take a photo of a subject that is close to the lens — preferably between four inches and twenty inches away — but more than twice that distance from the background. You then open the photo and choose whether to apply near focus, far focus, or pan focus, which makes both the subject and its background stand out.

Using Selective Focus

1 Tap the Home button.

The Home screen appears.

2 Tap **Camera** (⬤).

Ⓐ If Camera (⬤) does not appear on the Home screen, tap **Apps** (▦) and then tap **Camera** (⬤).

The Camera app opens and shows where the camera lens is pointing.

3 Tap the Selective Focus button (▨ changes to ▨).

Ⓑ The Selective Focus message appears briefly.

4 Compose your shot with your subject close to the lens and the background more than twice as far from the subject as the subject is from the lens.

5 Tap the subject to specify the focus.

6 Tap ⬤.

The Camera app captures the shot.

7 Tap the photo's thumbnail.

The photo appears.

8 Tap the Edit Selective Focus button ().

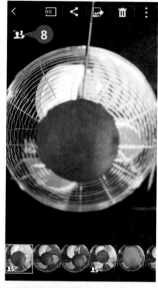

The screen for choosing Selective Focus appears.

C The highlighted icon shows the current focus.

9 Tap **Near focus** ( ), **Far focus** ( ), or **Pan focus** ( ), as needed.

Note: This example uses Far Focus ( ).

The focus changes.

10 Tap **Done** to save your changes.

TIP

How do I work around the "Subject not detected" error when using Selective Focus?

If the Camera app displays the message "Picture saved, but unable to apply Focus contrast effect. Subject not detected," try changing the distance between your Galaxy S 5 and the subject and between the subject and the background. Even a small change in one or other distance — or both distances — can make the difference between Selective Focus failing and working. Keep trying the shot with small variations until it works.

Choose Settings for Taking Photos

To help you shoot correctly exposed photos that look the way you want, the Camera app enables you to configure a wide range of settings. Beyond switching modes, as explained in the section "Using Other Camera Modes" earlier in this chapter, you can choose the resolution for photos and for videos, turn stabilization off for videos, and choose among three light-metering modes: Center-Weighted, Matrix, and Spot.

Choose Settings for Taking Photos

1 Tap the Home button.

The Home screen appears.

2 Tap **Camera** (⊙).

Ⓐ If Camera (⊙) does not appear on the Home screen, tap **Apps** (▦) and then tap **Camera** (⊙).

The Camera app opens.

3 Tap ⚙.

The Settings panel appears.

4 Tap **Picture size**.

The Picture Size dialog box opens.

5 Tap the picture size that you want (⊙ changes to ◉).

6 Tap **Burst shots** (▭) to turn burst shooting on or off.

7 Tap **Picture stabilization** (✋) to turn stabilization on or off.

8 Tap **Face detection** (☺) to turn face detection on or off.

9 Tap **ISO**.

Note: The ISO button is unavailable when Picture Stabilization is on.

The ISO dialog box opens.

10 Tap the ISO rating that you want to use.

11 Tap **Tap to take pics** (📷) to enable or disable taking photos by tapping the screen.

Note: The preceding section, "Using Selective Focus," explains the Selective Focus feature.

12 Tap **Metering modes** (◉).

The Metering Modes dialog box opens.

13 Tap **Center-weighted**, **Matrix**, or **Spot** (◉ changes to ◉).

14 Tap **Audio zoom** (🔊) to turn audio zoom on or off.

15 Tap **Video stabilization** (📹) to turn video stabilization on or off.

16 Tap **Recording mode** (🎥).

TIPS

What picture size and video size should I use?
For photos, use the highest resolution available — 5312 pixels × 2988 pixels — unless you require a different aspect ratio, such as 4:3 or 1:1. For video, unless you actually need Ultra High Definition (UHD) resolution, shoot at Full HD resolution, 1920 × 1080, which takes up only a quarter as much storage space as UHD video.

Should I use picture stabilization and video stabilization?
Use both forms of stabilization unless you have mounted your Galaxy S 5 on a tripod or you need another feature that applying stabilization makes unavailable.

continued ▶

For recording video, your Galaxy S 5's Camera app enables you to not only choose the video resolution but also record in fast motion, slow motion, or smooth motion. You can also use the Limit for MMS feature to shoot short, low-resolution videos that you can send via the Multimedia Messaging Service (MMS).

Your Galaxy S 5 enables you to apply effects to photos to make them look different. You can apply effects either when taking photos with the Camera app or afterward with the Gallery app.

Choose Settings for Taking Photos (continued)

The Recording Mode dialog box opens.

17 Tap the recording mode that you want to use (⬤ changes to ⬤).

18 Tap **Video size**.

The Video Size dialog box opens.

19 Tap the video resolution that you want to use (⬤ changes to ⬤).

20 Scroll down to display the lower part of the Settings panel.

21 Tap **Flash** (⚡) to cycle through the three flash settings: On (⚡), Auto (⚡A), and Off (⚡⊘).

22 Tap **Timer** (⏱).

The Timer dialog box opens.

23 Tap **Off** or the timer delay that you want to use (⬤ changes to ⬤).

24 Tap **Location tags** (◉) to turn location tagging on or off.

25 Tap **Review pics/videos** (▶) to turn instant review on or off.

26 Tap **Storage** (▤).

The Storage dialog box opens.

27 Tap **Device** or **Memory card**, as appropriate (◉ changes to ◎).

28 Tap **Exposure value** (☒) to adjust the exposure value.

29 Tap **Guide lines** (⊞) to toggle the display of guide lines.

30 Tap **Voice control** (🎙) to turn voice control on or off.

31 Tap **White Balance**.

The White Balance dialog box opens.

32 Tap **Auto**, **Daylight**, **Cloudy**, **Incandescent**, or **Fluorescent** (◉ changes to ◎).

33 Tap ⚙.

The Settings panel closes.

TIP

How can I make the Camera settings easier to choose?

You can customize the Settings bar at the top of the Camera app by tapping ⚙ to display the Settings panel, tapping and holding an icon to make it mobile, and then dragging it to the Settings bar. If you need to restore the Settings bar to its default settings, tap ⚙, tap **Reset** (↺), tap **Include shortcut layout** (■ changes to ☑) in the Reset dialog box, and then tap **OK**.

Take Photos on a Remote Camera

The Camera app includes a feature called *Remote Viewfinder* that enables you to send what the camera is seeing to another device. For example, say you have a Samsung Galaxy Note 3 as well as your Galaxy S 5. You can set up Remote Viewfinder on the Galaxy S 5 and then view the camera feed on your Galaxy Note 3.

To make Remote Viewfinder work, the two devices must be connected via Wi-Fi Direct. If both devices support Near Field Communication (NFC), you can use that to establish the connection.

Open the Camera App

Start by opening the Camera app on the device that will share its camera feed via Remote Viewfinder. This section assumes that your Galaxy S 5 is the device that will share its camera feed and that another device will view the feed.

On your Galaxy S 5, tap the Home button to display the Home screen and then tap **Camera** (◉) to open the Camera app.

Set Up Remote Viewfinder

With the Camera app open, aim the camera lens at what you want to watch. You may want to use a stand or tripod to hold the Galaxy S 5 steady and pointed at the subject.

You can now set up Remote Viewfinder. First tap ⚙ to display the Settings panel, scroll down if necessary to display the Remote Viewfinder icon, and then tap **Remote viewfinder** (▤). The Remote Viewfinder dialog box opens, and you can choose how to connect, as described next.

Choose How to Connect

The Remote Viewfinder dialog box lets you choose between using NFC to establish the Wi-Fi Direct connection and establishing the connection manually. If both devices have NFC, and you can easily bring them together, tap **Easily connect via NFC**; if not, tap **Wi-Fi Direct settings**.

If you have already established a Wi-Fi Direct connection between the two devices by this point, the Remote Viewfinder dialog box enables you to choose between using the existing connection and ending the connection so that you can set up a different connection.

Establish the Wi-Fi Direct Connection via NFC

If you choose to use NFC to set up the Wi-Fi Direct connection, your Galaxy S 5 prompts you to bring the devices back to back. Position the devices back to back with their NFC chips in close proximity; with a tablet, you may need to move the devices around to establish the connection. Tap **Touch to beam**, which appears on your Galaxy S 5. The devices then establish a Wi-Fi Direct connection. The Camera app automatically opens on the viewing device and displays what the camera connected via Remote Viewfinder is showing.

Establish the Wi-Fi Direct Connection Manually

When you cannot use NFC, you can establish the Wi-Fi Direct connection manually. When you tap **Wi-Fi Direct settings** in the Remote Viewfinder dialog box, the Wi-Fi Direct screen appears on your Galaxy S 5. On the other device, navigate to the Wi-Fi Direct screen by pulling down from the top of the screen, tapping and holding **Wi-Fi** (🛜) on the Quick Settings bar, and then tapping **Wi-Fi Direct** on the Wi-Fi screen. On your Galaxy S 5, tap the other device in the Available Devices list to send an invitation. On the other device, tap **Connect** in the Invitation to Connect dialog box. The Camera app automatically opens on the second device and displays what the camera connected via Remote Viewfinder is showing.

Use the Camera and End the Connection

With the connection established, you can use the Camera app on the other device to view and control the Camera app on your Galaxy S 5. You can zoom in and out, tap to change the point of focus, or tap 📷 to take a photo. You can also take videos, manipulate the flash, and apply effects.

When you are ready to end the connection, tap 🔧 to display the Settings panel and then tap the Remote Viewfinder button (📱 changes to 📱). On the Wi-Fi Direct screen, tap **End connection** to end the connection.

Edit Your Photos

Your Galaxy S 5 enables you to edit your photos easily by using the Gallery app. You can apply artistic effects, such as sepia or fish-eye, to change the overall color balance or look of the photo. You can apply borders in various styles, and you can draw on a photo to annotate it.

You can straighten a photo, crop it, rotate it, or flip it either horizontally or vertically. You can apply a wide range of adjustments, such as correcting the photo's exposure or modifying its color temperature.

Edit Your Photos

Open the Gallery App

1 Tap the Home button.

The Home screen appears.

Note: You can also start from the Camera app. Tap the thumbnail of the last photo to open it for editing. You can then navigate to other photos.

2 Tap **Apps** (▦).

The Apps screen appears.

3 Tap **Gallery** (🖼).

The Gallery app opens.

Open the Photo That You Want to Edit

1 Tap the album that contains the photo that you want to edit.

The photos in the album appear.

2 Tap the photo.

The photo opens.

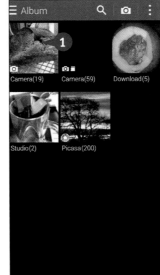

Display the Editing Controls

1 Tap the photo.

The controls for manipulating photos appear.

2 Tap the Edit button (⊡).

The editing controls appear.

Ⓐ You can tap **Enhance** to enhance the colors in the photo.

Ⓑ You can tap the Undo button (↺) to undo the last edit.

Ⓒ You can tap the Redo button (↻) to redo the last undone edit.

Straighten, Rotate, or Flip a Photo

1 With the photo open for editing, tap **Adjustment**.

2 Tap **Rotate** (↺).

Ⓓ You can tap the Rotate Counterclockwise button (↺) or the Rotate Clockwise button (↻) to rotate the picture.

Ⓔ You can tap the Flip Horizontal button (⇋) or the Flip Vertical button (⥮) to flip the picture.

TIP

How do I resize a photo in the Gallery app?

1 Tap the photo to open it.

2 Tap ⊡ to display the editing tools.

3 Tap **Adjustment** (↺).

4 Tap **Resize** (⊡).

5 Either drag the sizing handles to contain the appropriate area or tap **10%**, **25%**, **50%**, or **75%** to resize to that proportion.

6 Tap **Done**.

continued ▶

Edit Your Photos (continued)

The Gallery app enables you to crop a photo either to a specific aspect ratio, such as the square 1:1 aspect ratio or the widescreen 16:9 aspect ratio that many computer screens and TVs use, or to a freehand area that you draw on the screen. You can also adjust many aspects of a photo's tone, including the red, blue, and green balance; the brightness and contrast; and the color temperature, hue, and saturation.

Edit Your Photos (continued)

3 Place two fingers apart on the screen and rotate them to straighten the photo.

A You can tap the Mirror button (⬚) to apply a mirroring effect to the photo.

4 Tap **Done**.

The Adjustment tools appear again, and you can edit the photo further if needed.

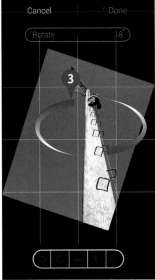

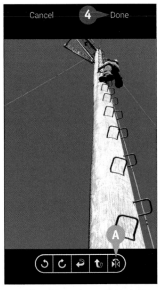

Crop a Photo

1 With the photo open for editing, tap **Adjustment** (⬚).

2 Tap **Crop** (⬚).

B You can tap ⬚, ⬚, or ⬚ to crop to a specific aspect ratio.

C Tap ⬚ to crop to a freehand area you draw.

3 Drag the white crop handles to encompass the area that you want to keep.

4 Tap **Done**.

236

Adjust the Tone of a Photo

1 With the photo open for editing, tap **Tone** (⬤).

Note: In Portrait orientation, scroll the Tone controls bar left to display further controls.

2 Tap the tone button that you want to use.

Note: This example uses **Temperature** (🌡).

3 Slide your finger right to increase the temperature or left to decrease it.

4 Tap **Done**.

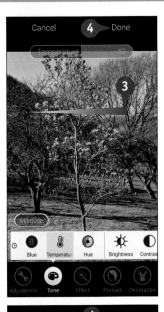

Use the Portrait Tools

1 With the photo open for editing, tap **Portrait**.

The Portrait tools appear.

2 Tap the tool that you want to use.

Note: This example uses the **Remove red-eye** tool (👁).

3 Tap each offending eye to remove the red.

4 Tap **Done**.

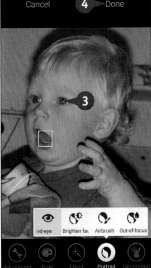

TIP

How do I apply an effect to a photo?

1 In the Gallery app, tap the photo to open it.

2 Tap 🖼 to display the editing tools.

3 Tap **Effect** (✳) to display the effects bar.

4 Scroll the effects bar as needed and then tap the effect that you want to apply.

5 Tap **Done**.

continued ▶

The Portrait editing tools in the Gallery app enable you to remove red eye, brighten faces, airbrush blemishes, or apply an out-of-focus effect. These tools work only with photos that contain faces that the Gallery app can detect. For example, you cannot use the Airbrush tool to remove blemishes from a photo that does not contain a detectable face.

The Decoration tools in the Gallery app enable you to add stickers, labels, or frames to your photos. You can also draw on a photo or inset an image on a photo.

Edit Your Photos (continued)

5 Tap **Brighten face** (⊞).

6 Slide your finger across the screen to the right to increase the brightness.

A The Brighten Face readout indicates the degree of brightening on a scale of 1 to 20.

7 Tap **Done**.

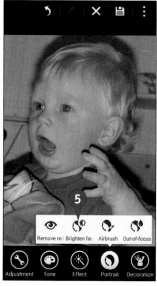

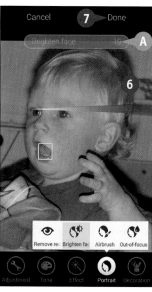

Add Decoration to a Photo

1 With the photo open for editing, tap **Decoration** (☙).

The Decoration tools appear.

2 Tap the decoration type that you want to apply.

Note: This example uses **Frame** (▢).

3 Tap the appropriate tab button.

4 Tap the frame that you want to apply.

A preview of the frame appears.

5 Tap **Done**.

Gallery applies the frame to the photo.

B You can apply other types of decorations if you want to.

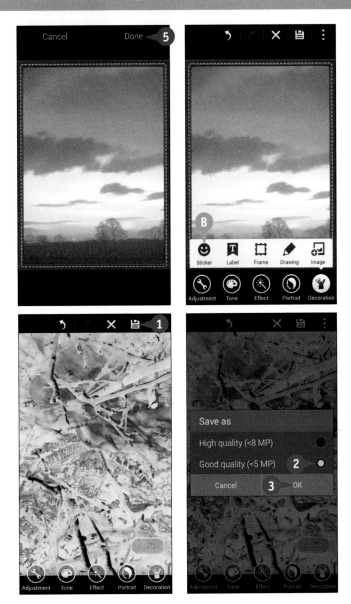

Save Your Edits to a Photo

1 After editing a photo, tap the Save button (💾).

The Save As dialog box opens.

2 Tap **High quality (<8 MP)** or **Good quality (<5 MP)** (⚫ changes to ◉), as appropriate.

3 Tap **OK**.

Gallery saves the edited photo in the Studio folder. The original photo remains in its current folder, unchanged.

TIP

Can I undo my edits to a photo after I have saved them?
No — after you save the edits, you cannot undo them in the photo. But because Gallery saves the edited photo in the Studio folder, you can return to the original photo by opening it from the folder in which it is stored. You can then edit the original photo as needed.

Capture Video

Your Galaxy S 5 can capture video as well as take photos. The rear camera can capture high-definition video, whereas the screen-side camera can capture lower-resolution video suitable for online chat and similar uses. To capture video, you use the Camera app in Video mode. After taking the video, you can review it on your Galaxy S 5. You can also share the video with other people or play it back on your TV, as described in the next section, "View Your Photos and Videos."

Capture Video

1 Press the Home button.

The Home screen appears.

2 Tap **Camera** (📷).

Ⓐ If Camera (📷) does not appear on the Home screen, tap **Apps** (▦) and then tap **Camera** (📷).

The Camera app opens.

3 Aim the lens at your subject.

4 Tap the Video button (📹).

The Camera app starts recording video.

Ⓑ The upper readout shows the time elapsed.

Ⓒ The lower readout shows the amount of space consumed and the amount of space available.

Note: You can zoom in by placing two fingers on the screen and pinching apart. You can zoom back out by pinching inward.

Ⓓ You can tap 📷 to take a still photo while the video is recording.

5 Tap the Pause button (⏸).

The recording pauses.

6 When you are ready to resume recording, tap the Record button (■).

The recording resumes.

7 Tap ■.

The recording stops.

The video's thumbnail appears.

8 Tap the thumbnail.

The video appears, and you can play it back.

TIP

Can I record videos with the screen-side camera?

Yes, you can. Tap **Camera** (◉) on the Home screen to open the Camera app and then tap 📷 to switch to the screen-side camera. Tap ▭ to start recording video.

When using the screen-side camera, you can control recording by tapping ▐▐, ■, and ■, as with the main camera, but you cannot zoom in and out.

View Your Photos and Videos

You can view your photos and videos using the Gallery app. The Camera app saves your photos and videos into a folder called *Camera,* which you can access via the Album screen in the Gallery app. You can also access the Camera folder directly from the Camera app.

When you want to view your photos and videos at a larger size, you can connect your Galaxy S 5 to a TV or monitor. This is great for enjoying your photos or videos with other people.

View Your Photos and Videos

1 Tap the Home button.

The Home screen appears.

Note: You can also start from the Camera app. Tap the thumbnail of the last photo to view it. You can then navigate to other photos.

2 Tap **Apps** (▦).

The Apps screen appears.

3 Tap **Gallery** (▨).

Gallery opens and displays its home screen.

4 Tap the navigation button (▤).

5 Tap the item by which you want to browse.

Note: This example uses **Album**, which gives you easy access to the Camera folder.

The Album screen appears.

6 Tap the album that you want to view.

Thumbnails of the photos in the album appear.

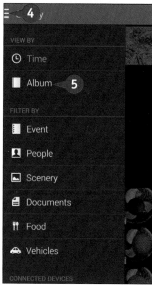
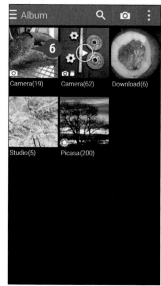

Ⓐ You can tap another album's thumbnail to display that album.

Note: You can scroll up and down to display other thumbnails of photos in the album.

7 Tap the photo that you want to view.

The photo opens.

Ⓑ The controls and a thumbnails bar appear at first and then disappear if you do not use them for a few seconds.

Ⓒ You can tap a thumbnail to display that photo.

8 If the photo is in Portrait orientation, turn your Galaxy S 5 sideways.

The photo appears in Landscape view, enabling you to view it better.

Note: You can swipe left or right to move through the photos. You can tap the screen to display the controls and thumbnails bar.

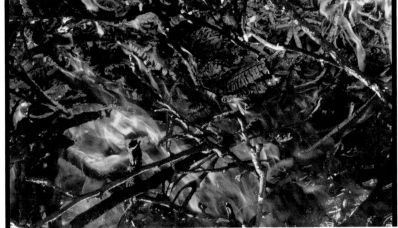

TIP

How do I view my photos and videos on my TV?

You can view your photos and videos on your TV in two ways:

- Connect your Galaxy S 5 to your TV via a cable that has a micro-USB connector at one end and an HDMI connector at the other. Plug the micro-USB connector in to the multipurpose jack on the Galaxy S 5 and the HDMI connector into the HDMI port on the TV.

- Use the Screen Mirroring feature to display content on a TV that supports the Wi-Fi Miracast feature.

Share Your Photos and Videos

Your Galaxy S 5 and its Camera app include a wide range of features for sharing the photos and videos that you take. You can attach them to e-mail messages, include them in text messages, or post them to your accounts on social networks.

You can share photos and videos when you are browsing in the Gallery app, but you can also share them straight from the Camera app — even immediately after you take them.

Share Your Photos and Videos

1 Tap the Home button.

The Home screen appears.

Note: You can also start from the Camera app. Tap the thumbnail of the last photo to open it. You can then navigate to other photos.

2 Tap **Apps** (▦).

The Apps screen appears.

3 Tap **Gallery** (▨).

Gallery opens and displays the last screen used, such as the Album screen.

4 Tap the album that you want to open.

The photos in the album appear.

5 Tap the photo that you want to share.

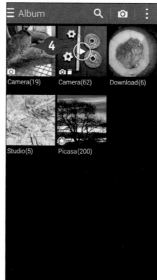

244

The photo opens.

6 Tap the photo.

The controls appear.

7 Tap the Share button ().

The Share Via dialog box opens.

8 Tap the app that you want to use for sharing.

Note: This example uses **Email**.

A new message opens with the photo attached.

9 Start typing the recipient's name.

The list of matches appears.

10 Tap the recipient's name.

11 Tap **Subject** and type the subject for the message.

12 Tap the body and type the body of the message.

13 Tap the Send button (📧).

Email sends the message and the photo.

TIP

How do I post a photo to Facebook?

1 With the photo open, tap ◁ to display the Share Via dialog box.

2 Tap **Facebook** to start a new post containing the photo.

3 Type any text that you want to post with the photo.

4 Tap **Location** if you want to add the location.

5 Tap **Post** to post the photo.

CHAPTER 11

Using Maps and Other Built-in Apps

Your Galaxy S 5 includes the Maps app for finding your location and getting directions, the Clock app for tracking and measuring time, and various other apps that you may find useful.

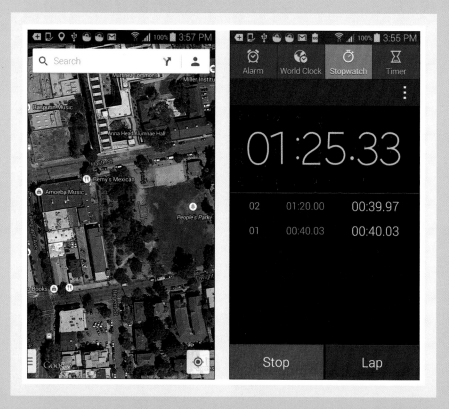

Find Your Location

The Maps app on your Galaxy S 5 enables you to pinpoint your location by using the Global Positioning System (GPS) or known wireless networks. You can view your location on a road map or a satellite map, or you can switch quickly to the Google Earth map to view a terrain map. You can add different layers of map information to make the map display exactly what you want. To help you get your bearings, you can rotate the map to match the direction that you are facing.

Find Your Location

1 Press the Home button.

The Home screen appears.

2 Tap **Apps** (▦).

The Apps screen appears.

3 Tap **Maps** (▨).

The Maps screen appears.

Ⓐ The blue dot shows your current location.

Ⓑ The arrow next to the blue dot shows the direction your Galaxy S 5 is facing.

4 Place two fingers apart on the screen and pinch inward.

The map zooms out, showing a larger area.

5 Tap ▤.

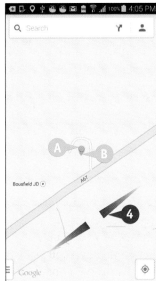

6 Tap **Satellite**.

The map switches to the Satellite view, showing an overhead view of the area consisting of satellite photos with road names and place names overlaid.

7 Tap ▤.

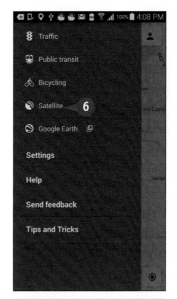

c The darker shading indicates that Satellite is turned on.

8 Tap **Traffic**.

d Colored lines indicating traffic flow appear on the major roads.

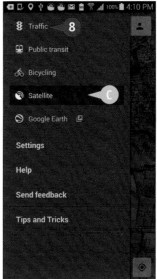

What is the best view to use in Maps?

It depends on what you are doing in Maps. When you need straightforward street navigation, use the regular map instead of the satellite photos; you may want to add layers such as Traffic, Public Transit, or Bicycling to provide extra information. When you want to see a picture of the area, open the menu and tap **Satellite** to display the Satellite view. When you want to see the lay of the land, open the menu and tap **Google Earth** to display the location in the Google Earth app.

Get Directions

The Maps app enables you to get step-by-step directions to exactly where you want to go. Maps can also show you current traffic information to help you identify the most viable route for a journey and avoid getting stuck in congestion.

Maps displays driving directions by default, but you can also display public transit directions and walking directions. It is wise to double-check that public transit directions and schedules are up to date before you use them.

Get Directions

1. Press the Home button.

   The Home screen appears.

2. Tap **Apps** (▦).

   The Apps screen appears.

3. Tap **Maps** (▨).

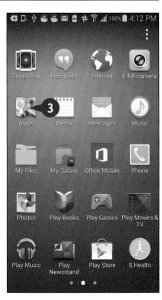

   The Maps app opens.

4. Tap the Directions button (⌐).

   The Directions screen appears.

5. Tap the type of directions that you want: driving (🚗), public transit (🚉), bicycling (🚲), or walking (🚶).

Ⓐ The upper box shows **My Location** as the suggested starting point.

6. To use another starting point, tap the upper box.

7 Type the starting point.

A list of suggestions appears.

8 If a suggestion is correct, tap it. Otherwise, type the entire address.

9 Tap **Choose destination** and enter the destination.

Note: If the Directions screen shows a choice of routes, tap the route that you want to view.

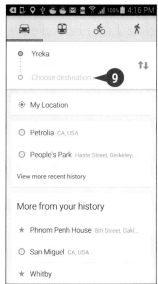

The directions appear on the map.

B A button showing the starting point, destination, and direction type appears at the top of the map.

10 Tap **Preview**.

The first direction in the route appears.

11 Tap the Next button (▶) to display the next direction.

Note: Tap the Back button to return from the directions to the map showing the entire route.

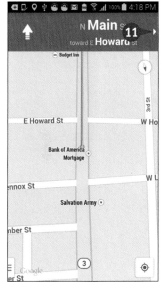

How can I get directions back to where I started?

After getting directions for a route, tap the button containing the starting point, destination, and direction type. The Directions screen appears. Tap the Reverse Start and End button (⇅) to switch the starting point and destination. The Maps app gets directions for the return trip. If the Directions screen shows a choice of routes, tap the route that you want to view.

Display Different Layers in the Maps App

The Maps app enables you to view different layers of information about a location. For example, instead of viewing a conventional street map, you can display the Satellite layer so that you see satellite photos as well as the roads. You can then add the Public Transit layer to see where public transit runs on the map or add the Bicycling layer to display designated bike routes in the area.

Display Different Layers in the Maps App

1 Press the Home button.

The Home screen appears.

2 Tap **Apps** (⊞).

The Apps screen appears.

3 Tap **Maps** (▨).

The Maps app opens.

4 Tap ▤.

5 Tap **Satellite**.

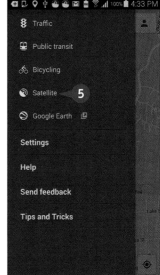

The map switches to the Satellite view.

6 Tap ▤.

7 Tap **Public transit**.

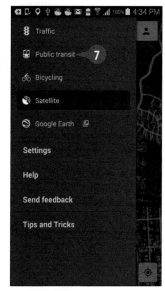

Ⓐ Public transit lines appear.

8 Tap ▤.

9 Tap **Bicycling**.

Ⓑ Designated bicycling routes appear in green.

Note: The Traffic layer, Public Transit layer, and Bicycling layer are mutually exclusive. Displaying one of these three layers hides any other of the three that is displayed.

TIP

How can I remove places and routes from the list of suggestions?

1 Tap ▤ to open the menu panel.

2 Tap **Settings** to display the Settings screen.

3 Tap **Maps history** to display the Maps History screen.

4 Tap the Delete button (⊗). The Delete dialog box opens.

5 Tap **Delete**. Maps deletes the item from your history.

Rotate, Zoom, and Tilt the Map

The Maps app enables you to rotate, zoom, and tilt the map to make it easier to use. By rotating the map, you can align it with the direction in which you are looking, which helps you to identify your location and get your bearings. Zooming the map enables you to move from viewing a large area at a small scale to viewing a small area at a large scale. Tilting the map gives you a better idea of the lay of the land. You can combine the three movements to explore the map in great detail.

Rotate, Zoom, and Tilt the Map

Open the Maps App

1 Press the Home button.

The Home screen appears.

2 Tap **Apps** (▦).

The Apps screen appears.

3 Tap **Maps** (▨).

The Maps app opens, and you can navigate to the place that you want to explore.

Rotate the Map

1 Place two fingers apart on the map and then rotate them in the direction that you want to turn the map.

The map rotates.

Ⓐ The compass arrow (▼) appears. The red end points north, and the white end points south.

2 Tap ▼ when you want to make the map point north again.

The compass arrow disappears.

Zoom the Map

1 Place your thumb and index finger together on the screen and pinch outward.

The map zooms in, showing the area at a larger size.

2 Place your thumb and index finger apart and pinch together.

The map zooms out, showing a larger area.

Note: You can zoom in by increments by double-tapping the area. Double-tap with two fingers to zoom out in increments.

Tilt the Map

1 Place two fingers near the bottom of the screen and draw them up.

The map tilts away from you, giving a flatter perspective instead of a straight-down perspective.

2 When you finish using the tilted map, place two fingers near the top of the screen and draw them down.

Maps restores the straight-down perspective.

How can I see the scale of the map that I am viewing?

Place your thumb and index finger on the screen and start to pinch them outward or inward. Maps displays a scale at the bottom of the screen. The scale disappears a few seconds after you stop pinching.

How do I change the measurement units that Maps uses?

Tap ☰ and then tap **Settings**. Tap **Distance Units** to display the Distance Units dialog box and then tap **Miles**, **Kilometers**, or **Automatic** (◯ changes to ◉).

Explore with the Street View

The Street View feature of the Maps app enables you to get the view from ground level of places on the map. The Street view displays images from Google's vast database of city streets and rural areas. You can pan around the area at which you enter the Street view; you can move along some streets almost as if you were walking along them; and you can look upward or downward to see more.

Explore with the Street View

1 Press the Home button.

The Home screen appears.

2 Tap **Apps** (▦).

The Apps screen appears.

3 Tap **Maps** (▨).

The Maps app opens.

4 Navigate to the place that you want to explore.

5 Tap and hold the place where you want to enter the Street view.

Ⓐ A dropped pin (▼) appears.

The banner at the bottom of the screen shows the location of the dropped pin.

6 Tap the banner.

The card for the dropped pin appears.

The Street view picture shows a preview of the Street view for the location.

7 Tap **Street View**.

The Street view appears.

Note: The images in the Street view may be several years old, so what you see may be significantly different from reality.

8 Tap a white arrow to move in the direction indicated.

9 Drag left to look right or drag right to look left.

10 Drag up to look downward or drag down to look upward.

11 When you are ready to return to the map, tap the Back button.

Maps exits the Street view and displays the card.

12 Tap the Back button again.

Maps displays the map in the view that you were using before.

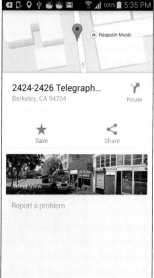
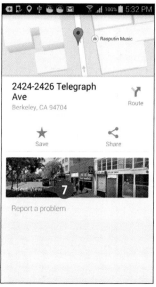

TIP

What does the button with curling arrows do?
This button () is the Compass Mode button. Tap it (changes to) to turn on Compass mode, enabling you to control what the Street view displays by panning and tilting your Galaxy S 5. Compass mode is especially useful when you are using the Street view to explore your current location, as it helps you to orient yourself to your surroundings. When you finish using Compass mode, tap (changes to) to turn it off.

Share a Location

The Maps app enables you to share any location quickly and easily. This feature is great for when you want to let others know about a particular location, such as where you are holding an event or an interesting place that you have found. You can share the location in a wide variety of ways, depending on the apps installed and configured on your Galaxy S 5. For example, you can share via e-mail using Gmail or Email, post to Facebook, tweet on Twitter, or send a text message via Messaging.

Share a Location

1 Press the Home button.

The Home screen appears.

2 Tap **Apps** (▦).

The Apps screen appears.

3 Tap **Maps** (▨).

The Maps app opens.

4 Navigate to the area containing the location that you want to share.

5 Tap and hold the location.

📍 appears.

6 Tap the banner for the dropped pin.

The card for the dropped pin appears.

7 Tap **Share**.

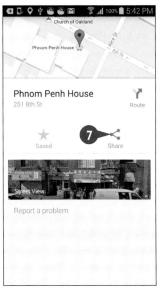

The Share Via dialog box opens.

Ⓐ If the app that you want to use does not appear in the dialog box, drag up to scroll down and display other apps.

⑧ Tap the app that you want to use.

Note: This example uses **Gmail**.

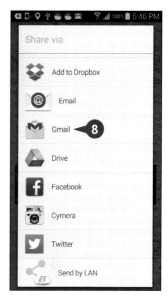

The Gmail app opens and displays a new message.

⑨ Tap the **To** field and add the recipient.

⑩ Tap the body field and type any explanatory text needed.

Ⓑ The address and URL appear in the message.

⑪ Tap the Send button (▶).

Gmail sends the message containing the location.

TIP

How can I mark a place so that I can easily find it again later?

In the Maps app, navigate to the area that contains the place and then tap and hold until 📍 appears. Tap the banner for the dropped pin to display the place's card and then tap the **Save** button (Save ☆ changes to Saved ★).

To return to the place, tap **Account** (👤) to display the Account screen. In the Nearby Saved Places list or the Saved Places list, tap the place that you want to display.

Explore the Clock App

Your Galaxy S 5 includes a powerful Clock app with many features. The Alarm feature enables you to set as many alarms as you need, and the World Clock features enables you to track the time in multiple locations simultaneously. The Stopwatch feature makes it easy to time events to within hundredths of a second, and the Timer feature provides a countdown of the duration that you set with a warning when the time elapses. The Clock app also includes a Desk Clock feature for displaying the time and the current month's calendar.

Launch the Clock App

You can launch the Clock app by pressing the Home button, tapping **Apps** (▦), and then tapping **Clock** (◔) on the Apps screen.

Set Alarms

To work with alarms, tap **Alarm** (◔) on the tab bar. On the Alarm screen, tap **Create alarm** to start creating a new alarm. You can then set the time for the alarm, choose the days on which to use it, and control whether it repeats weekly. You can set the alarm type, the alarm tone, and other options, such as choosing whether to allow snoozing the alarm. Tap **Save** when you have made your choices.

Use the World Clock

To use the World Clock, tap **World Clock** (◔) on the tab bar. Tap **Add city** to display the Add City screen, on which you can either pick from an alphabetical list of cities or start typing a city name and search for matches. Tap the city that you want to add, and it appears on the World Clock screen. You can change the order of the cities on the World Clock screen by tapping the Menu button, tapping **Change order**, and then working on the resulting screen.

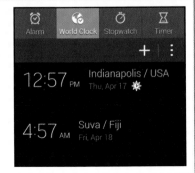

Use the Stopwatch

To use the Stopwatch, tap **Stopwatch** () on the tab bar. You can then tap **Start** to start the stopwatch running, tap **Lap** to mark a lap time, and tap **Stop** to stop timing. After stopping the stopwatch, you can tap **Restart** to restart it from the current time total or tap **Reset** to reset it to zero.

Use the Timer

To use the Timer, tap **Timer** () on the tab bar. Tap **Hours** and then tap the number buttons to set the number of hours; then tap **Minutes** and **Seconds** in turn and set the number of each. Tap **Start** to set the timer running. You can then tap **Stop** to stop the timer or **Reset** to reset it.

To change the sound the Timer plays, tap the Menu button and then tap **Settings**. On the Settings screen, tap **Alarm tone** to display the Alarm Tone dialog box. Tap the tone that you want to play (■ changes to ●) and then tap **OK**. On the Settings screen, you can also drag the Volume slider to set the volume at which the Timer plays the alarm.

Explore Other Apps

Your Galaxy S 5 comes with a host of specialized apps that you likely want to try in order to get the most out of your phone. These apps include Calculator, S Health, Voice Recorder, Earth, Smart Remote, and Samsung Apps. You can run each of these apps by tapping its icon on the Apps screen.

Calculator

In Portrait orientation, Calculator displays a set of buttons that enable you to do simple calculations, such as addition, subtraction, multiplication, and division. In Landscape orientation, Calculator displays its full set of buttons, enabling you to perform more complex calculations. You can hide the keys by tapping the horizontal bar that separates them from the calculations. With the keys hidden, you can tap **Clear history** to clear the details of the calculations that you have performed.

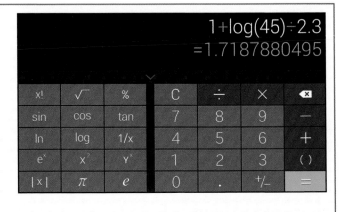

S Health

S Health aims to help you manage your health by defining fitness goals and measuring your progress. After accepting the extensive terms, conditions, and disclaimers, you set up a profile of your condition and your aims. You can then use tools such as Exercise Mate, Food Tracker, and Walking Mate to help achieve your goals.

Voice Recorder

Voice Recorder gives you an easy and effective way to record voice memos or other informal audio. You can start a recording quickly by tapping the Record button (⏺) and stop it by tapping the Stop button (⏹).

To choose settings, tap the Menu button and tap **Settings**. You can choose to store files on your Galaxy S 5 or on a memory card, switch between High and Normal recording quality, and turn noise reduction on or off.

Earth

Google Earth is an information service that shows a virtual globe and detailed maps supplemented by geographical information. On your Galaxy S 5, the Earth app enables you to explore an amazing variety of places around the world in impressive depth. After launching Earth, you can scroll to where you want to start exploring and then double-tap to zoom in. You can rotate the view by placing two fingers on the screen and rotating them, and you can tilt the view by placing two fingers on the screen and dragging them up or down.

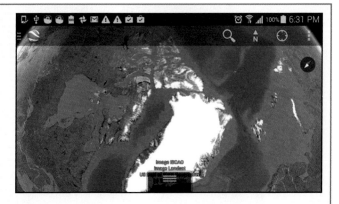

Smart Remote

The Smart Remote app enables you to use your Galaxy S 5 as a remote control for your TV and other electronic devices. To use Smart Remote, launch it from the Apps screen, and then follow the steps for selecting your country or region, finding your service, and selecting the content that you want to view.

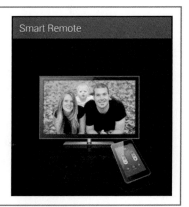

Samsung Apps

The app called *Samsung Apps* enables you to purchase, download, and install apps from Samsung's online store. The store offers a wide variety of apps designed for Samsung devices, so if you cannot find the apps that you want on Google Play, try looking in Samsung Apps. You can browse the store's offerings in various ways, such as by displaying the Category screen and then tapping the category of apps that you want to browse.

CHAPTER 12

Playing Music and Videos

You can pack a huge amount of music and many hours of video on your Galaxy S 5, enabling you to enjoy music and videos wherever you go.

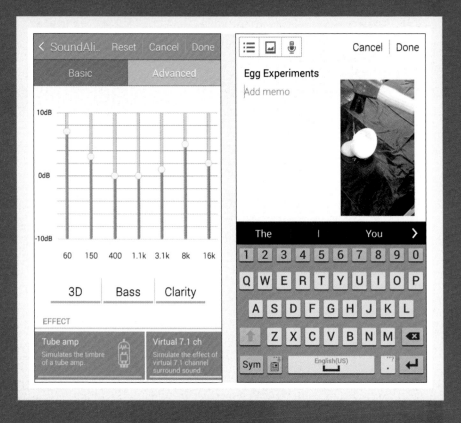

Copy Your Music and Videos to Your Galaxy S 5

If you already have music files, you can add them to your Galaxy S 5 so that you can play them anywhere. Your Galaxy S 5 has only a modest amount of built-in storage, part of which is occupied by the operating system and included apps, but you can give yourself plenty of space for media files by inserting a memory card.

The easiest way to get your existing music files and videos onto your Galaxy S 5 is to copy them from your computer using Samsung Kies. You can use either a Windows PC or a Mac.

Copy Your Music and Videos to Your Galaxy S 5

Connect Your Galaxy S 5 and Open Kies

1 Connect your Galaxy S 5 to your PC via USB.

Note: If your screen is locked, unlock it.

The Kies driver recognizes your Galaxy S 5, and Kies opens automatically.

Note: If Kies does not open automatically, click **Samsung Kies** on the Start screen or Start menu to launch it.

Ⓐ Your Galaxy S 5 appears in the Connected Devices list.

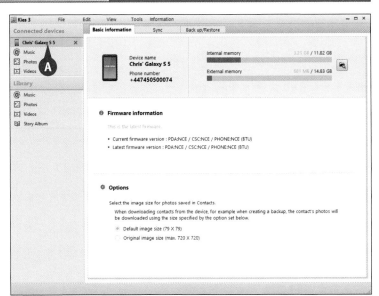

Copy Files from Kies to Your Galaxy S 5

1 Click **Music**.

Your Kies Music list appears.

2 Click each song that you want to copy (☐ changes to ☑).

3 Click 🔁.

4 Click **Internal memory** or **External memory**, as needed.

Kies copies the files to your Galaxy S 5.

Note: To copy video files to your Galaxy S 5, use the same method but click **Videos** in the Library list.

Copy Files from Windows to Your Galaxy S 5

1 Click **Music**.

Your phone's Music list appears.

2 Click **File**.

3 Click or highlight **Add file** or **Add folder**, as appropriate.

Note: This example uses **Add folder**.

4 Click **Internal memory** or **External memory**, as appropriate.

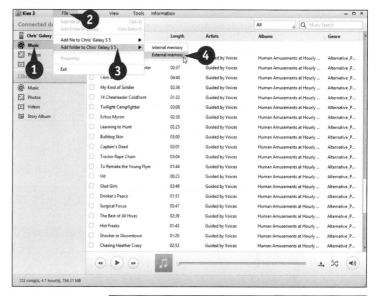

The Open dialog box opens.

5 Click the folder that you want to add.

6 Click **Select Folder**.

Kies copies the files to your Galaxy S 5.

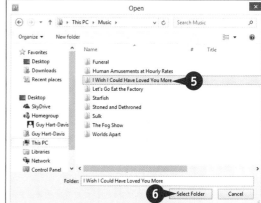

TIP

How do I copy music files to my Galaxy S 5 on the Mac?

You can use the Samsung Kies app in much the same way on the Mac as on Windows. Kies should launch automatically when you connect your Galaxy S 5 to your Mac via USB; if not, click the Launchpad icon (🚀) on the Dock and then click **Kies** (🅺). After your Galaxy S 5 appears in the upper-left corner of the Kies window, select the music files that you want to load and then click **Transfer to device**.

Buy Music Online

Google's Play Store offers millions of songs for sale, making it easy for you to buy music online. To access the Play Store, you use the Play Store app, which comes loaded on the Galaxy S 5. Songs you buy in the Play Store become available both on your Galaxy S 5 and on any other computers and devices that you have linked to the same Google account.

You can also buy music from other online stores, such as Amazon's MP3 Store, or download music from sources such as an artist's website.

Buy Music Online

1 Press the Home button.

The Home screen appears.

2 Tap **Play Store** (▶).

Ⓐ If Play Store (▶) does not appear on the Home screen, tap **Apps** (▦) and tap **Play Store** (▶).

The Play Store app opens and displays the Play Store Home screen.

3 Tap **Music**.

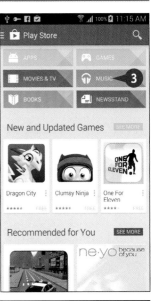

The Music section of the Play Store appears, displaying the Home page.

4 Tap **Genres** or swipe right once.

The Genres screen appears.

5 Tap the genre that you want to browse.

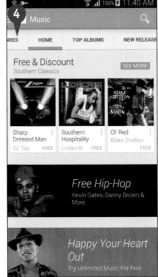

The Top Albums screen for that genre appears.

Note: You can tap **Top Songs** or swipe left once to display the Top Songs screen. You can tap **New Releases** or swipe left again to display the New Releases screen.

6 Tap an item that you want to view.

The screen for the item appears.

7 Tap the Play button (▶) to play a sample of a song.

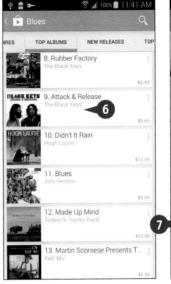

8 Tap ⏸ to pause playback.

9 Tap the price button to buy an item.

10 Follow the prompts to pay for the item.

Your Galaxy S 5 downloads the item.

TIP

What music formats can the Music app play?
The Music app can play a wide range of music formats including MP3, AAC without digital-rights management protection, FLAC, Ogg Vorbis, and WAV files. The one widely used music format that the Play Music app cannot play is Apple Lossless Encoding, a format Apple provides in iTunes. If you have Apple Lossless Encoding files on your computer, use iTunes to create AAC versions of the music and put the AAC files on your Galaxy S 5. You can also create MP3 files from the Apple Lossless Encoding files, but AAC gives slightly better audio quality than MP3 at the same file size and thus is usually a better choice.

Play Music with the Music App

You can enjoy the music on your Galaxy S 5 any place or time by using the Music app. This app enables you to browse your music by songs, artists, albums, playlists, or folders. You can browse the Recently Added playlist to find new music, the Recently Played playlist for songs that you have enjoyed recently, or the Most Played playlist to find songs to which you have listened a lot. You can also mark any song as a favorite, which makes it appear in the Favorite playlist.

Play Music with the Music App

1 Press the Home button.

The Home screen appears.

2 Tap **Apps** (▦).

The Apps screen appears.

3 Tap **Music** (◉).

The Music app opens.

4 Tap the tab for the screen that you want to display.

Note: For example, tap **Albums** to display the Albums screen, which lists all the albums available.

Note: Scroll the tab bar to display other tabs. The tabs are Playlists, Tracks, Albums, Artists, Music Square, Folders, and Devices.

The associated screen appears.

5 Tap the album that you want to open.

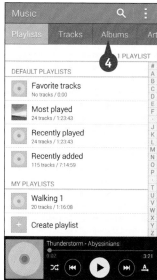

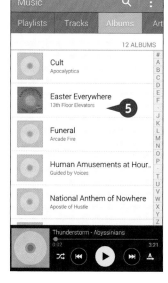

6 Tap the song that you want to play.

The song's screen appears, and the song starts playing.

7 Tap ⏸ to pause playback.

Note: You can then tap ▶ to resume playback.

8 Tap ⏮ once to go back to the beginning of the current song.

Note: You can tap ⏮ again to go to the previous song.

9 Tap ⏭ to skip to the next song.

A You can drag the playhead to move through the song.

10 Tap 🔀 to turn on shuffling.

Note: Tap 🔀 to turn off shuffling.

11 Tap ⭐ to mark the song as a favorite.

12 Tap 🎵.

The song list appears.

13 Tap the song that you want to play.

The song starts playing.

14 Tap the album thumbnail.

The album art appears again.

TIPS

What does the A button do?

This is the Repeat button. Tap it (🔁A changes to 🔁) to turn on repeating for all songs. Tap 🔁 (🔁 changes to 🔂) to turn on repeating for the current song. Tap 🔂 to turn off repeating.

How can I prevent some songs from playing much more loudly than others?

In the Music app, tap the Menu button and then tap **Settings**. On the Settings screen, tap **Smart volume** (■ changes to ✔). The Music app then "normalizes" the volume of songs, making the overall volume more consistent at the cost of some dynamic range.

Adjust the Sound with the SoundAlive Equalizer

The Music app includes the SoundAlive feature, an equalizer that enables you to adjust the sound balance to your liking. You can apply an equalization by tapping the appropriate square on a grid of different balances or create a custom equalization that suits your ears and your speakers or headphones by adjusting the frequency bands. You can also add an effect such as Tube Amp, Small Room, or Concert Hall.

Adjust the Sound with the SoundAlive Equalizer

1 Press the Home button.

The Home screen appears.

2 Tap **Apps** (▦).

The Apps screen appears.

3 Tap **Music** (◐).

The Music app opens.

4 Start some music playing so that you can hear the effect of the changes that you make.

5 Tap the Menu button (⋮).

6 Tap **Settings**.

The Settings screen appears.

7 Tap **SoundAlive**.

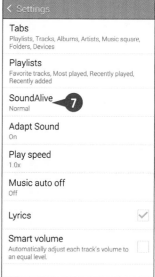

The SoundAlive feature appears, showing the Basic screen.

Ⓐ You can tap **Auto** (☐ changes to ☑) to apply an equalization automatically based on each song's genre.

Ⓑ You can tap a square on the grid to apply that preset equalization.

Ⓒ You can tap an effect on the Effect bar to apply that effect.

Ⓓ You can tap **Reset** to reset the equalization.

⑧ Tap **Advanced**.

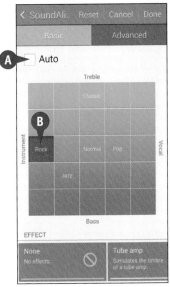

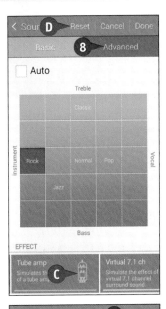

The Advanced screen appears.

Ⓔ You can drag the frequency sliders to set the equalization.

Ⓕ You can tap **3D** to add a 3D feel.

Ⓖ You can tap **Bass** to add bass.

Ⓗ You can tap **Clarity** to increase clarity.

Ⓘ You can tap an effect to apply that effect.

⑨ Tap **Done**.

The Settings screen appears.

⑩ Tap the Back button.

The music appears.

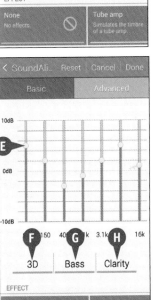

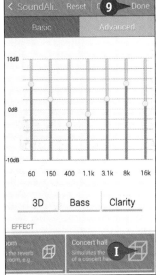

TIPS

What is the Adapt Sound feature in the Music app?
Adapt Sound applies a custom sound configuration for you. First, create your Adapt Sound configuration as discussed in the section "Customize the Audio Settings for Your Headset" later in this chapter. Then, in the Music app, tap ▤, tap **Settings**, tap **Adapt Sound**, and then tap **On** (☐ changes to ⦿).

How do the frequency sliders in SoundAlive work?
The sliders are arranged from the lowest frequencies on the left to the highest frequencies on the right. Drag a slider up to increase the amount of that frequency or down to decrease it.

Create a Playlist

The Music app enables you to create playlists that contain the songs you want to hear in your preferred order. Playlists are a great way to enjoy music on your Galaxy S 5. You can easily create as many playlists as you want by working on the Playlists screen.

After creating a playlist, you can add songs to it as needed, remove existing songs, and rearrange the remaining songs.

Create a Playlist

1 Press the Home button.

The Home screen appears.

2 Tap **Apps** (▦).

The Apps screen appears.

3 Tap **Music** (◧).

The Music app opens.

4 Tap the tab by which you want to browse your music and then navigate to the songs.

5 Tap ⋮.

6 Tap **Select**.

The Music app displays a check box to the left of each song.

7 Tap each song that you want to add (☐ changes to ☑).

8 Tap the Add to Playlist button (▤).

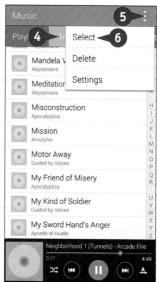

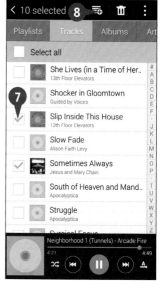

The Add to Playlist screen appears.

9 Tap **Create playlist**.

A You can tap an existing playlist to add the selected songs to it.

The Create Playlist dialog box opens.

10 Type the name for the playlist.

11 Tap **OK**.

The playlist's screen appears.

12 Tap 🔡.

13 Tap **Change order**.

The Music app displays a dotted handle (🔡) to the right of each song.

14 Tap and hold 🔡 and then drag the song to its new position.

15 When you finish editing the playlist, tap **Change order**.

The playlist's screen appears again.

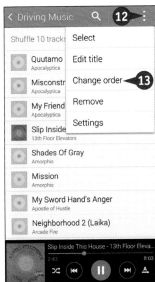

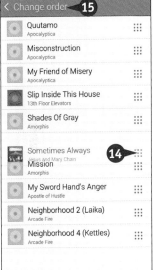

TIPS

How else can I add a song to an existing playlist?
While playing a song, tap 🔳 in the lower-right corner of the screen. You can then tap the name of the existing playlist to which you want to add the song; alternatively, you can tap **Create playlist** to start a new playlist.

How do I rename a playlist?
Tap **Playlists** to display the Playlists screen and then tap the playlist that you want to rename. On the playlist's screen, tap 🔳 and tap **Edit title**. In the Edit Title dialog box, type the new name for the playlist and then tap **OK**.

Customize the Audio Settings for Your Headset

Your Galaxy S 5 includes an innovative feature called *Adapt Sound* that enables you to create a custom audio configuration for listening to music or taking phone calls. First, you go through the process of configuring Adapt Sound to suit your hearing and choose which features may use your Adapt Sound configuration. Then you turn on Adapt Sound in the Music app when you want to use the configuration — for example, when you are listening through headphones.

Customize the Audio Settings for Your Headset

1 Connect the headset or headphones that you will use with the Adapt Sound feature.

2 Put on the headset or headphones.

3 Press the Home button.

The Home screen appears.

4 Tap **Apps** (▦).

The Apps screen appears.

5 Tap **Music** (◑).

The Music app opens.

6 Tap ⋮.

7 Tap **Settings**.

The Settings screen appears.

8 Tap **Adapt Sound**.

The Adapt Sound dialog box opens.

9 Tap **On** (◯ changes to ◉).

Note: If you have already set up Adapt Sound, tap **Check Adapt Sound again** to reconfigure it.

The Adapt Sound screen appears.

10 Tap **Start**.

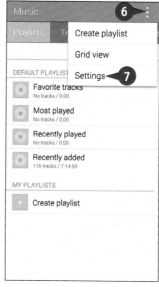

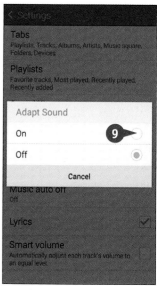

The Set Up Adapt Sound screen appears.

Adapt Sound plays a sequence of sounds at different pitches to test each ear's hearing.

11 At each prompt, tap **Yes** if you can hear the sound or **No** if you cannot hear it.

When you finish the sequence, the Adapt Sound screen appears.

12 Tap **Left** to see the hearing profile for your left ear or **Right** to see that for your right ear.

13 Tap **Preview**.

14 Tap **Left**, **Right**, or **Both** to choose which configuration to hear.

15 Tap **Personalized** to hear your personalized sound.

16 Tap **Play Adapt sound sample**.

17 Tap **Call sound** to use Adapt Sound for calls.

18 Tap **Music sound** to use Adapt Sound for music.

19 Tap **Frequently used side** and tap **Left** or **Right** to indicate your phone ear.

20 Tap **Done**.

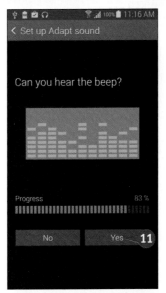

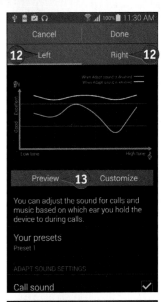

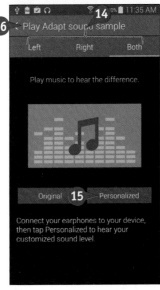

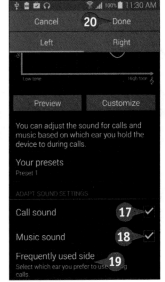

 TIP

How do I customize Adapt Sound?

On the Adapt Sound screen, tap **Customize** to display the screen for customizing Adapt Sound. Tap **Left** to configure the left channel or tap **Right** to configure the right one. On the histogram for that ear, tap the + button or the − button to increase or decrease the amount of the frequency, much like setting a custom equalization for music. Tap **Done** when you are satisfied with the sound.

Play Music through Other Devices

Your Galaxy S 5 can play music through other devices that use the Digital Living Network Alliance (DLNA) standard. For example, you might enable DLNA on your TV so that you can play music through it from your Galaxy S 5 using the Music app.

Via DLNA, your Galaxy S 5 can also access content on other devices and share its content with other devices. For example, you can use your Galaxy S 5 to play music stored on your computer via the speakers connected to your TV.

Play Music through Other Devices

Enable Nearby Devices

1 Pull down from the top of the screen.

The Notifications panel opens.

2 Tap ⚙.

The Settings app opens.

3 In the Connect and Share section, tap **Nearby devices** (🔲).

The Nearby Devices screen appears.

4 Set the **Nearby devices** switch to **On**.

5 Tap **Shared contents**.

Ⓐ You can tap **Allowed devices** to deny any currently allowed device.

Ⓑ You can tap **Denied devices** to allow any currently denied device.

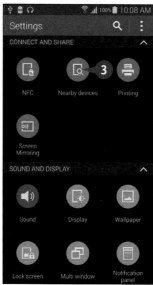

The Shared Contents dialog box opens.

6 Tap each item that you want to share (■ changes to ☑).

7 Tap **OK**.

8 When the Nearby Devices dialog box prompts you to allow a device to access your Galaxy S 5, tap **OK** or **Cancel**, as appropriate.

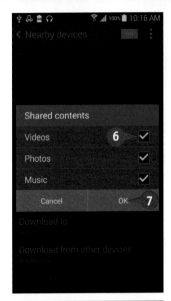

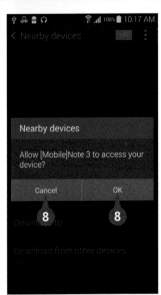

Play Music on a Nearby Device

1 In the Music app, navigate to a song and start playing it.

2 Tap 🔲.

The Select Device dialog box opens.

3 Tap the device through which you want to play music (◯ changes to ◉).

C You can tap **Refresh** to refresh the list of devices if necessary.

The Music app starts playing the music through the device that you selected.

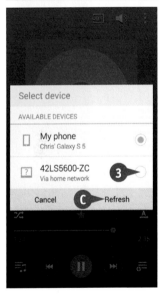

TIP

How can I troubleshoot the Nearby Devices feature?

Make sure that each wireless device is connected to the same wireless network and to the same Wi-Fi access point. To determine which Wi-Fi access point your Galaxy S 5 is using, pull down from the top of the screen to open the Notifications panel, tap and hold **Wi-Fi** (📶), and then look for the **Connected** readout on the Wi-Fi screen.

When each device is connected to the same access point, display the Music app, tap the Select Device button (🔲), and then tap **Refresh**.

Watch Videos

Your Galaxy S 5 includes the Video app for playing videos. The Video app can play videos using either Portrait orientation or Landscape orientation and provides straightforward on-screen controls for controlling playback.

The Gallery app gives you an easy way to browse your photos and videos together and enables you to open a video in either the Photos app or the Video Player app. This section demonstrates this method. You can also open the Video Player app directly from the Apps screen and then open a video from within the app.

Watch Videos

1 Press the Home button.

The Home screen appears.

2 Tap **Apps** (▦).

The Apps screen appears.

3 Tap **Gallery** (▦).

Note: You can tap **Video Player** (▶) on the Apps screen and then open a video from within the app.

The Gallery app opens.

Ⓐ You can change the view by tapping ▤ and then tapping the view that you want, such as **Time** or **Album**.

4 Tap the item that contains the video you want to view.

The item's contents appear.

5 Tap the video that you want to view.

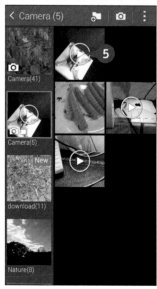

The Gallery app displays a preview of the video.

6 Tap the Play button ().

The Complete Action Using dialog box opens.

7 Tap **Photos** (📷).

8 Tap **Just Once**.

B Tap **Always** if you want to use Photos each time you open a video from the Gallery app.

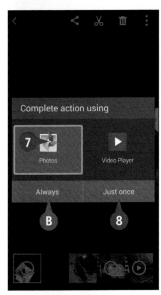

Photos opens and starts playing the video.

9 Turn your Galaxy S 5 to Landscape orientation to view the video full screen.

10 Tap anywhere on the screen when you need to display the controls.

11 Use the controls to pause, rewind, or fast-forward the video.

Note: The controls disappear automatically a few seconds after you stop using them.

TIP

How do I play a video from my Galaxy S 5 on my TV?

If your TV has DLNA, tap 📶 to display the Select Device dialog box and then tap the device that represents your TV (⚪ changes to ◉). If your TV does not have DLNA, either connect a DLNA dongle to it or use an HDMI-to–micro-USB cable to connect the multipurpose jack on your Galaxy S 5 to the HDMI port on the TV. Switch the TV's input to that port, and the contents of your Galaxy S 5's screen appear on the TV screen.

Using the Pop-up Video Player

Your Galaxy S 5 includes a pop-up video player that enables you to keep watching a video in a small window that appears in front of whatever else is on the screen. You can adjust the size of the pop-up window and reposition it on-screen so that you can continue watching the video while you work or play in other apps.

Using the Pop-up Video Player

1 Press the Home button.

The Home screen appears.

2 Tap **Apps** (▦).

The Apps screen appears.

3 Tap **Video** (▶).

The Video app opens.

4 Tap the video that you want to open.

The video starts playing.

5 Tap the screen.

The controls appear.

6 Tap the Pop-Up Player button (▣).

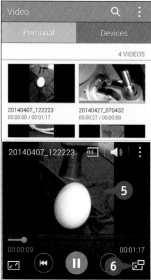

The Video app displays the video in the pop-up player, still playing.

The Home screen appears.

7 Drag the pop-up player to where you want it to appear.

Note: You can pinch inward or outward with two fingers to resize the pop-up player to your preferred size.

8 Tap **Apps** (▦).

Note: Alternatively, press and hold the Home button.

The Apps screen appears.

9 Tap the app that you want to launch.

Note: This example uses **Memo** (▭).

The app opens.

10 Work in the app, watching the video in the pop-up player.

11 Tap the video to pause it. Tap again to restart it.

12 With the video paused, to exit the player, tap ⊗.

The pop-up player window closes.

How do I return from the pop-up player to the Video app?

You can return quickly to the Video app from the pop-up player by double-tapping the pop-up player. Tap 🖼 if you want to go back to the pop-up player again from the Video app.

Explore YouTube

Your Galaxy S 5 includes the YouTube app, which enables you to watch videos on YouTube, Google's video-sharing website. YouTube contains a wide variety of videos that you can browse freely and watch. To use some of YouTube's features, such as rating videos or flagging them for unsuitable content, you must log in to your Google account.

Open and Navigate the YouTube App

To launch the YouTube app, press the Home button, tap **Apps** (▦), and then tap **YouTube** (▶).

At first, the YouTube app displays the What to Watch screen. From there, you can tap the Search button (🔍) to search for videos by keyword or tap **YouTube** (▶) to display the navigation panel, which gives you quick access to different aspects of your user account, your subscriptions, and the Best of YouTube list.

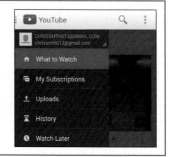

Browse Videos

Browsing is a good way to explore the millions of widely varied videos that YouTube contains. You can browse simply by scrolling down the What to Watch screen, which contains current content that is proving popular. From the navigation panel, you can tap **Popular on YouTube** to browse the Popular on YouTube list. Tap the **Home** tab, the **Videos** tab, or the **Playlists** tab first, and then scroll down as needed to find videos that interest you.

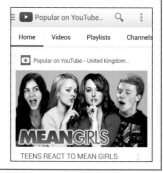

Search for Videos

Searching enables you to quickly locate videos that have specific keywords. Tap 🔍 at the top of the screen and then type your search terms in the Search box that opens. You can also tap 🎤 and dictate your search terms.

As you enter search terms, the YouTube app displays suggested matches. Tap a match to view the search results, or finish typing and then tap 🔍 at the lower-right corner of the keyboard. YouTube displays the search results.

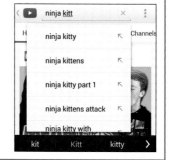

Look at a Video's Information

When you find a video that looks interesting, tap it to display its information screen. The video starts playing automatically. You can tap ▭ to display the text description of the video, which you can read to determine whether you want to view the video. You can tap ▦ to display the Add To dialog box, which enables you to add the video to your Watch Later list, to your Favorites, or to a new playlist. You can tap ⬔ to switch the video to full screen in Landscape mode.

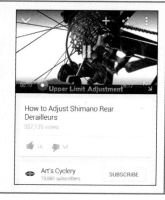

Watch a Video Full Screen

On the video's information page, rotate your Galaxy S 5 from Portrait mode to Landscape mode to switch to full-screen viewing. Tap the screen when you need to display the video controls, which enable you to pause the video and scrub through it.

Flag a Video for Inappropriate Content

If you find a video to be offensive, you can flag it to help YouTube identify problems with it. For example, if the video shows sexual content or dangerous acts, you can flag it for review.

To flag a video, tap the Menu button (▤) on the video's screen and then tap ⚑. In the Flag This Video dialog box that opens, tap the appropriate option, such as **Hateful or Abusive Content** (◯ changes to ◉), and then tap **Flag**.

Flag this video

◉ Sexual Content
◯ Violent or Repulsive Content
◯ Hateful or Abusive Content
◯ Harmful Dangerous Acts
◯ Infringes My Rights
◯ Spam

If you are the copyright owner of this video and believe

Cancel   Flag

CHAPTER 13

Using Your Galaxy S 5 for Work

Your Galaxy S 5 is as good for work as it is for play. You can set up and use Private mode, connect to your work network and Exchange Server, install digital credentials, and work on memos and documents.

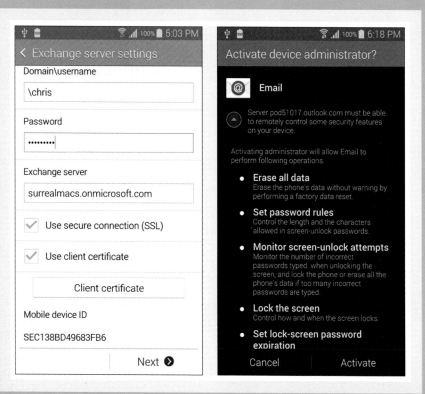

Understanding the Options Available for Work

Your Galaxy S 5 can be highly useful as a work tool as well as a device for managing and enjoying your personal life. The Galaxy S 5 includes various options that you can use to work securely, connect to work networks and servers, and create and share office documents.

Securing Your Documents with Private Mode

Your Galaxy S 5 includes a feature called *Private mode* that enables you to secure your sensitive files against intrusion. You can use Private mode for any files — including documents, music, and videos — that you want to protect for either work reasons or personal reasons. For example, if you use your Galaxy S 5 for work and bring it home, you can use Private mode to hide files that you want to keep away from others who can access your phone.

Installing and Using Credentials

To keep their precious data and money safe, many work-related networks require stronger security measures than passwords. One widely used security measure is to use a *digital certificate,* a piece of encrypted computer code, to identify a computer or device. Android enables you to install digital certificates, which it refers to as *credentials,* on your Galaxy S 5 and use them to authenticate its identity to servers. Credentials are typically used for securing virtual private network connections and connections to Exchange Server.

Connecting Securely via Virtual Private Networking

For work, you may need to connect your Galaxy S 5 to your company's network across the Internet. Android includes a feature called *virtual private networking* (VPN) that encrypts data to create a secure connection between your Galaxy S 5 and the VPN server on the remote network. By using VPN, you can connect your Galaxy S 5 securely to your company's network anywhere you can establish an Internet connection.

Connecting to Exchange Server

If your company or organization uses Microsoft's Exchange Server software, you likely want to set up your Exchange account on your Galaxy S 5 so that you can send and receive work-related e-mail, access contact data, and sync calendar events no matter where you go. You can set up your Exchange account using the Email app on your Galaxy S 5. You may need to use a digital certificate to authenticate your Galaxy S 5 to the Exchange Server.

Working on Microsoft Office Documents

If your company, organization, or colleagues use Microsoft Office, you likely need to read and edit Word documents, Excel spreadsheets, and PowerPoint presentations as part of your work. You can work on Microsoft Office documents on your Galaxy S 5 by using either the free Office Mobile app from Microsoft, supplementing it with an Office 365 subscription if you need to edit and create documents, or a third-party app that can open Office documents. You can transfer documents to and from your Galaxy S 5 in various ways, including connecting to a SharePoint server.

Working Securely with Samsung KNOX

For corporate security, your company or organization may install the Samsung KNOX software on your Galaxy S 5 to give you an easy and effective way to separate your work data from your personal data. After installing KNOX, you launch it from the Apps screen like any other app. KNOX then opens a secure area running secure versions of system apps, such as Camera, Memo, Email, S Planner, Phone, and Internet. While KNOX is running, you can switch between the secure KNOX area and the regular apps by using the Notifications panel. At this writing, KNOX is available only for corporate use, not individual use.

Set Up Private Mode

If you plan to use your Galaxy S 5 for work, it is a good idea to use Private mode to keep your sensitive files safe from intrusion. Private mode provides a secure storage area in which you can keep any file that you do not want other people who can access your Galaxy S 5 to be able to find or open. In Private mode, you can use a limited selection of apps securely, such as Gallery, Video, Music, Voice Recorder, and My Files.

Set Up Private Mode

1 Pull down from the top of the screen with two fingers.

The Quick Settings panel opens.

2 Tap **Private mode** (🔒).

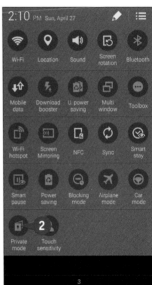

The Private Mode Welcome screen appears.

3 Tap **Next**.

The first Using Private Mode screen appears, showing a list of the apps available in Private mode.

4 Tap **Next**.

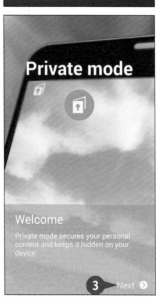

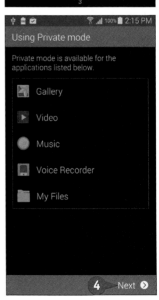

The second Using Private Mode screen appears, providing instructions on how to move content to and from Private mode.

5 Tap **Start**.

The Select Unlock Method screen appears.

6 Tap the unlock method that you want to use.

Note: This example uses **Fingerprint**.

Note: To secure your files effectively, do not use the Pattern unlock method.

7 Swipe your finger over the Home button multiple times, following the prompts on the screen.

8 Type a password of at least four characters, containing at least one letter.

9 Tap **Continue**.

The Confirm Password screen appears.

10 Type the password again.

11 Tap **OK**.

Your Galaxy S 5 turns on Private mode.

The Private mode icon (🔒) appears in the status bar.

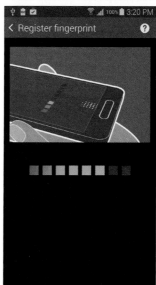

TIP

How does Private mode protect my web browsing?
Private mode does nothing to protect your web browsing. Instead, you should use Incognito mode in the Internet app or the Chrome app when you need to browse without the history recording the pages that you visit. To use Incognito mode in the Internet app, tap ⋮ and then tap **Incognito mode**. To use Incognito mode in the Chrome app, tap ⋮ and then tap **New incognito tab**.

Using Private Mode

Afterter setting up Private mode for the first time, as explained in the previous section, "Set Up Private Mode," you are ready to use it to keep your sensitive files secure.

After enabling Private mode, you can move files to the Private storage area, making them accessible only when Private mode is turned on. After using Private mode and working with the files you have stored in the Private area, you turn Private mode off again, making those files inaccessible to others.

Using Private Mode

Turn on Private Mode

1 Pull down from the top of the screen with two fingers.

The Quick Settings panel opens.

2 Tap **Private mode** (⬛).

Your Galaxy S 5 prompts you to provide your unlock method.

Note: This example uses the Fingerprint unlock method, for which the alternative unlock method is entering a password.

3 Swipe your finger down over the Home button.

A Alternatively, tap **Alternative password** and then type the password.

Your Galaxy S 5 turns on Private mode.

B The "Private mode turned on" message appears briefly.

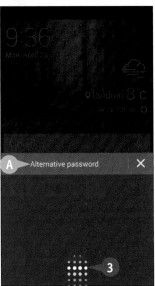

Move Files to the Private Storage Area

1 Press the Home button.

2 Tap **Apps** (▦).

3 Tap **My Files** (□).

The My Files app opens.

4 Navigate to the folder that contains the files that you want to move to the Private storage area.

C When Private mode is on, the Private storage area appears in My Files.

5 Tap ⋮.

6 Tap **Select**.

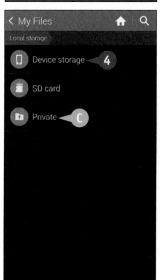

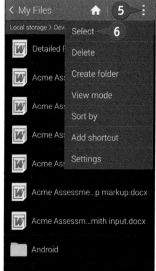

How do I move files to the Private storage area in the Music app?

In the Music app, tap the **Tracks** tab to display the list of tracks. Tap ⋮ and tap **Select**. Tap each track that you want to move (■ changes to ☑). Tap ⋮ and tap **Move to Private**.

How do I move photos and videos to the Private storage area?

In the Gallery app, tap ⊟ and tap **Album** on the navigation panel. Tap ⋮ and tap **Select**. Tap each album that you want to move (☑ appears on the album). Tap ⋮ and tap **Move to Private**.

continued ▶

hen you finish using Private mode, you turn it off. The easiest way to turn Private mode off is by tapping its icon in the Quick Settings panel, but you can also open the Notifications panel and tap the Private Mode notification to go directly to the Private Mode screen in the Settings app, which includes a switch for turning Private mode off.

Using Private Mode (continued)

7 Tap each file that you want to move to Private mode (■ changes to ☑).

8 Tap ⋮.

9 Tap **Move**.

The Move screen appears.

10 Tap **Private**.

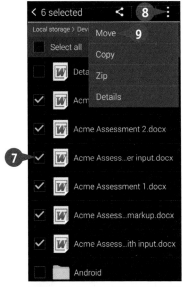

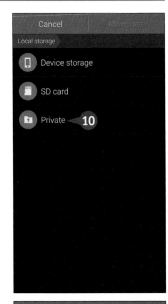

The contents of the Private storage appear.

11 Navigate to the folder in which you want to store the documents.

Ⓐ You can tap **Create folder** to create a new folder.

12 Tap **Move here**.

My Files moves the files to the Private storage.

Turn off Private Mode

1 Pull down from the top of the screen with two fingers.

The Quick Settings panel opens.

2 Tap **Private mode** ().

The Private Mode dialog box opens.

B You can tap **Do not show again** (■ changes to ✔) to prevent the Private Mode dialog box from appearing again.

3 Tap **OK**.

C The "Private mode turned off" message appears briefly.

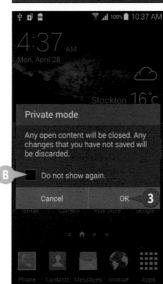

TIP

How do I move files back from the Private storage area to regular storage?

To move files back from the Private storage area to regular storage, you use a similar method as when moving files to the Private storage area:

- In My Files, select the files, tap **⋮**, and then tap **Move**. On the Move screen, navigate to the appropriate folder on Device Storage or SD Card and then tap **Move Here**.
- In Music, select the files, tap **⋮**, and then tap **Remove from Private**.
- In Gallery, select the files, tap **⋮**, and then tap **Remove from Private**.

Connect to a Work Network via VPN

Android includes the capability to connect to a remote network securely across the Internet. It uses a technology called *virtual private networking* (VPN) that encrypts data to create a secure connection between your Galaxy S 5 and the VPN server on the remote network.

By using VPN, you can connect securely to your work network from anywhere you can establish an Internet connection. Before you set up a VPN connection, you must apply a lock screen PIN or password to your Galaxy S 5.

Connect to a Work Network via VPN

1 Pull down from the top of the screen.

The Notifications panel opens.

2 Tap the Settings button (⚙).

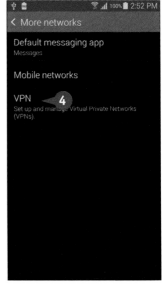

The Settings app opens.

3 In the Network Connections section, tap **More Networks** (▣).

The More Networks screen appears.

4 Tap **VPN**.

Note: If you have not yet set a lock screen PIN or password, the Enable Screen Lock dialog box opens. Tap **OK** to display the Screen Unlock Settings screen, tap **PIN** or **Password**, and follow the prompts.

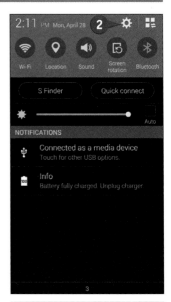

The VPN screen appears.

5 Tap the Add button (⊞).

The Add VPN dialog box opens.

6 Type a descriptive name for the connection.

7 Tap the **Type** pop-up menu and then tap the VPN type.

8 Type the server address.

9 Type the security information.

10 Tap **Save**.

The VPN screen appears.

11 Tap the VPN's name.

12 Type your username.

13 Type your password.

14 Tap **Save account information** to save your credentials.

15 Tap **Connect**.

A The Connected readout appears. You can now work with network resources such as e-mail and network folders.

16 When you are ready to disconnect, tap the VPN's name.

17 Tap **Disconnect**.

What VPN type should I choose?
Ask your VPN's administrator what VPN type to use. PPTP, the Point-to-Point Tunneling Protocol, and L2TP, the Layer 2 Tunneling Protocol, are the most widely used VPN types, but it is hard to guess what type you need.

What is the pre-shared key?
The *pre-shared key,* or PSK, is a group password for the VPN. The pre-shared key is shared among a group of users instead of being specific to a single user. The pre-shared key is also called a *shared secret.*

Connect to Exchange Server

Microsoft Exchange Server is widely used server software that provides e-mail, contact management, and scheduling. If your company or organization uses Exchange Server, you can connect your Galaxy S 5 to it and work with your e-mail messages, contacts, and calendars.

To connect to Exchange Server, you set up an account in the Email app. Depending on the Exchange Server setup, Email may be able to set up the account automatically. If not, you can configure the account manually. You must also use manual configuration if you need to authenticate using a digital certificate.

Connect to Exchange Server

1 Press the Home button.

The Home screen appears.

2 Tap **Email** (⊚).

The Email app opens.

Note: If you have not yet set up an account in the Email app, the app automatically displays the Set Up Email screen on launch. Go to step **7**.

3 Tap ▤.

4 Tap **Settings**.

5 Tap **Manage accounts**.

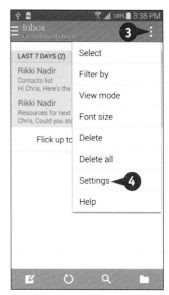

6 Tap ⊞.

7 Type your e-mail address.

8 Type your password.

A You can tap **Show password** (☐ changes to ☑) to display the password characters.

9 To make this your default account, tap here (☐ changes to ☑).

10 Tap **Manual setup**.

B You can tap **Next** to try automatic setup. If it works, go to step **18**.

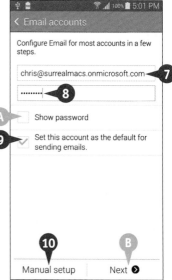

The Add Email Account: What type of Account? screen appears.

11 Tap **Microsoft Exchange ActiveSync**.

The Exchange Server Settings screen appears.

12 Edit the contents of the **Domain\ username** field if necessary.

13 Edit the server name if necessary.

14 If your account requires a secure connection, tap **Use secure connection (SSL)** (☐ changes to ☑).

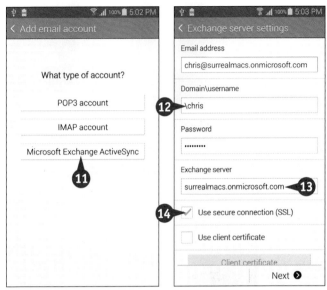

15 If your Galaxy S 5 must use a certificate to authenticate to the server, tap **Use client certificate** (☐ changes to ☑). If not, go to step **18**.

16 Tap **Client certificate**.

The Email Certificate screen appears.

17 Tap the certificate that you want to use.

C If the certificate does not appear, you can tap ➕ and follow the prompts to add it from your Download folder.

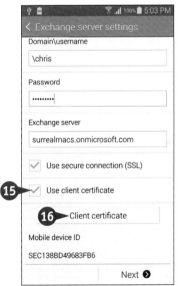

TIPS

How do I know whether to enter a domain for my Exchange account?

Ask your Exchange Server administrator whether to enter a domain and, if so, which one. Exchange Server systems tend to be complex, and you stand little chance of guessing the correct information.

Is my Exchange username the same as my e-mail address?

Your Exchange username may be the same as your e-mail address, but it may also be different — for example, just the part of your e-mail address before the @ sign. Ask your Exchange Server administrator what your username is.

continued ▶

Whadn setting up your Exchange account, you need to know your e-mail address and password. You may also need to know the Exchange domain name and the name of the Exchange Server to use. You can get this information from your Exchange administrator or systems administrator.

Some Exchange Server connections require your phone to use a *digital certificate,* a unit of encrypted computer code used to identify a device. Normally, if you need to use a digital certificate, an administrator will provide it and install it on your Galaxy S 5.

Connect to Exchange Server (continued)

The Exchange Server Settings screen appears again.

⑱ Tap **Next**.

The Activation dialog box opens.

Ⓐ You can tap **Do not show again** (☐ changes to ☑) if you want to suppress the dialog box in the future.

⑲ Tap **OK**.

The Email app attempts to contact the appropriate Exchange Server. If so, it selects suitable settings automatically.

The Remote Security Administration dialog box opens.

⑳ Tap **OK**.

The Account Options screen appears.

㉑ Tap the **Period to sync Email** pop-up menu and tap the period, such as **3 days** or **All**.

㉒ Tap the **Sync schedule** pop-up menu and tap the schedule, such as **Push** or **5 minutes**.

㉓ Tap the next three pop-up menus and set the peak schedule, e-mail retrieval size, and period to sync Calendar.

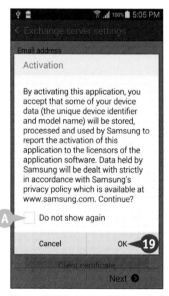
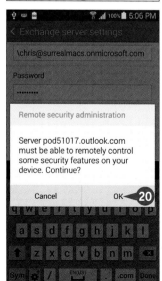
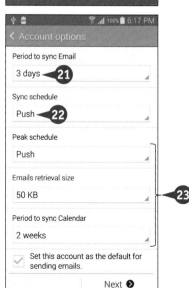

24 Tap **Notify me when e-mail arrives** (☐ changes to ☑) to receive notifications.

25 Tap the **Sync** options (☐ changes to ☑) to choose what to sync.

26 Tap **Next**.

The Activate Device Administrator? screen appears.

Note: This screen explains the remote-control features that Exchange can exercise over your Galaxy S 5. For example, an Exchange administrator can remotely erase all your data.

27 Tap **Activate**.

The Set Up Email screen appears.

28 Type the name that you want to assign to the account.

29 Tap **Done**.

Your Inbox appears, and you can start using your Exchange account.

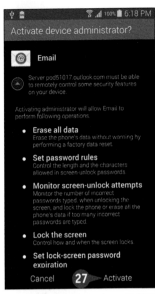

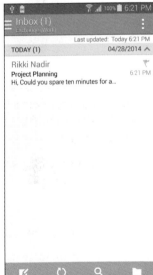

TIPS

What is Push syncing, and should I use it?
Push is a sync technology in which the server notifies your phone whenever new mail is available. Use Push if you want to receive your messages as quickly as possible and do not mind sacrificing some battery power to get them.

Should I turn on the Use Secure Connection option?
You will probably need to select **Use secure connection (SSL)** (☐ changes to ☑) in order to log in to the Exchange Server. SSL is the abbreviation for *Secure Sockets Layer,* a communications technology for establishing a secure connection. In this case, the connection is between your Galaxy S 5 and the Exchange Server.

Install Credentials

When connecting to Exchange Server systems or establishing a VPN connection, you may need to provide credentials to authenticate your Galaxy S 5's identity and — by implication — your own identity. Android enables you to install digital certificates containing credentials on your Galaxy S 5.

You can install a digital certificate either by opening a digital certificate attached to an e-mail message or by copying the digital certificate's file to your Galaxy S 5's Download folder and then using the My Files app to install it.

Install Credentials

Install a Digital Certificate from an E-mail Message

1 In the Inbox of your e-mail app, tap the message that contains the digital certificate.

Note: This example uses the Email app. You can also install a digital certificate from the Gmail app.

The message opens.

2 Tap the Attachment button.

3 Tap **Preview**.

4 Type the digital certificate's password.

5 Tap **OK**.

The Name the Certificate dialog box opens.

6 Edit the name for the certificate as needed.

Note: Give each certificate you install a descriptive name so that you can easily distinguish it from other certificates.

7 Tap the **Credential use** pop-up menu and tap **VPN and apps** or **Wi-Fi** to specify the uses for the certificate.

8 Tap **OK**.

A A message says that the certificate has been installed.

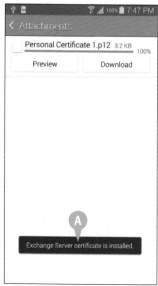

302

Install a Digital Certificate from Your Download Folder

1 Press the Home button.

The Home screen appears.

2 Tap **Apps** (▦).

The Apps screen appears.

3 Tap **My Files** (▭).

The My Files list appears.

4 Tap **Device storage**.

The Device Storage list appears.

5 Tap **Download**.

The Download list appears.

6 Tap the certificate file.

The Extract From dialog box opens.

7 Follow steps **4** to **8** in the preceding subsection to complete the installation.

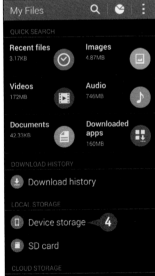

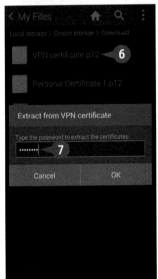

How else can I install a digital certificate?
You can use Settings. From the Apps screen, tap **Settings** (⚙). In the System section, tap **Security** (🔒) and scroll down to the Credential Storage section. Tap **Install from phone storage**, tap **Downloads** if Android offers a choice of folders, and then tap the certificate's button.

How do I remove a certificate from my Galaxy S 5?
Normally, if you do not use a certificate, you can simply leave it on your Galaxy S 5. But if you want to remove it, you must remove all credentials. Follow the instructions in the preceding tip to display the Security screen and then tap **Clear credentials**. In the Attention dialog box that opens, tap **OK**.

Work on Microsoft Office Documents

The three key apps in Microsoft Office are Microsoft Word, the word-processing app; Microsoft Excel, the spreadsheet app; and Microsoft PowerPoint, the presentations app. Your Galaxy S 5 may have an app installed, such as Polaris Office Viewer, that can display Office documents. You can install Microsoft's Office Mobile app and use it to view or edit documents, or you can install third-party software.

Get Your Office Documents onto Your Galaxy S 5

If you have only a few Office documents that you need on your phone, you can transfer the files via e-mail or Bluetooth. But in most cases, you want to connect your Galaxy S 5 to the network server or Internet service on which you store your Office documents. For example, you can connect to your company's network via VPN to access documents on a server, or you can store your documents on an online service such as Dropbox, www.dropbox.com, or Microsoft's OneDrive, https://onedrive.live.com.

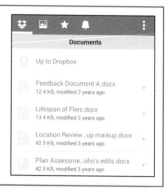

Use an Included Office-Compatible App

Your Galaxy S 5 may have an Office-compatible app installed, such as Polaris Office or Polaris Office Viewer. You may be able to find this app on the Apps screen. If you cannot see an icon for such an app, tap **My Files** (▢) on the Apps screen. Browse to an Office document and tap it. The Complete Action Using dialog box opens, showing you the compatible apps on your Galaxy S 5. Tap the app that you want to use, such as **Polaris Office Viewer** or **Docs To Go**, and then tap either **Just once** or **Always**, as appropriate.

Install Docs To Go

If your Galaxy S 5 does not have a satisfactory Office-compatible app, try the free version of Docs To Go. You can download and install this app from the Play Store and then run it from the Apps screen.

Docs To Go enables you to view, edit, and create Word documents, Excel workbooks, and PowerPoint presentations. The free version is supported by ads, but you can purchase the Docs To Go Premium Key to remove the ads and give yourself access to all the features.

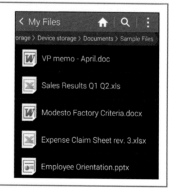

Install Office Mobile

Office Mobile is a free app that you can download and install from the App Store. On its own, Office Mobile enables you to view Word documents, view Excel workbooks, and view and present PowerPoint presentations, but it does not let you create new documents or edit existing ones. By adding to Office Mobile a suitable subscription to Microsoft's Office 365 service, you unlock the capabilities to create and edit documents. You can set up an Office 365 subscription by browsing to http://office.microsoft.com and following the Office 365 links. Microsoft offers various subscription types, so read the small print closely before you buy.

Connect Office Mobile to OneDrive, Office 365, or SharePoint

After installing Office Mobile, you can connect it to OneDrive, Office 365, or your company's SharePoint server, enabling yourself to access documents stored on those services or that server. In Office Mobile, tap ⬜ to display the Open screen and then tap ⬛. On the Add a Place screen that appears, tap **OneDrive** (⬛), **Office 365** (⬛), or **SharePoint** (⬛) and follow the prompts to provide your credentials. You can then open documents from and save documents to that place.

Create New Documents with Office Mobile

If you add an Office 365 subscription to your Office Mobile installation, you can create new documents using Office Mobile on your Galaxy S 5. In Office Mobile, tap ⬜ to display the New Document screen. You can then tap the appropriate template in the Blank Documents list, the Word Templates list, the Excel Templates list, or the PowerPoint Templates list to create a new document based on that template. For example, tap the **Report** template in the Word Templates list to start a new report document.

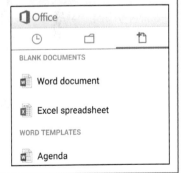

CHAPTER 14

Troubleshooting Your Galaxy S 5

To keep your Galaxy S 5 running well, you should update its software, keep backups in case of disaster, and learn essential troubleshooting steps, such as closing apps that have stopped responding and solving wireless connection problems.

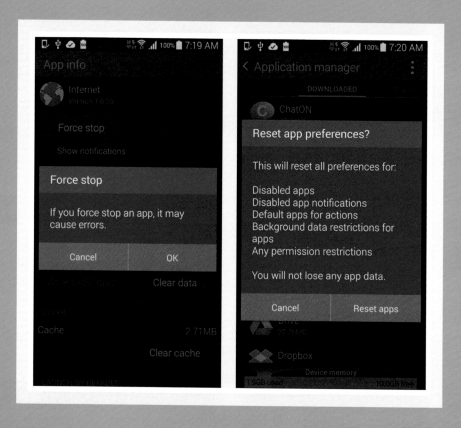

Close an App That Has Stopped Responding

Sometimes you might find that an app on your Galaxy S 5 has stopped responding to your input. When this happens, you need to close the app and then restart it before you can continue using it.

Your Galaxy S 5 enables you to close apps quickly from the Recent Apps screen. From there, you can either close individual apps or close all the apps that your Galaxy S 5 is running. You can also display the Application Manager, which enables you to stop apps or system services.

Close an App That Has Stopped Responding

Display the Recent Apps Screen and Close Apps

1 When you notice that an app has stopped responding, tap the Recent Apps button.

The Recent Apps screen appears.

2 Swipe the app that has stopped responding to the left or right.

Android closes the app and removes it from the list.

A You can tap the Close All button (⊟) to close all the apps.

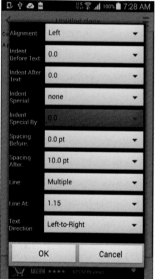

Force an App to Stop

1 On the Recent Apps screen, tap and hold an app.

B You can tap **Remove from list** to close the app and remove it from the list.

2 Tap **App info**.

The app's App Info screen appears.

3 Tap **Force stop**.

The Force Stop dialog box opens.

4 Tap **OK**.

Android stops the app.

Open the Application Manager and Stop Apps or Services

1 Pull down from the top of the screen.

2 Tap ⚙.

The Settings screen appears.

3 In the Applications section, tap **Application manager** (▦).

The Application Manager opens.

4 Swipe left or right one or more times until the Running tab appears.

5 Tap the app or service that you want to stop.

The Active App screen appears.

6 Tap **Stop**.

The Stop System Service? dialog box opens.

7 Tap **OK**.

Android stops the app or service.

8 Tap **Active app**.

You are returned to the Running tab.

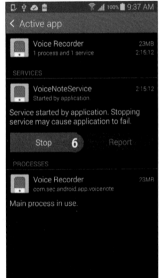

TIP

What else can I do in the Application Manager?

On the Running tab, you can tap **Show cached processes** to display the processes that your Galaxy S 5 has cached. These processes are apps and services that you are not currently using but which the operating system has stored so that it can load them again quickly if you ask to use them. You can then tap a process to display the Active App screen, which shows information about the process. On the Active App screen, you can tap **Stop** to stop a process, but usually this is not necessary. Tap **Show services in use** to display the list of running services again.

Update Your Galaxy S 5's Software

Samsung periodically releases new versions of the Galaxy S 5's operating system and TouchWiz skin to fix problems, improve performance, and add new features. To keep your phone running quickly and smoothly, you should update its software when a new version is available.

You can update your Galaxy S 5's software either "over the air" — by downloading it wirelessly — or by using Samsung Kies on your computer.

Update Your Galaxy S 5's Software

1 Press the Home button.

The Home screen appears.

2 Tap **Apps** (▦).

The Apps screen appears.

3 Tap **Settings** (⚙).

The Settings app opens.

4 In the System section, tap **About device** (ⓘ).

The About Device screen appears.

5 Tap **Software update**.

The Software Update screen appears.

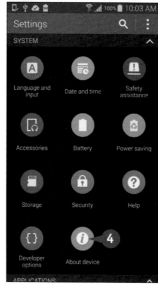

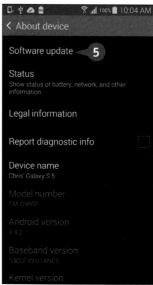

Ⓐ You can tap **Auto update** (■ changes to ☑) to check for updates automatically.

Ⓑ You can tap **Wi-Fi only** (■ changes to ☑) to download updates only via Wi-Fi, not via cellular.

6 Tap **Update now**.

Note: If no updates are available, a dialog box shows the message, "The latest updates have already been installed."

Another Software Update screen appears.

7 Tap **Install**.

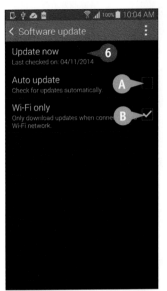

The Software Update dialog box opens, warning you that your device will restart and install updates.

8 Tap **OK**.

Your Galaxy S 5 restarts and installs the updates.

The lock screen appears.

9 Unlock your Galaxy S 5 as usual. You can then resume using it.

TIPS

How do I update my Galaxy S 5 using Samsung Kies?
Connect your Galaxy S 5 to your PC via USB and unlock the phone's screen if necessary. After Kies launches and connects to your Galaxy S 5, Kies displays a dialog box telling you that an update is available. Click **Update** and then follow the process of installing the update.

Should I update my Galaxy S 5 over the air or using Kies?
Normally, updating your Galaxy S 5 over the air is easier, but make sure that your phone uses Wi-Fi rather than its cellular connection when downloading the updates. Occasionally, an update may not be available over the air; in this case, you must use Kies.

Extend the Runtime on the Battery

To keep your Galaxy S 5 running all day long, you can turn on Power Saving mode to reduce power usage. Power Saving mode can throttle back the processor, dim the screen, and shut off haptic feedback to save power. You can choose which of these settings to use.

For greater power saving, you can turn off Wi-Fi and Bluetooth and set a short screen timeout. When the battery runs dangerously low on power, you can use Ultra Power Saving mode, which is discussed in the next section.

Extend the Runtime on the Battery

Configure Power Saving Mode

1 Pull down with two fingers from the top of the screen.

The Quick Settings panel opens.

2 Tap and hold **Power Saving** (◨).

Note: To save power, set a short screen timeout. In the Settings app, tap **My device**, tap **Display**, tap **Screen timeout**, and then tap the appropriate time, such as **15 seconds** (◉ changes to ◯).

3 Set the **Power saving mode** switch to **On**.

4 Tap **Block background data** (■ changes to ✔) to block data transfer by apps other than the one you are currently using.

5 Tap **Restrict performance**.

The Restrict Performance screen appears.

6 Set the **Restrict performance** switch to **On**.

7 Choose other options as needed.

8 Tap the Back button.

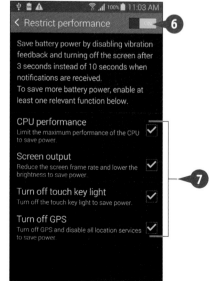

You are returned to the Power Saving Mode screen.

9 Tap **Grayscale mode**.

The Grayscale Mode screen appears.

10 Set the **Grayscale mode** switch to **On**.

The screen switches to grayscale.

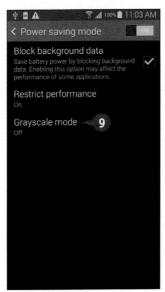

Turn Power Saving Mode, Wi-Fi, and Bluetooth On or Off

1 Pull down with two fingers from the top of the screen.

2 Tap **Power Saving** (🔋 changes to 🔋 or 🔋 changes to 🔋).

3 To turn Wi-Fi off or on, tap **Wi-Fi** (📶 changes to 📶 or 📶 changes to 📶).

4 To turn Bluetooth off or on, tap **Bluetooth** (📶 changes to 📶 or 📶 changes to 📶).

TIP

What else can I do to increase the runtime of my Galaxy S 5?

Your Galaxy S 5 has a removable back that gives easy access to the battery compartment, so you can carry a spare battery with you and swap batteries when your Galaxy S 5 runs low on power. Some third-party batteries offer higher capacities than Samsung's batteries, but before using such a battery, verify that doing so will not void your phone's warranty. If you need more power while you are on the move, buy a case with a built-in battery or a charger for charging the battery in a car.

Using Ultra Power Saving Mode

As well as Power Saving mode, discussed in the preceding section, "Extend the Runtime on the Battery," your Galaxy S 5 offers Ultra Power Saving mode. This mode enables you to eke out the remaining battery life by switching to a spartan black-and-white interface, limiting the apps that you can run, and preventing you from using power-hungry features.

You can use Ultra Power Saving mode at any time, but it is normally best kept for emergencies.

Using Ultra Power Saving Mode

Turn On Ultra Power Saving Mode

1 Pull down with two fingers from the top of the screen.

The Quick Settings panel opens.

2 Tap **U. power saving** (🔲).

The Ultra Power Saving Mode dialog box opens.

Ⓐ The Estimated Max. Standby Time readout shows the maximum standby time that Ultra Power Saving mode may be able to deliver.

3 Tap **OK**.

Your Galaxy S 5 switches to Ultra Power Saving mode.

Ⓑ You can tap an app to launch it.

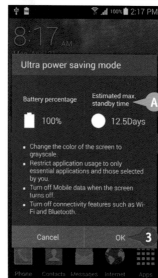

Add an App to the Home Screen

1 Press the Home button.

The Home screen appears.

2 Tap one of the Add buttons (⊕).

The Add Application screen appears.

3 Tap the app that you want to add.

The app appears on the Home screen.

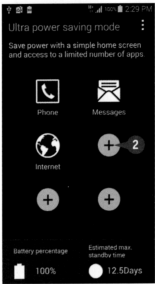

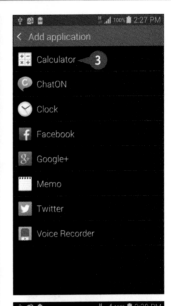

Turn Off Ultra Power Saving Mode

1 Press the Home button.

The Home screen appears.

2 Tap the Menu button (▮).

3 Tap **Disable Ultra power saving mode**.

The Ultra Power Saving Mode dialog box opens.

4 Tap **OK**.

Your Galaxy S 5 turns off Ultra Power Saving mode.

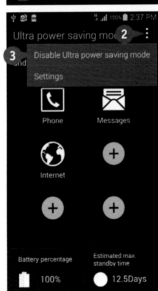

TIP

How do I remove an app from the Home screen in Ultra Power Saving mode?

1 Press the Home button to display the Home screen.

2 Tap ▮ to open the menu.

3 Tap **Remove**. A Remove icon (⊖) appears next to each app that you can remove.

4 Tap the app that you want to remove.

5 Tap **OK**.

Reset Your App Preferences

If the software on your Galaxy S 5 becomes unstable, you may be able to sort out the problem by resetting all your app preferences to their default settings.

After resetting all the preferences, you can set the preferences for any individual app the way that you want them. You may also find resetting your app preferences useful when you have been experimenting with the settings for different apps but cannot find the settings needed to undo the changes that you have made.

Reset Your App Preferences

1 Press the Home button.

The Home screen appears.

2 Tap **Apps** (⊞).

The Apps screen appears.

3 Tap **Settings** (⚙).

The Settings app opens.

4 Swipe up the screen to scroll down to the Applications section.

5 Tap **Application Manager** (⊞).

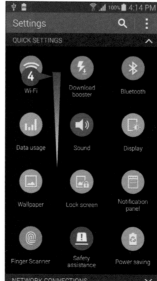
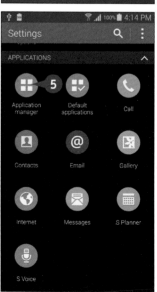

The Application Manager screen appears.

6 Tap the Menu button (▤).

7 Tap **Reset app preferences**.

The Reset App Preferences? dialog box opens.

8 Tap **Reset apps**.

Android resets the app preferences.

9 Press the Home button.

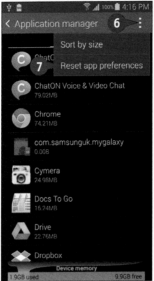

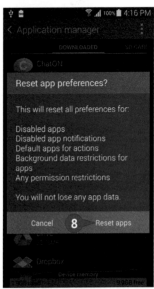

The Complete Action Using dialog box opens.

10 Tap **TouchWiz home**.

11 Tap **Always**.

The Clear Defaults dialog box opens.

12 Tap **OK**.

The Home screen appears.

You can now launch an app from the Home screen or the Apps screen to verify that resetting the app preferences resolved the problem.

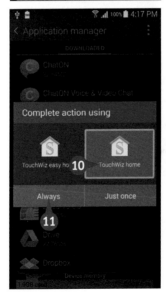

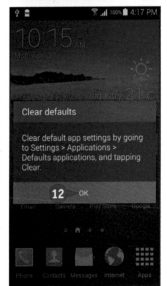

TIP

What other effects does resetting app preferences have?

As well as from resolving instabilities, resetting app preferences also removes the associations that you have made between particular file types and apps. So if you had associated a given file type with an app by clicking the **Always** button in the Complete Action Using dialog box, making Android always use that app for that file type, you will need to make that choice again after resetting the app preferences. This is why the Complete Action Using dialog box opens when you press the Home button after resetting app preferences, giving you the choice between TouchWiz Easy Home and TouchWiz Home, the regular version of the TouchWiz user interface.

Check Free Space and Clear Extra Space

If you take your Galaxy S 5 everywhere, you probably want to put as many data and media files on it as possible so that you can carry them with you. When you do this, your phone may become low on free space, which can cause it to run slowly or unstably. To avoid problems, you can check how much space is left on your Galaxy S 5. When free space runs low, you can clear extra space to help avoid running into problems.

Check Free Space and Clear Extra Space

1 Press the Home button.

The Home screen appears.

2 Tap **Apps** (▦).

The Apps screen appears.

3 Tap **Settings** (◉).

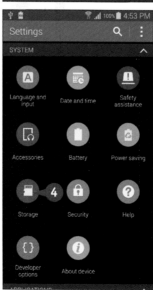

The Settings app opens.

4 In the System section, tap **Storage** (▤).

The Storage screen appears.

Ⓐ Device Memory shows how much memory is in use.

Ⓑ Total Space shows the total storage space, minus the space taken up by the operating system and included apps.

Ⓒ Available Space shows how much space is free.

5 Tap **Used space**.

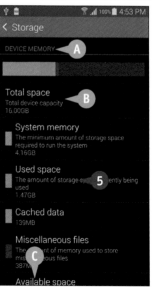

The Used Space screen appears.

6 Tap **Applications**.

The Application Manager opens, showing the apps listed in descending order of size.

7 To remove an app, tap its name.

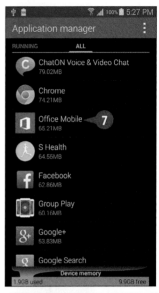

The App Info screen appears.

8 Tap **Uninstall**.

A confirmation dialog box opens.

9 Tap **Uninstall**.

Android uninstalls the app.

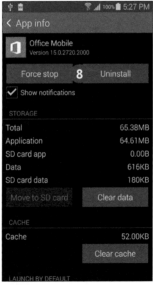

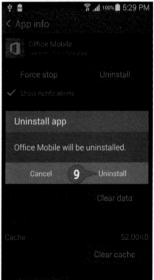

TIP

What other items can I delete to free up space on my Galaxy S 5?
You can delete cached data, miscellaneous files, and media files. On the Storage screen, tap **Cached data** to display the Clear Cached Data? dialog box and then tap **OK**. Next, tap **Miscellaneous files** to display the Miscellaneous Files screen. You can then tap the option for each file that you want to delete (■ changes to ✓) and tap 🗑.

Although the Used Space screen contains Pictures, Video, and Audio buttons, it is easier to remove pictures, video, and audio files using Samsung Kies on your computer than directly using Android.

Back Up and Restore Online

You can back up your Galaxy S 5 to your Google account to keep your data and settings safe. If your Galaxy S 5 subsequently suffers problems, you can reset it to the factory settings and then restore your data and settings to it from your Google account. Similarly, if your phone gets broken, lost, or stolen, you can restore your data and settings from your Google account to a new phone. Restoring your data and settings enables you to implement your preferred setup on a new phone without laborious customization.

Back Up and Restore Online

1 Pull down from the top of the screen.

The Notifications panel opens.

2 Tap 🔧.

The Settings app opens.

3 In the User and Backup section, tap **Backup and reset** (▤).

The Backup and Reset screen appears.

4 Tap **Back up my data** (■ changes to ✓).

Note: If you have already set your Galaxy S 5 to back up to your Google account, you do not need to change the settings.

5 Tap **Backup account**.

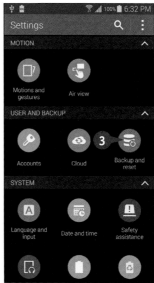

The Set Backup Account dialog box opens.

6 Tap the appropriate account if it appears.

A If the backup account that you want to use does not appear, tap **Add account** and follow the prompts on the Add a Google Account screen.

7 Tap **Automatic restore** (■ changes to ✓) if you want to restore your settings and data when you reinstall an app.

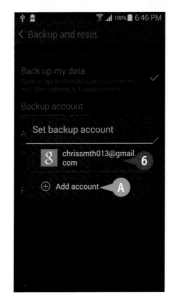

8 Press the Home button.

The Home screen appears.

Your Galaxy S 5 is now set to back up your data periodically to the account that you designated.

TIP

What settings does Android back up to my Google account?
Android backs up your personal data, such as your contacts, web bookmarks, and Wi-Fi passwords. Android also stores the list of apps that you have bought or downloaded from the Play Store and your customized settings — for example, your Display settings and Sound settings.

Back Up Your Data with Samsung Kies

Samsung Kies, the companion app that Samsung provides with the Galaxy S 5 and other devices, enables you to back up your phone to your PC or Mac for safety. You can choose between backing up all the contents of your Galaxy S 5 and backing up only selected items.

This section shows Kies running on Windows, but the app works in a similar way on OS X.

Back Up Your Data with Samsung Kies

1 Connect your Galaxy S 5 to your PC via USB.

Note: If your Galaxy S 5's screen is locked, unlock it.

The Kies driver recognizes your Galaxy S 5, and Kies opens automatically.

Note: If Kies does not open automatically, click **Samsung Kies** on the Start screen or Start menu to launch it.

A Your Galaxy S 5 appears in the Connected Devices list.

2 Click **Back up/Restore**.

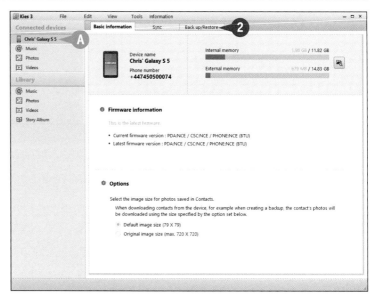

3 Click **Data backup**.

B You can click **Select all items** (□ changes to ☑) if you want to back up all the items.

4 Click the option (□ changes to ☑) for each item that you want to back up.

Note: You can click **Applications (internal memory)** to back up apps. To back up only some apps, click **Select individually**, make your choices in the Select Application dialog box, and click **Confirm**.

5 Click **Backup**.

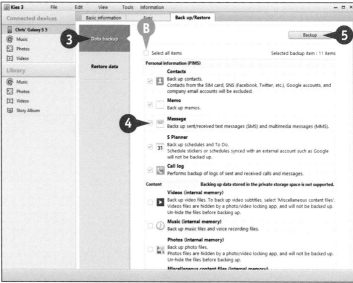

The Backup dialog box opens.

Kies backs up your data.

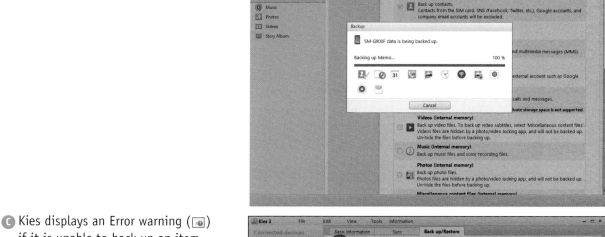

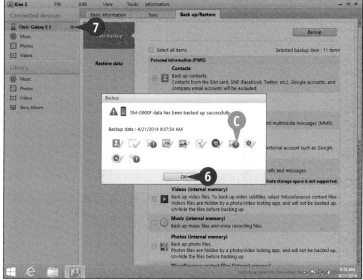

C Kies displays an Error warning (⊡) if it is unable to back up an item.

6 Click **OK**.

7 Click the Disconnect button.

Kies removes your Galaxy S 5 from the Connected Devices list.

8 Disconnect your Galaxy S 5 from your PC.

TIP

Should I back up all the contents of my Galaxy S 5 to my computer?
Provided your computer has plenty of space, you can back up as many items as you want. But normally it is not worth backing up any files that already exist on your computer. For example, if you have synced music files from your computer to your Galaxy S 5, you need not back up those same files from the Galaxy S 5 to your computer. Similarly, you may choose not to back up any apps that you can easily reinstall by downloading them from the Play Store.

Restore Your Data with Samsung Kies

I f you have backed up some or all of the data from your Galaxy S 5 to your computer using Samsung's Kies app, you can restore data to your phone if it suffers a software or hardware failure. When restoring data, you can choose which of the available backups to use. Within the backup that you choose, you can select which items to copy to your Galaxy S 5.

This section shows Kies running on Windows, but the app works in a similar way on OS X.

Restore Your Data with Samsung Kies

① Connect your Galaxy S 5 to your PC via USB.

Note: If your Galaxy S 5's screen is locked, unlock it.

The Kies driver recognizes your Galaxy S 5, and Kies opens automatically.

Note: If Kies does not open automatically, click **Samsung Kies** on the Start screen or Start menu to launch it.

Ⓐ Your Galaxy S 5 appears in the Connected Devices list.

② Click **Back up/Restore**.

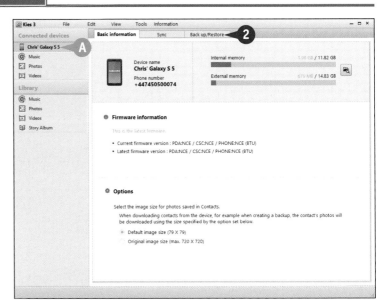

The Back Up/Restore pane appears.

③ Click **Restore data**.

The Restore Data pane appears.

④ Click the **Select the backup file to restore** pop-up menu.

⑤ Click the backup file to use.

Ⓑ If the Select the Backup File to Restore pop-up menu does not show the correct backups, click **Select folder** and select the folder that contains the backups.

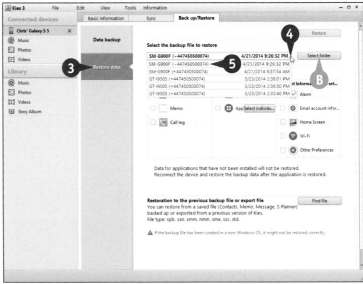

The contents of the backup file appear.

6 Click the option (☐ changes to ☑) for each item that you want to restore.

C You can click **Select all items** (☐ changes to ☑) if you want to restore all the available items.

7 Click **Restore**.

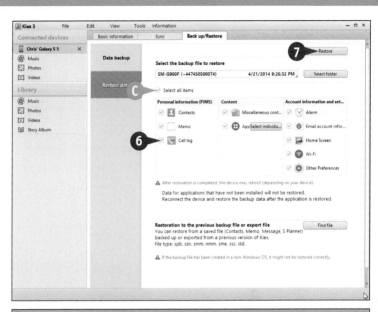

The Restore dialog box opens.

Kies restores the data that you selected.

8 Click **OK**.

Your Galaxy S 5 restarts.

Your Galaxy S 5 reappears in the Connected Devices list.

9 Click the Disconnect button.

Kies removes your Galaxy S 5 from the Connected Devices list.

10 Disconnect your Galaxy S 5 from your PC.

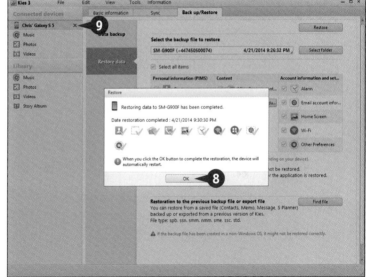

TIP

Which items should I restore to my Galaxy S 5?

This depends on what problem your Galaxy S 5 has suffered and how you are trying to resolve it. If only some of your data has become corrupted, try restoring only the affected data and see if that fixes the problem. If you need to replace a wide variety of data, you may choose to restore everything in the backup. But even when you do this, look quickly through the files involved and verify that you want to have them all on your Galaxy S 5. For example, you may not need to restore many gigabytes of video files, especially if you have already watched them.

Reset Your Galaxy S 5 to Its Factory Settings

Samsung makes your Galaxy S 5 and the customized Android OS it runs as reliable as possible, but even so, the phone's software can become corrupted. If your Galaxy S 5 has severe problems and cannot communicate with Samsung Kies on a computer, or if you do not use Kies, you may need to reset your phone to its factory settings in order to resolve the problem. After resetting to the factory settings, you can restore your data and settings to your Galaxy S 5 from your Google account.

Reset Your Galaxy S 5 to Its Factory Settings

1 Press the Home button.

The Home screen appears.

2 Tap **Apps** (⊞).

The Apps screen appears.

3 Tap **Settings**.

The Settings app opens.

4 In the User and Backup section, tap **Backup and reset** (▣).

The Backup and Reset screen appears.

5 Tap **Factory data reset**.

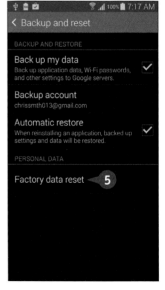

The Factory Data Reset screen appears.

6 Tap **Reset device**.

The Confirm PIN screen appears.

Note: If you use a different security method than a PIN, your Galaxy S 5 displays the appropriate screen.

7 Type your PIN.

8 Tap **Continue**.

9 Tap **Delete all**.

Android resets your Galaxy S 5 to its factory settings.

Your Galaxy S 5 restarts and goes into setup.

10 Follow through the setup steps, selecting your language and signing in to your Google account.

11 On the Google Services screen, tap this option (■ changes to ✔).

12 Tap the Down button (■), tap the Next button (▶), and allow setup to finish.

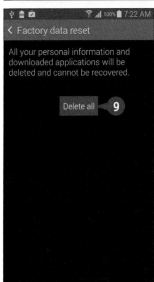

TIP

What are other reasons for resetting a Galaxy S 5 to its factory settings?
Other than software problems, there are two common reasons for resetting to the factory settings. First, if you have encrypted your Galaxy S 5, you can reset it to remove the encryption. Second, if you plan to give or sell the phone to someone else, you can reset it to remove all your data and settings.

Troubleshoot Wireless Network Connections

Your Galaxy S 5 enables you to connect easily to wireless networks, and you should use them instead of the cellular network whenever possible. This is especially important if your phone has a meager data plan.

Normally, your Galaxy S 5 establishes and maintains Wi-Fi connections without problems. But you may sometimes need to tell it to forget a network and then rejoin the network manually, providing the password again. You may also need to find your phone's IP address or its MAC address, the unique hardware address of its wireless network adapter.

Troubleshoot Wireless Network Connections

Reestablish a Faulty Wi-Fi Connection

1 Pull down from the top of the screen.

The Notifications panel opens.

2 Tap **Wi-Fi** (📶 changes to 📶) to turn Wi-Fi off.

3 Tap **Wi-Fi** again (📶 changes to 📶) to turn Wi-Fi on.

Android attempts to reestablish the connection to the last wireless network that your Galaxy S 5 used.

Note: If the Wi-Fi connection is now working satisfactorily, skip the remaining steps.

4 Tap and hold **Wi-Fi** (📶).

The Wi-Fi screen appears.

5 Tap the network marked **Connected**.

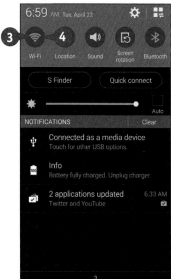

A dialog box opens showing the connection details, including the IP address.

6 Tap **Forget**.

Android forgets the network.

7 Tap the network's button again.

A dialog box opens.

8 Type the password.

A You can tap **Show password** (■ changes to ☑) to display the password.

9 Tap **Connect**.

Your Galaxy S 5 connects to the wireless network.

Find Out Your MAC Address

1 On the Wi-Fi screen, tap ⋮.

2 Tap **Advanced**.

The Advanced screen appears.

3 Check the MAC address readout.

Note: *MAC* is the acronym for *Media Access Control*. It does not refer to Apple's Macintosh computers, although those also have MAC addresses.

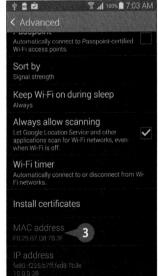

TIP

Why might I need to know my Galaxy S 5's MAC address?

Many Wi-Fi networks use a whitelist of MAC addresses to control which computers and devices can connect to the network: Any device with a MAC address on the list can connect, whereas devices with other MAC addresses cannot. A MAC address whitelist is a useful security measure, but it is not foolproof. This is because, although each network adapter has a unique MAC address burned into its hardware, an unapproved device can run software that *spoofs* — imitates — an approved MAC address.

Index

A

B